Bookplates in the News, 1970-1985

Related Gale Title

Bookplates - Audrey Spencer Arellanes. A comprehensive bibliography of more than 5,000 items. Illustrations. Published 1971.

Bookplates in the News, 1970-1985

A Collection of Sixty Issues of the Newsletter of the
American Society of Bookplate Collectors and Designers,
Including a General Index and an Illustrations Index
to Bookplate Artists and Owners

Audrey Spencer Arellanes,

Editor

GALE RESEARCH COMPANY • BOOK TOWER • DETROIT, MICHIGAN 48226

Editor: Audrey Spencer Arellanes

Indexes prepared by Richard H. Schimmelpfeng,
Director of Special Collections, University of Connecticut Library
Storrs, Connecticut

External Production Supervisor: Mary Beth Trimper
Senior External Production Associate: Dorothy Kalleberg

Internal Production Supervisor: Laura Bryant
Internal Production Associate: Louise Gagné

Publisher: Frederick G. Ruffner
Editorial Director: Dedria Bryfonski
Director, Indexes and Dictionaries Division: Ellen T. Crowley
Senior Editor, Research: Annie M. Brewer

Contents

Preface

Bookplates are attached inside the front covers of books to give information about the owner and are referred to in the library/literary world as "ex libris"—a Latin phrase meaning "from the books." The world's oldest ex libris dates back to the eighteenth dynasty of Egypt, when Amenhotep III ruled Thebes. Much later, when the form of the book was well established, bookplates became the most practical way to identify the ownership of a particular book. They are executed in many media: as woodcuts, engravings, lithographs, etchings, line drawings in both pen and pencil, and in calligraphy.

Fifteen Years of *Bookplates in the News* Reprinted

Bookplates in the News, 1970-1985 is a one-volume reprint of sixty issues of the official newsletter of the American Society of Bookplate Collectors and Designers, dating from July, 1970, through April, 1985. The newsletter provides information about bookplates, their artists and illustrators, bookplate owners, and bookplate exhibits, as well as including reviews of the literature on bookplates and annotated bibliographical references.

The newsletter also presents contemporary bookplates, the labels of identification used by individuals today for their private libraries, as well as the designs of established artists created for individuals and institutions. The ex libris has come a long way from its early development based on coats-of-arms, which only a limited number of families were privileged to use. Today many individuals have personal bookplates. A[lfred] Edward Newton (1863-1940), Philadelphia book collector, said that the use of a bookplate "is a way to a certain sort of immortality—the only sort of immortality within the reach of most of us." Commissioning a personal bookplate is also a way to be a patron of the arts and is within the means of any dedicated book lover.

More Than 250 Illustrations Included

An outstanding feature of the newsletter is the bookplates themselves. In the issues that subscribers receive, it is possible to have many of the original bookplate prints tipped-in, which gives the readers a chance to see the color and feel the beauty of an original print, whether the paper was etched, engraved, or embossed. Many of the plates have been designed by famous artists, many owned by famous literary people; and both artists and owners were generous in sharing. Tipping-in of bookplates was, of course, not feasible for this reprint; however, among the bookplates reproduced in black and white are those of Robert Frost, Bill Griffith, Edwin Markham, and Lytton Strachey. Among the artists represented are Philip Hagreen, Leo Wyatt, Frederick Remington, and Rockwell Kent.

This 1970-1985 collection also allows one to trace the development of the first fifteen years of the newsletter. It shows the evolution of the publication from a single sheet printed on one side to ten or more pages in the later editions. Enhancements to the masthead and page layout may also be noted.

I have purposely maintained the 8 1/2" by 11" size throughout the life of the newsletter. The periodical that changes size, whether owing to the editor's whim or in the guise of progress, creates a nightmare for the subscriber who wishes to bind the issues of a particular journal. In addition, the decision to present the text in its typewritten form has been deliberate, as this method permits me most control over the final copy.

Indexes Provide Easy Access

A special thanks is due Richard H. Schimmelpfeng, Director of Special Collections, University of Connecticut Library, for the development of the indexes featured in *Bookplates in the News, 1970-1985.*

The General Index covers the authors and the titles of articles that appear in *Bookplates in the News,* the names of people and institutions mentioned in those articles, titles of books, names of libraries and universities, and generally any topic that would be suitable for an index. The names of exhibits, auctions, and events that would be of interest to bibliophiles are indexed as well. Under the heading "Book Reviews," the title and author of the book reviewed are given. Under the heading "Periodical Literature," titles of magazines and periodicals that are mentioned in *Bookplates* appear, forming an unusual and excellent bibliography within the General Index.

The Illustrations Index concentrates upon the unique feature of *Bookplates in the News*. The name of the artist or illustrator of each bookplate that was tipped-in or that was shown as a facsimile is indexed, as well as the individual or institution owning each bookplate.

Both of these indexes greatly enhance the reprinted newsletters by giving full access to the many nuggets of information that might otherwise have remained buried in the text. Uniform folios have been added to all the pages in the reprint to aid in using the indexes.

The Joys of Bookplate Collecting

My own interest in bookplates was first aroused while reading the John Fleming and Edwin Wolf biography of A.S.W. Rosenbach, the flamboyant antiquarian bookseller who was a prime mover in the formation of the libraries of Henry E. Huntington and William Andrews Clark. Along with intriguing tales about rare books, large paper copies, limited editions, and suppressed publications, there were in biographies occasional mention of bookplates. Some plates were designed for a specific library by well-known artists, some were created and placed in books at the time of their sale, such as the Hoe and Jerome Kern auctions. As a possible subject to study and collect, the ex libris had considerable merit in my eyes. Bookplates would not shatter easily if dropped, as would bone china teacups, nor would they take as much space to display or store, although, if collected in quantity, they may fill a trunk!

For me, another appeal of bookplates is that an interest in them does not restrict the enthusiast to a particular time period or to any one geographic location. The common denominator may be bookplates, but the time frame ranges from the early centuries of the clay tablet to the present. The country may be anywhere there are books. And owners, artists, and collectors of bookplates may also be authors, physicists, historians, computer scientists, librarians, teachers, doctors, or from nearly any profession.

My approach to bookplates was through the literature of the book world, both books and periodicals, but especially the periodicals. After ten years of Saturdays during which I read and annotated articles about bookplates in all sorts of periodicals in the hallowed stacks of the Huntington Library, *Bookplates*, my bibliography of bookplate periodical literature, was published in 1971 by Gale Research Company. And I was ready for the next phase.

Development of the Society's Newsletter

Since 1963 I had been a member of the American Society of Bookplate Collectors and Designers. Carlyle S. Baer was Secretary and guiding light of the Society from its founding in 1922 until his death in 1969. During the time Baer directed the activities of the Society, he edited thirty-three volumes of the *Year Book* and issued an occasional *Bulletin* (actually, sixteen in forty-seven years). There was a strong possibility the Society would not long survive the demise of its Secretary and sole officer. From my extensive reading of bookplate literature, I was well aware of the transitory nature of publications devoted to bookplates. Three years was about the limit of endurance, financially and otherwise, for the editor of such journals—journals that were usually sustained by the enthusiasm, creativity, and persistence of one individual, with only the occasional help of like-minded fellow enthusiasts. So when the Society seemed about to become inactive as the result of Baer's death, I volunteered to carry on the tradition of the Society by publishing the *Year Book*. I also hoped to add a more frequently issued communication. I had often wished there were a means of knowing what was taking place in the world of bookplates on a current basis.

A newsletter seemed a good way to keep in touch with Society members, to bring word of books, articles, and exhibitions featuring bookplates while these publications and events were current. A quarterly publication would be often enough to generate interest for the membership and not so often as to be a burden for the editor. The timing was nearly perfect, as I had just completed my bibliography and had available time to devote to an on-going project.

Origin of the Title

What to name the new quarterly so that it would not be confused with the bookplate journals, bulletins, chronicles, and magazines of the past? This was in 1970, when there was a weekly program on American television that tickled the funny bone and poked fun at many aspects of the establishment. Among the targets of its humor was newscasting. The program was "Laugh-In," and one of the weekly specialties was "Laugh-In Looks at the News." There was the making of a title, one that announced the subject in the first word and was not a duplication of any previous bookplate publication - Bookplates in the News!

The title expressed the desired feeling of being current and non-stuffy. The newsletter was to feature contemporary bookplates, designed and used today by people for their libraries, and to include news of exhibits, books, and periodicals mentioning ex libris. The quarterly was a vehicle in which to continue my bibliography by annotating articles as they appeared and to include any citations that escaped my attention the first time.

"A Passport to Friendship"

Bookplates in the News is now international in scope, with readership throughout the world where interest in books and art blend in the bookplate enthusiast. The bookplate art from these many countries represents the "passport" in the Society's motto: "Bookplates Are a Passport to Friendship." The added dividends for the bookplate enthusiast are the many friendships that evolve from the correspondence carried on in the pursuit of ex libris.

Whether you are just discovering bookplates in the contemporary scene or have come to their study through the literature of the Golden Period, 1890-1920, *Bookplates in the News, 1970-1985* will bring you many happy hours of reading and viewing, facts and fantasy, and a revisit to some of the classics of the past. This reprinted collection will appeal not only to bookplate collectors, but also to printers, typographers, calligraphers, artists, illustrators, and librarians developing their rare book collections.

And to close, a quotation from Laurence Hutton, who wrote a series of articles on American bookplates for *Book Buyer* in 1886: "997 out of 1,000 book owners don't know what a bookplate is, though all of them know about fashion-plates, boiler-plates, armor-plates, and soup plates...." After reading *Bookplates in the News, 1970-1985* you will surely be among the three knowledgeable individuals out of that 1,000.

Audrey Spencer Arellanes

Bookplates in the News, 1970-1985

SERIF, Kent State publication, has a continuing bookplate article each quarter. Mrs. Mary DeVolld selects a plate, usually of historical or literary interest, which is illustrated and gives details about the owner and artist. A. Edward Newton was featured in March 1970.

While not specifically a bookplate article, the January issue of *AMERICAN BOOK COLLECTOR* used a bookplate to illustrate an article titled "Huckelberry Finn: A Copy Inscribed in 1903," by John Hakac. Illustrated is a scarab-beetle bookplate of New York actress, Blanche Bates.

While the auction item below came to my attention too late to be of help to any members who might wish to bid, it will at least show another area where bookplates are featured and should be of interest to the collector who wishes to add to his collection as well as the person who may want to sell. The catalog was priced at $2 and prior notice appeared in *ANTIQUARIAN BOOKMAN (AB)*, which incidentally is a good source for notices about bookplate exhibits, auctions, etc.

Charles Hamilton Auction 43
Waldorf Astoria, July 23, 1970

89 BOOKPLATES. Remarkable collection of more than 500 bookplates, English and American, mostly 18th and 19th centuries, but with a few 20th century examples, many ornately engraved with armorial designs, some flat printed. Includes examples of: OLIVER WENDELL HOLMES, DAVID GARRICK, EDWARD EGGLESTON, WM. BYRD OF WESTOVER, JONATHAN BELCHER, WILLIAM HAMILTON and BENNETT A. CERF, with many British nobility (Earls of Aulie and Arran, 4th Duke of Wellington) and lesser luminaries, also a considerable number of library bookplates. Some mounted, but all in good to very good condition. See separate listing under WASHINGTON, GEORGE and BUSHROD. With three A.Ls.S. of English noblemen presenting bookplates: Lord Wellington (1933), the Earl of Arran (1933) and Lord Aulie. A fascinating, colorful collection. In all, more than 500 pieces. ------------------------------(80.00)

90 BOOKPLATES. Collection of 117 handsome bookplates, American and English, 18th to 20th centuries, many engraved with armorial designs and some flat printed, a few in colors. Of various sizes and shapes ranging from 8vo to about 2" x 1½". Includes examples of Sir Robert Peel, William Howard, William Cowper, Cadwallader D. Colden, Maria Seymour, John Murray, Samuel L. M. Barlow, Beverley Robinson, Robert Gracie, John V. L. Pruyn, the Grolier Club, and numerous institutions. Some wear, mounting traces and minor defects, but mostly very good. In all, 118 pieces. ------------------------------(35.00)

354 (WASHINGTON, GEORGE). His original 16mo engraved bookplate, bearing his arms, family motto in Latin and his name (slightly trimmed, with one marginal tear, else a fine example of a rare bookplate). With original engraved bookplate of BUSHROD WASHINGTON (different design but bearing the same arms and motto), a choice example with a heavy plate impression. Two desirable pieces. ------------------------------(75.00)

With your help it would be possible to issue B O O K P L A T E S in the NEWS quarterly or more frequently if sufficient material is submitted. There must be many local items or articles in specialized journals which various members could send along for inclusion. If interest is expressed, note could be made of booksellers' catalogs which include books about bookplates, as example the recent Heritage Bookshop's Fine Printing and the Illustrated Book which offered *THE HUMAN SIDE OF BOOKPLATES* by Louise Seymour Jones (1951) at $10.

An exchange/want list could be included if there is sufficient expressed interest.

American Society of Bookplate Collectors & Designers
429 North Daisy Avenue, Pasadena, California 91107

Doris Frohnsdorff's catalog of children's
books was spotted at the Los Angeles
Antiquarian Book Fair. Its cover reproduced
a design to be used as a bookplate for her
collection of children's books. The artist
is Donald Hendricks, a California illustrator.
Our thanks for permission to reproduce it for
our newsletter.

Dr. Radbill furnished the following clipping
which is quoted in full from PHARMACY IN
HISTORY, 12:#3:122, 1970 - Exhibit, Ex Libris.
An unusual exhibit focusing on bookplates having pharmaceutical themes and associations was
shown in Exhibit Hall at the annual meetings
under the sponsorship of AIHP's Committee on
Exhibit and Pictorial History, headed by J.
Hampton Hoch of Charleston, S.C. Although a
fascinating variety of bookplates, it represented only a special selection from among
thousands collected by Samuel X. Radbill, M.D.,
of Philadelphia, who is internationally known
for his collection and his writings on medical
ex libris (e.g., see his Bibliography of
Medical Ex Libris Literature, Hilprand Press,
Los Angeles, 1951, 40 pp.)

DORIS · FROHNSDORFF

Another exhibit was at the Courville-Abbott
Memorial Library during June, 1970 which
featured the bookplate collection of Milton
W. Castle, a "well-known theatre personality
and reconteur" of North Hollywood. An article with two illustrations appeared in
TELSTAF (White Memorial Medical Center, Los Angeles), "Library Display," 2:2 unnumbered pages, June 14, 1970.

While few articles are devoted exclusively to bookplates, the artists who design
them, their owners, or collectors, bookplates are a frequent part of the larger
literary and art scene. Such an instance is the article in BOOK COLLECTOR, "Contemporary Collectors - The Charlecote House Library. II: Provenance and Peregri-
nations," by Douglas Gordon, 19:185-93, Summer 1970. This excellent article shows
in part how bookplates play an important role in documenting provenance.

Passing reference to bookplates is made in the TIMES LITERARY SUPPLEMENT, "Achievement of Arthur Waley," No. 3477:1051-52, September 18, 1970. A review of Madly
Singing in the Mountains, an appreciation and anthology of Waley, a scholar of
worldwide fame for his translations from Chinese and Japanese; he is quoted as
claiming to have undertaken the study of these two languages "simply to escape
from German bookplates" while working at the British Museum.

William R. Holman, who printed BOOKPLATES FOR LIBRARIES, has designed the new
series of LIBRARY CHRONICLE, issued by the University of Texas at Austin. It
contained "J. Frank Dobie on Libraries," New Series Number 1:53-60, March 1970.
The article is a reproduction of Dobie's handwritten comments on the La Salle
County Library which doesn't get "as much a year as one - just one - good Brahma
bull sells for." The illustration is Frank Dobie's bookplate which features a
roadrunner and his signature.

The actual prices realized at the Charles Hamilton Auction on July 23, 1970 in each instance exceeded the reserve. Lot 89 brought $110; almost double was bid for lot 90, $60; and the George and Bushrod Washington bookplates brought $85. See the last newsletter for full descriptions of the lots.

UCLA LIBRARIAN - "Acquisition of the Ewing Library," 23:33-4, June 1970. Majl Ewing, professor of the Department of English at UCLA, had an extensive collection of first editions of Aldus Huxley, D. H. Lawrence and Osbert Sitwell. One of the illustrations accompanying the article pictures a simple bookplate using printer's ornaments which was designed for the collection.

Some of you are already familiar with the LITERARY REPOSITORY (published by the antiquarian bookseller Stevens-Cox, Mount Durand, St. Peter Port, Guernsey, C.I. via Britain) which occasionally includes bookplate items. The most recent issue No. 2/1970 offers a dozen 19th or 20th century plates for $1.

Catalog Seven of Deval & Muir (T keley-Bishop's Stortford, Herts, England) listed four bookplates by Joan Hassal, well-known wood engraver. The J. G. Dreyfus was priced at $7.80, the remaining at $8.40 each.

With all the publicity given the Thomas W. Streeter sale, it was interesting to note reference to bookplates in AB BOOKMAN's YEARBOOK, part two:7-8, 1970 in "A Memoir of T.S.W. by Archibald Hanna, Jr." Some 15 years ago Streeter's Texas collection was acquired by Yale and a special bookplate designed "so that future generations of scholars and collectors would be able to identify his books."

Thanks are due Kurt Schnitzer, M.D., for a reprint of a well-written article from CHICAGO MEDICINE - "Ex Libris in Medicine," H. W. Kienast, M.D., 73:445-47, June 6, 1970. It gives the historical background of medical bookplates with specific reference to some of the early books relating to bookplates in general. An illustration shows Dr. Kienast at Spring 1970 Midwest Clinical Conference with his display.

Louis Ginsberg has volunteered to handle an Exchange List and the first list is enclosed with this newsletter. This presents an excellent method by which exchanges may be made and long sought bookplates or books about them obtained.

The Society has recently been given the bookplate collection of Mrs. Alexander Nichols Cook of Brooklyn, New York. Though small in size the collection is rich in "Little Masters" and other bookplate artists of great skill. Thanks for this bequest are due the late Mrs. Cook's daughter, Miss Marion Belden Cook, who was told of the ASBC&D by the New York Public Library. In time this collection will be added to the Society's collection in the Library of Congress where it is available to interested collectors and scholars.

The response to the questionnaire for the Member's Directory has been very good, and several members have already furnished 200 copies of their bookplates to be tipped in - Carl Junge, Dr. Midlow, Mrs. Mishkin; others are promised. However, there are some members from whom I have never heard - won't you please take or make the time to write and/or complete the questionnaire?? We have several new and prospective members. By the next issue, it is hoped to have an updated mailing list.

Won't you please share the bookplate references you discover by sending them to the editor for publication in the newsletter? Magazine articles, exhibits, newspaper items, books (occasionally a biography will illustrate the person's bookplate).

American Society of Bookplate
  Collectors and Designers
  429 North Daisy Avenue
  Pasadena, Calif. 91107

B O O K P L A T E S in the NEWS
Number Three   January 1971

Editor - - - - - Audrey Arellanes

Probably the first ex libris exhibition in sub-Saharan Africa was held during the spring of 1970 at the Haile Sellassie I University Library. Over five hundred bookplates, representing English armorials, American colleges and universities, early American plates, and the work of Carl S. Junge, were displayed. The collection was the gift of Francis W. Allen, who was associated with the library for several years.

ILLUSTRATED ESSAYS ON JEWISH BOOKPLATES by Philip Goodman, scheduled for publication in April 1971, will be the first book to treat the subject in depth and on a comprehensive scale. It opens with an essay on the earliest bookplates of Jewish interest, including some of the Christian Hebraists of the 16th century. This is the first volume to present more than one hundred reproductions of Jewish bookplates, many of them rare and a goodly number created by noted artists for outstanding personalities; it also includes "Jewish Bookplate Literature: An Annotated Bibliography" which records over one hundred items. The volume will prove fascinating to bibliophiles, librarians, art enthusiasts, historians and genealogists. It will be published by Ktav Publishing House, 120 East Broadway, New York, New York 10002, price $12.50.

Former ASBC&D member Mrs. Mary Alice Ercolini is the author of an article, "The Cat in Ex-libris Design," which appeared in SVENSKA EXLIBRIS FORENINGENS, 1967-68 (published in 1970). The article was in English with an abstract in Swedish. One illustration is a tipped in woodengraving by Mark Severin of Belgium, the other a woodcut by Padre Oriol of Spain.

"Enough to Keep a Byrd Alive," by Ulrich Troubetzkoy includes an illustration of the William Byrd bookplate (VIRGINIA CAVALCADE, XI:36-41, Autumn 1961).

CHILDHOOD AND YOUTH, a catalog of books for, by and about children issued by Peggy Christian of Los Angeles included a copy of Wilbur Macey Stone's SOME CHILDREN'S BOOK-PLATES, a signed presentation copy from L. C. Woodworth, "who was the Brothers of the Book, to Bertram Grosvenor Goodhue, architect and designer of type, books & bookplates, in a presentation binding." It was marked "sold" before the catalog issued.

Larry Edmunds, Hollywood dealer in material pertaining to the movies and the film industry, listed two books in a recent catalog under the autograph section by virtue of the bookplates they contained - one for Monte Blue, the other Colleen Moore.

About one-third of the ASBC&D membership have responded by completing and returning the questionnaire for the Membership Directory. If another questionnaire is enclosed with your newsletter, it is a hint that the editor has not received your reply.

If you have information about exhibits, articles, collectors or artists - any news concerning bookplates - please send the details to the editor, so that she may share it with the entire membership.

New member Roy Jensen (Harrisburg, Pa.) will have about 800 bookplates on exhibit during January and February at the International College of Surgeons Museum of Surgical Science and Hall of Fame, Chicago.

In its continuing series on bookplates, SERIF, issued by Kent State, had the following articles: "Book-Plate of Paul Louis Feiss," 7:inside cover, June 1970. Illustration is the plate of Paul Louis Feiss, who inherited a Cleveland clothing manufacturing company, was an organizer of the Cleveland Symphony; member of the Grolier, Aldine and Rowfant Clubs. At his death, his private library of 5,000 volumes was purchased by Kent State. -- "Book-plate of B. George Ulizio," 7:inside cover, September 1970. Illustration is the bookplate designed by noted game bird illustrator, Richard E. Bishop, for his friend B. George Ulizio; it appears in the nearly 1,500 volumes of English and American literature acquired by Kent State from Mr. Ulizio, who counted A. Edward Newton among his friends.

Herbert Cahoon, Director of Library Services, Pierpont Morgan Library, brought the following articles to the attention of your editor: COLUMBIA [University] LIBRARY COLUMNS, 45-6, December 1970. Illustrated is the bookplate of David Garrick which was included in the gift of the James Mark Baldwin Collection of Bookplates made to Columbia by his daughter, Mrs. Elizabeth B. Stimson. "Of special interest is the plate done for Dr. Baldwin by the English painter-etcher Charles William Sherborn; the collection contains the proofs, prints with remarques on various sizes and types of paper, and the correspondence relating to the designing and production of the plate." -- HARVARD ALUMNI BULLETIN, 57-9, December 7, 1970. A lively, well-written article about "bookplates, bookplate collecting, and bookplates in the Harvard University Library" with nearly 30 illustrations one-half actual size.

The KENNEDY QUARTERLY (X, December 1970), devoted to Primitive, Folk and Native Arts from the 18th, 19th & 20th centuries, listed item #215 as a bookplate for Margretha Wotringin, 1788, a 6" by 4" watercolor. "Although small fracturs of this type and size are frequently described as bookplates, it is possible that this piece may have been instead a school reward for a prize pupil."

Among a wide variety of catalog references to bookplates are the following: Edward P. Rich & Co., Box 295, Haverford, PA. 19041 - #393 Bookplate. Harvard College, engraved by N[athanael] Hurd, silversmith and engraver, fl. 1730-1777. Fine sharp silver plate impression, small tear repaired. $22.50 -- Bennett & Mar hall, Los Angeles - Catalog #10, item 9, Hardy, Book-Plates (1897), 2nd edition, $12.50 and item 15, Allen, Classified List of Early American Bookplates (Grolier Club Exhibit) $27.50 (1894) 350 copies. -- Brick Row Book Shop, Texas. #457, Rockwell Kent, Later Bookplates & Marks (1937), 1250 numbered copies $15.

Another reminder to please return your questionnaire and two copies of your bookplate to the editor for the Membership Directory. The deadline will be February 15, 1971. In addition to current members, it is hoped to picture the bookplates of early members of the ASBC&D. If you will lend any such plates, they will be returned to you.

The typescript for the next Year Book is being prepared for the printer now. Thanks to those who sent correspondence from Carlyle S. Baer from which quotations could be used, they will add to the tribute. However, doesn't anyone have letters from the early years with quotable paragraphs?

Your suggestions are needed for future articles for the Year Book.

Publication of my bookplate bibliography is scheduled for Spring 1971. Full details soon.

Preliminary membership list enclosed. See notes on second page; any information you can supply will be helpful. 5

American Society of Bookplate
    Collectors and Designers
429 North Daisy Avenue
Pasadena, Calif. 91107

B O O K P L A T E S in the NEWS
Number Four   April 1971

Editor . . . . . Audrey Arellanes

The Boston Public Library
_____

PURCHASED
FROM THE FUND
ESTABLISHED
BY
*James
Lyman
Whitney*

Bibliographer & Sometime Librarian

The Boston Public Library has offered our
members a selection of 20 of their bookplates
on receipt of a check for $2 made payable to
the Trustees of the Boston Public Library and
addressed to the Keeper of Rare Books (John
Alden), Boston Public Library, Boston, Mass.
02117. They range from period pieces of the
late 19th century to work by contemporary
artists, calligraphers and typographers.

List #92 (January 1971) of bookseller Craig
W. Ross, Medina, New York had the following
item: "With Portrait Bookplate of Harry Houdini
ATTIC MISCELLANY, AND MIRROR OF MEN AND THINGS.
London 1791. With 12 copperplates, mostly handcolored. Half calf. 8vo, covers detached. Plates
of theatrical interest. Interesting folding plate
from Cruickshank (colored). Orig. marb. covers,
worn. $22.50."

Dawsons of Pall Mall, Kent, England, Catalogue
No. 6, listed two books - #44 Castle, Egerton.
ENGLISH BOOK-PLATES ANCIENT AND MODERN. 2nd
edition. £4.50. #100 Hardy, W. J. BOOK-PLATES. 1st edition. £6.50. Both
are given in the new decimal system of pounds and new pence effective on
February 15, 1971. (£ = $2.40)

Thanks to the skill and generosity of designer-member Carl S. Junge, our
Society will have a new letterhead and masthead for our publications. It
will be introduced in the Year Book which will be distributed late April or
early May.

Dan Burne Jones, another designer-member, furnished reference to an article
in READING AND COLLECTING. (1) 2:#1, December 1937, pages 9-10, "Collecting
Bookplate Prints," which he wrote. He quotes A. J. A. Symons: "The
addition of a bookplate print to a book is its final grace." Dan Burne Jones
made a statement of considerable importance in this article, especially for
those who may question the relevance of bookplates to 20th century living:
"Art, as we know, recognizes no race, creed, or border demarcations; bookplate
collecting and bookplate societies have, then, the express purpose of exchanging that which is ideal, noble, and good between the nations of men; and keeping that art and its ideal active, dynamic and purposeful. And so, if you
need a reason beyond the fun of it, the collecting of bookplate prints may
serve a worthwhile end."

In a subsequent issue of READING AND COLLECTING was "Why I Collect Rockwell
Kent," Emma R. Martin, 2:11-12, February-March 1938. While there is no
mention of bookplates in the article, an accompanying bibliography lists
both his 1929 and 1937 volumes on bookplates.

Edward Gordon Craig, a bookplate artist to most of us is doubtless better known generally for his theatre work. His son, Edward Craig, has written his biography simply called GORDON CRAIG. As the long-time editor of the MASK, he wrote much about stage craft but only one bookplate appeared in the many volumes of this publication - "Bookplate for William Goble," 6: 108, October 1913. Designed and engraved by Gordon Craig, it represents a bookworm "many times enlarged, struggling . . Beauty it has not, even when compared with the Ant or the Crab. Poor little beast."

Noted artist Rockwell Kent died late in March at his home in Plattsburg, New York. He held a prominent position as an illustrator of classics issued in limited editions which became collectors' items; Kent also had a considerable reputation as a bookplate artist. There will be many articles concerning Rockwell Kent in art, literary, and general interest magazines; please let your editor know about any you see, so that they may be shared with the membership.

The YEAR BOOK will soon be ready for distribution. It contains a tribute to Carlyle S. Baer by George Swarth; comments by his brother; excerpts from his letters to members; the story of the California Book-Plate Society authored by Christine Price; an article by Dr. Enrico Molnar concerning an Aztec design. Please be certain to complete and return the postal enclosed with your copy of the YEAR BOOK. If you are interested in being on the exchange list, please type or print the information as requested on the postal so that your exchange listing will be correct.

To celebrate the 100th anniversary of the birthday of San Francisco printer John Henry Nash, the Rounce & Coffin Club of Los Angeles sponsored an evening at the Williams Andrews Clark Library where Professor Robert D. Harlan spoke about Nash. The University of California Press has published Harlan's biography of the flamboyant printer. It was very appropriate that the talk was given in the Clark Library, since Clark was Nash's patron. On display that evening were many of the luxurious Christmas books Nash printed for Clark to distribute to his friends. The lecture was accompanied by slides of some Nash ephemera including several bookplates.

Gale Research Company of Detroit mailed all members a copy of their Date Book for 1971 which was illustrated by ex libris. Included in the mailing was an announcement and order form for BOOKPLATES: A Selected Annotated Bibliography of the Periodical Literature by Audrey Arellanes, $15.00; publication is anticipated about May, 1971.

Robert B. Hitchman, a Seattle member, was one of two new councillors added to the governing board of the American Antiquarian Society at its 158th annual meeting on October 21, 1970.

In addition to current members, it is hoped that the Membership Directory will include early members of the Society. If you have bookplates of early members which you would lend, please write the editor. If you have not completed and returned your own questionnaire for the Membership Directory, please do so and remember to enclose two copies of the bookplate you want to represent you (or 200 if you want them tipped in).

Please send information about any bookplate activity to your editor for inclusion in the newsletter.

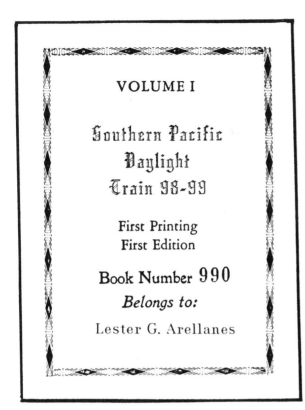

VOLUME I

Southern Pacific
Daylight
Train 98-99

First Printing
First Edition

Book Number 990
Belongs to:

Lester G. Arellanes

An unusual and magnificent opus of railroad history has become available with the publishing of SOUTHERN PACIFIC DAYLIGHT, TRAIN 98-99 authored by Richard K. Wright. Containing 656 pages, it is Volume I of a series to be done on each of Southern Pacific's "name" trains, containing literally hundreds of fine pictures, official diagrams, drawings, etc. as well as thoroughly researched text which recounts the career of "the most beautiful train in the world" from her antecedents, her birth, her great days to her present twilight, forty-eight years later. Unusual, too, as will be seen by the illustration, is the use of a bookplate that indicates the number of the limited edition and allows space for the owner to enter his own name.

Philo Press, Postbox 806, Amsterdam 1000, Holland has issued a flyer on reprints in preparation which include: Leiniingen-Westerburg on German bookplates; Walter Hamilton's DATED BOOK-PLATES (3 parts in one volume), FRENCH BOOK-PLATES: and J. B. L. Warren's A GUIDE TO THE STUDY OF BOOK-PLATES.

AMERICAN BOOK COLLECTOR, 21:3, February 1971 - bookreview - The Bewick Collector: A Descriptive Catalogue of the Works of Thomas and John Bewick, by Thomas Hugo. This is a reissue of the 1866 volume plus the 1868 supplement from Singing Tree Press (Detroit); $16 for the base volume and $12.50 for the supplement which is available separately. John R. Payne in his review says: "Professional and business men were quick to utilize the skills of Thomas Bewick for the production of bookplates, memorial cuts, notices of exhibitions, billheads, shop-cards, bar bills, coal certificates, etc."

Heraldry Today (10, Beauchamp Place, London S.W.3, England) has numerous bookplate items in their catalog for New Year 1971: JOURNAL OF THE EX LIBRIS SOCIETY, Vol. IX-XII, 1895/1902, £27. ANGLO-JEWISH COATS OF ARMS, Alfred Rubens, accompanied by a list of·Armorial Bookplates, 1900, £3. In their list of new books: AMERICAN BOOK-PLATES, the 1968 reprint of Allen, £5.25. BOOKPLATES OF GEORGE TAYLOR FRIEND, P. C. Beddingham, 1963, duplicated, limited to 75 copies, £1.50. HERALDIEK IN HET EXLIBRIS, 1967, Amsterdam, text in Dutch, £2.25. SOUTH AFRICAN BOOKPLATES, R. F. M. Immelmann, 1955, limited to 500 copies, £2.75. EX LIBRIS, Arvid Bergman, 1956, Sweden, £4.20. (Prices are in the new English decimal system)

Plandome Book Auction, Box 395, Glen Head, New York 11545, Sale #57 lists a half dozen or more books about bookplates included in the mail auction for April 26th. There should still be time for those interested to obtain a catalog and send in a bid.

The Adelphi Book Shop, 822 1/2 Fort Street, Victoria, British Columbia,
Canada had several bookplate items in their catalog received in March.
#328 was a two-page autograph letter and three-page enclosure giving
details of designs and prices for bookplates by William Edgar Fisher,
Fargo, North Dakota, December 1903. In addressed envelope, $6.50.
#373 Frederick Starr, WASHINGTON BOOKPLATES (six articles reprinted from
THE TOWN CRIER, 1925-6, Seattle, 1927, 72 pages, 17 plates and illustrations. $6.50.
#376 Wilbur M. Stone, JAY CHAMBERS: HIS BOOK PLATES with XXVII examples
& an Essay Concerning Them. New York, 1902. $7.50.
#379 Henry M. Vaughan CATALOGUE (with Notes) OF THE ANEURIN WILLIAMS
COLLECTION OF BOOK PLATES. Aberystwyth, National Library of Wales, 1938.
(limited to 500 copies), $7.50. -This catalogue was also listed in #17
issued by Lea Valley Books, Hastings, England, late in 1970 at £2.10.

ILLUSTRATED ESSAYS ON JEWISH BOOKPLATES by member Philip Goodman may be
ordered through the publisher, Ktav Publishing House, 120 East Broadway,
New York, New York 10002 at $12.50 a copy. Full details were given in
Number Three of this newsletter.

The indefatigable Roy Jansen of Harrisburg, Pennsylvania currently has
two bookplate exhibits, one in Chicago and the second at the Harrisburg
Area Community College.

The World of Books, catalog 226 issued Winter 1970/71 by Zeitlin & Ver Brugge
of Los Angeles, contained a number of bookplate items. While most entries
from any catalog will have been sold by the time you receive news of it, it
is hoped the sources will prove helpful and the prices will keep you aware of
current values. #505 PRIVATE BOOKPLATES. 1939 Annual Volume. Bookplate
Collectors Club. Spiral bound. $2. - #508 Radbill, Samuel X.,M.D.
BIBLIOGRAPHY OF MEDICAL EX LIBRIS LITERATURE. Los Angeles: Hilprand Press,
1951. $10. - #581 Starr's WASHINGTON BOOKPLATES. $8.50. - #596 Clare Ryan
Talbot, IN QUEST OF THE PERFECT BOOKPLATE. No. 21 of 300 copies signed by
the author. $15. - #619 George H. Viner, DESCRIPTIVE CATALOGUE OF BOOKPLATES
DESIGNED AND ETCHED BY GEORGE W. EVE. American Bookplate Society, 1916.
Limited to 250 copies. $22.50. - #638 THE WHITE HOUSE LIBRARY. A SHORT-TITLE
LIST, 1967. White House Library bookplate tipped in. No. 47 of 300 copies
signed by Mrs. Lyndon B. Johnson. $35. - #660 ZAMORANO 80. No. 3 of 500
with bookplate of J. Gregg Layne, one of the compilers; copy signed by all
the compilers including Henry R. Wagner, Homer D. Crotty, Phil Townsend
Hanna, Robert J. Woods, Leslie E. Bliss. $100. - #787 FACETIAE OF POGGIO THE
THE FLORENTINE. The Roxburghe Club, 1962. Contains bookplate of Ed Ainsworth, noted author of the Southwest. $15. - #800 (Indiana Kid Private Press)
Walter Klinefelter, A PACKET OF SHERLOCKIAN BOOKPLATES. One of 150 copies.
$10.

An original bookplate for Frederick Locker, designed by Kate Greenaway, and
printed in sepia was offered in catalog #10 of Deval and Muir, Herts, England,
for $12.60. It is described as "A charming design shewing two children seated
beneath a tree-of-knowledge, from which is suspended Locker's family crest. An
owl perched on a rustic fence behind the two figures."

Another English dealer in Kent, Keith Hogg, listed M. F. Severin, MAKING A
BOOKPLATE (£1.15s) and W. J. Hardy, BOOK-PLATES, 2nd edition (£2.15s).

ANTHONY F. KROLL · ENGRAVER

The Leon Kibort plate is primarily for the owner's historical collection about the Grand Duchy of Lithuania. This Coat of Arms was used by an old Polish clan. Upon election of Yogiala, Grand Duke of Lithuania, to the throne of Poland in 1386, it was adopted by several Lithuanian families. The symbols shown on the pages of the open book - the charging knight with the double-barred cross on the shield and the so-called "Gates of the Grand Duke Gedinias of Lithuania" - represent national emblems of the ancient Grand Duchy of Lithuanians. The oak leaves in the vignette point to the reverence in which the oak tree was held by the pagan Lithuanians.

Thanks are due Mr. Kibort for his kind permission to use his bookplate and to our member, Anthony F. Kroll, who furnished prints of this ex libris which he engraved and blind embossed.

Mrs. Homer Strong, a Society member since about 1935, died in Rochester, New York, on July 17, 1969. She was born March 20, 1897 in Rochester, the daughter of Alice Motley and John C. Woodbury. From both parents Margaret inherited an urge to collect - from her mother the appreciation and love of bookplates and eventually her mother's collection of them. Her aunt Maude Motley's collection of ex libris was willed to the University of Rochester. Mrs. Strong's own collection, which numbered approximately 85,000, was willed by her to the Pierpont Morgan Library in New York City, together with the sum of $60,000 "which sum I request, but do not direct, the Library to expend in providing facilities for the better care and display of bookplates." The Margaret Woodbury Strong Museum of Fascination in Rochester (which will be open to the public in the near future) will exhibit many of her other major collections - toys, miniatures, shells, oriental art, the world's largest and finest doll collection, hundreds of dolls' houses, buttons, minerals, china, etc.

Madame Paulette Colin-Gury, copper engraving artist, has written from Paris: "I created a lot of ex libris a few years ago. My son, a student in an engineering school, 23 years old, is going to visit the US next July and August. I shall give him most of my works which may be of interest for exchange among your members." The examples which she sent of her work are beautiful. She mentions in particular that her son will visit Rochester, Buffalo, Cleveland, Chicago, Boston, Indianapolis, St. Louis, Memphis, Jackson, New Orleans, Houston, San Antonio, El Paso, Tucson, San Diego, San Francisco, Portland or Seattle. Perhaps you will receive a call from Madame's son or you may wish to write her directly at 11 Rue Guillaume-Tell, Paris 17e, France.

EX-LIBRIS

Attention Bookplate Collectors

GRAY'S INN LIBRARY
SOUTH SQUARE, GRAY'S INN
LONDON, WC1R 5EU

With regard to the forthcoming visit in July of American lawyers, it has occured to me that among those who are coming to London there may well be a few who are interested in the history and study of bookplates. As I am a collector, I would be particularly pleased to meet them.

In the course of my duties as Librarian at Gray's Inn, I shall be seeing many of your members, but there may not be an opportunity to discuss personal interest. I would, therefore, be delighted if anyone who does follow this interest would contact me so that we could make arrangements to meet outside working hours....

P. C. BEDDINGTON

Old bookmen walk, as walk they must
    Through life's grim stacks that end in
        dust;
Unless they walk physicians say
    The sooner their story's writ on clay.
Old bookmen talk, as talk they must
    To other bookmen they can trust;
Without such talk then sad to say
    Loneliness hastens their final day.
Old bookmen dream as dream they must
    Until death gives his last page thrust
To end sweet tricks that memory plays
    And futile hopes for happier days.

Ed Sterne

The above poem is quoted from ANTIQUARIAN BOOKMAN, 47:1832, May 31, 1971.

Philip C. Beddington's letter appeared in the AMERICAN BAR ASSOCIATION JOURNAL, 57:396, May 1971. Many of you may be familiar with Mr. Beddington's articles which were featured in BOOKPLATE COLLECTORS NEWS, edited by the late A. B. Keeves, and his ex libris monographs.

ANTIQUARIAN BOOKMAN, 47:1612, May 17, 1971, noted the passing of member "Frank [Patrick] Clune, 77, in Sydney on March 11. Prolific Australian author, he was at work on his 68th book when he died." Francis Clune had a woodcut ex libris by Adrian Feint which was illustrated in the 1929 YEAR BOOK; in 1932 the Palmtree Press, Sydney, printed an edition limited to 30 copies of THE CLUNE BOOKPLATES BY ADRIAN FEINT, which was 20 pages containing five signed plates. Plates for other Clune family members (Thelma C. and Anthony Patrick) are included in "The Final Check-List of the Bookplates of Adrian Feint," by Thelma Clune, YEAR BOOK 1963/64. As a youth Frank Clune was befriended by Carlyle S. Baer.

"Rockwell Kent, Controversial Artist, Is Dead," headlined four column article in NEW YORK TIMES, Sunday, March 14, 1971. Illustrations include portrait, the painting "Winter" (1907), and one illustration from MOBY DICK. Mention is made of his paintings, watercolors, lithographs and woodcuts, but no specific reference to his bookplate work.

Yet another compliment for the Gale Research [Book Tower, Detroit, Michigan 48226] Ex Libris Calendar in AB, 47:1142, April 5-12, 1971.

In THE COWBOY IN ART, Ed Ainsworth said: "A special artistic brand has been burned on history's hip by Don Louis Perceval." This painter and illustrator is interested in the lore of the West, particularly cattle brands. It is fitting, therefore, that his bookplate includes several. The cowboy mounted on a mustang along with the cattle brands are taken from the heading he designed for "The Vanishing Mustang" which is chapter 17 of the Ainsworth book. Perceval's drawings and water colors appear in A NAVAJO SKETCH BOOK; he also assembled 164 sketches and the text for MAYNARD DIXON SKETCH BOOK; both are beautifully published by Northland Press of Flagstaff, Arizona. It is interesting to note that at one time he owned and occupied the Dixon home in Tucson. We are indebted to Don Louis Perceval for permitting us to use his ex libris and to Anthony F. Kroll who engraved the plate and furnished the prints.

Don Louis Perceval

His Book

The Knave feature of the Oakland TRIBUNE for Sunday, April 18, 1971 headed "Bookplates Offer Absorbing Study" describes the exhibit from Clare Ryan Talbot's collection at the main Oakland Public Library, for National Library Week through May 9th. The four column, full page coverage included an enlarged illustration of the Herbert E. Bolton bookplate; he was the late director of the Bancroft Library at the University of California. This plate is a prime example of the scriptorial as it contains not only the signature of Bolton but also five additional historic autographs: Father Kino, Don Juan de Onate, Juan Bautista de Anza, Athanese de Mezieres y Clugny, and Antonio de Arredondo. The Knave quotes Mrs. Talbot: "Finding pleasure in your work is the only genuine Fountain of Youth."

Auctioned at Sotheby's late in 1970: "Bookplates. A collection of over 750 armorial bookplates, the majority eighteenth and early nineteenth century, mounted in an album, many of the owners identified, with a description of the arms on opposite pages, index at end, black morocco, metal clasps, g.e. 4to. £38." From BOOK COLLECTING & LIBRARY MONTHLY [Sussex, England], No. 36 April 1971.

The Public Library of Altadena, California had an exhibit of bookplates assembled by Adurey Arellanes, June 7-28, 1971. Featured were the many plates of Elizabeth Watson Diamond and J. Edouard Diamond, and a selection from the Canadian ex libris collection of Willo S. Singer, member from London, Ontario, Canada.

George Washington's bookplate illustrates the cover of BOOKFINDERS' VALUE GUIDE published by Universal Books [Ardmore, Pa. 19003], a 48 page paperback price guide, alphabetical by author; no reference other than the illustration to bookplates.

POSTERS IN MINIATURE With an Introduction by Edward Penfield [R. H. Russell & Sons Publishers, New York, 1896]. To quote the cover: A Collection of Well-Known Posters Together with some Portraits of the Artists. A surprising number of these artists are well-known also in the field of bookplates: E. A. Abbey (portrait), Aubrey Beardsley (self sketch), E. B. Bird (autographed portrait), Will Bradley (autographed portrait), Claude Fayette Bragdon, Walter Crane, George W. Edwards, Phil May (self sketch), Maxfield Parrish, Louis J. Rhead (portrait), Wilbur Macey Stone. The posters, reduced almost to the size of a bookplate, in many instances closely resemble ex libris. The book is a fitting addition to a collection of bookplate literature.

COMMUNIQUE (Claremont Colleges, California), May 14, 1971 - "DENISON EXHIBIT - Bookplate designs offer clues to hidden traits of their owners, the late Louise Seymour Jones said. Mrs. Jones studied thousands of bookplates before she stated her theory in THE HUMAN SIDE OF BOOKPLATES. Denison Library at Scripps is exhibiting selections of bookplates from Mrs. Jones' and other collections. These include books owned by universities and colleges, politicians and historical figures. The work of well-known engravers is also on display." Thanks to Dr. Enrico Molnar for bringing this to our attention.

Childs Gallery, 169 Newbury St. Boston, Mass., issued catalog recently with three bookplate prints - sale prices were:
  #34 - $ 70.00
  #35 - $200.00
  #36 - $ 70.00

34. Theodore Atkinson Bookplate — engraved by Nathaniel Hurd, Boston — circa 1755 — line engraving 3" x 2" cropped to printed border — very good impression, excellent condition. *Allen* 38. Plate still in *The Works of Shakespear* London 1747 Vol. VIII. This fine, engraved cartouche by Hurd has the unique feature of a shell pouring water into an overflowing two-handled basin. Atkinson was Secretary of the Colony of New Hampshire in 1741 and its Chief Justice in 1754.

35. Isaiah Thomas Bookplate — engraved by Paul Revere — circa 1797 — line engraving 3⅜" x 2⅝" plus margins — excellent impression, excellent condition. *Allen* 853 (misattributed). *Brigham* Pl. 53, no. 3. A.P. 47a, illus. This is the second of the two bookplates cut by Revere for Isaiah Thomas, the first being known in only one impression. This print comes directly from one of Thomas' library books.

36. Robert L. Livingston Bookplate — unknown American engraver — circa 1795 — line engraving 3" x 2¼" plus full margins — very good impression, excellent condition. *Allen* 498, *The Curio.* 1887 p. 64.

Robert Hitchman, Seattle, brings to our attention a chapter on bookplates in FIFTY YEARS OF COLLECTING AMERICANA FOR THE LIBRARY OF THE AMERICAN ANTIQUARIAN SOCIETY, 1908-1958, Clarence S. Brigham [Worcester, Mass. 1958]. The collection started with 3400 examples presented to the Antiquarian Society by Rev. Herbert E. Lombard, 1915; additions of other famous collections include those of James Terry, Henry C. Eno, Frank Evans Marshall, John P. Woodbury. Their plates are mounted on separate cards to make them easily accessible for consultation and display. The article states: "A new 'Allen' is much needed by collectors. We have considerable material to aid such a list." Who will accept the invitation?

LITERARY SKETCHES, XI:8, January 1971. Gnome's News notes the Gale Literary Date Book with the ex libris theme illustrated from the collections of the Detroit Public Library and Frederick G. Ruffner. The editor, Mrs. Mary L. Chapman, says in the February 1971 issue: " . .what I meant to tell you about the Gnome is that he's an original with the Antioch Bookplate Company and they have given us permission to use him for our Gnome's News column. If you would like to have Gnome Bookplates, ask your bookseller for Antioch #M-90. And, if you'd like paper bookmarks with the Gnome in color, ask us [Box 711, Williamsburg, Va. 23185]." The bookmarks are charming in muted colors.

B O O K P L A T E S in the NEWS
429 North Daisy Avenue
Pasadena, Calif. 91107

Editor . . . . Audrey Arellanes
Annual   ) $1.00 U. S. A.
Subscription)···· $1.50 Foreign

American Society of BOOKPLATE Collectors and Designers

BOOKPLATES in the NEWS   Number Six   October 1971

Anne Nagel, bookdealer in Albuquerque, New Mexico, writes: "The Rocking A was my grandfather's cattle brand in 1893. It was registered in Stevens County, Texas where he was a pioneer in the Amarillo area. Grandfather W. S. McNabb and his brand were known throughout the panhandle in the early days.

"I was born on the ranch; was an army wife for 25 years; started in the book business after my husband's retirement from the Air Corps; used the Rocking A brand as the name of my company.

"I sell southwestern art books, specializing in autographed and first editions of books on the Southwest Indian. My business is strictly mail order."

Whether brand or bookplate, the Rocking A is a distinctive mark.

The Private Libraries Association [41 Cuckoo Hill Road, Pinner, Middlesex, England] announce their free book for 1971 will be ENGRAVED BOOKPLATES: EUROPEAN EX LIBRIS 1950-1970 by Mark Severin and Anthony Reid. Work is now well underway and copies should be available in the spring of 1972. Membership is $8.50 which includes an excellent quarterly. The ex libris volume will be profusely illustrated - probably 500 plates will be reproduced - and will have notes on all the artists represented.

THE WEST COAST PEDDLER, a tabloid-size antique publication, for August 1, 1971 contains a page article titled "Books and Book-Binding" with 11 illustrations of which six are ex libris for George Washington, Alfred P. Sloan, Jr., Calvin Coolidge, Pierre S. du Pont, Abby and John Rockefeller, Jr., and Walter Crane.

Yale University is offering among its greeting cards with envelope, the Brandenburg Angel bookplate for Hildebrand Brandenburg, woodcut ca. 1470 from the Yale University Library Bookplate Collection. It is in four colors, 4 1/4" x 6 1/2", 12 for $2.75.

BOOKPLATES IN THE NEWS
429 North Daisy Avenue
Pasadena, Calif. 91107

Published Quarterly - January, April, July, October
Audrey Arellanes -   Editor

UNESCO GIFT COUPONS FOR LITERACY

This book belongs to

_____

The purchase of this bookplate has helped a
man, woman or child somewhere in the world to
learn to read and write.

UNESCO Bookplates for Literacy -
ex libris like the one pictured are
available through the UNESCO Gift
Stores, 10 for $1

Beginning with the July 1971 issue
of NEW SERIAL TITLES, published by
the Library of Congress, BOOKPLATES
IN THE NEWS will be listed as a
new periodical.

The University of Rochester Library
has brought to our attention six
items from the FORTNIGHTLY BULLETIN
as follows: "A Collection of Bookplates," vol. 12, No. 9, January 13,
1934. Exhibit from the collection
of the late Miss Maude Motley rich
in examples of work by Edwin Davis
French. Australian ex libris from
collection of Donald B. Gilchrist
also on display.

"Donald Bean Gilchrist,"
vol. 18, No. 1, September 23, 1939. Notice of sudden death of Mr. Gilchrist, who
was Librarian of the Unviersity of Rochester for 20 years. His widow and son David
have given his bookplate collection to the Library; selections from it were displayed
in the Welles-Brown Room.

"Gilchrist Book-Plate
Collection," vol. 18, No. 2, October 7, 1939. Among plates on display is a group
consisting of "labels used by Rochesterians or those made by Rochester artists.
Claude Bragdon, Norman Kent, Elmer Adler, and James Havens are among the artists
represented . ."

"Bookplate Proofs by
Famous Engravers," vol. 19, No. 11, February 11, 1941. On exhibit are E. D. French
plates from the Maude Motley collection; other engravers represented are A. N.
Macdonald, Sidney L. Smith, William F. Hopson, and J. Winfred Spenceley.

"Bookplates from the
Strong Collection," vol. 21, No. 6, November 14, 1942. "Mrs. Strong's collection,
which has been thirty years in the process of formation, is one of the largest collections of ex libris in this country, and contains more than thirty-five thousand
items. . . . The bookplate, admittedly, is one of the smaller arts, but in the
hands of master artists it has achieved a distinction of its own. As a hobby,
bookplate collecting holds an important place; and as a record of artistic trends
and processes, this place is an important one."

"A Gift of Bookplates
by Mrs. Homer Strong," vol. 23, No. 15, January 13, 1945. A gift of 264 bookplates
includes forty-nine by E. D. French, nearly one hundred by A. N. Macdonald, and one
hundred early American plates bearing names of Bushrod Washington, Charles Carroll,
DeWitt Clinton, George Bancroft. The Gilchrist and Motley collections contain more
than six thousand bookplates. All of these articles from the FORTNIGHTLY BULLETIN
bear the initials R. F. M. as author.

Gale Research Company announces October 1, 1971 as the publication date for
BOOKPLATES, the annotated bibliography by Audrey Arellanes [$15, 474 pages].

LOS ANGELES
PUBLIC LIBRARY

The Los Angeles Library Association [630 West Fifth Street, Los Angeles, Ca.90017] will shortly be distributing gratis to their members a booklet authored by Joan West, librarian at Pasadena College, on the bookplates of the Los Angeles Public Library. Ten or twelve bookplates will be reproduced in this 24 page cloth-bound book. Physical production of the book is in the capable hands of Richard Hoffman, California State College, and Bela Blau, noted bookbinder. With the permission of Ernest Siegel, Director of the Los Angeles Public Library, and through the generosity of Glen Dawson, we present a plate designed by distinguished Southern California publisher Ward Ritchie. No copies of the book will be for sale, but you may obtain one as part of membership in the Los Angeles Library Association for $10.

The Yale University GAZETTE for July 1971 lists among books in print one by member Francis W. Allen - BOOKPLATES OF WILLIAM FOWLER HOPSON: A DESCRIPTIVE CHECK LIST. Yale University Library, 1961, 65 pages, $15.

MAYO CLINIC PROCEEDINGS, "Of Bookplates, Books, and Their Owners," Ruth J. Mann. (6) 46:358-60, May 1971. "Plates in which beauty of design is combined with a famous name . . . are sought after by collectors." Illustrated are plates of Oliver Wendell Holmes, Sir Frederick Grant Banting, Frank Sadleir, Andrew Dickson White, Thomas Clifford Allbutt, and Donald Church Balfour.

The Spring 1971 issue of THE PRIVATE LIBRARY has several articles of interest to our membership. - "Thomas Sturge Moore, Wood-Engraver," Malcolm Easton. Second Series (7) 4:1:24-37, Spring 1971. The symbolism is explained of the artist's bookplate for poet W. B. Yeats; also one for Mrs. Yeats. A plate commissioned for their daughter Anne was sketched but probably not completed. A scrap book in the possession of the family contains proofs of Moore's work, "six rice-paper pulls made by Sturge Moore himself" are in color - orange, orange verging on rose, blue-grey, mustard; this is of particular interest as his woodcuts are not usually associated with color. No ex libris are among the illustrations. - "Check-List of Books Illustrated by T. Sturge Moore," David Chambers. (4) 4:1: 38-46, Spring 1971. Seventy-one of Moore's engraved blocks presented by his daughter to St. Bride Printing Library, London. Only specific reference to bookplates is an article "T. Sturge Moore" edited by Cecil French in MODERN WOODCUTTERS No. 3 published by Herbert Furst, 1921. A catalog of the exhibit is available from the University of Hull, Yorkshire, England. - "Gleeson White, ENGLISH ILLUSTRATION: The Sixties 1855-1870." Review by Rigby Graham. 4:1:46-7, Spring 1971. Some of these illustrators were also bookplate artists and Gleeson White wrote extensively in the field. This is a Kingsmead Reprint (£3) of a hard to find and expensive first edition. - "Collecting Yeats and Publishing Lady Gregory," Colin Smythe.

(7) 4:1:4-24, Spring 1971. Brief mention on page 13 of acquiring copy of Maxwell's bibliography of Cuala Press containing Maxwell's own bookplate.

UCLA LIBRARIAN, "Books from Professor O'Malley's Library." 24:26, June 1971. Some 850 volumes from C. D. O'Malley's library have been given to the History and Special Collections Department of the Biomedical Library at UCLA. The collection is marked by a special bookplate.

EVERGREEN REVIEW, "Erotic Bookplates," (23) 91:48-49, July 1971. The 23 stamp-sized illustrations are from "the newly published volume EROTIC BOOKPLATES by Drs. Phyllis and Eberhard Kronhausen, published by Gala Verlag, Hamburg, Germany.

Antiquarian Bookseller, Charles B. Wood III, Inc. [South Woodstock, Conn. 06267] has issued a broadside on American Bookplates - a collection to be sold en bloc - $6,000. Many of the 600 pieces came from two collections formed many years ago - that of R. T. Haines Halsey, long associated with the Metropolitan Museum of Art, and Albert Carlos Bates, formerly librarian of the Connecticut Historical Society. Among the bookplates used to illustrate the announcement are those of Gardiner Chandler, Isaiah Thomas. William P. Smith, Henry Dawkins, Benjamin Greene, William Wetmore, Jeremiah Hull, Joseph Winship, Anita B. Clemens, Harold May Elwood, Lucy Anne Kirk, Elbert Hubbard.

During the month of August, the Pasadena Public Library had an exhibit, The Evolution of a Bookplate - from Idea to Print. On display were steel die engravings made by Anthony F. Kroll and bookplates from the collection of Audrey Arellanes featuring the work of Cleora Wheeler, Dorothy S. Payne, Carl Oscar Borg, and a Bookplate Zoo. A sampling of periodical literature in the field of the ex libris filled one case.

It is with sadness that we report the death of Christine Price on August 17, 1971. Miss Price was born in Rutherford, New Jersey; attended Simmons College where she took library training; and spent the major portion of her professional career as custodian of the Rare Book Department at the Unviersity of California at Berkeley. Over the years she was not only instrumental in keeping the California Book-Plate Society alive, but has long been a member of ASBC&D, has authored a number of articles on bookplates. Probably her crowning achievement is the CATALOGUE OF THE ROYAL BOOKPLATES of Louise Winterburn. Her own collection of bookplates and the accompanying literature have found a home at the San Diego College for Women, and her files from the California Book-Plate Society are to be given to the University of California at Berkeley as another segment of the California story.

INTERNATIONAL COLLEGE OF SURGEONS, July 1971, "Bookplates, Attractive and Useful," tells of Roy Jansen's collection on exhibit in the manuscript library of the Museum of Surgical Science and Hall of Fame in Chicago. Particular note is made of ex libris used by celebrities such as Hal Foster whose plate features the smiling figure of his creation, Prince Valiant; David K. E. Bruce, negotiator at the Paris Peace talks; writer Erle Stanley Gardner; Olympics mentor Avery Brundage. Currently Roy Jansen is concentrating on acquiring bookplates from foreign countries including Seoul, Singapore, Tehran and Shanghai.

A collection of over 600 German bookplates of the 15th to 18th centuries, including the first German plate and a number of Durers, about 75% of which are Warnecke checklist numbers, is being offered by C. A. Stonehill, Inc., 282 York Street, New Haven, Conn. 06511. For additional details and a checklist, write directly to Robert J. Barry at the above firm.

UNIVERSITY OF SOUTHERN CALIFORNIA

NORRIS MEDICAL LIBRARY

SALERNI COLLEGIUM

FAR WESTERN MEDICAL COLLECTION

Named after the sole private donors, the Eileen and Kenneth T. Norris Medical Library serves primarily the faculty and students of the University of Southern California School of Medicine. Mr. Norris, chairman of Thermador Corp., is a Trustee of USC and Occidental College.

The Norris Medical Library houses a collection of approximately 80,000 volumes emphasizing medical and related subjects. Among its collections is the Salerni Collegium History of Medicine Library established and maintained through donations of the School of Medicine support group.

The Far Western Medical Collection, part of the History of Medicine Library, has a special bookplate which was commissioned by Dr. Alden H. Miller, a physician interested in Western art and the history of far Western medicine.

Artist Ken Mansker made a pen and ink sketch which was then engraved by Anthony F. Kroll. Mansker, an Indian from the Flathead area of Montana, has particular empathy for the Medicine Man, who is a spiritual leader perhaps more akin to the White Man's minister than a doctor. When an Indian feels the "call", he meditates, fasts and undergoes various ordeals before becoming a Medicine Man. He selects a symbol or totem. The Medicine Man in the bookplate has the buffalo skull as his totem; below the skull is a shield, and a horn which may be used to blow herbs down a patient's throat; next is a fan of an eagle's wing, both white and dark. Opposite the buffalo skull is his warrior's shield, a horn spoon and a block of wood on which is cut the ceremonial "tobacco". The medicine pipe is always held in the left hand, nearest the heart.

From the Periodical Literature -

WESTWAYS, 64:55, January 1972, briefly mentions the Los Angeles Library Association keepsake, THE BOOKPLATES OF THE LOS ANGELES PUBLIC LIBRARY.

YANKEE, "I'd rather believe in inspiration . ." Wade Van Dore. (5) 116-9, 204, 207, November 1971. The author of this article was befriended by the poet Robert Frost; in addition to revealing first person insight about Frost, he tells of a "Christmas card" house which in the 1920s artist J. J. Lankes pictured in the snow. Later it was printed as a bookplate. Van Dore says, "A packet of these had been lying around for a number of years, and one day when Frost murmured that Lankes might get mad if he didn't use them, I volunteered to do the job." Thanks are due Mrs. Anna Marie Hager for bringing this article to your attention; among the illustrations are the original Lankes design as well as the bookplate print.

AUCTION, "Tauromaquia: The Bullfight Library of Lester and Edythe Ziffren," Jerry E. Patterson. (5) 5:41-3, October 1971. Among the illustrations Lester Ziffren is pictured surrounded by mementoes of his years in Spain and South America; the arms of Sir William Stirling-Maxwell are shown emblazoned on a rich calf binding; Ziffren's own simple bookplate depicts a bull pierced with three banderillos.

COLORADO COLLEGE MAGAZINE, Colorado Springs, Colorado 80903, vol. 6, #4, 1971. A brief paragraph tells of two new coordinated bookplates in white and gold which will acknowledge donors in one case and donors and designees of memorial books in the other; these bookplates were adopted for the Charles Leaming Tutt Library by Dr. George V. Fagan, librarian. The plates bear the College seal, the name of the library, and an inscription from John Milton: "A good book is a precious life blood of a master spirit, embalmed and treasured up on purpose to a life beyond life."

NORTHWESTERN UNIVERSITY BULLETIN, "Peter Christian Lutkin Memorial Library." (1) 33:17-8, May 1, 1933. Pictured is the bookplate to be used for the Memorial Library, the nucleus of which consists of the former private library of Peter Christian Lutkin, Dean of the School of Music, strong in literary and choral works.

* * * * * *

It is with sadness that we report the death of Dr. J. Herman Schauinger on September 26, 1971. His widow writes that their daughter, an art-history graduate student, intends doing an Independent Study Project on some phase of bookplate collecting during her next quarter at the university. Hopefully we will soon have a new young member to welcome to the Society.

From the Catalogues -
Dawsons of Pall Mall (Cannon House, Folkestone, Kent, England), Catalogue No. 7-#11 Allen, AMERICAN BOOK-PLATES £10. #165 Dixson, CONCERNING BOOK-PLATES £8. #238 Hall, BOOK PLATES BY FREDERICK GARRISON HALL £6. #241 Hamilton, FRENCH BOOK-PLATES £8. #512 Slater, BOOK PLATES AND THEIR VALUE £8.
Plandome Book Auctions (113 Glen Head Road, Glen Head, N.Y.) sale on Jan. 13, 1972 - #42 THE DOLPHIN, Fall 1940, Winter 1941, Spring 1941 (there are three bookplate articles in this periodical).
American Library Service (New York City) - DATED BOOK-PLATES, Hamilton, in three parts, 1895, uncut for rebinding, $29.50.

MARION
HOLLAND
Her Book

Marion Holland, born in the old French Hospital in Los Angeles, was in the first freshman class at St. Agnes Central High School. Graduated from the University of Southern California with a degree in Education, certificated in Social Welfare, Group and Recreation Work, she married Elwood W. Holland, a civil engineer, also graduated from USC, whose special interest is Western history. Mrs. Holland's book collecting goes hand-in-hand with her hobbies which are miniature books, crewel embroidery, flower arranging, gardening, and cooking (she says, "I particularly like collecting cookbooks published by women's clubs and church groups."). Her bookplate was designed by Tyrus Wong and engraved by Anthony F. Kroll. It was printed in her favorite color - blue.

ATTENTION MEMBERS - Individuals or Institutions: We would welcome bookplate prints to be tipped-in future issues of the quarterly newsletter. Two hundred prints are needed together with a few details about the artist, the owner, and the design.

A Review of the Classics of Bookplate Literature. Each quarterly will contain a different classic, in a generally chronological sequence. Our reviewer is Francis W. Allen, Physical Sciences Librarian at Western Michigan University, Kalamazoo. He is the author of BOOKPLATES, A Selection from the Works of Charles R. Capon and BOOKPLATES OF WILLIAM FOWLER HOPSON: A Descriptive Check List.

A GUIDE TO THE STUDY OF BOOK-PLATES (ex-libris), Warren, John Byrne Leicester (Lord de Tabley, 3rd Baron, 1835-1895). London, The Bodley Head, 1900, 2nd edition (first published in 1880).

Warren is without doubt the "Old Testament" for English speaking collectors of ex libris as perhaps is Leiningen zu Westerburg for our German speaking brethen.

The first real analyst of types of bookplates, Warren is more than that - he is a master of the English language and a pleasure to read in this latter day of ignoring basic rules of grammar.

The GUIDE outlines the types of English ex libris and establishes a pattern for classification for collectors. Most early English bookplates were, of course, armorial in nature. Warren divides these between Jacobean and Chippendale according to their style of mantling. In addition he devotes separate chapters to allegoric types, landscapes, mottoes and plates of purely historic interest. He deals also with those he calls "foreign", in this context meaning continental European plates.

From the twentieth century and more ecumenical point of view,

Warren is perhaps old fashioned. But still he furnishes a point of departure, and as such should be read by all devotees of the art as a "taking off place" as well as for purely historical interest.

* * * * * *

Thanks to the generosity of one of your fellow members, Christmas greetings were sent in the name of the Society by the Brandenburg Angel bookplate card. The Society's name was handset in Caslon type and printed on the Yale University Library's 1830 Albion handpress by Dale Roylance, Curator of their Collection of Printing and the Arts of the Book.

The Private Libraries Association (41 Cuckoo Hill Road, Pinner, Middlesex, England) announces for Spring 1972 publication - ENGRAVED BOOKPLATES: European Ex Libris 1950-1970, by Mark Severin and Anthony Reid, 160 pages, quarto, cloth boards with reproductions of 500 of "the finest plates by contemporary European engravers." This is a free presentation volume for PLA members for 1971; copies are available to non-members at £5 or $12.50. A special edition in quarter morocco with twelve extra plates by some of the principal European engravers mounted at the back will cost $37.50.

Mrs. J. G. Edison (133 Dunvegan Road, Toronto 7, Canada) is preparing a book on the graphic work of Thoreau MacDonald, who has designed over forty bookplates, some of which have been shown in the exhibits of the Bookplate Association International of Los Angeles. Mrs. Edison would appreciate information by Xerox from collectors who have catalogues listing Thoreau MacDonald and copies of bookplate designs by this Canadian artist.

Member Clare Ryan Talbot is known to us primarily for bookplates, but to the world of antiques, she is known as the Books Editor of SILVER (Box 1208, Vancouver, Washington), now in its fifth year of publication. Of interest to bookplate collectors would be the review for Martha Gandy Fales' EARLY AMERICAN SILVER which appeared in the issue for November, 1970. Clare writes that while she was preparing the review a welcome fact emerged in the lively text - the relationship of bookplates to silver; this relationship has long been known to devotees of Charles Dexter Allen and is explored further in the Fales volume with thirty-six entires under the Hurds, father and son, and even the endpapers for the book contain a quasi-bookplate reference. Clare would welcome hearing from members about their bookplate-silver adventures.

Mrs. Ione Wiechel, of Sandusky, Ohio, frequently gives bookplate lectures which are illustrated by color slides from her own collection. The bookplates are mounted on cards with explanatory material and then photographed and prepared as slides. A few colonial bookplates introduce the subject, followed by plates of some of Sandusky's pioneer citizens. As Sandusky is part of the Connecticut Western Reserve, the bookplate of Ebenezer Lane, used while he was a student at Harvard, provided an interesting transition. Another early Sandusky ex libris has the same type border as the 1812 plate for the Library of Congress. The story was brought to the present with bookplates of local personages and a few plates of national importance. In addition to local organizations, Mrs. Wiechel has spoken before the Collectors Society of Cleveland and the Western Reserve Historical Society.

BOOKPLATES IN THE NEWS   Published Quarterly - January,
429 North Daisy Avenue   April, July, October
Pasadena, Calif. 91107   Audrey Arellanes   -   Editor

American Society of BOOKPLATE Collectors and Designers

CARL STEPHEN JUNGE - A Tribute

It is with sadness we report that Carl Stephen Junge died on January 17, 1972 at the age of 91. Carl Junge will be fondly remembered and greatly missed by his many friends. The Society is greatly privileged to have a letterhead and symbol designed by this exceptional artist in 1970; the design is also used as the masthead for our newsletter and the YEAR BOOK.

Some of the details which follow are from a tribute which appeared in OAK LEAVES, January 26, 1972, written by his friend Mrs. W. R. Mahoney.

Carl Junge was born June 5, 1880 in Stockton, California, the son of Conrad and Mary Junge. He completed a course at Hopkins Art Institute of California before he was 17; he went to work for the San Francisco EXAMINER in 1897 and later headed the art department of the Out West Co. in Los Angeles. His art education was continued at the Julien Academy in Paris and the London School of Art.

Active in both fine and commercial art, he designed type faces, illustrated books, drew maps and cartoons, painted in oil and watercolor, was expert in pen and ink, and was noted for his beautiful lettering. Junge received international fame for his bookplates, winning five awards from the American Bookplate Society (1916, 1917, 1921, 1922, 1925), and two from the Book Plate Association International. He was the author of BOOKPLATES (1916) and EX LIBRIS (1935).

On February 25, 1908, Carl Junge married Fannie J. Corbett. A veteran of World War I, he served in the 472nd Engineers. He was an expert golfer and swimmer; loved gardening and travel; collected books, bookplates and autographs. He had a keen sense of humor, a quick wit, and was a delightful companion and correspondent. He lived in Oak Park, Illinois, more than 60 years. He taught printing at the Senior Citizens Center at Mills House and was active and working until last Thanksgiving when a heart attack began his first and final illness. He was a truly happy man, who enjoyed life, work, family and friends.

GRAPHIC ARTIST, Robert Corey

The new bookplate for the San
Fernando Valley State College
was designed by Robert Corey
and introduced to the public in
an exhibit of ex libris during
the month of February in the library. It depicts an Indian
rock painting from the China Lake
area of California; it will be
used for gift books and other
materials housed in Special Collections.

Robert Corey has operated his own
graphic communications business,
BOB COREY ADVERTISING DESIGN, for
the past nine years. He has gained international awards and recognition in the advertising field.

Although born and raised in Los
Angeles, he obtained his degree
from the Art Institute of Chicago.
Bob's interests are varied and include travel, archeology, photography, fine
art, bow hunting, fishing, mineralogy and river running. His extensive trav-
els have taken him to such remote and diverse areas as the headwaters of the
Amazon River, the Andes in Peru, the jungles of middle America, and into
North Africa to film the Berbers.

Norman E. Tanis, Director and College Librarian at San Fernando Valley State
College, furnished the information here quoted about his Corey designed bookplate:

My bookplate consists of a rep-
presentation of the desert big
horn sheep. The design is inspired by a very similar drawing painted on rock in the
China Lake district by California Indians several hundred
years ago. It symbolizes for
me tenacity and persistence in
in the face of adversity.

The representation done by Bob
Corey has an amusing but unre-
lated similarity to Picasso's
famous goat. I attribute this
to the fact that Picasso draws
much of his inspiration from
aboriginal abstract art.

The bookplate will be used in a
special collection of books and

23

pamphlets which either belonged to or are associated with the famous American publisher, Emanuel Haldeman-Julius. The Norman Tanis bookplate is reproduced on the inside back cover of the Library's 1970/71 annual report.

A Review of the Classics of Bookplate Literature, by Francis W. Allen, Physical Sciences Librarian at Western Michigan University, Kalamazoo.

BOOK-PLATES, W. J. Hardy. London: Kegan Paul, 1897, 2nd edition. (First edition published in 1893 as volume II of BOOKS ABOUT BOOKS.)

Hardy is one of the most popular of the late nineteenth century works on ex libris now known to us as classics in the field. Somewhat lighter in style than Warren, Hardy does an adequate piece of work on English, German and American plates, with appropriate acknowledgment to Egerton Castle and Charles Dexter Allen (the standard Leiningun zu Westerburg had not yet appeared). His treatment of French plates is sketchy, and he barely mentions the ex libris of other European countries.

The introductory chapter is largely an apologia, both for the use of bookplates and for the avocation of collecting them. It is very well written and is quoted extensively in more modern and lesser known literature. Following this is a history of the use of bookplates in England and a chapter on styles, wherein he follows, generally, the Warren classification. The chapters on allegory, "picture" plates, inscriptions condemning book stealing, and on personal particulars appearing on bookplates are among the most interesting.

Other sections include one on ladies' plates, acknowledgely superseded by Miss Labouchere's LADIES BOOK-PLATES, a brief discussion of some of the more prominent engravers of English plates, and a chapter called "Odds and Ends," a delightful mishmash of miscellaneous information.

Hardy is by no stretch of the imagination a scholarly treatise. It is, however, a reasonably well written introduction to our field and should be read, if not owned, by all serious collectors.

ARTISTS AND ENGRAVERS OF BRITISH AND AMERICAN BOOK PLATES, A book of reference for book plate and print collectors, Henry W. Fincham. New York: Dodd, Mead, 1897.

Fincham is a standard reference work in the field indicated in the title. Its chief value today is in its illustrations, which are many and superb.

It is an alphabetical arrangement, by artist, owners listed alphabetically under artist. The second column identifies the signature of the artist, the third the style of the plate. The fourth column attempts to assign a date for each plate and is woefully full of errors and inadequacies (see my "Notes on the Bookplates of Amos Doolittle," in OLD TIME NEW ENGLAND, vol. 29, No. 2, October 1948, pages 38-44). A complete index by owner adequately cross references the main body of the work.

Fincham's main fault is in its inaccurate fourth column. Otherwise it is a most useful tool for collectors, especially for its myriad illustrations and should rank along with the Franks Catalogue (to be reviewed later) in the modern collectors' reference library.

*   *   *   *   *   *   *   *   *   *   *

Elmer J. Porter recently presented a bookplate lecture illustrated with slides from his collection to the local chapter of the D.A.R. in Terre Haute, Indiana.

The Nippon Ex Libris Association, Yuge P.O., Okayamaken, Japan, issues each year a calendar with each month printed on a separate sheet and a bookplate tipped-in. Many of the artists are well known print makers. $2 in cash.

EX LIBRIS

THE

THEODORE

PAYNE

FOUNDATION

THEODORE PAYNE FOUNDATION

The Theodore Payne Foundation, formed in 1960, was named in honor of Theodore Payne, who devoted most of his life to the native flora of California. He was born in England in 1872 and showed an early interest in botany. Following an apprenticeship of three years in a nursery business, he sailed to the United States and arrived in California in his twenty-first year. Madame Modjeska, the famous Polish actress, hired him as a gardener for her estate in Santiago Canyon, Orange County, where he first became interested in California native plants. After two and a half years at the Modjeska ranch, he was employed by the Germain Seed Company; he left them in 1903 to enter the nursery business for himself. In June of 1961, he retired at the age of 90.

On January 28, 1961 the County of of Los Angeles honored Theodore Payne by the dedication of 320 acres near Llano on the Mojave Desert as a wild flower sanctuary.

The Theodore Payne Foundation, 10459 Tuxford Street, Sun Valley, California, is carrying on his work by making available to the public native trees, shrubs and plants not generally found through commercial sources. In addition to the 22 acre garden site maintained by the Foundation, it sponsors a free lecture series at the Los Angeles State and County Arboretum in Arcadia and Descanso Gardens in La Canada. (Thanks are due Mrs. Marion Holland and Anthony F. Kroll for making this bookplate print available.)

14th INTERNATIONAL EX LIBRIS CONGRESS

The 14th International Ex Libris Congress is to be held in Elsinore, Denmark from August 24 through 27, 1972. Enclosed with the current newsletter is a reproduction of the postal invitation issued by the Dansk Exlibris Selskab which details the activities to be celebrated at the Marinelyst Badehotel. The delegates meet the morning of August 24, general registration is in the afternoon, with the official welcome at 4:30 and dinner at 6:30. The following day the bookplate exhibit will open and prizes will be distributed. After lunch an excursion by ship to Sweden is planned. Dinner that evening will be followed by a lecture. On Saturday the Congress will visit Kronborg Castle and drive through Helsingor. The Gala-Dinner will be Saturday evening. After lunch on Sunday, the group leaves Marienlyst for Copenhagen and a farewell drink at the Tivoli Gardens. - Several of our artist members have sent prints of their work for the exhibit. - A report on the Congress will appear in the fall issue of BOOKPLATES IN THE NEWS.

From the Periodical Literature:

AMERICAN ARTIST, "Thoreau MacDonald, Canadian Illustrator," Norman Kent.
(2) 10:22-5, January 1946. MacDonald's career as an artist started in
1922 "when three of his linoleum cuts appeared in the February issue of
the CANADIAN FORUM." (Hal Wright of Toronto is to be thanked for bringing
this article to the attention of Mrs. J. G. Edison in response to her request for additional data on the artist; she is still seeking a print of
the H. W. Hardy bookplate listed in the Bookplate International exhibit
of 1933. - The author of the above article, Norman Howe Kent, died January 27, 1972, at the age of 68 in Mamaroneck, New York. ANTIQUARIAN BOOK-
MAN, 49:584, February 21, 1972 indicates this artist and teacher "had retired last year as editor of AMERICAN ARTIST, and was completing his many
books on art and watercolor techniques.")

University of Rochester LIBRARY BULLETIN, "George Eastman: A Bibliographical Essay of Selected References," Karl S. Kabelac. (1) 27:33-8, Winter
1971-72. The illustration is the bookplate of George Eastman; it measures
5" x 6½" and pictures one side of his library with books, a large mirror, logs
burning in the fireplace, and he sits in a wing chair reading. (Thanks
to Robert L. Volz, Head of the Department of Rare Books, Manuscripts and
Archives of the University of Rochester Library and editor of the LIBRARY
BULLETIN. It is hoped other librarians and editors will follow his lead
and send material for inclusion in the newsletter. This article is a fine
example of the dividends collected by the bookplate enthusiast who reads
and learns about people, places, and things he might not encounter were it
not for the connection, however slim, with bookplates.)

The Cleveland Public Library has mounted a bookplate exhibit in honor of
the International Book Year 1972, and issued a leaflet "The Bookplate, An
Historical Review," which contains a brief history of the ex libris and
suggested reading limited to bookplate literature on its shelves with
the Dewey decimal number for ease in finding them. The illustrations include the Paul Revere plate for David Greene, Bennett A. Cerf, and one
bearing a thumb print. (Dean H. Keller, Curator of Special Collections,
Kent State University Library, sent the brochure to your editor.)

SATURDAY NIGHT, "Bookplate Exhibition," Maxwell Hamilton Noll, June 13,
1936. Annual exhibit of bookplates designed during the preceding year
sponsored by the Bookplate Association International held in the art gallery
of the Los Angeles Museum in Exposition Park. - The same page contained
Mr. Noll's ad as a "Bookplate Designer - Heraldic Specialist, Hand-Letterer,
Illuminator." (Mrs. Anna Marie Hager discovered this article.)

THE AUGUSTAN, "The Augustan Society Exhibit," Joseph A. Lubecki. 13:187-
90, May-June 1970. During the month of March 1968, the Public Library,
History and Travel Department, Chicago, had an exhibit featuring Heraldry
and Orders of Knighthood. The Rev. James Parker displayed representative
examples from his collection of heraldic bookplates from the United States,
Great Britain and Poland.

THE AUGUSTAN, "Reviews," 14:169-70, July-August 1971. The JOURNAL OF THE
EX LIBRIS SOCIETY reprinted by the Greenwood Press ($595.00) is reviewed
by the Rev. James Parker, who says: "the evidence in these reprints shows
it to have been a wholly undeserved demise."

LIBRARY OF CONGRESS INFORMATION BULLETIN, "Bookplates Displayed in E&G," 31:77, February 25, 1972. The Exchange and Gift Division exhibited the bookplates used by LC and other Federal libraries as well as a few plates belonging to the Staff. Reference is made to a notice in the FEDERAL LIBRARY COMMITTEE NEWSLETTER (August-September 1971) requesting copies of bookplates from all Federal libraries; since many such libraries are now using "simpler methods of affixing marks of ownership and the Library considers it important to collect for historical and preservation purposes samples of these bookplates while they may still be available. One copy of each bookplate has been sent to the Library's Prints and Photographs Division for its collections." (Sent in by E. A. Thompson, an enthusiastic non-member from Santa Barbara.)

Lester Ziffren writes that while he was stationed in Chile in the late 1950's his bookplate was designed by British artist, Peter Sinclair. (The print for reproduction arrived too late to be included with the periodical reference to AUCTION in our last newsletter.)

To quote the NEW YORK TIMES, February 2, 1972: "Rockwell Kent's personal collection of 3,300 of his working drawings and sketches has been given to Columbia University. An exhibition of 100 works from the Collection of Mr. Kent, who died last March at the age of 88, will be on exhibit for six weeks. Included are sketches for furniture, alphabets, postage stamps, posters, calendars, silverware, menus and bookplates for prominent persons."

LOS ANGELES HERALD-EXAMINER, "The Gossip Column," Robin Adams Sloan, February 6, 1972, had a question and answer on the Los Angeles Public Library which said in part: "During the Los Angeles Public Library's centennial celebration, the original bookplates from the first 750 volumes will be displayed in the Central Library, 630 West Fifth Street."

FOREBEARS, An International Journal of Things Historical, Heraldic & Genealogical (formerly THE AUGUSTAN) is the new quarterly publication of the Augustan Society, which was founded in 1957. Now celebrating its 15th anniversary, the Augustan Society has grown from 34 members to over 500 and has a notable record of publication during the period that includes newsletters, bulletins, journals and four occasional publications, two of which were books. The new format of FOREBEARS includes a section on ex libris which will be conducted by the Rev. James Parker, F.A.S. - "Ex Libris - Introduction to Bookplates," James Parker. (2) 15:26-7, Winter 1972. This initial article contains brief reviews of Charles Dexter Allen's AMERICAN BOOK-PLATES, BOOKPLATES FOR LIBRARIES by Edward H. Shickell, the Greenwood reprint of the JOURNAL OF THE EX LIBRIS SOCIETY, and the Arellanes bibliography, BOOKPLATES, published by Gale Research. Two heraldic bookplates are detailed listing the Authority, arms, motto, the artist and printer, and paper and ink used. An unusual feature has the two ex libris printed on the page and additionally a loose print of each is furnished for the collector to mount as he wishes, a welcome dividend! FOREBEARS (18002 Faysmith Avenue,

Torrance, California 90504, annual subscription $7) and the Rev. Parker's ex libris department are a welcome note in the bookplate field.

GREENWICH VILLAGE, "The Book-Plate of 5153." (1) 2:25, June 23, 1915. See entry for BRUNO'S WEEKLY, March 26, 1916.

GREENWICH VILLAGE, "Troubadours and Book-Plates," Guido Bruno. (4) 2:67-71, July 15, 1915. "The man who finds something which others overlook, the man who appreciates what otherswith less receptive minds for beauty discard, loves to show it to the world, to link his name with it, and label it with his own individuality so that he may point it out as a part of him . ." In Bruno's tale a prince claimed the troubadour as his property and presented the poet with a golden chain bearing his portrait embossed in gold. "And wasn't this gold chain, placed upon the neck of the ancient troubadour, the fore-runner of the book plate of days to come?" Three of the illustrations are bookplates, two by Clara Tice and one courtesy of Winward Prescott.

BRUNO'S WEEKLY, "Book-Plate Auction," 2:357, January 8, 1916. The Collectors' Club was the site of the auction of the bookplate collection of a "well-known resident of Greenwich Village, Mr. Henry Blackwell," who was writing a book on American Book-Plates Previous to the War of Secession.

BRUNO'S WEEKLY, "Bookplates of John E. and Samuel Pepys," 2:418, January 29, 1916. "Howard C. Levis' new work" has chapters on Evelyn's own etchings on the bookplates.

BRUNO'S WEEKLY, "Book-Plate Notes," (1) 2:544-5, March 11, 1916. The bookplate reproduced was drawn by and for Adelaide Helen Page in April 1898 when she was 5½ years old. It was accepted by the Museum of Fine Arts in Boston. American Art Association is to conduct a public auction of Dr. Eno's collection; Coulton Waugh will arrange an ex libris exhibit "in the near future." "Book-plates are not an ornament. Just a visible sign of proprietorship."

BRUNO'S WEEKLY, "Book-Plate Notes," (1) 2:580, March 25, 1916. Pictured is a unique plate designed and printed in a prison by a prisoner for a prisoner to be used in books on penology.

All of the items from GREENWICH VILLAGE and BRUNO'S WEEKLY, both published by Guido Bruno, were provided by Richard Schimmelpfeng, Director of Special Collections, University of Connecticut Library.

An article on "Guido Bruno's Greenwich Village Magazine," appeared in the SADAKICHI HARTMANN NEWSLETTER, 2:1-2, Winter 1971, published by the University of California at Riverside. Bruno's various ventures into publishing are referred to by Frederick J. Hoffman in his THE LITTLE MAGAZINES: A History and A Bibliography, published by Princeton in 1946.

HARRISBURG SUNDAY PATRIOT-NEWS, February 6, 1972, "Ex Libris Around the World, Foreign Book Plates Are on Exhibit," M. W. Milliron. Harrisburg's Roy Jansen has compiled a gallery of bookplates from almost fifty countries and has them on display at the State Library. The bookplates illustrating the article are from Japan, State Library of East Germany, Queen's University of Belfast, Tel Aviv University, Welding Library of University of Cape Town.

CARL HAVERLIN - Another Robert Corey design is the bookplate for Carl Haverlin, who for twenty years was the president of Broadcast Music, Inc. He describes his road runner bookplate:

CARL HAVERLIN

"Anyone born in Arizona and reared in Southwestern and Mexican mining camps remembers the road runner with affection and respect. Like all desert children, I feared rattlesnakes and actually believed the audacious little birds killed sidewinders for my personal protection. For these reasons I welcomed Bob Corey's road runner bookplate which he adapted from an ornament on an Acoma Pueblo pot. I find its simplicity and desert colors especially appealing. I am grateful, too, that Corey avoided using my suggestions to curve the name, enclose the design or otherwise gussie it up. The road runner will be used in the books of my general library. For my Lincoln collection I have asked Mr. Corey to design another plate to be printed from an original woodblock of the President's portrait which I own. It has not been reproduced since its appearance in the assassination issue of the Washington CHRONICLE on April 20-22, 1865."

From the Catalogs:

Jeff Dykes/Western Books, Box 38, College Park, Maryland 20740. No. 18, Winter 1972, $2. Devoted to Charles M. Russell, it is illustrated by the bookplate of Frederick G. Renner, "the greatest Russell scholar and buff of them all." The bookplate featuring 'The Trail Boss' is present in the hard cover duplicates in the catalog (it is also one of the illustrations in the Arellanes bibliography). Item #7 is the Charles M. Russell Library, catalog No. 152 of Dawson's Book Shop, Los Angeles, February 1941, which reproduced the so-called Russell Bookplate fashioned by Dawson to identify the books of the Russell library, $10.

Heraldry Today, 10 Beauchamp Pl., London SW3. #1406, Hardy, BOOK-PLATES, 1893, £2.50, #1550, Eve, DEOCRATIVE HERALDRY, 1908, £4. and many more.

Dawson's Bookshop, 535 N. Larchmont, Los Angeles, Ca. Catalog #407, 1972. Item #296, a file of 20 issues of ASBC&D YEAR BOOK, $150, #297, Arellanes bibliography, $15.

There isn't space this issue for all the bookplate items in catalogs. If you are especially interested in purchasing, let me know and I will send you a list of booksellers and titles.

BOOKPLATES IN THE NEWS
429 North Daisy Avenue
Pasadena, Calif. 91107

Published Quarterly - January, April
July, October - $3 U.S./$4 Foreign
Editor - - Audrey Spencer Arellanes

ROBERT W. BREWER

Robert W. Brewer of Pasadena, California, writes: "I made this bookplate quite a few years ago while working as a steel and copper plate engraver. I am a member of a camera club, The Pack Rats, of which I was one of the founders in 1930. This is a club specializing in desert photography. Most of the members, like myself, are now retired. I chose this design because at that time I spent a great deal of time exploring desert regions which were not built up as they are now."

Born in the rural area of LaPorte, Texas, Robert Brewer came to Pasadena at the age of six. While working as a letter carrier and engraver, he continued his art studies at Pasadena City College. A member of the Mid-Valley Arts League and the Artists of the Southwest, presently he is doing oil painting and sculpture.

KATHARINE OLIVER STANLEY-BROWN

On April 15, 1972, Mrs. Katharine Oliver Stanley-Brown died in Boston; she was 79. A native of Philadelphia, she graduated from Vassar in 1915. She wrote for literary magazines and taught music in New York before marrying architect Rudolph Stanley-Brown, the only grandson of President James A. Garfield, in 1922.

Mrs. Stanley-Brown was the author of more than 200 articles and five books, the last of which, CARP AMONG MINNOWS, was published in 1962. She was a member of the Cosmos Club, The American Society of Bookplate Collectors and Designers, American Society of Architectural Historians, Thornton Society of Washington, and Artists Association of Nantucket. The ASBC&D YEAR BOOK for 1957 contained an article on Rudolph Stanley-Brown and his bookplate designs.

She is survived by a son, daughter and seven grandchildren. Her many friends in the Society will miss her.

The Classics Revisted and reviewed by Francis W. Allen, Physical Sciences Librarian at Western Michigan University, Kalamazoo.

AMERICAN BOOK-PLATES, A Guide to Study with Examples, Charles Dexter Allen, with a bibliography by Eben Newell Hewins. New York: Macmillan, 1894.

Allen (no relation to the reviewer) is the standard bible of collectors on the western side of the Atlantic Ocean and should probably need no review. However, he certainly must be included in any survey of the older literature. "Allen No. _" is now and always has been a standard description of American plates, as has "not in Allen."

His lists, primarily the numbered list of early American bookplates, the chronological list of dated plates, the alphabetical list of signed plates, and the list of mottoes are invaluable to all collectors of American plates. Often disregarded is the bibliography by Mr. Hewins, the most important forerunner of the 1926 Fuller bibliography (hopefully to be updated by this reviewer within the next two years).

Allen should be the primary reference tool of all American collectors, after Franks.

ENGLISH BOOK-PLATES, Ancient and Modern, Egerton Castle. London: George Bell, 1893. (First edition December 1892. New and enlarged edition, November 1893.)

One of the familiar green cloth, gold stamped entires in the Ex-libris Bell series, Castle is the standard reference on English bookplates. His arrangement and description are traditional by style. He lists English plates as follows: Early Armorial: Tudoresque, Carolian, Restoration; Eighteenth Century: Queen Anne-Jacobean, Middle Georgian - Chippendale or Rococco, Later Georgian - Festoon; Pictorial: Literary, Portrait, Allegoric, Landscape; Modern plates: Modern armorial - die sinker, Seals, Printers' marks, Heraldic - allegoric, Heraldic - symbolic, Pictorial non-heraldic.

Perhaps the most interesting section of Castle is his last chapter - on the choice of a bookplate and bookplate collecting. This is the work of a scholar, well and humorously written. I recommend it highly to all collectors.

Reviews of Current Literature

ILLUSTRATED ESSAYS ON JEWISH BOOKPLATES, Philip Goodman. New York: Ktav Publishing House, 1971.

Favorable reviews appeared in JEWISH NEWS, Detroit, January 28, 1972 -- NEWS AND VIEWS for March-April 1972 which is published by the Federation of Jewish Philanthropies. Reviewer Charles Angoff says: "There are many other fascinating pages, plus an annotated bibliography of bookplate literature and a generous number of first-rate illustrations, all adding up to a unique, valuable, and charming book." -- JEWISH BOOKLAND, February 1972. Reviewer Alfred Werner says: "The scholarly text is filled to the margins with fascinating bits of information."

BOOKPLATES: A Selective Annotated Bibliography of the Periodical Literature, Audrey Spencer Arellanes. Detroit: Gale Research Company, 1971.

Reviews appeared in AMERICAN BOOK COLLECTOR, March-April 1972; LIBRARY JOURNAL, June 15, 1972; MINIATURE BOOK NEWS, March 1972; LIBRARY BULLETIN, March 1972.

AMERICAN ARTIST for May contained a delightful review by Fridolf Johnson in which he said: "Mrs. Arellanes obviously pursued her quarry with love, enthusiasm, and wit. Browsing through her annotations is a delight; they are replete with fascinating bits of bookplate lore, apt quotations and intimate sidelights on graphic designers and bookplate owners."

RADBILL PLATE BY BLAKE

EX LIBRIS

FRANCES·RADBILL

Dr. Samuel X. Radbill writes as follows about Sara E. Blake, the artist who did the original dry point engraving of the Frances Radbill ex libris:

"I am not at liberty to tell you the year that Miss Blake was born, but I can tell you that she is sprightly, with undimmed wit and friendly spirit. A native of Boston, she was Librarian at Tuft's Medical and Dental College for many years. Her bookplates were created during her spare time as a hobby. She exhibited in 1949 at the Printmaker's Club in such company as Rockwell Kent and Thomas Nason; her work has also been exhibited at the University of Rochester and Western Reserve as well as in Milan, Italy, and Amsterdam, Holland.

Among the rarest of collector's items is the first GARLAND OF BOOK-PLATES. This contains a group of early plates by Sara Eugenia Blake which her friends, Jack and Elizabeth Diamond of Cleveland, gathered in 1944 to publish in their basement private press as the sixteenth 'blossom' of the Hyacinth Press. The checklist of Miss Blake's ex libris which Dr. Radbill prepared for the ASBC&D YEAR BOOK 1952/53 listed about eighty plates, but by the time Mrs. Mary Alice Ercolini published an article on Miss Blake's work in the Bulletin of the Portuguese ExLibris Association in 1960, the list had grown to 109.

Miss Blake lives as 204 Hemmenway Street, Boston, Massachusetts 02115, and I am certain she would enjoy correspondence from fellow philibrists.

Dr. Radbill, a specialist in the pediatric field, is best known to Society members for his comprehensive MEDICAL EX LIBRIS BIBLIOGRAPHY printed by the Hilprand Press. The print here tipped-in is a steel intaglio reproduced by photogravure from the original dry point engraving.

*　　*　　*　　*　　*　　*

Society Member Willo Singer, London (Ontario, Canada) Teachers' College reported on an International Conference at Loughborough in ONTARIO LIBRARY REVIEW for March 1972.

The Bookplate Society of London has recently affili-
ated itself with the Private Libraries Association.
Previously known as the Bookplate Exchange Club, the
Bookplate Society was formed in 1897 as part of the
Ex Libris Society, itself founded in 1890.

Membership of the Bookplate Society in future will
be restricted to members of the Private Libraries
Association. At present no extra subscription cost
is involved, and any P.L.A. members interested in
joining should write the Hon. Secretary, Brian Lee,
32 Barrowgate Road, London W4, England, for details.
U.S. membership is $8.50, which includes the P.L.A.
quarterly. The Exchange Club will continue to be
limited to 25 residents of the United Kingdom.

Their bookplate and letterhead was designed by Diana
Bloomfield, whose work was presented by Philip C. Beddingham in the 1969/70
YEAR BOOK.

To coincide with the publication of the P.L.A. book, ENGRAVED BOOKPLATES: 1950-
1970, by Mark Severin and Anthony Reid, there was an exhibition of bookplates
in conjunction with the National Book League from June 7th to 16th, in the
Library of the National Book League on Albemarle Street, London.

From the Catalogs:
The Ashley Library, A Catalogue of Printed Books, Manuscripts and Autograph
Letters collected by Thomas J. Wise, in 11 volumes, London 1922-36, was privately printed in an edition of 250 copies. By courtesy of the British Museum
a new edition of 250 sets is being printed to include the shelf-numbers. The
flyer from Dawsons of Pall Mall is illustrated by the handsome Ashley Library
bookplate.

The Elegant Library of Celia Tobin Clark, removed from the Library, House-on-
the-Hill, Hillsborough, California, was sold in two parts at California Book
Auction Co., San Francisco, during early June. The catalog was illustrated
by Mrs. Clark's calligraphic ex libris, white lettering pleasingly spaced in
a black square inch. California Book Auction (224 McAllister Street, San
Francisco, CA.. 94102) frequently features bookplates as catalog illustrations.
A series of 12 catalogs is $10 or $1 each.

The Gleeson Library Associates, University of San Francisco, used the ex libris
designed by Leo Wyatt for Norman Strouse in their announcement of the lecture
to be given at their annual meeting by Mr. Strouse.

Catalog #48 of E. P. Goldschmidt, London, illustrated item #53 with a bookplate
and detailed footnote for the printed bookplate to "commemorate the acquisition
of books by Faber for donation to the College of St. Nicolas, Vienna," dated
September 1, 1540 and priced at $225.00.

Plandome Book Auctions, Glen Head, New York, continues to have occasional bookplate items as in Sale No. 74 - A bookplate by Bruce Rogers in Rockwell Kent's
SALAMINA.

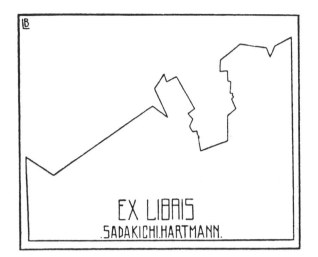

EX LIBRIS
.SADAKICHI.HARTMANN.

SADAKICHI HARTMANN

Carl Sadakichi Hartmann was born in 1867 on the island of Desima in Nagasaki harbor. After his mother, Osada, died in childbirth Sadakichi and his elder brother were taken to Hamburg and brought up by a wealthy uncle and their grandmother. In 1882 he came to America; after years of association with literary and artistic communities and lecturing across America, Hartmann settled in Southern California in the early 1920's.

The bookplate here illustrated is by Lillian Bonham, Hartmann's second wife. She designed it for his private library when they were at Elbert ("The Fra") Hubbard's Roycroft colony in 1907; she was in the bookbinding department and her advertisements indicated she was a "Designer of Bookplates, Monograms, Artists' Signatures, Ring Designs and Trade Marks."

Hartmann's daughters Wistaria Hartmann Linton and Dorothea Atma Gilliland donated most of the material in the Hartmann Archives at the University of California Riverside Library. Dr. George Knox edits a newsletter, issued three times a year, concerning this author; additionally two books jointly authored with Harry Lawton were published in 1971 dealing with Hartmann and his writings. Gene Fowler in GOOD NIGHT SWEET PRINCE tells of Hartmann's friendship with John Barrymore. In 1944 at the age of 77, Sadakichi Hartmann died while visiting a daughter in St. Petersburg, Florida. Thanks are due Professor George Knox for the Hartmann ex libris and biographical details.

HARDING BOOKPLATES EXHIBITED AT DEDHAM PUBLIC LIBRARY

Recently the bookplates designed by Dorothy Sturgis Harding were on display in the Children's Room and lobby of the Dedham (Massachusetts) Public Library. Mrs. Harding's art studies began at the age of ten under the instruction of Frederick Garrison Hall, the etcher who was a Harvard classmate of her brother. Later study at the Boston Museum of Fine Arts was under C. Howard Walker, and private lessons were taken from Elizabeth Shippen Green Eliot, who had studied under Howard Pyle. She was encouraged by her father, R. Clipston Sturgis, Fellow and former President of the American Institute of Architects. Examples of her work will also be on exhibit during the 14th International Ex Libris Congress in Denmark during August.

PERSONALIZED BOOKPLATES BY CLEORA WHEELER

The ST. PAUL PIONEER PRESS for March 25, 1972 had a warm, human interest article by Carole Nelson about bookplate designer Cleora Clark Wheeler, who over the last 64 years has been commissioned by organizations and individuals to create ex libris to immortalize something meaningful and bearing the owner's name in Miss Wheeler's precise lettering.

PENNSYLVANIA STATE LIBRARY

Gilt stamping was used to identify books in
the Pennsylvania State Library in 1767, a
simple typographic label was used during the
1890's, and the current plate follows the
design of the seal drawn by Dr. Robert Bray
Wingate in 1962.

Dr. Wingate is the Head of Rare Books and
Special Collections of the State Library,
and also is a medical illustrator of considerable note. He wrote a detailed article
in the PLA BULLETIN of November 1970 about
the Pennsylvania State Library, which was at
that time celebrating 225 years of service.
In the Proceedings of the House of Representatives for December 5, 1745, it was ordered
"that the Clerk send to England for the best
Edition of the Statues at large for the Use
of the House, and also for some large Maps
. . "   Thus Benjamin Franklin, who was
Clerk of the Assembly, became instrumental in creation of the Pennsylvania State
Library. The first Assembly Library was on the second floor of what is now Independence Hall in Philadelphia.

ASBC&D member Roy Jansen has exhibited his extensive bookplate collection at the
Pennsylvania State Library.

GILL COLLECTION AT CLARK LIBRARY

The bookplate of the Eric Gill collection at the
William Andrews Clark Memorial Library, University
of California at Los Angeles, was commissioned in
1963 by the then Director, Dr. Lawrence Clark
Powell, and was designed and cut in two sizes (the
smaller of which is shown here) by David Kindersley
of Cambridge, England. As an apprentice of Eric
Gill, and later a journeyman in his studio, David
Kindersley was uniquely qualified for the task. His
bookplate is based on the handsome cipher with
which Gill signed his work. The Clark Library's
collection, which developed from an interest in the
illustrations which Eric Gill provided for certain
Golden Cockeral Press books, includes drawings,
blocks, prints, and books representing the full
range of his work as an artist, sculptor, author,
printer, and type designer.

BOOKPLATES IN THE NEWS

Published Quarterly - January,
April, July, October

Number Nine   July 1972

$3 U.S./$4 Foreign
Editor - Audrey Spencer Arellanes

American Society of BOOKPLATE Collectors and Designers

429 NORTH DAISY AVENUE, PASADENA, CALIFORNIA 91107

BOOKPLATES IN THE NEWS   Number Eleven   October 1972

NATIONAL PARKS YEAR

America's first national park, Yellowstone, was established by legislation signed by President Ulysses S. Grant in 1872. In observation of this 100th anniversary, the Post Office Department issued a commemorative stamp showing Old Faithful. Additional stamps in the series to honor National Parks Year will feature Cape Hatteras, City of Refuge in Hawaii, McKinley in Alaska, and Wolf Trap Farm for the Performing Arts in Virginia.

A series of thrity-six medals, silver dollar size, each commemorating one of the thirty-six national parks, is being designed by Frank Hagel, an artist interested in Western Americana. The medals will be struck by the Medallic Art Company of New York City and distributed by Roche Jaune, Inc. (yellow stone in French) of Kalispell, Montana.

Finds tongues in trees
Books in the running brooks
Sermons in stones
And good in everything

LIBRARY of
MARDY & OLAUS MURIE

Over the years bookplates, too, have shown the beauties of some of our parks, as well as nature in general. Particularly appropriate is the plate of Olaus J. Murie (1889-1963), president of the Wilderness Society from 1950 to 1957.

Murie was field biologist for the U.S. Biological Survey (now the Fish and Wildlife Service) from 1920 to 1946; then a director and later president of the Wilderness Society. He was the author of THE ELK OF NORTH AMERICA, A FIELD GUIDE OF ANIMAL TRACKS, and monographs on the coyote, bear, caribou, and other large mammals.

Mrs. Marie writes: "The plate was designed and drawn by my late husband, Olaus J. Murie. Since I was raised in Alaska, and that is where we met, and since he was a biologist and traveled much in the north, and our honeymoon had been a dog team trip to Northern Alaska, where we often saw the snowy owl, it seemed a natural choice for our bookplate.

"We returned to Alaska several times, on scientific expeditions, even after our permanent base became Jackson Hole, Wyoming, where my husband was sent in 1927 to make a life history study of the Jackson Hole elk. Two expeditions were to explore and

36

recommend the great area of the Brooks Range which has become the Artic National Wildlife Range. The background for the snowy owl, mountains and the curve of a river, were taken from a favorite spot on the Sheejek River in the heart of this beautiful area. And the quote from Shakespeare's "The Tempest" seemed to harmonize with that background and express our own philosophy."

GREGORY KROLL

"Climb the mountains and get their good tidings.
Nature's peace will flow into you
    as sunshine flows into trees.

    The winds will blow their own freshness into you,
    and the storms their energy,
    while cares will drop off like autumn leaves."
                                JOHN MUIR

Gregory, 24, is at present living in La Macarena, a jungle in Colombia, South America. About two years ago he was sent by the Peace Corps to assist in the development of Colombian national parks and the relocation of squatters in these potential park areas.

He graduated with honors from Humboldt State College with a major in Natural Resources. For two summers he was a ranger at Jedediah Smith State Park. He is a Board member of the Redwood Chapter of the Sierra Club, with a special interest in saving the California coast redwoods; he testified at the Congressional hearings for the preservation of these trees.

In 1969 he participated in the John Powell Centennial Colorado River Expedition that recreated Powell's original journey from Portola Valley through the Grand Canyon. Martin Litton lead this group; Francois Leydet was one of the oarsmen.

Gregory was a counselor for the Wilderness Foundation at Elk, Wyoming and Mammoth, California. The Foundation teaches individuals how to survive in the wilderness.

Gregory Kroll's bookplate is from an Olaus Murie print showing the Grand Tetons as you look west from Jackson Hole, and the John Muir quotation is especially fitting for someone interested in the California redwoods in particular and nature in general.

CLEORA CLARK WHEELER

Another artist who frequently uses nature as a theme for the bookplates she designs is Cleora Clark Wheeler. Born in Austin, Minnesota, educated at the University of Minnesota and the New York School of Fine and Applied Art, Miss Wheeler has lived in St. Paul during her long professional career. Her varied activities have included organizing the St. Paul Vocational Bureau for Trained Women, designing Christmas cards, writing songs and poems; she is also a designer and illuminator of books and other publications, and a photographer.

EX ·LIBRIS·

·FITZHUGH·BURNS·

Miss Wheeler designed the Fitzhugh Burns ex libris, which is #17 in her checklist, for his personal library of 5,000 volumes. This young, St. Paul bachelor attorney spent his vacations at Crow's Nest Mountain in British Columbia, Canada, and wanted it pictured on his ex libris to look impregnable. The plate is a copper intaglio with prints by hand - a rare treat for the current collector!

Cleora Wheeler has well earned her listings in Who's Who in America, Who's Who in American Women, Who's Who in the Mid-West, and Who's Who in American Art. She is active in the National League of American Pen Women in which she has served as vice president (1938-40) and president (1940-42) of the Minnesota branch and on the national committees for design, inscriptions, illumination, and heraldry at various times between 1944 and 1966. She is a life member of the American Association of University Women and belongs to the National Society of Magna Carta Dames and the Daughters of the American Revolution.

From the Periodical Literature:

BOOK COLLECTOR, "Book Reviews," 21:275-6, 279, Summer 1972. J. D. Fleeman in his review of A CATALOGUE OF HORACE WALPOLE'S LIBRARY, by Allen T. Hazen, with HORACE WALPOLE'S LIBRARY by Wilmarth Sheldon Lewis, says, "Collectors of bookplates have much to answer for in the havoc they have played with the records of provenances and Walpole's books have suffered both by the frequent removal of his plate, and by the shifting of bookplates from 'uninteresting' books into those with greater appeal. Here at last is an authoritative guide to the inquirer who is faced with an ambiguous bookplate or an enigmatic press-mark. There are now several tests which can be applied to any alleged Walpolean provenance for the title must be right, as well as the pressmark, and the bookplate must be in the right state."

GAZETTE of the Grolier Club, "Great American Book Collectors to 1800," Edwin Wolf, 2nd, Number 14:3-69, June 1971. Twelve collectors are discussed : Winthrop, Mather, Prince, Byrd, Logan, Norris, Franklin, Adams, Jefferson, Mackenzie, Bentley, and Wallcut. The 153 printed labels for the accompanying exhibition "are concise, weighty, and frequently witty essays on the varieties and vagaries of provenance, studded throughout with matter of scholarly, historic and bibliophilic interest." Eleven bookplates or labels are illustrated.

CONNECTICUT ALUMNUS, March 1968, has an article on the Special Collections in the University of Connecticut's Wilbur Cross Library. One of the illustrations is a picture of ASBC&D member Richard H. Schimmelpfeng, Assistant Librarian at that time who was organizer and curator of the Library's Department of Special Collections.

SOUNDINGS, Collections of the University Library, University of California at Santa Barbara, "English Bookplates as Reflections of English Life," Michael Heskett, 4:23-31, June 1972 ($1). "One of the smallest, yet most significant, parts of any collection on the art of printing and the book is that on the study and appreciation of ex-libris." UCSB has collection of E. D. French plates in eleven volumes.

SERIF - "Bookplate of Algernon Charles Swinburne," 9:inside cover, Summer 1972, and "Bookplate of Charles Dickens," 9:inside cover, Spring 1972. No text.

Additional reviews of BOOKPLATES: A Selective Annotated Bibliography of the Periodical Literature, Audrey Spencer Arellanes, appeared in BOOK EXCHANGE for March 1972; CAR-DEL SCRIBE, April 1972; NEWSLETTER OF THE AMERICAN SOCIETY OF HERALDRY, March 1972; AMERICAN REFERENCE BOOKS ANNUAL.

LALA LETTER issued by the Los Angeles Library Association, June 1972, notes publication of THE BOOKPLATES OF THE LOS ANGELES PUBLIC LIBRARY by Joan West, $10 with membership in the Association; also mentioned in January 1972, UCLA LIBRARIAN.

Mansell Information/Publishing Limited, London, is publishing a series titled, "Sale Catalogues of Libraries of Eminent Persons." The next library will be that of William Dodd, author, preacher and forger. Two of his bookplates will be shown, both reproduced from the Yale University Library collection; the first reading simply "W. Dood, M.A." would have been used before 1763 when Dodd became Chaplain to the King, and this title was added to the later plate

AMERICAN BOOK COLLECTOR, "The Rev. Thomas Price and the Price Library," Peter Knapp, 22:19-23, October 1971. "The name Price selected for his collection is recorded on one of the bookplates found in many of his books: . . . The New-England Library, ...collected by Thomas Price, upon his entering Harvard-College, July 6, 1703.

AMERICAN BOOK COLLECTOR, "Book Collecting in the Field of Children's Literature," Justin G. Schiller, 22:11-23, Summer 1972. This excellent article contains one ex libris among the illustrations which reads: From the Bewick Collection of the Rev. Thomas Hugo, and Described in "The Bewick Collector," No. (33).

E X H I B I T S
The University of Pittsburgh, Hillman Library, will feature the bookplate collection of Roy Jansen during October, 1972.

The Brand Library, Glendale, California will have a bookplate exhibit during November from the collections of Audrey Arellanes and Anthony Kroll.

Philip C. Beddingham, President of the Bookplate Society, London, sent notice of an Exhibition of Bookplates at the National Book League, Albemarle Street, Piccadilly, London, from September 11 to 22, 1972. Admission free, illustrated catalogue 10p. Over 400 bookplates ranging from the 17th century to the present were on display from England and twelve other countries. In addition to stimulating interest in bookplates the exhibit was to help launch ENGRAVED BOOKPLATES 1950-1970 by Mark Severin and Anthony Reid. Next year the London Society will publish THE BOOKPLATE DESIGNS OF REX Whistler, by Brian North Lee with 34 illustrations.

BOOKPLATES IN THE NEWS - Issued quarterly in January, April, July, and October - $3 Audrey Spencer Arellanes, Editor -- Contributing Editors: Francis W. Allen, Review of the Classics -- Anthony F. Kroll, Engravings -- Louis Ginsberg, Exchange List

SIDNEY D. GAMBLE

Sidney D. Gamble was born in Cincinnati, July 12, 1890, the son of David Berry and Mary Huggins Gamble; he was a descendant of James Gamble, who with William Procter, founded Procter and Gamble in 1837.

In 1912 he graduated from Princeton where he was elected to Phi Beta Kappa; he received a Master's degree from the University of California in 1916 and stayed to teach in the economics department prior to going to China.

Sidney Gamble served as secretary of the International Committee (now the National Council) of the Young Men's Christian Association in 1918-19, 1924-27, and again before 1932, in China where he completed a number of social and economic studies. From 1949 to 1957 he served on the executive committee of the organization's National Board.

Some of his publications were: "Peking: A Social Survey," the first such survey of an Oriental city, 1921; "How Chinese Families Live In Peiping," 1933; "Ting Hsien : A North China Rural Community," 1953; "North China Villages: Social, Political and Economic Activities Before 1933," 1963, and "Chinese Village Plays," which was in preparation at the time of his death, March 30, 1968.

Mr. Gamble served as president of Princeton in Asia and of the Princeton-Yenching University Foundation, Treasurer of the Y.M.C.A. World Student Service Fund, Church Committee for China Relief and National Committee on Material Health.

His bookplate reflects this interest in the Orient, also drama and photography, and includes the seals of both the University of California and Princeton.

The David B. Gamble House in Pasadena, California, is the most complete and best preserved example of the work of Charles Sumner Greene and Henry Mather Greene, California architects famed for their California Bungalow style. Sidney David was 18 when construction was started on the house in 1908 and the second upstairs bedroom was designed for Sidney and his brother, Clarence. An extremely interesting article on the Gamble House has been written by Randell L. Makinson, and appeared in PRAIRIE SCHOOL REVIEW, volume V, number 4, 1968.

COLLECTIONS FOR SALE

John Howell - Books, has the famed Louise Winterburn Collection of Royal Bookplates, which is described in his Cat. #43 - for details & price write - 434 Post Street, San Francisco, Ca. 94102. A second collection, priced at $3,000, is mounted in two volumes of 195 and 193 leaves respectively, and includes 75 European plates (1580-1800), 250 modern plates (1850-1950), 43 ex libris eroticis, and numerous others.

Don E. Burnett, P. O. Box 178, East Greenwich, R.I., is offering a "magnificient collection of bookplates and owners labels dating from 1679 to the early 1900's" numbering 2,682 for which the price is $12,500.

E. Helene Sherman of Sudbury, Massachusetts, excells in the field of Medieval illumination. Her interest dates from early childhood when she first used a paint brush. She is the grand-daughter of Louis Prand, artist and pupil of Lippi, and also related to the Boston publisher and lithographer, Louis Prang, who is best known for introducing the Christmas card.

Miss Sherman was the subject of an article by Cynthia Elyce Rubin, in the December, 1971 issue of NATIONAL ANTIQUES REVIEW, which tells of the numerous testimonials, bookmarks, bibles, books for rare book collectors and alter cards illuminated by this highly esteemed artist. She has been honored by the American League of Pen Women, exhibited at the Smithsonian Institution, and drew the color citation presented to Dr. Albert Schweitzer for his 85th birthday in 1960.

Her bookplate indicates various talents and interests including designing, illumination, calligraphy, miniature books, and lecturing. Her poodle Sookie is often a model for miniature designs; monastic scribes often pictured demons or animals in the flowery margins of their manuscripts and Miss Sherman in a similar fashion shows Sookie prancing with a bit of foliage through the myriad letters of a word. She collects owls, the symbol of the Pen Women, and bookplates. Inquiries concerning bookplate commissions would be welcome and may be addressed to - 328 Goodman Hill Road, Sudbury, Mass. 01776.

G. HARVEY PETTY

To quote this Indiana typographer, "I'm just an average person with a hankering to be a bit better than that, a sixth-generation American, a third-generation Hoosier, a dyed-in-the-wool Mid-westerner, a bug for details, and a lover of everything that has to do with the graphic arts."

After a long career as printer and nationally known, award-winning typographer, Petty entered a second field - calligraphy. He tells of his discovery of this art and his romance with it in his completely calligraphed little book, "Calligraphic Antics." A three-part article appeared in SIGNS OF THE TIMES, December, 1971 through February, 1972, and gives illustration of several alphabets from his pen, and discusses with wit and humor other calligraphers whom he admires, such as Don Margo and Raymond Da Boll, who have also designed bookplates.

Harvey Petty created the bookplates in DEVICES AND VICES entirely from type and ornaments for forty-eight famous people in history, literature, and legend including such diverse characters as Theda Bara, Huck Finn, and Santa Clause. This charming book was printed by the Private Press of the Indiana Kid, alias James L. Weygand. Those interested in expert calligraphic design for an ex libris, letterhead or other creative graphics may write...

G. H. Petty
5305 East Tenth Street
Indianapolis, Indiana 46219

American Society of BOOKPLATE Collectors and Designers

Number Eleven-A   BOOKPLATES IN THE NEWS   January 1973

14th INTERNATIONAL EXLIBRIS CONGRESS
by Charles Midlo, M.D.

One hundred and sixty collectors and designers of bookplates from twenty-two countries of Europe and North America met at the famous Marienlyst Badehotel in Helsingør, Denmark, from August 24 through 27, 1972, to participate in the 14th International Exlibris Congress. The host, the Danish Exlibris Society, under the leadership of Klaus Rodel, arranged a comprehensive program of exhibitions, lectures and entertainments. There were ample opportunities for exchanging bookplates and meeting old and new friends. Lucullan feasts, rather than meals, added to the feeling of good fellowship which prevaded the congress.

An initial function of the assembly was the meeting of delegates of the Federation Internationale des Societes d'Amateurs d'Exlibris (FISAE). Of the existing twenty-two ex libris associations, all but four are now members of FISAE. The Federation plans to establish a central EXLIBRIS-INSTITUTE which will coordinate and record the various activities of its member-groups.

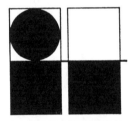

14. INTERNATIONALE
EXLIBRIS-KONGRES
HELSINGÖR-DANMARK
24.-27. AUGUST 1972

Several exhibits graced the Congress: 1) at the Marienlyst Castle, eleven Danish artists showed some of their recent work. 2) The Helsingør Bibliotek displayed ex libris contributed by 166 designers of bookplates from eighteen countries. This exhibit evinced an engrossing renewal of the art of the bookplate. The number of artist-contributors from each country could well be a measure of the interest given to this Kleingraphik by the country in question. Well represented were Hungary, Czechoslovakia, Poland, Lithuania, Estonia and France. One may well ponder the reasons for the upsurge of ex libris interest in the countries behind the "iron curtain," all of which presented examples of bookplates with modern tone and, at times, with exciting experimental techniques. 3) At the Marienlyst Hotel were shown the contributions by 130 international artists in a competition for the best Congress ex libris. The judges were: Helmer Fogedgaard, Vagn Clemmensen, Jorgen L. Rasmussem Kaj W. Riis, Otakar Hradecny, Norbert Ott and Paul Pfister. Prizes were awarded to Lenke Diskay (Hungary), Ladislau Feszt (Romania), and Anatoli Kalaschnikow (USSR).

The participants to the congress were literally showered with gifts of bookplates, prints, and booklets donated by ex libris societies and artists. Also, a "tombola" gave several fortunate winners the opportunity to acquire a new personal bookplate by artists who will generously donate its design and execution.

The assembly enthusiastically accepted the invitation extended by Dagmar Novacek of the Exlibris Sloveniae to hold the 15th International Exlibris Congress (1974) in Bled, Yugoslavia.

The first day of the Congress was devoted to a meeting of the delegates; presiding was Klaus Rodel. The agenda was available to each of the 33 delegates in the form of a bound folder printed in four languages: Danish, German, French and English. Rodel stated in his welcoming address that in spite of obstacles (lack of public interest and support), he feels the program of exhibitions, excursions, and opportunities for discussion and exchange of bookplates will be eventful and rewarding. The presiding officer gave a report of the activities of FISAE; officers are: Klaus Rodel, president; Carlo Chiesa (Lugano), vice president; Poul A. Anderson (Helsingør), secretary; Knud Fougt (Copenhagen), treasurer. An international ex libris periodical would be desirable, especially to cover a bibliographic survey of the international publications in the ex libris field; therefore, it was suggested that a permanent secretaryship of the FISAE be formed to coordinate various efforts of member societies concerning data of universal interest. At the Exlibris Congress in Budapest during 1970, the Centre of Documentation was initiated by Madame Meyer in Nancy. This was the basis of the establishment in Frederikshavn of the Exlibris Institute in connection with the publishing house of Exlibristen. In the past five years, Exlibristen has issued 80 publications in the realm of bookplates. Helmer Fogedgaard, who with Klaus Rodel is enthusiastically cooperating in the founding of the Exlibris Institute, has promised to place at its disposal, at a later period, his extensive collection of ex libris and his library. Mr. Rodel seriously solicited the cooperation of the member societies in supplying bibliographic ex libris material for annual publication; he requested contributions of copies of all ex libris publications to the Institute. He will endeavor to compensate the senders with publications of his own as they appear in Exlibristen; he further suggested that a modest fee be donated annually to FISAE to meet certain expenses.

With all sincerity we can consider our attendance at the Congress to be the highlight of our European journey. We made many friends, fully enjoyed the events of the Congress, met collectors and artists with whom I had corresponded for many years. Everyone was friendly, gracious, and generous, forming a cordial and fraternal group with a common though esoteric interest. Very little commercialism was apparent, even though some of the artists attending were not adverse to being given commissions for ex libris. To Mrs. Midlo and myself the affair was an extraordinarily pleasant and memorable experience.

FOREIGN EX LIBRIS SOCIETIES

The various ex libris societies outside the United States offer opportunities for exchange of bookplates, friendship and in most instances publications. While not being able to read foreign languages limits the information to be gained, all the journals are well illustrated and can thus be enjoyed for their visual aspects. The following list gives the name, address and subscription (in their currency) for the known bookplate societies outside of the United States.

Graphia, c/o Leo Winkeler
Boudewijnstratt 97
2000 Antwerpen, BELGIUM (200,00 Bfr)

Nippon Ex Libris Assoc., Taro Shimo
Kumenancho, Yuge P.O.   (Calendar)
Okayamaken 709-36, JAPAN($2U.S.)

Dansk Exlibris Selskab
Box 1519
2700 Copenhagen Brh., DENMARK (30,00 Kr)

Mario Lourinho Rodrigues Vinhas
R. D. Joao da Silva 4- Restelo
Lisboa 3, PORTUGAL

Suomen Exlibris-Yhdistys, c/o Verho
Ylakiventie 2F
Helsinki 92, FINLAND (10,00 m)

Associacao Portuense de Ex Libris
Rua de Santa Catarina 461
1 Porto, PORTUGAL

L'Assoc. Francaise des Collectionneurs
 et Amis d'Ex Libris et de Gravures
Palais Ducal, Grande Rue 43
F59 Nancy, FRANCE (25,00 Fr)

Associacion de Exlibristas de
 Barcelona
Mario Aurelio 4, pral.,
Barcelona 6, SPAIN (240,00 Pesetas)

Exlibriskring der W.B.-Vereniging
Minervalaan 26
Amsterdam 9, HOLLAND (15,00 Guilder)

Svenska Exlibrisforeningen
Observatoriegata 3, IV
11329 Stockholm, SWEDEN (30,00 Kr)

Associazione Italiana del Collezionisti Artisti e Amatori dell Ex Libris
c/o Aldo Galli, 22100 Como
Via Rusconi 27, ITALY (3000,00 Lire)

BIBLIOTHECA SANCTI FRANCISCII ARCHDIOECESEO

by Joan West

The Bibliotheca
Sancti Franciscii
Archdioeceseos is
over 100 years old,
yet its bookplate
dates less than half
a decade. The Col-
lection arrived in
California in 1850
as the personal li-
brary of Rev. Joseph

S. Alemany, Archbishop of California, at San Francisco. During the next
century the collection was to have several homes, first at Monterey, then
San Francisco. In 1883, it was moved to the seminary at Mission San Jose
and finally, shortly before the turn of the century, it was moved to
Saint Patrick's Seminary in Menlo Park where you will find it today. Of
the 2,700 volumes noted in the collection in 1878 by Flora Apponyi, only
1,612 remain. Most of these bear the inscription "Joseph Sadoc Alemany,
O.P." or "Diocesis Sancti Francisci." While the Rev. Francis J. Weber,
Archivist of the Los Angeles diocese, was cataloging the collection, a
special bookplate was created using the same decorative border as that
for the Biblioteca Montereyensis-Angelorum Diocecéseos housed at Mission
San Fernando. Our thanks to Rev. Weber for making available the necessary
copies for this tip-in.

GERALD T. BANNER is librarian at
the University of Maine, Portland-
Gorham. His bookplate hobby grew
out of a general interest in the
graphic and printing arts. Portland is fortunate to have had two
men noted in the book arts: Thomas
Bird Mosher (1852-1923), publisher
and Fred Anthoensen (1882-1969),
printer. Both were outstanding
book designers. Upon Mr. Anthoensen's death, the clerk of his corporation gave a collection of im-
prints from the press to the University of Maine Library.

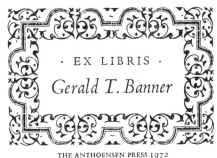

THE ANTHOENSEN PRESS 1972

"A characteristic of the Anthoensen Press is the fine use of type ornaments ("flowers") which fascinate me," writes Gerry Banner. "This bookplate, designed by Harry Milliken, manager of the press, is intended to
reflect these interests and be my memorial to the artistry of a local
genius."

E X H I B I T S - Robert A. Hawley, who does calligraphy and scribal
writing, reports: "An exhibit of AS of BC & D YEAR BOOKS, newsletters &
information was displayed during the Simsbury Historical Society's fall
semester course in Genealogy & Heraldry and at the Oct. 21 meeting of
the Connecticut Society of Genealogists at the Simsbury Society's Historic Center. The exhibit, with ones of the American Society of Heraldry
and the Augustan Society, drew crowds - comparatively, that is: the class
averaged ten, the meeting had around 25. Practically all showed interest."
A new artist-member, Robert Hawley lives on South Road, East Hartland, Conn.

An exhibit arranged jointly by the Bookplate Society and the Private
Libraries Association was held at the National Book League during September 1972 to coincide with the publication of ENGRAVED BOOKPLATES: European
Ex Libris 1950-70 by Mark Severin and Anthony Reid. A catalog has been
issued with excellent annotations for the historical plates noted in items
1 through 115, additionally items 116 through 366 list bookplates by country, owner and artist. The catalog (8" x 10", 15 illustrations, typed and
reproduced) may be ordered for $1.25 including postage through BOOKPLATES
IN THE NEWS.

Brand Art Center Library, Glendale, California will have a bookplate exhibit from the collection of Audrey Arellanes and show the Evolution of
A Bookplate through the engraving tools and plates of Anthony F. Kroll;
originally planned for November, the display is now scheduled for the
month of January, 1973.

FROM THE PERIODICAL LITERATURE -
Mn U BULLETIN, "Some Comments on Bookplates," Cleora Wheeler. (5) 3:65-70,
July 1972. This is a condensation of six articles which appeared in
MINNESOTA MEDICINE from June through November 1957. Illustrated are five
bookplates designed by Miss Wheeler, including her own.

SKETCH BOOK (Chicago) "The Bookplate," M.E.C. (28) 1:3,5,7,13-4,21,23,25,
May 1902. Work of numerous artists including F. W. Goudy.

THE HORN BOOK, "The May Massee Collection," Ruth Gagliardo. (2) XLVIII: 220-22, April 1972. Illustrated is the bookplate designed by Valenti Angelo for the Massee Collection: Creative Publishing for Children at Kansas State Teachers College, William Allen White Library.

THE HORN BOOK, "Bertha Mahony Miller Collection," 557, October 1971. Mrs. Miller's collection of children's books is housed at Horn Book, Inc., Boston; Nora S. Unwin designed a special ex libris for the collection.

YANKEE, "All About E. B. Bird and Bookplate Collecting," Curtis B. Norris. (15) 156-9,206,209-12, October 1972. An informative, lively article by a nephew of artist Bird, who was one of four then living American book-plate men included by the American Antiquarian Society in their collection during the 1920's.

PRIVATE LIBRARY, "Bookplate Collecting and the Bookplate Society," Brian North Lee. (4) 5:88-95, Summer 1972. Background on the reactivated Book-plate Society and basic aspects of collecting. "Anyone wishing to join the Bookplate Society must be a member of the Private Libraries Associa-tion. Membership is $8.50 U.S. a year and the Hon. Membership Secretary is Peter Hall, 10 Garford Crescent, Chievely, Newbury, Berkshire, England. The Hon. Secretary of the Bookplate Society (Brian North Lee, 32 Barrowgate Road, Chiswick, London, W.4, England) should then be contacted for regis-tration."

SERIF, "Bookplate of Edwin Gordon Craig." (1) 9:inside cover, Fall 1972. The tipped-in plate is a reproduction of Craig's own bookplate printed by a steel engraving made from a pull from the original boxwood block a gift from Craig to John Wesley Swanson.

SERIF, "Edward Gordon Craig, Father of Contemporary Theatre Art: An Exhi-bition of the John Wesley Swanson Craig Collection, Kent State University, 1971," Orville K. Larson. (2) 9:14-35, Fall 1972. Interesting details concerning versatile talents of Craig. Among 119 items annotated from the exhibit are numerous references to bookplates and Craig's publications in the field.

NEW YORKER, "Printer." XLVIII:31-2, October 21, 1972. Bernard Roberts, managing director of the John Roberts Press, London, who lectured before several bibliophile groups, mentioned distinctive ephemera they printed which included letterheads, bookplates, programs, menus, and book jackets.

AMERICAN ARTIST, "Rockwell Kent," David Preiss. (16) 36:64-9, 84-7, No-vember 1972. Among illustrations are bookplates for Carola Zigrosser and Stephen Morgan Etnier, once a student of Kent's.

SKETCH BOOK (Chicago) "The Pictorial Book Plate," H. E. Townsend. (3) 1: 10-1, February 1902. Illustrated are plates for Thomas Wood Stevens and Benjamin F. March.

SKETCH BOOK (Chicago) "Book Plate Design," J. W. Norton. (2) 1:25, March 1902. Illustration only of plate for Dorothea Barnett Drews.

SKETCH BOOK (Chicago) "Book-Plate," Jaren Hiller. (1) 1:27, March 1902. Bookplate featuring lion and pirate illustrated.

University of Pittsburh LIBRARIES, "Exhibit," Vol. 3, #9, October 1972.
Over 500 bookplates from Roy Jansen's collection on display through the
10th of November, including over 40 by Rockwell Kent.

ATLANTA JOURNAL and CONSTITUTION, "Art in Miniature - Bookplates Beg
Attention," John Mebane.(1) December 10, 1972. Illustrated is the John
Dudley dated (1754) bookplate engraved by Nathaniel Hurd which measures
5" by 6½". Comments on the Hacker Art Books reprint of Charles Dexter
Allen's AMERICAN BOOK-PLATES.

"She Strives to Keep Art of Calligraphy Alive," is a newspaper item from
Sandusky, Ohio, which features Ione Wiechel and numerous fine examples of
calligraphy which she has collected. Illustrated is a bookplate for Irene
Pace with an oriental design, probably by Sara E. Blake.

LOS ANGELES TIMES, "Canon Molnar, Monastic Group Founder, to Talk." November 18, 1972. Notice of guest sermons at St. Mark's Episcopal Church in
Downey, California, by Canon Molnar, ASBC&D artist-member.

Census of Bookplate Collections Donated by ASBC&D Members - Charles Midlo,
M.D., of New Orleans has given his extensive bookplate collection to the
Rare Book Section of Tulane University Library. If you have already given
your collection to a library or institution or have made provision for
such a bequest, please send full details about the collection (mounted,
cataloged, including periodical literature and books, etc.) and its des-
tination. This information will be presented in a future issue of BOOKPLATES
IN THE NEWS as valuable sources for research and reference.

EX LIBRIS for tip-in. The Editor would welcome bookplate prints (200), together with biographical data about the owner and artist, to be featured
in BOOKPLATES IN THE NEWS.

New York Public Library

STOCK BOOKPLATES

While "stock bookplates" are not usually sought by the discriminating collector, such plates have been designed
by highly esteemed artists, notably
Rockwell Kent and Lynd Ward. Perhaps
the real importance of the stock plate
is the indication it gives of general
public interest. Two diverse sources
currently offer stock plates: New York
Public Library and Hallmark Cards. The
Library features reproductions from
fine and graphic arts, Hallmark offers
a variety of ten styles ranging from
Snoopy and Raggedy Ann to a quotation
from Seneca. For many years SATURDAY
REVIEW had a Bookplate section with ads
by Antioch in Yellowsprings and Berliner-
McGinnis in Nevada City, California.
Current interest in astrology is reflected in stock plates using the Signs
of the Zodiac.

IN MEMORIAM
Dr. Kurt Schnitzer

It is with sadness we note
the death of Kurt Schnitzer
on September 20, 1972 at
age 64. He was a 27-year
resident of Santa Ana, California, where he was an
artist and author as well
as a practicing physician.

Dr. Schnitzer was a native
of Austria and studied medicine at the University of
Vienna. He and his wife,
Lilli, who survives him,
fled Austria in advance of
Hitler's legions and reached the Dominican Republic
in October, 1938. As an im-
migrant he was forbidden by
law to practice medicine,
so with the help of his wife
Dr. Schnitzer launched a career as a photographer. He
received critical acclaim
for his prints and had as-
signments from National
Geographic, Saturday Evening
Post, and the New York Times.

In 1945 the Schnitzers with
their son George came to the
United States and he began a year of internship at the Orange County General
Hospital. The Schnitzers became citizens, and Dr. Schnitzer resumed the
private practice of medicine with offices in Santa Ana.

In addition to affiliation with numerous medical organizations, he was a
member of American Physician's Art Association, American Medical Writers
Association, and the American Society of Bookplate Collectors & Designers.
During the transition period following the death of Carlyle S. Baer, Kurt
Schnitzer was a staunch supporter in keeping the Society alive.

EMBLEM of 14th INTERNATIONAL EXLIBRIS CONGRESS

The emblem, which is tipped-in to accompany Dr. Midlo's article about the
congress, was designed by Peter Thrane of Rødovre, Denmark. The design was
conceived to combine two basic elements: the impression gained when observ-
ing the reflection of the full moon over the Øresund (the sound connecting
the Baltic Sea with the Kattegat), and the capital letter H standing for
Helsingor, the upright columns and cross-bar of the letter signifying the
bridged landmasses of Denmark and as well the ties of friendship and soli-
darity that binds its people.   This is a free translation by Dr. Midlo
from a portfolio issued by the Dansk Exlibris Selskab for participants of
the Congress.

THE CLASSICS REVISTED - Reviewed by Francis W. Allen, Physical
Sciences Librarian, Western Michigan University, Kalamazoo.
FRANKS BEQUEST: CATALOGUE OF BRITISH AND AMERICAN BOOKPLATES bequeathed
to the Trustees of the British Museum by Sir Augustus Wollaston Franks
by E. R. J. Gambier Howe. London, 1903-04, 3 volumes. British Museum,
Prints and Drawings Department.

The Franks catalog, as this title is familarly known, lists over
15,000 British and American bookplates arranged alphabetically by owner
(anonymous plates are assinged names by reference to the heraldic design)
gives the date, engraver and style where this information is possible.
An informative preface is written by Sidney Colvin, the late great British
librarian (whom this reviewer once had the honor to meet). Following the
main listing are library and society lists, and, of inestimable value to
the collector, an heraldic index to the anonymous plates.

The Franks catalog is not a tome to retire with on a cold winter's
night, but as most plates offer the Franks number when listed for sale
or exchange, and as the heraldic index is of great value for identification, this three-volume title deserves a prominent place on the serious
collector's bookshelf. Unfortuantely at this point in time, some seven
decates after publication, it is a difficult item to obtain. This reviewer has had, over the years, only three copies pass through his hands,
and considers himself fortunate to have obtained his current copy at
Quaritch in London for some £20 about three years ago. Collectors should
have this catalog, but they will have a rough time finding one.

GERMAN BOOK-PLATES: An Illustrated Handbook of German and Austrian Ex
Libris, Karl E. P. Franz au Graf Leiningun-Westerburg. Translated by
G. Ravenscroft Dennis. London: Bell, 1901 (Ex-libris series). American
edition published by Macmillan.

Leiningen-Westerburg is the standard work on German bookplates to
1900 even though the preface states there is no attempt to provide complete lists of these plates. One of Bell's familiar gold stamped, green
cloth ex-libris series, this volume occupies an honored place on the book
shelves of most serious collectors.

The author opens this treatise with a description of reproduction
methods, followed by a discussion of the differences between German and
English heraldry. He devotes some time to inscriptions, size and varieties
and then launches into a well illustrated catalog of German plates, arranged chronologically. There is a separate chapter on ecclesiastical
plates from the fifteenth to the nineteenth centuries and the final section
is devoted to special plates, i.e. military, children's, medical, etc.

For the collector limiting himself to American bookplates, Leiningen-
Westerburg may be of only peripheral interest, but for the more general
collector or for the ex libris historian, it is an invaluable addition to
the reference library.   *   *   *   *

Editor's Note: The October issue of BOOKPLATES IN THE NEWS was mis-num-
bered Eleven; it should have been Ten; the January 1973 issue bears the
Number Eleven-A.

BOOKPLATES IN THE NEWS   Issued Quarterly - $3/U.S.-$4/Foreign
429 North Daisy Avenue   January - April - July - October
Pasadena, Calif. 91107   Editor -   Audrey Spencer Arellanes

American Society of BOOKPLATE Collectors and Designers

ASBC&D

| BOOKPLATES IN THE NEWS | Number Twelve | April 1973 |

FRITZ EBERHARDT - Bookbinder and Designer

Ellen V. Becker

Writing about the bookplate he designed for Ellen V. Becker, Fritz Eberhardt says: "Mrs. Becker became one of our students in the art of bookbinding. This bookplate illustrates what this meant after Mrs. Becker had dedicated herself to the cello since high school years. She achieved recognized perfection on this demanding instrument and could have left well enough alone. To commit oneself to bookbinding is the next best thing to self-sacrifice this side of the Inca culture. Becoming a good bookbinder means endless practicing of a variety of intricate techniques, a 24-hour a day commitment, and the readiness to realize a hopelessly long lapse of time between a beginning and a noticeable result. The eventual achievement of this effort and recognition by the outside world is a very specific phenomen. It is expressed by a great number of bibliophiles and bibliographers who in full view of a number of remarkably good bookbinders travel the lecture circuit and proclaim that bookbinding is a dying or better yet a dead art. To survive and to keep working in this field while having been put to rest by one's own historians is a task that demands a special brand of cheerfulness and stamina. This bookplate is a salute to Mrs. Becker, who possesses these qualities."

The September 1956 issue of AMERICAN BOOK COLLECTOR contains an excellent, though brief, article by Lawrence S. Thompson on Fritz Eberhardt. Born in 1917 in Beuthen, Silesia (now part of Poland), Eberhardt was apprenticed to a bookbinder in Silesia at an early age; after passing his apprenticeship examination in 1935 he studied further in Leipzig both binding and calligraphy. The war years in Europe were not only difficult politically but bookbinders' supplies including leather, gold leaf, rag paper and adhesives were in short supply or non-existent.

In 1950 Fritz met Trudi, a teacher of bookbinding, who became his wife while they were in Sweden. By 1954 they arrived in New York. Fritz soon secured a position with the Library Company of Philadelphia, and Trudi did free-lance work. They now teach, do fine binding and design work from their studio in Old Sumneytown Pike, R.D. 1 Harleysville, Pa. 19438.

The Stephen Ballentines - by Elmer J. Porter

Mrs. Ballentine (Sally Porter) is my daughter and a 1970 graduate of Earlham College with a major in biology. She taught biology for two years at Choate-Rosemary Hall, a girls' school in Connecticut. Now connected with Marine Research, Inc. she is doing oceanographic research in Woods Hole, Massachusetts. Her husband, Stephen, a graduate of Wentworth Institute of Technology in Boston, is now assistant manager of Ballentines Marina on Buzzards Bay, North Falmouth, Massachusetts. Both are very much interested in sailing.

I have been a member of the ASBC&D for many years and have designed a number of plates for various people. However, my own plate was a gift from a former classmate, Dan Burne Jones.

While still attending high school in Richmond, Indiana, where we were neighbors of Esther Griffin White, author of INDIANA BOOKPLATES published in 1910, I started collecting bookplates. I, too, attended the Quaker college, Earlham, later graduated from the Chicago Art Institute, and have an M.A. degree from Ohio State University. I taught art in Cedar Rapids and Cincinnati before becoming Professor of Art and Chairman of the Department at Indiana State University, Terre Haute.

The 1951 YEAR BOOK of the ASBC&D contains my article on the bookplates of Ernest Haskell. I am a member of the Honorary Men's Educational Fraternity Phi Delta Kappa, and International Secretary of Kappa Pi, Honorary Art Fraternity.

CHARLES F. PRICKETT

Charles F. Prickett was the business manager of the Pasadena Community Playhouse from 1920 to 1930 and was General Manager of the Pasadena Playhouse Association from 1930 to 1954. Born March 2, 1900 in Centralia, Illinois, he moved at an early age with his family to Pasadena where he graduated from Pasadena High School and later the University of Southern California. In 1941 he maried Maudie Marie Doyle in Denver, Colorado. She has kindly furnished the following information about his bookplate:

"Charles designed his own book-plate and you will see his CFP in the lower right hand corner of the plate under the last prism. Charles had wood-work and photography as hobbies and these are reflected in the design as well as the figures with which he had to work in balancing the budget of the Play-house. He loved the design of the old Colorado Street Bridge as well as the skeleton of the sycamore trees which were in the patio of our old house. In the lower right hand corner above the PRICKETT are actors on a stage. Charles started at the Playhouse in 1917 as an actor when he was in high school, and he always loved scenic designing. This is the reason for the stage flats in back of the actors."

His widow is a character actress under the name of Maudie Prickett.

FRED THOMPSON - Artist

The 1931 YEAR BOOK contained an article about "Fred Thompson, Designer and Bookplate Engraver, 1851-1930," which was an appreciation by his friend and contemporary, John Hudson Elwell. A checklist of his work covered the years 1881 through 1925 and named 28 owners, among them H. J. Thompkins. Unfortunately no details where furnished about Mr. Thompkins, whose plate presents a variety of elements that hint at a personality of wide interests. Fred Thompson had his studio on the beautiful Charles River in Waltham, Massachusetts. He was also the subject of a brief article in the BOOKPLATE Quarterly, December 1917, which had a chronological list of 20 bookplates. Thanks are due Francis W. Allen for furnishing the prints to tip-in.

This is my book - Who are you?

One of the interesting ecological disasters along the Maine Coast is U.S. 1 from Kittery to Portland; with ticky tacky beach towns on the ocean side and take-out stands and junk antique shops along the highway, this 50 mile stretch has been a vacationer's haven since WWI. Rummaging in one of these shops, I came across a box of ex libris. Does any one know who was Copelin Roe Day or recognize the artist's initials - JMR? Any information leading to the identification of this plate will be gratefully received - Jerry Banner, 5 Ricker Park, Portland, Maine 04101.

<u>Review</u> by P. W. Filby

ENGRAVED BOOKPLATES: European Ex Libris 1950-1970. by Mark Severin & Anthony Reid. Private Libraries Association, Pinner, England, 1972. Quarto. 176 pages, illustrated. $17.00.

The brilliant idea carried out under the auspices of the Private Libraries Association is a delight to bookplate collectors, artists, calligraphers, and to bookmen. Over 500 bookplates selected from the work of the finest engravers in Europe are shown, and with the excellent introduction this is a collector's item. But it is more than this. Combined with the beauty of the selections are technical symbols, advice on commissioning a bookplate and on collecting bookplates, a list of bookplate societies and a select bibliography. Finally there is a comprehensive gazetteer of 400 practitioners with addresses. Twenty countries are represented, including Russia, Latvia, and Estonia. Most of the bookplates shown tend to pictorial representation, and it is only in Britain that lettering is to the fore. Much depends on whether the owner wants a plate to illustrate his own love or the content of his library, or whether he wants just a beautiful label. This reviewer's love for calligraphy tends to a bias in favor of calligraphic bookplates, and though the authors' admiration for Reynolds Stone "whose use of the letter is shatteringly perfect" is well founded, the reviewer would like more consideration for Leo Wyatt. The Breasted example given is far from being his best; there are many finer examples to his credit. The omission of Eric Gill and the inclusion of Stephen Gooden is not easy to understand, since both are pre-1950, but again it is a question of personal taste. Some of the European samples appear too heavy and often without much merit, but it is good to see a change whereby armorial bookplates seem to have gone out of fashion; surely a move for the better. But in all there is something for everyone; not a single reader will close the book without registering delight in some artists' work. The design of David Chambers is masterly. It is a pity, of course, that America could not have been included. There is no one to approach Wyatt or Stone, but the lettering of James Hayes and Byron Macdonald, and Alexander

Nesbitt in a different way, would be worthy of inclusion in any bookplate listing. Perhaps the American Society can produce a similar work which will show the European counterparts that bookplate design in America is not without considerable merit. The Private Libraries Association is to be congratulated on making this beautiful book available to members and to the general public. It is amazing what the Association has done for members on a mere $8.50 annually. The address is 41 Cuckoo Hill Road, Pinner, England.

From the library of   Elwood William Holland

E·W·HOLLAND

Born and raised in Los Angeles, California, E. W. Holland was educated in local schools and received a B.S. degree in Civil Engineering from the University of Southern California. A course in California history increased an already existing interest in the southwest which resulted from several summer vacations in the Mojave and Sonoran deserts.

His professional career started with the Metropolitan Water District in surveys and mapping, followed by construction. During 1940 service with the Army Engineers included topographic surveying in San Diego, Imperial and Riverside counties. The years 1942-45 were spent in mapping in Alaska and the Southwest Pacific. Postwar employment was with the City of Glendale ending with retirement as City Engineer in 1971.

The bookplate indicates areas of interest and routes of some of the early explorations; the surveyors represent the topographic activity. Mr. Holland indicates Dutch is a nickname of many years standing, in fact some people seem unaware of the E.W. He is a member of the Historical Society of Southern California (President 1972-73), California Historical Society, Conference of California Historical Societies, and Associate Member of the Los Angeles Corral of the Westerners. Anthony F. Kroll designed and engraved this plate.

FROM THE PERIODICAL LITERATURE

SERIF, "The Bookplate of Richard Brinsley Sheridan," (1) 9:inside front cover, Winter 1972. Illustration only.

GIFT OF
THE CLASS OF 1895

ANTIQUARIAN BOOKMAN, "Samford University Bookplate." 51:front cover, Feb. 26, 1973. Design inspired by replica depicting College President Samuel S. Sherman rolling a wheelbarrow through Marion, Alabama, rounding up books.

THE LANTERN'S CORE, "The University Library Bookplate," Rolf Erickson. (13) 3:5-8, January 10, 1973. Over 140 different bookplates have been used by Northwestern University since 1856, and their librarian has furnished three to be tipped-in our newsletter. The Class of 1895 is one of the earliest dated plates used by the library (see page 54).

THE LANTERN'S CORE, "Bookplates in Brief," Claudia Tonella. (9) 3:1-4, February 7, 1973. "Development of the art of the book plate parallels history. The early use of heraldry is an example. The art of the book plate changes, and by changing remains alive. It will continue to exist as long as men revere learning and books."

TIMES LITERARY SUPPLEMENT, "Engraved Bookplates." 1440, November 24, 1972. Review of the Severin/Reid book which makes you want to add this excellent volume to your library.

PRINT COLLECTOR'S NEWSLETTER notes an exhibit organized by Peter Wick of the Houghton Library for the Toulouse-Lautrec Festival which included a miniature bookplate.

ETOBICOKE GUARDIAN (Canada), "Bookplates reflect owners' interests," December 7, 1972. Pictured is our Canadian member, Emil Eerme, whose collection was on display at Richview Library.

L'EX LIBRIS FRANCAIS, issue for October 1972 includes a brief reference to the 50th Anniversary Keepsake of the ASBC&D.

COLLEGE & RESEARCH LIBRARIES, 33:498-9, November 1972, includes a review of BOOKPLATES, A Selective Annotated Bibliography of the Periodical Literature by Audrey Spencer Arellanes. "This book, then, is much more than a bibliography for collectors. It is a well edited and compact source book in cultural and social history."

THE LIBRARY, Transactions of the Bibliographical Society (London), 4:367, December 1972, also reviews BOOKPLATES and adds ten entries from Stuart Guthrie's THE BOOKPLATE (1920-22) which were not in the bibliography because copies of the periodical were not located in the United States. The reviewer has numbered and annotated the entries as follows:

    THE BOOKPLATE (Stuart Guthrie, editor. English Bookplate Society)
  657a "In the matter of exchange." 1:7-8, September 1920. On need for

system of arranging exchange of bookplates.

657b "Bookplates in the magazines." 2:3-4, December 1920. The state of criticism of bookplates in magazines.

657c "The serious question of progress." 3:1-3, September 1921. "We have still to admit the existence of the bookplate."

657d "A grateful note upon the engraved bookplates of Ida M. Swaine," James Guthrie. 3:4-8, September 1921.

657e "Soul and the bookplate," H. J. Stock. (1) 3:9-10, September 1921. "A bookplate design must have an idea."

657f "The bookplate in society." 3:19-20, September 1921. Parody of society column on subject of bookplates.

657g "Two bookplate collectors." 3:21-22, September 1921. A poem.

657h Review of THE BOOKPLATE annual for 1921. 3:23-25, September 1921.

THE BOOKPLATE, new series (Stuart Guthrie, editor. English Bookplate Society)

657i "The traditional style in bookplates," Henry Daniell. 1:5-7, December 1922. On early armorial style.

657j "The bookplates of Walter Kampmann," William Giles. 1:9-10, December 1922.

FOREBEARS,"Ex Libris."15:226-7, Fall 1972. Illustrated and described are the bookplates of Rev. Enrico Molnar, Dr. John B. Umhau, William F. Freehoff and Jose Miguel Quintana. In addition there are two loose prints of the Quintana plates for each subscriber to mount in his own collection.

The Bookplate Society (England) Newsletter No. 2, includes "An American Calligraphic Artist," by James Wilson which tells of the fine work by James Hayes of Colorado and reproduces illustrations of four of his plates for Moravian College, Johns Hopkins, Abel Berland, and Beloit College.

MAINE SUNDAY TELEGRAM,"Are You A Collector of Bookplates?"headlines the column, Clearing House, by Fran Hapgood, January 14, 1973. Gerald T. Banner is interested in collecting plates used by Maine residents and libraries; he also asks what became of the Oliver Clement Sheehan collection.

Anchorage Historical and Fine Arts Museum NEWSLETTER, January 1973, "Museum to Receive Rockwell Kent Painting," pages 2 and 3. The featured speaker was Dan Burne Jones, ASBC&D member from Oak Park, Illinois, whose slide illustrated talk concerned "The Many-Faceted Career of Rockwell Kent." The painting was titled "Resurrection Bay." Additional coverage was given the presentation in the ANCHORAGE DAILY TIMES, January 8, 1973, which included a picture of the 175 patrons attending the ceremonies and a portrait shot of Mr. Jones.

ANTIQUARIAN BOOKMAN, "SPB American Week." 50:1582, November 20, 1972. The Sotheby Parke Bernet auctions during October 1972 included C. M. Russell's BACK-TRAILING (1922) with the CMR bookplate - it brought $225.00.

THE PRIVATE LIBRARY, "Reviews," 5:167-8, Autumn 1972. Brian North Lee in reviewing the Arellanes bibliography BOOKPLATES gives praise for the useful index it provides to the JOURNAL OF THE EX LIBRIS SOCIETY, MISCELLANEA GENEALOGIA ET HERALDICA, and BOOKPLATE COLLECTORS NEWS and takes her to task for "inadequate comments on Mr. Beddingham's various articles for the P.L.A. . . . But it would be churlish to draw attention to such details at the expense of so comprehensive and rewarding a piece of research."

PHILIP REED
by Nancy Reed

Born in Park Ridge, Illinois, 17 January 1908, Philip Reed was graduated from the Art Institute of Chicago in 1930, and in that same year, set up his printing office. Except for several years' service with the U. S. Army Corps of Engineers during World War II, he maintained his business in the Chicago area until 1956, when he moved to St. Joseph, Michigan.

Primarily an illustrator and designer of books, Mr. Reed has been awarded many honors by the American Institute of Graphic Arts, the Chicago Society of Typographic Art, the Chicago Book Clinic and other organizations. His books have been chosen fourteen times among the Fifty Books of the Year and were shown in the American National Exhibition in Moscow as typical of American art at its finest. Mr. Reed's works are in the Library of Congress, the Victoria and Albert Museum in London, The Morgan Library, the National Library of Scotland, The Huntington Library, the New York Public Library, the Newberry, the Art Institute of Chicago, and in the permanent collection of the Institutet Grafiska in Stockholm, as well as in many university libraries and private collections.

You are respectfully invited
to return this book to
Eric Tack

In St. Joseph he continues to work at illustration; serves as Art Director of Consulting Engineer magazine, and with his wife, Nancy, operates a woodcut stationery and bookplate business. His medium is the color wood engraving, often printed in as many as seven colors, and though time does not permit him to accept commissions right now, this may change in the future. Special commissions involving color cuts usually cost $350 to $400, for the blocks and the printing of 250 plates.

Nineteen stock bookplates are now available, as well as nineteen stationery designs, similar in feeling, and samples will be furnished on request. The charge for stock bookplates if $7 per 100 imprinted, and $4 for each additional 100 with the same imprint, same order. Design only, without imprint, $4.50 per 100. The plate tipped-in above is one of the stock designs.

  E X H I B I T S - "This Book is Mine: Bookplates of famous people" titled the exhibit at the Currier Galley of Art, Manchester, New Hampshire, from January 20 to February 25, 1973.

"Bookplates Make Ornate Display," wrote Harold Klopper of the Glendale, California, News-Press, in describing the exhibit installed in the Brand Library during the month of January, 1973, by Audrey Arellanes and Anthony Kroll.

Review by Clare Ryan Talbot - D. QUIXOTE NO MUNDO DOS
EX-LIBRIS, Manuel da Cruz Malpique. Porto, Portugal, 1964.
     For sheer ex libris delight and artistic wonder, this book is hard
to equal. It is the distillation of ex libris experience since it
covers the work of some of the great bookplate artists of the past 100
years, as well as some of the great owners, collectors and bookplate
personalities. As a feat of publishing it defies description since the
varying sizes, colors and insets represent the most tricky in bookplate
publishing. Add to these the exquisite tip-ins and etchings, and one
posses a dazzling array of technological triumph.

     Furthermore, the volume represents an opus in literature, philosophy
and art, for the immortal Cervantes' eccentric hero could well be *l'homme
universel*. Most collectors have achieved a Quixote plate or two in the
course of their acquisitions, but so many versions of the one figure will
come as a surprise to many. The language problem for this reader is provoking indeed, but the patchy attempts to unravel the text reveal a
literary style of a college Professor; one of his books is a biography,
CREVANTES: CIDADAO do MUNDO.

     Let the reader not take this review as adequate in scope, for the book
should be reviewed by one knowing the language. Suffice it to say that the
bookplate here fulfills its true mission in the world of art: the picture
transcends the word.

     Copies may be purchased for $15 from A. M. da Moto Miranda, Caixa
Postal 413, Lobito, Angola (Portuguese West Africa) or (between July and
December 1973) Casa do Outeiro, Celerico Baste, Portugal.

     Review by Richard H. Schimmelpfeng - FILOSOFIA AMENDA do
EX-LIBRIS, Manuel da Cruz Malpique. Braga, Livraria Pax Editora, 1960.
139 p. illus. 750 copies.
     FILOSOFIA AMENA do EX-LIBRIS, the author's second excursion into the
world of bookplates, is a charming series of essays concerning the psychological side of ex-libris and their owners and collectors.

     Dr. Malpique, a noted Portuguese psychologist and author (incidentally
not a bookplate collector) begins with an explanation of what an ex-libris
is, treats briefly of the whys and wherefores of collecting in general and
then more specifically of bibliophiles and thereby their bookplates. The
author develops the thesis that true bibliophiles will also have excellent
bookplates: pride in ownership of books extends to the plate proclaiming
that ownership.

     The bookplate may be read as a biographical statement of the owner
with presumably a psychological character reading implied. To support this
concept, Dr. Malpique quotes various owners' descriptions of their plates,
and gives a number of requirements for a successful bookplate. Although
not stated, one assumes that the bookplates illustrated are representative
of these requirements.

     The book is well-printed on art paper and contains 113 facsimiles, the
etched and engraved plates being reproduced by the half-tone process. Each
illustration is captioned by the name of the artist, and in the case of two
names, the first is the name of the artist, the second the name of the en-

graver, etcher, etc. An artist index is included, although no owner index is given. The reproductions are mostly European, with a large number of Portuguese and Spanish plates. Since the chief interest of this book to non-Portuguese readers will be the illustrations, it is a pity that the numerous etchings and engravings suffer from the reproductive process. The wood engravings reproduce satisfactorily. The comparison between this volume and the author's D. QUIXOTE no MUNDO do EX LIBRIS is perhaps unfair, but after seeing the excellent illustrations in the latter, those in the former must come a poor second. The book, in spite of the above remarks, is definitely worthy of inclusion in any serious collection of bookplate literature.

Copies may be obtained through Mr. Miranda either by purchase at $3.00 or by writing to arrange for exchange of other bookplate literature.

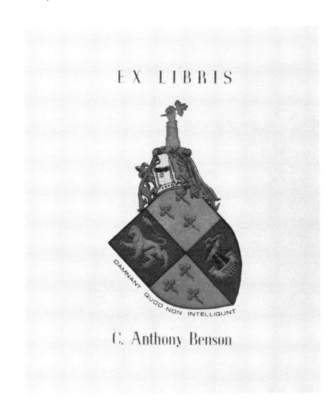

C. ANTHONY BENSON and the HERALDIC REGISTRY

"My appetite for the printing process led to part-time work on a newspaper, and in a job printing plant, then to general office manager in a photography studio, and eventually to a hobby-business under the name of Heraldic Registry," writes Mr. Benson. "I do designing and printing of heraldic items."

The full color plate here tipped-in is one of his own designs printed by letterpress from photoengraved plates. The coat of arms is a 1958 American creation copyrighted the same year and registered in his own Heraldic Registry in 1962.

A new member of ASBC&D, Mr. Benson also belongs to the Heraldry Society of England, Augustan Society and the Hammenhill Guild of Printers. His address is P. O. Box 4729, San Francisco, California 94101.

SPECIAL NOTE: This special edition to celebrate the completion of three years of publication of BOOKPLATES IN THE NEWS was made possible through funds provided by the Dorothy Sturgis Harding Proof Set Auction.

Enclosed with this newsletter is a copy for each member of his own entry for the MEMBERSHIP DIRECTORY. If there are any corrections or changes, they must be made on the copy and returned immediately to the Editor. The DIRECTORY will be YEAR BOOK 1971/72. Articles are also ready for the 1973 YEAR BOOK. An index for the YEAR BOOK 1951-1972 will be ready for the printer shortly.

BOOKPLATES IN THE NEWS
429 North Daisy Avenue
Pasadena, California 91107

Published – January - April - July
October - $3 U.S./$4 Foreign
Editor - Audrey Spencer Arellanes

American Society of
BOOKPLATE
Collectors and Designers

ASofBC&D

Number Thirteen   July 1973

429 NORTH DAISY AVENUE, PASADENA, CALIFORNIA 91107

BOOKPLATES IN THE NEWS . . . . .Editor, Audrey Arellanes

WILLIAM & GLADYS SUNDAY

William and Gladys
Sunday, ex libris
enthusiasts, were
members of ASBC&D
from 1952 to 1960.

William, born Octo-
ber 1, 1889, at
Scranton, Pa., at-
tended art school
as a young man. In
1950 he designed an
ex libris for his
wife (tipped-in on
page 61) showing
their 12 year old
dog in their garden,
and her interests in
music and button
collecting. Over a
25 year period she
was fortunate in
acquiring 29 out of
a possible 33 George
Washington Inaugural
buttons.

William spent a year
in New York City and
three in the Philip-
pines before return-
ing to the U.S. in
1914. He served over-
seas in World War I.

Mr. Sunday was a numis-
matist, who started
collecting as a boy,
then seriously in 1912,

60

and in 1917 became the youngest member of the Rochester Numismatic Association. By 1924 he was president of RNA, and in 1928 when Rochester hosted the national organization, American Numismatic Association, Mr. Sunday was asked to be on the Board of Governors of the national soiety. He also wrote a weekly newspaper column on coins which his wife helped him research.

Gladys was born in England and attended school there. Her early interest in antiques may have developed from exposure to the beautiful furniture, rugs, and crystal in the homes of her English grandparents. At one time Mrs. Sunday was an appraiser of oriental rugs. Collecting old buttons and antiques eventually lead to ex libris. William and Gladys attended country auctions where they purchased trunks of books which often contained artistic or otherwise interesting bookplates.

Gladys came from a family which for three generations had been medical professionals, and she went into nursing. The Botel and Vannuccini plates each note her R.N. degree. Mrs. Sunday was one of many ex libris enthusiasts who assisted European artists during World War II by sending clothing and food in exchange for bookplates. Her Botel is such an exchange plate. She explains it "depicts the tree where life overcomes death; in another not shown, a fountain was used as his idea of my overflowing kindness. Mr. Sunday sketched the design for the Angel of Mercy plate executed by Vannuccini."

While Mrs. Sunday is no longer active in collecting, she would welcome letters from old friends. Her address:
700 - 50th Street North
St. Petersburg, Florida 33710

EX LIBRIS ALBRECHT DURER

In December of 1971, Mexico issued a commemorative stamp for the 500th anniversary of the birth of Albrecht Durer, German painter and engraver.   It is a two peso air mail featuring the Durer coat of arms.

Albrecht Durer was born in Nuremberg on May 21, 1471, one of 18 children. His father was a goldsmith and the son was trained in the same trade. However, Albrecht wanted to be a painter, and in 1486 he was apprenticed to Michel Wolgemot.

In WOODCUTS OF ALBRECHT DURER, T. D. Barlow says, "Durer was a highly intellec- tual artist with widely varying interests and astonishing powers of work and of concentration. This was the universal feeling of his contemporaries, who write and speak of him with deep affection. The journal of his Netherlands tour ob- viously written as a personal record with no eye to publication, unaffectedly pleased by the honour with which he was received, but friendly and companionable to all."

He is best known for his major works such as the Apocalypse, The Great Passion, Life of the Virgin, The Little Passion, Nuremberg Chronicle, and the Flight in- to Egypt, and perhaps known only to the specialist for his ex libris.

Durer was from the Hungarian family of Ajtos, derived from "ajto" (door); it signifies the same as the German Thurer or Durer, and Durer used the same arms - the open door under a pent-house roof - shown above.

IN MEMORIAM - Rev. H. Leach Hoover

The Rev. Homer Leach Hoover, former Rector of St. Bartho- lomew's Episcopal Church in Hartsville, South Carolina, died February 9, 1973.

He was born in Davidson County, North Carolina, in 1879. He attended the Univer- sity of North Carolina and the University of the South at Sewanee, Tennessee. In 1905 he was ordained to the ministry of the Episcopal Church and served churches in North Carolina, Oklahoma, Cincinnati, Ohio before moving to Hartsville in 1926, where he was Rector for 21 years. Upon his retirement in 1947, he became rector- emeritus.   In 1917 he was commissioned a lieutenant in the infantry and served in the American Expeditionary Force; later he was a member of the South Carolina na- tional Guard for 10 years. He served as chaplain of the 30th Division and retired in 1941 with the rank of Lt. Colonel. He was also active in the American Legion and Rotary.

Rector John Prior of St. Bartholomew's wrote: "Some of our newer members missed a great deal in not having known our Rector Emeritus, who died last week. We as a Parish are grateful for him and his delightful sense of humor and also his amazing vitality which stayed with him until not too long ago. We do not mourn his passing. When a man reaches the age of 94, each day becomes a little more of a burden. We shall miss him." His bookplate friends will miss him, too; his charm, humor and vitality were very evident in his letters. He also had a collection of over 200 Rubaiyats and was starting a nucleus of books on Francois Villon.

MOGENS EILERTSEN
Private Press Printer/Artist

Private press printers, no less than bookplate enthusiasts, know no language barrier and reach across international boundaries to form friendships. Such a friendship has developed between Mogens Eilertsen and Audrey Arellanes, who met through the Private Library Association's listing of private press books and subsequently discovered a mutual interest in ex libris.

Mogens Eilertsen, who lives in Kastrup, Denmark, is headmaster of Nordegardsskolen, a secondary school founded in 1804. A booklet on the school shows a multi-level structure built about 1967. Mr. Eilertsen specializes in mathematics and physics and has published four textbooks.

Printing and drawing are his hobby interests, and while he has had no formal training in either, his work is very professional. He has printed about twenty books, including ten since 1961 which have appeared in the Private Library listing. Almost all contain illustrations executed by Mogens by various methods - relief etching, linocuts, drawings reproduced by offset lithography and woodcuts. One was a family project with seven linocuts of birds executed by Ellen and verse captions by Anne Marie, his wife and daughter. One publication, issued in 1964, was a presentation for the Copenhagen Rotary Club. Ellen and Mogens collaborated on SORT HVIDT OG LIDT FARVE ET PAR NYE EX LIBRIS; it contained 15 illustrations and the tipped-in bookplates were in various colors. Most publications are in editions of 50 copies and are only for exchange, not for sale.

Mogens Eilertsen has designed about 60 bookplates for friends and in exchange for private press books. Some of his personal ex libris include several Ex Nicotica for a collection on smoking; some show the graver, brayer and other engraving tools; one here tipped-in depicts his graver and printing press. Mogens has designed two ex-libris for Audrey Arellanes. One with an A-slug of type atop a book and a more recent plate with a view from Mogens' studio with trees, hills and clouds in the distance. Some of his bookplate prints are in as many as four colors. A three color plate showing a potter's wheel was made for Ella Engel, former ASBC&D member.

PHILIP METZGER/CRABGRASS PRESS

The Crabgrass Press was started in 1957 with the purchase of a small, treadle-operated letterpress manufactured some time before 1906. Like many another private pressman, Philip Metzger originally housed his press in the basement of his home. After mastering the basic skills of printing, he acquired a larger treadle press and a motorized press, both of ancient vintage. By 1969 he felt he possessed enough expertise to justify the purchase of a demi-folio English Albion handpress built in London in 1900, the last in its line of a press invented in 1820.

Philip Metzger has been fortunate in the number of talented people who have become interested in his press and worked with him to produce handsome examples of printing. Among these was Harald Peter of Hallmark Cards who designed the Crabgrass pressmark, and Hermann Zapf, the famous type designer and calligrapher, who has taken a great interest in the work of the Press and designed some of the printed pieces exhibited during July 1970 at the Watson Library, University of Kansas. To quote from the combination brochure/exhibit catalog printed for the occasion, "The story of the Crabgrass Press would not be complete without an explanation of how it got its name. Every homeowner knows that if he neglects his lawn it soon will be overrun with crabgrass. Since becoming a private press addict the owner has wasted no time on his lawn. Therefore the lawn is solid crabgrass. Ergo: The Crabgrass Press." (Address: 4900 Tomahawk Road, Prairie Village, Kansas 66208)

From the PERIODICAL LITERATURE

NEWS-JOURNAL (Kent, Washington), April 11, 1973 - "Ex Libris Exhibition Part of Library Week," headlines an article about the collection of ASBC&D member Leon Thompson. The display included ex libris from the Lenin State Library in Moscow, USSR, and a plate designed for Pablo Picasso.

TRI-STATE TRADER (Knightstown, Indiana), June 2, 1973 - "Oldest Known Bookplate," Leon Thompson. King of Sweden's plate pictured. Mr. Thompson, a comparative newcomer to the field of bookplates, is an enthusiastic collector not only of ex libris but old greeting cards.

THE BOOK COLLECTOR (London), Spring 1973. Review by Percy H. Muir of BOOKPLATES: A Selected, Annotated Bibliography of The Periodical Literature by Audrey Spencer Arellanes.

ANTIQUARIAN BOOKMAN, February 19, 1973, contained a full page Obituary Note on Clara Tice, 84, who died on Feburary 2, 1973 in Forest Hills, New York. Some of her bookplate designs appeared in Bruno Guido's publications.

A ARTE DO EX-LIBRIS, publication of the Portugese Association of Ex Libris, now includes in each issue a full page summary in English.

The Alcuin Society (P. O. Box 94108, Richmond, British Columbia, Canada), a book collector's society formed in 1965, printed a keepsake, A SELECTION OF OLD CANADIAN BOOK PLATES, with notes by Neil Brearley ($5).

MILTON CASTLE

Milton Castle, well-known theatre personality, reconteur, and poet, and his charming wife, Claire, recently returned from a tour of the Orient. Along with the other more expected adventures of traveling, Mr. Castle discovered a number of interesting ex libris in Hong Kong and the various British consulates to add to his large collection of institutional plates.

Mr. Castle, who was born in New York City at the turn of the century, engaged in the stock bookplate business about 1925 and a business interest evolved into a hobby. He became even more active in the field of bookplates while one was being designed for his collection of humor which was given to the University of Louisville during the 1960's.

The Courville-Abbott Memorial Library at the White Memorial Medical Center, Los Angeles, featured Mr. Castle's bookplate collection during June of 1970. His personal bookplate, which is here tipped-in, was designed by Roma Van Rosen about 1930 as a canting plate with Milton holding a castle, the jester's cap bespeaks of his professional vocation, and the glasses and big ears are personal characteristics. "Aus Unseren Buchern" translates as "out of our books".

SANTA BARBARA BOOKPLATE EXHIBIT

The main branch of the Santa Barbara Public Library will have an ex libris exhibit from June 30th through the end of July from the collection of Audrey Arellanes, Director of the American Society of Bookplate Collectors and Designers. Included will be engraving tools and plates of Anthony F. Kroll, and material featuring the work of early Santa Barbara artist, Henry Sawe, will be on display from the collection of Helan Halbach. Sawe is represented in Clare Ryan Talbot's HISTORIC CALIFORNIA IN BOOKPLATES by the plate he designed for his daughter, Elizabeth Brainerd Sawe, which shows an Indian youth as the bringer of fire. Among manuscript materials held by Ms. Halbach from another Santa Barbara bookplate artist, Margaret Ely Webb, are references to Henry Sawe, whom she found fascinating when he spun tails of earlier times.

A SONG
IN A MEADOW
Henry J. Sawe

American Society of
BOOKPLATE COLLECTORS AND DESIGNERS

429 North Daisy Avenue · Pasadena · California 91107

BOOKPLATES IN THE NEWS   Number Fourteen   October 1973

NEW MASTHEAD CREATED BY LEO WYATT

It is with pleasure and pride that the Society introduces its new masthead for the newsletter created by English engraver Leo Wyatt.

At an early age Leo showed an ability to draw and was apprenticed to Dacier Baxter of London as an engraver. While training as a commercial engraver, he attended the Central School of Arts and Crafts in London evenings and was most fortunate to be tutored by the well known engraver George Taylor Friend. He was also at this time made aware that in addition to the traditional copperplate script, there were new letter forms being developed by such artists as Johnston and Gill.

In his early thirties, Leo married and the marriage was blessed with two daughters. Following World War II, the family moved to South Africa for health reasons, as one child needed lots of sun. Wyatt freelanced as designer engraver in South Africa between 1947 and 1961. One of the bookplates designed during this period was for his wife Betty, who was working as verbatim Inquiry Reporter for the Jockey Club of South Africa in Cape Town. The ex libris shows a spiral shorthand book across the top of which is written in Pitman, "Increase your speed". The book is supported by her pen and behind a racehorse is a veiw of Table Mountain from Milnerton Race Course. Wyatt wrote about his bookplates and annotated a dozen of them in the YEAR BOOK 1961/62.

Since 1963, he has been lecturing at Newcastle College of Art and Industrial Design. His incomparable work was exhibited in "2,000 Years of Calligraphy" (USA 1965), "Exhibition of Alphabets" (1969 at Chapin Library, Williamstown, Massachusetts), Designer Craftsmen Exhibit (London, 1969), "The Art of the Letter" (Scottish National Gallery of Modern Art), "The English Art of the Book" (Chapin Library, Winter 1970); examples of his work are in the Victoria and Albert Museum in London as well as in museums in Canada, Australia, South Africa, Spain, Brazil and the United States.

Work has recently been commissioned by the Maryland Historical Society, Boston Athenaeum, David Godine, National Portrait Gallery, Smithsonian Institution, Worshipful Company of Stationers (London). Leo Wyatt's work is well represented in ENGRAVED BOOKPLATES, European Ex Libris 1950-70, and articles about him have appeared in BLACK ART (1962), CONNOISSEUR (July 1970).

The Society is indeed indebted to Leo Wyatt for the beauty of his wood engraved letterhead. Inquiries concerning commissioning a bookplate may be directed to him at 15 Devonshire Place, Jesmond, Newcastle on Tyne NE2 2NB, England.

SARA EUGENIA BLAKE

EX LIBRIS
SARA EUGENIA
BLAKE

Sara Eugenia Blake died on June 16, 1973 at the age of 87. Lively, energetic and charming to the end, she will be mourned by a wide circle of ex libris friends in all parts of the world. She carried on a brisk correspondence with fellow philibrists in this country and abroad over a period of four decades. Gifted with a unique talent for etching bookplates of great beauty, she was noted for the delicacy of the plates she designed as a labor of love for so many of her friends. Known to her friends as Sally, she captured the hearts of all the collectors and designers of bookplates whom she met.

For many years Miss Blake was librarian at Tufts Medical College in Boston. She developed a liking for philately early in life, and out of this hobby she veered to her amateur interest in bookplates. Greatly attracted by all beautiful art objects, she purchased some equipment, took art lessons, and plunged into her avocation of designing ex libris. When arthritis hindered her using the printing press, medical and dental students kindly came to her aid. She was a perfectionist who was never satisfied until the print looked perfect to her.

A short, but agreeable, account of her activities was published in 1963 by M. H. Leight in a small magazine, SUCCESS, volume X, No. 6, June-July 1963, pages 15-9. It reproduced a photograph of Miss Blake in company with Warren Lowenhaupt at the 1958 Congress de Ex Libristas, convened in Barcelona, Spain. In 1953, Mary Alice Ercolini published a short, illustrated note concerning Miss Blake in the circular distributed among the members of the Asociacion de Ex Libristas de Barcelona, III, No. 6, pages 84-5; and in 1960 Mrs. Ercolini wrote a more extensive article which appeared in the Portugese journal, BOLETIM A ARTE DO EX LIBRIS, V, No. 6, pages 113-8. Encouraged by Carlyle S. Baer, former Secretary of the ASBC&D, about 1953 I worked up a checklist of bookplates designed by Sara Eugenia Blake which appeared in the YEAR BOOK 1952/53, volume 25, pages 26-7 (published in 1955). More recently BOOKPLATES IN THE NEWS had a short note about Miss Blake accompanied by the tipped-in plate she designed for Frances Radbill, wife of Dr. Samuel X. Radbill.

J. Edouard Diamond and his wife, Elizabeth, both avid collectors of ex libris, set up the Hyacinth Press as a hobby in the basement of their Cleveland home. One of the earliest productions of this limited edition press, published in 1944, was A GARLAND OF BOOKPLATES ETCHED BY SARA EUGENIA BLAKE.

Sally Blake was a vivacious, cheery person who liked the good things in life and enjoyed doing things for others. A host of medical and dental students at Tufts, who spent long hours of study in her library during the three decades she was there to assist them, were much indebted to this benevolent soul. In the past 40 years ex libris neophytes have likewise been beholden to her for encouragement which was always so cheerfully bestowed. We have all of us lost a good friend. Vale!

July 14, 1973   Samuel X. Radbill, M. D.

JUSTIN HARVEY SMITH

The American historian Justin Harvey Smith was born January 13, 1857 in Boscawen, New Hampshire. He was the youngest of three sons born to Cynthia Maria (Egerton) and Rev. Ambrose Smith, a Dartmouth graduate and Congregational minister. In 1877 Justin graduated with honors and B.A. from Dartmouth and two years later received his M.A. From 1879 to 1881 he was a student at Union Theological Seminary in New York.

He spent some time at the Paris Exposition as private secretary to John D. Philbrick, who was in charge of the American Education Exhibit. He entered the publishing business in 1881, first with Charles Scribner's Sons, then Ginn & Co., text book publishers. Justin was in charge of the editorial department until 1898 when he retired with a "satisfactory" fortune.

At this time he started his second career as professor of Modern History at Dartmouth, where he served until 1908, when he resigned to devote his entire time to historical research. He wrote TROUBADOURS AT HOME; a critical study of Benedict Arnold's march from Cambridge to Quebec with a reprint of Arnold's JOURNAL; OUR STRUGGLE FOR THE FOURTEENTH COLONY, a study of Canada and its relation to the American Revolution; and in 1919 published two volumes on WAR WITH MEXICO, for which he received the Pulitzer Prize in 1920. The following year he was awarded the first Loubat Prize of $1,000.

Although he called himself "unmarried" he married Mary E. Barnard of Chico, California in May 1892. They separated two years later, and the marriage was terminated by a Paris divorce. Justin Smith served as chairman of the Historical Manuscript Commission of the American Historical Association from 1917 to 1923. He traveled through forty countries plus Alaska and the Philippines.

In November of 1929 he was injured in a taxicab accident. Then on March 21, 1930 he suffered a heart attack in front of Brooklyn's Borough Hall and died instantly just two months after his 73rd birthday. He is described as having been tall, with sharp eyes and a full beard; for recreation he cruised in power boats from his own plans.

It is thanks to Francis W. Allen that copies of Justin Harvey Smith's bookplate are available to be tipped-in. Perhaps another member will be able to furnish information about the artist who designed the plate?

GEORGIA A. DIEHL
YOUNG PEOPLE'S ROOM

SOUTH PASADENA PUBLIC LIBRARY

SOUTH PASADENA PUBLIC LIBRARY

On October 28, 1946 the South Pasadena Public Library dedicated a new young adults' reading room named in honor of Georgia A. Diehl, who had recently retired after 15 years as head librarian.

A special bookplate was designed by South Pasadena artist Mildred Bryant Brooks. The original etching measured about 6" x 8" and was then reduced in size for use in books for the special reading room. A print of the etching was presented to the bookplate collection of Scripps College.

Thanks are due the Board of the South Pasadena Public Library for permission to reproduce the Diehl bookplate and to City Librarian, Mrs. Mary Helen Wayne, for her help.

In a following issue, there will be an article on Mildred Bryant Brooks and her etched ex libris.

REVIEWS - -

THOREAU MacDONALD, A CATALOGUE OF DESIGN AND ILLUSTRATION, Margaret E. Edison. University of Toronto Press, Toronto, 1973. 204 pages, illustrated, 8x10. $15

Canadian artist Thoreau MacDonald did line drawings, oil paintings, book illustrations, calligraphy & designed book jackets, end papers and other ephemera. This book is a pictorial and bibliographical record of MacDonald's work, based on Margaret E. Edison's collection, which was started in the thirties.

There is an autobiographical note by Thoreau MacDonald and an assessment of his work by Mrs. Edison. The catalogue is divided into sections on the artist as writer, books wholly illustrated and catalogue designs, books containing designs or lettering, designs for and in periodicals, joint work with his father, J. E. H. MacDonald, and ephemera. It is within the ephemera section that fifteen of his ex libris are reproduced.

This is a handsome volume, profusely illustrated, with a dust jacket reproducing one of his landscapes. It will especially appeal to all who are interested in the graphic arts.

A special limited edition with a signed MacDonald print and a different binding is priced at $50.

During July and August 1973 there was an exhibit from the Edison collection at the Thomas Fisher Rare Book Library of the University of Toronto.

FREDERICK GARRISON HALL, ETCHINGS, BOOKPLATES, DESIGN (with a biographical sketch by Ariel Hall & a personal memoir by Henry P. Rossiter), Elton Wayland Hall. Boston Public Library, Boston, 1972. $15

Illustrated are many of Hall's etchings, bookplates, representative drawings, cover designs and paintings. The text also includes two reprinted articles on his etchings and one on "The Little People of F. G. Hall," the catalogue of the Memorial Exhibition at the Museum of Fine Arts in the spring of 1947, which included four ex libris.

Fifty-two of Hall's bookplates, designed between 1901 and 1919, are illustrated. They were generally photomechanically reproduced from drawings. Almost all of them have what Ralph Bergengren described as "the distinctive characteristic of the little picture . . its combination of fantasy and plausibility."

This volume is a valuable addition to the library of the collector whose interest centers on the bookplate artist.

MY LIVES, Francis Meynell. Random House, New York, 1971. 332 pages, illustrated.

This is the autobiography of a man who excelled in a number of fields, though perhaps he is most frequently associated with typography and the Nonesuch Press,

Of interest to bookplate enthusiasts will be the illustration of the wood engraved ex libris Eric Gill designed for Francis Meynell, engravings by Reynolds Stone, and references to Aylmer Valance, Gordon Craig, Lovat Fraser, Stephen Gooden.

PRINTS BY E. REITSMA-VALENCA with an introduction by Louis Ginsberg. Petersburg. Virginia, 1964. $5

This forty-page booklet was a keepsake celebrating Mrs. Rietsma-Valenca's 75th birthday. Among the thirty reproductions of her work is a self-portrait and nine ex libris.

AN OPEN LETTER TO A BEGINNER BOOKSELLER, Louis Ginsberg. Glade Press, Wormley, England, 1972. $3.50

"The most important tools for the antiquarian bookseller are the study of book-plates, bibliography, and booksellers' catalogues. But why book-plates? The field of book-plates is a study in miniature of the book as a human artifact."

LABEL DESIGN, EVALUATION, FUNCTION AND STRUCTURE OF LABEL, Claude Humbert. Watson-Guptil Publications, New York, 1972.

One thousand labels from the 17th century to the present are tri-lingually captioned. Simple labels for practical identification and elaborate graphics, all sizes, shapes, and various methods of reproduction - cigar bands, labels for wine, biscuits, booksellers, liquor, propaganda, and thirteen ex libris examples.

N O T E - Edward R. Roybal has introduced to the House of Representatives (July 18, 1973) a resolution to proclaim October 1974 as HOBBY MONTH.

"Elmer Belt at Eighty: A Tribute," was presented April 12, 1973 at the UCLA Center for Medieval and Renaissance Studies. Included on the program was an illustrated talk by Suzanne B. Larson, "The Ex-Libris of the Belt Library." The Belt Library of Vinciana bookplate shows a vignette from a sheet of technological drawings in the Codex Altanticus dating about 1480.

FROM THE PERIODICAL LITERATURE:
PLAYBOY, New Sexual Life Styles, 20:73-et seq., September 1973. A panel discussion titled, A Symposium on emerging behavior patterns, from open marriage to group sex, included among the twelve panelists Phyllis and Eberhard Kronhausen, psychologists who authored a book on erotic bookplates and are the founders of the International Museum of Erotic Art in San Francisco.

Reviews of BOOKPLATES, the annotated Arellanes bibliography appeared in: HERALD OF LIBRARY SCIENCE, January 1973; UNESCO BULLETIN FOR LIBRARIES, March-April 1973; PAPERS OF THE BIBLIOGRAPHICAL SOCIETY OF AMERICA, 66:#4, 1972.

CONNOISSEUR, 155:51, January 1964, a review by Ruari McLean of "Concerning Booklabels" by P. C. Beddingham, W. Carter, and R. Stone; 29 labels are reproduced.

EQSUIRE, Manhattan Round-Up, Ex Libris. 13:2 pages, May 1940. Exhibit at Bitter and Loud in New York City devoted to bookplate work of Dorothy Sturgis Harding, who "at the moment is at work on a plate for Jack at 21 . . . ."

MnU BULLETIN, An Essay on Bookplates, John Jensen. (5) 1:90-9, July 1970. Interesting biographical essay on Edwin Davis French with five ex libris reproduced and annotated, and a selected bibliography.

SERIF, Bookplate of William Wardsworth. (1) 10:inside front cover, Spring 1973. Illustration only.

PRIVATE LIBRARY, The Perez Collection of British Bookplates, Keith Clark. (4) 6:22-8, Spring 1973. Illustrations include plate for Queen Victoria, and plates by R. Anning Bell, Paul Nash, and Sherborn. Perez, the Cuban delegate to the International Sugar Council in London, donated duplicate prints to the Cuban National Library.

FOREBEARS, Ex Libris. (2) 16:188, Spring 1973. Details and reproduction of bookplates for Harrison Monroe and Arthur Melville Clark.

FOREBEARS, 16:190, Spring 1973. Request by P. W. Filby for assistance in preparing the second edition of AMERICAN & BRITISH GENEALOGY & HERALDRY.

FOREBEARS, A Heraldry Bibliography, Rev. James Parker. 16:288-302, Spring 1973. The foreword is by L. G. Pine and Rodney Hartwell has written a biographical sketch of Rev. Parker. Both Hartwell and Parker are ASBC&D members.

BOOKPLATE SOCIETY NEWSLETTER, No. 3, July 1973. Artist Diana Bloomfield was the speaker for their third meeting. - "Notes and Queries" was a manuscript book circulated among Bookplate Exchange Club members in 1942. It is intended that some of the more interesting and significant articles be edited for printing in the current newsletter. - P. C. Beddingham mentions the following English periodicals: ART AND ANTIQUES WEEKLY, February 10, 1973, has a three page article by C. G. L. Du Cann, The Mark of the Well Read Man, which includes ex libris for Arnold Bennett, a joint plate for Benjamin Britten and Peter Pears by Reynolds Stone, and Earl Mountbatten by G. T. Friend. - THE LADY, March 29, 1973, Collecting Bookplates, Keith Clark. Author is the librarian of the National Book League, which has a bookplate collection of note. - COUNTRY LIFE, CLIV:1596-7, June 7, 1973, This Belongs To... Time for an Ex Libris Revival? Christopher Neve has written a well-illustrated article which includes illustrations of a Phil May plate by William Nicholson, neo-rococo collotype by Rex Whistler for Osbert Sitwell, Millais' allegorical for Sir Christopher Sykes, Italo Zetti plate featuring a vintage Bugattis and can-can girls. - COUNTRY LIFE, CLIV:36, July 5, 1973, Bookplate Revival, P. C. Beddingham. The Bookplate Society has twenty-five new members.

CONNOISSEUR, Leo Wyatt - letter engraver on Wood, James Moran. (15) 174:192-5, July 1970. " . . . it is hoped that his endeavors will, in an age of mass-production, help to restore a much needed elegance to the small but important intimate pieces of printed matter by which we announce ourselves and our possessions to the world."

SAMFORD TODAY, Drive Seeks Resources. (1) 9:6, December 1972. While the entire issue is devoted to the library, one page particularly features the bookplate designed by Marlene Rikard, Head of Reader Services at Harwell G. Davis Library and designer of SAMFORD TODAY, and Lee C. Ketcham, assistant to the librarian.

PACIFICULTURE-ASIA MUSEUM

The Pacificulture-Asia Museum, in Pasadena, California, is a new museum situated in an ageless Chinese Palace that was built in 1924 by Grace Nicholson to house her collection of American Indian and Oriental art. The new museum opened on October 29, 1971 and is staffed entirely by volunteers; however, the sponsoring foundation was created in 1960 when about 25 Americans of both Caucasian and Japanese descent met with a common goal in mind - to provide a center where Asians and Americans could be brought together through art and cultural activities.

This Chinese Treasure House was built in 1924 by noted architects Marston, Van Pelt, and Mayberry, who received an award from the National American Institute of Architects for it in 1929. The authenticity of the Imperial Palace Courtyard style was assured by having all of the decorative

Library of
Pacificulture-Asia Museum
46 North Los Robles
Pasadena

roof tiles, finials, wood, stone, and marble carvings made in China. The only Western element was the cement fire-proof steel beam construction. This building was one of the first structures to be designated by the Cultural Heritage Board as an historical monument of Pasadena.

The bookplate created by Anthony F. Kroll incorporates the design used by Grace Nicholson for her library at 46 North Los Robles and the red chop mark of the Pacificulture. We are indebted to the Pacificulture-Asia Museum for permission to use their bookplate, and in particular to Ruth C. Scherrer, Registrar.

N O T I C E -
E. M. LILIEN, BOOK PLATES 1897-1907. This small booklet contains 38 bookplate prints, briefly annotated, and a one page biographical sketch. The edition is limited to 375 copies, of which 150 copies were for members of the Wynkyn de Worde Society. Copies may be obtained from the artist's son, Otto M. Lilien, whose address after November 1, 1973 will be 18, Hess Street, Rehovot, Israel. $6.00

WHO'S WHAT - Enclosed with this newsletter is a questionnaire to be completed by any individual or institutional members who may wish to be listed in THE COLLECTOR'S DIRECTORY which is published in Paris, France.

EX LIBRIS EXHIBIT at Cal-State Long Beach (California) - Five glass display cases in the Fine Arts Library of Cal-State Long Beach are filled with bookplate prints from the collection of Audrey Spencer Arellanes. One case depicts the Evolution of a Bookplate - From Idea to Print and features the engraving tools, steel die engravings, and final bookplate prints designed by Anthony F. Kroll. The exhibit is scheduled from September 17th to mid-October.

<u>R E V I E W   by V. R. Filby</u>

EKLIBRISY KHUDOZHNIKOV ROSSIYSKOY FEDERATSII (Ex Libris of Artists of the Russian Federation), by E. N. Minaev. Izdatel'stvo "Sovetskaya Rossiya" ("Soviet Russia" Press), Moscow, 1971. Octavo. 319 pages, illustrated.

In his introductory essay, Evgeniy Minaev sketches the history of ex libris in Russia from the earliest book marks, found several years ago in manuscripts of the Solovetskiy monastery dating to 1493-94, to the work of Soviet artists today. Societies of bookplate collectors have existed in the USSR for many years, but the author credits Moscow artists for a renewed interest in ex libris during the 1960's. Collectors in over fifty Soviet cities exchange bookplates. Three collectors, S. P. Fortinskiy, the late B. A. Vilinbakhov, and Estonian art critic Paul Ambur, are internationally known, and their collections, says the author, each numbers 35,000 or more.

The author explains that his task as compiler was to acquaint lovers of miniature graphics with the ex libris of artists of the Russian Federation, and since hundreds of artists make ex libris he had to limit himself to the best known masters. He chose forty-five, the earliest birthdate being 1881 and the latest 1939.

Most of the 500 bookplates illustrated are grouped in "albums" arranged alphabetically by the artists' names. Each album includes a list of the owners of the ex libris shown, a photograph of the artist or artists (there is one husband and wife team), a brief biographical sketch. The pages are handsomely laid out, most of them with color, usually gray and cedar, but some with ivory-yellow, and a few with a soft blue or pink or vivid green to surprise and please the viewer leafing through the pages.

This attractive book should be an interesting addition to any bookplate collector's library. It is good looking and on good paper, with a pleasing rough gray cloth cover, but the binding is not very sturdy, and the book would probably not stand heavy handling.

RICHARD BALCH

Prints of the Balch ex libris have been furnished through the generosity of the owner, the printer (Anthony F. Kroll), and ASBC&D member Helan Halbach. Little is known as the origin of the bookplate except that it was probably "done years ago in Chicago".

Richard Balch is proprietor of the Curious Book Shoppe in Los Gatos, California and specializes in rare and out of print books.

- - - - - - - - - - - - - - - - - - -

BOOKPLATES IN THE NEWS -Published January - April - July - October $3. U.S./$4 Foreign

Editor - Audrey Spencer Arellanes

American Society of
BOOKPLATE COLLECTORS AND DESIGNERS

429 North Daisy Avenue·Pasadena·California 91107

BOOKPLATES IN THE NEWS   Number Fifteen   January 1974

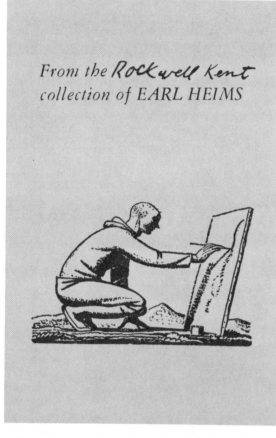

*From the Rockwell Kent
collection of EARL HEIMS*

One of the larger collections of the works of Rockwell Kent is located in Portland, Oregon, because of the Great Depression.

It belongs to Earl Heims, presently head of Heims & Turtledove Advertising Agency.

He became an avid collector of bookplates and a bookplate bibliophile because during the depression he needed to stretch the meager earnings of a young advertising novice. He was inspired by Rockwell Kent ex libris designs to create twelve bookplates for commercial selling. And that started him as a bookplate collector.

In recent years Earl has concentrated on his collection of Rockwellkentiana. Today, with appreciated assists from ASBC&D member Robert Hitchman and George S. Keyes, his collection includes 67 books - most of them autographed first editions - written or illustrated by Kent, and ephemeral material.

In designing a bookplate for his collection, Heims had many choices - particularly difficult with the many Kent bookplate designs available. He believed that it should be "personal" and that narrowed his choice to two designs: the frontispiece drawing from IT'S ME, O' LORD and the selected drawing from Kent's THIS IS MY OWN. The first drawing was not typically Kent, although it inspired a perfect bookplate title: "It's Mine, O' Lord - the Rockwell Kent Collection of Earl Heims." A facsimile of Kent's signature is used in the final plate which has been printed on stock of various colors and textures.

Issued Quarterly - January - April - July - October
BOOKPLATES IN THE NEWS   Editor: Audrey Spencer Arellanes
Subscription: Regular - $3 U.S./$4 Foreign
    Contributing: $10 (includes newsletter + additional ex libris prints)
     Sustaining: $25 (includes newsletter + additional ex libris prints from YEAR
                    BOOK and newsletter)

CLARE RYAN TALBOT
Honorary Member

It is with pleasure and pride that we name Clare Ryan Talbot an Honorary Member of the American Society of Bookplate Collectors and Designers. Mrs. Talbot has well earned this distinction with her many contributions to the field of bookplates.

She wrote in QUEST OF THE PERFECT BOOKPLATE, which was published by the Ruth Thompson Saunders Press in 1933. This was followed in 1936 by HISTORIC CALIFORNIA IN BOOKPLATES for which the noted California bibliographer, Robert Ernest Cowan, wrote the introduction. Throughout the years she has written a prolific number of articles for periodicals revealing her extensive research into the history of the ex librs.

Mrs. Talbot's Hilprand Press scored a first in specialty bibliography with the publication in 1951 of Dr. Samuel X. Radbill's BIBLIOGRAPHY OF MEDICAL EX LIBRIS LITERATURE.

In addition to being an author, historian, and publisher of ex libris material, Mrs. Talbot has long been a dealer and appraiser of bookplates, and founder of the Society of Ex Libris Historians.

Earlier recepients of Honorary Membership in ASBC&D were David Ellsworth Roberts of the Library of Congress, Mrs. Joseph C. Egbert, Dr. Frederick Starr, Edmund Hort New, John W. Evans, James Guthrie, and Mrs. William F. Hopson.

Mrs. Talbot was a charter and honorary member of the Bookplate Association International, Los Angeles; also an honorary member of the California Book-Plate Society. It is fitting that the First Lady of Bookplates now be an Honorary Member of ASBC&D.

The Winged Victory bookplate etched by Australian artist, Ella Dwyer, has been photoengraved in intaglio on steel by Anthony F. Kroll for special use on this occasion.

Contemporary Lithuanian Bookplates were exhibited during 1973 at the University of Missouri; Forrest R. Polk Library in Oshkosh, Wisconsin; Albrecht Gallery-Museum of Art, St. Joseph, Missouri; Karl E. Mundt Library, Dakota State College, Madison, South Dakota; Luther College, Decorah, Iowa; and Illinois State University. This traveling exhibit, which originated at the Octagon Center for the Arts in Ames, Iowa, is from the collection of a new ASBC&D member, Dr. Vitolis E. Vengris.

Please send news of your bookplate exhibit or other ex libris activity to the Editor.

RAYMOND F. DABOLL, Calligrapher

Ray DaBoll is that rare individual - an artist with a sense of humor. Anyone fortunate enough to exchange letters with him soon is aware of his skill with words both as calligrapher and correspondent.

Born in 1892, Mr. DaBoll has been a leading American calligrapher since the late 1930's. In 1939 the Newberry Library held an exhibit of the work of Johnston and his pupils which sparked DaBoll's interest in lettering. He attended the Art Institute in Chicago and R.I.T. For many years he was an advertising artist and art director. Even when moving to "forty acres" in Newark, Arkansas, the change of address announcements heralded the "Ozark headquarters for calligraphy, typographic design and layout." More recently he and his wife moved to Batesville, Arkansas.

One of the earliest bookplates Ray designed was about 1913 "for a gal I was nuts about... Mildred Sykes Whitford." The design included a comic mask, a Grecian urn, and Pan, all showing the influence of Franklin Booth to whom he was devoted; Ray still treasures a scrapbook with just about everything F. Booth ever did. A second plate in similar style was created in 1915 for John Koehl, a Chicago art director, showing his ship outward bound which might come in some day and a castle in the air. While free lancing in 1926 DaBoll designed an ex libris for Egbert Jacobson, art director of the Container Corporation of America, and "included the whole Jacobson family of five brothers and one sister - all devoted to some branch of the arts - five brothers represented as jay birds perched in the branches of the family tree bearing five sun flowers - the sister Lily is also a jay bird peering into a lily."

Three calligraphic plates have been designed: a joint one for John and Jean Michel, art director of Johns-Manville Co. and his pianist wife; in 1942, for Richard Nall, and in 1953 a plate for F. Dean Russell, IV. These show the influence of English designer, Reynolds Stone. About 1963 DaBoll designed a memorial plate which was given to the Library of Dobbs College.

The artist's own ex libris was designed in 1967 and originally printed by Antioch Bookplate Company. The copy here tipped-in was printed specially for the newsletter.

MEMBERSHIP DIRECTORY
The long awaited MEMBERSHIP DIRECTORY being published as YEAR BOOK 1971/72 is now scheduled for January mailing. It will contain over 100 pages with information on more than 150 members, both individual and institutional, with 115 bookplates of which 44 will be tipped in. $20 to members appearing in the DIRECTORY; otherwise $25. No directories will be mailed without a signed order form.

FROM THE PERIODICAL LITERATURE:
FRIENDS OF THE LIBRARIES (Case Western Reserve University), Outstanding Bookplate Collection Here. (3)1:1,3,4,Autumn 1973. The collection is primarily the result of gifts from Miss Clara Prentis Sherwin, Paul Lemperly, and Miss Alice S. Tyler.

SERIF, Book-plate of Bilibaldi Pirckheimer, X:inside cover, Summer 1973. Illustration only of Albrecht Durer design. (Incidentally, this bookplate was on display recently at the Walton Galleries in San Francisco during an exhibit of fifty Durer engravings and etchings which ranged in price from $150 to $10,500; the Pirckheimer was on loan.)

QUARTERLY JOURNAL of Library of Congress, A Book from Garfield's Library, The Preface to a Preface, Madeleine B. Stern. (1) 30:205 et seq., July 1973. "Garfield's library motto was 'inter folia fructus' - fruit among the leaves. His interest in libraries was great, and he made the Library at the Capitol the recipient of his large annual collection of pamphlets."

BULLETIN OF THE NEW YORK PUBLIC LIBRARY, Library of Grand Duke Vladimir Alexandrovich (1847-1909), A Recent Accession. (3) 35:779-82, November 1931. One illustration is the Grand Duke's ex libris.

BULLETIN OF THE NEW YORK PUBLIC LIBRARY, Sidney Lawton Smith (1845-1929). 35:783-4, November 1931. Notice of memorial exhibit of prints by Sidney L. Smith during December 1931 and January 1932 "with special stress on his bookplate work."

EVENING SENTINEL, New Display at Spahr, September 28, 1973. "Roy Jansen, an ex-newsman and retired publicist for the Pennsylvania Medical Society, recently donated his wide assortment of personalized bookplates to the Pennsylvania State Library in Harrisburg. . . which in turn loans portions of the collection to other interested libraries for exhibition." Such was the exhibit at Spahr Library of Dickinson College, Carlisle, Pennsylvania.

EX LIBRIS, Simplistic Press, Vol. 1, No. 6, November 1, 1971. Four illustrations of possible bookplates for D. M. Gardner who is interested in fishing. Dick Ulrich (P.O. Box 206, Cambridge City, Indiana 47327) is a hobby printer with a sense of humor. His wide variety of cuts coupled with type could be used to create bookplates.

AMPHORA III (Alcuin Society, Canada), Book Reviews. (4) 11-12, Fall 1968. Neil Brearley reviews U.S.S.R. EX-LIBRIS by Evgueni Minaiev which was apparently published in connection with Expo'67 with text in Russian, English, German, and French. "The book is an eloquent testimony to the craftsmanship and fertility of imagination of the Soviet artists currently producing bookplates - and to the way in which the ordinary citizen must presumably care about books in order to support their output."

STAR-NEWS, Pasadena, Library Gets Fund from Coffin Estate, October 29, 1973. Longtime Pasadena resident, Clifford L. Coffin, left the Pasadena Public Library $113,881.81 for the purchase of books dealing with all phases of the fine arts. A special bookplate is to be commissioned which will be placed in each item purchased through the trust as a means of providing a continuing acknowledgment of the bequest.

THE BOOKPLATE SOCIETY, Newsletter No. 4, October 1973. The major article is one never previously published by the late G. H. Viner, Bookplates Engraved by David Loggan. In addition to the Isham plated engraved in 1673, Viner concluded there were at least nine other plates attributable to Loggan, some of which closely follow designs of Michel le Blon (1590-1656).

AMERICAN LIBRARIES, January 1974, carries a notice that by writing Library of Congress, Central Services Division, Publications Distribution Unit, Washington, D.C. 20540, you may obtain an illustrated brochure containing bookplates & prices.

DECORATIVE PAPERS AND FABRICS (Van Nostrand Reinhold, 1971) by Annette Hollander, wife of ASBC&D member William V. Hollander, may interest collectors who would like a simple method for binding bookplate ephemera, single signature periodical literature, or covering storages boxes for ex libris prints. In addition to the book, supplies and magazines on the subject can be obtained by writing Bookcraft, Box 6048, Hamden, Ct. 06517.

NEW MEMBERS who have joined ASBC&D since the MEMBERSHIP DIRECTORY deadline:
Mrs. Barbara Anne Abele, 215 Belmont Court, Redlands, Ca. 92373
Mrs. Ruth C. Bowen, 8 Penn Terrace, Chatham, N.J. 07928
Hebrew Union College, Jewish Inst. of Religion, Cincinnati, Ohio 45220
Mrs. Ruth Hermann, 2304 Riddle Ave.-#2, Wilmington, De. 19806
John R. Jenson, 3121 Cedar Ave. South-#201, Minneapolis, Mn. 55407
Mrs. Katherine Day Kamuck, 113 Buxton Road, Bedford Hills, N.Y. 10507
Mrs. Gertrude H. Mahony, 201 Linden Ave., Oak Park, Ill. 60302
J. P. O'Beirne, 23 W. Holly St., Santa Barbara, Ca.
Katsuyoshi Ohmoto, 137-23-306 Ueda Yahon, Omiya City, Saitama Prefecture, Japan
Tom Owen, 6157 Glen Oak, Hollywood, Ca. 90068
G. Thomas Tanselle, 410 W. Washington St., Lebanon, Ind. 40652
Dr. Vitolis E. Vengris, 6018 Pratt St., Baltimore, Md. 21224
Richard D. Wells, 16 South St., Mobile, Al. 36606
Thoreau Willat, 4723-F La Villa Marino, Marina del Rey, Ca. 90291

EUROPEAN BOOKPLATE LITERATURE

EXLIBRIS WERELD, edited by G. J. Rhebergen, Jr., Amsterdam, December 1973, has an illustrated article on Guild Hall ex libris, which include those for Master Wardens Assistants and Company of Gardeners of London, Institute of Masters of Wine, Company of Clockmakers, Worshipful Company of Glaziers and Painters of Glass (8 pages, 7½ x 5 1/8).
NORDISK EXLIBRIS TIDSSKRIFT, edited by Helmer Fogedgaard, Copenhagen, #3, 1973, has articles on artists from Hungary, Sweden, and Holland. Each issue has about a quarter page summary in English (20 pages, 7 5/8 x 10½).
A ARTE DO EX-LIBRIS, edited by Artur Mario da Mota Miranda, Portugal, #62, 1973, has a wealth of material including two pages of English summary of the articles (40 pages, 8 x 10 3/4).
EXLIBRISTEN, P.O. Box 109, DK-9900 Frederikshavn, Denmark, is the name of Klaus Rodel's firm devoted to the publication of books relating to bookplates. Write him for details of subscribing to his publications. Tentatively planned for 1974 Bibliography of European Exlibris 1972, Modern Polish Exlibris, Modern Czech Exlibris, and artists Mart Lepp, Leida Soom, Jaroslav Svab, Rastislav Michal and Josef Nechansky. Past volumes have been well illustrated and represent good graphic design.

You are missing out if you are not subscribing to any of the European ex libris journals or acquiring some of the literature being published on European artists. While a reading knowledge of the European languages would naturally enrich your enjoyment, all the publications are profusely illustrated, often with tipped in plates, and the visual pleasures alone are worth the purchase price. For addresses of European associations, see BOOKPLATES IN THE NEWS for January 1973.

The Architect of the Capitol

The device now used by the Architect of the Capitol on letterheads has also become the emblem for bookplates.

The device was designed by George M. White, FAIA, who is Architect of the Capitol, in 1971 and was executed by Gustav Veres. It won first place in the 7th Annual Exhibition of the Society of Federal Artists and Designers in 1971.

LIBRARY OF CONGRESS GOUDY COLLECTION

"It is natural that great libraries should have an abiding interest in all aspects of typography. The Library of Congress has given effect to this interest by attempting to keep its collection on the book arts as complete as possible: the acquisition of the Goudy Collection is the first serious attempt to include within it examples of the art of type design." Thus wrote David Judson Haykin, Chief of the Subject Cataloging Division, in the QUARTERLY JOURNAL OF CURRENT ACQUISITIONS, 1:#3, 1944.

In February of 1944, Archibald MacLeish as Librarian of Congress wrote to Frederic W. Goudy: "It would be most appropriate that the bookplate that will distinguish the Frederic and Bertha Goudy Collection bear some mark of your genius, and I am happy to learn that you will try to find time to design one."

The actual bookplate print is in two colors: black and sienna for the initials within the ruled frame.

"Goudy's interest in type design quite naturally grew out of his interest in the art of printing. By 1894 he had advanced so far as to embark upon a short-lived venture known first as the Booklet Press and presently as the Camelot Press. In 1903 he founded the Village Press in which he and his wife continued to produce beautifully printed books from types of his own design. Not being satisfied to design the types, Goudy eventually began to cut the matrices and cast the type, so that after the Village Press had been moved into an old mill at Deepdene, the Goudy's home near Marlborough, New York, the name of the press was extended to include the words "and Letter Foundery". When in 1939 fire destroyed the old mill and everything in it, Goudy's printing activity came to an end," though he continued his work as a designer.

EXHIBITS

"In the village-hall of Doorn, a village in the centre of the Netherlands, an exhibition has been held of bookplates from the collection of the German artist Hermann Huffert. Also exhibited were bookplates by Huffert. Ending date for the exhibit was October 15, 1973." (Thanks to Henk G. van Otterloo, the Netherlands.)

The Friends of the Mobile Public Library will feature an exhibit from the collection of Audrey Arellanes from March 22 to April 2, 1974.

American Society of BOOKPLATE COLLECTORS AND DESIGNERS

429 North Daisy Avenue · Pasadena · California 91107

BOOKPLATES IN THE NEWS   Number Sixteen   APRIL 1974

ERNIE PYLE MEMORIAL LIBRARY

The white clapboard house which was Ernie Pyle's home in Albuquerque, New Mexico was given to the city and in 1947 became the first branch of the public library system. Pyle won wide readership during World War II as spokesman for the GIs and met his death at 44 from Japanese machine gun fire while driving to a forward command post on a tiny Pacific isle on April 18, 1945 (born August 3, 1900, Dana, Indiana).

The library is filled with Pyle mementos including his notebooks, Stetson hat, the Jo Davidson bust of him, photos of him in the African, European and Pacific war areas where he served as correspondent. In 1944 he won the Pulitzer Prize for distinguished reporting and was pictured on the cover of TIME MAGAZINE. In a recent article by Los Angeles TIMES staff writer Charles Hillinger, the librarian at the Ernie Pyle Memorial Library, Anne McRedmond is quoted: "Every day they come - these men whose lives were brushed by Mr. Pyle. They recall the day they met him or what he said about them or about their company, battalion or ship in a column so many years ago."

The bookplate for this special library was designed by Lloyd Lozes Goff, who has received considerable acclaim for his oils, watercolors, and his new balloon paintings on wood exhibited in Albuquerque during the recent International Balloon Meet there.

Born in Dallas, Texas, Goff moved to Albuquerque with his parents at 17, graduated from the University of New Mexico, and was assistant professor of art and acting head of the UNM Art Department for several years. He has traveled extensively throughout Europe, painting wherever he went. Goff is well represented in private and museum collections. Flo Wilks of the Albuquerque JOURNAL interviewed the artist in 1971 when he gave his impressions of ecological deterioration in the Southwest and again in February '74 during the International Balloon Meet.

FRIDOLF JOHNSON/The Mermaid Press
        (Excerpts from a letter)
"The collection of Mermaid lore has been an absorbing interest of mine for many years, and when I set
up my own press in 1957 I naturally christened it
The Mermaid Press. The oval device I drew for it also
serves as a bookplate for my books on printing and
typography. The mermaid holds an open book in one
hand. The fish symbols on the left-hand page refer
to my interest in marine biology; the smiling sun on
the opposite page is a reminder to be as optimistic
as conditions permit.

"As a designer in love with books, my interest in
bookplates came easily and early. I began collecting them seriously in 1941, and for about ten years
carried on an extensive exchange of correspondence with collectors in America
and Europe.

"Soon after setting up the Mermaid Press in 1957 I took part in forming the
New York Chappel of Private Presses, a strictly informal group of printers
which cooperated in producing some interesting and quite admirable small books
and calendars.. The Mermaid Press has turned out a great variety of small items
including a few booklets. The earlier pieces have all been dissipated except
for personal copies. My most ambitious project was a miniature book - NASTY NANCY
& HER CAT, A HORRID ABC BOOK, 1962."

Fridolf Johnson studied at the Art Institute of Chicago, then entered the commercial art field and became art director of an advertising agency. A chance to
illustrate some children's books led him to Los Angeles, where he eventually
joined Universal Pictures as an advertising artist. During a two-year period
in San Francisco as a freelance designer, he developed his practice of calligraphy. In 1951 he was again in New York; late in 1962 he became Executive Editor of AMERICAN ARTIST. His well illustrated article, "The Art of the Bookplate," appeared in the May 1965 issue. Though theoretically retired, he says,
"I have my hands full with numerous commissions and though I resigned from the
AMERICAN ARTIST in 1969, I continue to write reviews for it, chiefly upon books
of interest to graphic artists."

FROM THE PERIODICAL LITERATURE . . .

AMPHORA XIV (Alcuin Society, P.O. Box 94108, Richmond, B.C. Canada), "The Symbolism of the Staff of Aesculapius as Illustrated by Medical Bookplates," Samuel
X. Radbill. (24) 28-41, Fall 1973. Reprinted from the 1962 issue of JOUNRAL of
the Albert Einstein Medical Center. Anyone interested in the graphic arts would
enjoy the Alcuin Society publications.

UNDAUNTED BOOKMAN (Friends of Langsdale Library, University of Baltimore), "The
A. Edward Newton Collection of B. George Ulizio," Dean H. Keller. (1) 2:9-16,
Winter 1974. Tipped in as illustration is the special bookplate Mr. Ulizio used
for his Newton Collection; it has a border of two pine trees and pine cones - the
Ulizio home was called Pine Valley. This collection comprizing 33 items went to
Kent State University Library in 1969.

BIBLIOGRAPHICAL SOCIETY OF AMERICA PAPERS, 67:485, October-December 1973, brief
review of ENGRAVED BOOKPLATES: EUROPEAN EX LIBRIS 1950-70, by Severin and Reid.

THE PRIVATE LIBRARY, "A Problem for the Bookplate Collector," Brian North Lee. (5) 6:123-32, Autumn 1973. "Had it been customary for bookplates to bear the legend 'ex libris' the collector would undoubtedly have been saved a great deal of research and sometimes unfruitful speculation. As a result of the general omission of these blessed words one has to ask oneself, "When is a bookplate not a bookplate?" What I am implying by this apparently contradictory question is that a pictorial plate bearing a name or a heraldic design has all the appearance of a bookplate may but in fact be something else.

BIBLIO TALK (Friends of the University of Rochester Libraries), "Bookplates in the Collections." (1) Volume 1, No. 1, January 1974. Illustrated is the bookplate for the Hubbell Collection of Books Illustrated with Original Photographs, which was presented in memory of Walter Sage Hubbell, 1871, by Robert F. Metzdorf in 1965. The plate was designed by Milton Punnett and printed by Robert Hart, Inc.; it shows a box camera resting on an open book. Dr. Metzdorf was a member of ASBC&D for many years and compiled the YEAR BOOK Index 1922-1949/50. - - "The Rochester List." Book purchased with the help of a Friend will be marked with a special bookplate.

NEWS-JOURNAL (Kent, Washington), "He's Expert on 'Paper Americana'," Steve Beaty. Newspaper article on ASBC&D member, Leon Thompson, who collects post cards and Valentines as well as bookplates; several examples illustrated, also Mr. Thompson is pictured. This was a two-page spread in the NOW section, November 18, 1973.

WELLSVILLE DAILY REPORTER, "A Successful Artist," December 31, 1913. William Edgar Fisher is the artist, and the article quotes from an illustrated story in GRAPHIC ARTS by Oliver Hereford. The David A. Howe Public Library in Wellsville, New York, has a considerable amount of material on Fisher, who was born in Wellsville in 1872. Notice of his death on November 3, 1956 was also carried in the DAILY REPORTER; he is buried in his birthplace.

E X H I B I T S and Other Things . . .

Contemporary Lithuanian Bookplates from the collection of Vitolis E. Vengris were a loan exhibit at Chapin Library, Williams College, from February 25 to March 15, 1973. Twenty-three artists were represented by 116 bookplates. In the foreword to the handlist of the exhibit, Dr. Vengris said, "Modern Lithuanian artists have developed a richly varied number of styles and techniques for this fascinating miniature art form, and have been recognized with numerous awards in international exhibits of bookplates."

To celebrate the 400th anniversary of the Vilnius University, founded in 1570, a competition was held to design a new bookplate. A miniature book was printed in 1970 by Vaga Publishers (Vilnius, Lithuania) titled BOOKPLATES OF LIBRARY OF THE VILNIUS STATE UNIVERSITY. It contained all the bookplate designs submitted revealing a great variety of treatments; the winning design was also issued as a commemorative stamp, Scott #3772. The imaginative artists have also imprinted their designs on envelopes much in the manner of a commemorative First Day Cover.

The Southern California Chapter of the Manuscript Society had a meeting to honor Lincoln at which one of the speakers was Larry Burgess, librarian of the A. K. Smiley Public Library, Redlands. He told of the many treasures at the Redlands Lincoln Memorial Shrine and had copies of the special bookplate used in the collection which features the bust of Lincoln by sculptor George Grey Barnard and a quotation from the Gettysburg Address.

The Pennsylvania College of Podiatric Medicine in Philadelphia will have an April exhibit of bookplates featuring plates from the the their own colleges as well as material from the extensive collection of Dr. Samuel X. Radbill.

OLIVE T. SPRONG

"Many years ago, Mr. Noguchi from Japan visited the Art Department of the Los Angeles Public Library. He was greatly interested in bookplates, and after his return to Japan I corresponded with him for several years. He had several bookplates made for his own collection, and he, too, had the 'iris bookplate' made for me. I never knew the name of the artist who made it. He used the 'iris motif' because I had told him that I had iris in my garden." Thus wrote Miss Olive T. Sprong recently in response to an inquiry concerning her bookplate here tipped in.

Born in Leavenworth County, Kansas, in 1896, Miss Sprong moved with her family to Des Moines when she was five.

After graduating from Drake University and teaching for five years, she attended the Los Angeles Public Library School (later affiliated with USC). She was a librarian at the Los Angeles Public Library for many years, 28½ of which were spent in the Art and Music Department. During that time she accumulated a small portfolio of bookplates which were given to the library accompanied by a short preface annotating the collection.

15th INTERNATIONAL BOOKPLATE CONGRESS will be held in Bled, Yugoslavia, September 19-22, 1974. The central theme will be discussion of the oldest bookplates of various countries. Also featured will be a lecture on Slovenia by Dr. Valter Bohinec, a talk on Slovenian bookplates by Prof. Janez Logar, and the customary ex libris exchange session.

Three special exhibits are planned: the first being bookplates created during 1972, 1973 and 1974; the second having the special theme "Books Bring Nations Together" with special awards; and the third an ehxibition of illustrations appearing in publications of Mladinska Khjiga, the publishing house in Ljubljana.

A highlight of the Congress will be two excursions to visit Slovenian landmarks; following the Congress will be a two-day excursion into the mountain country. Artists wishing to submit exlibris for either exhibit must submit their work before July 1st. In the case of the second exhibit, the design must be tied to its theme and plates submitted in five copies. Work should be addressed to: Drustyo Exlibris Sloveniae, 61000 Ljubljana, Trubarjeva 14, Jugoslavia. (Thanks are due Richard Schimmelpfeng for his translation of the multi-language notice.)

GIFT TO THE LIBRARY FROM

ARIZONA STATE UNIVERSITY ■ TEMPE, ARIZONA

ARIZONA STATE UNIVERSITY GIFT PLATE

Bonnie D'Agostino, a staff member of the Arizona State University at Tempe in 1966, designed this bookplate used to designate volumes given to the Library. It was selected as the winner in a library contest for bookplate ideas.

The university is represented in the recently published MEMBERSHIP DIRECTORY (Year Book 1971/72) by a plate designed in 1973 by Christian A. Rosner for the Pablo Casals International Cello Library. A silhouette of Casals after a photograph by Albert Kahn is superimposed over an excerpt of "Oratorio del Pessebre" by Casals and a facsimile of his autograph is found in the title.

EXHIBIT AT MOBILE PUBLIC LIBRARY

Among the festivities scheduled during the period of the Historic Homes Tours in Mobile from March 19th through April 2nd is an exhibit of bookplates at the main Mobile Public Library, which was made possible through the efforts of the Friends of the Mobile Public Library under the able direction of Richard D. Wells. The idea of a bookplate exhibit developed after Mr. Wells read an article about the work of Cleora Clark Wheeler ("A work of art for the front of each book," Margaret McEachern in CHRISTIAN SCIENCE MONITOR, July 17, 1973); he subsequently made contact with the ASBC&D and made the necessary provisions to obtain loan of sufficient materials for an exhibit of the art of the bookplate. Coverage of the exhibit has been included in the Festival of the Arts Calendar, PRESS REGISTER (March 3, 1974, Fine Arts Page), VOICES (February 1974), and the Sunday Magazine of the MOBILE PRESS REGISTER (March 10, 1974).

* * * * * * * *

WILL BRADLEY (1868-1962) is among the designers whose work has been adapted to stock bookplates by the Library of Congress. The one tipped in was taken from a poster Bradley designed for his periodical BRADLEY, HIS BOOK, published during 1896 and 1897; at least one bookplate was illustrated in the January 1897 issue. Bradley was a boy printer in Ishpeming; an art student in Chicago; a designer, printed and publisher at the Wayside Press, art director in periodical publishing, and spent interludes devoted to stage, cinema and authorship. The Typophile Chap Book #30, published in 1955, was a tribute to Will Bradley.

* * * * * * * *

BOOKPLATES IN THE NEWS   Published Quarterly
$3 U.S./$4 Elsewhere   January/April/July/October
Editor - Audrey Spencer Arellanes

YEAR BOOK 1971/72 (Membership Directory) available.

For the 33rd year the Rounce & Coffin Club has made a selection of Western books printed during the prior year which will be exhibited at public and university libraries. Dates already scheduled during 1974 and 1975 include libraries at California State (L.A.), the Book Club of California, Sutro, Chaffey, Idaho State, University of Iowa, Texas, California, Slippery Rock State College and public libraries in Long Beach, Riverside, Seattle, Portland, Denver and the Los Angeles County Medical Association.

Thirty-two books were selected representing private, university and commercial presses. While many books were not only printed by Westerners but also had subject matter concerning the West, others were about Ezra Pound and T. S. Eliot, wines and spirits, Turner and Shakespeare, and Copernicus. The bookplate which will identify these volumes was designed and printed letterpress by Pall Bohne, a member of the organization.

In TEN YEARS (ALMOST) OF ROUNCE & COFFINISM, a paper read October 8, 1940 by Lawrence Clark Powell, he said the organization was founded "by an itinerant book-peddler and a band of starveling printers - Jake Zeitlin, abetted by Gregg Anderson, Grant Dahlstrom and Ward Ritchie - back in the bitter autumn of 1931 . . . This little band (was) augmented very early by Saul Marks and Paul Landacre . . ." Membership included printers, designers, writers, artists, librarians, bookdealers, students and collectors. Thanks are due William E. Conway, Librarian of the William Andrews Clark Library and Secretary of the Rounce & Coffin Club, for his assistance, and to Pall Bohne for the prints to tip in.

GERRY BANNER PLATE BY H. D. VOSS - Gerry Banner's latest bookplate, completed the last day of 1973, is a wood-engraving done by H. Detlev Voss, a Dutch graphic artist and printer who has lived in Canada for the past 20 years. Voss' work is represented in many publications including the Mark Severin/Anthony Reid book, ENGRAVED BOOKPLATES 1950-1970.

Gerry writes, "I met the Voss' this past summer when they were passing thru Maine. The tree in the plate is the northern white pine, Maine, of course, being the Pine Tree State. Unfortunately I had only a limited number printed, but I will send a 'live' copy to anyone who requests it from me (a signed copy will be sent to anyone who sends me their ex libris)."

MEMBERSHIP - New Members
Peggy Christian, 769 N. LaCienega Blvd., Los Angeles, Ca. 90069
Robert Homer, 20160 Center Ridge Rd., Rocky River, OH. 44116
Michael Murphy, 4304 McCausland, St. Louis, Missouri 63109
V. O. Virkao, Art Dept. Geo. Williams College, 555 - 31st St., Downers Grove, Ill. 60515

Change of Address
Kenneth R. Barrie, 127 Gaslight Dr.-#5, South Weymouth, Mass. 02190
Milton Castle, 6338 Denny Avenue, North Hollywood, Ca. 91606
Mrs. Doris Frohnsdorff, P. O. Box 2306, Gaithersburg, Maryland 20760
Ernest Huber, 6 Rue Chopin, 67000 Strasbourg, France
Mrs. J. Herman Schauinger, 1760 Fernwood, St. Paul, Minn. 55113 - RESIGNED
PLEASE notify us immediately of a change of address so publications will reach you.

American Society of BOOKPLATE COLLECTORS AND DESIGNERS

429 North Daisy Avenue · Pasadena · California 91107

BOOKPLATES IN THE NEWS   Number Seventeen   July 1974

KIRK MARTIN: ARTIST-ENGRAVER
by Ardis M. Walker

My first view of the wood engraving art of Kirk Martin was a revelation!

During my years in New York when the graphic arts enjoyed a high level of public interest, I haunted the galleries which featured them. They interested me because they offered a young man seeking a career the opportunity to collect worthwhile items at prices he could afford. I attended exhibits of etchings from Rembrandt to Bauer, lithographs from Daumier to Grant, and wood engravings from Holbein to Nason.

Upon returning to my native Sierra Nevada to settle down and write, I lost much of my contact with the world of art. What I did see caused me to conclude that the graphic arts had gone into an eclipse.

Then one day at an art show, I spotted Kirk Martin's Trail Ride. The impact of that engraving caused me to exclaim, "Here is a man who can match the masters!" Immediately, Kirk and I became good friends. Later while preparing Sierra Nevada Sequence for publication, one of the sonnets was selected for publication in the Los Angeles Westerners' Brand Book with decoration in black and white by another fine Western artist, Don Perceval.

I had not thought of illustrating my sonnet sequence until I received the tear sheet from the Brand Book. Then I sent it to Kirk suggesting that we collaborate. The result was that Sierra Nevada Sequence came out at $50 per copy with illustrations for all thirty-two sonnets and page decorations done in original wood engravings by Kirk Martin. Since then the price has risen to $500, because the engravings show Kirk to be a sensitive and highly skilled artist with a matchless sense of design.

What some of Kirk's friends may not know is that he enjoys a special genius for printing. He has done a series of broadsides for me in which he combines engraved blocks and handset type to create designs that automatically become collector's items. In fact, in addition to other select repositories, the William Andrews Clark, Jr. Memorial Library constantly adds Kirk Martin's work to its magnificent collections of fine prints and printing.

Anthony F. Kroll of Pasadena produced the joint Gayle and Ardis Walker bookplate featuring a Martin woodengraving. The author is certain it will justify all the plaudits contained herein.

BIOGRAPHICAL NOTES on Author and Artist - -

RAINBOW CHASERS   KIRK MARTIN

ONE OF THE BOOKS OF

Audrey Spencer Arellanes

Born in Colorado in 1906, Kirk Martin comes by his love of printing naturally, said Ed Ainsworth in THE COWBOY IN ART. His father, a country printer, taught Kirk the trade from the age of ten. The qualities of patience and exactitude are required for both a printer and a wood-engraver. Martin was inspired to do wood block carving by the late Paul Landacre, a Los Angeles artist whose bookplates are well-known. Western subjects, particularly horses, are a Kirk Martin specialty. His prints, originally created as illustrations for books, poems or for framing, adapt beautifully to ex libris as demonstrated by the prints Tony Kroll created for the Walkers and Audrey Arellanes. Any members interested in commissioning a bookplate may write Kirk Martin, P.O. Box 542, Yucca Valley, California 92284.

Ardis Walker, born April 9, 1901, is a native of Kernville, California. He attended Fresno State College, UCLA, and in 1927 received his B.S. from the University of Southern California. His checkered career has included being a member of the technical staff of Bell Telephone Laboratories, a free-lance writer and researcher, Judicial Court judge in Kernville (1938-48), Kern County supervisor (1948-52), and public relations consultant. He is a member of the National Wildlife Federation and California Historical Society. Among his writings are QUATRAINS, SIERRA PROLOGUE, FRANCISCO GARCES: PIONEER PADRE, SIERRA NEVADA SEQUENCE.

— — — — — — — — — — — — —

The Private Libraries Association announces the publication of THE BOOKPLATE DESIGNS OF REX WHISTLER by Brian North Lee. The book contains a descriptive essay, fully annotated checklist, 42 illustrations, 128 pages, Royal octavo, cloth boards, 1,000 copies of which 350 in a slip case have a tipped-in frontispiece bookplate, $25 ($12.50 to PLA members); the balance have a printed frontispiece, $20 ($10 to members).

FOLLOWING BERNHARDT WALL by Francis J. Weber is a miniature book published by Dawson's Bookshop, printed by William Cheney and with four intaglio reproductions of Wall's etchings by A. F. Kroll. Among Wall's publications were several which included bookplates: WALL'S ETCHED MONTHLY and QUARTERLY, ETCHT MINIATURE MONTHLY MAGAZINE. One of the illustrations shows Wall at his etching press; another is a photoreduced copy of his ex libris with a cowboy on a horse below which is his name and profession - etcher.

Whitney T. Genns

Even if one did not know that Whitney T. Genns
was born in New Orleans, one would immediately
recognize him as a gentleman who combines charm
with scholarship. In his early years he was a
newspaperman of some distinction who served in
New York; Washington, D.C.; New Orleans; and
Atlanta. He specialized as a writer, and later
as a bookseller, in the Confederacy and Lincoln
material. In 1938 he established the Albatross
Bookstore in San Francisco and was a charter
member of the Civil War Roundtable in that city.

In later years he moved to Santa Barbara where
he still flourishes as a bookseller. A member
of the Westerners (Los Angeles), he helped start
a Santa Barbara "corral". His current specialization as a book dealer centers on Western
Americana and fine bindings.

Mr. Genns bookplate reflects his interest in the Confererate States of America.

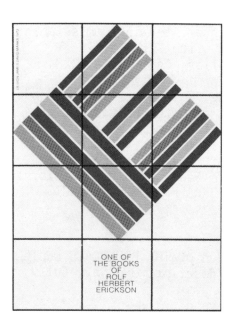

Rolf Herbert Erickson

Rolf Erickson, Head of Circulation Services Department at Northwestern University Library, writes as
follows about his new ex libris:

"The bookplate design was conceived and executed by
my very good friend James David Marks, an Art Director for an advertising agency in Milwaukee. The
design came out of several conversations about what
I wanted in a plate. I wanted something colorful,
fresh, and youthful. I also insisted on "One of the
books of" since, as a librarian, I am reluctant to
term my loosely organized collection of books a library. The middle name (my father's name) appears
since in the rural area of Shawano where I come from
my father and his family are well known. In addition
genealogy is one of my strongest interests.

"The plate is printed on 70 lb. suede coated offset
paper. It is printed in full color using process colors which means that four
colors (red, yellow, blue and black) were used in screen combinations. The type
used for the main legend is 6 point all caps Helvetica. The same type in 3 point
size is used for the signature in the upper left corner."

FROM THE PERIODICAL LITERATURE . . . .

METMENYS, "Apie Knygos Zenkla," by Vitolis E. Vengris. (45) #27:37-64, 1974. The
article, about bookplates, is written in the Lithuanian language and printed in
a Lithuanian cultural magazine published in Chicago. There are 45 illustrations

in the article and an additional seven scattered throughout the magazine; all are by Lithuanian artists from the 16th century through 1973.

ANTIQUARIAN BOOKMAN (AB), March 24, 1974, 1205. Notice of Lithuanian Bookplate exhibit at Chapin Library, Williams College, Williamstown, Massachusetts. The work of twenty-three contemporary Lithuanian artists was represented.

ANTIQUARIAN BOOKMAN (AB), April 29, 1974, cover. The cover picture is composed of postage stamps with the theme of books from various countries. Included is the stamp with the bookplate design commemorating the 400th anniversary of the Library of the Vilnius University of Lithuania.

AMERICAN HERITAGE, 6:109, June 1955. "Seeing and Hearing History," William G. Tyrell. "Remington's sketches and his library of books on the West - complete with bookplate of a longhorn's skull - are in the Remington Memorial in Ogdensburg, New York." The ex libris is reproduced with Frederic Remington's signature.

A NEWBERRY NEWSLETTER, #2, Spring 1974, mentions the Newberry's Rosenthal Fund ex libris, the work of Giovanni Mardersteig of Verona, who is considered by many the greatest living printer. Their Burgess Fund bookplate is designed by Sue Allen and her husband Greer Allen printed it. A third plate is in preparation by Mrs. Eugene A. Davidson for the Mark Morton Fund. The Associate Director writes: "I would be grateful if you would stress in anything you write about it that we cannot exchange or present copies of our bookplates to collectors. . . . We're sorry to be stuffy, but we are stuck with having too little time, staff, or money to be as generous as we would like to be." (Editor's note: I know members will respect the request expressed by the Newberry; this same situation holds true for many other institutions, too. We do want to mention all bookplate periodical literature, so your cooperation will help.)

THE NEWBERRY LIBRARY
The
Samuel R. & Marie-Louise
Rosenthal Fund

AMERICAN BOOK COLLECTOR, "A Book Collector in Mid-Appalachia," Charles Carpenter. (1) 24:27-30, January-February 1974. Books and bookplates are often found in unlikely places as Mr. Carpenter points out in his interesting article. Illustrated is the ex libris with "John Quincy Adams 1831" at the bottom and "Charles Francis Adams 1905" at the top.

CALLIGRAFREE, "Bookplates." (23) 1:#4:1-9, July 1974. Brief text with accompanying details about bookplates in the calligraphic hand of editor Abraham Lincoln. Calligraphic bookplates feature the work of Cullen Rapp, Raymond F. DaBoll, Jerry Jablon, G. Harvey Petty, Leo Wyatt (represented by the masthead of the ASBC&D as well as ex libris), Byron J. Macdonald, John Shyvers, Jackie Jones, Barbara Getty, Fridolf Johnson, and James Hayes. Single copies of periodical are $2.75.

A ARTE DO EX-LIBRIS. "The Heraldic Bookplate in England," D. M. A. DeNoronka De Paiva Couceiro. (16) No. 64,263-9, 1973. Bi-lingual article (Portugese and English). "The bright colours and distinct patterns on his shield were designed to identify the bearer to all viewers. . . . In this manner was born the language of Heraldry." - "The Bookplates of an English Artist - Diana Bloomfield," Philip Beddingham. (13)No. 64,271-7, 1973. One illustration shows the artist at work. This article supplements prior one by Beddingham in YEAR BOOK 1968/69 of the ASBC&D.

ENCYCLOPAEDIA JUDAICA, 1972, contains almost a full page on bookplates with special emphasis on Jewish designs, artists, owners; reference is made to Philip Goodman's article on Marco Birnholz in YEAR BOOK 1952/53 of the ASBC&D.

A. I. Kalaschnikow

Because member Charles Midlo's wife, Natalie, is interested in archaeology and art history, Russian artist Anatoli Ivanovitch Kalaschnikow chose the design here tipped-in as a motif for her bookplate which was engraved in 1973. The owner is a serious student of the Sumerian and Babylonian cultures. She owns a representative collection of Mesopotamian cylinder seals and gemstone carvings from the Aegean regions. Themes referring to her collection form the subject matter of other bookplates made for her by Jurgen Dost of Germany and Anatanas Kmieliauskas of Lithuania.

Kalaschnikow was born in Moscow (1930) and entered the Moscow Academy of Art in 1947. Among his teachers were Ivan Pawlow and Michail Matroin; he mastered wood engraving and devoted his efforts mainly to miniature designs.

In the late fifties, he was active in the Ministry of Postal Affairs, where he designed and engraved postal papers and numerous postage stamps. He made his first ex libris in 1964; since then he has created scores of bookplates. At the 14th International Exlibris Congress, held in Denmark in 1972, he was awarded a prize for his commemorative bookplate design. For the same Congress he prepared a folio of color engravings as a keepsake which was presented to each of the participants. Dr. and Mrs. Charles Midlo represented the American Society of Bookplate Collectors and Designers at the Congress in Denmark.

* * * * * * * * * *

A special "thank you" to our member P. W. Filby for sponsoring the commission of the masthead by Leo Wyatt which first appeared on our October 1973 issue. Though a comparative newcomer to the Society, his enthusiasm, encouragement, and support have indeed changed the face of the newsletter!

NEW MEMBER:
Gintautas Vezys, 6349 South Artesian Avenue, Chicago, Illinois 60629.
A Membership Application is enclosed - perhaps you have a friend who would like to join the American Society of Bookplate Collectors and Designers.

EGDON H. MARGO BOOKPLATE: Designed and printed in his favorite & inimitable Caslon by the late Herbert Simpson (The Feather Vender Press, Evansville, Indiana) and presented as a surprise natal day gift to EHM by HWS, writer, designer, printer, calligrapher, scholar. Margo is himself a calligrapher and graphic arts designer whose work gives frequent evidence of his wit and humor. One plate is printed "Egdon H. Margo: Creative Brooder." He further describes it: "A fun bookplate using a Thomas Bewick wood-engraving from the T B Collection of THE PEN & PRESS. Executed in a spirit of ribaldry and impressed on the Columbian Numero Duo."

TULANE UNIVERSITY EX LIBRIS

EX COLLECTIONE DR CHARLES MIDLO

TULANE UNIVERSITY-NEW ORLEANS

The Rare Book Department of the Tulane University Library in New Orleans houses the Midlo Collection of Ex Libris. It consists of close to 11,000 bookplates acquired mainly by exchange during the past sixty years. The plates, in dust proof file boxes, are individually mounted and cataloged according to subject, artist, and owner. There are also approximately three hundred items of bookplate literature: books, booklets, bound journals, among which are the YEAR BOOKS of the American Society of Bookplate Collectors and Designers, BOEKCIER, NEDERLAND-SCHE EXLIBRIS-KRING, and many other European ex libris periodicals.

The bookplate for the Midlo Collection is characteristic of the style and technique of artist Wojchech Jakubowski, who executed it in 1973. Jakubowski was born in 1929 in Starogard, Poland. He studied art under Professors Jerzy Hoppen and Kuczynski in Torun. In 1953 he became a teacher in his specialty: copper engraving. He has made numerous bookplates distinguished by exquisite workmanship. Often he uses a mere symbol as in the plate for Leopold Stokowski, which depicts a rose which has one of its outer petals metamorphosed into a human ear, the whole design conveying the beauties and joys of music.

PERIODICAL LITERATURE (continued)
STRIDES, "Dr. Radbill Shows Collection at PCPM," 11, #4, April 1974. Dr. Radbill chose material relevant to podiatry from his extensive collection to exhibit at the Pennsylvania College of Podiatric Medicine, April 15 to May 15, 1974. - On March 12, 1974 a dinner was held in honor of Dr. Samuel X. Radbill by the Section on Medical History of the College of Physicians of Philadelphia.

MOBILE PRESS, May 17, 1974, "Homes Tour A Success," R. D. Wells. In connection with the Historic Mobile Tours of historic homes, the Friends of the Library sponsored an exhibit of bookplates furnished by the American Society of Bookplate Collectors and Designers.

BOOKPLATES IN THE NEWS
$3 U.S. & Canada /$4 Overseas

Editor - Audrey Spencer Arellanes
Quarterly - January/April/July/October

American Society of
BOOKPLATE COLLECTORS AND DESIGNERS

429 North Daisy Avenue · Pasadena · California 91107

BOOKPLATES IN THE NEWS   Number Eighteen   October 1974

Santa Anita Station
and Jack McCaskill

It is fitting that the Santa
Anita Station should be featured on Jack McCaskill's ex
libris since this historical
monument is on the grounds of
the Los Angeles County & State
Arboretum where he works.

Jack, born in Pasadena, went
through the Rose City schools,
attended California State Polytechnic University, Pomona and
majored in horticulture. His
father had a camellia nursery
where Jack helped out while attending school and after service
in the Navy during the Korean
conflict. He joined the American Camellia Society, is an ac-
credited Camellia judge, and a
member of the Southern California Camellia Society. Jack is
also interested in California history and belongs to a number of local as
well as state-wide historical societies, and collects books on Southern
California History.

The bookplate of the Santa Anita depot will be used for this collection.
Since 1932 Jack has lived about a mile from the station, and for the past
16 years has worked at the Arboretum where the station was moved when it
was saved from destruction by the Arcadia Historical Society, Arcadia
Chamber of Commerce, California Arboretum Foundation, & concerned citizens
who banded together to raise the necessary funds. The original drawing by
Charles H. Owens (NUESTRO PUEBLO, Los Angeles - City of Romance, Joseph See-
werker) was reduced and photoengraved by Tony Kroll. The station, originally
built about 1890, was closed in 1940. For a time it had a woman stationmistress,
Nora Higginson (1895-1898). The station was originally used by Lucky Baldwin
to ship produce from his ranch, local people would pick up their mail there,
and take the Santa Fe train to Los Angeles.

GLENN WYATT WOLCOTT

The Wolcott arms on the plate are the same as the Oliver Wolcott plate, one of the Signers of the Declaration from Connecticut, which date back to about 1400. A literal translation of the motto is: Accustomed to swear in the words of no master.

There is a Society of Descendants of Henry Wolcott, who emigrated from England, at the age of 52; he settled first in Dorchester, Massachusetts, and later moved to Windsor, Connecticut. Henry was elected a member of the committee of twelve which constituted the first general assembly held in Connecticut in 1637.

Glenn Wolcott's plate was designed by Ann Newton, a friend and neighbor who illustrated children's books. He attended both Syracuse University and Yale Law School, where he was associated and a member of Delta Kappa Epsilon social fraternity and Phi Delta Phi legal fraternity. He served during World War I as a sergeant in the 78th Division. For the past 45 years he has been associated with the Aetna Life Insurance Company, is a member of the University Club, Yale Club of Central New York, and past president of the Society of Descendents of Henry Wolcott.

BOOK ARTS PRESS -- A broadside printed by the Book Arts Press states that it was "founded by Professor Terry Belanger in April, 1972, at the School of Library Service of Columbia University as a bibliographic laboratory for the training of students in the rare books and special collections librarianship program of the school. The Columbia University Library's Special Collections loaned the Press two of its handpresses: an 1830 Imperial (platen size 9 x 13:) and an 1843 R. Hoe & Co. Washington (platen size 14 x 19"), the former bought in 1941 as part of the American Type Founders library, the latter a gift from the American Bible Society in 1953. . . . as of July 1973 seven present students or recent graduates have become Printers of the Book Arts Press. . . . The Press regularly produces announcements of lectures for the School of Library Service and for the Friends of the Columbia Libraries."

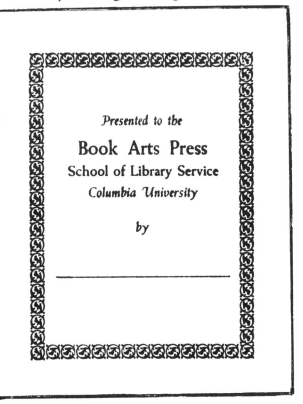

Presented to the

Book Arts Press
School of Library Service
Columbia University

by

_____

FROM THE PERIODICAL LITERATURE

CALLIGRAFREE, Bookplates. (23) 1:1-9, July 1974. An interesting variety
of bookplates by calligraphers Raymond F. DaBoll, Jerry Jablon, G. Harvey
Petty, Leo Wyatt, Byron J. Macdonald, John Shyvers, Jackie Jones, Barbara
Getty, Fridolf Johnson, and James Hayes.

CALLIGRAFREE, Designer: James Hayes. (9) 1:16, 19, September 1974. The
plates illustrated reveal the variety of this artist's design abilities
as well as his calligraphic skill and subtle use of color.

AMPHORA XV (Alcuin Society, Richmond, B.C., Canada), Karl Michel: An Artist of the Roaring Twenties, Geoff Spencer. (14) 11-16, Winter 1974. In
his delightfully witty style, Spencer relates the bookplate dividend resulting from a mail order bid for a couple of old PENROSE ANNUALS!

THE PRIVATE LIBRARY, A Fearful Joy, Diana Bloomfield. (14) Second Series,
7:4-18, Spring 1974. This is a transcript of a talk given to the Bookplate
Society (London) which reflects the personality of the artist as well as
detailing her techniques in wood-engraving. There is also a checklist of
nine books illustrated by her and a checklist of her engraved bookplates
compiled by Philip Beddingham for his article on Diana Bloomfield in ASBC&D
YEAR BOOK 1969/70.

THE PRIVATE LIBRARY, An Open Letter to a Beginner Bookseller, Louis Ginsberg. 7:28-32, Spring 1974. "The most important tools for the antiquarian
bookseller are the study of book plates, bibliography, and booksellers'
catalogues. But why book-plates? The field of book-plates is a study in
miniature of the book as a human artifact." (This paper available through
the author at Box 1502, Petersburg, Virginia 23803.)

BiN, Free Book. 2:2, July 1974. Note on ASBC&D member Louis Ginsberg's
A. HART, PHILADELPHIA PUBLISHER (1828-54), 53 page publication issued in
1972.

BiN, New Books. 2:3, May 1974. Jim Hayes' THE ROMAN LETTER, a 56 page
booklet is available from the Lakeside Press of R. R. Donnelley & Sons,
2223 Martin Luther King Dr., Chicago, Ill. 60616. Hayes is a designer
member of the ASBC&D.

BiN, Publications. 2:7, September 1974. Among Gale publications is noted
BOOKPLATES: A SELECTED, ANNOTATED BIBLIOGRAPHY OF THE PERIODICAL LITERATURE
by Audrey Spencer Arellanes.

SERIF, Bookplate of Paul Louis Feiss. (1) XI;Inside front cover, Spring 1974.
"The first important rare book collection acquired by the Kent State University Libraries came from the noted Cleveland, Ohio, collector in 1952."

TIMES LITERARY SUPPLEMENT, Osbert Sitwell Ex Libris. (1) 805, July 26, 1974.
Illustration from BOOKPLATE DESIGNS OF REX WHISTLER by Brian Lee North which
is described as "typical example of Whistler's early work, dating from 1929."

YALE UNIVERSITY LIBRARY GAZETTE, A Color Bibliography, Robert S. Herbert.
(1) 49:3-49, July 1974. Illustrated is the bookplate used to identify a
group of 226 books on color serving as a core for research and teaching.
It is worded: Books on Color/Faber Birren Collection/Art Library/Yale
University.

CALIFORNIA FREEMASON, Masonic Bookplate Lore, James Fairbairn-Smith. 21: 132-4, Summer 1974. "A number of prominent eighteenth century engravers were Masons, among whom may be mentioned John Pine, William Hogarth, Francesco Bartalozzi, John Baptist Cipriani, Benjamin and John Cole, the poet Goethe and Paul Revere."

BOOKSELLER WEST, Collecting Bookplates, Joan West. 4:1,2,5, July 9, 1974. Personalized approach to collecting with good hints for the beginner; reprint of article which appeared in earlier issue of this same publication.

L'EX LIBRIS FRANCAIS, No. 112, May 1974. English synopsis tells of exhibit on Revival of Ex-Libris in Eastern Europa held in the Fine Arts Museum in Nancy from February 23 to April 1, 1974; 57 artists from 9 countries represented. Memorial for Artist Alfred Selig (1907-1974).

THE INNOCENT BYSTANDER (newsletter of the University of Connecticut Library)
- Bookplate of Marco Birnholz, November 2, 1973. Illustration only.
- J. Karasek ex libris reproduced from GRAPHIC, No. 166, "Ex Libris, A Dying Art Form?" October 26, 1973.
- Gift to the Library, February 8, 1973. A special bookplate is to be designed to denote purchases made from the Meyer X. Zarrow Memorial Fund.

Bookplate Society NEWSLETTER, No. 6, 1974
- Correspondence, 1-2. James Wilson recounts finding four ex libris one atop the other in a single book; in descending order: E. G. Godfrey; Gladstone Library; National Liberal Club; Symond's Circulating Library.
- Publications, 2-3. Notice of ex libris publications in England, Italy, Poland, and in Holland where Hamilton's DATED BOOKPLATES and FRENCH BOOKPLATES and Warren's GUIDE TO THE STUDY OF BOOKPLATES are being reprinted.
- Oxford Bookplates by William Jackson, New Light on the Brighton Collection, Anthony Pincott, 3-10. Well documented sleuthing into the identification of plates by Jackson for Cambridge and Oxford (1700-1704); early collection of account books furnishes some dates and prices.
- Bookplate Query, 11. American collector, Arthur Goldsmith, asks about methods of mounting and cleaning bookplates.
- Annoymous Bookplate, 11. Ascribed to Seaman; data on plate mentioned in Newsletter No. 5.
- Exhibit, 11. Request is made for loan of plates by Frank Brangwyn, L. Leslie Brooke, Thomas Heath Robinson, Charles Robinson, Francis D. Bedford, Marion Reed, or Byram Shaw for October exhibit.

E X H I B I T S -
Guitautas Vezys exhibited over 300 ex libris at the Balzekas Museum of Lithuanian Culture from April 19 to May 10, 1974. It is expected same display will be in the main Chicago Public Library during October.

"Bookplates by Book Illustrators, 1880-1940" is title of the Bookplate Society's second London exhibit at the National Book League, October 9 - 19, 1974. Fifty artists are represented, most well-known to bookplate enthusiasts. An attractive poster/announcement has been printed illustrating a bookplate for Phil May and a joint plate for Arthur and Jessie Guthrie by Henry Ospovat.

The ASBC&D is preparing an exhibit for National Library Week (April 1975) which will feature public library bookplates. It will be appreciated if members will send copies of the bookplates used by their local public libraries for the exhibit; details about the library and artist desirable.

"Rare Books and Bookplates from Atheneum Collections" is the title of an exhibit to be held at the Austin Gallery of the Wadsworth Atheneum, Hartford, Connecticut, from October 15 to November 3, 1974. An attractive postal announcement of the exhibit has been printed featuring the bookplate W. F. Hopson designed for the Atheneum in 1910. The ex libris are from the museum's Hettie Gray Baker Collection which were given by Miss Baker between 1927 and 1935. Miss Baker had a variety of careers from a position at the Connecticut State Library to a distinguished post with Fox Films, and authored numerous books about cats. The bookplate exhibit was organized by Katherine Collens Bartholomew, a scholar and designer of bookplates.

JAMES HAYES, Calligrapher

The elegant simplicity of Gerald Banner's name label is the calligraphy of James Hayes, whose subtle use of color gives an added dimension to the basic label of identification. A future issue of this newsletter will feature a partial Hayes checklist and biographical sketch.

Banner, a resident of Portland, Maine, was born in Brooklyn, New York. He majored in history at Goddard College and the New School for Social Research where he received his B.A. in 1965; subsequently he attended Pratt Institute for his MLS. Gerry is Reference Librarian at the University of Maine where he is also an instructor in the Graduate School Department of Library Service. He is an enthusiastic and active bookplate collector.

VILNIUS UNIVERSITY LIBRARY
1570 - 1970

To celebrate the 400th anniversary of the Scientific Library of the Vilnius V. Kapsukas University a competition was held for the design of a new ex libris. The oldest identifying design in the library is a super-ex libris of the Grand Duke of Lithuania, Zygmunt August (1520-1572), pressed on the leather cover of a volume. His collection was the basis for the library formed in 1570.

Forty-six designs were submitted by twenty-nine different Lithuanian artists. Awards were made for two designs: a special one for the anniversary and another for permanent use. The anniversary award was to Antanas Kucas, the second to Petras Repsys. The anniversary award ex libris was also issued in a reduced size as a commemorative stamp in 1970. A small tri-lingual book was published giving all the artists' names and illustrated the forty-six designs. (The stamp appeared on the cover of ANTIQUARIAN BOOKMAN for April 29, 1974 as one of several using books as a theme.)

— — — — — —

Dr. Samuel X. Radbill was honored by the Section on Medical History of the College of Physicians of Philadelphia on March 12, 1974; dinner was followed by a talk on "Medicine and Pharmacy in French Political Prints."

- - - - - -

BOOKPLATES IN THE NEWS   Editor - Audrey Spencer Arellanes
$3 U.S. & Canada/$4 Overseas   Quarterly - January/April/July/October

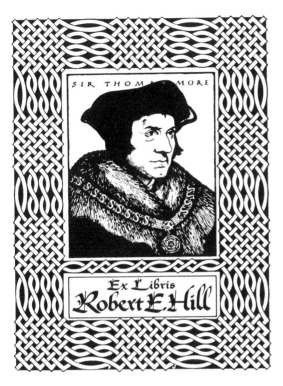

Dr. Robert E. Hill
by Michael Murphy

The Thomas More bookplate was created for Dr. Robert Hill by New York graphics designer and author, Fridolf Johnson.

Dr. Robert E. Hill is Executive Director of the National Center for Voluntary Action, Washington, D. C. He is an internationally known economist, former President of California State University, Chico, and a frequent lecturer and guest instructor in economics.

His cultural interests are dominantly focused on the life and times of Sir Thomas More, and he maintains an active interest in several Thomas More organizations, both in this nation and abroad. An ardent Anglophile, Dr. Hill is constantly adding to his personal library of English history, particularly in the sphere of Henry VII and his court. His favorite text, he readily confesses, is THE LIFE OF SIR THOMAS MORE, KNIGHTE by his son-in-law William Roper. Among Dr. Hill's treasures is the rare Golden Eagle Press edition of this work.

ARTIST/PRINTER'S OWN PLATE

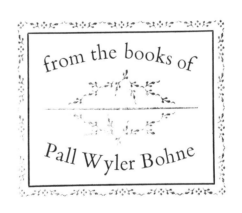

Among the advantages of being an artist and printer is the pleasure of designing your own bookplate and then printing it - in this instance in two colors plus black. More recently Pall Bohne demonstrated his dual talents at the Book Fair held in the Ambassador Hotel, Los Angeles, where a drawing he made of a restored Columbian Press had been transferred to a zinc cut, was printed on the very hand press it depicted, and then he hand-tinted the prints. An early issue of A ARTE DO EX-LIBRIS will feature an article on the bookplates of Pall Bohne with several illustrations including tipped-in plates.

- - - - - - - - - - - - - - - -

EXCHANGE or Sell - Joint bookplate of M. G. and E. A. (Edwin Austin) Abbey (1852-1911), American muralist, illustrator and painter. Please quote for lot of 14 or for individual plate to Mr. Alexis Pencovic, Ass't Conservator, Asian Art Museum of San Francisco, Golden Gate Park, San Francisco, Ca. 94118.   - - - - - - - - - - - - - -

NEW MEMBERS --
John J. Ahern, 107 Boston Avenue, Medford, Mass. 02155
Antonio J. Molina, Apartado 1361, San Juan, Puerto Rico 00902
Mary Peterson, Route 2, Box 5093, Escondido, Ca. 92026
Mrs. Mary Pew, 210 E. Fern Avenue, Redlands, Ca. 92373

Attention: PLEASE NOTIFY IMMEDIATELY OF CHANGE OF ADDRESS

15. medhnarodni ekslibris kongres 19.-22.9.1974 bled-slovenija jugoslavija

BLED CONGRESS - Enclosed with the current newsletter is a Keepsake published for ASBC&D members. A limited number were sent for distribution to participants at the 15th International Ex Libris Congress in Bled. We hope to have a report about the congress in the January issue from one of our European members who attended.

The theme of our Keepsake is "Bookplates are a passport to friendship (in any language)" and the phrase was translated into the various languages of most countries which publish bookplate periodicals including Japanese, Dutch, Swedish, Danish, Hebrew, German, French, Italian, Polish, Spanish, Lithuanian, Czech, Russian, Portuguese, and Yugoslavian.

— — — — — — — — — —

Bicentennial Seal Inc. (18th & Franklin, Columbia, Pa. 17512), is offering an edition limited to 1776 sets of four plates with the Peale portraits of George Washington, John Adams, Thomas Jefferson and Alexander Hamilton ($225). The Seal of Approval is an adaptation of the Washington ex libris.

- -

THE DUN EMER PRESS, LATER THE CUALA PRESS, Liam Miller ($7.50). Published as Chap Book Number 50 by the Typophiles (140 Lincoln Road, Brooklyn, N. Y. 11225), this excellent book not only details the development and history of each press, spanning the period 1903 to 1946, but includes checklists of books, broadsides and ephemera. Illustrated are the bookplates of W. B. Yeats engraved by T. Sturge Moore and Lily Yeats by Jack Yeats; also mentioned are plates for John Quinn, Lennox Robinson, and others by Elizabeth Yeats. -

COPELIN ROE DAY (Bookplate tipped in Number Twelve, April 1973) - Gerry Banner had asked for information concerning this plate. The following is quoted from a reply he received from Henry L. P. Beckwith, Jr.: "The Day plate is a puzzle, which my researchers only wrap in an enigma (as they are fond of saying). It is a pirated Vinycomb design, almost line for line (see plate facing page 174 of Egerton Castle's ENGLISH BOOKPLATES). The original, done for Robert Day, F.S.A., etc., of Cork, Ireland, and a bookplate collector himself, is only different in the placing (and text) of the lettering . . . I am certain that the design was lifted - close examination shows that 'J.M.R.' carefully copied the plate by eye; probably as a pen and ink sketch from which the letterpress line-cut was made. The arms are probably valid, but I don't understand them, that is to say they make no sense in an heraldic/genealogical context. The arms of the Robert Day plate are valid, and were confirmed about 1880 (when the plate was cut) to Robert and his two brothers, Richard and William T. (The pedigree is listed from GENERAL ARMORY, Sir Bernard Burke, Ulster King of Arms, London, 1884, page 270.) Now, this pedigree has all the earmarks of an 'Ulster Confirmation'. That is to say the custom in Ireland was, and is, that any family that can show either three generations or 100 years of use of a coat may have the coat confirmed to them. Most unscholarly, to my mind, and completely unsound practice. It is my <u>tentative</u> opinion that C. R. Day may have claimed but not been able to prove a connection with the Days' of

Youghal, got arms granted as close as possible to theirs, and then had the Vinycomb ex libris copied by "J.M.R.', of whom I know nothing (he does not appear in Fincham)."

— — — — — — — — — —

CONFEDERATE COLLECTION - The Rev. James Parker (Saint Mark's Rectory of Albany, Georgia) identifies his collection of books on the Confederacy with the plate here tipped-in which has been appropriately printed on gray paper. On occasion Rev. Parker has written articles on bookplates for the Augustan Society publication.

EX LIBRIS

JAMES PARKER

AS of BC & D
Bookplates in the News
429 NORTH DAISY AVENUE, PASADENA, CALIFORNIA, 91107
AUDREY SPENCER ARELLANES, *Editor*

Number Nineteen   January 1975

HELMER FOGEDGAARD
by Ella Engel

Helmer Fogedgaard, a well-known European ex libris collector, lives in
Denmark. He was born July 21, 1907
and has a business education. Most
of his life he was president of a grain
and seed company, but is now retired.
He feels happy in his retirement, because now he can devote his full time
to his hobbies which are far from business. His most loved hobbies are art
and books, especially ex libris and
graphic arts. He has been an ex libris
collector since 1942 and is now in possession of more than 40,000 artistic and
beautiful bookplate prints. Since he is
a citizen of Denmark, he collects all
kinds of Danish ex libris, but he selects
and keeps only artistic, valuable copies
of foreign productions. All nations of
importance are represented in his collection, both old and modern ex libris, and
the United States is generously represented.

In spite of the fact that Denmark is a
small nation (slightly over 5,000,000
citizens), there are many Danish collectors. Dansk Exlibris Selskab, the Danish
bookplate society, has about 350 members of which several are from other countries.
The large influx of non-Danes is due to NORDISK EXLIBRIS TIDSSKRIFT, an internationally oriented periodical. Helmer Fodegaard took the prime initiative to start this
periodical in 1946, and he has been its chief editor for 21 years. He has been on
the Board of Directors of Dansk Exlibris Selskab for several decades and is now an
Honorary member of the Society.

Helmer has edited fifteen books on ex libris and published them through his own
company, Grafolio. Together with his collector friend Johnny Køhler he has published during the past 16 years each year a booklet called BOOKPLATES IN COLOR.
Each small book contains ten beautiful, colored tipped-in ex libris. They can

100

only be acquired as gifts. Further, Helmer publishes the periodical INTER-
NATIONAL GRAFIK together with another well-known collector, Klaus Rodel. This
periodical limits itself to publishing original prints pulled from the wood
or linoleum blocks borrowed from the artists. This periodical is entering
its sixth year of publication; during the first five years, 81 artists from
21 nations have been represented with their works in many colors.

Helmer Fogedgaard loves beauty and has a strong preference for bibliophile interests. In this field, the focus of his interest is the ex libris which brings
him much pleasure, partly by handling the prints themselves and partly through
the many beautiful publications in the field. He has a large library which includes key international works on the ex libris and complete runs of many of the
periodicals. A lover of beauty and an eager collector are united in one person
- Helmer Fogedgaard.

(Note Concerning the Author - Ella Engel: Helmer writes:"Ella is my old friend.
We have known each other from childhood." For many years Mrs. Engel was a member of ASBC&D and through a happy instance of serindipity your editor discovered
she was in Santa Fe, New Mexico, and enjoyed the gracious hospitality of Ella and
her charming husband in their home perched on a bluff above the city which offers
an unobstructed view of the desert. In addition to the pleasant surprise of discovering a bookplate enthusiast where perhaps least expected, a Santa Fe bookstore
had two of the bookplate volumes found during a trip from coast to coast and as far
north as Montana!)

VINCENT STARRETT
by Fridolf Johnson

Vincent Starrett and I were friends from 1941
or earlier. He was a fantastically knowledgable book collector, especially in late 19th
and early 20th century books, and had a keen
nose for exploring the by-ways of literature.
He took me book hunting many times and taught
me that his kind of collecting was much more
rewarding than paying high prices for items
everyone else was collecting.

One of his interests was "The Night Before
Christmas," and I made an illustrated manuscript book of it for him. He had collected
Sherlockian stuff for years, and I drew the
bookplate for his collection in 1931. The
first batch were printed in black on Japan
Vellum; these are all in his books or in collectors' hands, including members of ASBC&D
and the Nederlandsche Exlibriskring. Later
Starrett had another batch printed in brown
on buff stock. The plate has been reproduced several times, notably as the frontispiece and cover design for Walter Klinefelter's A PACKET OF SHERLOCKIAN BOOK-
PLATES, Private Press of the Indiana Kid (James Lamar Weygand), 1964, Nappanee,
Indiana, 150 copies. A charming book with reproductions of six other Sherlockian
bookplates. The original cut was damaged in printing something, possibly the
brown ink plate. Starrett gave me the cut on one of my visits to Chicago. I had
repros made from it and made some slight corrections, including the addition of
my name in small type at the bottom. The original black and the brown plates have

my name in reverse across the bottom of the panel. This change will help to identify the new from the original plate.

(Editor's Note: The following is quoted in part from the Obituary Note which appeared in PUBLISHERS WEEKLY, February 4, 1974: Vincent Starrett, a writer and bookman who was an authority on Sherlock Holmes and one of the leaders of the Chicago Literary Renaissance, died January 5, 1974 in Chicago at age 87. Born in Toronto, Canada, Starrett, from 1906 to 1917, was a crime reporter, feature writer and foreign correspondent for the Chicago Daily News. His column, "Books Alive," appeared in the Chicago Tribune for over 25 years. With Christopher Morley he founded the Baker Street Irregulars in 1934.

ASBC&D member Michael Murphy, who delivered the Eulogy for Starrett, is the author of VINCENT STARRETT: IN MEMORIAM, published by Pontine Press (Luther Noris, P.O. 261, Culver City, Ca. 90230, 28 pages, 8½x5½, 9 illustrations, $5). A limited number of the last book published during his lifetime and signed by Starrett titled LATE, LATER AND POSSIBLY LAST, Essays by Vincent Starrett, are available through Michael Murphy (7144 Murdock, St. Louis, Mi. 63119) at $10. Mr. Murphy arranged for the printing of the Sherlock Holmes plate tipped-in our newsletter.)

DR. CHARLES MIDLO - It is with sadness we report the death of Dr. Charles Midlo on December 6, 1974.
Dr. Midlo, born on Febraury 27, 1899 in Poland, was a New Orleans physician. He was a member of ASBC&D from 1937 and he and his wife Natalie represented our Society at the International Congress in Denmark during 1972 and carried our Keepsake for the participants. It was your editor's pleasure during this period to talk with this gentleman who even via telephone radiated old world charm.
His bookplate collection is in the Howard Tilton Memorial Library of Tulane University. The collection of 11,000 ex libris prints are mounted on standard sized cards and housed in 103 dustproof library file boxes, classified according to design; there are ten file cabinets containing 3x5 cards that catalog and index the bookplates according to owner and artists. There are 250 books on ex libris, 101 volumes of periodicals, 850 transparencies, 12 catalogs listing exhibits or sales of bookplates, 4 volumes of personal memoirs, hundreds of news items, brochures, announcements all on bookplates, and his extensive correspondence with Professor Friedrich Schlager, his teacher in Germany who introduced him to bookplates at age 10.
We have been privileged in past issues of our newsletter to feature ex libris of both Dr. Midlo and his wife Natalie.

MASTHEAD DESIGNED BY JAMES HAYES

At last BOOKPLATES IN THE NEWS has its own masthead which has been designed by ASBC&D member James Hayes, a calligrapher of note now retired in Woodland Park, Colorado.

The newsletter during the past four years has used the Society's letterhead-first as designed by the late Carl Junge and more recently by English artist Leo Wyatt. The Society will continue to use the woodengraved letterhead by Wyatt.

An article about James Hayes and a checklist of his bookplates (numbering about sixty) is now in preparation for a future YEAR BOOK.

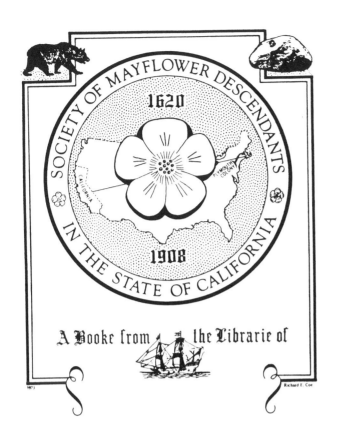

The aims of the Society of
Mayflower Descendants are to perpetuate to a remote posterity the
memory of our Pilgrim Fathers, to
cherish and maintain the ideals
and institutions of American freedom, and to discover and publish
original matter in regard to the
Pilgrims, together with existing
data known only to antiquarians,
and to authenticate, preserve, and
mark historical spots made memorable by Pilgrim association.

The Society of Mayflower Descendants in the State of California
has a bookplate which was designed
by Richard E. Coe, who is also the
editor of CALIFORNIA MAYFLOWER.

The following quotes in part a
thumbnail sketch of Richard Coe:
" . . by profession an adman and
a color photographer, and his avo-
cation is genealogy. However, in recent years the avocation has threatened to
take over as his profession, as he becomes more involved in the tracing of
family trees . . . not his own, for he hasn't the time for that . . . He is
also interested in heraldry, is a Fellow of the American Society of Heraldry,
and is the Herald of the National Genealogical Society."

BOOK REVIEW by Clifford Wurfel, Riverside - IVENSKII, Semen Georgievich.
                                              MASTERA RUSSKOGO EKSLIBRISA.
(Masters of Russian Bookplates) Leningrad, Knudozhnik RSFSR, 1973. 331 pages,
illustrations, some in color. Available at Four Continent Book Corp., 156 5th
Avenue, New York 10010. About $4.60 including postage.

Since the book is entirely in Russian and does not include summaries in English
or French, I give a rather full outline of its contents for the readers' information.

In the Introduction (66 pages), the author describes 20th century bookplates. He
complains that the artists frequently do not sign their works. There is a very
short history of bookplates up to the 19th century, then a longer history of
Russian ex libris from about 1880 to 1970.

Many artists belonged to the "Mir Iskusstvo" (the world of art), an association
of artists formed to advance art for art's sake; they often designed bookplates
for each other. There is a discussion of each artist who designed bookplates in
this period and of his esthetics. Bookplates and their design flourished up to
the early 1930's, and after a lapse it was not until the mid-1950's that the art
was taken up again after the Second World War.

The illustrations are arranged alphabetically by artist, giving a thumbnail biography and several examples of his work, citing the legend, the name of the owner, date of design and medium of reproduction (woodcut, line engraving, lithograph, etching, engraving or pen and ink drawing). Eighty-seven artists are represented, and for almost all of them two or more plates are pictured. There follows a bibliography, whose entries are arranged chronologically (1905-71) of Russian publications about bookplates and individual artists.

BOOK REVIEWS IN BRIEF -

THE DOHENYS OF LOS ANGELES (A talk before the Zamorano Club, with a bibliography by Francis J. Weber), by Ward Ritchie. 50 pages, 11 illustrations, decorative boards, printed by Richard J. Hoffman, California State University, Los Angeles, for Dawson's Book Shop, 1974. $10. This volume's primary interest to bookplate enthusiasts is that the front paste-down endpaper reproduces the ex libris of Edward L. Dohney which pictures his wife Estelle, their three children, their homes, yacht, and oil wells.

NORSKE EXLIBRIS, Thor Bjorn Schyberg. Published by ExlibRisten, 1974. This is a list of 8,650 ex libris of Norwegian owners which includes when known the city of residence, the artist, and the year designed. There are a dozen tipped-in ex libris prints. There is a tri-lingual introduction in Norwegian, German and English. The book has been printed on one side of the page only from typewritten text; the binding is an interesting paper with linen corners and spine, and a paper title label. A copy of this limited edition may be ordered from Klaus Rodel, Postbok 109, DK-9900 Frederikshavn, Denmark.

A VISIT WITH RFD, "Ozarkalligrapher" - text and scribal writing by G. Harvey Petty. This tribute to Raymond F. DaBoll is beautiful both visually and in the warmth of feeling it expresses. All of the text and captions are by Harvey Petty and many examples of RFD's versatile calligraphic skills are illustrated including one bookplate.

BOOKPLATES OF THOSE OF THE SIXTIES, published by Ukrainian Orthodox Church, P.O. Box 495, South Bound Brook, N.J. 08880, 1972, $15.00. An inch thick, square volume with printed cloth cover and endpapers illustrated with ex libris (back and front are different). This volume about young Ukrainian artists has the introduction printed in English, French, German and Spanish. The works of thirteen artists are illustrated including a few multi-color tip-ins. The introduction states: "Most of the ex libris of these artists aim at fusing creatively the traditional Ukrainian artistic imagery with the modern aesthetic vision." Mykola Viruk, author of the introductory article, is a well-known man of letters. The Art Gallery of the Archdiocesan Center in South Bound Brook has a special section devoted to ex libris drawings from Ukraine and Europe.

PRIVATE PRESSES AND AUSTRALIA, Geoffrey Farmer, published by the Hawthorn Press, 601 Little Bourke Street, Melbourne, 1972, $10 Australian. Twenty pages of introduction are followed by a Tally of Press Names and Owners, and a Check-List for each press. Surprisingly a large number of the private presses have bookplate association, such as the Australian Ex Libris Society, presses of Jack and Norman Lindsay, H. B. Muir, P. Neville Barnett, Adrian Feint, Fisher Library of the University of Sydney, John Gartner of Hawthorn Press. This is a handsome, well printed volume with paper printed cover and dust jacket with the same design.

TECHNIQUE OF WOOD ENGRAVING, John O'Connor, published by Watson-Guptil/B. T. Batsford, New York-London, 1971. $10. A how-to book for either the person who wants to learn to engrave on wood or wants to know about the process in order better to understand wood engravings. The text is supplemented with photographs of techniques and processes, diagrams, and the works of numerous artists are illustrated. While no ex libris are among the illustrations, some artists in the field are represented: Thomas Bewick, John Buckland Wright, Audrey Beardsley. And the following statement is made: "In the early part of this century, Lucien Pissarro made small bookplates. . . "

MAXFIELD PARRISH, Coy Ludwig, published by Watson-Guptil, 1973, $25. Following a biographical introduction there are separate chapters devoted to various phases of Parrish's work: book illustrations, magazine illustrations, posters, murals and paintings, landscapes, and a catalog of selected works in which a small section is a checklist of bookplates designed by this turn-of-the-century artist:
    Ethel Barrymore - Her Book. (Bookplate appeared in THE CRITIC, June 1905.)
    Bookplate for John Cox. (John Cox, a fictitious name, was replaced with Dean
       Sage when the bookplate was sold to Mrs. Sage for her husband in 1904.
    Bookplate for the Meeting-House. (Finished November 1909)
    Be Good - Ellen - Her Book. (Bookplate for Ellen Biddle Shipman, appeared in
       CENTURY, July 1912.)
    Bookplate for Frank Van Derlip. (Drawn in December 1899-January 1900. Size:
       stretcher 15" x 20", composition 14" x 12".)
    Bookplate for Frank A. Vanderlip. 1902. (Size: stretcher 14 3/4" x 21"; cir-
       cular composition 7½" diameter.)
    Bookplate for Thomas C. Watkins. 1899. (Size: stretcher 16" x 20"; composi-
       tion 12¼" x 12¼".)
    This Is The Book Of (Bookplate for THE KNAVE OF HEARTS by Louise Saunders.)
The only bookplate illustrated is that of Ethel Barrymore, which was reproduced from a photo from the Library of Congress.

A book of "coffee table" proportions, its cover Parrish blue protected by a pictorial dustjacket, lavish with color reproductions of his work, it evokes some of the best of the nostalgia art, and gives extensive documentation of a wide variety of ephemeral material such as calendars, menus, greeting cards, etc. A Maxfield Parrish design was included in the bookplate exhibit recently held at the Wadsworth Athenaeum in Hartford.

THE BOOKPLATE DESIGNS OF REX WHISTLER, Brian North Lee, published by Private Libraries Association for the Bookplate Society, 1974. 128 pages, royal octavo, cloth boards, gilt. Limited to 1000 copies, 350 with tipped-in frontispiece at $25 ($12.50 to PLA members), 650 with printed frontispiece at $20 ($10 to PLA members). (Bookplate Society, Ravelston, South View Road, Pinner, Middlesex, England.) A full scale review by W. P. Filby is scheduled for publication in the April issue. Meanwhile, we highly recommend this book with Brian Lee's delightful essay on bookplates and in particular the work of Rex Whistler. The essay is followed by a list of the eighteen ex libris Whistler designed with specifics as to size, type of reproduction, whether or not signed and dated, and there are 41 illustrations which include the finished plate as well as sketches and designs. David Chambers designed the volume thus assuring visual as well as reading pleasure.

OSWIN VOLKAMER, Paul Pfister, published by ExlibRisten, 1974. Multi-lingual text introduces fourteen tipped-in engravings including a self-portrait of the artist at work. Volkamer, born in Germany in 1930, became an engraver working especially with postal stamps and bank notes. About his ex libris work, Pfister says, "As few other artists of his time, he masters the indispensable demand, to maintain in the bookplate the utmost accuracy, no matter whether it concerns the beauty of the nude, the harmony of the human body, the delicacy of an animal or a flower, the elegance of a building or elucidation of an allegory."

A. K. SMILEY LIBRARY

The A. K. Smiley Library was
dedicated and given to the
City of Redlands, California
on April 28, 1898. Albert K.
and his twin brother Alfred H.
developed the library from its
earliest public reading room
aspect in the local YMCA until
it was housed in the showplace
Moorish or Mission style building designed by T. R. Griffith.
Of particular interest is the
vaulted ceiling with its many
handcut wood trimmings, the
winding staircase, sculptured
heads at the base of each wood-
en arch, and stained glass windows.

The bookplate used by the
Smiley library was designed in 1905 by an unidentified artist with the initial
"H".

15th INTERNATIONAL EXLIBRIS CONGRESS IN BLED
by Klaus Rodel

The 15th International exlibris congress has now become history, mainly part of
the European exlibris movement's history. More than 200 participants from a
dozen countries attended this congress which took place from 19th to 22nd September in Bled, the picturesque little town in the heart of Slovenia. Despite the
fact that the congress was held rather late in the year, the interest and participation was very good, so good in fact that perhaps a congress held during the
tourist season would attract so many participants that the arrangement would get
out of control.

Wednesday, which was the day of arrival for several guests from far away, there
was this typical congress-atmosphere with reunion of collectors and artists. Another characteristic thing was that several East-european participants, who had
been unable to attend the congress in Elsinore, here had an opportunity to meet
their West-European friends after a period of four or six years since Budapest
and Como.

While Wednesday brought lovely mild autumn weather with sun and a clear view of
the mountains surrounding Bled, the first day of the congress started with mist
and rain, which unfortunately went on til the end of the congress. However, this
did not spoil the atmosphere, and when the congress and exhibition in the beautiful building started, everybody felt that also this congress was "in the bag". As
practically all previous exhibitions, this one showed that during the past period
several beautiful exlibris had been created and that new names had been added to
those already known and appreciated. There were some East-german "novelties" which
we are bound to hear more about during the years to come. The Yugoslavian hosts
had really managed beautifully in preparing the congress, and one felt that here
the young Slovenian exlibris society passed its test and came out with flying
colors.

The first evening, with its exchanging of exlibris and renewal of old friendships and making of new ones, passed almost too quickly, and it proved again that the congresses could easily last for an entire week without anyone getting bored. The following day the delegates from several exlibris societies met in the conference room of the Golf Hotel, and a number of problems in connection with the work of the societies were discussed. The most important problem was to assure the arrangement of the next congress, and everyone was anxiously waiting for Portugal to confirm its initial promise of arranging the congress in 1976. This confirmation met with applause and the Portuguese delegate even promised they would try to publish the next FISAE volume.

Furthermore the undersigned presented the first edition of an international EXLIBRIS-NEWS, i.e. FISAE - MITTEILUNGEN. This first attempt naturally had certain shortcomings, among others the introductory text being in German only. All the same, all delegates seemed to be interested. The first number had, in the original languages, a short statement of the activities in each country (society) during the period since the congress in Elsinore; unfortunately, not all countries had responded. It was agreed in one of the coming numbers to ask the societies for better cooperation and assistance with information.

The lectures on the oldest exlibris of each country were very good, but unfortunately not all speakers could stick to the subject - and the time. This meant that the Slovenian lecture had to be left out; however, the participants plan these as a beautiful publication. It proved once more how difficult it is on the various congresses to make all participants interested in lectures due to the rather serious language problems. It helps that the committee will publish the lectures. During the evening there was a folklore entertainment of top class.

The banquet, as in many previous congresses, was the climax of the congress. Many beautiful words were spoken to Aunt Dagmer and her faithful team, not least her super-secretary, Rejko Pavlovits, and Gerhard Kreyenberg, who little by little has undertaken a certain duty to "print" the work describing the congress; he called this 15th congress - "Kongress der Liebe" (Congress of Love) - a very convincing expression. So once again thank you to everybody - and see you in 1976 - the first week of September in Lisbon!

ZDRIZENE PAPIRNICE LJUBLJANA
(Association of Paper Mills)

The following is part of an announcement given to participants at the Bled Congress:

Invitation to the Exlibris Making

Our Association, one of the oldest of its kind in Jugoslavia, bids a warm welcome to all the participants of the 15th International Congress of Exlibris, wishing them a lot of success and a pleasant stay in our country.

We avail ourselves of this opportunity to invite you to take part in the exlibris making contest. The conditions of participation are the following:

1 - The exlibris will serve as a printing pattern for wall-papers (length of 53 cm).
2 - The choice of motives remains unlimited, provided the exlibris remain simple and their colours clear and impressive. A special cliche will be made for printing, therefore all small details and half-tones are to be avoided.
3 - The exlibris must be devoid of the owner's name; it must not be published or used previously.
4 - Two versions of each exlibris are to be presented to the jury - one for a a single colour reproduction, one for the four-colour reproduction.

5 - Only the exlibris arriving to the below mentioned address will be taken
into account:

ZDRUZENE PAPIRNICE LJUBLJANA
Vevce, 61260 Ljubljana - Polje, Jugoslavija

They must reach the above address by January 31, 1975. The envelope must
bear the note "NATECAJ EKSLIBRIS".

The three best ex libris will be purchased for 4.000 dinars, 3.000, and 2.000.

FROM THE PERIODICAL LITERATURE

PUBLISHERS WEEKLY, Book plates, featuring art by Clancy Kralicek, 32, October 28,
1974. Ms. Kralicek's depictions of lions, featured in Joy Adamson's THE ELSA
WILD ANIMAL APPEAR, is used for a worldwide fund-raising project. (See article
on the artist and tipped-in plate on page 114.)

FORTUNE, On Your Own Time: Those Who Leave No Tome Unturned, Charles G. Burck
and Joseph A. Zebrowski, Jr. XC:79 et seq, November 1974. Among the book collectors featured is Frazer Clark whose library contains 30,000 pieces of Hawthorn-
eana, including the stencil Hawthorn used as a customs agent to paint his name on
imported goods. Mr. Clark has adapted it to function as a bookplate.

TRANSACTIONS & STUDIES OF THE COLLEGE OF PHYSICIANS OF PHILADELPHIA, The History of
Cardiology and the Cardiac Motif in Ex Libris, Norman Shaftel, M.D. (9) 4th Series,
42:#1, 98-104, July 1974. A well documented article of interest to both the physician and the philibrist, a term coined by A. B. Keeves, editor of BOOKPLATE COL-
LECTORS NEWS, in 1957. Dr. Shaftel details the development of cardiology from the
earliest noted stylized heart in the ex libris of Johannes Raceberg of Weimar (ca.
1570) to the prediction that future plates will feature open-heart surgery. He
also touches on his association with Dr. Radbill, dating from WWII.

TIMES LITERARY SUPPLEMENT, The Golden Age of the Ex-Libris, Brian North Lee. (14)
No. 3,787, 1065 et seq. The article was occasioned by the exhibit of the Bookplate
Society at the National Book League (October 9-19) of the work of book illustrators
working between 1880 and 1940 who also created bookplates. "Apart from the intrin-
sic beauty of many of them, their chief interest lies in the fascinating insight
which they give into the artistic preoccupations of their times, and into the
vagaries of fashion."

SERIF, Bookplate of Patricia C. Ulizio. (1) 11:inside front cover, Summer 1974.
"In a number of books in the B. George Ulizio Collection in the Kent State
University Library will be found the bookplate of Mr. Ulizio's daughter, Patricia."

ANTIQUARIAN BOOKMAN, Book Plates, October 21, 1974. Notice of the 20th anniversary exhibition of the bookplates of members of the Book Club of California.

UCLA LIBRARIAN, David Kindersley's Bookplate for the Alice Espey Memorial Fund.
(1) 27:#9, September 1974. The first bookplate Kindersley designed for special
libraries at UCLA was for the Eric Gill Collection at the Clark Library in 1963;
the second was commissioned in 1966. Mrs. Espey was head of a section of the
Technical Services Department in the University Research Library until late 1972.

ANTIQUARIAN BOOK MONTHLY REVIEW, Gawain Press. (1) #7, August 1974. This press (at
14 Gray's Inn Road, London WC1) designs bookplates and will furnish 500 prints for
£15. For local clients, the artist will "ring up to make certain he has the feel" of
you concerning background and hobbies to be represented.

ANTIQUARIAN BOOK MONTHLY REVIEW, Collecting Whistlerana, John S. Kinross. (2) 1-3, #9, October 1974. Interesting article on Rex Whistler who died in a tank battle during WWII. Good list of publications by and about Whistler, though the latest volume on his bookplates by Brian North Lee is not mentioned.

ABOUT ARTISTS AND BOOKPLATES, Number 4, July 1974 (#113 published by Willametta Keffer, Shady Acre, Rt. 5, Box 606, Roanoke, Va. 24014). Two bookplates for Betsie Diamond are reproduced as well as one for Sonja Strube. Mrs. Keefer and her husband bid on the Diamond library and acquired much of the equipment of the Diamonds' private press, The Hyacinth Press.

TIMES LITERARY SUPPLEMENT, Irish Earls. 1164, October 18,1974. Letter to the editor corrects description accompanying bookplates designed by Jack Yeats. It is the Earl of Desart (not Dorset) according to R. T. Hines.

NEWS LETTER No. 71 (Private Libraries Association), Autumn 1974. An item notes that William R. Holman is making a special offer to PLA members on his 1968 pub-lication, BOOKPLATES FOR LIBRARIES. Regularly $14.95, it is offered to PLA mem-bers at $10. (Holman, 4305 Cat Hollow, Austin, Texas 78731)

EXHIBITS - CATALOGS - Etc.

The Calendar of Events at the Cultural Center, Chicago Public Library, October 1974, listed an exhibit of The Lithuanian Contemporary Book Plate Collection, lent by Gintautas Vezys. Forty-three artists are represented by approximately 400 ex libris, among them ASBC&D member Vytautas Virkau. Mr. Vezys (6349 S. Artesian Ave., Chicago, Ill. 60629) is interested in future exhibition opportunities for his collection

California Design - 1910 was the title of an exhibit at the Pasadena Center from October 15 to December 1, 1974. A catalog ($7.50) was issued, edited by Timothy J. Anderson, Eudorah M. Moore and Robert M. Winter, which contains ref-erence to the bookplate of Olive Percival, "poet and book collector" who lived on the banks of the Arroyo (in Pasadena).

James Hayes was represented by five original pieces, including a mount which had the original drawing for the Johns Hopkins Sidney Painter bookplate, in the calligraphy exhibit which opened at the Dallas Public Library on November 4, '74. The exhibit featured the work of North American Calligraphers only.

Graphic Arts Unlimited, Inc. (225 5th Ave., New York) has a print by Michael Lyne titled "Ex Libris". It is a signed artist proof at $80.

Heritage Bookshop (847 N. La Cienega Blvd., Los Angeles, Ca. 90069) recently had a dozen standard reference bookplate volumes reasonably priced from $12.50-$22.50.

Dawson's Book Shop (535 N. Larchmont Blvd., Los Angeles, Ca. 90004) issued a catalog on Printing which was from the collection formed by Jackson Burke. The cover has his bookplate aptly designed for the subject collection.

Graf Books (717 Clark St., Iowa City, Iowa 52240) continues to list an occasional bookplate item. The November 1974 catalog contained Dr. Samuel Radbill's BIBLI-OGRAPHY OF MEDICAL EX LIBRIS LITERATURE, Hilprand Press, 1951, at $17.50 and THE BOOK-PLATE BOOKLET, vol. 1, #2, February 1907 for $4.

PLEASE SEND IMMEDIATE NOTIFICATION OF ANY CHANGE OF ADDRESS - - - - - -

WERNER R. EILERS - California Engraver

Werner Eilers entered the trade of engraving within three days of graduation from high school in 1923. He recounts that during the bleak days of 1929 there was a time when the employees in the shop where he worked were paid a dollar bill at the end of each day; it was by such drastic action that the firm survived and so did the employees!

The ex libris tipped-in was designed while Eilers served in the navy during WWII. It is used for his collection of books concerning heraldry and the graphic arts. At times the plate has been printed in blue, green or sienna.

Mr. Eilers is a very modest person, whose dedication to his work is well-known by those privileged to work with him such as Gene Dodge, who printed the edition of Eiler's ex libris used for this newsletter. His precision engraving is almost legendary, says Gene, and he enjoys good music and collects fine art.

Gene has a beautiful letterhead designed by Werner which depicts his engraving press and proclaims his profession as "Printer in Intaglio". It is printed handsomely in brown and gold. Gene, too, is a native of Los Angeles where he was born 44 years ago. His printing apprenticeship was served with a Hollywood firm. He especially enjoys working on his vintage hand pull intaglio press. He is married to a wonderful "Italian girl who makes the best pizza this side of heaven", and they are the happy parents of six sons. For those seeking a printer capable of the intricate precision of intaglio printing, Gene Dodge may be the answer (12521 El Oro Way, Granada Hills, Ca. 91344).

VOLUME TO BE PUBLISHED BY FISAE -- The international bookplate organization to which ASBC&D now belongs is planning to publish its third volume. Below are the particulars and deadline for any who may be interested in contributing an article.

1 - All articles will be written in Portugese, French, Spanish, English or German.
2 - The volume will be limited to an edition of 500 numbered copies.
3 - Each article will be illustrated; it is hoped each will have 8 ex libris prints.
4 - Each association member of FISAE will publish only one article about an artist of your country.
5 - There will be a copy of the volume for the author of the article, the artist, and the association member of FISAE.
6 - Articles and ex libris prints for tipping-in must be received by December 31, 1975. Send to: A. M. DaMota Miranda, Casa do Outeiro, Celorico de Basto, Portugal.

So that our efforts may be coordinated, it will be appreciated if any who want to write an article or who have suggestions about an artist will get in touch with me. It takes time properly to write and polish an article, to provide the necessary prints, and mail overseas. A snapshot of the artist would be desirable.

LINCOLN SHRINE OF REDLANDS
by Barbara Abele

The bookplate of the Lincoln Shrine of Redlands, California was designed by Leo Sarkadi from the George Grey Barnard cararra bust of Abraham Lincoln which occupies the place of honor in the lovely Lincoln Shrine. The symbolical interpretation incorporated by the artist used the plant life, humbly rooted in the soil, yet ever climbing that it might reach the sky - there to mingle with the stars and comets. Lincoln's phenomenal rise to great heights is admirably represented in Sarkadi's bookplate. Emblazoned across the heavens is the ending of Lincoln's Gettysburg address, which the artist has used to suggest the whole.

Leo Sarkadi (1879-1947) was Hungarian by birth but American by adoption and is classed as a member of the American School of Art.

THIS BOOK PRESENTED TO
REDLANDS LINCOLN MEMORIAL SHRINE
BY

The tipped-in ex libris prints are provided through the generosity of Larry Burgess, Curator of the Lincoln Shine. The original bookplates read "This Book Presented to Redlands Lincoln Memorial Shrine by Robert Watchorn" and the donors name is a facsimile signature. Subsequent prints have a space left blank for the name of a donor. Robert Watchorn (1858-1944) was born in England where he worked in the coal mines beginning at age 11, and in 1880 he came to the United States where his life closely paralleled that of a Horatio Alger hero. His varied career included being the first secretary of the United Mine Workers Union; Chief Factory Inspector of Pennvylvania (1891-95); Commissioner of Immigration on the Canadian frontier (1898-1905); U.S. Commissioner of Immigration at Ellis Island (1905-09); treasurer of Union Oil (1909-15) and president of Watchorn Oil and Gas Co. (1916-44). Early in his life he became fascinated with Lincoln and the Civil War period; in the 1920's Watchorn formulated plans for construction of a memorial and selected Redlands, his winter home, as the site for the Lincoln Shrine, the only one in existence west of the Mississippi River - monument, museum, library and archives, located at 120 Fourth Street, Redlands, California 92373.

NEW MEMBERS - -
Henry Lyman Parsons Beckwith, Six Villa Avenue, Providence, R. I. 02906
Rev. Kenneth O. Eaton, 11695 S.W. Park Way, Portland, Oregon 97225
Jack McCaskill, 25 South Michillinda Avenue, Pasadena, Ca. 91107

CHANGE OF ADDRESS - -
Mary E. Michenfelder, 1205 W. Cypress Avenue #204, San Dimas, Ca. 91773
Dr. Enrico Molnar, P. O. Box 1027, Visalia, Ca. 93277
Dana Pinizzotto, 30 Brocadero Place, Pasadena, Ca. 91105
Gretchen M. Potter, 1007 West John, Champaign, Ill. 61820

Joy Adamson, author of BORN FREE, has called
Clancy Kralicek one of the greatest living artists
of exotic cats, namely lions. The bookplate print
tipped-in is a copy of a Kralicek original and
part of the proceeds from the sale of these plates
is donated to animal wildlife conservation groups.
The ex libris, 50 to a box, may be obtained from
Simba Limited, 27 Jackson Street, Los Gatos, Ca.
95030, for $2.98.

Clancy has had an interesting background, having
traveled extensively while her husband was in the
career airforce. Now that her family is grown she
devotes her full time to producing paintings for
the enjoyment of her growing audience. Expressive
eyes are a distinctive feature of her animals.

In writing about her in the SAN JOSE MERCURY, Jose
Stell said, "The combination of charcoal as a
medium and animals as subject matter has enabled her to revert to drawing - her first
love - and to execute far more detail than is practically possible with brush and
palette." Stell quotes Clancy as saying, "All animals do not look alike. Some are
moody, some are contented. Some are beautiful and some are quite homely, but each
has its individuality." She has received commissions from Guide Dogs for the Blind
including illustrating their 1973 Christmas card series.

REV. JAMES PARKER - The Confederate bookplate of Rev. Parker was featured in Number
Eighteen of BOOKPLATES IN THE NEWS, but space did not permit including a few details
about the owner and the ex libris. - The bookplate was "lifted" from the design
of a Confederate monument which appears on the visitor's flyer at Shiloh National
Battlefield. Rev. Parker states that while he uses an armorial plate in most of his
books, he has a great interest in the History of the War Between the States and
quite naturally he wished to mark his books on the subject with an appropriate ex
libris. This drawing seemed to show that proud heritage of his Southern background.
The gray paper, of course, alludes to the Confederacy.

The Rev. James Parker is a priest in the Episcopal Chursh and is presently rector
of a parish in Albany, Georgia. He was born and grew up in Charleston, South
Carolina, and has lived in Indiana, Virginia, Illinois (Chicago), and Tennessee.
He is vice-president and a Fellow of the Augustan Society and occasionally contrib-
utes material on bookplates to its quarterly journal THE AUGUSTAN. Father Parker
is a graduate of the University of South Carolina, has a Master in Divinity degree
from Virginia Theological Seminary, and a Master of Arts in Library Science from
Rosary College in Illinois. In addition to his parish work, he has also been a
seminary librarian. He and Mrs. Parker are the parents of two teen-aged daughters.
A member of ASBC&D for several years, his principal interest is in heraldry and thus
heraldic ex libris. — — — — — — — — — — —

Dawsons of Pall Mall (16 Pall Mall, London SW1Y 5NB) has a large collection of
approximately 1,600 English bookplates, principally armorial and mostly 18th or
early 19th century, for sale at £650.

BOOKMAN, San Francisco, New Series No. 1, December 1974. This is a catalogue from
John Howell - Books which illustrates in reduced size the ex libris Dorothy Sturgis
Harding designed for John Howell.

BOSTON ATHENAEUM PLATE BY LEO WYATT

The ex libris used by the Boston Athenaeum for the Ames Collection was designed by English artist Leo Wyatt in 1972. The original edition of plates was printed in England, but the subsequent edition was printed by the Anthoensen Press of Portland, Maine. The Ames family gave the Commonwealth of Massachusetts their large country estate in Easton but first gave the Athenaeum the opportunity to select books from its library. General Butler of Civil War fame was related to the Ames family and among the books acquired were a few Civil War and Confederate items reflecting General Butler's time in the South.

The Boston Athenaeum has an old and interesting history, which dates back to 1805; today it is a proprietary library owned and maintained by 1049 shareholders. In 1850 it was one of the five largest libraries in the United States; today, with approximately half a million volumes, it makes no pretense of competing with the large public and university libraries as to size and completeness. Law, medicine, theology and the sciences have long since been substantially abandoned to the care of more specialized libraries, and the Athenaeum's field restricted to a judicious choice in history, literature, and the arts.

An article on the history of the Boston Athenaeum says that during the period beginning in 1837 "it became a common practice for women to visit the Library, although such a concession would occasion frequent embarrassment to modest men." Two librarians who contributed much to the science of librarianship also served on the staff of the Athenaeum: William F. Poole (of Poole's Index) and C. A. Cutter.

Our thanks to Rodney Armstrong, Director and Librarian of the Boston Athenaeum, for providing the Leo Wayatt prints. It is interesting to note that Rudolph Ruzicka, who also designed bookplates, did the illustrations for A BOSTON ATHENAEUM ANTHOLOGY, 1807-1972 by Walter Muir Whitehill; these illustrations were first issued in 1952 in color in a portfolio.

PUBLIC LIBRARY EX LIBRIS EXHIBIT - An exhibit of ex libris used by public libraries is planned for National Library Week at the Pasadena Public Library. If each ASBC&D member would send a print of a bookplate used in the public library of your city it will make this exhibit a great successs. Please send your prints to Audrey Arellanes, 429 North Daisy Avenue, Pasadena, Ca. 91107, immediately.

HARTFORD COURANT, Sunday, October 20, 1974, A Look at Art - Bookplates at the Atheneum, Jolene Goldenthal. One ex libris illustrated is that of Theda Bara. The exhibit, held at the Wadsworth Atheneum, combined rare books and bookplates; the ex libris are from the collection of Hettie Gray Baker, who donated them to the library when she became associated with the film industry. The exhibit was mounted by ASBC&D member Katherine Collens Bartholomew.

PUBLICATIONS READY - Order YEAR BOOK 1973/74 ($10) and INDEX 1951-1972 ($5). Make checks payable to the American Society of Bookplate Collectors and Designers.

AS of BC & D
Bookplates in the News
429 NORTH DAISY AVENUE, PASADENA, CALIFORNIA, 91107
AUDREY SPENCER ARELLANES, Editor

Number Twenty   April 1975

A MODERN BOOKPLATE BY THOMAS BEWICK
by George S. Swarth

Thomas Bewick, most noted of English wood engravers, was born at Cherryburn, near Newcastle-on-tyne, on August 12, 1753. Without formal instruction, he early showed a natural talent for drawing, and at the age of fourteen he was apprenticed to a Newcastle copperplate engraver, Ralph Beilby or Bielby.[1] By 1770 he was doing most of Beilby's wood engraving. After his apprentice- ship he was in London briefly, then returned to Newcastle where be became Beilby's partner and was later joined by his son, Robert Elliot. He died at Gateshead, near Newcastle, on November 8, 1828.

Before Bewick's time, wood cuts were incised with a knife on a slab cut with the grain like a plank. As described in Edward Almack's BOOKPLATES [1903], page 3: " In modern times - about 1785 - a revolution took place in wood en- graving, when Bewick began to engrave on a piece of wood cut endwise, and with a graver instead of a knife . . . . Sometimes to distinguish the old art from the new, the former is called a woodcut and the latter a wood-engraving."

Bewick illustrated many books, including GAY'S FABLES [1779], SELECT FABLES [1784], and Goldsmith's DESERTED VILLAGE. His own most noted productions, A GENERAL HISTORY OF QUADRUPEDS [1790] and THE HISTORY OF BRITISH BIRDS [1797- 1804], showed his very considerable attainments as a naturalist as well as an artist. His final work, which occu- pied him for six years, was a set of illustrations for AESOP'S FABLES.

Although best known for his book illustra- tions, Bewick also made many bookplates-about a hundred, ac- cording to W. J. Hardy, BOOKPLATES [1897], page 3. At least 41 are iden- tified as Bewick's

George Selwyn Swarth

work in E. R. Gambier Howe's CATALOGUE OF THE FRANKS COLLECTION OF BRITISH AND

AMERICAN BOOKPLATES [1903-4].[2] Besides his more numerous wood engravings, Bewick did some work on copperplate. Examples of both appear in BEWICK GLEANINGS [Julia Boyd, editor, 1886], and Hardy says [op. cit., page 112], "There are a great many more copper-plate book-plates by Bewick than is generally supposed." He lists six, apparently corresponding to Nos. 907 [Buddle Atkinson], 20781 [Edward Moises, A.M.], 5620 [James Charlton], 5862 [A. Clapham], 205 [J. H. Affleck, Newcastle-upon-Tyne], and 5213 [Thos Carr, Newcastle], respectively, in the Franks catalogue. The catalogue itself does not describe the medium, except for No. 205, nor does it identify the first two as Bewick's work, but it refers to Hardy's attribution of No. 907.

Bewick's bookplates were mostly pictorial, chiefly landscape, or landscape or pictorial armorial, the latter types having an armorial element, usually a shield but sometimes a crest, introduced rather extraneously into the composition. A few were purely armorial. Bookplates by Bewick are illustrated in Egerton Castle's ENGLISH BOOK-PLATES [1894] at pages 147 [John Anderson, Jun.] and 148 [Geroge Hawks] and Hardy, op. cit., at page 111 [Robert Southey]. Besides these and similar reproductions of bookplates as such, a great many of the ordinary bits of landscape which Bewick used for book-plates he afterwards utilized as tailpieces for various books illustrated by him." [Hardy, op. cit., page 110.]

Bewick's talent was particularly adapted to the creation of bookplates of great charm. As Hardy says [op. cit., pages 112-3], "One reason why Bewick was so successful as an engraver of book-plates lay in the fact that his ability was most conspicuous in a small design. The work of such men as Hogarth or Bartolozzi seems cramped when it appears on the small scale which alone a book-plate can admit; but with Bewick, the smaller the size of the scene he desired to represent, the greater was his skill in introducing into it both originality and beauty."

Perhaps because of his preoccupation with outdoor life, Bewick seems to have appealed more to men than to women. None of the plates attributed to Bewick in the Franks catalogue appears to be for a woman, though the use of initials rather than full names in some cases makes it impossible to say with certainty. Nora Labouchere's LADIES' BOOK-PLATES [1895] gives only one by Bewick, that of Jane Hewitt [so in the text, pages 67-8; "Jane Hewitson" in the index, page 290], dated April 24, 1800.

A relatively large number of Bewick's wood blocks survive, and from time to time some of them come into the market. Recently Mr. George S. Swarth, a member of the ASBC&D, took advantage of such an opportunity to buy from Dawson's Book Shop in Los Angeles the block shown here, evidently a bookplate that never found an owner, as the central space intended for a monogram or armorial identification remains uncut. It was illustrated in BEWICK GLEANINGS, which says of it [page 68], "We have been unable to find impressions from this fine block. It is evidently Thomas Bewick's work." The block is dated in ink on the back "I Sept 23" [i.e. September 1823].

Because of differences in printing techniques, most Bewick blocks offer great difficulties to modern printers. In Bewick's time, blocks were inked with a ball, which tended to ink too heavily along the edges of the raised portions. To avoid this, those edges were "lowered" or rounded down slightly; but a block so treated does not ink properly with a modern roller, which touches only the most elevated plane surface. Printing from such a block requires careful hand inking and the use of heavy padding under the paper to secure a satisfactory impression. Fortunately, edges of the present block had not been lowered [perhaps because the block was never completed], and Pall Bohne, of Rosemead, California, who is particularly skilled in fine hand printing, has been able to produce from the original block the excellent impression shown on the left on page 114. At Mr. Bohne's suggestion, a zinc reproduction of the block has also been made, in which by photographic process he inserted Swarth's family coat of arms in the unfinished central oval, thus producing a completed bookplate, as contemplated by Bewick, shown on the right.

Mr. Swarth is a native of Berkeley, California, a graduate of Stanford University and Stanford Law School, who retired from the United States Department of Justice in 1971 after 26 years in Washington, D.C. He now lives in Denver. In the Department of Justice, Mr. Swarth was associated for a time with Carlyle S. Baer, then Secretary of the ASBC&D, who stimulated Mr. Swarth's long-standing interest in bookplates, introduced him to the Society, and generously assisted in building his collection. In 1960 Mr. Swarth was able to give to Carlyle Baer, who was always interested in memorabilia and in items punning on his name [he was proprietor of the Bruin Press], Bewick's wood block of the European brown bear, which had come into the market at that time. Mr. Swarth's library does not include any specific group of books in which he plans to use his new Bewick bookplate, but he expects to use it in any books the subject matter or period of which makes it seem appropriate.

(Footnotes: [1] "Beilby" according to ENCYCLOPEDIA BRITANNICA, 1944 edition, vol. 3, page 489, s.v. Bewick, and W. J. Hardy, BOOK-PLATES, 1897, page 109; "Bielby" according to the CENTURY CYCLOPEDIA OF NAMES, 1914, page 154, s.v. Bewick. [2] Vol. 1, Nos. 169, 205, 487, 494 & 495, 497, 658, 1402, 2123, 3795 & 3796, 4148, 4155, 4764, 5213, 5606, 5612, 5620, 5862, 6254, 6685, 6957, & 58, 8854 & 55, and 9922; Vol. 2, Nos. 14171, 14978, 15664, 21425, 23982, and 24693; Vol. 3, Nos. 26058 & 59, 26755, 26756, 27623 & 24, 27689, 28289, 28336, 29038, 29239 & 40, 29356, 24265, 24339, and 34398. (Numbers here linked by an ampersand denote two examples of the same design.) Besides the completed plates there is a frame, No. 34439. Additionally, four plates are conjecturally attributed to Bewick: Vol. 1, Nos. 720, 2464, and 5899; Vol. 2, No. 14634. These lists may not be complete. Hardy (op. cit., page 112) also attributes to Bewick, Franks No. 907 and plates that apparently correspond to Franks Nos. 8812 and 20781, not attributed in the catalogue. In Vol. 3, No. 32123 was attributed to "Bewick" by Sir Wallaston Franks, but Howe observes that the initials "I.B." appear on the urn, from which he conjectures that the plate may be by John Bewick. In the same volume, No. 29409 was engraved by "T. Bewick & Son" and No. 33937 was by R. E. (Robert Elliot) Bewick.]

— — — — — — — — — — — —

MINIATURE EX LIBRISEK, Karoly Andrusko; Budapest: Egyetemi Nyuomda, 1974, with an introduction by Ferenc Galambos, 184 pages, 65 illustrations, 2-1/4 x 1-1/8, in Hungarian, Russian, English, and German. This small book contains reproductions of 65 woodcut ex libris, in actual size, by Karoly Andrusko, a noted Hungarian artist presently residing in Yugoslavia. Andrusko began his career as a typographer and gradually extended his talents to art and design. Well known in eastern Europe, Andrusko's artistic efforts include approximately 2,000 miniature bookplates, and he is said to have executed the world's smallest woodcut [8 x 7 mm]. The ex libris miniatures presented in this book vary in size from 20 x 17 mm to 25 x 30mm.

Published in an edition of 250 numbered and 250 unnumbered copies, the book was designed by Janka Gyula, a bibliophile residing in Budapest and probably best known for his annual bibliographies of miniature books.[Reviewer: John Lathourakis]

From the Collection of
EDWARD W. ALLEN

ALLEN PLATE BY JACKSON
by Robert Hitchman

Edward W. Allen, Seattle attorney, has distinguished himself as a member of the bar, as an author, a book collector and as a public servant. Why, then, should his bookplate carry a picture of a North Pacific halibut schooner? The answer is logical: for 41 years Mr. Allen served his country as a member of the International Fisheries Commission (1932-55), the International Pacific Salmon Commission (1937-53), and the International North Pacific Fisheries Commission (1954-73). He represented the United States on these bodies, which also included delegates from Canada and Japan and often observers from the Soviet Union. The Commissions' work in the promotion and support of study and research, and the promulgation of treaties and international agreements has been responsible for the conservation and development of halibut and salmon in North Pacific waters. At the time of Mr. Allen's resignation from this work (for which, incidentally, he received no compensation), the President of the United States referred to him as "the leader and senior statesman of the American fisheries community."

The map of the North Pacific that serves as the background on Mr. Allen's ex libris refers to the area of concern of the three Commissions, to his remarkable collection of Pacific Northwest Americana, and to the rich and unique collection of maps of this region that he has built up over the years. Chief among the books he has written are NORTH PACIFIC and THE VANISHING FRENCHMAN: THE MYSTERIOUS DISAPPEARANCE OF LAPEROUSE.

The bookplate is the work of Hewitt R. Jackson of Bellevue, Washington, an artist who has gained an international reputation for his maritime research and pictures of historic vessels. In 1974 he received the Captain Robert Gray Award, the highest honor bestowed by the Washington State Historical Society. This was given "in recognition of distinguished contributions to Washington State and Pacific Northwest history."

———— —— —— —— ——

FROM THE PERIODICAL LITERATURE .. .. ..
ANTIQUES JOURNAL, Collecting Bookplates, G. R. & P. K. Dalphin. (10) 14-5, 33, February 1975. Highlights of bookplate history, especially in America. "Collectors of American bookplates continue to identify examples by the Allen number or proudly note when their own example is not listed by Allen." The illustrations for this article are thus identified, including two "not in Allen."

PRINTING ART, Bookplates, Kendall Banning. (10) 6:359-63, February 1906. "Yet of all the so-called fads few have more practical value and more historic interest than that of bookplate collecting, and none can offer better opportunities for getting in touch with congenial spirits; for when the significance of a bookplate is understood, and one acquired, the step (continued next page)

An exhibit of ex libris designed by
Vytautas Virkau, associate professor
of art at George Williams College in
Downers Grove, Illinois, went on display in the college's library during
February. The forty bookplates are
executed in mixed media/offset technique, and were designed as part of a
recent sabbatical project. The artist
has signed each print of the Pilka ex
libris tipped-in our newsletter.

Stasys Pilka is by profession a theatre
director and actor. His original book
collection, which he had in Lithuania
after the second WW, was dispersed and
ended up in Moscow and Leningrad. He
started a second collection for which
many artists have designed bookplates
and says Vytautas Virkau, "It was my pleasure to join their ranks. The inscription 'We are such stuff as dreams are (made of)' is from THE TEMPEST.
The angel in the ex libris was originally used on a farewell recital program
to commemorate Pilka's 50th anniversary with the theatre."

The artist Virkau was born in Lithuania in 1930; he studied in Munich from
1946 to 1949; upon his arrival in the United States in 1951 he attended the
University of Chicago and the School of the Art Institute of Chicago, where
he received his Master of Fine Arts degree in 1956. Virkau has had at least
two one-man shows where his oil paintings received critical acclaim; Franz
Schultze, art critic of the Chicago DAILY NEWS described him as a "landscapist,
moreover of abstract proclivities. . ." His ex libris work was exhibited at
the 15th International Ex Libris congress in Bled during 1975, and the jury
for the VII International Ex Libris Biennale in Malbork, Poland, has accepted
his work for an exhibit opening June 7, 1975. "They tell me," says Virkau,
"in both cases it is the first time an American was represented with his bookplates."

PRINTING ART (continued)
from bookplate owner to collector is brief." Illustrations are plates by William Jordan, third member of the Triptych headed by Wilbur Macey Stone and Jay
Chambers.

Miniature Books List #60-1975 from Dawson's Book Shop announces
SOME MINOR BOOK PLATES printed by William M. Cheney with a selection of 23 miniature bookplates designed by Cheney and an
appropriately brief introduction by Audrey Arellanes. The edition
is "somewhat under 200 copies," bound in grey cloth, measuring
1-1/4 x 1-3/4".

PUBLISHERS' WEEKLY, A Bibliography of Bibliographies of Book Plates. 88:633-
5, September 4, 1915. Reprint from Boston TRANSCRIPT "of a few weeks ago" of
checklist by Winward Prescott under classifications including Artists in General, Individual Artists, and by country (American, France, Holland, Russia,
Portugal, Italy, Sweden, Switzerland, Belgium), and bibliographies.

VINCAS KISARAUSKAS
Lithuanian Artist
by Dr. V. E. Vengris

Lithuania, a small country of 3.2 million inhabitants at the Baltic Sea, today is one of the leading countries in the world of ex libris art. With history dating back to the 16th century, the ex libris in Lithuania is a highly developed and popular art; contrary to many other countries, modern bookplates are created by professional artists. They have developed a richly varied number of styles and techniques for this fascinating miniature art form and have been recognized with numerour awards in international exhibits. Lately, Ms. G. Didelyte and Mr. A. Kmieliauskas were awarded first prizes at the 15th International Congress of Ex Libris held in Bled during September 1974.

I would like to introduce our readers to the work of Mr. Vincas Kisarauskas, who is one of the leading Lithuanian artists and is very active in bookplate art. Kisarauskas, born in 1934, is living in Vilnius, the capital city of Lithuania. He studied at the Vilnius Art Institute, graduating in 1959. Since then, he has been very active in oil painting, graphics, mosaic, scenography, bookplates and book illustration. V. Kisarauskas is one of the most original of Lithuanian artists. He is beset with heavy moods and is a dour expressionist. The rough, unpolished shapes of his art bring to mind Lithuanian folk art in which most primitive forms are highly expressive.

V. Kisarauskas made his first bookplate in 1957, and since then he has created more than 500 of them using etching and linoleum block techniques. His bookplates have been exhibited in Argentina, Belgium, Bulgaria, Czechoslovakia, France, Denmark, Holland, Hungary, Japan, Italy, Poland, U.S.A., USSR, and Yugoslavia. He received awards at the 12th International Congress of Exlibris held in Como (Italy) in 1968 as well as at the 13th Congress held in Budapest in 1970.

V. Kisarauskas does not use symbols in his bookplates to tell us about the owners, their hobbies or interests. His approach is a modern one. The bookplate is being used as an example of miniature graphic art with the purpose of decorating the books and the means for the graphical expression of the artist. The tipped-in bookplate was made for Dr. V. E. Vengris of Baltimore in 1972. (Note: the prints for this newsletter were printed by Pall Bohne at his Bookhaven Press.)

NEW MEMBERS:
Fred W. Lagerquist, Jr. 2575 Peachtree Road NE, Atlanta, Georgia 30305
John Lathourakis, 3055 Oneida Street, Pasadena, Calitornia 91107
Egdon H. Margo, 19143 Schoolcraft Street, Reseda, California 91335
Internationaal Exlibriscentrum, Zamanstraat 49, 2700 Sint Niklaas, Belgium

THE LIBRARY

STR. DELTA QUEEN

FOUR TIMES A MAIDEN,
YET ALWAYS A QUEEN
by Lester Glenn Arellanes

The date was advertised as the maiden voyage. But Queens cannot falsify their age and for others to do so borders on lèse-majesté. For in truth, her birth began in 1924 in the Isherwood Shipyard on the bonnie banks of the River Clyde in Scotland. Here her steel hull, along with that of her sister, DELTA KING, was fabricated, each part numbered, then knocked down for shipment. Meanwhile, at the Denny Works in closeby Dumbarten, her engines were built and likewise tested and disassembled for shipment. Simultaneously, at the famous Krupp steel foundries in Germany, her wheel shafts and cranks were being turned out to last, if not for a thousand years, at least much longer than the Third Reich. The first maiden voyage then took place when all the disassembled parts of hull, engines, shafts and cranks were shipped from Europe to San Francisco where they were transferred from the steamship to a barge for the final voyage up the San Joaquin River to Stockton, California.

Here, in a temporary yard, the hull was reassembled and other mechanical parts were machined and installed. Then four decks, largely of oak, teak, mahogany, walnut and Oregon cedar were built by American shipbuilders to give the QUEEN spacious staterooms, a social hall, dining room, stained glass dome, and every facility to make these vessels the last word in luxurious inland liners. Each ship was 285 feet long overall and 58 feet wide, registered at 1837 gross tons, carried 2000 tons of freight, over 200 passengers and cost $875,000.

The first real maiden voyage took place on a sunny day in 1926 when daily overnight service commenced between San Francisco and Sacramento by the new ships, a service that was to last for 15 years until DELTA QUEEN was withdrawn in November of 1941. She was sold, but before her new owners could claim her, the U.S. government took her over early in 1942 for war service in the San Francisco Bay area conveying personnel to and from ocean vessels. War ended, she was once again laid up and offered for sale in 1946.

Purchased November 20, 1946 for $46,250 by Captain Tom Rae Green (1905-50), he started her April 19, 1947 on still yet another maiden voyage, this time a 5,261 mile odyssey on salt water from San Francisco Bay via the Panama Canal to New Orleans, a feat deemed impossible by many. She survived without a scratch, and later she would survive a five year Congressional battle to remain on the river. But now it was June 2, 1948, and time to make her fourth (and last?) maiden voyage. It was the beginning of a ten day cruise from Cincinnati to Muscle Shoals on the Tennessee River. Happily, 27 years later, at the age of 49 years, the great sternwheel river steamboat DELTA QUEEN still reigns on the river. Long live the Queen!

120

DELTA QUEEN BOOKPLATE   The library of the DELTA QUEEN has a bookplate
by Harvey Simmonds   which is a woodcut done by Harlan Hubbard, an
artist who lives with his wife Anna on the Ken-
tucky bank of the Ohio River, a few miles downstream and across from Madison, Indiana. Harlan and Anna married in middle years - he a painter, she
until that time Fine Arts librarian at the Cincinnati Public Library. They
built together a shantyboat, an unpowered platform with a cabin, and for
seven years lived upon it, floating down to New Orleans and then traveling
the bayou country. Harlan wrote of this experience in SHANTYBOAT [Dodd,
Mead, 1950] and more recently Eakins Press published his book, PAYNE HOLLOW,
about their twenty years living on and with the land and river at Payne Hollow .
The DELTA QUEEN's bookplate was cut in wood, on a block left from local lumber
used in the building of the Payne Hollow house. It was printed in the fall of
1972 on paper cut from a roll that Harlan salvaged from the river, so tightly
wound that the water had not damaged the interior, the only marks of its bump-
ing journey being a kind of natural deckle.

REVIEW by P. W. Filby, Director, Maryland Historical Society - THE BOOKPLATE
DESIGNS OF REX WHISTLER, by Brian North Lee. Private Libraries Association
for the Bookplate Society, 1973. 39 pages, 41 plates. 650 copies with printed
frontispiece; 350 copies with frontispiece bookplate tipped-in.

This handsomely produced and designed book contains a good survey of the
bookplate as a whole in England. Mr. Lee notes that Rex Whistler's bookplates
are remarkable and most individual, and this they surely are. He also avers
that Whistler was unquestionably an artist of great originality and charm,
and this too is agreed. It is perhaps a little surprising that Whistler claims
to have a lack of knowledge of the methods of reproduction (nowadays no one
would dare to contemplate graphic work without such knowledge), and therefore
it is probable that some bookplates have suffered from this. The reviewer
also suffers somewhat from a complete lack of enthusiasm for much of the pre-
World War II work on bookplates. They are usually (in his opinion) too florid,
and often fail to convey the owner's interests, whereas nowadays the bookplate
designer tends to show this in most of his or her works. To be sure, there is
a delicacy and harmony and a fine show of good taste about Whistler's plates,
but so often they are too busy. There is no doubt that Whistler had great command when involved in designs, but the effect of many of his bookplates is
rather outdated. It is noted that many are reduced, and yet the reproduction
is almost 5 x 4"! It is astonishing how booklovers of the past ever allowed
their books to be cluttered by such huge plates.

However, the book, beautifully designed by David Chambers and lovingly
written and compiled by Brian North Lee, is a must for all bookplate collectors,
and for any library graphics collection. The reviewer has a predeliction for
small bookplates, where the owner's interests are shown, where there is beautiful lettering with the minimum of illustration, making him perhaps not the
best person to review Whistler!

BOOKPLATE SOCIETY, Newsletter No. 8, December 1974. Contains news on the ex
libris exhibit at the National Book League in October 1974; quotes from the
NOTES AND QUERIES (a manuscript of the Bookplate Exchange Club, 1952) of G. H.
Viner on the Clifton family coat of arms which is illustrated; announces a
talk to be given by Mark Severin on April 15, 1975; mentions availability at
nominal cost of the Viner notes for "Bookplates for Identification" from the
JOURNAL OF THE EX LIBRIS SOCIETY; tells of the bookplates of Robert Austin
with illustration of one for Margaret Helen Mackenchnie; suggests members send
a copy of their bookplate and details of its commissioning; and reproduces the
plate for the Prime Minister's Library showing the door at No. 10 Downing Street.

KLAUS RODEL & ExlibRisten

EXL·INGE RODEL

Though a small country, Denmark has probably published more ex libris literature than any other primarily due to the initiative of one individual - Klaus Rodel.

The first separate publication on ex libris in Denmark was published in 1913; it was a small leaflet of 24 pages. Called ARETé, it appeared about once yearly until 1952, when publication was accelerated. However, until the end of 1966 only 96 ex libris publications had been issued in Denmark; therefore, it is quite impressive that commencing in 1967 and to the present, Klaus Rodel has issued 100 publications devoted to the bookplate art.

Klaus relates that he started collecting books during his school years and his desire to indicate ownership of volumes lead to his first bookplate, a small printed sticker with the "pompouse text KLAUS RODEL LIBRARY."

Klaus states he began his own publications after making a table of contents for NET, a periodical which ran for 18 years. A chance remark that this enormous work should be made available for more people led to the printing of 75 copies. Everything was "night work and a one-man show." The result, he states, was not "exactly bibliophile" but it was very useful. Following this in 1966 he made opus lists, also first of all for his own pleasure, but then printed 50 to 100 copies. Thus started EXLIBRISTEN, the publishing firm of Klaus Rodel. He gives great credit to his printer, Vagn Clemmensen, not only for his expertise in the physical aspects of printing and design but for his cooperation in planning the publications as economically as possible and still maintain the exacting graphic standards set for all the EXLIBRISTEN publications.

The art of the bookplate is of particular interest in several countries which for currency reasons are least able to purchase books, i.e. Poland, Lithuania, CSSR, and Hungary; however, often exchanges can be made. Many bookplate collectors are not interested in the literature on the subject, but fortunately there are a sufficient number who are to help support an important publication program such as that carried on since 1966 by Klaus Rodel. A dozen publications are in various planning stages and subscribers are sought, either to the entire series or to individual volumes. To assure your copy of these limited edition ex libris publications write directly to Klaus Rodel, Smedevej 20, Postboks 109, DK-9900 Frederikshavn, Denmark.

The bookplate tipped-in above is for Rodel's wife, Inge, and was designed by Russian artist Lew Beketow in 1972.

— — — — — — — —

1975 Subscription to BOOKPLATES IN THE NEWS - U.S. & Canada $3/$4 Overseas

122

CROWN CITY EXHIBIT
Centeno & Coffin Ex Libris
     by Betty Powell 
Pasadena Public Library's ex-
hibit of library bookplates,
in celebration of National Library Week (April 13-19, 1975),
will feature the first public
showing of a new commemorative
bookplate designed by PPL's
display artist, Ruth Fitzer.

The new bookplate will be placed
in library materials purchased
with funds from two generous be-
quests. Mrs. Fitzer's design: an
embossed crown - representing
Pasadena, the Crown City - over
a stylized embossed book; the
library name is engraved in copperplate Gothic capital letters;
the gift designation engraved in
italic Roman upper and lower case.
Anthony F. Kroll produced the
design on 40# vellum paper, with
cocoa brown letters and a plate
marked edge.

Elizabeth Centeno, who with her
husband was a longtime patron of
the Pasadena Public Library, be-

PASADENA
PUBLIC
LIBRARY

queathed to the library her collection of books and records as well as a
cash gift "for the acquisition of materials pertaining to Spanish and
Latin American culture." The bookplate in materials purchased with these
funds is engraved: "The Elizabeth and Augusto Centeno Collection."

Clifford L. Coffin, a regular patron of the Central Library, and particularly the Fine Arts Division, bequeathed a portion of his estate for the
"purchase of books dealing with all phases of the fine and creative arts,
excepting music." Purchases from this fund will be designated by the new
bookplate engraved: "The Clifford L. Coffin Collection."

Public and private libraries across the nation have responded to PPL's invitation to enter the bookplate exhibit, and several ASBC&D members generously sent plates from their home towns or from their collections. The exhibit will be on view in the Library's Main Hall and Reference Division at
285 East Walnut Street, Pasadena, California, April 1-30, 1975.

MORE FROM THE PERIODICAL LITERATURE .. .. ..
HERALDRY IN CANADA, Bookplate Collecting, A Many Splendour'd Thing, John D.
Light. (14) 8:6-12, December 1974. A charming, well-illustrated article.

REPRODUCTIONS REVIEW & METHODS, Many Uses for the Hand Press, C. Owen Brantley.
(2) 25:44, March 1975. In addition to the commercial uses to which a 6x10"
Sigwalt or any similar handpress may be put, Brantley used it to print individual
names on a specially designed bookplate.

AS of BC & D

Bookplates in the News

429 NORTH DAISY AVENUE, PASADENA, CALIFORNIA, 91107
AUDREY SPENCER ARELLANES, Editor

Number Twenty-One

July 1975

PAUL McPHARLIN
by   Ione Wiechel

THE
LIBRARY ASSOCIATION
OF SANDUSKY

The bookplate of the Library Association of Sandusky was designed as a gift for the library in 1947 by Paul McPharlin. This plate is a typographic label, the border being an unusual geometric design printed in grey, with an inner red line as accent. The typographic label has a history of long and distinguished use in this country. When Henry Dunster, the first president of Harvard, came to this country in 1640, he brought his library; some of the books contained a label printed in England. The Harvard students saw them and took up the idea. The Stephen Daye plate of 1642 is considered the first and most interesting of American bookplates; it believed to have been printed on the first Cambridge press. While this type of book label is often considered of lesser interest than the pictorial bookplate, this typographic book label is eminently suitable for use by the Library Association for its simplicity and taste as well as for its historical significance.

Paul McPharlin also designed the Ione plate for Ione K. Weichel, a member of the American Society of Bookplate Collectors and Designers. The calligraphic design is placed in a French type border dated 1812.

Paul McPharlin was a noted artist and illustrator, as well as a well-known writer on the graphic arts. His book illustrations and designs have frequently appeared among the Fifty Books of the Year selected by the American Institute of Graphic Arts. He illustrated the SATIRICAL DICTIONARY OF VOLTAIRE which he translated for a new English version. In the world of books Paul McPharlin was very active. As a publisher he issued several classics under the imprint of the Fine Book Circle. He designed trade books for Hastings House, Scribners, and Random House. For the Limited Editions Club he designed the seven volume DECLINE AND FALL OF THE ROMAN EMPIRE with the Piranesi etchings. His untimely death in 1948 was a loss to all those interested in the graphic arts as well as to groups concerned with puppetry, as he founded the Puppeteers of America. His History, THE PUPPET THEATRE IN AMERICA, was published posthumously.

BOOKPLATE

by

Vincent Starrett

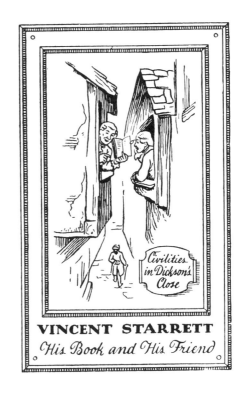

VINCENT STARRETT
His Book and His Friend

Ah, what a happy scene is this
Of self-effacing bibliobliss!
This ancient paramour of print,
Who takes his pleasures "fine to mint,"
Turns pages with divine content
Nor thinks one shilling badly spent;
While all around on floor and table
Rise books like little towers of Babel.

The cat that purrs upon his knees,
The leaping flame, the slippered ease,
The stocking cap, the mild distraction,
All mark a seemly satisfaction;
And yet one ventures to assert
This gentle soul would sell his shirt
For some small fugitive in binding
That somehow still escapes his finding.

[Michael Murphy, who furnished the above poem, states it was first published
in Vol. 11, No. 1, January 31, 1965 of PENNY POEMS FROM MIDWESTERN UNIVERSITY.
The Starrett bookplate is from IN MEMORIAM Vincent Starrett, 1886-1974 published by the Green Escape Press, Houten, The Netherlands, 1974. This is the
press of ASBC&D member Henk van Otterloo. In addition to the bookplate which
is printed in a soft green, Vincent Starrett's distinctive signature is printed
in turqoise, and there are two brief contributions which this famous bookman
made to a 1931 Dauber & Pine Bookshops catalogue and a Marshall Field catalogue
of 1942. Henk van Otterloo printed his tribute by hand on deckle edge paper,
using black and three colors, in a limited edition as a New Year's greeting to
friends. - The Sherlock Holmes bookplate of Vincent Starrett, executed for
him by Fridolf Johnson and which was tipped-in the January issue of BOOKPLATES
IN THE NEWS, is one of six Starrett bookplates which will be featured in a special monograph to be published later this year by the Starrett Memorial Library.
Legal representatives of the Starrett estate caution that permission for use of
the plate in exhibition or for reproduction must be granted through written permission of the Starrett Memorial Library; deceptive use or reproduction could
subject such user to legal action. This is for the protection of collectors of
both books and bookplates.]

— — — — — — — — —

BOOKPLATES IN FICTION -- THE COLFAX BOOK-PLATE, A Mystery Story, by Agnes Miller,
published by the Century Co., New York, 1926, 375 pages. There is a paper label
on the front of the book similar to an ex libris with the title of the book at
the top, then a fireplace and library table are pictured, with the name of the
author below. This is a pleasant mystery story in the more leisurely pace of 1926
with romantic interest but none of the more explicit excitement usually present
in the current genre. This volume is in the Rare Book Room at the Huntington Library! A brief death notice in the New York TIMES for November 19, 1951 states
Agnes Miller had celebrated her 100th birthday on October 25th and died November
18, 1951, in North Plainfield, New Jersey. "For thirty years she was a governess
in the home of Right Rev. Paul A. Matthews, retired Episcopalian Bishop of Tren-
ton Diocese. She was survived by a sister, Mrs. W. S. Mayers, Fairmount, Va."

FROM THE PERIODICAL LITERATURE . . . BOOKS and EPHEMERA . . .
COLLECTOR'S WEEKLY, January 21, 1975, The Observer notes, "With a little imagination a willing collector can find a hobby that won't chew up too much of his budget. Take bookplates. In Europe, packets of a hundred different 19th-century bookplates can be bought in hobby shops for a few dollars."

SERIF, Book Pile Bookplate, (1) 11:inside front cover, Winter 1975. "For the bookplates in this final issue of the SERIF, we felt this fine example of a book pile bookplate would be appropriate."

TEXAS QUARTERLY, "Saber Para Obrar: Know in Order to Act." Nettie Lee Benson. (2) 2:194-202, Spring 1959. "Genaro Garcia used both a book mark and a book plate in his library. The book mark was stamped on the reverse side of the title page or on the colophon to indicate that the item was rare. He used the book plate to indicate that he valued the book not necessarily for its rarity but for its importance and significance to him. . . . in the 1518 Rotterdam edition of Sir Thomas More's UTOPIA, he used both book plate and book mark. . . Saber para Obrar, Know in Order to Act, was Genaro Garcia's motto, which he had engraved on his book plate. The motto now appears on the reproduction of the book plate over the entrance to the Latin American Collection of the University of Texas." The library was purchased from the Garcia estate in Mexico during the 1920's.

AB, A.B.A. Delegation Meets with Ford. (2) 55:cover, 1211, March 17, 1975. A gift of 250 books was presented by the American Booksellers Association to the White House Home Library. A reduced size copy of the bookplate used in these volumes is illustrated; the plate was produced by Peter Pauper Press, printed on light buff stock, showing a green border and black type. The library resulted from a comment made by President Herbert Hoover shortly after inauguration in 1929 that there were no books in the White House.

SLOVENSKI EKSLIBRIS by Emilijan Cevc and Janez Logar was published for the international congress in Bled during September 1974 by Drustvo Exlibris Sloveniae. The two articles are printed bilingually with 16 pages for the English version of "Exlibris in Slovenia" and "The Artistic Importance of Exlibris in Slovenia." While the pattern of the bookplate's development is much the same in all countries, it is especially interesting for the American enthusiast to read of "firsts" in Slovenia, and for the names of the artists and owners to be new. The text shows some roughness in translation, but it reads smoothly enough not to detract from the facts.

THIRTEEN WAYS OF LOOKING AT WALLACE STEVENS was the title of a special exhibition catalog issued by the Henry E. Huntington Library in Spring 1975 ($1). Of particular interest to bookplate enthusiasts is the ex libris shown on the catalog cover which was made by Victor Hammer in 1946 from a design by James Guthrie. Wallace Stevens, born in 1879, was admitted to the New York State Bar in 1904. In 1914 he began to publish poems in magazines, the following year he joined the Hartford Accident and Indemnity Co. where he became a vice president in 1934. Concurrent with his career as an insurance executive, he continued to write poetry. He won the Bollinger Prize in Poetry in 1949, in 1951 the National Book Award in Poetry, and perhaps the highest honor, the Pulitzer Prize in Poetry, in 1955, the year he died.

EL ARTE DEL EXLIBRIS by Antonio J. Molina, ASBC&D member from Puerto Rico. This 8 page leaflet in Spanish is dated April 1975 and has 14 bookplates illustrated, one in two colors plus black is tipped in. There is also a picture of the handsome author/bookplate collector. Among the illustrations are plates for Brandenburg, Lady Charlotte Schreiber, Herr Adolph von Trott, Enrico Caruso, Herbert and Norbert Ott.

THE BOOKPLATE SOCIETY, Newsletter No. 9, March 1975 (9 pages). ASBC&D member Rev. Kenneth O. Eaton asks for exchange of pictorial bookplates. - Bookplates of members includes notes about and illustration of those for Horace E. Jones (wood cut by Barbara Jones); K. F. Langford (handprinted plate with arabesque border); Peter Stockham (Leo Wyatt wood engraving); Brian North Lee (Joan Hassall engraving, Leo Wyatt engraved label in edition of 200 printed by Will Carter; pictorial wood engraved plate by Reynolds Stone also printed by Will Carter limited to 100 copies; wood engraved label by Philip Webb limited to 50 copies); G. J. Bord (three plates by Polish graphic artist Plciennik with prints of one tipped in); Peter Summers (armorial by Reynolds Stone; pictorial by Joan Hassall; calligraphic label by Leo Wyatt); Norman Searle; Bookplate Society bookplate which is a device by Diana Bloomfield. - The Clarke Coat of Arms with a salient unicorn crest illustrated. - A Seventeenth Century Armorial is illustrated which is suspected of being in fact a frontispiece as its size would preclue use in any volume much smaller than a folio.

— — — — —

NEW MEMBERS:
Harold Berliner, 224 Main Street, Nevada City, Ca. 95959
George R. Kane, 114 Royce Street, Los Gatos, Ca. 95030
Cand. med. Illmar Laan, Institute of Experimental & Clinical Medicine, Tallinn,
   Hiiu St. 42, Estonian S.S.R. 200015
Alexander S. Mikhalevsky, Box 584, Alexandria, Va. 22313
Joseph Sodaitis, 287 Forest Dr., Union, N.J. 07083.

— — — —

ROBERT FREDERIC MEDZDORF died April 16, 1975 at his home in Colebrook, Conn. after a long illness at the age of 62. Herman W. Liebert wrote a tribute to him in AB (55:1498, March 31, 1975 and 55:1867-8, April 21, 1975) from which this brief summary is taken. Metzdorf was born in Springfield, Massachusetts. He received three degrees from the University of Rochester: A.B. (1933), M.A.(1934), Ph.D.(1939), and he continued there until 1949 in various capacities in the library and English department; in 1967 he became a trustee. For four years he was a cataloguer at the Houghton Library, Harvard University, and in 1952 became curator of manuscripts at Yale University and later was archivist. In 1961 he left academe to join Parke-Bernet Galleries in New York and in 1964 became an independent appraiser. As an individual collector he was principally interested in Victorian bindings, books and manuscripts of Queen Victoria, and editions of Samuel Johnson's RASSELAS. He was co-founder and partner of the Shoe String Press; editor of the Papers of the Bibliographical Society of America (1959-67). Among the numerous organizations to which he belonged and the many publications to his credit, Mr. Liebert did not mention the ASBC&D to which Metzdorf belonged from 1941-1972, and that he compiled the Index 1922-1950 of the ASBC&D YEAR BOOK.

FROM THE CATALOGS -- -- Bookplates continue to reap attention by catalog annotators when either the artist or owner, or both, are worthy of attention as in the entries which follow: George S. MacManus Co. (1317 Irving Street, Philadelphia, Pa. 19107), catalog 226, item 80, announced as "The Forger's Own Copy" a copy of Charles Dickens' TO BE READ AT DUSK - $350. "The forger's own copy with his book-plate; . . There is no evidence, according to Mr. John Carter, that a stock of (Thomas J.) Wise's bookplates existed after his death or was used by anyone other than him and, indeed, there are several books in the Wrenn collection at Texas with Wise's book-plate that he sold as duplicates." The plate is illustrated in what appears to be reduced size. -- -- Kekker & Nordemann B.V.(O.Z. Voorburgwal 239, Amsterdam-C. Holland), catalog 1, item 2 "With 15th-Century Ex Libris" and item 4 with "16th-Century Woodcut Ex-Libris" both of which are stated as unrecorded. -- -- Goodspeed's (18 Beacon Street, Boston, Mass. 02108), catalog 580, item 78 by Jonathan Swift described as "An association copy of great American interest, from the library of John Wentworth, last Colonial Governor of New Hampshire, with his autograph, dated 1755, the year of his graduation from Harvard College, his book-plate, engraved by Nathaniel Hurd . . . Though ten years his senior, Hurd became a protege of the Governor, whose secretary he became in 1770 . . . Unlike his patron who remained loyal to the Crown, Hurd threw his lot in with the revolutionary cause and became a substantial citizen of Boston. . . . The book-plate, engraved by John Hurd's younger brother Nathaniel, is of particular interest. Hurd was Paul Revere's senior and his work evidently had considerable influence on that of Revere, though Hurd's work is superior to that of the more famous silversmith. Hurd engraved two Wentworth plates, this being the one with the scroll below a shell through which a stream of water falls." The annotator quotes from Hollis French who wrote a monograph on Nathaniel Hurd for the ASBC&D YEAR BOOK 1940/41. The Wentworth plate is illustrated.

MARIO LOURINHO RODRIGUES VINHAS
Director Da Revista Ex-Libris

Mario Vinhaus, born October 1, 1915 in Lisbon, capital of Portugal, founded a Portugese ex libris publication in 1951. Without the support of any bookplate society, he created a quarterly publication which he has now published for over 20 years.

Vinhaus from his youth has been in the banking business. He is also an eager sportsman with particular interest in swimming, shooting, and fencing. He shares an interest in fencing with another man famous in the field of the ex libris: Egerton Castle, author of ENGLISH BOOK PLATES. Mario has a personal ex libris depicting fencing designed by Spanish artist Juan Anglada Villa in 1951.

In 1943 Mario Vinhaus began collecting bookplates. During the years he has arranged many exhibits and written about ex libris for his journal, EXLIBRIS PORTUGAL, and a book titled A PAISAGEM e os MONUMENTOS NO EX-LIBRIS. He is a member of numerous European ex libris associations as well as the ASBC&D.

XVI EX LIBRIS INTERNATIONAL CONGRESS - CONTEST FOR ORIGINAL EX-LIBRIS

In connection with the XVI Congress in Lisbon in September of 1976, there is a contest open to artists from all over the world for an original ex libris based on a specific motif. The Sun has been selected as the symbol of the Congress, and the motto is: Sol Lucet Omnibus. Entries must include: name of the owner, "ex libris" or the equivalent, and optionally the contest motto. While all techniques are acceptable, three will be considered for rating purposes: (1) metal engraving, (2) wood, linoleum and plastic engraving, lithography and serigraphy, and (3) drawing to zinc or photogravure. More than one entry may be submitted but all must be technically finished. Two copies of each entry should be addressed to Comissao do XVI Congresso Internacional de Ex-Libris, Rua Freitas Gazul 21, 20.- Lisboa 2, Portugal, together with a note stating: name, (continued overleaf)

DON MARGO -
Calligrapher

The work of Egdon
H. Margo has been
featured in LETTER-
ING TODAY by John
Brinkley [1964] and
CALLIGRAPHY TODAY by
Heather Child [1963].
Major exhibits in
which his work ap-
peared are Two Thou-
sand Years of Callig-
raphy and Calligra-
phy & Handwriting in
America 1710-1962.
The last exhibit was

assembled and shown by the Peabody Institute Library in Baltimore and a catalog
printed by Italimuse, Inc.

A graduate of Boston University, Don later studied under J. Albert Cavanagh at the
Art Students League in New York. To quote from his entry in the Peabody catalog:
"At the outbreak of World War II he was called to Washington to become Chief Visual Information Designer for the U.S. Public Health Service. In 1942 he enlisted
in the 8th Air Force and served as interpreter to the French Army. During an air
raid in London he took shelter in the doorway of a bookshop, and even as the bombs
fell around he was fascinated by a calligraphic display in the shop window. This
chance encounter was followed by another, with a London bobby who guided him to
the right books and implements for his new interest. A third lucky find was the
publicity piece FROM BACH TO GERSHWIN with calligraphy by Raymond DaBoll, which became his pin-up for the duration and the model for his calligraphic exercises and
his V-mail. On his return he served for four years as Art Director and Promotion
Specialist for the Marine Corps. Since 1948 he has lived in Los Angeles, where he
operates a private press, At the Sign of the Pen and Press, devoted to the art of
design in printing, executes many calligraphic commissions, and teaches privately."

nationality, and complete address of artist
and owner of the ex libris; technique used
as described in (1), (2) or (3) . The contest-
ant's name and nationality, as well as the
technique used should be noted on the reverse
side of the entry. All entries should be received not later than July 31, 1976. No entries will be returned. Three cash prizes be
awarded to each class of work: 1st $400, 2nd
$250, 3rd $150. Entries will be judged by
two juries. Winning entries will be exhibited during the Congress and will be printed
in A ARTE do EX LIBRIS.

The tipped in plate is the official ex libris
for the Congress.

Let's see American artists represented in the
contest!

JAMES H. FINCKEN [1860-1942] by Maurice Frederick Fincken [1887-1972]

It is indeed gratifying that a life of integrity, artistic skill in all the
graphic arts, and a nature so sensitive to beauty and spiritual discernment
should meet with appreciation on every hand, for invariably he was kind and
patient and gave freely of his knowledge and skill, without hope of reward.

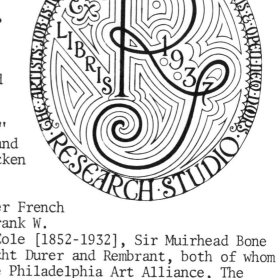

The son of a sugar baker, James Horsey Fincken was
born in Bristol, England, and educated in Manchester. When his father failed in business,
he began the study of engraving at the Manchester Academy of Art, when he was 19.
After he married he moved to London. There,
among many works, he engraved on steel superb portraits of Prime Minister Gladstone
and Charles Dickens. In 1892 he moved to
Philadelphia, Pennsylvania, where he shared
a studio with John Sloan at 804 Walnut St.
Sloan went to New York where he became one
of "The Eight" known as "The Ashcan School,"
because these artists emphasized the slum and
night life of the city. In 1900 James Fincken
became a U.S. citizen.

Fincken was a contemporary of Daniel Chester French
[1850-1931], Joseph Pennell [1857-1926], Frank W.
Benson [1862-1951], wood engraver Timothy Cole [1852-1932], Sir Muirhead Bone
[1876-1953]. He studied the work of Albrecht Durer and Rembrant, both of whom
he greatly admired. He was a member of the Philadelphia Art Alliance, The
Print Club, The Philadelphia Sketch Club and The Graphic Sketch Club. A frequent exhibitor at the Pennsylvania Academy of Fine Arts, he was awarded their
John Gribbel Prize in etching. His work is represented in major institutions:
New York Public Library, Metropolitan Museum of Art, The Montclair (New Jersey)
Public Library, etc. Fincken did aquatints, mezzotints, lithographs, wood engravings, steel engravings, and etchings on copper and zinc. Many of his bookplates breathe an atmosphere of exquisite delicacy of conception and skill in
execution. His richest and most productive period was after the age of 50. He
executed over 109 separate ex libris in an amazing range of designs.

The Fincken family had a modest
vacation cottage in Arden, Delaware, a single-tax colony where
many artists, writers and ideal-
ists of his time lived.

[Editor's note: A checklist of
22 of Fincken's ex libris appeared
in BOOK-PLATE BOOKLET, May 1909.

The checklist which follows was
compiled by his granddaughter,
Rhondda Fincken Cressman, from
the collection of his work in her
possession, of which #1 to #67
are available for purchase.]

1. Colonel Mason Whitney Tyler (A)
2. "Absque Labore Nihil" (A)
3. Henry Lee Mason (A)
4. J. Gibson McIlvain, Jr. (A)
5. Roland Gideon Curtin, M.D. (A)
6. Missouri HIstorical Society (A)
7. Mayor Simon Williard (A)
8. Caroline Hampton Cochran (A)
9. Horace Magee Memorial Book Fund (A)
10. Thomas Willing Balch (A)
11. Robert M. Janney (A)
12. Rudolphe Meyer de Schauenesee (A)
13. Catherine Bohlen (A)
14. John Bakewell Phillips (A)
15. William S. Vaux (A)
16. Arthur Edwin Baiocis (A)
17. Ward W. Pierson (A)
18. St. Andrew's Society of Philadelphia
19. Edwin S. Potter, M.D. (A)
20. Bernard Penn-Gaskell McGrann (A)
21. Argus George Bullock (A)
22. Percy Kierstede Hudson (A)
23. Franklin D. Murphy, M.D. (H)
24. George W. Mears, M.D. Memorial Med.Lib.
25. Calvin Collidge Lib.,Alpha Chi Chapter
26. William Clyde Wilkins (H)
27. John Burton Foley (E)
28. W. P. Lea (E)
29. John Additon Robb (E)
30. Ada and William Moore (E)
31. Mabel Potter Lewis (E)
32. Dorothy S. Wiggins (E)
33. Emily Francis Witney
34. Grace P. Perkins (E)
35. Dorothy McCormick/Cyrus McCormick(E)
36. James G. Hunter (E)
37. Spencer K. Mulford (E)
38. Emory Leyden Ford (E)
39. Patricia Ulizio (E)
40. Mary Gwinn (E)
41. Milicent Barrett Estabrook (E)
42. W. Elwell Lake (E)
43. Edward Larned Ryerson (E)
44. Elizabeth Wardell Smith (E)
45. Gamma Alpha Chapter, Chi Omega,Swarthmore
46. Frank Sydelotte (E)
47. Warner Windom Brackett (E)
48. Lewis Cass Scheffey, M.D. (E)
49. Joseph Earle Moore, M.D. (M)
50. Florence Purdy Burns (M)
51. Research Studio (M)
52. Otto W. Helbig (M)
53. Isabel Ingram Barbier (M)
54. Guy M. Nelson, M.D. (M)
55. J. Paul Haughton (M)
56. Edward Shirley Borden (M)
57. Frank Fichardson (M)
58. Gordon and Anna Johnston (M)
59. Walter Scott Mitchell (M)
60. Agnes Lisle Brown (M)
61. Amelia Donovan Pitcairn (M)
62. Mary S. Collins (M)
63. Robert Bentley (M)
64. Charles W. Burr, M.D. (M)
65. FJP (M)
66. William S. Eaton (M)
67. Mary Slizabeth McCulloch (M)
68. Fisher Corties Morgan, Esq.
69. Leila Weeks Wilson
70. University Club, Philadelphia
71. Wm. C. Readio
72. Walter Scott Mitchell
73. Eben C. Hill
74. James A. and Nora Culbertson
75. Alexander Boteler Shepherd
76. George P. Pope, Esq.
77. Norris Stanley Barratt
78. Frank Downs
79. Keene Harwood Addington
80. Walter Newbold Walmsley
81. John Frederick Lewis
82. George Tucker Bisham, Esq.
83. Elizabeth R. Brackett, M.D.
84. John G. Lynch
85. Edward Goodrich Acheson
86. William Abraham Haskell
87. Caroline Hampton
88. James S. Young - Pittsburgh
89. Albert Arnold Sprague, 2nd
90. Henry Dibblee
91. University Club of Chicago
92. Darlington Library-Allegheny Preparatory Sch.
93. Clarence Stanley McIntire-Memorial Lib. Soc.
94. J. McD. Bryer
95. H. Darlington
96. Maitland Alexander
97. John G. Shedd
98. Robert Garrett
99. J. Wesley Ladd
100. B. W. Lewis
101. Charles Calvin Jenks
102. Henry W. Moore
103. C. M. E.
104. Gladys Stout
105. Abram C. Mott, Jr.
106. Ellem M. Whitney
107. Walter J. McBride
108. Isaac M. Loughhead, Haverford, Pennsylvania
109. Regina M. Downey

Note: (A) armorial, (E) environmental
  scenes, (H) human figure, (M) miscellaneous.

EX LIBRIS
GLEN
DAWSON

<u>Dawson Family Bookplates</u>   The Dawson family has had several bookplates and at least two of them picture a High Sierra scene. In 1925 Charles Joseph Rider designed a plate for Ernest Dawson with his wife and children in silhouette within a border of verbena; it was described at length in the article by Marion Carmichael in the 1925 ASBC&D YEAR BOOK. It was also illustrated and included in the text of "Ex Libris California," in the October 1965 CALIFORNIA LIBRARIAN. Ernest Dawson, who established Dawson's Bookshop which just celebrated its 70th anniversary this year, gave a collection of books to George Washington High School, Los Angeles, so that students might have first hand knowledge of "rare books". A contest was held to design a plate for the collection. Dorothy M. Drake wrote about "The Dawson Collection" for PACIFIC BINDERY TALK in January 1935.

The plate tipped in is for one of Ernest Dawson's sons, Glen. It was reproduced in slightly reduced form in Clare Ryan Talbot's HISTORIC CALIFORNIA IN BOOKPLATES with the following description: "The leopard lily is also to be found in the bookplate of Glen Dawson, youthful member of the Sierra Club. The plate further depicts a group of Sierra clubbers taking their noonday tea about a campfire in front of a large pine, Pinus ponderosa, or Western yellow pine." The original drawing for the plate by Marjorie Dichieson is currently framed and hanging in the Glen Dawson home.

REPRINT OF FULLER -- Gale Research Company announces the reprint of A BIBLIOGRAPHY OF BOOKPLATE LITERATURE, edited by George W. Fuller; bibliographical work by Verna B. Grimm, with an introduction by Winward Prescott. It was originally published in Spokane in 1926, 151 pages, with subject index. The reprint is $13.00.

ARTIST'S MARKET, 480 pages, 50 illustrations, $8.95 (9933 Alliance Road, Cincinnati, Oh. 45242). Primarily of interest to the free-lance artist, craftsperson, or photographer seeking markets; however, it also offers sources for the individual who wants art work commissioned, ideas for exhibits, etc.

BOOKPLATES IN THE NEWS-$ 5 U.S. & Canada
                      $ 6 Overseas
                      $10 Special Subscription
                          with extra prints

132

HERMANN ZAPF DESIGN

Harold Peter, Director of Book Design and Development at Hallmark Cards for some ten years, had a blind embossed bookplate designed for him by Hermann Zapf in 1973. Peter graduated from the Kunstgewerbe Schule in Munich with high honors in 1961 and immediately joined Hallmark as a designer. All the books issued by Hallmark were conceived by Peter, especially the original Hallmark Editions. Now at 35 he has decided to free lance until determining what direction his career will take.

Hermann Zapf, who studied under Rudolf Koch in Frankfurt, is a world-famous type designer. Type faces he has created include Palatino, Melior, Optima, Sistina, and Greek and Arabic types. He has served as an advisor to European and American type foundries. Zapf is a notable engraver and calligrapher who has designed a few calligraphic ex libris. He was the recepient of the prestigious international Gutenberg Prize in 1974.

Peter's friend, Philip Metzger, has printed his blind embossed bookplate on Japanese Hosho paper and comments that some of the embossings are slightly canted because each had to be fed individually into a contraption somewhat like a corporate and notary seal which meant he had no guide to assist in placing each ex libris accurately. Further, the pieces of paper are not uniform in size as Metzger wanted to obtain the maximum number of embossings from the Hosho available.

— — — — — —

RADEK KUTRA, VISITING ARTIST
by Mrs. Zdenka Pospisil

A former Czechoslovian artist, Radek Kutra, will be visiting in Oregon and possibly Northern California this summer. Currently he paints and teaches painting in his own private school in Lucerne, Switzerland.

Mr D. GILTAY VETH

His most recent exhibit was held in Zurich-Dietikin during May, 1975; another is scheduled for October in St. Galen. Primarily a painter, Kutra first became interested in graphic arts and particularly bookplate design some fifteen years ago. He began designing ex libris for collectors in his own and other European countries. Many of his more recent designs have a tortured realism which, I believe, shows the influence of the death of his best friend, a bookplate collector and the man who first introduced Kutra to the field of ex libris design.

[During his visit the artist may be reached care of Mrs. Pospisil, 1909 E. 17th Avenue, Eugene, Oregon 97403. His permanent address: Fluhmattstr. 26, 6004 Lucerne, Switzerland.)

— — — —

SIXTH YEAR OF PUBLICATION - The July 1975 issue of BOOKPLATES IN THE NEWS commences the sixth year of publication for this quarterly newsletter.

AS of BC & D
Bookplates in the News
429 NORTH DAISY AVENUE, PASADENA, CALIFORNIA, 91107
AUDREY SPENCER ARELLANES, Editor

Number Twenty-Two   October 1975

CLARE LEIGHTON DESIGN
by Harvey Simmonds

HARVEY SIMMONDS

In 1963 I began working in the library
of the New York Botanical Garden in
Bronx Park. The librarian, Robert Jones,
became a good friend, and was helpful
in introducing me to much that I might
otherwise not have known in the way of
botanical and horticultural literature.
Clare Leighton's works had a particular
appeal for him, and came to have for me;
and it wasn't long after beginning to read
them that I found from the jacket text of
a book she had illustrated, THE FLOWERING
HAWTHORNE, that Miss Leighton lived in
Woodbury, Connecticut. Robert Jones had
recently bought land in Roxbury, and was
of course interested to learn of his neighbor. He went to see Miss Leighton and
asked if she would undertake a commission
to design a bookplate for me, using Cal-
tha palustris, Marsh Marigolds or Kingcups,
 a wildflower of which I am especially
fond. This must have been in April or May
of 1965, as she did the studies for the block from living flowers. The block
was completed; and I was told; and Clare and I met -- and became, and have re-
remained, dear friends. The bookplate appears here, with the name set in type
and printed at the Shiver Mountain Press, Washington Depot, Connecticut.

Years later, while working toward a degree in librarianship at Columbia University, I arranged an exhibition of the bookplates Clare Leighton has designed and
cut in wood. In the spring of 1967 the exhibition was mounted; a handlist was
designed and its printing supervised by Melvin Loos of the Columbia University
Press. An introductory historical note was provided by Dale Roylance, Curator
of the Arts of the Book collection in the Sterling Library at Yale University.

Clare Leighton was among those artists who shaped the revived art of wood engraving in the years following the First World War. The daughter of literary
parents who moved easily in the heady social milieu of Edwardian England, she
studied at the Brighton School of Art, the Slade School, and the Central School
of Arts and Crafts, and soon came to recognition through her mastery in individ-

ual prints and notable suites of such varied subjects as age-old English farming traditions, Mediterranean folk life, and the American northwoods. During the period of her marriage to the English journalist H. N. Brailsford, she combined her abilities as engraver and writer in the first of a series of books celebrating the rhythms of life found when man works with and comes to fulfillment through nature: FOUR HEDGES and COUNTRY MATTERS; followed after her coming to live in America by SOUTHERN HARVEST, GIVE US THIS DAY, and WHERE LAND MEETS SEA. In TEMPESTUOUS PETTICOAT and SOMETIME, NEVER she reflects upon her mother's life and her own; and in two books for children, THE MAGICAL BOX and THE WOOD THAT CAME BACK, she has brought a mythic quality into tales for the young. During recent years she has expanded her vision as an artist into new media, designing and supervising through each stage the monumental stained glass windows of St. Paul's Cathedral, Worcester, and several other churches, and creating mosaic murals on a grand scale for the Convent of the Holy Family of Nazareth in Monroe, Connecticut, while continuing her work as writer and illustrator.

Harvey Simmonds' work as librarian and horticulturist at the New York Botanical Garden was followed by positions on the staffs of the Manuscript Division, Berg Collection, and Editor's Office of the New York Public Library, and a term of duty as Librarian of the Grolier Club. During two years spent as a crew member on the Steamer DELTA QUEEN he developed the library for which Harlan Hubbard designed and printed the bookplate described in the April 1975 issued of BOOKPLATES IN THE NEWS. Simmonds now lives in New York City, where he is associated with the Eakins Press Foundation.

— — — — —

ARTUR MARIO DA MOTA MIRANDA
President of 16th Congress in 1976

The next international bookplate congress will be in Lisbon, Portugal, September 2 to 5, 1976, and Artur Mario Da Mota Miranda will be the president. He was born in Porto, Portugal, January 1, 1928. Married, he has five sons and a daughter. In addition to being an ardent bookplate collector with more than 20,000 ex libris in his collection and more than 1,000 volumes of bookplate literature, he edits A ARTE DO EX-LIBRIS, the magazine of the Associacao Portuense De Ex-Libris. He is the author of several books on ex libris including one published in Denmark on Portugese artist Pais Ferreira. Mr. Miranda has over 70 personal ex libris. The example tipped in was designed by Belgian artist Raymond Verstraeten in 1963. If you are interested in exchanging bookplate prints or literature, write him at Casa do Outeiro, Celorico de Basto, Portugal.

Phil Dike, N.A., A.W.S.
by William F. Kimes

The bookplate of William F. Kimes was
commissioned as a surprise birthday
gift by a bibliophile-colleague, Vernon
Patterson of Orange Coast College.
It was designed by Phil Dike, distinguished California artist whose long
friendship with the Kimes family
uniquely qualified him to design an ex
libris that would characterize Mr. Kimes'
life-long love of nature and his devotion
to education.

Phil Dike, National Academician, was born
in Redlands, California. His painting reflects his love of people and the life
around him. His major subject interest
has been the coastal environment of California. Of this he writes: "The sea is
a master. The beach is a learning place,
a place that touches all the senses, a
place of great personal pleasure. . . .
The beach is surrounded by shifting light,
blazing or falling away in mysterious envelopment - sounds, smells, and movement of the shore life add to the flow of living patterns and sensations. This
is the elegance that is nature." It is in this "framework of reference and
search" that Phil Dike has achieved national acclaim.

Early in his career he was a color specialist for Walt Disney Productions. In
the years that followed he devoted his talents to not only his own painting,
but in addition to teaching at which he became an important influence on thousands of art students - at Chouinard, later as Professor of Art at Scripps
College and Claremont Graduate School. Upon his retirement in 1970 from Scripps
he was designated Professor Emeritus. He has received numerous awards in major
exhibits from coast to coast, and his work hangs in galleries and museums such
as the Metropolitan Museum of Art, National Academy of Design, Library of Congress Pennell Print Collection, Pasadena Art Museum.

The tipped-in plate above is the only one Dike has designed - done in genial
compliance to a request by a friend. He explains the symbols used in the design
as follows: Book: The World of Truth and Authority - Bird: Peace and Limitless
Space - Tree: Growth and the Wonders of Nature - School: Knowledge and Understanding - Sun: Light of the World.

William F. Kimes, well-known authority on John Muir, in conjunction with his
wife Maymie, is currently nearing completion of a bibliography entitled JOHN
MUIR: A CHRONOLOGICAL BIBLIOGRAPHY OF HIS PUBLISHED WRITINGS, Compiled and
Annotated with Quotations. It will first be published by Tamalpais Press of
Berkeley, California, in a very limited collectors' edition, handbound in
leather, illustrated with some unpublished Muir drawings and letters as well
as numerous photographs including some of very rare editions. William and
Maymie reside at their Rocking K Ranch in the Mariposa foothills within easy
access to the Yosemite country that John Muir loved so well.

SPECIAL BOOKPLATE FOR
COLLECTION OF HERBALS
by Robert Hitchman

Here is a copy of my most recent bookplate, designed especially to go into
my collection of herbals and books on
herbs. The design is reproduced from
ORTUS SANITATIS, published in Mainz by
Jacob Meydenbach in 1491. The type face
dates back to about 1840 (Black #400
from the type collection of William O.
Thorniley). Fortunately I had a quantity of late XVIII or early XIX century watermarked paper, so we used that
for plates that go into old, old herbals.

I am an advocate of special bookplates
for special collections and - in fact -
have a small but interesting collection of such bookplates. The practice
of using special plates for special
collections is common in libraries and
institutions - not so common with private book collectors - and yet it seems
a logical practice to follow.

Robert
Hitchman: his book.

In my own case I use special plates for my collection of Pacific Northwest
Americana, of books on place names, on bookplates, for miniature books and
now for the herbals. And all this adds up to having more plates for exchange.

EX LIBRIS

Antonio J. Molina

EX LIBRIS OF ANTONIO J. MOLINA

Antonio J. Molina is a critic of art for
EL MUNDO, an important newspaper in Puerto
Rico, and is a painter whose works are in
museums in La Habana, Miami, New York,
Bonn, Bern, and Barcelona.

Molina was born in Cuba in 1928 and now
lives in San Juan. He is president of
Puerto Rico's UNESCO, president of the
Association of Bookplates, and Friends
of the Carnegie Library. He collects
pre-hispanic ceramics and ex libris. Any
one wishing to exchange with him may write
Box 1361, San Juan, Puerto Rico 00902.

His bookplate was designed by Guillermo
Serrano, a young Cuban painter who lived
in San Juan and studied at Escuela de
Artes Plasticas del Instituto de Cultura
Puertorriquena. His exhibit last May in
Las Americas Gallery received critical acclaim from Jose Gomez Sicre, a spe-
cialist in Latin American art.

Thure Hindstrom designed the bookplate of Finnish collector Esko Ronka, who was born in Viipuri (Vyborg) in 1918. On the Gulf of Finland, this port belonged to Finland until 1917 when it became part of the USSR. Ronka and his family moved to Vassa, a Finnish port city of over 40,000 population. He is a painter employed by the city of Vaasa which is indicated on his bookplate by tools of the trade, and his hobbies are represented: photography and music. As a young man he belonged to a band in which he played the mandolin.

If you would like to exchange with Esko Ronka, you may write to: Urheilukatu 7D42
65220 Vaasa 22, FINLAND

ECCLESIASTICAL EX LIBRIS

The Reverend James Parker of Albany, Georgia, is an avid student of heraldry. This is evident in his newest bookplate. His own arms in the center are shown with the black ecclesiastical hat of a priest in the Episcopal Church. Under the shield suspended on their ribbons are the decorations of a Knight Commander of the Royal Order of St. Sava of Yugoslavia (given to Father Parker by the late King Peter II), Knight of the Military and Hospitaller Order of St. Lazarus of Jerusalem, and the maltese cross of a Knight Commander of the Order of St. John of Jerusalem (Knight Hospitaller). The border is lined with the devices of arms of several Church bodies and organizations with which Father Parker is connected; the escallop or shell at the bottom alludes to St. James the Apostle for whom he is named and the golden bee is the spe-

cial badge of the Emperor Napoleon in whom he has a great interest. This ex libris is a pen and ink drawing by the well-known heraldic artist the Chev. T. Alan Keith-Hill of Chester, England, and the original illustration is reduced and printed by offset. The coat of arms in the center is so drawn that all the other material can be masked off and the arms used for letterheads, etc.

From the PERIODICAL LITERATURE . . . . .

AMERICAN PRINTING HISTORY ASSOCIATION, Letters, #5, 5, May-June 1975. Frank
J. Anderson of the Kitemaug Press is looking for a publisher for his manuscript tentatively titled PRIVATE PRESS WORK. A BIBLIOGRAPHIC APPROACH TO
PRINTING AS AN AVOCATION. The contents include such subjects as bookbinding,
typography, printing history, bookplates, letterforms, etc.

PROOF: THE YEARBOOK OF AMERICAN BIBLIOGRAPHICAL AND TEXTUAL STUDIES, vol. 3,
1973. This reference volumes includes BOOKPLATES: A SELECTIVE ANNOTATED BIB-
LIOGRAPHY OF THE PERIODICAL LITERATURE by Audrey Spencer Arellanes.

THE BOOKPLATE SOCIETY, Newsletter No. 10, June 1975.
  Members' Evening was held at Grays Inn Library during June with Philip C.
Beddingham as host.
  Mark Severin's Talk: In April Mark Severin spoke about continental book-
plate artists and illustrated his talk with excellent slides.
  Bookplates mentioned in literature: WYNDHAM AND CHILDREN FIRST by Lord
Egremont (1968) referes to a bookplate "consisting of an imposing coat of
arms . . ."
  Green Shield bookplates! - Mr. Beddingham noted an ad in the TIMES LITER-
ARY SUPPLEMENT, May 9, 1975, offering 15 personal bookplates free finely
printed with your name with orders of £9 from Bibliagora of Hounslow.
  Michael Renton by Keith Clark. (4), pages 2 & 3 - "Although Renton's architectural bookplates are fine examples of well-designed and engraved pictorial composition, it is a pity that more of his bookplate commissions
have not enabled the artist to use his talent for landscape drawing, for he
has cut some exceptional landscapes, full of detail and feeling."
  Famous Bookplates and Forgeries: The Washington Bookplate by J. Henderson
Smith and The Bookplate of William Cowper the Poet by G. H. Viner, pages 4
& 5 - Both of these short articles are from the manuscript "Notes and Queries" of the Bookplate Exchange Club in 1943. The Cowper forgery was also
discussed by Thairlwall in JOURNAL OF THE EX LIBRIS SOCIETY in the 1890's.
  Bookplates of Members, pages 6 & 7 - Illustrated and described are the
ex libris of Phillip Beddingham by Anthony Christmas; Otto M. Lilien's book
label; Sir Harry Page is represented by a flying owl design by Pauline Marsh,
a modern version of his arms by S. L. Harley, and an oval armorial by the
heraldic designer to the College of Arms.
  Angelica Press Bookplates, page 8 - Four woodengravings and four typographic
stock bookplates offered by Brooklyn, New York firm.
  Exlibristen 1967-1974, page 8 - Over 100 publications offered by Klaus
Rodel concerning bookplate artists, bibliographices, etc.
  Exhibition of bookplates at Colchester, page 8 & 9 - A report of the display at the Colchester Public Library appeared in the ESSEX COUNTY STANDARD,
April 18, 1975. Brought to light is a collection of 300 or so bookplates at
the Essex Record Office, Chelmsford.
  Federation Internationale des Societes D'Amateurs D'Exlibris, page 9 - The
1976 Congress will be hosted by the Portuguese association in Lisbon.
  An interesting association copy, page 9 - Raymond DaBoll reported buying a
copy of J. Leicester Warren's A GUIDE TO THE STUDY OF BOOK-PLATES which con-
tained a number of family ex libris bound in at the back: an armorial of John
Fleming, Baron De Tabley; Tabley Library; J. B. Leicester; Catherine Lady De
Tabley; George Warren, 2nd Lord De Tabley; and John B. L. Warren, 3rd Lord
De Tabley.

AMERICAN PRINTING HISTORY ASSOCIATION, Bruce Rogers. #4, 8, March-April 1975.

S. R. Shapiro plans publication of a Check List of Bookplates designed by Bruce Rogers which will include facsimiles of all bookplates extant designed by BR.

EXLIBRIS-REVUE (Unofficial Bookplate-News for F.I.S.A.E.), Volume 1, #1, 1975. This is a new publication edited by Klaus Rodel (P.O. Box 109, DK-9900 Frederikshavn, Denmark), who plans four issues per year. U.S. Subscription is $8 per year or $10 for air mail delivery. The first issue has 12 pages. This is a multi-lingual journal, measuring 8¼ x 11 3/4 inches, three columns to a page. The paper resembles card stock in an eggshell shade which offers sharp contrast for the bookplates illustrated, photos, and clear type. The text is in four languages including English. A foreword is followed by a Report of the Congress in Bled. - Jaroslav Vodrazka 80 Years: This Czechoslovankian artist is pictured and two of his latest multicolored lino-cuts are tipped-in. - In Memoriam Albrecht Durer: Polish artist Zbigniew Dolatowski designed four bookplates celebrating Durer-year (1971); each is illustrated. - Eugene Schmidt: Leipzig engraver excelled at portrait, armorial and nude ex libris. "May the exlibris shown here contribute to keeping the memory of this artist and friend who died too early." - Wojciech Luczak: Born in 1946, this artist has already created 250 wood engraved ex libris. - Existing Book-plate Societies: Twenty-two are listed with their addresses including the ASBC&D.

ANTIQUARIAN BOOK MONTHLY REVIEW, Bookplates For All Sorts and Conditions of Men, Brian North Lee. (24) 2:2-12, August 1975. The fascination of collecting bookplates is captured in the cover photo by Mark Mason and nearly half of the magazine is devoted to this major article about ex libris which indicate the profession, occupation, or post of their owners. "The small size of the bookplate is in no way the measure of its importance, and one must repeat that many aspects of its history still call for investigation and recording. Yet beyond purely genealogical and artistic usefulness and significance the subject provides a record of all sorts and conditions of men who loved and collected books, a record which would have been lost had they not endowed their books with the dignity of a bookplate."

AUSTRALIAN BOOKPLATE LITERATURE, Klaus Rodel ($2.50). 34 pages, 4 tipped-in ex libris prints. This bibliography covers the period 1900-1950 and gives credit to H. B. Muir, A CHECKLIST OF EX LIBRIS LITERATURE PUBLISHED IN AUSTRALIA. The 99 items are in chronological order with brief descriptions, alphabetical index and artists listed separately.

THE MODERN POLISH BOOK-PLATE, Jerzy Druzycki, published by Exlibristen, Klaus Rodel, Postbox 109, DK 9900 Frederikshavn, Denmark, $25.00, 8½x11 3/4. This multi-lingual volume is profusely illustrated with the work of more than thirty artists, many of them women. There is a photograph of almost every artist and numerous tip-ins with a variety of techniques, some in color. While the English text is brief, it is interesting and will introduce you to artists currently creating bookplates in Poland.

NORDISK EXLIBRIS TIDSSKRIFT, quarterly publication of the Danish Exlibris Society, it contains numerous illustrations as well as tipped-in prints, many in color. Edited by Helmer Fogedgaard; about 16 pages with a quarter page English summary.

GRAPHIA, is published in Antwerp with Antoine Rousseau as editor. About 12 pages to the quarterly issue, with both illustrations and tipped-in prints. None of the text is in English.

HERALDRY IN CANADA, The Heraldic Bookplate. (2) 9:28-9, June 1975. Illustrated and described are the ex libris for Richard Ernest Bolton and Rev. Graham Allan David.

THE PRIVATE LIBRARY, My Engraved Work, Joan Hassall. (26) 7:139-164, Winter 1974. A delightful article by Joan Hassall, a superb engraver. One illustration is from the nature calendar she engraved for the British Transport Commission; others include bookplates for A. P. Polack, Henry & Sybil Birkbeck, Kathleen Finlay Horsman, J. G. Dreyful, Max Ward, Charles & Enid Dreyfus, two for Girton College, The Marine Society, Seafarers Education Service, David Keir, Brian North Lee, and Margaret Howatson.

THE PRIVATE LIBRARY, Open Letter Two, To A Beginner Bookseller, Louis Ginsberg. 7:165-69, Winter 1974. ASBC&D member Ginsberg says: "When I first became interested in book-plates, one of the world's greatest collectors, the late Marco Birnholz, advised me to begin by collecting all types."

AMERICAN COLLECTOR, The Ex Libris Craze: Bookplates, William Rodger. (4) 6: 12-3, April 1975. "Name a collectible that dates back 500 years, is universal, comprises work of the great artists, and weighs on the average a quarter of an ounce. Stand in the corner unless you said bookplates. These mighty mites, once a great fad in the hobby world, are coming back."

COLUMBIA LIBRARY COLUMN, Our Growing Collections, Kenneth A. Lohf. 22:#2, February 1973. Lohf mentions gift made by Mr. and Mrs. Dan Burne Jones of Rockwell Kent materials including a six-piece dinner service with designs from SALAMINA, drapery material featuring the wheatfields near his Au Sable Forks farm, and among ephemeral items several bookplates.

ITALIC NEWS, Rich Cusik: Young Calligrapher. #5:9-14, 1974. Picture of the artist and numerous examples of his work. Artist acknowledges assistance of Lloyd Reynolds, James Hayes, and Maury Nemoy; influenced by Don Margo, who is quoted: "Calligraphy is all! It is ability to lay out a job, whether it's a stone-carving, an inscription, postage stamp or bookplate . . ."

THE LIBRARY (Transactions of the Bibliographical Society), Recent Books. 29: 248, June 1974. EX LIBRIS bibliologie si bibliofilie, by Dima-Dragan, published in Rumania in 1973, containing 400 pages and illustrated. By a leading Rumanian bibliographer, bibliophile and exlibrist, this volume gives a history of the book, libraries, and book collecting.

YALE GAZETTE, The Charles J. Rosenbloom Bequest, Herman W. Liebert. 49:309-10, April 1975. The cover of the GAZETTE illustrates the bookplate used for this special collection which is a simply printed label. Rosenbloom's personal ex libris features his favorite painting by Edward Hicks, The Peaceable Kingdom.

Dawson's Bookshop (535 N. Larchmont, Los Angeles, Ca. 90004), List B-1975 has 41 books about bookplates mostly from the collection of Edith Emerson Spencer. List C-1974 has 40 books from the library of Olive Percival, each with one of her several bookplates.

— — — — — —

NEW MEMBERS –
Mrs. Rhondda F. Cressman, 1948 Maywick Court, Lexington, Ky. 40504
Emerson G. Wulling, 613 North 22nd Street, La Crosse, Wi. 54601

AS of BC & D

Bookplates in the News

429 NORTH DAISY AVENUE, PASADENA, CALIFORNIA, 91107
AUDREY SPENCER ARELLANES, Editor

Number Twenty-three

January 1976

Dan Burne Jones'
The PRINTS of ROCKWELL KENT
A Catalogue Raisonne

The visual delights of the Kent prints are enhanced by the carefully researched text of Jones, who is himself an artist, writer, collector, and was appointed official bibliographer to Kent by the artist prior to his death.

The main body of the catalogue details 156 prints giving title, medium, size, date, number of proofs in the edition, known locations of related sketches and drawings, known watermarks, reproductions, collections, writings related to the print, and most interesting of all are the small facts which Jones has ferreted out which might otherwise be lost to history. It is this aspect of the text which makes the book not only a major reference source magnificently illustrated but also a pleasure to read. The considerable use of sketches and preliminary drawings gives a feeling of seeing the artist at work.

Separately listed and illustrated are twenty-two small wood engravings and woodcuts, print patterns and designs for cloth, twenty-eight drawings by Kent which were cut in wood by J. J. Lankes, prints done in color; a list of variant print titles, chronology of prints; and a bibliography divided into works having original or reproductions of Kent's prints, works by Kent, and works about Kent.

Dan Burne Jones in this catalogue raisonne has provided a definitive work on Kent's prints which scholars, collectors, and artists will long use and enjoy; he has also provided the best possible tribute to his friend Rockwell Kent by bringing together in one volume graphic reproductions of the prints along with detailed specifications further illuminated by a scintillating text.

142

THE PRINTS OF ROCKWELL KENT is published by the University of Chicago Press in a large format which gives ample space for each page to be laid out attractively with the prints presented in actual or only slightly reduced size. The unjustified right-hand margin is visually harmonious with the overall appearance of the page. The text of the body of the book is supplemented by the Foreword of Carl Zigrosser, leading authority on prints who did the first checklist and bibliography of Kent's prints, written and illustrated works in 1933; and by Dan Burne Jones' Introduction which fleshes out Kent the artist to Kent the man who "knew what he believed about life and politics and was in the forefront of battle fighting for those beliefs when they were least popular." The index gives ready access to finding specific prints, and the material in the appendices gives much valuable additional information; the bibliography furnishes a wealth of further material to read for in-depth study of Kent. The pine tree pattern used for the endpapers is the same as that used by the Kents for draperies in the dining alcove of their home before it was destroyed. A poem, "Farewell, Great Friend," by Jones is the epilogue in this lasting tribute of a friend and artist. Until December 31, 1975 the price was $27.50; subsequent to that date, $32.50. The cloth cover has a pasted label of the Rockwell Kent mark which during the late 1920's he used on his personal letterheads; this mark was used as the endpiece for Jones' "Genesis of a Rockwell Kent Bookplate Design," the 1969/70 YEAR BOOK, American Society of Bookplate Collectors and Designers.

There are six full-page bookplate entries and an additional dozen are noted in Appendix 1 as small wood engravings and woodcuts. Appendix 3 covers drawings by Kent which were cut in wood by J. J. Lankes, who has done considerable bookplate designing of his own.

Congratulations to ASBC&D member Dan Burne Jones! (Review by Audrey Arellanes)

HARRIS EX LIBRIS BY EUWER

The bookplate of Edward Norman Harris, missionary in Burma, was designed by Anthony Euwer in the early 1930's. Pictured in the center is the driveway to the Harris home in Burma which is lined by Banyan trees. Immediately above is the elaborate headdress of a native dancer. Leogriffs, which frequently guard the entrance to pagodas, ornament the top of the plate. Peacocks are the national bird of Burma, and elephants, which are used in the teak industry, are also represented.

This bookplate from the family of Mrs. Raymond Boese, Redlands, California, is very fitting, for members of the Harris family served in outlying mission stations in Burma continuously from 1846 to 1932.

In addition to being a bookplate artist and illustrator. Euwer authored RICK-E-TY RIMES AND RIG-MA-RO, nonsense verse illustrated with his own drawings.

143

WORTH A CONTINENTAL ?
By Frank W. Allen

Of eighteenth century book-plate engravers the best known and most often collected are, of course, Hurd, Doolittle, Callander, Maverick, and Revere. But others, less known and less skillful with the burin are of interest, too, for a variety of reasons. Among these minor artists may be found the name of Henry Dawkins.

Dawkins probably emigrated from England but was known in New York as early as 1754 as an ornamenter of buttons, and this also is the year of his only dated book-plate, that of John Burnet. Fincham credits him with twenty-three plates and dates most of them as 1770, although Fincham's dates are never to be trusted. Allen lists twenty-two signed plates and attributes two more to Dawkins.

Allen also describes Dawkins' work as "Chippendalism run wild," a reasonably mild comment when compared with that of others. Thieme-Becker says, "Er war ein Stecher von geringer Originalitat," and Stauffer says of some disputed, unsigned plates, "the work is poor enough, and it is possible that he engraved them."

Other than book-plates Dawkins' best work is probably the large plate of Nassau Hall at Princeton. His one known portrait plate is that of Benjamin Lay of Philadelphia, "atrociously drawn and poorly engraved." Benezit mentions a plate called Ruins Palmyra and of Balbec, but the writer has seen no other mention of this. And Dunlay (HISTORY OF THE ARTS OF DESIGN) attributes to Dawkins a very poor portrait of the Rev. Mr. Ogilvie at the Historical Society of New York.

In his book-plate work Dawkins was very largely a copyist, the majority of his plates being variations of one general plan apparently borrowed from an English-made plate and embellished in outrageous Chippendale style. Only the Jones, Yates, and Stringer plates confine themselves to the legitimate Chippendale with no extraneous material introduced. The Bushrod Washington plate has been ascribed to Dawkins by some collectors, but Allen comes to the conclusion that Dawkins had seen the plate, probably by an English artist, and copied his Whitebread plate from it.

By 1758 Dawkins had moved to Philadelphia and was associated for some time in that city with James Turner. He returned to New York in 1774. It was engraving and probably the poor quality of such which proved his downfall. According to Peter Force's AMERICAN ARCHIVES (Washington, 1851), Dawkins was arrested in May 1776 and charged with engraving, printing, and issuing counterfeit Continental paper money. At the trial he confessed to engraving, but implicated Rivington the printer, who by that time had fled to England. It also appears from the evidence that Dawkins had been previously imprisoned in New York for counterfeiting. Why anyone would want to counterfeit currency of such dubious integrity as the Continental dollar is anyone's guess.

At any rate on October 19, 1776, Henry Dawkins was still in jail in White Plains and on that date petitioned the Committee of Safety of New York for "the termination of his sorrows by a death to be inflicted in what manner the Honourable House may see fit." Exit Henry Dawkins. He is not heard from again, and his ultimate fate is uncertain. Stauffer thinks he was probably hanged. Allen thinks the evidence of bookplates in a later style indicates that the petition was not granted. Readers of this sketch may decide for themselves.

JOSEPH SODAITIS · Artist
by Maria E. Reventas

Joseph Sodaitis first became interested in ex libris some 30 years ago while he lived in Germany as a World War II refugee from his native Lithuania. Upon arriving in the United States in 1949, he attended several schools and now works for the City of New York as an architect who specializes in subway graphics.

Sodaitis got his art training at Brooklyn Museum Art School, the Art Students League in New York, and has studied privately with artists in Europe and the United States. He has had four one-man shows and has won more than 20 awards.

Renewing his interests in ex libris Sodaitis began to build his bookplate collection in 1975 and at the same time started designing ex libris for his friends and others. His bookplates are done mostly in mixed media - offset technique. The tipped-in print for Zigmas Raulinaitis was created in the same manner; each print for the newsletter has been signed and dated by the artist. Its owner, a former army officer, is very much interested in military history, is editor of a veterans' magizine, and an author of several publications of war histories.

The little emblem of the mounted warior on the Raulinaitis bookplate represents a modern version of a Lithuanian state seal. Since its loss of independence in 1940, any reference to pre-communist days, including this emblem, has been prohibited in Lithuania.

Joseph Sodaitis created over 40 bookplates in a very short time this year. An exhibition of his bookplates is planned in New York during the early part of 1976.

BOOKPLATES IN THE NEWS – Issued: January/April/July/October – $5 US/$6 Overseas
$1.50 Single Copy
Copyright 1976 by Audrey Spencer Arellanes

145

Random Notes on Jean
Hersholt's Bookplate
by Anna Marie Hager

In that most valuable book
on bookplates authored by
Clare Ryan Talbot, HISTORIC
CALIFORNIA IN BOOKPLATES,
appears the following de-
scription of the Hersholt
bookplate: "Jean Hersholt
is a Thespian whose proper
classification here has
caused difficult editorial
problems. Perhaps he should
have been placed in the
Artists' chapter, for he
has designed his own plate
which possesses a world of
personal significance. The
Danish flag for the land of
his birth and the flag of
his adopted country are
crossed beneath a mask which
is not the conventional, but
a copy of the oldest Greek
Mask in existence. Burning
tripods suggest the adora-
tion of the Greeks for arts
and sports. As Mr. Hersholt
pointed out, 'the arts were
as integral a part of the
Olympic Games as were sports
and burning tripods were given as prizes in the Olympic Games.' The rose is
his favorite flower, and the palette is the sign of his avocation."

In a letter to Mrs. Hager, Mr. Hersholt indicated that the palette represented
his status as an amateur painter and his hobby, and the old Greek mask, "being
an actor by profession."

Hersholt was born in Copenhagen, Denmark, July 12, 1886 and came to the United
States to pursue a career in motion pictures. Before his death on June 2, 1956,
at the age of 70, he had appeared in more than 400 motion pictures. Among this
large number he had notable roles in THE FOUR HORSEMEN, TESS OF THE STORM COUN-
TRY with Mary Pickford, STELLA DALLAS, OLD HEIDELBERG, MEN IN WHITE, GRAND HOTEL
with John Barrymore and Greta Garbo. He is perhaps best remembered for his
characterization of doctors, particularly the role of Dr. Dafoe to the Dionne
Quintuplets in COUNTRY DOCTOR and the title role in DR. CHRISTIAN, which Hersholt performed in the screen and radio series. In addition to acting, he also
served as President of the Motion Picture Relief Fund and was always an ardent
supporter of the various Danish-American societies in this country.

(The Hersholt bookplate print tipped-in above has been printed specially for
BOOKPLATES IN THE NEWS on a colored paperstock to avoid its being mistaken for
an original bookplate used in his library.)

EX LIBRIX NAPOLEONICIS

LESLIE HENRI KUEHNER
MEMPHIS, TENNESSEE

No._____
Date_____

LESLIE HENRI KUEHNER
Ex Libris Napoleonicis
by
The Reverend James Parker

Leslie Henri Kuehner is a good friend, who has a particular interest in the Emperor Napoleon; some years ago he used illustrations cut from books about Napoleon, title page frames, etc., and the person who prepared the layout for offset printing misspelled ex libris. At the time of printing the bookplates were numbered consecutively with red numerals, so Kuehner has a running count of books in this collection; space is also provided to add the acquisition date.

At the top center of the plate is the complete armorial bearing of Napoleon designed when he became Emperor of the French. In the borders are the Hand of Justice, Staff of the Imperial Eagle, Staff of Charlemagne, a sword or two, a flaming torch - all emblems of the First Empire which are influenced by classical history, as are the soldiers of the Roman Legions and an eagle in the bottom portion of the plate. Within the borders are six golden bees, which were Napoleon's special badge. Under the central familiar portrait of the Emperor dressed in the uniform of a colonel of the Imperial Guard is the imperial crown device, and at the very bottom a Napoleonic medallion. The Emperor wears the medal and breast star of the Legion of Honor and the medal of the Order of the Iron Crown, both of which he founded early in his reign.

NEW MEMBERS . . . .
Klaus Rodel - P.O. Box 109, 9900 Frederikshavn, Denmark

Jørgen Vils-Pederson - Box 2094, DK-1013 Copenhagen K, Denmark

JOHN SYKES, DESIGNER
by Helan Halbach

John Joseph James Sykes, a bachelor in his mid-forties, a native of up-state New York, came to California a few years ago on an extended visit while recuperating from a near-fatal accident. Enticed by family stories of an unrepentent bachelor great uncle with the same name, who came to California a century before and was never heard from again, and who was something of an artist, JJ employed his Irish luck and well-founded intutition in lingering in Santa Barbara long enough to contact someone interested in his pursuits, which led him to me and my Studio 3. I suggested that the now immortalized "Itinerant Mission Artist, John Sykes," whose works can still be found in Southern California Missions, historic societies, and lesser known places, was very likely his lost great uncle.

For something to do in between bouts of tourism and investigating, JJ exhibited many remarkable skills and soon found himself so employed he nearly lost sight of his original purpose. During the course of the years he has produced some excellent wood carvings, three Sherlockian bookplates, one western ex libris and one with an Omar theme. As a result of designing my personal Coat of Arms,

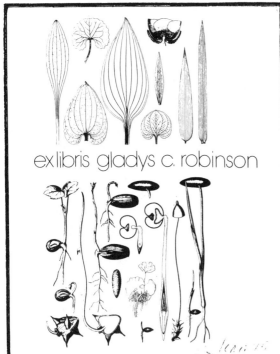

which passed through two necessary Boards of Heraldists, being then accepted and registered, making me "armigerous," he absorbed considerable heraldic knowledge which has proved useful on other occasions.

Vezys Exhibit

From November 14 to 30, 1975 there was an exhibit of Contemporary Lithuanian Ex Libris at the Lithuanian Youth Center in Chicago. This is the sixth exhibit from the collection of Gintautas Vezys. V. O. Virkau has 36 plates in the exhibit including the Robinson print. Vezys prepared a catalog with 23 prints illustrated in black and white; brief text in Lithuanian. Vezys lectured opening day; was interviewed for daily newspapers DZAUGAS and Voice of America. Exhibit had 618 ex libris by 77 artists, from Lithuania and US. The Sodaitis print on page 145 is reproduced in catalog in reduced size.

AN EGYPTIAN BOOKPLATE: Bookplate of the
Patriarchal Library of the Coptic Orthodox Church
by Dr. Enrico S. Molnar

Christianity was introduced into Egypt by St. Mark
towards the end of the first century. Alexandria
became the first patriarchate of the early church.
The patriarchate inherited the Alexandrian library,
reputed to have been the largest library of antiquity, until its destruction by the Moslems in the
seventh century.

Egyptian Christianity became Monophysite after the
Council of Chalcedon in A.D. 451. The Coptic Patriarchate moved its see to the new capital of Moslem
Egypt, Cairo. Known as the See of St. Mark, it is
the spiritual center for some four million Copts,
who are the descendants of pre-Moslem Egyptians;
the Coptic language, used exclusively in liturgi-
cal worship and literature, is the direct descendant of the Pharaonic Egyptian. Today the Coptic
Church has thirty Metropolitans and Bishops, headed by the Pope of Alexandria, who resides in Cairo.
The above bookplate is the official ex libris of
the Patriarchal Library.

SEE of St MARK

(Reference: Anba Gregorius, ST. MARK AND THE COPTIC CHURCH. Cairo: The Coptic
Orthodox Theological University College, 1968.)

VYTAUTAS O. VIRKAU, by V. E. Vengris. (Published by Exlibristen,
Klaus Rödel, P.O. Box 109, 9900 Frederick-
shavn, Denmark.)

EX LIBRIS
ALGIRDAS
NEVERAVIČIUS

This attractive, nearly square, small book
has a picture of the young artist, and a
brief biography in four languages, including English. Nineteen of his recent bookplates are tipped-in; each is signed and
dated.

V. O. Virkau was born in Lithuania in 1930.
Following his arrival in the United States,
he attended the University of Chicago and
the Art Institute of Chicago where he received a Master of Fine Arts degree in 1956.
Virkau is on the art faculty of George Williams College in Downers Grove, Illinois.

Virkau designed his first bookplate in 1970
and has nearly sixty to his credit now. There is an ever-present theme of
nature in his ex libris, with flowers, blossoms and leaves appearing frequently. His plate for Gladys C. Robinson, reproduced on page 148, is an excellent
example of his continuing concern with nature. Vengris states Virkau's ex
libris are executed by the rarely used collage-offset technique which is especially suitable for reproduction. The Algirdas Neveravicius plate, designed in
1976, is not in this book, but the Robinson plate is.

149

BOOKPLATE LITERATURE . . . . .

NORSK EXLIBRISIANA, Thor Bjorn Schyberg. Published by Exlibristen (Klaus Rodel,
P.O. Box 109, 9900 Frederikshavn, Denmark). This multi-lingual volume is a
Check List About Norwegian Bookplate Literature; there is a brief foreword by
the author, introduction by the publisher, and an index in English. The lists
include books, periodicals, house organs, encyclopedias, newspaper articles,
Norwegian artists, lectures sponsored by the Norwegian Exlibris Society, literature in Denmark and Sweden on Norwegian ex libris. Eight prints are tipped
in and several title pages reproduced. This is a large format (8 x 11), 89
pages printed one-side only; paperbound; subscription or 55 Dkr. separately.

INTERNATIONAL EXCHANGE LIST, Jørgen Vils-Pedersen (Box 2094, DK-1013 Copenhagen K, Denmark), price 25 d.kr international money order. The essay on Collecting Bookplates is reprinted with the permission of Mark F. Severin and
Anthony Reid from their ENGRAVED BOOKPLATES, European Ex Libris 1950-70. The
key to the technical symbols used in exchange lists as approved by the International Congress of Ex Libris at Barcelona in 1958 is included, as well as a
listing of eighteen bookplate societies which gives the address, publications,
and membership fees for each. In addition to furnishing the name and address
of collectors by country, some entries indicate the artists whose work they
have for exchange. Under Art Literature there are 172 items including title,
author, publisher, and price; also a list of artists and their addresses. IN-
TERNATIONAL EXCHANGE LIST is an excellent source for a variety of information
useful to the collector seeking exchanges or searching for an artist to design
a new ex libris.

BIBLIOGRAPHY ABOUT CZECHOSLOVAKIAN BOOKPLATE LITERATURE, Lubomir Vanicek. Published by Exlibristen, it is similar in format to NORSK EXLIBRISIANA, which is
#113 in Klaus Rodel's bookplate publications. There are eleven tipped-in ex
libris prints and several title pages reproduced. There are 289 bibliographic
entries which have been selected from a list of over 2,500 started by Dr. Jaro-
mir Maly, Vanicek completed. Special subscription available or 55Dkr. separately.

JANUSZ SZYMANSKI - en polsk exlibrissamler, Klaus Rodel. Yet another monograph published by Exlibristen during 1975, this is devoted to a single artist
with a portrait, brief biographical profile, and a checklist of 61 bookplates
designed since 1962. Six prints are tipped in, including one for the artist
himself which presents an unusual treatment of St. George and the dragon, using two colors and embossing.

THE BOOKPLATE SOCIETY (London), Newsletter No. 11, September 1975.
   Death of T. E. Owen, first president of Bookplate Society, noted by B.N. Lee.
   Engraved Bookplates of Simon Brett, Keith Clark. Brief biography, checklist
of 25 plates, and details about four which are reproduced.
   "Crudes" is reprinted from "Notes and Queries" of the Bookplate Exchange Club
of 1943. These were notes by G. H. Viner on badly engraved plates accompanied
by an alphabetical list; five are illustrated.
   Otto M. Lilien's book label, printed in grey and red, is tipped-in.
   Horace E. Jones will be new president of Society.
   Owen collection being offered for sale to Bookplate Society members.
   "Bookplates for all sorts and conditions of men," is an article by Brian
North Lee which appeared in the August issue of ANTIQUARIAN BOOK MONTHLY RE-
VIEW; copies available from the Secretary of the Bookplate Society, price 35p.

WHO'S WHAT, the collectors' directory, edited by Jean-Claude Baudot, is now available. Over 15,000 active and enthusiastic collectors worldwide are included, also associations; there is a complete index of 700 themes in English, Dutch, German, Spanish, Italian; the body of the text is in French. There are two volumes priced at FF 115, shipping charges included, or FF 121.20 for registered mail. A numbered edition limited to 4,000 copies is FF 170. Please add FF 5 for banking charges to all orders.

THE COLLECTOR, Art, History Combined in Bookplates, Helen Langworthy. (2) p. 24, December 1975. A few paragraphs for those unfamiliar with bookplates in this hobby, tabloid-format magazine. John Cox plate by Maxfield Parrish and E. D. French's for the Club of Odd Volumes are illustrated.

SAN FRANCISCO CHRONICLE, Ex Libris - A Collectible for Book Lovers, Anne Gilbert. (1) p. 25, December 11, 1975. Ann Gilbert appears to have a series on "Antiques and Stuff" which appears in a number of newspapers across the country, for almost the identical article was in the BOSTON SUNDAY ADVERTISER on November 30, 1975.

LOS ANGELES TIMES, Book Plate Exhibit, November 6, 1975. Kennedy Library North at Cal State Los Angeles had an exhibit of ex libris printed in the 1920-35 period in the US, Japan, Britain, and Czechoslovakia; exhibit was from sometime in October through December 20, 1975.

EXLIBRIS-REVUE, #2, 1975 (Unofficial Bookplate-News of F.I.S.A.E., edited by by Klaus Rodel, Frederikshavn, Denmark). This second issue continues the multilingual text, generous illustration, and excellent graphics which are associated with all publications under the direction of Klaus Rodel.
    Exlibris International Congress Rules for the Contest for Original Exlibris. Deadline for entries is July 31, 1976. Any interested artists may write BOOKPLATES IN THE NEWS for details.
    Zbigniew Janeczek - Young artist, native of Lodz, who has learned copper engraving and etching. In about 4 years he has created 70 bookplates.
    Notes about the International Congress in Lisbon during September 1976; letter from the Bookplate Society in London; officers listed for the Federation Internationale Des Societes D'Amateurs D'Exlibris; details about publications of ex libris societies in Belgium, CSSR, Portugal, Holland.
    Eva Papai - Hungarian graphic artist is pictured.
    Forty-six bookplates are among the illustrations, of which two are tipped-in.

Foreign Ex Libris Societies Publications (Because of the language barrier, it is impossible to review these journals; however, all of them offer a wealth of reproduced and tipped-in ex libris prints which can be enjoyed by anyone).
EX LIBRIS PORTUGAL, Libson, Mario Lourinho Rodrigues Vinhas.
GRAPHIA, Amsterdam, Leo Winkeler & Antoine Rousseau.
EXLIBRISWERELD, Amsterdam, G. J. Rhebergen, Jr.
L'EX LIBRIS FRANCAIS, Nancy, Daniel Meyer.
A ARTE DO EX-LIBRIS, Porto, Artur Mario Da Mota Miranda.
NORDISK EXLIBRIS TIDSSKRIFT, Copenhagen, Helmer Fogedgaard
EXLIBRIS-NYT, Copenhagen, Skolegade.
SVENSKA EXLIBRISFORENINGEN, Stockholm, B. S. Nordin-Pettersson
NIPPON EXLIBRIS ASSOCIATION, Okayamaken, issues a calendar with tipped-in prints.

REMINDER - 1976 membership dues now payable. Your support is needed. The YEAR BOOK 1975 is ready for mailing - send $13 for your copy!

AS of BC & D

Bookplates in the News

429 NORTH DAISY AVENUE, PASADENA, CALIFORNIA, 91107
AUDREY SPENCER ARELLANES, Editor

Number Twenty-Four   April 1976

MY BOOK
& HEART
SHALL NEVER
PART

added to the
George Williams College
Library during the
Bicentennial Year

THE BICENTENNIAL - NOW and THEN

COMMEMORATIVE COLLEGE EX LIBRIS

George Williams College (Downers Grove,
Illinois) was established in 1890 and
named in honor of Sir George Williams,
founder of the YMCA. The college has a
complete liberal arts program with special emphasis on human service profes-
ions.

The commemorative bookplate was designed
to be used in books added to the college
library during the bicentennial year.
The profile of a man is Sir George Williams. The ship refers to the vessels
bringing colonists to the new shores.
The phrase "my book and heart shall never
part" is from the NEW ENGLAND PRIMER
(earliest edition, 1737). The bookplate
was designed by Vytautas O. Virkau as
a collage and printed offset on dry gummed paper.

JAMES TURNER by Frances W. Allen

Another rather minor American engraver of the eighteenth century was James
Turner of Boston and Philadelphia. Perhaps the most interesting thing learned
about him by this writer is that the description by Fielding (DICTIONARY OF
AMERICAN PAINTERS, 1926) was lifted in its entirety from Stauffer's earlier
work, although Thieme-Becker lists both sources.

In the BOSTON EVENING POST Turner advertised as follows in 1745: "James
Turner, Silversmith and engraver, near the Town-House in Cornhill Boston.
Engraves all sorts of Stamps in Brass or Pewter for the common Printing Press,
Coats of Arms, Crests, Cyphers, etc. on Gold, Silver, Steel, Copper, Brass
or Pewter. He likewise makes Watch Faces, makes and cuts Seals in Gold,
Silver or Steel : or makes Steel Faces for Seals, and sets them handsomely
in Gold or Silver. He cuts all sorts of Steel Stamps, Brass Rolls and Stamps

for Sadlers and Bookbinders, and does all sorts of work in Gold and Silver. All after the best and neatest manner and at the most Reasonable Rates."

While in Boston Turner did a view of Boston appearing in the AMERICAN MAGAZINE for 1744, the three large folding maps used in a "Bill in Chancery of New Jersey" published by James Parker in New York in 1747, and his well known and rather well engraved portrait of the Rev. Isaac Watts. He removed to Philadelphia some time before 1758 and is there best known for his large map of the "Province of Pennyslvania" published in 1759 in Philadelphia by Nicholas Scull and the Penn coat of arms used by the PENNSYLVANIA GAZETTE of this period.

Of Turner's ex libris work there are four signed plates, the most interesting being the rare and ornate plate of John Franklin of Boston, brother of Benjamin. The plate is illustrated in Allen. Fincham illustrates the plate of John Ross of Philadelphia, Jacobean in style, and that of Isaac Norris, Speaker of the Pennsylvania Assembly from 1751 to 1766, is reproduced in ART AMATEUR, February 1894, page 93. No published illustration of the plate of Sir John St. Clair (#751 in Allen) is known by this writer. In addition, the unsigned plate of James Hall is attributed to Turner by Allen. The Stauffer checklist (numbers 3329-36) notes Turner prints, maps, book illustrations, and the Watts portrait, but no bookplates.

Turner died in late 1759, and there is a notice of the sale of his household effects in the December issue of the PENNSYLVANIA GAZETTE. Among these effects were engraving tools, perhaps purchased by Henry Dawkins for his work on Continental currency?

HELEN AGNES GAFFNEY

The original Helen Agnes Gaffney bookplate was engraved and presented as a gift by the librarian of Hamilton College to a member of his staff when she resigned to study at the University of Buffalo. The plate was conceived by the donor and executed by Mary Elizabeth French, a graduate of the Fine Arts College at Syracuse University. The reading woman is Correggio's ST. CATHERINE OF ALEXANDRIA, patron saint of Librarians and women students. The Renaissance border is in keeping with the period of the painting. It embodies wheels, representing those which were miraculously destroyed at Saint Catherine's touch. The initials of the donor (which also stand for Library Science or Service) and the seals, greatly reduced, of Hamilton College and the University of Buffalo are also in the border. The plate is dated and signed. The original prints were in brown ink on cream colored paper; the prints tipped-in were run offset for use in BOOKPLATES IN THE NEWS.

BOOKPLATES IN THE NEWS - Issued January/April/July/October $5 US/$6 Overseas
Copyright 1976 by Audrey Spencer Arellanes $1.50 Single Copy

PAM G. RUETER
by G. Jan Rhebergen

On the 18th of February, 1976 Pam Reuter
celebrated his 70th birthday. He is the
most important Dutch ex libris artist of
today, and not only of today but the best
Holland ever had. Born the son of a great
Dutch painter, Professor Georg Rueter,
Pam has art in his veins. He studied
at the Rijksacademie voor Beeldende Kunst
(national academy of art) at Amsterdam
and started his career as an assistant
of the famous dutch architect H. Th.
Wijdeveld. Later he worked for several
years as a designer for a textile mill; he explored the world of the theatre
both as a set designer and an actor. In the 1960's he was asked to become a
professor at the Technical University of Delft, where he remained until he retired in 1970.

In addition to bookplates, Pam did illustrations, occasional graphics and all
types of commercial graphic designs. His ex libris work reaches the number of
600; only a few early plates were made by lithography, the rest are all wood-
engravings. His bookplates are elegant and very decorative. The round and
oval forms are appropriate to his kind of work, and an essential part of his
ex libris is the lettering. He gives great attention to his lettering as it
is often the most important part of the composition. His love for nature is
also reflected in many of his bookplates with flowers and animals.

Pam is a very good amateur cook, who serves the finest meals, and he often invites friends to join him and his wife. The superb wines he serves are famous!
His wife, Nini, is a great musician, who plays several instruments ranging from
the flute to the harp; she has many music students. In the Rueters' home you will
find a little, 18th century church organ and the finest collection of old wine-
glasses you ever saw.

At 70 Pam is still very active as an artist. He works daily. It seems that in
spite of the hundreds of bookplates he has created, his work continues to be new
and fresh and has lost nothing of the superb techniques of his woodengraving,
which is Pam's "trademark".

Editor's Note: The tip-in above is one of many plates commissioned by Norman
Shaftel, M.D., a physician practicing in Brooklyn, New York. Dr. Shaftel has
personal plates designed for him by American and European artists; as the Rueter
represents excellence in the calligraphic name label, his other bookplates are
unusual and original in design, executed in various mediums (woodcuts, engravings, etc.), and all examples of superior graphics by the standards of any counyry.
A checklist of Dr. Shaftel's personal ex libris would present a good cross section of artists highly skilled in the miniature art of the bookplate during recent decades. His collection centers on medical ex libris, including those of
notable physicians such as Rene Laennec (1781-1826), who introduced the use of
the stethoscope which Osler rated as one of the eight to ten greatest contributions to the practice of medicine.
G. Jan Rhebergen, editor of the Dutch ex libris journal, will be featured soon
in the continuing series about editors of bookplate publications.

FORD ASHMAN CARPENTER

While no information is available about the bookplate tipped-in to the left, considerable is known about Ford Ashman Carpenter, who was born in Chicago, March 25, 1868. He received his early education at Dilworth Academy and went on to the Carson Astronomical Observatory and the U.S. Balloon and Airship Schools. He received an LLD from Whittier College in 1913 and a degree of Sc.D. from Occidental in 1921.

From 1888 to 1919 he was assigned to various stations with the U.S. Weather Service; he was manager of the department of Meteorology & Aeronautics of the U.S. Chamber of Commerce from 1919-1941. During this latter period he was also an honorary lecturer at the University of California, attended the Monterey Military Encampment 1916-17, was associated with the U.S. Army Aviation School in San Diego during 1915, and served in a faculty capacity to Columbia, Cornell, West Point, and several other institutions.

Carpenter's unusual talents brought him employment with such varied companies as TWA 1927-30; Santa Fe Railroad 1922-35; American and United Airlines 1927-8, Los Angeles Municipal Airport 1927; Hollywood Bowl 1928; Goodyear-Zeppelin Co. 1926-9; American-Hawaiian Steamship Company 1934-40; he was a radio broadcaster 1923-41. During World War II he served in Intelligence; he held International Balloon pilot license #913. He wrote numerous monographs and pamphlets in the technical fields of his proficiency and a book, GENERAL "BILLY" MITCHELL AS I KNEW HIM. Ford Ashman Carpenter died in November of 1947.

If you have information about the bookplate - who designed it, when, the meaning of the motto and heraldic symbol on the cross cut of the redwood, please write the editor, who will include the details in a future issue of the newsletter. The lower right hand corner of the plate has three initials, probably those of the artist, but identification has been unsuccessful.

BOOKS FROM THE LIBRARY OF LESLIE VICTOR SMITH   Recent correspondence from Richard L. Smith, son of the Canadian bookplate artist, made known that books about ex libris from the library of Leslie Victor Smith are for sale. Among these is a complete set of the 18-volume JOURNAL OF THE EX LIBRIS SOCIETY, the three volumes on the Franks collection, and many other standard reference books in the field. If you are interested, write Richard L. Smith, 151 Libby Boulevard, Richmond Hill, Ontario, Canada L4C 4V5.

Leslie Victor Smith was a member of the ASBC&D for many years before his death at 72 in 1952. Born in Canada, he studied art in London where he joined the Langham Sketch Club. Among his fellow students was Arthur Rackham. His personal bookplate collection numbered 17,000, of which 4,500 were Canadian plates. William Colgate's BOOKPLATES OF LESLIE VICTOR SMITH is among volumes for sale.

EX LIBRIS

mr. & mrs.

walter

Ferguson

WALTER FERGUSON
by Sister Mary Joachim, O.S.B.

Walter Ferguson, now deceased, was a prominent banker in Tulsa, Oklahoma. He was brought to Oklahoma Territory in a covered wagon when his parents left Kansas in 1892. Walter's family settled in Watonga and immediately established a newspaper, THE WATONGA REPUBLICAN. They had brought with them a second-hand army press. There was much to record in this pictuersque period, and Mrs. Ferguson did much of the work from writing editorials to folding the finished papers. Walter became involved in politics and was eventually Governor of the Territory.

Edna Ferber, in her novel CIMMARON, built her story around the experiences of Mrs. Ferguson and her newspaper. Although much fiction is intertwined with fact in the novel, the background is authentic.

The bookplate depicts Mrs. Ferguson's trip to Oklahoma, about which she explains: "I came in a covered wagon with my husband and two babies ... to carve a home and a newspaper out of the raw, far from a railroad. In one wagon, which my husband drove, were an army press, type, a few cases a hand job press, some chases, wooden quoins, a shooting stick (no, I do not mean a gun) and other necessary materials for getting out a small newspaper. In the other, which I drove, were our household supplies and camp outfit. In my lap was one baby and on the seat was another, just old enough to ask questions." She wrote a book, THEY CARRIED THE TORCH, which told of the early newspapers in Oklahoma.

Walter Ferguson's bookplate attests to the pride he held for his mother, who represented the finest type of pioneer woman. Walter's wife was also a newspaper woman; her column, "A Woman's Viewpoint", appeared daily for many years in the Scripps-Howard syndicated newspapers.

XVI INTERNATIONAL EX LIBRIS CONGRESS -- Lisbon, August 11-14, 1976

An announcement of the program to be held in Lisbon is enclosed with this issue. If you plan to attend write directly to Mr. Eugenio Mealha Costa.. ..Treasurer Rua Coelho da Rocha, 122 - r/c Esq., Lisbon 3, Portugal.

Artists from all over the world are invited to participate in the exhibition to be held on the occasion of the Congress. Each artist who is interested should send eight to ten recent and different ex libris to the President of the Congress, A. M. da Mota Miranda, Casa do Outerio, Celorico de Basto, Portugal.

If you plan to attend, please notify the editor of BOOKPLATES IN THE NEWS.

156

BOOKPLATE HOAX   An article by Ernest Dickinson, Professor Carberry Was Here, appeared in READERS DIGEST, 106:21 +, April 1975, which told of books being given to Brown University in the name of Josiah S. Carberry and a bookplate designed for these gift volumes. It also appeared that the good professor was a non-existent character.   Thanks to Arnold Van Benschoten we have the following additional information.

"Yes, there is actually such a bookplate, very similar to the Brown seal, but with the added words attributed to Horace, Dulce et Decorum Est Desipere in Loco - It is sweet and fitting to unbend upon occasion; or, if you prefer, a little nonsense now and then is relished by the wisest men.

"You will note on the Carberry plate that the 13 under F is printed in red to indicate the custom of donating to the Fund on Friday the 13th. This reminder is posted: 'On every Friday the 13th, it has been the custom of Brown students, faculty, and staff to donate to the Josiah S. Carberry Fund.   The Fund was anonymously established by Professor Josiah S. Carberry in memory of my future late wife Laura Carberry with an initial donation of $101.01 presented on May 13, 1955.' A little brown jug for collections is placed nearby.   An average of $100 is given annually, and recently American Express has used Professor Carberry, 'the world-wide traveler', in radio advertising.   The faculty club at Brown University has a small private dining room called the Carberry room in which is a large portrait of the professor going down College Hill, showing the back of him.

"The YORKTOWNER, June 19, 1974, carried under Community News a headline 'Dr. Carberry Tours with Nixon', and someone else conceived of Josiah in the bullring. I tend to the opinion that the professor fills a void in college life left by the demise of college humorous publications, such as the BROWN JUG and HARVARD LAMPOON."

WILLIAM WILKE - Checklist and Biography - Clare Ryan Talbot is at work on a checklist and biography of William Wilke, who was associated with John Henry Nash as artist and illustrator from about 1923; he also did some splendid bookplates which were included in Talbot's HISTORIC CALIFORNIA IN BOOKPLATES.   Among those he designed are plates for William Randolph Hearst, Dr. Aurelia Reinhardt of Mills College, Yehudi Menuhin, and John Francis Neyland, a Hearst attorney.   Mrs. Talbot requests owners of Wilke bookplates write to her at 1438 Cottage Street, Alameda, Ca. 94501. She would welcome biographical details on this competent artist who contributed much to the deserved fame of Nash, and would appreciate hearing from members of the Wilke family.

- - - NEW MEMBERS - - - - - - -

Warren R. Johnston, 10706 Kenilworth Avenue, Garrett Park, Maryland 20766
Gary E. Switzer, 73 Ravine Park Crescent, West Hill, Ontario M1C 2M5, Canada

THE PRIVATE LIBRARY, The Bookplate Designs of Walter Crane, Keith Clark. (1) 8: 58-74, Summer 1975. " . . . bookplates by Crane illustrate the interests or professions of their owners, always a difficult task for a conscientious designer as so often those who commission this type of bookplate require every one of their interests to be depicted. . . . he was applauded in his own lifetime as much for his furniture and furnishing design, his mosaics, stained glass, ceramics, pottery, gesso and oil paintings as he was for his book illustrations. "Excellent descriptive checklist of ten plates designed by Crane.

ANTIQUARIAN BOOK MONTHLY REVIEW, Walter Crane Revived, Keith Nicholson. (2) 3:46-9, February 1976. Three items on Walter Crane (1845-1915) have recently been published: Isobel Spencer has written a biography on Crane as "a visionary artist in all fields, as painter, designer, author, radical socialist, and illustrator." Rodney K. Enger has approached Crane as a book illustrator; and Keith Clark gives a scholarly account of his bookplate designs. Nicholson indicates two additional bookplates were designed by Crane which were for Caroline Miller Parker and H. E. Widener.

RHODE ISLAND HISTORICAL SOCIETY, Heraldry: Theory, Design, Uses. 4:#10, February 1976. A four session course is offered by ASBC&D member Henry L. P. Beckwith and is "geared to the needs of designers, the antiquarian, and the collector of these products" which include ex libris.

A ARTE DO EX LIBRIS, Pall Bohne, Amateur Bookplate Designer, Audrey Spencer Arellanes. (9) 9:227-30,1975. Article in English and Portugese; portrait of the artist, two tipped in prints and six reproduced of which three have color. Checklist of eleven bookplates created from 1960 to 1974 using a variety of mediums, including an etching and woodengraving.

SOUNDINGS (University of California, Santa Barbara), The Pear Tree Press: Addenda, Christian Brun. 7:77-85, September 1975. This additional archive of the press of James Guthrie (1874-1952) contains a number of related bookplate items such as a prospectus of the BOOK-CRAFTSMAN, A Review of Fine Printing, Bookplates, Poetry, etc., and bookplates produced at the press in various proof states.

EXLIBRIS I FARVER, Helmer Fogedgaard and Johnny Kohler. This is the seventeenth publication privately printed by these two Danes. A short introduction is followed by ten tipped-in bookplate prints, each by a different artist, all printed in several colors, a few lines of text for each plate.

BOGEN FORENER FOLKENE, 3 EXLIBRIS BY CHRISTIAN BLAESBJERG. Publisher: Klaus Rodel, Denmark, 1974. Multi-lingual text, including English, concerning three exlibris which incorporated in their composition the motto of the International Congress in Bled: "The book unites the peoples." Three prints tipped-in, each in at least two colors. At the Bled meeting the American Society of Bookplate Collectors and Designers was welcomed to membership in the International Federation of Exlibris Amateur Societies (F.I.S.A.E.).

HENRY SCHJAERVEN EXLIBRIS, Thor Bjorn (EXLIBRISTEN, 1974). Text in three languages including English. There are six tipped-in bookplate prints, a checklist of 196 ex libris for this Norwegian artist (1900-1972). Excellent graphic design displayed in this small volume.

EXLIBRIS REVUE, Vol. 1, #3, 1975: 7th Biennial held during June in Malbork during which 800 bookplates were exhibited; note on artists Herbert Ott and Kazimierz Nekanda-Trepka; 21 bookplates illustrated including two tipped-in. Vol. 1, #4 - Helmer Fogedgaard's article on ex libris of the period spanning 1892 to 1910 has 16 illustrations; as with other art forms the art nouveau-jugendstil ex libris is now receiving renewed attention. - In Memoriam Karl Blossfeld - Evald Okas - News from various European bookplate socities. (Subscription to this quarterly is Danish kroner 30,oo annually. Klaus Rodel, P.O. Box 109, DK-9900 Frederikshavn, Denmark)

NORDISK EXLIBRIS TIDSSKRIFT, #4, 1975. One paragraph English summary indicates articles on Wilhelm Richter whose bookplates feature humorous animal motifs, graphic artist Premysl Rolcik, collector Vaclav Krupka describes visit to an artist, Flemish artist Edward Pellens, and review of bookplate literature; 21 illustrations plus five tip-ins.

EXLIBRIS WERELD. While there is no English summary, the illustrations are well produced. The issue for June of 1975 noted the article by Norman Shaftel on "The History of Cardiology and the Cardiac Motif in Ex Libris."

L'EX LIBRIS FRANCAIS, October 1975. To quote from the English summary: "As 1975 is "The Wife's Year", we desired, under Jacques Bois' signature to bring our contribution to this tribute with "The Feminine Ex Libris." The subject is a very vast one, so the author limited himself to the French ex libris."

THE TOWER (Oak Park, Illinois), 13, February 1976. Dan Burne Jones was honored at a "Meet the Author" event in Oak Park where he autographed copies of his new book, THE PRINTS OF ROCKWELL KENT. Reviews of his book have appeared in SUNDAY SUN-TIMES, February 22, 1976; PACIFIC SUN LITERARY QUARTERLY, Winter 1975

EARLY PRINTED LABELS, A Catalogue of dated personal labels and gift labels printed in Britain to the year 1760, Brian North Lee. (Private Libraries Association and Bookplate Society, 1976. Ł12.50, Ł10 PLA members. Royal 8vo, 207 pages) Book labels have been much neglected. Hardy dismissed them as numerous and uninteresting; Hamilton listed quite a few but with inadequate annotations; and only in the JOURNAL OF THE EX LIBRIS SOCIETY did Sir Arthur Vicars mention their fashion up to 1690 and stated "over twenty dated labels are known to that date." Brian North Lee has extended the period covered to 1760 which more nearly represents the time of their popular use and has recorded over 500 dated labels. The 100 illustrations give visual evidence of the wide variety of labels which can be created from borders, type ornaments, and type, and the uneven inking impression of many of the printed labels reproduced indicates the lack of uniformly skilled pressmen working with the presses of that period. In addition to describing each label, the location of the label is given when known, such as from the Viner and Franks Collection, or the Julian Marshall Collection, or from a volume in a specific library; biographical data on the owners are furnished. The biographical tidbits make these early book owners come alive, and perhaps in some cases will elicit enough curiosity to send the reader in search of greater details (i.e., Samuel Radcliffe, #147, "was Principal of his College from 1614 until he was ejected in 1647/8." His death followed in June of 1648; one wonders why he was ejected from office and if these circumstances had any bearing on his death following so soon thereafter.) EARLY PRINTED LABELS will be the standard reference for this specialty, and as such belongs in the library of bookplate collectors regardless of their own specific period of specialization. (You may place your order through Private Libraries Association, Ravelston, South View Road, Pinner, Middlesex, England. At the current rate of exchange the price is about $24.)

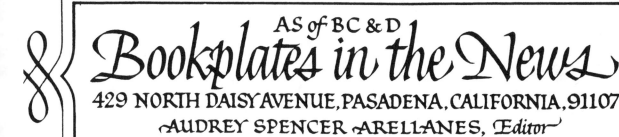

AS of BC & D

Bookplates in the News

429 NORTH DAISY AVENUE, PASADENA, CALIFORNIA, 91107

AUDREY SPENCER ARELLANES, Editor

Number Twenty-five   July 1976

THE GREAT DOOLITTLE MYSTERY by Frank W. Allen

Amos Doolittle, New Haven silversmith and engraver, is now known chiefly for
his "Four Views of the Battle of Lexington, Concord, etc.", which he engraved.
This engraving also served as a model for the original drawing or painting by
Ralph Earle. Doolittle and Earle were both members of the New Haven Cadets
who, under Captain Benedict Arnold and later General Israel Putnam, marched to
Cambridge upon news of Lexington being received at New Haven. A reproduction
of the "Four Views," engraved by Sidney L. Smith, was published in seventy-five
numbered sets by C. E. Goodspeed in 1903. They have been redrawn in several
other places, notably the Rev. E. G. Porter's FOUR DRAWINGS OF THE ENGAGEMENT
OF LEXINGTON AND CONCORD, Boston, 1883, and reduced in part three of the DOO-
LITTLE FAMILY IN AMERICA, Cleveland, 1903.

Amos is well known and his prints highly prized by bookplate aficionados.
Seventeen plates are known to have originated from his burin, most from Connecticut, three from Yale College society libraries. One other society plate,
Allen No. 676, the Phoenix Society may very well be a Doolittle. (Fincham's
claim that the Vassall plate, Allen No. 888, is a Doolittle we shall disregard
from internal evidence.)

In the year 1806 there was organized at Yale a new society called Phoenix. It
was apparently the brain child of the gifted and controversial Thomas Smith
Grimké of South Carolina, who was at Yale from 1805 to 1807 when he graduated.
Although this society did not succeed in outliving its sponsor, being absorbed
by the Linonian the next year, it did issue a broadside catalogue of the books
in its library. None of these books has been found. Were one to turn up, with
its plate intact, the relationship of the Society and the plate would be definitely proven. Allen's statement that the plate is from South Carolina may be
partially accepted, as Mr. Grimké was a South Carolinian and may very well have
taken the entire Phoenix Society library with him when he graduated from Yale.
The plate itself is unsigned, but the style of engraving is not incompatible
with that of Doolittle, and the fact that he engraved ex libris for all the
Yale societies is certainly a point in his favor. The design is better than
usual for Doolittle, but not impossible. It compares favorably with the designing of the Social Library Company and is not as well   done as his engraving
in the 1811 edition of Joel Barlow's Hasty Pudding.

Currently a trained researcher is studying the Grimké papers at the College of
Charleston looking for references to the Phoenix Society and possible proof
of the origin of its bookplate. Will, perhaps, the symbol of immortality one
day arise yet again from its own ashes and settle our doubts once and for all?

NOTES FROM A DESIGNER by Philip Sperling

What to tell you - that I must be a "designer" from birth, because I can remember from my earliest days delighting in creating, changing, sketching, doing the unexpected and the unusual with the usual, etc. But to come first and directly to the typographic bookplates - these were designed by me just after World War II when I was stationed in Bad Canstatt, a lovely spa just across the river from Stuttgart. When the War in Europe was over, the Generals did not know just what to do with all those G.I.'s so they sent us on "vacation trips" all over Europe, to schools, etc. We were pretty much on our own. Can you imagine how excited I was when I discovered just a block or two from my apartment (I was a Staff Sergeant in the 325th Medical Battalion attached to the 100th Infantry Division) a fully equipped (bombed but still in working order) printing house. I was an early reader and lover of type! The U.S. soldier was "king" then, and I must confess I pulled my rank and just about appropriated that shop. What pleasure I had pulling type and ornaments from the boxes and then slowly and laboriously pulling proofs from the hand press. Everything was done and learned by the hit and miss process, but I had lots of time and was going nowhere, certainly not home yet. I did have some help from a young, disabled German who was very competent in all phases of printing. As I recall, he had been an employee there before the war, and for some reason was allowed to live there and work the equipment. This shop did a great deal of wine label printing, and discovered from "snooping" around that they also did printing for the great library in Stuttgart which was almost totally destroyed.

About some of the bookplates: The one for the Vigdermans was inspired, I know, by the ornate plastic work of a ceiling in a Schloss and by their German name and heritage. The basis for the Keats label for Sylvia and Philip Sperling was the desire to do a label for my wife and myself using the same text as I had on the bookplate before my marriage. Others had their origins in a play of the imagination generated by the small pieces of type - just examining them slowly and at great length and thinking what to do with them.

When I returned home, a wife and family took all my time as well as an association with a large and growing industrial corporation that lasted until I retired just a couple of years ago; printing and designing were put aside for a while. When I tried to putter around some time later in a print shop, I ran into "union" restrictions. My designing talents were exercised within the company with which I was associated for 30 years, creating their letterheads, catalogues, and mailing pieces. From time to time I have created bookplates for friends, sketched designes that others have brought to completion. And, of course, it was most exciting when Louise Seymour Jones discovered my bookplates at the Huntington Library (how they got there I do not remember) and asked me to send copies to Scripps College; she was most flattering when referring to me in her book, THE HUMAN SIDE OF BOOKPLATES!

(Editor's Note: Recently Philip Sperling completed a three-year project with the Grolier Club Library, which has a Graphic Arts Room whose holdings include almost a complete run of the YEAR BOOK OF THE ASBC&D.)

EMANUEL HALDEMAN-JULIUS
by Norman E. Tanis

The new bookplate with the legend "from the personal collection of Emanuel Haldeman-Julius" was designed and produced to be affixed to publications that came directly from the personal collection of the famous printer of the Little Blue Book.

The bookplate was designed for use at California State University Northridge, Kansas State College, my own personal collection, and that of Gene De Gruson. It was produced from a photograph by Amanda Blanco and the graphic design, which was imposed upon it, was by Lydia Wilde. It was meant to follow the spirit of a sketch of Leonardo Da Vinci entitled "Proportions of the Human Firure," after Vitruvius, c. 1485-1490, pen and ink, in the Academy, Venice. The photograph is of model Vincent Van Bok of Malibu. The Da Vinci sketch and the present bookplate are intended to suggest the balance and symmetry of man in his world. I think this is an appropriate symbol for an American writer, thinker, publisher, and promoter such as Emanuel Haldeman-Julius.

From the
Personal Library
of
Emanuel Haldeman - Julius

With his overnight success of the BALLAD OF READING GAOL, published in 1919 in Girard, Kansas, a new era of good books for the millions for the price of a few pennies was ushered in. In 1929, a set of 1,500 Little Blue Books accompanied Admiral Richard E. Byrd on his scientific expedition to Little America in Antarctica. It was to continue this tradition that Norman E. Tanis and Gene De Gruson sent twenty-two selected Little Blue Books to the U.S. astronauts.

Called the Henry Ford of publishing, Haldeman-Julius was the first to mass-produce quality books cheaply and efficiently, to offer a vast range of subjects, to advertise widely in newspapers and magazines, and to make his little books easily available by mail order. Like Ford, the Kansas publisher was thoroughly familiar with the product he sold. "As editor and publisher, I've always known my public intimately--it's myself," he claimed. "I judge a manuscript by only one standard--do I like it? I'm Mr. Public--E.H.J., multiplied hundreds of thousands of times." His outstanding achievement, earning him an important place in American publishing, was that he made it possible for the worker to afford books by the giants of western culture. Through the Blue Books, authors reached a wider reading public. For a nickel, a person could buy the works of Thoreau, Hawthorne, Shakespeare. "The genuine Popularization of excellent literature has now emerged from the heart of Kansas as an established fact," wrote John Cowper Powys, English novelist, essayist, and critic, in congratulating Haldeman-Julius on the publication of his 500th Little Blue Book title in 1923.

Asked how the idea got started, he replied, "I got the idea when I was about 15 years old, in Philadelphia, my home town. There, on a freezing November day, I picked up a pamphlet edition of THE BALLAD OF READING GAOL for 10¢ at a small book-store . . . I'd been lifted out of this world - and by a 10¢ booklet. I thought then how wonderful it would be if thousands of such booklets could be picked up easily and inexpensively whenever one wanted to buy them." Fifteen years later (1919) when Haldeman-Julius bought THE APPEAL TO REASON printing plant in Girard, he worked to make his publishing dream a reality and, at the same time, raise money to pay off his debt on the plant. The first two little paperbound books, offered at 25¢ each to the 175,000 subscribers of his weekly newspaper, THE APPEAL TO REASON, were THE BALLAD OF READING GAOL and THE RUBAIYAT OF OMAR KHAYYAM. These sold rapidly; thus encouraged, he decided to publish a series of fifty es-tablished classics to be sold for $5. Within a week he received 5,000 orders, enough to insure the success of his venture. [This article is taken for the most part from a pamphlet written by Lenore Anderson entitled, "Fiftieth Anniversary Celebration of the First Little Blue Book," issued April 26, 1969.]

THE REVEREND JAMES PARKER

Father Parker uses this book-plate in his various religious and theological books. The scene shows four Deacons of Honor carrying the figure of Our Lady of Walsingham (Mary) un-der a processional canopy. In 1061 the Mother of Christ appeared in a vision to a no-ble lady in the little English village of Walsingham. The Lady Recheldis erected in that place a special shrine in honor of Mary's visit, and it soon be-came a very popular place of Medieval pilgrimage rivalling even Canterbury and Compostella. But in the 16th century, the evils of religious controversy fell upon Walsingham; King Henry VIII destroyed the shrine and its church, taking its mon-ies into his treasury. In 1921 the vicar of the Anglican Church in Walsingham had the image of Our Lady rebuilt from a design on an ancient seal, and once again the shrine is restored. Regular pilgrimages are now flourishing in this Church of England "Holy Village". Father Parker is a Priest-Associate of the Shrine and displays its arms on his heraldic ex libris.

The artwork for this bookplate is by the noted English illustrator Enid M. Chad-wick, who lives in Walsingham, and has done a great deal of the decorative work in the Shrine church.

VLADAS ZILIUS - Lithuanian Artist

by Gintautas Vezys

Vladas Zilius is a talented Lithuanian artist, who emigrated with
his wife in March 1973, and temporarily resides in Rome while he
waits for his immigration visa to
the United States. Vladas was born
in 1939; graduated from the Institute of Art in Vilnius in 1964, he
is a painter, graphic artist, and
book illustrator. Since his paintings deviated from the official
social realism school promulgated
by the state, he was forbidden to
participate in exhibitions during
the last 12 years.

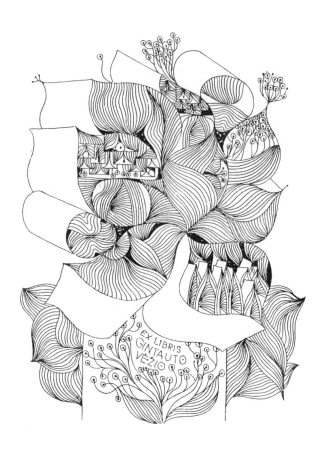

The art of Zilius is very precise,
and he possesses a highly developed drawing technique. In graphic
arts and ex libris designs he uses
architectural, folkart, and religious motifs. His paintings are
abstracts with escape symbols and
geometrical forms. In 1967 he
participated in the III International Bookplate Biennal in Malbork, Poland; he has created more
than 50 ex libris.

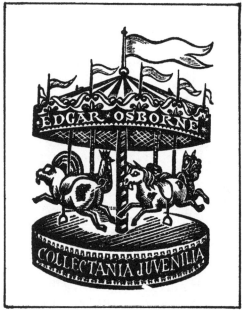

FRIENDS of the EDGAR OSBORNE and LILLIAM H. SMITH COLLECTIONS, Toronto Public Library

At a Colloquium held at Boys and Girls House in
October 1965, when children's book collectors
from the United States, England, and Canada gathered to meet Dr. Edgar Osborne and Miss Lillian
H. Smith, the decision was made by the Toronto
Public Library Board to take steps to institute
an organization of Friends of these two collections.

In 1949 Dr. Edgar Osborne, a British librarian
and book collector, presented his collection of
about two thousand children's books published in
England to the Toronto Public Library as a memorial to his wife. A printed catalogue was published by the Toronto Public Library in 1958 and
it was reprinted in 1966 with minor corrections.
A new Boys and Girls House in 1964 replaced the original house built in 1875.
The oldest book in the collection was published in 1505, and the terminal date is

1910, the year that marks the end of Dr. Osborne's boyhood and the end of the Edwardian era.

Miss Lillian H. Smith was appointed as Toronto's first children's librarian in 1912. To celebrate the fiftieth anniversary of the children's libraries in Toronto the Board inaugurated The Lillian H. Smith Collection of Children's Books, to be comprised of books published in English for children since 1910 that exemplify the standards of book selection set forth by Miss Smith in THE UNRELUCTANT YEARS; sub-titled A Critical Approach to Children's Literature, it was published by the American Library Association in 1953 and in paperback by Viking Press in 1967.

An appropriate bookplate has been designed for each collection. The material for this article was furnished by ASBC&D member Willo Singer and the Toronto Public Library.

The
LILLIAN H. SMITH
COLLECTION
BOYS AND GIRLS HOUSE

FROM the BOOKPLATE LITERATURE . . . . .

POLAND ILLUSTRATED MAGAZINE. For Five Centuries, Professor Andrzej Ryszkiewicz. (6) 19-21, May 1976. "Such a large group of outstanding artists who designed book plates, as well as the very good atmosphere around our ex libris (many exhibitions and publications, active groups of ex libris fans in a variety of towns) were bound to lead to the development of a "Polish School" of this art in Poland rather different from others in the world in its ambitions and achievements. This Polish school obviously is not uniform: its strength lies precisely in its diversity, which suits the nonconformist nature of the Poles."

AMERICAN LIBRARIES. Paul C. Richards-Frost Collection. (1) 226; April 1976. A woodcut by J. J. Lankes, who illustrated many Robert Frost books, is used as the ex libris for the Frost collection given by Paul C. Richards in memory of his parents to the Boston University Libraries.

GENTLEMAN'S QUARTERLY. Pulse, Rosemary Kent. (2) 12, May 1976. Whimsical animals and printer's ornaments featured on unusual stock plates designed by Marilyn and Dennis Grastorf.

ON ANTIQUES. Bookplates: Look Between the Covers - Collecting Bookplates (Ralph & Terry Kovel). (3), 1 page, June 1976. "[Bookplates] are enjoying a new surge of popularity in the United States (they've always been popular in Europe) now because they are easy to collect, relatively inexpensive and fasinating records of history."

JAAP KUIJPER, John J. Hanrath [1975, Exlibrisking W. B. Vereeniging.] Brief biography, checklist of 80 ex libris designed from 1932 to 1975, and eleven bookplates illustrated in black and white. Variety in style, occasional humor.

OTTO KUCHENBAUER, Klaus Rodel [1975, Exlibristen]. Multi-lingual text including English; 15 multi-colored prints tipped in, and portrait of the artist. In Denmark designers and advertising artists lead in ex libris production; in Holland, Belgium, France and Germany, it is the lithographic artists.

THE LURE AND LORE OF BOOKPLATES
by Mrs. Leonard C. Mishkin

The Yeshiva Women of the Hebrew Theological College, Saul Silber Memorial Library, Skokie, Il., held a special program on April 28, 1976. The librarian, Mrs. Leonard C. Mishkin, gave a slide lecture on "The Lure and Lore of Bookplates." The lecture was developed around colored slide reproductions of thirty bookplates. Emphasis was placed on the personal story of the individual ex libris owner with much reference to the historical period and the artist.

An exhibit was arranged in the reference reading room; six plates were displayed in each picture frame (37"x7") mounted on white matting with a thin gold border frame. Explanations on gold poster board the same dimensions as the frame were placed next to picture and were typed in brown ink on white cards. A center display housed the most valuable plates, mounted on brown Strathmore paper: famous collectors with catalogs of their collections and early, rare, and handwritten bookplates.

LIFE NEWSPAPERS [Skokie, Illinois], April 15, 1976, pictured Mrs. Mishkin holding a book with the family crest embossed on a fine leather cover with the family bookplate inside, and the JEWISH UNITED FUND NEWS, April 1976, pictured ex libris indicating the profession of the owner.

Dr. Solomon Levadi designed the Hebrew Theological College bookplate in 1953. The crown of Torah tops the tablets of law, and they point with the yad to the symbolic tree of knowledge. The motto, taken from Avoth, implies that all sources of knowledge are to be found in the Study of Torah which will enlighten the world.

The CHICAGO SENTINEL, April 22, 1976, had a longer article on Mrs. Mishkin, who started collecting bookplates in 1951 and has close to 3,000.

— — — — — — — — — — — —

EUROPEAN BOOK PLATES. BIBLIOGRAPHI EX LIBRIS 1974, Klaus Rodel. Exlibristen, 1976. 107 pages, 83 illustrations of which 62 are tip-ins, Dkr. 80.00. Order from Klaus Rodel, Smedevej 20, Postboks 109, DK-9900 Frederikshavn, Denmark. This is an alphabetical listing of practicing bookplate artists which includes the address, sequencial numbering of ex libris, owner's name, size of plate and whether etching, engraving, zinc, etc. Numerous artists listed from Russia and Czechoslovakia as well as other European countries. A useful volume for all ex libris enthusiasts and helpful to those wishing to commission a bookplate.

— — — — — — — — — — — —

MICHAEL FINGENSTEN EXCHANGES SOUGHT - Heinz-G. Hintze, Chem. Eng., 2116 Hanstedt, Nordheide 4, Nindorf, Germany, will exchange YEAR BOOKS of the German Ex Libris for ex libris or other graphics of Michael Figensten.

AMERICAN PLANT SOCIETY BOOKPLATES

V. O. VIRKAU has designed an unusual series
of ex libris for American plant societies
and for individual collectors interested in
plants. Each society is devoted to the propagation, collecting, breeding, etc. of a particular plant. The artist, himself an amateur collector of a variety of plants including rare fruit trees, thought it would
be interesting to create ex libris for each
society. The series is distinguished by an
oval frame within which is the flower or
plant for that society, reproduced and a-
dopted for the design from a herbal or an
old book. The societies represented are
those for the daffodil, hemerocallis, iris,

lily, peony, and primrose. Individuals for whom plates have been similarly
designed are:
  Louis Smirnow, peony collector and breeder, Long Island, New York.
  D. K. Ourecky, small fruit breeder, Cornell University.
  R. A. Nitschke, rare and old fruit varieties collector, near Detroit.
  Dorothy Stemler, collector of old scrub roses, Watsonville, California.
  H. F. Jason, collector of rare fruit varieties, Toronto, Canada. (*)
  Isaac R. Hunter, collector of rare fruit varieties, specifically Mountain
                        Ashes, Dowagiac, Michigan.
  A. Miseviciute, strawberry and small fruit breeder, State Research Station,
                        Lithuania.
  (*) Editor's Note: Would anyone be interested in writing a short article
about bookplates devoted to fruit motifs for NORTH AMERICAM POMONA.

WANGENHEIM ROOM of the San Diego Public Library

Julius Wangenheim, born April 21, 1866 in San Francisco, graduated from the
University of California in 1887 . After college he became a bridge engineer

for the Southern Pacific Railroad. In
1895 he became a partner in the Klauber-
Wangenheim Co., wholesale grocers in San
Diego. Among his many civic activities
was helping to develop Balboa Park. In
1892 Julius Wangenheim married Laura
Klauber, and their home was the center
of San Diego's cultural life for more
than half a century. Following her
death in 1947 an offer of $10,000 to
furnish a reading room in the proposed
new San Diego Public Library was made by
the estate of Mrs. Laura K. Wangenheim;
a large portion of the private library
she and her husband had collected was
given to the city for use in the reading
room. The Wangenheim plate was designed
by his wife's sister, Alice Klauber. The
library has a scrapbook of plates designed
and collected by Alice Klauber.

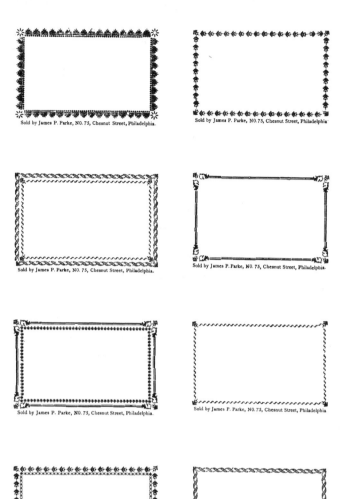

Sold by James P. Parke, NO. 75, Chesnut Street, Philadelphia.

AN AMERICAN PRINTER'S OFFER
of Borders for Bookplates, Circa 1811
by John Swingle

Recently I acquired a sheet of eight different borders, probably meant as borders for bookplates, which are reproduced to the left about half size. Under each border is the single line of type: Sold by James P. Parke, No. 75, Chesnut Street, Philadelphia.

All the borders measure approximately 1 3/4 x 3 inches, with some a bit more and some a bit less.

Through the courtesy of Mrs. Lillian Tonkin, Reference Librarian, The Library Company of Philadelphia, Parke has been placed at 75 "Chesnut" (as Parke spells it) as a bookseller and stationer in the year 1811.

Has anyone seen these borders used as bookplates? Please write John Swingle, at 422 North Coast Highway, Laguna Beach, Ca. 92651.

LIBRARY OF
WESTERN AMERICANA

THIS BOOK PROPERTY OF
E. A. BRININSTOOL
LOS ANGELES, CAL.

DATE.................... VALUE....................

DAWSON'S BOOK STORE Catalogue 438 was issued on the hundredth anniversary of the Battle of the Little Big Horn, Montana, June 25-26, 1876. E. A. Brininstool was one of the major authorities on this event, the others being Fred Dustin, Col. W. A. Graham, and Charles Kuhlman. The catalogue notes that Earl Alonzo Brininstool was born in Warsaw, New York, October 11, 1870. In 1895 he came to Los Angeles where he worked for the LOS ANGELES TIMES, LOS ANGELES RECORD, and LOS ANGELES EXAMINER. He wrote over 5,000 poems, mostly about cowboy and ranch life. The wide scope of his interests and contacts is shown in his personal library. He died in 1957.

A BIBLIOGRAPHY OF BOOKPLATE LITERATURE, George W. Fuller. Republished by Gale Research Company, Took Tower, Detorit, 1973. $13. This is an attractively bound reprint of the original Spokane Public Library volume published in 1926 with the bibliographical work by Verna B. Grimm and Some Random Thoughts on Bookplate Literature by Winward Prescott. The wide-margin format of the original volume has been retained but in slightly reduced size. While Fuller's bibliography did not include all the bookplate literature to 1926, it is still the best available for books. Fuller and the Arellanes bibliography of the periodical literature [also published by Gale Research, 1971, $15] are both useful reference tools.

GAYFIELD SHAW'S "FIRST AMERICAN COMMISSION" by Dean Keller

Among the papers which came to the Kent State University Libraries in 1969 with the acquisition of the library of the late B. George Ulizio of Haddonfield, New Jersey, was a letter from the Australian artist and engraver Gayfield Shaw. In this hand-written letter of two pages, dated September 11, 1933, Shaw described in detail two designs for a bookplate which Mr. Ulizio has commissioned him to design and engrave. Evidently Shaw sent sketches of both designs to Ulizio, but he asked that they be returned, and they are not now with the letter.

From the letter we learn than Ulizio wanted Shaw to engrave a bookplate as a gift for Ulizio's friend L. Berry. Unfortunately, we do not know who L. Berry was, nor do we know if Shaw ever actually executed a bookplate for this person. No copy of the bookplate was among the papers which came to Kent State, and it does not appear on the list of bookplates by Shaw which was published in YEAR BOOK 1939 of the American Society of Bookplate Collectors and Designers, Sewanee, Tennessee, The University Press, 1940, pages 13-14.

Shaw began his letter to Ulizio by expressing his regret that he did not know personally the person for whom he had submitted designs for a bookplate, for "To me book plates are more than mere labels and I like them to be as personal as possible and embody the aims, ambitions, etc. of my clients." Shaw then goes on to describe the designs he sent with the letter: "That in the left has as a base the initials L.B. worked into Rococco scrolls, combined with acanthus leaves & surrounded with flowers, symbolising the beauty of Life; whilst the trumpet, pipes & tambourine represent the music of Life--or song--or happiness; the torch stands for the Immortal Flame, Learning & the Passions or of Knowledge. Literature is represented in the bottom scroll of the letter B. No. 2 I have left or suggested a portal or porch for which can be substituted Mr. Berry's own home school or university, or any particular view. The Snuffed Candle is to point out you cannot burn the candle at both ends; the Quills for Writing or Correspondence."

Shaw then asks Ulizio to select the sketch he likes better adding that he and Mrs. Shaw favor the first design. He concludes the letter with the following: "I would like to add that it is my desire to make this, my first American commission, the best example of my work to date."

As a footnote to this fragmentary account of Gayfield Shaw's "first American commission," it may be of interest to note the bookplates by Shaw in Mr. Ulizio's collection. Ulizio was not an avid collector of bookplates, but among the books was a ledger in which he had placed those he had acquired over the years. Among the plates in this collection are nine engraved by Shaw. No doubt Mrs. Shaw was the source of these examples, for in a letter from her to Mr. Ulizio dated August 26, 1933, also in Kent State's collection, she wrote that she was "enclosing more prints for your collection. These are later plates of Mr. Shaw. . . ." She singled out the Francis Clune bookplate and her own bookplate for special notice. Here then is a list of the Shaw bookplates in Mr. Ulizio's collection in the Kent State University Library. If the bookplate is dated, the date is given, and this is followed by the number assigned to the plate in the 1939 YEAR BOOK cited above; the page in Mr. Ulizio's ledger on which the bookplate will be found is given in brackets.

Berckelman, Colin B. 27/5/33, #35 [17]   Ingram, W. W. Jan. 30, 1933, #33 [35]
Clune, Francis. Oct. 17, 1932, #25 [35]   O'Conor, Icey. Oct. 7, 1932, #19
Cowie, Rev. Geo. June 27, 1932, #21 or   Shaw, Gayfield. Mar. 20, 1933, #36 [33]
                          #24 [27]   Shaw, Gayfield. Undated, #37? [33]
Fitzpatrick, George. Dec. 22, 1932, #30 [35] Shaw, Jane. Nov. 20, 1932, #27 [51]

AS of BC & D

Bookplates in the News

429 NORTH DAISY AVENUE, PASADENA, CALIFORNIA, 91107

AUDREY SPENCER ARELLANES, Editor

Number Twenty-Six   October 1976

FEDERATION INTERNATIONALE des SOCIETES d'AMATEURS d'EX-LIBRIS
XVI Congress - 11 - 14 August 1976 - Lisbon
Reported by Frank W. Allen

The formal proceedings of the Congress were accomplished in one day, the second day of the meeting. Simultaneous translation into and from French, English
and Portuguese was available as was translation from German. The President of
this Congress, Senhor Artur Mario da Mota Miranda, gave the report to the Congressistes, including the proposal to affiliate FISAE with UNESCO and the admission to the Federation of the Societies of Finland and Canada.

There was a proposal to add a reporter as the sixth member of the Secretariat,
a permanent member of this body with the duties of encouraging member societies
and publishing a newsletter (REVUE EXLIBRIS) from Denmark. All proposals will
be taken up and decided upon by the Secretariat before the next Congress.

A jury of five members was selected as judges to determine winners of the three
categories of entries in the design competition held by the Portuguese Society
in connection with the Congress (your reporter was one of the five jury members).

The Czechoslovakian Society is not able yet to confirm its invitation to hold
the XVII Congress in Prague in 1978. It was given until December 31, 1976 to
do so. If at that time it is still unable to confirm, The Belgian Society offers
to host the Congress at the International Center for ExLibris in Sint Niklaas,
near Antwerp.

The afternoon portion of the meeting was devoted to papers; first a soliloquy
on the meaning of an ex libris read for a prominent Portuguese artist, who
could not be present; second, an historical note on an important early German-
Portuguese plate, and third and featured, an illustrated paper on "The Golden
Age of American Bookplate Design," by your reporter. The proceedings were concluded with a talk and film on Portugal from the ministry of tourism.
- - - - - -   - - - - - -   - - - -- - -   - - - - - -   - - - - - -

Lisbon - 1976, A Personal View by Verna M. S. Nescheler

Any ex librist fortunate enough to be present at an International Ex Libris
Congress will find it interesting and stimulating. The Congress is several
days of reports, addresses, exhibits, tours, dinners, and, like a conglomerate,
held together by constant exchanges and greetings of friendly people with a
pronounced empathy. I have attended two - the latest in Lisbon, and one in
Como, Italy in 1968; both were refreshing experiences.

The speech by Dr. Frank Allen was closely followed and well received, the first representative of the United States on the platform. The Calouste Gulbenkian Foundation is well suited to these activities. We toured the museum within the building. It houses exceptional art from ancient civilizations to the most recent. I was especially delighted with the Oriental rugs, oil paintings, and rare books.

We toured the city by bus stopping by the Tower of Belem, the very moving monument to Henry IV, the Navigator, where there is a colored marble sidewalk map of the world showing the places to which the Portuguese had voyaged and the ships they used. We visited the Jeronimos Cathedral with its remarkable columns of ancient but unknown origin. Then we bused to a high point over the city to see, at this hour, the city lights below us. From there we went to an older section where we had dinner while listening to Fado singers and watching north Portuguese dancers.

On the last day we visited the ocean resorts of Cascais, Estoril, and the most western edge of Europe - AND we all have a certificate with seal to prove it! The next stop was the Royal Palace of Sintra with its unusual mixture of styles symbolizing the peoples who had influenced Portugal. The very last event was a trip to St. George Fortress-Castle, which is directly above the city; here a buffet was prepared. Several speakers addressed the Congress and were answered by Senhor C. Chiesa of Lugano. The Mayor of Lisbon gave a speech of felicity, asserting the satisfaction of having the Ex Libris Congress in Lisbon. Afterward he sought out the Americans; he spoke with the Allens and me. I'd say he was greatly interested in the United States, having been here to visit relatives in southern New England a number of times. We spoke of many things about America, sports, highlights of his visits here and my visit to Lisbon. I'm certain his relatives are among our most enthusiastic citizens, he was so well oriented to the U.S.

Parting is ever nostalgic but harbors the hope of another meeting. The next Congress in 1978 is scheduled to meet in Prague with an alternate place near Antwerp, Belgium. There one wishes/thinks - "Could this happen in my country? Could the United States host such a Congress?" Europeans are interested.

- - - - - -   - - -   - - - - -   - - -   - - - - - -

EXCHANGES at the LISBON CONGRESS
by Frank W. Allen

As you will hear of other features of the XVI International Ex-Libris Congress from a different reporter, I shall confine myself to the single aspect of exchange. It is an important aspect - perhaps the most important and certainly the most time consuming of the entire Congress. Although there were three definite exchange sessions provided in the official program, the practice went on constantly - at lunch, in the bus taking us to see historic spots, even at the historic spots themselves!

Before leaving the States, our esteemed editor asked me to report on the mechanics of exchange and the formality involved. Let me assure you - it could not be much more informal or much more varied in execution. May I urge you, dear readers, when you attend the next Conference to go armed with as many copies of as many plates as you have available for this purpose, particularly your own plate or plates. It really matters little how many varieties you have (it is not a piece for piece deal), but you should have enough copies of each plate you bring - I would suggest 200 as an adequate number.

171

Participants use any variety of methods to exchange ex libris. Some have one copy of each plate they have available neatly boxed, and the box labelled as for the Congress. Others do the same, but use an envelope instead of a box. Still others carry albums with items neatly numbered - one chooses what he or she desires and is furnished with them on the spot, or on the next day, or even by mail after the Congress has adjourned and the congressistes have returned to their various countries.

Some have brief cases full of plates, with copies of each plate in separate envelopes (your reporter used this method). Some carry plates in their pockets, a different ex libris in each pocket. And one man, from Czechoslovakia, I believe, carried a cardboard carton 30" x 24" x 18" everywhere he went! So any way you want to make your exchanges available is acceptable.

Above all, do not be bashful. You will be buttonholed constantly, and urged to choose as many plates as you want, even though you may have only a few to offer yourself - you will have plates urged on you even when you are carrying none of your own for exchange. This happened to us on two occasions, but happily we were able to find the donors again and return the favor. But the common correspondence process of piece for piece exchange is just ignored at the International Congress.

Language is a problem, of course, but not an insurmountable one. We wished many times we were fluent in more languages, but still we managed; most west Europeans can converse in French, the Scandinavians and many Hungarians speak English. Even our very bad French was enough for purposes of exchange. And even when there is no common language (our German, for example, is execrable and our Portuguese non-existent) interpreters are readily found to willingly act as intermediaries. Without a doubt, exchange is the most important single activity of the Congress. It is the reason most participants attend. And it is a truly great way to make new friends.

- - - - - - -

O. PAUL KELLOW MEMORIAL EX LIBRIS

About a year ago, Paul Kellow fell to his death while rappelling on the Matterhorn near Zermatt, Switzerland. Paul was a great reader and had a large collection on mountaineering. Many of his friends sought to honor his memory by purchasing books to be given to the Sierra Club, Angeles Chapter library. The Kellow family donated his mountaineering books to the library. The Sierra group felt it appropriate to have a limited edition bookplate printed for both the purchased and donated collections. The plate was designed by Michael McKinney of Sierra Madre, Ca. The project was completed under the able direction of Louanne Kalvinskas.

This book, from the library of

O. PAUL KELLOW

has been given to the Sierra Club,

Angeles Chapter Library,

in his memory.

BOOKS of SCOTTISH INFLUENCE
and SIGNIFICANCE, A Special
Collection in the Library of
Florida State University

FROM SCENES LIKE THESE OLD SCOTIA'S GRANDEUR SPRINGS

THAT MAKES HER LOVED AT HOME, REVERED ABROAD.

A special collection to honor the Scottish folk
who conquered the wilderness of Northwest Florida

(Material for this article was gleaned
from the comments of John M. Shaw at
the dedication ceremony in Moore Auditorium, October 9, 1975, Florida
State University, Tallahassee.)

Soon after I came to Tallahassee fifteen years ago, I became aware of the
many families in this region who bear
the names with which I had been familiar in my boyhood home in western Scotland. They were the names that had
their origin in the Highlands and especially in the islands in which my
Gaelic-speaking mother and father were born, MacDonalds, MacDougalls, Campbells,
Monroes, MacLeods, MacKinnons, Mackays, Mackenzies, and more than a few Shaws.
After some discreet inquiry, I learned that this resulted from an influx of
Highland Scots, chiefly from North Carolina, into Quincy, Mariana and other
parts of Northwest Florida more than a hundred years ago. Since I knew that
whole families of Shaws and MacDougalls had left my father's native isle of
Jura for North Carolina in the last half of the 18th century, I had a strange
feeling that fate had brought me back in my old age to live among my own kin-
folk.

A year or so ago, while going through the storage shelves of this library in
search of books that might be added to my collection, I came upon quite a number of books of Scottish interest - history, genealogy, biography and other
similar subjects. I brought these to the attention of our new director, Mr.
Charles Miller, who agreed with me that these books should be made more accessible. I told him that if he would bring them together in one place, I would
make a gift to the University of my own Scottish collection. This has been
done. The collection is now shelved in my room in the special collections area.

The gift includes a distinctive bookplate designed by my sister Nan, who has
used her skill with pen and pencil to depict the house in which our grandmother,
Annie MacIsaac, was born. Her father, Alexander MacIsaac, was the miller and
piermaster on the island of Jura, and the scene shows the pier from which I am
convinced the ancestors of many Northwest Florida people started off on their
momentous journey to the new life in North Carolina. As an expression of our
confidence that the collection will grow, we have provided five thousand bookplates, and I expect it will not be long before we have to order another supply.

—   —   —   —   —   —   —   —

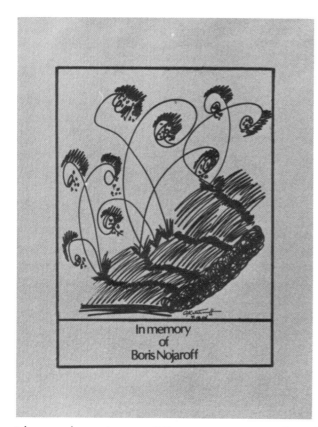

In memory
of
Boris Nojaroff

BORIS NOJAROFF MEMORIAL EX LIBRIS
by Norman E. Tanis

This bookplate, containing the drawing of an abstract figure, was inspired
by a period during 1964 when artist
Atanas Katchamakoff devoted two weeks
to listening to recordings of music
from different historical periods, particularly the modern and baroque. After digesting these sounds he created
twenty-nine acrylic crayon representations based on his listening experiences.
These works were drawn very quickly using
only one line each. The form and style
of the musical compositions were reflected in the drawings: close musical harmonies might be depicted by parallel
crayon lines, forte entrances of individual instruments might be designated
by brilliant jabs of color, angular lines
might reflect the neoclassicism of Stra-
vinsky. Katchamakoff, primarily a sculptor and painter, considers these drawings
his most important graphic work up to this
time, since he could never repeat the rhapsodic spontaneity.

He has chosen one of these twenty-nine drawings to decorate the bookplate commemorating the memory of his adopted son, Boris Nojaroff, who died in 1975. Boris
had been a United Nations translator, was well read, and an insatiable bibliophile. His collection of over two thousand books was given to California State
University, Northridge. All of the books from his collection, added to the permanent University collection, will bear this bookplate.

Atanas Katchamakoff was born in the village of Leskovertz, in the valley of the
Yantra, in Bulgaria. Always his work has been colored by the folklore, myths,
epics, and legends of Byzantium, Rome, Asia, and Slovakia. He recalls vividly
the traveling professional storytellers reciting the narrative of Alexander, the
Macedonian, and the Bulgarian hero-kings. His family home was a Byzantine house
filled with icons, locally woven rugs and tapestries; his father was a successful farmer. As with many creative artists, his first encouragement and opportunities came through his mother. It was she who convinced his father the boy
should be allowed to paint pictures on the white-washed walls of their home. At
his father's insistence, he completed law studies at the University of Sofia.
After passing the bar examination, he entered the Academy of Arts in Sofia, and
while a student married artist Alexandra Najarova. The couple moved to Paris,
and in 1924 moved to New York. Eventually they continued westward to Los Angeles
and La Quinta, between Palm Springs and Indio.

The Katchamakoffs founded the first art gallery and art school in Palm Springs.
In 1931 they became American citizens. Always a partner in her husband's activities, Alexandra Najarova shared Atanas' desire to give the Boris Nojaroff
Collection to California State University, Northridge. (Norman Tanis, Director
of University Libraries at Northridge, based his article on an exhibition catalog written by Diane Gordon.)

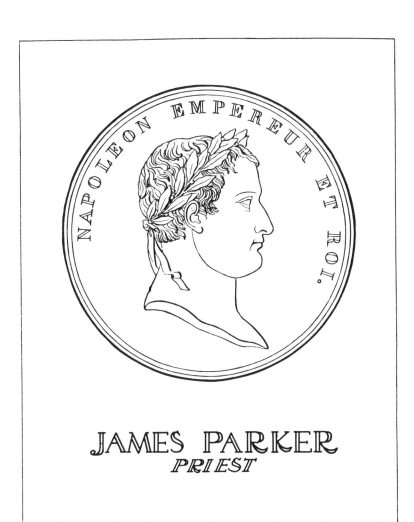

JAMES PARKER
PRIEST

In addition to an armorial plate used in his general library of books, Father James Parker has a special interest in Confederate history, and also is a student of Napoleon and things Napoleonic. The tipped-in ex libris is used in his comparatively large book collection dealing with the Emperor of the French. The seal design shows Napoleon in the classic bust profile wearing a laurel wreath. The French inscription refers to his thrones as Emperor of the French and King of Italy. The bookplate was printed offset on ivory paper.

- - - -- - - -

INDEX Available Shortly To
BOOKPLATES IN THE NEWS

Orders are now being accepted for the INDEX to the first five years of BOOKPLATES IN THE NEWS. The INDEX covers Number One through Twenty and is $5. The INDEX is divided into four sections: subject, author, artist, and the illustrations are defined as tip-ins or facsimiles. Richard Schimmelpfeng, Special Collections Librarian at the University of Connecticut, Storrs, has compiled the INDEX. The ASBC&D is much indebted to Mr. Schimmelpfeng for his generous use of time and professional skill in providing this useful key to finding specific references in the Society's quarterly newsletter. Our hope is for an INDEX of Number Twenty-one through Twenty-six, and a yearly index thereafter. Only a limited number of the INDEX will be published, including a title page - so place your order now.

YEAR BOOK 1976 - Bicentennial Edition . . . Orders now being accepted
Articles -
. Mary Alice Ercolini's personal ex libris
. More Diamond Lore by Verna Neuscheler
. Calligrapher James Hayes by Louis Ginsberg
. Rockwell Kent letters to Harry Geller
. Rockwell Kent by Dan Burne Jones
. Checklists: Hayes / Kent
. Tip-ins: 10 + many illustrations

for delivery in

November 1976

$19.76 to Members Only

($25.00 to non-members)

BOOKPLATES IN THE NEWS - 1976 / $5 U.S. & Canada / $6 Overseas
- - - - - - - - - - - - - -
BOOKPLATES IN THE NEWS, copyright 1976 by Audrey Spencer Arellanes . . . . .

THE BOOKS and BOOKPLATES
of B. GEORGE ULIZIO
by Dean H. Keller, Curator of
Special Collections, Kent
State University Libraries

B. George Ulizio was a name well known
in book collecting circles during the
1920s, '30s and '40s when he formed his
great collections of English and American literature. Since Mr. Ulizio did
not write about his collections or
otherwise seek publicity of them, he is relatively unknown today. He was born
in New Haven, Connecticut, in 1889, and he died in Haddonfield, New Jersey, in
1969. He was a business man whose diverse interests took him to New York City,
Atlantic City, and Philadelphia. By 1931 he was settled comfortably at Pine
Valley, New Jersey, moving later to Haddonfield. He numbered A. Edward Newton,
John Eckel, and Morris Parrish among his friends.

During his lifetime Ulizio assembled at least three major collections of books.
The first was sold in four sessions on January 28 through 31, 1931 and the second
in two sessions on October 30 and 31, 1935;
both sales were at the American Association
Anderson Galleries in New York. The third
collection was acquired by the Kent State
University Libraries, Kent, Ohio, in 1970.
Among the 1084 lots in the four sessions
of the 1931 sale were substantial collections,
including some manuscript and association material, of such English authors as James M. Barrie,
Lord Byron, Charles Dickens, Rudyard Kipling,
Thomas Hardy, Henry James, Robert L. Stevenson,
William Makepeace Thackary, and Oscar Wilde.
A prime Pickwick in the original parts that once
belonged to George Barr McCutcheon was in the sale,
as were Hardy's anonymous first book Desperate

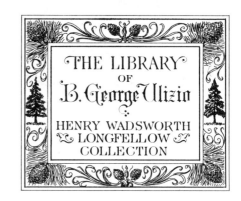

Remedies, the manuscript and corrected galley proofs of "New England" by Henry
James, Stevenson's The Pentland Rising, and Oscar Wilde's first book, The Newdi-
gate Prize Poem. Scattered through the sale were a number of rare works that
are not strictly literary, such as a leaf from the Gutenberg Bible, Blackstone's
Commentaries on the Laws of England, Darwin's On the Origin of Species, Smith's
An Inquiry into the Nature and Causes of the Wealth of Nations, and others.

While the 1931 sale was made up almost exclusively of English authors, the sale
of 1935 in 344 lots contained both English and American authors, with emphasis
on the Americans. The third of Mr. Ulizio's collections, that acquired by Kent
State University Libraries in 1970, follows the pattern of the first two collections. It consists of approximately 1500 volumes of English and American literature. From the collection now at Kent State it is evident that one of the
methods used in his collection was the list, such as those provided by Merle
Johnson in his High Spots of American Literature and Jacob Blanck in From Peter
Parley to Penrod. Association copies were also of great interest to Mr. Ulizio,
as they were to other collectors of the period. Of this group one of the most interesting books is the Wakeman copy of Robert Dinsmoor's Incidental Poems (1828),
notable because it contains a tribute to Dinsmoor by John Greenleaf Whittier and
is his first poem to appear in a book. The book contains a long letter from Dinsmoor to A. W. Thayer dated December 10, 1827, with the writer's comments on a
poem by Whittier, and it bears the bookplate of Whittier.

Mr. Ulizio liked very much the idea of collecting author's first books, and he
assembled a very impressive group of them. Another element of special interest

in the Ulizio collection at Kent State is a group of fifty-six copyright deposit copies of American and English literature dating from 1809 to 1906.

Like many book collectors, Mr. Ulizio identified his books with a bookplate. For the several author collections he developed, he had designed a standard border of pine trees and pine cones to represent his home at Pine Valley, no doubt. The border enclosed the words "The Library / of / B. George Ulizio" followed by the name of the author collected. We have been able to identify bookplates in this style for the following author collections: James M. Barrie, Wilkie Collins, Ralph Waldo Emerson, George Gissing, H. Rider Haggard, Thomas Hardy, Bret Harte, Nathaniel Hawthorne, Washington Irving, Rudyard Kipling, Henry Wadsworth Longfellow, James Russell Lowell, George Meredith, A. Edward Newton, Charles Reade, George Bernard Shaw, Robert Louis Stevenson, A. C. Swinburne, Mark Twain, John Greenleaf Whittier, and Oscar Wilde. The names are given here as they appear on the bookplate. A copy of one of these ex libris accompanies this article.

Mr. Ulizio also commissioned the noted nature artist Richard Evett Bishop to design a bookplate for him that he could use in his general collections. Evidently Ulizio admired Bishop's work, for he owned a number of signed prints of waterfowl by him, some of which are now at Kent State, and he had a copy of the de luxe edition of Bishop's Birds: Etchings of Waterfowl and Upland Game Birds, Philadelphia, 1936, in his library. The bookplate depicts a scene in a living room with a fire in fireplace and a dog reclining on the hearth. The full plate was made in at least two sizes, 4 3/4" x 3 1/4" and 2 3/4" x 1 3/4", and details from the drawing were used on small blue and maroon leather plates, lettered "Ex Libris / B. George / Ulizio" in gilt.

Mr. Ulizio's daughter Patricia was also interested in books and book collecting, and some of the books in the collection bear her bookplate. It was designed for her by J. H. Fincken in 1939.* The plate has a border of books and names of authors surrounding a center panel containing books, a lamp, lyre, hour glass, artist's palette and brushes, and laurel leaves. Two pine trees are seen through a window, and there is the following motto: "Beauty is truth, truth beauty."

(Editor's note: * - There is an article about J. H. Fincken with a checklist of his bookplates in BOOKPLATES IN THE NEWS, Number Twenty-one, July, 1975.)

— — — — — — — — — — —

EXHIBITS Contemporary Lithuanian Bookplates, September 19 to October 20, 1976, at the 2nd Street Gallery in Charlottesville, Virginia, presents a selection of the work of twenty Lithuanian artists from the collection of Vitolis E. Vengris. An attractive flyer, with two illustrations, has been printed which gives a few biographical details about each of the twenty artists represented including ASBC&D member Vytautas O. Virkau.

The Ottawa (Canada) Public Library exhibited Bookplates by Vytautas O. Virkau from September 15 to October 31, 1976. THE CITIZEN newspaper of Ottawa, September 27, 1976, had an interesting article by Martha Scott, "Exhibit of bookplates - Artful prints in miniature," with two illustrations, which resulted from the library exhibit. Referring to Virkau's work, she writes: "The detail in the graphics, in scale and in technical expertise, is substantial, but even more rewarding are the whimsical dream-like images they depict. .... Virkau's personal concerns for nature are reflected in each bookplate. However, as each was designed for a specific person, each contains a separate spiritual identity."

Exhibit at Philosophical Research Society (3910 Los Feliz Boulevard), Los Angeles, September 12 through October 31, 1976. While the library is small, it is well porportioned, with ample exhibit area spaced between the leaded glass, recessed book cases. Additional exhibit space has been utilized on a shelf beneath the cases running the length of the library; bevel edged glass keeps prints flat and protected. This is the first time the Society has exhibited its collection which is well represented by the "Little Masters". A varied selection was made to include armorial, large European ex libris which assume the dimensions of framable prints, proof states of plates Barrett designed for Queen Alexandria and Queen Mary of England, and ex libris of the famous and the infamous.

\-   \-   \-   \-   \-   \-   \-   \-

PETER RUSHTON MAVERICK
by Frank W. Allen

Seldom does a bookplate engraver match his name. Doolittle, for example, actually did quite a lot. But Maverick is the exception. Although mentioned in all the standard reference works (Thieme-Becker, Benezit, Dunlap, Stauffer and Fielding) and easily the most prolific of American engravers of the period, he is probably the least collected and least considered of all, truly a maverick among his peers.

Peter Rushton Maverick was born in England in 1755 and came to New York about 1774 where he lived, worked, and taught until his death in 1807. Like so many other bookplate engravers, he was originally a silversmith and was descended from a long line of ancestors practicing the same craft. Carrying on the tradition he taught his own sons, Peter and Samuel, and was also the genesis of the knowledge for William Dunlap and Francis Kearney.

There exists a very interesting collection of proofs kept by Maverick, and now in the library of the New York Historical Society, which contains thirty-eight varieties signed by him as well as others unsigned but undoubtedly his work, and also examples by Dawkins, Hutt, and Child.

Fincham lists sixty-eight plates by Maverick, Allen records fifty-six signed and sixteen attributed to him as well as five which he believes to have been executed by the younger Peter. The great majority of Maverick's plates are Ribbon and Wreath style, but there are examples of Jacobean and Chippendale, and he did (rather badly) one or two pictorial and allegorical designs. In his delineation he used the same features over and over, and gives the impression of a rapid, perhaps careless worker.

\-   \-   \-   \-

FROM THE BOOKPLATE LITERATURE

JAROSLAV SVAB, published by ExlibRisten (Klaus Rodel, P.O. Box 109, 9900 Frederikshavn, Denmark), September 1975. A tri-lingual introduction is followed by thirty-six illustrations, all but eight of which are ex libris, and a chronological vita which mentions some of his special honors. Many of the ex libris are printed in color or at least have some small touch of color. Svab was born in 1906 in Moravia. He has been active in the artistic life of Czechoslovakia, both as a creative artist and as an educator. From 1935 to 1948 he was the leader of the important private school of art, Officina Pragensis in Prague. There is a portrait of the artist in his studio. This soft-bound book, 7½" x 9½", maintains the fine standards to be expected of a Rodel publication.

EX-LIBRIS REVIE. Vol. 2, #2, 1976. The program of the Lisbon Congress is presented tri-lingually; only one other article has a brief English summary, that on Polish artist Jerzy Piotrowicz, born in 1943. Four of his plates are illustrated. There are about eighteen ex libris illustrated to accompany an article on Max Kislinger; nine beautiful black and white ex libris by Daniel Meyer, and twenty plates by Anatoli Kalaschnikow, USSR, who uses white lines on black to superb effect.

(Editor's Note: TRANSLATORS WANTED - Are there any members, who read any of the European languages in which the foreign ex libris journals are published, who would volunteer to furnish a summary in English to be printed in BOOKPLATES IN THE NEWS?? Please contact the editor if you are interested.)

THE ILLUSTRATIONS OF ROCKWELL KENT, Selected by Fridolf Johnson. New York: Dover Publications, 1975. Two hundred and thirty-one examples from books, magazines, and advertising have been selected with the collaboration of John F. H. Gorton, Director of the Rockwell Kent Legacies; the large format of the book permits full size reproduction of book illustrations and advertising art. A generous number of bookplates are also reproduced. In his introduction, Fridolf Johnson says: "Kent also had the gift for creating simple, compact vignettes of strong design admirably adaptable to page decorations, signets, and bookplates." A chronological list of the books from which the illustrations are drawn is excellent as it includes full bibliographical reference with edition limitation.

PRINTING IMPRESSIONS, "Typographically Speaking: It's Time to Bring Back the Colophon," Alexander S. Lawson. 18:38, May 1976. "If the bookplate is to the book what the collar is to the dog - as the artist Edward Gordon Craig is reputed to have remarked - then the colophon is to the book what the hallmark is to the silversmith."

— — — — — — — —

EX LIBRIS CONGRESS IN THE U.S. ??   The question of having the International Ex Libris Congress in the United States was raised by Verna Nescheler, who has just returned from attending the most recent congress in Lisbon. Such a meeting would entail a considerable amount of planning. Of almost equal importance would be to determine who would actually attend - both from abroad and within our own country - and where the meeting could be held which would be easily accessible to those coming from Europe as well as our own members and would be in an environment hospitable to the ex libris artist, collector, and enthusiast. If an Ex Libris Congress in the United States is to be anything more than a wish, it will require committment of time and energy by individuals and institutions to make such an event a success. Let's hear from you!

— — — — — —

NEW MEMBERS   CHARLES ANTIN, 50 East 89th Street, New York, NY 10028; THE EVERGREEN PRESS, Malcolm Nielson, P.O. Box 4971, Walnut Creek, CA 94596; HELEN A. GAFFNEY, 322 East Withrow Ave., Oxford, OH 45056; CHRISTOPHER HARTMANN, Kanawha County Public Library, Extension Dept., 123 Capitol St., Charleston, W.VA 25301; LINDA HERMAN, Box 4150, Fullerton, CA 92634; KNUD HOLAR, Skvadronsgatan 8, S-217 52 Malmo, Sweden; HELEN HUREWITZ, 353 Hempstead Ave., Rockville Centre, NY 11570; PETER JOHNSON, Circle Gallery, 315 South Main, El Dorado, KS 67042; EDWARD KRISCH, 3160 Grant Ave., Philadelphia, PA 19114; Ralph 7 Terry Kovel, 22000 Shaker Blvd., Shaker Heights, OH 44122; JOHN E. WILSON, 1117 Lee St., Wyandotte, MI 48192.

AS of BC & D

Bookplates in the News

429 NORTH DAISY AVENUE, PASADENA, CALIFORNIA, 91107
AUDREY SPENCER ARELLANES, Editor

Number Twenty-seven   January 1977

Jørgen Vils-Pedersen, who lives in Copenhagen, Denmark, was born September 17, 1936. He dates his interest in ex libris to a large exhibition held in the spring of 1966; since that time he has put together a collection of 10,000 to 15,000 ex libris and other graphic works. Jørgen regularly corresponds with more than two hundred collectors and artists, with as many as 2,000 exchanges during the year. In addition to collecting bookplates, he is interested in ex libris literature. To quote his recent letter, "Besides the exchanging of ex libris and graphic things, I find the personal contact both in letters and by ex libris meetings around the world very important."

Vils-Pedersen works in the Royal Library in Copenhagen. Besides books and ex libris, his interests include music, film making, travel.

As with most bookplate collectors, Jørgen has special designs which he collects in depth; these include: flowers, birds, music, books, cats, erotica, wine, acting. The two plates tipped in feature birds. Below is one designed by Hungarian artist Moskal Tibor in 1975. Hans Michael Bungter of East Germany designed a plate for him in 1967 which also depicts a bird and a bar of music above with the notes of the bird's song. Both prints are multi-colored.

In 1974 Vils-Pedersen published INTERNATIONAL EXCHANGE LIST which contained the names and addresses of 240 collectors and 370 artists; the 90 pages included advertisements, a list of graphic books, and Jørgen's personal exchange list No. 8. Copies are still available at $5 (cash, no checks).

With about 260 personal bookplates, Vils-Pedersen would welcome exchanges and correspondence; his address is
 Box 2094
 DK-1013 Copenhagen K, Denmark

Jørgen was among those lucky enough to spend part of his 1976 holiday attending the Ex Libris Congress in Lisbon.

BOOKPLATES of GROLIER CLUB MEMBERS   The only other time the Grolier Club
            Charles Antin   exhibited anything about bookplates
                                         was in 1909, so this exhibit is long
overdue! Bookplates are often called <u>ex libris</u> from the Latin words meaning
"from the books of." Bookplates may be considered slight and insignificant
to the uninitiated but not to the book or bookplate collector. Lawrence Clark
Powell once wrote: "An old book which bears no plate or mark of ownership is
a book only half alive. It is the touch of a man's hand on a beloved object
which bestows immortality." Edward Gordon Craig, the actor and theatrical designer, supported himself during his lean years by designing, carving, and
printing woodcut bookplates. He said, "I always remember this and always feel
grateful toward the whole world of bookplates and bookplate collectors, users
and makers."

The exhibition, which opened in November of 1976 and
continues to March 31, 1977, features more than 200
personal ex libris of living members of the Grolier
Club, 47 East 50th Street, New York City. The bookplates have been designed and executed by many outstanding artists, typographers, calligraphers, and
printers; they have been arranged for display under
the headings of various styles - armorial, calligraphic, typographic, illustrative, those printed
on leather, and bookplates expressly designed by
Grolier members who have donated books to libraries

and institutions. Members also reveal how and why they came to select their ex
libris and who designed and executed them.

It has been a heartening experience to display this collection of bookplates
and to find so many designs revealing a love of books, homes, hobbies, family
traditions, and humanity in general. We hope they inspire you, the serious
collector and general reader, to desire a bookplate of your own.

(Editor's note: PRINTING NEWS, November 13
and 20, 1976, contained notices of the exhibit.)

—   —   —

BUNGTER DESIGNER OF VILS-PEDERSEN EX LIBRIS

Hans Michael Bungter, who designed the ex
libris tipped-in to the left, was born in
Leipzig on June 8, the son of a book printer.
He died September 21, 1969. Bungter designed
about 150 ex libris and many occasional
cards. When he was 14, he became the pupil of
a painter and he continued in art school until the war in 1915 changed his life to that
of a soldier. Following the war, he resumed
his studies with well-known artists such as
Tiermann, Kolb, Delitsch, and Buhe. He worked
with oil paints, water colors, and learned to
do woodcuts and etchings. Articles about this
artist have appeared in a number of European
graphic and ex libris journals, the earliest
dated 1930, the most recent 1965.

LANKES DESIGN for RICHARDS-FROST
COLLECTION at BOSTON UNIVERSITY

On September 3, 1975, Boston University dedicated a new collection of Robert Frost papers
which were the gift of Rev. Paul C. Richards,
retired antiquarian book and autograph dealer.
The Richards-Frost Collection, which is in the
Mugar Memorial Library, contains manuscripts,
letters, notebooks, and first editions of the
poet's works. This collection evolved as the
result of Richards meeting the poet in 1958
when Frost was giving one of his "evening read-
ings" at Hayden Hall; Richards was then a
sophmore at Boston University.

After Apple Picking   JJLankes

THE RICHARDS-FROST COLLECTION
GIVEN BY
PAUL C. RICHARDS
IN LOVING THOUGHT OF HIS PARENTS

A special bookplate was designed for use in
the collection, which was given by Richards
"in loving thought of his parents."   J. J.
Lankes, well known for his illustrations and
bookplate designs, did illustrations for a
number of early Frost publications; so it
was appropriate that his "After Apple Picking" should be selected for the commemorative ex libris. Lankes designed two bookplates for Frost during his lifetime; they
are #35 and #89 in A DESCRIPTIVE CHECKLIST
OF THE WOODCUT BOOKPLATES OF J. J. LANKES
published by Burl N. Osburn in 1937, with a foreword by Charles Harris Whitaker.
The earliest plate, designed in 1923, showed a "winter landscape with house";
the description seems to fit the ex libris tipped-in above; the second plate is
an apple tree and grindstone.

Lankes' work was written about by Wilbur Macey Stone in a 49 page booklet with
fifteen illustrations titled LANKES: HIS WOODCUT BOOKPLATES, published by the
Apple Tree Press of New York in 1922. He has also been the subject of a number
of periodical articles appearing in the BOOKPLATE ANNUAL, BOOKPLATE CHRONICLE,
PRINTING & GRAPHIC ARTS, and NEWS-LETTER OF THE LXIVMOS. The last journal, which
is devoted to miniature books, has an article by Wilbur Macey Stone on miniature
bookplates which uses as illustration the woodcut ex libris Lankes did for the
author. Ray Nash in his PAGA article mentions that Lankes has 1224 woodblocks
"enumerated and annotated in his forty-year record book." One article mentioned in Irving Lew's Catalogue of Books and Pamphlets Relating to Bookplates as
appearing in BOOK DIAL, Midsummer 1929, entitled "Bookplates by J. J. Lankes"
has been impossible to locate in that publication; if anyone knows the correct
citation, your editor would welcome the information.

— — — — —   — — — — —

ATTENTION UNIVERSITY / COLLEGE / MUSEUM LIBRARIES   The special collections of
                                                    many institutional librar-
ies undoubtedly have commemorative bookplates designed for collections they acquire much as Boston University in the article above. BOOKPLATES IN THE NEWS
would welcome the opportunity to feature a story about your library, the special collection, and the bookplate designed for use in its volumes.

FROM THE BOOKPLATE LITERATURE . . . . . .

THE BOOKPLATE, Journal of the American Bookplate Society (edited by Clifford N. Carver), two issues only for January and June 1914:

Membership, 10-26, January 1914. The names and address of 102 members listed.

Bookplates by Frank G. House, illustrations only for Rowland Winn (27), artists' (32), Phoebe Gregory (37), January 1914.

Announcements, 29, January 1914. THE BOOKPLATE is the first journal of the American Bookplate Society; thanks extended to Alfred Fowler for permitting use of his own journal as a medium for the Society during its first year of existence.

Correspondence, 31-2, January 1914. Letters printed from presidents of French and German societies to whom were extended invitations to be honorary vice presidents.

The Jabberwocky of the Bookplates, 35-6, January 1914. Clever parody with due apologies to Winward Prescott.

Victorian Bookplates, Clifford N. Carver, 39-42, January 1914. Chief fault of Victorian-era bookplates is a lack of character by which Carver meant lack of "expression of the owner's individuality."

Augustus Meredith Nanton, 43, January 1914. Illustration only.

The Extra-Illustration of Bookplate Books, Winward Prescott, 45-9, January 1914. ". . . the Bookplate Grangerite may extra-illustrate to his heart's content and never fear that unpleasant names will be applied to him . . . . (he) does not tear up or destroy any books but mounts his plates and extends his cherished volumes and leaves holes only in his Bookplate collection."

Recent Bookplate Literature, Clifford N. Carver, 50-1, January 1914. Mentioned are THEATRICAL BOOKPLATES by A. Winthrop Pope, "Bookplates, Ancient and Modern," by J. F. Badeley in COUNTRY LIFE for January 17, 1914, and MARQUIS von BAYROS printed in an edition of 25 copies for W. R. A. Hayes and Winward Prescott which is described as "for its sphere it is inimitable."

American Bookplate Society Constitution, 11-2; Officers, 13, June 1914.

Meeting, 15, June 1914. Fourth meeting held February 2, 1914 at the Hotel Wolcott in New York City with twenty members in attendance.

Thomas Kensett, William A. Beardsley, 16, June 1914. Firm of Shelton and Kensett in Cheshire, Connecticut, published a number of Amos Doolittle's plates. Kensett died June 16, 1829.

Cleaning Bookplates, 20, June 1914. Use three parts hot water to 1 part of chloride of lime. Bleach, then stand in water 24 hours, change water two or three times. If cockled, place hot iron on back to remedy.

Press Bookplates, H. Alfred Fowler, 21-5, June 1914. Several illustrations include ex libris for the Doves Press, Eragny Press plate designed by Pissarro.

Recent Bookplate Articles, 27, June 1914. An article in the SYDNEY MAIL on January 14, 1914 by P. Neville Barrett, "In the Library: Bookplates for the Art Gallery;" others in Baltimore EVENING NEWS, Brooklyn DAILY EAGLE, Boston EVENING TRANSCRIPT.

Notes, 28-30, June 1914. Mr. Carver will be in England at Trinity College.

Augustin Daly Bookplate, 31-2, June 1914. Daly was noted a theatre manager. His ex libris was printed in red on gray paper and made at least two years before his death. In reduced size it was affixed to china, etc. at his estate auction.

Dr. Radin's Bookplate, 33-35, June 1914. Ex libris engraved by Timothy Cole in December 1913; it shows book opened to title page of William Harvey's treatise on circulation of the blood.

Heartman Sale in New York, 36, June 1914. Auction held in February of 1914; due to inclemency of the weather the attendance was down.

Exhibition, 37-8, June 1914. Featured George W. Eve plates assembled by

Pierre la Rose of Cambridge for the print room of Fogg Art Museum at Harvard.
  Checklist of Bookplates Designed by Alfred J. Downey 1907-1914, 39-47, June 1914.
  Mrs. J. Winfred Spenceley, 49, June 1914. The artist's wife died March 1, 1914.

BAHUMIL KROTKY, (Klaus Rodel, Exlibristen, Postboks 109, DK-9900 Frederikshavn, Denmark). This painter, born in 1913 in Prague, studied art including a year at Ecole des Beaux-Arts in Paris. This book contains fourteen ex libris prints, each bears the plate mark, is numbered in an edition of 200, and signed by the artist. Most are printed multi-color, mostly in blue and red in muted shades which are reminescent of colored lithography earlier in this century. The fourteen prints, each mounted on a separate sheet, are housed in an attractive portfolio; there is a brief multi-lingual text. Price: Dkr 60,00.

EXLIBRIS GREETING, Klaus Rodel. In 1967 Rodel issued his first publication, an index of the first eighteen volumes of N.E.T., the Danish bookplate society's publication; the current volume is sent to subscribers to the subsequent volumes in appreciation. There are twenty-five ex libris prints tipped-in; they represent a wide variety of designs, methods of production, textures, colors. Most are for Klaus or his wife Inge.

BOOKPLATE DESIGNERS 1925-75, Catalogue of the Bookplate Society's Third Biennial Exhibition. The exhibit was held at the National Book League, London, October 16-28, 1976. There is an index to the catalogue, and the 292 plates in the exhibit was described; the catalogue is arranged alphabetically by artist, with a brief paragraph about each artist including vital dates. Among artists represented by several prints are Robert Sargent Austin, Henry John Fanshawe Badeley, Diana Bloomfield, Simon Brett, Will Carter, John Farleigh, George T. Friend, Eric Gill, John Buckland Wright, Leo Wyatt, David Kindersley, Michael Renton, Stephen Gooden, Joan Hassall, Leonard Ison, Mark Severin, Reynolds Stone, Rex Whistler. There are 78 plates reproduced.

SOL LUCET OMNIBUS. XVI CONGRESSO INTERNATIONAL de EX-LIBRIS, Lisboa-1976. This publication was dedicated to the participants of the Congress and contains the work of a highly esteemed Danish artist, Blaesbjerg. Each plate uses the motto of the Congress: Sol lucet omnibus (the sun shines over all the world). The plates, printed multi-color or at least black and gold, are tipped-in on the right-hand page, and on the left in four languages, including English, is a brief sentence warmly interpreting the design.

KRYSTYNA WROBLEWSKA by Bogna Jakubowska. (Published by Exlibristen, 1976). This is the tenth ex libris publication about this practioner of the minature graphic art of bookplate designing. Until a short time ago Bogna Jakubowska taught art in a polytechnical high school in Cracow, where she was professor of architecture. Fifteen woodcuts are illustrated. Her interest in music is frequently evident in her designs. This is an attractive oblong book with 16 pages of introduction presented in four languages including English. Price: Dkr. 35,00.

DANSK EXLIBRIS LITTERATUR by H. C. Skov (Exlibristen, 1976, price DKR. 55,00) is a bibliography of Danish ex libris literature in a volume about the same size as the Gale reprint of the Fuller volume. It comprises "all printed material about book-plates in Denmark. Thus, articles appearing in foreign yearbooks, periodicals are not registered." The bibliography covers 2,142 items in several categories which are basically in chronological order; 60 illustrations, of which 23 tipped-in. (H.C. Skov, Husarvej 13, I, DK-8900 Randers, Denmark.)

ANTIQUARIAN BOOK MONTHLY REVIEW, Fifty Years of Bookplate Design, Brian North Lee. (16) 3:246-52, September 1976. The Third Annual Exhibition sponsored by the Bookplate Society of England was held at the National Book League, October 16-28, 1976. Brian North Lee, who writes well and with authority, gives a wealth of material about bookplate designers from 1925-1975, all English except Mark Severin, a Belgian who worked many years in England.

THE PRIVATE LIBRARY, The Bookplate Designs of Walter Crane. (2) Second Series 8:164-5, Winter 1975. Liesel and Walter Schwab offer two more bookplates by Walter Crane in addition to the ten mentioned by Keith Clark (Second Series 8:#2).

FEDERATION INTERNATIONALE DES SOCIETES D'AMATEURS D'EX-LIBRIS, Artistas de Ex-Libris. (Published in Portugal, 1976, $15) This is volume III published by F.I.S.A.E., and is issued in conjunction with the recent 16th International Ex Libris Congress held in Lisbon under the presidency of Artur Mario Da Mota Miranda. An artist from each of seventeen bookplate societies is represented by a biographical sketch and up to eight tipped-in bookplate prints. The societies are in Portugal, Poland, France, Spain, Switzerland, Germany, Hungary, Italy, United States, Holland, Denmark, Belgium, Austria, Czechoslovakia, Yugoslavia, and Canada. The text of each entry is in the language of the society's home country. Anthony F. Kroll represented the ASBC&D with eight prints and the article was written by Audrey Spencer Arellanes. A partial checklist of Kroll's ex libris numbered seventeen, among them the armorial for Roberta Frank Watkins, here tipped-in. Other artists represented are Daniel Meyer, Oriol M. Divi, Aldo Patocchi, Isaias Peixoto, Zbigniew Jozwik, Oswin Volkamer, Nandor Lajor Varga, Italo Zetti, Lou Strik, Jørgen Lindhardt Rasmussen, Norbert Ott, Hedwig Zum Tobel, Andrusko Karoly, Frank-Ivo Van Damme, Vojtech Cinybulk, Sylvia Paradis, and Louis Frechette. The artists offer great variety in their approach to the bookplate - in design and in printing with colors and textures. However limited your reading knowledge of European languages, the visual delights of the tipped-in prints are well worth the price of the volume.

NEWSLETTER, The Bookplate Society. #14, June 1976. Meetings and Exhibitions, 9. The June meeting was held at Gray's Inn Library; Reynolds Stone gave an illustrated talk on his work in April. Philip Beddingham mounted an exhibition of bookplates in January at Colchester College and at the Ipswich Art School in May. Additionally Philip Beddingham and Freda Constable were interviwed briefly on Radio Orwell, the local commercial broadcasting service. A dozen drawings and finished bookplates by Kokoshka were on exhibit at the Victoria and Albert Museum mid-1976. - The Bookplates of EE Dorling, Arthur Dorling. (4) 10-13. Edward Earle Dorling (1863-1943) was a schoolmaster before he took holy orders. Two subjects which fascinated him were archaeology and heraldry; thus to bookplates. He created 70 which are given in an alphabetic list and briefly described. - Bookplate Designs of EH New(1871-1931). Anthony Pincott is preparing a monograph on Edmund Hort New and requests information about this bookplate artist. - Identification Queries, 14. This series of inqueries carries on the tradition of the JOURNAL OF THE EX LIBRIS SOCIETY in attempting to identify artists who sign only their initials, etc. - Books and Articles, 14. Philip Beddingham wrote on Essex bookplates in ESSEX COUNTRYSIDE. A half dozen free ex libris are being offered as a promotional item by Book Tokens; color advertisements appeared in WOMAN'S OWN, WOMAN'S JOURNAL, GOOD HOUSEKEEPING, READER'S DIGEST, and THE DAILY TELEGRAPH COLOUR MAGAZINE, THE BOOKSELLERS (all English publications). - Francis Carter's Bookplate, (1), 15. Carter, a well-known collector of Spanish coins and books, was elected a Fellow of the Society of Antiquaries in 1777. - Richard Ford's Bookplate, (1) 15-6. Ford was the first man to really bring the work of Velasquez to the notice of the British public. - Members' Bookplates, (9), 16-7. Those reproduced are for Christian F. Verbeke, M. G. J. Rhebergen, Philip Beddingham, John H. Orpen, and the Dean of Gloucester. - Tracking Down the Owners of Bookplates, (3), 19-20. Quotation from the Bookplate Exchange Club manuscript Notes and Queries in 1951. Mention is also made of an article by Charles Hall Crouch on Whitbread bookplates in THE HOUSE OF WHITBREAD, magazine of the Whitbread group of companies, 1949, volume 9, #4, pages 7-11. -New Members, 20. Two named.

NEWSLETTER, The Bookplate Society, #15, September 1976. Meetings and Exhibition, 21. The National Book League will be the site of the 1976 exhibit, Bookplate Designers 1925-1975. A catalogue may be ordered from Anthony Pincott, 3B, Hurlingham Court, Ranelagh Gardens, London SW6 3UN, England at a cost of 65 pence. It is well worth the cost. - Early American Bookplates, 22. The Victoria and Albert Museum had an exhibit "American Art: 1750-1800 Towards Independence," which contained eight early American ex libris; a catalogue may be ordered for £3. - Visit of M. Paul-Andre Fournier, 22. Canadian who formed Society of Canadian Amateurs and Collectors of Engravings and Ex Libris visited England on way to Congress in Lisbon. - New Members, 22. Six additional members. - Bookplates from the Owen Collection, 22-3. While all the modern plates by fine engravers are gone, there still remain Jacobeans, Chippendales, etc. in packets at £5 or £3. - Mr. Gilson's Book Label, 23. Designed by Reynolds Stone and printed by Will Carter. - Bookplates Signed 'W.P.B.', 23. Initials of William Phillips Barrett who was employed by J. & E. Bumpus & Co from about 1896 to 1928. - Bookplates Designed by C. Helard, 23. "C. Helard" was the "nom de guerre" of Mary Ellen Blanche, eldest daughter of Septimum Wilkinson Crookes. - Russian Prerevolutionary Bookplates by E. N. Minaev and S. P. Furtinskii, translated and adapted by William E. Butler, 24-34.(4) The article is reprinted from EKSLIBRIS, Moscow, izd-vo Kniga, 1970, in which it was chapter 2. - Offers and Requests, 35. Photocopy of THE BOOKPLATE COLLECTORS NEWS, edited by A. B. Keeves, is available from Peter Summers, % NEWSLETTER, 32 Barrowgate Road, London W4 4QY, England, at £3.75. - Aina Bjorck's Bookplates, 36. Miss Bjorck has seventeen personal bookplates, fourteen of which were designed and printed during 1976.

STUDIO, The Modern Spirit in the Art of the Bookplate. (23) 248-57, November 15, 1922. Most of the illustrations are ex libris by James Guthrie; others by Ida Swaine, Y. Urushibara, W. Giles, Ronald Simpson. "There is something to be said for any art which, in spite of all direct and insidious attacks upon its existence, not only continues in a traditional form but gathers new force and finds new grounds for continuance. . . . For, in our modern freedom from 'fabulous beasts and storied utensils,' there is no doubt about us being set a harder task if we would find for each person some device as truly his own as the old science of heraldry was able to construct by means of established and systematic blazonry."

EX LIBRIS for MORLEY COLLECTION
Herman Abromson

For quite some time I had been
dreaming of a bookplate for my
growing collection of Christopher
Morley books. However, the way the
bookplate finally came into being
was most unusual. I had done a
small favor for Harvey Dinnerstein,
one of America's outstanding illustrators and artists. In return
he offered me one of his pictures.
I selected a watercolor from a
series of illustrations he had done
for some Sherlock Holmes material
published by Macmillan.

Some years later, I was talking about those illustrations to Lew Feldman of the
House of El Dieff. He thought the University of Texas would want to buy the illustrations, but only if they could get the complete set, including the one in
my possession. Of course, I returned my illustration to Dinnerstein so he could
sell the series to the University. Now he asked me to choose another painting or
drawing to take the place of the one I had just returned. Instead of selecting
something from his studio, I asked the artist to do a drawing that I could use as
a bookplate for my Christopher Morley collection. Harvey asked all about Morley
and read his books. After he felt fully acquainted with the author, he drew the
design for the bookplate. I was delighted with it as soon as I saw it.

It refers to Morley's hero in his book PARNASSUS ON WHEELS, the story of an itinerant bookseller who travels about with horse and wagon, selling books from the
wagon and singing the praises of the great books of that era. In the drawing,
Dinnerstein pictured a horse and wagon, but added a caricature of Morley himself
as the bookseller. Morley, who was usually seen smoking his pipe, is portrayed
with pipe in mouth and some books in his hand, standing just outside the book
wagon. The ex libris is on the wagon, the artist's initials are in the corner of
the drawing, and there is a facsimile of Morley's signature just below the drawing. I have always felt that the drawing was just right, and enjoyed having this
bookplate in each item of my Morley collection.

— — — — — —   — — — — —

BOOKPLATE LITERATURE continued .   .   .

DARTMOUTH ALUMNI MAGAZINE, Bibliographical Branding Irons, David Wykes. (13) 69:
30-3, November 1976. The author, a transplanted Englishman who teaches English
at Dartmouth, has a flair for subtle wit and humor evident in his treatment of
the G.I.B.P. (Great Institutional Bookplate Problem). Wykes urges the use of the
pictorial ex libris rather than the book label, saying, "A label on a book is words
on words, and somehow it is the element of contrast between the picture and the
word which often makes the bookplate special." Wykes raised another interesting
point after reviewing the 1973 MEMBERSHIP DIRECTORY of the American Society of
Bookplate Collectors and Designers and noting that at the time there were 152 members, "which for a nation of joiners, is either small beer or great exclusiveness."
Most bookplate enthusiasts are not your average "joiner", but membership now nears
200 - still too few to fully support an expanded publications program.

SIMON BRETT - WOOD ENGRAVER

Simon Brett is a young wood engraver of considerable skill who is gradually gaining acclaim. He and his work were featured in the Bookplate Society's NEWS-LETTER No. 11, with an article by Keith Clark and a checklist of 25 ex libris.

In correspondence Brett told of visiting the United States: "I visited New Mexico in 1965, a year after leaving art school, at that "wanderjahr" period of one's life. I have an old great-aunt out there in Taos, Dorothy Brett, a last survival of the D. H. Lawrence generation; she accompanied Lawrence to Taos from England and stayed there when he left. She was a painter, having given over an academic training for a more natural, poetic approach that has found a spiritual home in New Mexico and in rather symbolist painting of the Indians. She's now very old, almost blind I gather, and has long since stopped writing; but we had corresponded for a few years in 1965, and I'd never met her, so she was the obvious goal for a pilgrimage. Apart from a three or four-month trip to Mexico, I spent about 18 months in New Mexico. It is a beautiful land, the impressions its indigenous cultures, Indian and Spanish Colonial, made will always be with me. It is a lovely land, but culturally too remote from the standards that mattered to me - symbolized then and now by Titian, even though I've never become deeply involved in his painting; it would have been so easy to make a success in that South-Western art, as many people told me I could, without having to become a very good painter. So I didn't stay, but, in considerable despair and frustration, came back to these smaller, rainy, dingier roots. I had learned engraving at art school, quite casually, in a course taught by Clifford Webb, and kept it up all through this time as a counterpart to painting. Since being here at Marlborough, with a permanent address, I've been able to build it up far more than I have been able to maintain painting - that is so full-time a work that it is difficult when one has to teach 3 days in the week.

"The bookplates are all from the last three or four years, therefore, and have built up as I've gotten in touch with the Bookplate Society here, through whom many of the commissions come. They are excellent practice, making one turn out designs on all sorts of subjects and acquire a mastery of letters - at which I have always been and still am very bad (the mastery is to come!). I hope to get back to larger, more ambitious engraving; it's no offense to anyone, surely, to recognise that bookplates are small fry; compared, for instance, to books. Or paintings or prints. Within the limited field, I come to realise that the more limits are observed, the better the work is. . . . Bookplates represent to me a balance of literary and visual things, but so often the literary seems to prohibit the visual sense. How people can stick on their books some of the stuff one sees, amazes me!"

Those interested in commissioning an exlibris may write Simon Brett at 12 Blowhorn Street, Marlborough, Wiltshire, SN8 1BT, England. His fees range from £40 to £75.

—   —   —   —   —   —   —   —   —   —

EX LIBRIS WITH JEWISH THEMES WANTED   Moshe Yaari and Avraham Frank are both collectors of bookplates printed for Jewish personalities, libraries, and institutions or depicting Jewish themes with or without Hebrew lettering. Write Moshe Yaari, 8 Ha'ari St., Jerusalem, Israel.

Kent State University Library

PRINCESS ILEANA DESIGNS A BOOKPLATE
Dean H. Keller
Curator of Special Collections,
Kent State University Library

On Sunday, October 28, 1951, Princess Ileana, daughter of Queen Marie of Romania and grand-daughter of Queen Victoria of England, was present at the Kent State University Library to dedicate a collection of books and other material about her mother. The collection, known as the Mariana Collection, was the gift of Ray Baker Harris of Washington, D.C.

It was through the efforts of a Kent State history professor, the late Dr. John Popa, and the University Librarian, John B. Nicholson, Jr., that this remarkable collection came to Kent State. That Kent was the geographic center of Romanians in America was also a factor in the decision. Ray Baker Harris was a writer, editor, and librarian whose interest in Queen Marie began when he was a schoolboy. A warm friendship between the Queen and Harris developed, and they corresponded until the Queen's death in 1938. Harris began to collect books and other material about Marie and Romania during her time, and the Queen aided him by sending copies of her books, appropriately inscribed. In 1942 Harris published a catalogue of his collection, and the books, pictures, and scrapbooks described in it form the basis of the collection dedicated by Princess Ileana in 1951.

Princess Ileana is a remarkable person in her own right, exhibiting the independence, resourcefullness, and strength we saw in her mother. She was born in 1908 and received part of her education in England. In 1931, she married Anton, Archduke of Austria, and they had six children. During World War II she opened a hospital on her estate in Romania and continued to operate it, working as a nurse. until the abdication of her nephew, King Michael, in 1947. Exiled from Romania, she went first to South America and then to North America, settling in New England in 1950. Princess Ileana is now known as Mother Alexandra, the founder of the Orthodox Monastery of the Holy Transfiguration at Ellwood City, Pennsylvania, the first English-speaking convent for Eastern Orthodox nuns in America.

When the Kent State University Library prepared to catalogue Mr. Harris' collection, it was felt that the books should be identified in a unique way, probably with an appropriate bookplate. It was Ray Baker Harris, perhaps inspired by the delicate pencil drawings made by the Princess to decorate the twenty-nine chapter headings of her autobiography, I LIVE AGAIN, published in 1952, who suggested that Princess Ileana design a bookplate for the collection devoted to her mother at Kent State. The Princess generously consented and delivered a pencil drawing to Harris in the spring of 1952. Harris sent the drawing to Librarian John Nicholson on May 19, 1952, with the following description: "I am sending herewith Princess Ileana's sketch for the bookplate for the Romanian Collection. . . . The design is of Castle Bran, which is in the heart of Romania near Brasov. It is a very old medieval fortress which was presented to Queen Marie after World War I, and was made into a private residence. A memorial chapel to the Queen was cut into the rock just below the castle, and this is represented in the design. Princess Ileana kept the sketch very simple, without decorations, so that it might be satisfactory when reduced in size. . . ." Princess Ileana's original drawing is 8" x 5 3/4", and it is interesting to note that she used the subject of Castle Bran and the chapel, in a somewhat different way, as the headings of chapters fifteen and eighteen, in I LIVE AGAIN. A bookplate was made from Princess Ileana's drawing, and it now is used to identify the books in the Mariana Collection in the Kent State University Library.

— — — — — — — —

EXHIBIT   Milton Castle, ASBC&D member, has prepared an exhibit from his book-
          plate collection which is at the Torrance (California) Public Library.
The ex libris will be on display through January 1977. Mr. Castle has traveled extensively and seeks bookplates in each country, thus the exhibit from his collection should be of great variety and interest.

— — — —

BICENTENNIAL YEAR BOOK of ASBC&D - 1976

The 1976 YEAR BOOK of the American Society of Bookplate Collectors and Designers celebrates the bicentennial of America with a cover designed by Dan Burne Jones using a Rockwell Kent drawing and is printed in red, blue, and black on white coverstock.

The 80-page book includes an article by collector Mary Alice Ercolini which is illustrated with six tipped-in plates pulled especially for the YEAR BOOK by Gene Dodge from the original etched plates; Louis Ginsberg writes about calligrapher James Hayes, whose checklist of bookplates is presented in his own working calligraphic hand; Verna Neuscheler adds a note to the Diamond lore; Rockwell Kent's work is represented in a major article by Dan Burne Jones and a complete checklist of his ex libris with many of the plates reproduced; the evolution of Harry Geller's bookplates is followed in the the letters written to him by Rockwell Kent.

Tipped-in above is a Kent design which has been in the Antioch Bookplate Company stock for many years. Antioch, formed in 1926, has featured the work of several noted bookplate designers including Rockwell Kent, Lynd Ward, Raymond DaBoll. In a future issue of the newsletter Antioch, which for years has represented the bookplate for the general public, will be featured.

— — — — — — — —

WHERE ARE THEIR COLLECTIONS TODAY? - Your editor seeks information on the great collections of the past, such as Alfred Fowler, W. R. H. Hayes, etc.

BOOKPLATES IN THE NEWS
429 North Daisy Avenue
Pasadena, CA 91107

$5 U.S. / $6 Overseas
January/April/July/October
Copyright 1977 by Audrey Spencer Arellanes

AS of BC & D
Bookplates in the News
429 NORTH DAISY AVENUE, PASADENA, CALIFORNIA, 91107
AUDREY SPENCER ARELLANES, Editor

NUMBER TWENTY-EIGHT   APRIL 1977

BOSTON UNIVERSITY
LIBRARIES

T.R.

THE THEODORE ROOSEVELT COLLECTION
GIVEN BY
PAUL C. RICHARDS
IN LOVING THOUGHT OF HIS PARENTS

THEODORE ROOSEVELT COLLECTION
at Brown University

The anniversary of Theodore Roosevelt's birth was marked at Boston University on October 26, 1976 when the world's third largest collection of the late President's papers went on display in the University's Mugar Memorial Library. The collection is the gift of Brown alumnus the Rev. Paul C. Richards, semi-retired antiquarian book and autograph dealer.

The contents of the collection illustrate the range of the late President's interests including natural history, ranching, hunting, civil service reform, naval history, Abraham Lincoln, Panama, and the Philippines. There are campaign materials such as buttons, music, posters, and ribbons dating from 1900, 1904, and 1912. Other memorabilia included three original recordings of Roosevelt's speeches, postcards, cartoons, inscribed photographs, videographs, unpublished letters, and original manuscripts of articles, books, and speeches many fully or partially handwritten.

The device for the bookplate was derived from the one used by T. R. on his stationery (in the 1800's) and on his own personal ex libris.

Paul C. Richards majored in American history and government at Boston University. His collecting interests were aroused while still a student. In addition to the Roosevelt Collection, he donated his Robert Frost collection to Boston; the Henry Wallace papers he gave to Iowa State University; and he continues his private collection of Baden-Powell materials.

ALBRECTSEN PLATE
by EDMUND PETER

As the result of a recent happy exchange of letters, P. Th. Albrectsen of Vejle, Denmark, sent prints of one of his ex libris and a few particulars about himself and the artist who designed his plate.

Edmund Peter, born in 1897 in Germany, was apprenticed in his father's art department in the textile business; later he moved to Sweden, then Copenhagen, Denmark, where he worked in the art department of a curtain factory. In his spare time he executed a large number of drawings, watercolors, and woodcuts. He is chiefly interested in nature. After his retirement he devoted much of his time to creating bookplates in lino and wood, sometimes a a combination as in the present example, made in 1971. The scene is from a park on the outskirts of Copenhagen.

P. Th. Albrectsen is a factory worker who is interested in the graphic arts, art books, etc. He is a member of the bookplate societies of Denmark, Belgium, Portugal, Japan, and Germany. Mr. Albrectsen would welcome correspondence and exchanging of ex libris; his address is: Grønnedalen 18 A, 2.mf, 7100 Vejle Denmark.

— — — — — — — — — — — —

INTERNATIONAL CONGRESS 1978 in LUGANO   The next International Ex Libris Congress is scheduled to be held during 1978 in Lugano, Switzerland. It is too early for any details, but they will be presented as soon as available or you may write Carlo Chiesa, Via Nosedo 8, 6900 Lugano-Massagno, Switzerland.

— — — — — — — — — — — —

BOOKPLATES IN THE NEWS
429 North Daisy Avenue
Pasadena, CA 91107

$5 US/$6 Overseas
January/April/July/October
Back Issues Available

PLEASE notify immediately of any CHANGE of ADDRESS

FROM THE BOOKPLATE LITERATURE . . . .

THE KENT COLLECTOR, A milestone for Bookplate Collectors! 3:22, Spring, 1977. George Spector, devoted editor of KENT COLLECTOR, reviews the 1976 Bicentennial YEAR BOOK of ASBC&D which contains an article by Dan Burne Jones on Kent and a master checklist of his ex libris, and reproduces several letters Kent wrote Harry Geller in the course of designing his bookplate. Spector says the YEAR BOOK "must surely rank as the handsomest of all the 39 issued in the history of the Society."

PRINTING NEWS, British Artist-Engraver Leo Wyatt To Be Speaker at Heritage on March 12, 1977. This was the first of numerous speaking engagements in the United States which included Yale, Harvard, and Dawson's Bookshop in Los Angeles on April 7th. Wyatt has executed countless blocks for ex libris and letterheads in wood and copper. His talk was illustrated with slides.

INNOCENCE

ANTIQUARIAN BOOK MONTHLY REVIEW, Book Reviews, C. W. Hill. 4:26, January 1977. In writing about John Lewis' COLLECTING PRINTED EPHEMERA, Hill stated: "it would have been pleasant to see more of the printed ephemera with a literary flavour such as bookmarks, bookplates and dust-jackets. One well-designed bookmark issued by the Zeeland Steamship Company whets the appetite for a fuller account of this subject but the other two topics are not mentioned."

MICROBIBLIOPHILE, Ex Libris. 1:3, March 1977. A new quarterly devoted to miniature books has been launched by Robert F. Hanson, editor and publisher. This first number contains an article on ex libris which mentions the American Society of Bookplate Collectors and Designers and discusses a number of miniature ex libris which are illustrated and/or referred to in the Arellanes bibliography of bookplate periodical literature. To subscribe write: Robert Hanson, P.O.Box 640, Mattituck, NY 11952.

FINE PRINT, Calendar of Events. 3:2, January 1977. Exhibition of Grolier Club Members' bookplates on view to March 31, 1977.

DESIGNING A BOOKPLATE, Hal W. Trovillion. Trovillion Press at the Sign of the Silver Horse, Herrin, IL, 1953, edition limited to 413 copies. The first two bookplates for the Trovillion's were designed by James Guthrie; for the second the block was cut by Howard J. Weis. The book consists of nine small pages.

THE LOST BOOKPLATE OF ARTHUR MACHEN, Nathan Van Patten, preface by Vincent Starrett; San Francisco, 1949 (Christmas), printed for Adrian Goldstone at the Greenwood Press in an edition of 50 copies for the Machen Society. Starrett mentions first seeing the ex libris in question about August 15, 1922 in a catalog of ex libris offered by Thomas Thorp, English bookseller, at 2 shillings. The etching is signed "JH", probably G. P. Jacomb Hood, who did etching for THE FORTUNATE LOVERS which Machen translated. Van Patten indicates he feels Machen only had a few proofs and never had the plate printed in quantity. The Latin motto on the bookplate is a variant of that for the U.S. Postal Service.

PENNSYLVANIA: AN ETHNIC SAMPLER, Daniel Walden, prepared for the Pennsylvania Public Television Network as a community service of the College of Liberal Arts, Pennsylvania State University, 1976, includes an illustration of the James Logan ex libris. "Scotch-Irish Quaker James Logan accumulated one of the finest libraries in the colonies. He acknowledged that 'books are my disease,' and, in a letter to a London bookseller, he wrote, 'It may seem strange to find an American Deerskin Merchant troubling himself with such books, but they have been my delight and will, I believe, continue my best entertainment in my advancing years.'"

PRINT TRADER, The Specialist Prints & Paper Collectibles Newsletter, The Return of Kentiana. (1) 2,#10, March 1976. Review of Dan Burne Jone's THE PRINTS OF ROCKWELL KENT. The reviewer feels the Catalogue Raisonne has "triggered major offerings, especially in prints which are reflected in the current Price Record, indicating a possible resurgence of trading in the work of this great artist in the prints and paper collectibles market."

PRINT TRADER, Collecting and Recollecting. 4,#10, March 1976. This is a condensation from an article by Bella C. Landauer in the New York Historical Society QUARTERLY, XLIII,#3, in which she relates the circumstances surrounding her first purchase of bookplates. There is also a list of booklets and articles by Mrs. Landauer which includes her "Bookplates from the Aeronautical Collection of Bella C. Landauer," Harbor Press, 1930.

BOOKCRAFT, Annette Hollander. New York: Van Nostrand Reinhold Co., 1974. An excellent how-to book with illustrations in color of the finished products, diagrams for construction of note pads, boxes, books, and other useful items. Many of the boxes would be ideal for housing bookplate prints or periodical literature and could be tailored to the specific dimensions required.

AMERICAN ADVERTISING POSTERS OF THE NINETEENTH CENTURY, Mary Black. Dover Publications, 1976 These posters are choice examples from the Bella C. Landauer Collection of the New York Historical Society (on exhibit early in 1977 at the Society). In the introduction, Mary Black gives some background on Bella Landauer's bookplate collecting, another aspect of printed ephemera which chronicles the life styles and graphic techniques of an era.

APARTMENT LIFE, The Self-Made Library. (1) 9:54-5, January 1977.
"And the fancy engraving overhead? It's nothing more than a
favorite bookplate, blown up at a photocopying studio and mounted.

BOOKPLATE SOCIETY, Newsletter No. 16:2:37-48, December 1976.
 - Exhibition and Meetings. A thousand visitors saw exhibit of
"Bookplate Designers 1925-1975" at which Will Carter was speak-
er at the opening; bookplate designers present included Joan
Hassall, Leo Wyatt, Richard Shirley Smith and Diana Bloomfield.
 - Members' Bookplates. Illustrated are those for William E.
Butler, Sir Harry Page, and Brian North Lee.
 - More About Richard Ford. Started Spanish collection in 1830.
 - 'W.P.B.' Bookplates. Horance E. Jones lists William Barrett
plates he would like to see to be able to describe for the de-
scriptive checklist he is preparing on this artist.
 - Sir John Betjeman's Book Label. Poet Laureate, who is presi-
dent of the Ephemera Society, contributed his bookplate to the
Society's second annual exhibition.
 - Three Crokatt Bookplates. This is an abstract of a talk given
by the late C. Hall Crouch at a meeting of the Walthamstow Antiquarian Society; two plates illustrated; family history given.
 - Bookplates of William McLaren, Brian North Lee. Five plates
are illustrated; the earliest engraved in 1944, the latest was
drawn in 1974. William McLaren (86 West Bow, Edinburgh, Scotland) is quite willing to undertake bookplate commissions.
 - Publications. THE BOOKPLATE DESIGNS OF REX WHISTLER is on
the verge of being out of print; still available through Private
Libraries Association. Philip Beddingham's THE BOOKPLATES OF
JOHN WILLIAM LISLE may be purchased for £2.40 from PLA (3B Hurlingham Court, Ranelagh Gardens, London SW6 3UN, England). The
YEAR BOOK and BOOKPLATES IN THE NEWS of the ASBC&D are mentioned as both being "to a consistently high standard."
 - SUNDAY TELEGRAPH Bookplate Competition. About 800 entries
were received from children in three age groups (7-9, 10-13,
and 14-16).

L'EX LIBRIS FRANCAIS, vol. 39, No. 122, December 1976. Includ-
ed are the conclusion of an article on Architecture in French
Ex Libris and "on the occasion of the Bicentenary of the United
States, J. Le Duchat d'Aubigny writes about Ex-libris in the U.S.:
its infancy, and what it is at the present time. (Perhaps by
July we will have a translation of the article for our readers.)

THE HOUSE OF WHITBREAD, Book Plates, Charles Hall Crough. (11) 9:
7-11, 1949. A brief, but good introduction to bookplates, and
ten Whitbread family plates are illustrated and described.

German Expressionist Art, University of California at Los Angeles
exhibit ending April 17, 1977, presented the outstanding print collection of Robert Gore Rifkin; it also included books, periodicals,
posters. It is apparent in viewing the exhibit the considerable impact the German Expressionists have had on bookplate art, particularly in the Iron Curtain countries. Josef Sattler and Lyonel Fein-
inger, both known for their ex libris, are among artists in the
catalog by Orrell P. Reed, Jr. issued for the Rifkin Collection.

ASA NEWSLETTER (Archaeological Survey Association of Southern California), New ASA Bookplate. (1) 23:12, Spring-Summer 1976. "The elements incorporated into this artistic work reflect the work of ASA: the terrain of the American Southwest desert, depicted by a stylized palm below unpolluted skies; dark recesses, suggesting areas such as Black Canyon where the bird petroglyph is found; the ASA bird glyph symbol itself; our interest in the American Indian shown by the basket; and archaeological activities indicated by the pick, one of the several types used in the field." The artist is Enrico Seeley Molnar, until recent years a ASBC&D member, who now devotes all his efforts to the Order of Agape and Reconciliation in Tajique, New Mexico, where he is the Prior of this Episcopal-sponsored semi-monastic modern religious order.

BAKER STREET JOURNAL, Wants & Offers. 26:55, March 1976. Among the offers are Sherlockian bookplates with "Holmesian design on pre-gummed stock . . ." In addition to stock ex libris, personalized or custom-made orders are accepted by Linda Finch, P.O. Box 46-125, Los Angeles, CA 90046.

Folio Fine Editions Limited, 202 Great Suffolk St., London SE1 1PR, England, recently issued a prospectus for THE BIRD PAINT-INGS OF HENRY JONES in a limited edition of 500 copies. Foreward by HRH The Duke of Edinburgh and introduction by Professor Lord Zuckerman, Secretary of the Zoological Society of London, which was the recepient of "over one thousand watercolours of birds left to the Society after his death in 1921 by Major Henry Jones." Each copy of the book contains a hand printed bookplate inserted loose, engraved in wood by Leo Wyatt, who also designed the engraved Folio Fine Edition colophon.

ANTIQUES, February 1977, contains an advertisement by Guthman Americana of Westport, Ct. 06880, for a bookplate collection; the prices are substantial.

— — — — — — — — —

I N D E X to BOOKPLATES IN THE NEWS

The INDEX to Numbers 21-26, July 1975 to October 1976, of BOOKPLATES IN THE NEWS has been compiled by Richard H. Schimmelpfeng. It follows the same format as the INDEX for Numbers 1-20 with four categories: Authors, Subjects, Titles; Artists, Engravers; Bookplates Mentioned or Discussed; Illustrations. The INDEX will be furnished with its own title page and a separate one for BOOKPLATES IN THE NEWS for $3.75. Send remittance to the Editor.

ASOCIACION CULTURAL de las
CALIFORNIAS MEMORIAL EX LIBRIS

The Asociación Cultural de las
Californias is an informal,
loosely knit, international
organization designed to foster the interchange of ideas
and better understanding among
the people of the Californias--
Alta, Baja, and Baja Sur. It
attempts to demonstrate that,
in spite of modern political
boundaries, the Californias,
not only geographically and
historically but in many other
ways as well, are closely tied
together, and especially is this
true of their respective peoples.
Toward this end, it sponsors
the annual Baja California Symposium, of which this year's
(1977) is the fifteenth.

Ing. Jose G. Valenzuela, a retired head of the state of Baja
California's public school system, helped to form the Asociacion and, from 1965 until his
death in December 1975, served

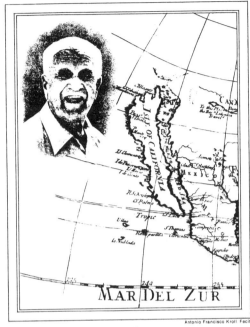

En memoria de
ING. JOSÉ G. VALENZUELA
(1894~1975)

Asociación Cultural
de las
Californias

as president of its Baja California Committee. A distinguished
and delightful gentleman, no one gave more unstintingly of time
and effort toward the organization's central purpose or toward
the work of the Symposium than he did. Consequently, at an homage ceremony given for Ing. Valenzuela during the 1976 Symposium,
William Hendricks, director of the Sherman Foundation Library in
Corona del Mar and president of the Alta California Committee,
proposed that, in honor of the memory of Ing. Valenzuela, the members of the Asociación donate books to the University of Baja
California Library; and, in order to emphasize the meaning behind
these gifts and make them distinctive, that a specially designed
bookplate, with the name of the donor added, be affixed to each
item.

Tony Kroll, who is a member of the Asociación and was present
that day, afterward volunteered to design and print the bookplate.
Providing him with a photograph of Ing. Valenzuela (taken, appropriately, during the La Paz Symposium, in 1974, by Sra. Anita
Alvarez de Williams) that seemed to capture the essence of the
man's effervescent personality, Dr. Hendricks proposed that perhaps it along with an old map from the period which showed the
Californias as an island might be incorporated into the design,
and in this way symbolize the continuing unity of the area for
which both Ing. Valenzula and the organization stood. Mr. Kroll
in an exercise of his considerable talents, took it from there,
and we have the resultant bookplate.

A recent letter from Karl Ritter indicated that he will be the subject of an article in the annual published by the German Ex Libris Society. Renewed interest in this artist's bookplate work was generated by the article and partial checklist of his ex libris in the 1975 YEAR BOOK of the American Society of Bookplate Collectors and Designers.

The bookplate illustrated to the left depicts a WWI vintage airplane which Karl also uses on one of his letterheads.

ELLERY QUEEN   An episode of Ellery Queen on TV (Sunday, May 9, 1976) featured Ida Lupino as an heiress who spent her final minutes alive reading an Ellery Queen mystery. Mention is made of the ex libris of the heiress' father in the novel.

W A N T E D: Bookplate News   Articles about artists, owners,
                and Tip-ins   and collectors of bookplates are
                                 wanted for BOOKPLATES IN THE NEWS.
Whenever possible prints of the bookplate discussed are desired; 225 prints are necessary for tipping-in. Please share your bookplate experiences with other ex libris enthusiasts!

NEW EXLIBRISTEN PUBLICATIONS   Two new publications are now available from Klaus Rodel's Exlibristen. They are RASTISLAV MICHAL and VOJTECH CINYBULK, both 1977 publications. The multi-lingual introduction by the artist in the Michal volume is accompanied by numerous black and white prints illustrated and eight tipped-in ex libris; some printed in color, some two color; price DKr. 75,00. Dr. Ottmar Premstaller provides the introduction for the Cinybuk portfolio of ten lithographic bookplates; unfortunately it is not in English. However, the plates themselves reveal an artist with a delightful sense of humor. VOJTECH CINYBULK is DRr. 75,00. Special reductions are offered to subscribers of Exlibristen publications which include EXLIBRIS-REVUE, a quarterly, which has now completed its second year. A cover for the first two volumes with the index printed on the inside back page has been issued for 1975 and 1976. The last number of EXLIBRIS-REVUE for 1976 contained a multi-lingual article on ASBC&D artist-member Vytautas O. Virkau accompanied by illustrations of 15 of his ex libris. Numerous other illustrations and articles, some of them in English.

AS of BC & D
Bookplates in the News

AUDREY SPENCER ARELLANES, Editor

Number Twenty-nine   July 1977

JACQUES HNIZDOVSKY

Since 1949 Jacques Hnizdovsky has lived in the
United States. He was born in the Ukraine in 1915,
studied at the Academy of Fine Arts in Warsaw, and
in Zagreb. His first exhibition was held in New
York in 1954. Since then more than fifty one-man
shows of his work, mostly woodcuts, have been held
throughout the United States, Canada, and Europe.
In 1971 a major retrospective of his woodcuts was
held at the Associated American Artists in New York.
In the same year a film on his work, "Sheep in Wood"
by S. Nowytaki, received first prize at the American
Film Festival in New York. Hnizdovsky's woodcuts are
included in permanent collections in Boston, Philadelphia and Cleveland Museums, the Library of Congress, the Winnipeg Art Gallery, and many other public and private collections. In 1976 a catalogue
raisonne of his woodcuts, HNIZDOVSKY - WOODCUTS 1944-
1975, complied by Abe M. Tahir, was published by
Pelican.

EX LIBRIS RECOLLECTIONS by Jacques Hnizdovsky

My interest in ex libris goes back to the early thirties. Bookplates were
popular at that time in Western Ukraine. While still in highschool, I had
the opportunity to see a collection of Ukrainian bookplates, compiled by
Pavlo Kovzhun, graphic artist and enthusiastic promoter of ex libris, that
had just been published in Lvov; several Ukrainian artists at that time took
part in international exhibitions including the large exhibition about 1931
in Los Angeles (probably the Bookplate International Association).

I did my first ex libris as a student at the Academy of Fine Arts in Zagreb
in 1942. Since then I have designed only about twenty-five bookplates, about
half of them, mostly recent, were executed in woodcut. In 1972 I did a woodcut for our daughter, then 13 years old. Children's bookplates are usually
of a short duration. With their growth, their interest in books changes and
with that the symbol of their ex libris, especially in the case of girls. With
their marriage and with the change of their name, usually arises the need for
a change in their ex libris.

At the same year, a newly established center for Ukrainian studies at Harvard commissioned me to design a bookplate for their library. As a symbol I have chosen the edifice of the Academy in Kiev, founded by Metropolitan P. Mohyla in 1632, the oldest institution of higher learning in the East that has long supplied the entire European East and to a certain extent Balkan with professors. I combined this edifice with the symbol of Harvard, three open books with the inscription: veritas. The bookplate has been executed in woodcut.

A music lover and an enthusiastic collector of records, Mr. Rostyslav Sonevytsky of New York has accumulated such a vast collection of records and albums that the real danger exists that under their weight they may land in the apartment below! In case it should really happen, Mr. Sonevytsky thought he owes it to the occupant of the apartment below to somehow indicate where the records came from and who their owner is. The bookplate could be the solution. But how to call the plate that has to be glued to the cover of a record album? Since we both have some familiarity with Latin and since the father of the record collector was a Latin teacher and I his student, so it came: "Ex discis". The bookplate has been executed in woodcut.

n o t i c e : CHANGE OF ADDRESS

Effective immediately there is a new address for BOOKPLATES IN THE NEWS and the AMERICAN SOCIETY OF BOOKPLATE COLLECTORS AND DESIGNERS.

It is -

    1206 N. Stoneman Ave. #15
    Alhambra, CA 91801

BOOKPLATES IN THE NEWS
Published Jan./April/July/Oct.
$5 U.S./$6 Overseas

Note: The translation by Rolf H. Erickson is from NORDISK EXLIBRIS TIDSSKRIFT, #3, 33-42, 1970.

THE UNITED STATES' BICENTENNIAL
AND THE EX LIBRIS IN THE U.S.A.
         by Jean d'Aubigny

(Note: This article appeared in
L'EX LIBRIS FRANCAIS, No. 122,
December 1976; it was translated
by George S. Swarth, a ASBC&D
member, for our readers.)

The idea of introducing some works of engraving into the commemoration
of the bicentennial of an independence to which France was intimately
connected can contribute to creating a climate of cultural activity and
of sympathy of a unique flavor.

America, in the world of ex libris, is the American Society of Bookplate
Collectors and Designers, of Pasadena, California, of which the editor
is A. S. Arellanes, and of which the bulletin, known to our subscribers,
matches the success of what is called in the U.S.A. YEAR BOOK, a truly de
luxe annual compilation issued for the past fifty-three years.

There has often been noticed, in the manner of the artists of this vast
land, and as typically American, a neoclassical style, of remarkable letters lovingly engraved; fine layout, and a taste seeking to link itself,
by the chosen themes, with the old world or long-vanished moments of American history.

Recently, we have seen in the bulletin of the ASBC&D an ex libris of the
personal library of Haldeman-Julies, called the Henry Ford of publishing.
This engraving represents a human silhouette inscribed in a circumference
and which, although in a newer technique, draws its inspiration from Leonardo da Vinci's "proportions of the human body in the world." It is an
indirect tribute to the great spirit of the XVth Century.

One could have feared, in view of the success and the enthusiasm that science evokes in America, a less lively consideration for the fine arts and
particularly engraving. It also is held in greet esteem. La Livaria ed-
itoria Pax LDA de Braga (Portugal) printed, on the occasion of the recent
International Ex Libris Congress, a superb volume which, among a number of
articles, gives some remarkable insights into the renewal and the freedom
on the contemporary American ex libris.

The article was written by A. S. Arellanes and recognizes at the outset
that many American artists, very different in this from the Europeans,
create only a small number of vignettes. Often a simple engraving for a
friend or a favored client, sometimes half a dozen. Seldom a number on
the order of the output of the French or Portuguese, for example.

The author expatiates on the case of A. F. Kroll, engraver on metal, born
at Chicago in 1914 and whose parents were born in Poland. This first generation American studied architecture four years, then, still in the same
city of Chicago, pursued the course of the Academy of Fine Arts.

Kroll adds a personal and original touch to certain ex libris that he begins by the process of photogravure. He also reproduced the features of
celebrated persons.

Leading up to the present progress of the ex libris, a less original ex-
uberance was seen about the time that society call the Belle Epoque (i.e.,

the opening years of the 20th century). We think it will interest our readers to extract a few lines at the beginnings of the American ex libris in a writing from that turn of the century.

The Beginnings of the American Ex Libris: In the number for the winter of 1898-9 of the revue THE STUDIO, an English publication that appeared in London in the neighborhood of Covent Garden, the subject is book plates, modern then, but which, somewhat lost in the distance of bygone time, have become old fashioned.

This number, rich in original notes, devotes an article to the ex libris in America, which deserves to be considered in the context of the Bicentennial of the United States.

Jean Carre, on the subject of sixteen reproductions of these vignettes, sets out some reflections of which we give an extract here: the general idea of his essay is the following: the American ex libris, especially those of the pictorial variety, have not yet acquired the individuality by which they could claim to be in a class of their own.

It seems indeed that the origin of the ex libris goes back to the times when the noble proprietors of great collections of books decorated their volumes with a representation of their arms. This hypothesis explains at all events the fact that the use of ex libris did not spread in America until quite recently. The old world also had an evolution, which passed through numerous phases and enables its quarterings of nobility to be traced back several centuries. It has served as expression of an idea, transmitted from generation to generation and modified from one time to another, according to the demands of general sentiment. Today we have arrived at the logical result of having a type of ex libris well defined, but still preserving numerous points that denote its origin and make its history easy to retrace.

In America, we find no trace of such an evolution. Formerly, at the time of the formation of the country, people were too much occupied with other matters to care much about heraldic bearings.

However, the works of the American designers are full of promise. Several artists have shown that this specialty might spread much more widely than could have been supposed at first, and their efforts, though limited, have given results of very appreciable importance. The better work comes from Boston. It is probably that the surrounding artistic atmosphere and the greater educational facilities tend to favor the progress of a branch of art that has more charms for an intelligent and cultivated elite than for the crowd avid for violent sensations.

We mention Mr. Bertram Grosvenor Goodhue, a designer in black and white. He has already drawn attention to himself at London by the borders and decorated letters of an altar Bible. An imagination of fine vigor is seen in his works. Harry B. Goodhue offers several specimens of ex libris, of a refined taste and a pleasing variety of design.

With time, one can expect from America more personal results, a newer feeling of the demands of this genre. The inventive spirit will assert itself among these people and a style, which probably will have no relationship to the character of the European works, will begin to develop.

H E L P! CAN YOU IDENTIFY?

In the tradition of ex libris publications in the past, especially
the JOURNAL OF THE EX LIBRIS SO-
CIETY, we welcome the occasional
request for help when a bookplate
owner and/or designer eludes identification. Such is the case as
described below.

Lewis Paul Kohrs (3876 Belmont
Ave., San Diego, CA 92116) seeks
the identification of an armorial
plate which he found on the inside front cover of each volume
of an incomplete set of OEVRES
COMPLETE of J.J. Rousseau (1793).
Each flyleaf has a "Bonaparte"
signature. Mr. Kohrs writes:
"This does not appear to be a bookplate of either Napoleon I or II
or their signatures; but Napoleon
III was exiled for a brief time
to the United States in late 1836
-early 1837, and may have left
behind part of his set of the complete works of Rousseau." We
hope to have an answer in the
next issue.

FRED W. LAGERQUIST

It is with regret we note the passing
earlier this year of Fred W. Lagerquist.
Though only a member of ASBC&D for a comparatively few years, he generously
printed the membership application used by the Society. Mr. Lagerquist was
president and counsel of several life insurance companies including two in
Atlanta, Georgia, and one in Providence, Rhode Island. He was a member of
the American Bar Association and the State Bar of Georgia, numerous insurance oriented associations, the South Carolina Historical Society, Society
of Cincinnati, Friends of the Emory University Library, and included his
membership in the American Society of Bookplate Collectors and Designers
among the many other organizations to which he belonged and lent support.

MARY ALICE ERCOLINI

We have just learned that Mary
Alice Ercolini died in June after
several weeks in the hospital. We would like to plan a tribute
to this lovely lady, who had many bookplate friends throughout
the world. As many letters as possible will be quoted in the
October issue of our newsletter. Mrs. Ercolini has been most
generous in her articles for the Society's YEAR BOOK which
were always beautifully illustrated with tipped-in ex libris,
most recently for 1976 when a number of her personal plates
were featured. Mary Alice was well-known for her interest in
cats, which frequently appeared in her bookplates; she also
had an unusual collection of cats in wood, glass, metal, etc.

EUROPEAN EXLIBRIS OF TODAY
Excluding Those of Scandinavia
by Klaus Rodel
Translated by Rolf H. Erickson
and Anette Norberg-Schulz

This article is a subjective discourse to give a short overview of the European exlibris of today. Subjective, because it is almost impossible to know all of the artists and also because there is too little space available to discuss them all. To produce "the Modern European Exlibris History" would be a large task - difficult to discuss the topic more exhaustively, as well as include information about respective experts in various countries. Perhaps the author of this article may undertake that challenge someday, but that is certainly very uncertain.

When one looks at the history of the exlibris, one observes periods of both high and low interest, ups and downs, dependent on economic conditions, and so forth. An exlibris society's "life" has often been dependent on the efforts of one individual or the contributions of a small group. The Second World War especially took its toll of many valuable collections and led to many broken collecting connections and friendships. In spite of this, the societies resumed publishing yearbooks or periodicals, the exchange of letters across borders increased, old friendships bloomed again and new ones were made.

To fully understand the pleasure of collecting, the enthusiams for the small graphic, and the international exlibris congresses, one really has to be an exlibris collector. I received help for this article from collector friends in two countries: in France - Paul Pfister, Versailles, and in Portugal - A. de Mota Miranda, Beira (Mocambique).

Let us begin with Holland. The Dutch exlibris history is rich in traditions and full of significance. There have always existed good artists and zealous collectors, and even today the Dutch exlibris periodical EXLIBRIS - WERELD exists in its characteristic format. The most well-known exlibris artists have created many good things, especially in woodblock prints and copper engravings. Unfortunately two of the most well-known artists, Lou Strik and Ru van Rossem, abandoned the exlibris circle, but there can still be found a score of fine artists. Here are some of the best: Cess Andriessen, Jan Battermann, Nico Bulder, Harry Corvers, Jan van Doorn, Dirk van Gelder, Maarten de Jong, Jaap Kuyper, Dirk van Luyn, Thijs Mauve, Emile Puettmann, E. Reisma-Valenca, Pam G. Rueter, Rein Snapper, H. D. Voss and Wim Zwiers (unfortunately not very active any more).

In neighboring Belgium are found some of the most active collectors and the very interesting typographical and exlibris periodical GRAPHIA - BULLETIN, certainly that periodical which gives the best "service" with their translations of articles and so forth. All articles are translated either to English or German on attached duplicated sheets. They, therefore, can be understood by many readers. Some of the well-known names are: Desire Acket, Frank-Ivo van Damme, Nelly Degouy, Karel ean Eeghem, Josef Hendrickx, Antoon Herckenrath, Andre Gastmans, Gerard Gaudaen, Lucien de Jaegher, Piet Janssens, Frans Lausure, Piet van Roemburg, Mark F. Severin, Gerard Schelpe, Victor Stuyvaert, Antoon Vermeylen, and Raymond Verstraeten.

The French exlibris demise has often been announced. It has, nevertheless, survived all storms, but that is all we can say about it. It is a shame. What the reason is for this deplorable situation is difficult to say, but there are possibly two main reasons: the lack of interested collectors to create demand, and the fact that many of the artists consider exlibris beneath them. Great artists such as Boullaire, Marianne Clouzot, Laboureur and Picasso have created a few exlibris, but generally they would rather busy themselves with more profitable graphics and book illustrations. There are, however, some well-known artists, among them are the late Valentin Le Campion, Henri Bacher, Andre Ballet, Philippe Burnot, Hansi, Henry-Andre, Andre Herry, Robert Louis, Edmond des Robert, Leo Schnug, and H. Solveen. Among those living artists known in collectors' circles are: Rene Barande, Jean Chieze (the most powerful graphic artist since Le Campion), Decaris, Charles Favet, Ernest Huber, Michel Jamar, Jean Lebedeff, Louis Maechler, Jocelyn Mercier, Daniel Meyer, Colette Pettier, Francois Rohmer, and Theo Vetter. The French exlibris periodical, L'EX LIBRIS FRANCAIS, appears regularly and is in its 32nd volume.

The two southwestern European countries, Spain and Portugal, have also brought forth a score of interesting exlibris artists. Especially the Spanish exlibris has had its periods where much exlibris art has been created and, not in the least, etchings. Today the following artists, among others, are known abroad: Frank Alpresa, Vicent Beltran, Juan V. Botella, Maria Josefa Colom, Juan Estiarte, Mercedes De Olanta, Julio Fernandex Saez, Antoni Gelabert, Antonio Olle Pinell, Elfi Osiander, Jaume Pla, E. C. Ricart, and Julio Salvatierra. The beautiful periodical AEB-CIRCULAR is now in its 20th volume.

In Portugal there are not so many well-known exlibris artists. Among those best known and most active is Joao Paulo de Abreu Lima, son of the well-known Antonio Lima, surely the most important exlibris artist in Portugal. Further there are: the designer and engraver Rui Fernandes, architect Eduardo Martins Beirrada, Jose Perez, Gouveia Portuense, and Jorge Nunes. The aristocratic designer D. Miguel Antonio de Noronha de Paiva Couceiro, the Comte de Paraty, has created many lovely heraldic exlibris, Portugal's most popular motif. Very active also is the engraver Antonio Pais Ferreira. Furthermore one can mention J. Bastos, Silva, and Isaias Peixoto. Occasionally exlibris come from Eduardo Malta, Lima de Freitas, Alberto Carneiro, Nunes Pereira, and Manuel Cabanas. The Portugese exlibris society is among the largest in Europe, and the very beautiful periodical, A ARTE DO EXLIBRIS, distinguishes itself mainly through the many examples of original engravings and etchings.

Looking at Italy, we find many well-known collectors and artists. Especially Gianni Manteros' name needs no further explanation - even the newest collectors get to know his name in a short time. The Italian exlibris periodical, BIANCO e NERO EX-LIBRIS, has a useful format and has brought out many original examples. Among those known abroad are Lorenzo Allessandri, Pier Luigi Gerosa, Armando Baldinelli, Guilio Cisari, Amleto Del Grosso, but the foremost names are: Maria Elisa Leboroni Pecetti, Tranquillo Marangoni, Virgilio Tramontin, Gian Luigi Uboldi, Enrico Vannuccini, Remo Wolf, and Italo Zetti.

Among the living artists in Switzerland, I know of only the monks from the monastery Engelberg, first and foremost Father Theodor Rutishauser.

In West Germany one finds the traditional German exlibris society, which can look back on several decades in the exlibris field. The yearbook D.E.G., rich with information, comes out each year with interesting articles and is richly illustrated. Just recently the German society succeeded in publishing their "Mitteilungen" in a bibliofile edition three times a year. Among the best well-known exlibris artists of today are: Ellen Beck, Karl Bedal, Ottohans Beier, Karl Blossfeld, Fritz Botel, Jurgen Dost, Wilhelm Geissler, Ernst Grunewald, Hermann Huffert, Rudolf Koch, K. E. Mersburger, Johann Naha, Herbert Ott, Norbert Ott, Friedrich Rasmus, Helmut Seehausen, and Peter Wolbrand.

In East Germany the exlibris situation is more or less well taken care of by Pirckheimer-Gesellschaft, who now and then has articles on exlibris in the bibliofile periodical MARGINALIEN. Several attempts to establish a society or a self-supporting division for exlibris have so far been unsuccessful. Among the best known artists, aside from the recently deceased Hans Michael Bungter and Heinrich Ilgenfritz, are: Gerhard Beyer, Ulrich Bewersdorff, Rudi Franke, H. G. Hirsch, Siegfried Hammermann, Th. P. Kassner, Fritz Kuhn, Heinz Olbrich, Richard Preusse, Wilhelm Richter, Eugen Schmidt, Hans Schulze, Gerhard Stauf, and Oswin Volkamer.

Austria also has a very old exlibris tradition and maintains this with success through the distinguished yearbooks, which are, however, only published every other year. Unfortunately "Mitteilungen" comes out only two times a year, too seldom to be a good contact between members. There are two categories of artists: the Cossman school's copper etchers, first and foremost in Vienna, and the folkloristic influenced graphic artists in the countryside. These latter mainly occupy themselves with wood and linoleum prints. Among known artists are: Gerhard Brandl, Fritz Cernajsek, Otto Feil, Hans Hauke, Karl Haselbock, Johannes G. Freund, Toni Hofer, Max Kislinger, Sylvia Penther, Harald Pickert, Ottmar Premstaller, Hans Ranzoni, Roland Roveda, Erich Schoner, Roswita Schoner, Franz Stummvoll, and Hubert Woyty-Wimmer.

In East Europe the exlibris art has had a powerful period of resurgence and is quantitatively superior to the West European exlibris without being poorer in quality. Polish graphics receive much attention abroad, and this is also true of exlibris art. Among the great number of those known outside the country's borders, these best known exlibris artists can be mentioned: Adam Mlodzianowski, Wojciech Barylski, Janusz Benedyktynowicz, Czeslaw Borowczyk, Andrzej Bortowski, Boguslaw Brandt, Tadeusa Cieslewski, Zbigniew Dolatowski, Stefania Dretler-Flin, Henryk Fejlhauer, Jozef Geilniak, Antoni Golebniak, Wojciech Jakubowski, Jerzy Jarnuszkiewicz, Alina Kalczynska, Andrzej Kandiora, Ryszard Krzywka, Wiktor Langner, Stanislaw Luckieqicz, Stefan Mrozewski, Boguslaw Marszall, Jerzy Napieracz, Henryk Plociennik, Tadeuxz Przpkowski, Gustaw Schmager, Stanislaw Szymanski, Konstanty Maria Sopocko, B. J. Tomecki, Kazimierz Wiszniewski, and Krystyna Wroblewska. In addition, Malbork-Biennaler has achieved a world wide reputation and has contributed to the popularity of the exlibris (this is an exlibris congress held every two years in Malbork, Poland).

In neighboring Czechoslovakia the exlibris is equally popular, and there are many collectors and artists. Also here the same is true as for most of the other East European countries, that is, that there might be good artists, but it is not possible to publish equally good periodicals or exlibris books; thus the societies lack this important link in their work. It is almost impossible to list a score of names without overlooking one or another artist, and I must beforehand ask for indulgence. The following exlibris artists are known abroad:

Alec Beran, Cyril Bouda, Olga Cechova, Dalibor Chatrny, Vojtech Cinybulk, Dusan Janousek, Kiri Jaska, Michael Florian, Ana Grmelova, Jan Halla, Jiri Hadlac, Stanislav Hlinovsky, Josef Hodek, Miroslav Houra, Oldrich Karel, Ladislav J. Kaspar, Bohuslav Knobloch, Jar. Lukavsky, Jindrich Mahelka, Zdenek Mezl, Rastislav Michal, Karel Oberthor, Frantisek Peterka, Ladislav Rusek, Pravoslav Sovak, Nadezda Synecka, Jaroslav Svab, Jiri Svengsbir, Karel Svolinsky, Jaroslav Uiberlay, Miroslav Vasa, Josef Weiser, Ladislav Vlodek, and Jaroslav Vodrazka.

The Hungarian exlibris, which we at the congress will surely meet in all possible variations, builds on a rich tradition, and there are a number of great ideals. Among the Hungarian artists are found copper engravers and woodblock artists, who attract much attention abroad. The Hungarian exlibris collectors belong to the Society of Small Graphics Collectors, which publishes its offset-printed membership paper with a French resume. Among those known abroad are the very productive Istavan Drahos, recently deceased, and: Ferenc Bordas, Lenke Diskay, Antal Fery, Gabor Gacs, Jeno Kertes-Kollmann, Marta Kopasz, Gyula Kohegyi, Jozsef Menyhart, D. A. Nagy, Arisztid Nagy, Ferenc Rakozy, Istvan Tempinszky, Bela Stettner, Zsigmund Sos, Lajor Nandor Varga, and Jozsef Vertel.

In Yugoslavia there is now a society which is growing steadily, and among the well-known artists, besides the unusually productive Karoly Andrusko are Jakac Bozidar and Pavel Meduescek.

The Soviet Union is today the country producing the most exlibris publications. There are many collectors, but they are not organized into a national society. A collectors' club in Moscow has produced some publications. Among the artists known abroad are: Igor and Lew Beketow, Ruben Bedrosow, Wadim A. Frolow, Eugen N. Goljachowski, Vlodimir Kadajlow, Anatoli Kalashnikow, German Ratner, and Wladimir Swalow.

The three northern border states, Estonia, Lithuania, and Latvia, are famous for their many active artists. Exlibris are in demand among many collectors. Paul Ambur is the main force in this circle, and we can thank him for many articles which have made us acquainted with the artists. It is difficult to list all the names among the large number of good artists, so I will only mention those who are listed in my annual bibliographies. Estonia: Juri Arrak, Richard Kaljo, Avo Keerend, Enn Kera, Raivo Kolka, Edith Kruus-Helwig, Jaak Kuusk, Lembit Lepp, Richard Mutso, Evald Okas, Imbi Ploompuu, Leida Soom, Vive Tolli, Vaino Tonisson, Silvi Valjal, and Edgar Valter. Latvia: Peteris Upitis amd Zigurds Zuze. Lithuania: Vincas Kisarauskas and Anatal Kmiliauskas.

In closing England should also be mentioned. Once it played a meaningful role in the exlibris movement, but today there is almost no activity - a confirmation of my opening words about the ups and downs which occur - often on account of one person. Among those exlibris artists known can be mentioned: John Buckland-Wright, Eric Gill, George Mackley, and Reynolds Stone.

This overview is not complete and could not be that; therefore, any possible critics must acknowledge this fact. I have merely made an attempt to describe the situation in this field which gives so many pleasure and is the reason for many friendships across many borders. Perhaps these lines can be regarded as a prelude to the thirteenth international exlibris congress in Budapest.

EXHIBIT : EX LIBRIS, Rolf Erickson

Charles Deering Library
Northwestern University

THE GIFT OF
FRIENDS OF
**THEODORE
WESLEY
KOCH**

IN REMEMBRANCE
OF WHAT HE DID
FOR THIS LIBRARY

An exhibit, "Ex Libris: Selected Bookplates and Bookplate Literature," was on display at Northwestern University Library from April 4th to 29th. It was prepared by Library staff members R. Russell Maylone, Sally Roberts, Anne Norton, Sandy Whiteley and myself.

The exhibit briefly treated the history of bookplates with examples of some of the various kinds of bookplates that have been created, and the themes into which many can be grouped such as: armorial plates, plates which give clues to owners' personalities or professions, and humorous plates. One exhibit case was devoted solely to some of the more than 150 plates used at the University Library in its 120 years.

Also on exhibit were bookplates on loan from the collections of Minnie Orfanos, Librarian of the Dental School Library, and Marcie Stibolt, Librarian of the Joseph Schaffner Library. Of special interest were plates from Theodore W. Koch's personal collection. Mr. Koch was University Librarian from 1919 to 1941 and, being very interested in all aspects of printing and typography, extended his interests to include bookplates. His own ex libris was included in the exhibit. After his death, it was thought there could be no finer tribute for Mr. Koch than a memorial book collection with its own plate.

Among the nineteen books of special local interest exhibited were the Caxton Club's AN EXHIBITION OF EX LIBRIS (Chicago, 1896) and Mr. Koch's own CONCERNING BOOKPLATES, published by the Bibliographical Society of America (PAPERS, 1915). Examples of bookplate periodical literature included issues of the JOURNAL OF THE EX LIBRIS SOCIETY (London, July 1891-November/December 1908), REVISTA IBERICA de EXLIBRIS (Barcelona, Seguida del inventari de exlibris ibericos, 1903-1906), NORDISK EXLIBRIS TIDSSKRIFT (Dansk Exlibris Selskab, 1946-   ), and, of course, BOOKPLATES IN THE NEWS.

— — — — — — — — — — — — —

FROM THE BOOKPLATE LITERATURE . . .

WEST ARCADIA HUB SHOPPER, Display at Library, 26:16, July 13, 1977. During July and August the American Society of Bookplate Collectors and Designers will have an exhibit at the Arcadia Public Library (California).

AMPHORA 28, The Bookplate Society's Third Biennial Exhibition: October 1976, G. A. Spencer. (7) No. 2, 17-20, 1977. This year's exhibit featured the work of modern designers between the year 1925-75. "There are not many book-men who commission bookplates these days. This is a pity because bookplate designers have never been better, and it is difficult to conceive of anything more gratifying than the commissioning of a personal bookplate, call it vanity if you will, but vanity gratified at bargain-basement prices which bear no relation to what the work should command in a truly civilized society. A wood engraving can be had for around fifty deflated pounds, and a copper... at 100."

WHO IS/WAS HARRY SMALLEY

The Carl Truman Batts ex libris has the artist's name in the upper left-hand corner-Harold Smalley but a preliminary exploration brought forth no record of this artist.

If you have information about either the artist or the owner, please let us hear from you, and we will share with other readers of BOOKPLATES IN THE NEWS.

— — —

INDEX - BOOKPLATES IN THE NEWS

The INDEX to Numbers 21-26 for July 1975 to October 1976 has been compiled by Richard H. Schimmelpfeng. It follows the same format as the INDEX to Numbers 1-20. Price - $3.75. Hereafter, the INDEX will be issued annually.

Carl Truman Batts

— — — — — — — — —

More BOOKPLATE LITERATURE . . .

EXLIBRIS-REVUE, vol. 3, #1, 1977. It is the custom for many graphic artists in Europe to design New Years cards, often woodcuts or lino-cuts. Klaus Rodel comments on those received and a variety are illustrated, some are tipped-in. - A young artist, Jana Kasalova, is pictured with her teacher, and some of her work, mostly etchings, illustrated. - A tribute to Gianni Mantero on his 80th birthday; illustrated is a portrait plate for him done by Oswin Volkamer. - In addition to numerous books and articles published in other than English, are listed the catalog published for the English Bookplate Society exhibit, Brian North Lee's article in ANTIQUARIAN BOOK MONTHLY REVIEW, and Philip Beddingham's THE BOOKPLATES OF WILLIAN LISLE (14 pages).

EXLIBRIS-REVUE, vol. 3, #2, 1977. Joseph Sodaitis, member of ASBC&D, is featured with nine plates reproduced and a picture of the artist. Lithuanian by birth, he has lived in the United States since 1949. - Charles Antin, ASBC&D member, writes about the exhibit of bookplates of Grolier Club members. - Articles about several other artists, each well illustrated.

L'EX LIBRIS FRANCAIS, the journal of the French ex libris society, will have an article by Audrey Arellanes on bookplate societies in the United States in the June 1977 (#124) issue. A somewhat different version of the article is scheduled for the next ASBC&D YEAR BOOK.

XVII CONGRESS IN LUGANO   The XVII International Congress of Ex Libris will be held in Lugano, Switzerland, August 16-20, 1978. As in the past there will be a publication featuring the work of an artist from the participating bookplate societies from each country. WHO WILL REPRESENT THE UNITED STATES? Do you know an American artist about whom you could write a short article and furnish 500 copies each of eight ex libris? Is there an American artist who will volunteer? It takes time to write and polish an article, time to have the necessary prints made available for tipping in, so please let us hear from you NOW. As details about the congress become available, they will appear in BOOKPLATES IN THE NEWS or you may write directly to the Congress, attention Harry Saeger or Carlo Chiesa, c/o F.E.S.A.E., XVII Congresso Internazionale Ex Libris, Via Pretorio 20, CH-6900 Lugano, Switzerland. The invitation to the Congress is extended through the Club Ex Libris Suisse.

— — — — —   — — — —

BOOKPLATE LITERATURE continued . . .

THE PRIVATE LIBRARY, James Guthrie, 9:1-48, Spring 1976. The entire issue is devoted to Guthrie: essays by Colin Franklin and Edward Thomas, "The Hand Printer and His Work," by James Guthrie and "Books from the Hand of Guthrie," by Frances Guthrie, a chronological list from 1895 to 1951 with the title of publication and the press name. A picture of Guthrie in the late 1930's is among the illustrations; no ex libris are reproduced, but the publications about them are mentioned and included in the checklist.

PAPERS OF THE BIBLIOGRAPHICAL SOCIETY OF AMERICA, Reviews, 71:#1, 127-8, 1977. EARLY PRINTED BOOK LABELS by Brian North Lee, published in 1976, records more than 500 dated labels and includes some hundred illustrations.

MARTIN R. BAEYENS, Prof. Dr. F. Vyncke. Published by Exlibristen (Klaus Rosel, P.O. Box 109, DK 9900 Frederikshavn, Denmark), 1977, in an edition of 350. This Belgium artist was born in 1943. About ten ex libris are reproduced and twenty-four larger graphics which fill the folio pages.

EXLIBRIS WERELD, Twentieth Century English Engraved Book Labels, Brian North Lee. (5) #1, 6-9, 1977. ". . . the woodengraved label was rare until the present century, and its flourishing has undoubtedly been due to its greatest innovator, Eric Gill." Later artists discussed are Reynolds Stone, Leo Wyatt and Diana Bloomfield, and emerging artists Peter Reddick, Simon Brett, and Michael Renton.

KENT COLLECTOR, Kentiana Wanted, 4:18, Summer 1977. Frank K. Tarrant, 6131 Powhatan Ave., Norfold, VA 23508, seeks the following Kent ex libris: Elmer Adler, Harvard Society for Contemporary Art, Figural Bookplates:Authors of America, Frederick Baldwin Adams, Jr., and Marjorie & Richard Damman. Also sought by two other collectors "relevant information" regarding a joint plate for Kathleen and Rockwell Kent (KENT COLLECTOR, 34-10 - 94th St., Jackson Heights, NY 11372). - Page 13 reproduces a letter from Herman Abromson with his Christopher Morley bookplate.

Number Thirty

October 1977

NEW BOOK ON EX LIBRIS BY FRIDOLF JOHNSON

We can heartily recommend to all bookplate enthusiasts the new volume just published by Dover, A TREASURY OF BOOKPLATES FROM THE RENAISSANCE TO THE PRESENT, selected and with an introduction by Fridolf Johnson.

This is a Dover paperback (8¼" x 11¼") which pictorially captures the essence of six centuries of the bookplate as designed and used throughout Europe, Japan, Australia, Great Britain, and the United States. Fridolf Johnson, former editor of AMERICAN ARTIST, has selected ex libris created by a variety of artists in each country which demonstrate visually the infinite variations in design for what is essentially a name label to proclaim ownership. Since it is generally accepted that the earliest bookplate, tentatively dated 1450, belonged to Johannes Knabensberg, called Igler from the German word for hedgehog, the volume begins with German ex libris including illustrations of plates by Albrecht Durer for Willibald Pirckheimer, Jost Amman, and continues into the twentieth century with Josef Sattler, Ellen Beck, Franz von Bayros, Alfred Cossmann, and many more.

As Fridolf Johnson mentions in his introduction, this volume does not attempt a definitive or scholarly treatment, but it will prove invaluable to a beginner or advanced collector. There are 761 illustrations which are identified by country, century, and artist. There is also an index of the artists which gives birth and death dates where known and country of origin.

The United States is well represented with the plates of early designers Henry Dawkins, Paul Revere, Nathaniel Hurd, Alexander Anderson, P. R. Maverick, Amos Doolittle, Joseph Callender; the beautiful work of Edwin Davis French, Sidney L. Smith, J. Winfred Spenceley, William F. Hopson, and more recent artists such as Carl S. Junge, James Hayes, Dan Burne Jones, Lynd Ward, Rockwell Kent, Dorothy Sturgis Harding, Mallette Dean, G. Harvey Petty, and Fridolf Johnson.

The field of bookplates has long needed a book to present a visual introduction to the ex libris. Such is A TREASURY OF BOOKPLATES as selected by Fridolf Johnson. And all for the unbelievably low price of $5!

ST. MICHAEL'S FOREST
VALLEY PRIORY EX LIBRIS

Recently your editor received in the mail a copy
of OARIFLAMME, an occasional newsletter of the
Order of Agape & Reconciliation for their mission
in Tajique, New Mexico, which is under the leadership of Father Enrico Molnar, who for many years
was a member of the ASBC&D. Among the news items
was a note about the trip Father Enrico had taken
to Europe, and that upon his return he underwent
open heart surgery. Thanks to the skill of the
physicians, the surgery was successful, and his
recovery was speeded by the tender nursing care
of his wife Sr. Patricia and the Companions of
the order.

Father Enrico continues to do graphics as well as
perform his many duties as Prior of St. Michael's.
The bookplate for St. Michael's is a pen and ink
drawing of the belfry, which is made of old railway ties. The bell is over 100 years old and comes
from Old Mexico. It is rung before the daily
eucharist and the other four daily offices, as well
as before mealtime when there are guests on retreat.

BONAPARTE PLATE IDENTIFIED

The response to the call for help in identifying the Bonaparte plate was most
gratifying as several people responded with a wealth of material. One reply
read: "My guess - and it is only a guess - would be that the plate is that
of Charles Lucien Jules Laurent Bonaparte, Prince of Canino and Musignano.
He was the son of Lucien Bonaparte, who was a brother of Napoleon I and was
made Prince of Canino in 1814. Charles was a noted naturalist; his works included AMERICAN ORNITHOLOGY (1825-1833). Bonaparte's Gull is named after him.
Walter Hamilton's FRENCH BOOKPLATES (2nd edition, 1896), page 131, shows the
bookplate of Lucien Bonaparte, with the same arms as the plate offered for
identification on page 203 of BOOKPLATES IN THE NEWS, but with mantling, without the Order, and with a seven-pointed crown rather than the nine-pearl coronet. According to Hamilton (p. 48), a sixteen-pearl coronet, of which only
nine pearls show in profile, denotes a count in French heraldry. I do not
know why Charles Bonaparte should have used a count's coronet, but Louis
Philippe d'Orleans (1838-1894), the Bourbon pretender to the French throne,
was called the Count of Paris and it may be that Charles Bonaparte used the
title of Count before his father's death in 1840. I should think that the
Smithsonian or the Library of Congress must have signatures of Charles Bonaparte, which could be compared with the one illustrated. The Order shown on
the Bonaparte bookplate is, of course, the Legion of Honor, with the old Imperial Crown above the Cross. After the collapse of the Second Empire, a
laurel wreath was substituted for the Crown." Another response included the
reproduction of several pages from the ENCYCLOPEDIA AMERICANA, which gives
the family tree and biographical sketches of major Bonaparte family members.
With this much interest shown in bookplates of the past, the editor will welcome other inqueries and/or articles with <u>new</u> material about <u>old</u> bookplates!

SCHIMMELPFENG PLATE BY HAWLEY

The first bookplate for Richard
Schimmelpfeng was designed by Robert
A. Hawley of East Hartland, CT. The
design is bases on his family name
and symbolizes a horse upon a coin.
The name itseld has two parts: "Schim-
mel" which means a white horse plus
"pfeng" which comes from "pfenning"
or penny or a coin, thus, white horse
penny. The design was created in pen
and ink, and reproduced by photolithog-
raphy.

Richard Schimmelpfeng is the Special
Collections Librarian at the University of Connecticut in Storrs. He
is interested both in bookplate prints
and the vast literature of the field.
His knowledge and professional approach have been applied in preparing the
INDEX for the YEAR BOOK 1950-1972 and more recently in the INDEX for BOOK-
PLATES IN THE NEWS #1-20 and #21-26. It is anticipated he will continue
indexing the newsletter on an annual basis.

A future article will tell of additional work by Robert A. Hawley.

CONTEMPORARY BOOKPLATES

Bookplate collectors will be interested to learn that they may add to
their collections by purchasing a
packet of twenty different ex libris
designed by Joseph Sodaitis.

Each packet includes designs of folk
art, flowers, nudes, sport, religion,
music, and other motifs; twenty different designs for $2.50. Write the
artist: Joseph Sodaitis, 287 Forest
Drive, Union, N.J. 07083.

BOOKPLATES IN THE NEWS
1206 N. Stoneman Ave. #15
Alhambra, California 91801

Published:
January/April/July/October

Membership for 1978:
$7.50 U.S. / $8.50 Overseas
(Production costs - paper, printing,
postage - necessitate increase.)
© 1977 by Audrey Spencer Arellanes

FROM THE BOOKPLATE LITERATURE . . .

EXLIBRIS-REVUE, vol. 3, #3, 1977. "Alena Antonova," article on artist born in Prague in 1930 who has studied ceramics, graphics, and other handcrafts. Her ex libris have a "very personal and almost folkloristic tradition" and achieve a sense of color with a slightly tinted background for the black and white prints. - "Frank-Ivo Van Damme," artist famous for his woodengraved bookplates was born in Antwerp; he studied under Mark Severin. Frank-Ivo also designs theatre scenery and costumes, creates film cartoons. He has over 180 ex libris designs to his credit. - "Gerardas Bagdonavicius," is a Lithuanian artist who recently celebrated his 75th birthday; he has created over 150 bookplates. He also "provides some 'microinformation' about the book-owner." This issue of EXLIBRIS-REVUE is twelve pages with numerous illustrations, a multi-color tip-in, and many multi-lingual articles. ASBC&D member V. E. Vengris submitted the article on Bagdonavicius.

L'EX LIBRIS FRANCAIS, vol. 39, #124, June 1977. The lead article, Les Societés D'Ex Libris Aux Etats-Unis, details the history of bookplate societies in the United States. The article, running five pages, is by Audrey Arellanes and has been translated into French by Françoise Bonnet. Mastheads, devices, and ex libris of the various societies are illustrated. (Essentially the same article will appear in the forthcoming YEAR BOOK 1977 of the ASBC&D.) Other articles feature the ex libris of Julien Benda, French philosopher and novelist (1867-1956); Daniel Meyer writes the obituary of Miss Madeleine Lagrange, who for long years was the devoted secretary of the French society; a general meeting was held in Toulon on May 21-22, 1977.

EUROPEAN BOOK PLATES 1975, published by Klaus Rodel, ExlibRisten, Denmark. This is the ninth volume in Rodel's continuing series. Artists throughout Europe are represented (291 artists) with their addresses, updated checklist for 1975, and illustrations in black and white and/or actualy tipped-in ex libris prints.

NEWSLETTER, The Bookplate Society (London), vol. 2, #18, June 1977. The annual meeting was held at Gray's Inn on June 15, 1977, which was also the second day of the Antiquarian Book Fair at the Europa Hotel. - Through the invitation of Dr. Anthony Ambrose, members were invited to attend the Ephemera Society's Summer Diversion at Minster Lovell on June 19th, which included an alfresco ephemera auction. - Professor Butler lectured on Kalashnivok's bookplates. A catalogue, containing a full checklist and an original ex libris tipped-in, is avaliable to members at 35 pence from the Private Libraries Association. - New members include several from the United States. - Tipped-in are two bookplates for Sir Harry Page; one with an owl is by Simon Brett. - "Bookplates of Orlando and Llewellynn Jewitt," with a three page text by Brian North Lee, ten plates are illustrated, and there is an annotated checklist of 50 plates designed. It is interesting to note that Orlando was considered by Dodgson as a possible illustrator for his ALICE IN WONDERLAND. - "Bookplates by the Earl of Aylesford," by Anthony Pincott list five plates designed by Heneage Finch, who became the fourth Earl in 1777. - Two Kinds of Bookplate Exchange: The Exchange Club, which has been in existence before the turn of the century, is limited to members in the United Kingdom and involves despatch of 30 bookplates for exchange six times a year. The other exchange will be open to all members of the Bookplate Society. - Book Tokens offers designs by Esme Eve in full color "based on a symbol of British history or legend - a dragon, unicorn and knight in armour."

This is an unusual ex libris. It has been "tested" under peculiar circumstances.

Its owner, a talented graduate from Tartu University (Estonia), soon became known among his colleagues abroad for his research work and brilliant articles on ornithology. His international contacts were among the main reasons for his arrest in 1959. He was sentenced to ten years at a Soviet labor camp. Deprived of everything, Mart Kiklus tried his best in order not to lose his scientific qualifications. While in the camps, he made full translations into Estonian of Darwin's THE ORIGIN OF SPECIES, Guy Mountford's BIRDS OF EUROPE, and several others. Unfortunately, although approved by experts, the translations have not been published.

In 1962 when many of his personal books arrived by post to the Camp Nr. 7 in Mordovia (about 450 km from Moscow), they all bore this ex libris. (The designer anticipated obviously the scientist's fate and put a barbed wire fence in the top right corner.) The camp guards had no idea what an ex libris really was. They started tearing them off in search of something "anti-revolutionary" hidden under those odd "pictures". Most books were badly damaged. Niklus protested immediately in his own way — he declared a hunger strike demanding at least punishment of the guards. He was fed artificially, and he didn't achieve anything except that two guards were transferred to another camp.

Niklus was released in 1966. He was not allowed to work as an ornithologist and had to make his living driving a truck. Now he is a teacher of foreign languages at an evening course.

On the 8th of October 1976, Mart Niklus, age 45, launched a hunger strike again, this time in protest of his illegal arrest on false suspicions. He was kept in prison Nr. 2 in Tallin for two months and again was fed artificially. On the third of December the charges against him were dropped, and he was released. This time he won. But what comes next? The barbed wire fence on his ex libris is not a mere symbol. To Mart Niklus it is a threatening reality.

— — — —   — — — — —

MORE BOOKPLATE LITERATURE . . .

TULSA WORLD, Exhibit of Bookplates, July 3, 1977. Newspaper coverage of the exhibit at the Tulsa City-County Library during July, which was cosponsored by Sister Joachim, librarian of the Monte Cassino High School in Tulsa, and the American Society of Bookplate Collectors and Designers. The text of the article indicated the wide variety of artists and collectors interested in bookplates; unfortunately the two plates selected for illustration were stock plates.

PLAN TO ATTEND THE INTERNATIONAL EX LIBRIS CONGRESS, Lugano, August 16-20, 1978.

The Margo ex libris uses a cartouche by the inestimable Thomas Bewick, redrawn by Charles Capon. Egdon set in Bembo type the names and ex libris. "All printed, con amore et cum labore, on our Columbian (Curtis & Mitchell, of Boston Town) this year, the Centennial of its birth," he wrote recently when generously furnishing the prints for tipping-in. All those fortunate enough to correspond with this talented gentleman, who is calligrapher, printer, bibliophile, are familiar with the witty content of his typed letters which are interlaced with calligraphic amendments. Examples of his work, including bookplates, appear in several volumes featuring calligraphic work.

EXHIBITS From now until the end of 1977, the library of St. John's Seminary, Camarillo, California, will have an exhibit of bookplates from the collection of Milton Castle. Mr. Castle has assembled his collection by extensive correspondence with people and institutions throughout the world, and has found many of them in the course of his travels. St. John's is a private institution, and permission to view the collection should be obtained in advance.

The PHILOSOPHICAL RESEARCH SOCIETY held its second bookplate exhibit during September and October, 1977. It is from the collection of P. Manley Hall, founder of the Society. The first exhibit concentrated upon the "Little Masters" and the second is devoted to later artists and groupings of pictorial plates around a central subject, such as: sporting, animals, portraits, etc. The PRS is in Los Angeles, so all ASBC&D members in the general Los Angeles area were notified of the exhibit. Several members viewed the display one Saturday morning and had an opportunity to visit with each other.

The Gleeson Library, San Francisco, used a bookplate to illustrate their recent postal announcement of an anniversary celebration of the Countess Bernardine Murphy Donohue Room (founded October 6, 1957) of Special Collections of the University of San Francisco. The occasion also celebrated the jubilee dinner at the Palace Hotel, October 6, 1937, when friends of Father Gleeson originated the idea of building the library.

Please send us news of your exhibits, new ex libris commissioned, finds in current or past bookplate literature for mention in BOOKPLATES IN THE NEWS.

FAREWELL TO A FRIEND
by Audrey Arellanes

Mary Alice Ercolini practiced the art of bookplate collecting on a world-wide basis and was beloved by all who knew her, either in person or by correspondence. Through her generosity of spirit many an artist in Europe during WWII received family CARE packages and many neophyte collectors were introduced to the bookplate world with a packet of ex libris prints by etchers, engravers, and calligraphers, so they might see the beauty of works of art often no larger than a postage stamp. In keeping with the etiquette of exchanging, Mary Alice sent two prints - one for the collector to keep and the other for further exchange.

He that hath the steerage of my course direct my sail

MARY ALICE ERCOLINI

Mary Alice practiced an "art" in the best sense of the word. She was not only a discriminating collector, but she was familiar with the vast literature of the subject. She supported the artists who created bookplates by commissioning numerous ex libris by artists around the world. Further Mary Alice wrote a number of articles which were published in the bookplate journals of ex libris societies in the United States and Europe. She was most generous to the American Society of Bookplate Collectors and Designers whose YEAR BOOK on more than one occasion carried her byline on an article, which was profusely illustrated with original prints, often many multi-colored printed or hand tinted. Mary Alice attended more than one of the International Ex Libris Congresses held throughout Europe every other year on the even dated year.

Mary Alice Ercolini was a native of Santa Clara, California, who died at the age of 74 on June 20, 1977, in Fairfax, California, where she and her husband Bruno had lived for 18 years. For thirty years Mary Alice taught the first grade in the San Francisco school system.

In addition to her many activities in the bookplate world, Mary Alice was very active as a member of the Society of Mayflower Descendants in the State of California; past regent of El Marinero Chapter of the Daughters of the American Revolution; past president of George H. Thomas Circle No. 32 of the Ladies of the Grand Army of the Republic; a member of branch 116 of the Italian Catholic

Federation, and the Tamalpais Women's Club in Kentfield. She is survived by
her husband, Bruno L. Ercolini, one son, Luciano J. Ercolini, and a grand-
daughter, Gina L. Ercolini. This lovely lady will live long in the hearts
of her family and in the hearts of the many collectors and artists who met
her through bookplates.

A FURTHER TRIBUTE TO
MARY ALICE ERCOLINI   "If anyone exemplified the statement 'Bookplates
                            are the passport to friendship,' it was Mary Alice
Ercolini. Our association ripened quickly, and I visited her and Bruno quite
frequently. She was responsible for changing my status from a novice collector
to a fledging one. She added greatly to my collection through purchases and
gifts of bookplates. Also my bookplate literature collection was enhanced.
She spent years developing her own personalized plates from commissions she
gave to the world's top artists - here and abroad. The lady had quality -
her bookplates had quality - her collection had quality. I personally will
miss her very much." From Earl Heims, Portland, Oregon.

— — — — —   — — — — —

MORE FROM THE BOOKPLATE LITERATURE . . .

ANTIQUARIAN BOOK MONTHLY REVIEW, "Ephemera," C. W. Hill. 4:#7, Issue 39, 295,
July 1977. Scottish Widows' Fund & Life Assurance Society, founded in 1815,
used bookmarks by Walter Crane as a promotional feature; Crane created a few
ex libris.

ANTIQUARIAN BOOK MONTHLY REVIEW, "Trade Notes," 4:#7, Issue 39, 296, July 1977.
The GLASGOW DESIGNERS is mentioned and illustrated is ex libris by Jessie Marion
King.

BOOKS WEST MAGAZINE, "The Green Tiger Press," Morrie Gelman. 1:#3, 17-8, Nov-
ember/December 1976. This San Diego press is a "quality graphics house (which)
rescues children's fantasy art from oblivion." They print books, posters, postcards, bookplates, etc.

ANTIQUARIAN BOOK MONTHLY REVIEW, "Book Chat," Paul Minet. 4:213, May 1977.
Bookplates accumulated from "deed books to loose boards" and . . . "now I
have progressed to the point which I am buying up small collections."

ANTIQUARIAN BOOK MONTHLY REVIEW, "Trade Notes," 4:262, June 1977. Jørgen Vils-
Pedersen (Box 2094, Copenhagen K, Denmark) has a new bibliography of 80 pages
with 1,500 titles which may be purchased for Dkr. 25.

AUSTRALIAN JEWISH HISTORICAL SOCIETY, "Bookplates of Jewish Interest," Louise
Rosenberg. (1) 8:Part 3, April 1977, Sydney, Australia. An interesting, well
documented article, primarily about the ex libris of Australian Jews which are
in the collection of the Australian Jewish Historical Society.

DANISH BOOK-PLATE LITERATURE, H. C. Skov. (ExLib Risten, 1976) A Bibliography
of Danish bookplate literature printed in Denmark; articles in foreign annuals
and periodicals are not included. A total of 2,142 items are noted. As the
editor notes it is seldom possible to consider such a bibliography "one hundred percent complete." For copies write the publisher: Kalus Rodel, Box 109,
Frederikshavn DK9900, Denmark, or the author if you have additional items: H.
C. Skov, Husarvej 13, I, DK-8900 Randers, Denmark.

Number Thirty-one   January 1978

WYATT DESIGNER
OF GRIFFITH PLATE

When English artist Leo Wyatt sent the prints to be tipped-in with this article, he wrote about the designing of the plate for Bill Griffith, "The copper plate is a genuine hand engraving. It is for a Warwickshire farmer, born and working in that county. Hence, the bear and staff, the symbols of the county which also is known for its fruit - so the apple and pear. Among the plate owner's interests are gardening, ornithology (blackbird, bull finch, bird of paradise, and owl shown), flowers, religion (fish symbol), writing and reading (scroll), and riding (horse). In addition to these interests is the collecting of Persian rugs. This gave me the idea of incorporating the above in the form of a rug with the traditional 'tree of Life' from which all springs. The top branches are in bud only, because the patron is of an age whereby he can expect many more years of fruitful and useful interests. These bookplates are machine printed which entailed my cutting sufficiently strongly to offset the harsh wiping this method entails."

1977 YEAR BOOK
FEATURES LEO WYATT

The 1977 YEAR BOOK, which was delivered from the printer between Christmas and New Year's Eve, features an article by Brian North Lee, Secretary of the Bookplate Society (London), on the "Bookplates of Leo Wyatt." Basically the same article appeared in A ARTE DO EX-LIBRIS, bulletin of the Portuguesa de Ex-Libris Association, during 1976. The bookplates used to illustrate the article in the ASBC&D YEAR BOOK were selected, as much as possible, on the basis not to duplicate those which appeared in the 1961/62 YEAR BOOK article the artist wrote about his own work. The Portuguese periodical reproduced many of her heraldic plates but had no tip-ins; the American publication is illustrated with tipped-in prints furnished by [continued page 225]

JEAN CHIEZE AND THE EX-LIBRIS
Daniel Meyer, President AFCEL
Translated by George S. Swarth
from LES TROIS BELIERS, Paris
September, 1977

Jean Chieze was born at Valence-sur-
Rhone in 1898, and he died in 1975 at
Granges-les-Valence, in Ardeche, where
he had retired. He lived at Saint-Cloud,
where from 1923 he combined the activities of wood engraver, of professor of
art and government and of member of the National Council of Engraving at the
National Library.

At a period when the French ex libris had neither association nor bulletin, Jean
Chieze, with Genevieve Granger, Jean Lebedeff, Valentin Le Campion, etc. worked
for its revival.

As illustrator of fine works for booklovers -- where the UNION LATINE d'EDITIONS
(Paris) has played so beneficial a role -- Jean Chieze, wood engraver of noble
inspiration and dazzling technique, was equally so in the realm of the ex libris
and of small engravings: occasional cards, New Year's cards, wedding announcements, baptismal cards, etc. But it is only regarding the realm of ex libris,
less well recognized, that we will address you.

On a reduced surface, he knew how to express himself with a minimum of lines,
all excess being regarded by him as a fault. How right he was!

Jean Chieze had a personal style, distinguishable from all others, but sometimes
he also liked to interpret his work in the manner of the medieval wood engravers,
without falling into a facile archaism again become fashionable. Very typographical, of an art always very lively and without eccentricities, his bookplates are
truly marks of ownership where only the essential is evoked. Jean Chieze had
taste and a feel for symbolism; thus, his great love for the sea was often expressed either by an utterly graceful siren or by robust high seas sailors or by
some Bretons in such typical costumes.

We point out especially in the bookplate work of Jean Chieze his four exceptional
pieces for a magician called ERIX. Artist and magician presented a rare conjunction of two personalities: that of the bibliophile and that of the engraver. The
fourth has a romantic inspiration: an imp, seated in a chariot drawn by a butterfly, flies away toward a dreamland in a sky strewn with twinkling stars.

The ex libris for Mathieu Varille, one of the handsomest we know of, shows at
once elegance and a rare vigor. A sun, with a smile filled with serenity, gilds
the grapes of Lourmarin, in Provence. In an aureole, the motto of the owner: "The
wine is his who rises betimes." The rooster is a wrought iron sign found at Saint
Maximin and which the engraver has incorporated in his composition in a very happy
way. It appeals to the fondness for folklore common to the owner and the artist.

These two masterpieces reveal and prove the whole extent of Jean Chieze's great
possibilities of conception, expression, and realization, for, as the excellent
art critic Claude Roger-Marx has so well defined it, "art is not a question of
dimensions." Think also of the medals, coins, postage stamps where likewise we
find such masterpeices.

In reading over the list of works illustrated by Jean Chieze, of his freelance
engravings, etc., such an abundance of creations leaves us bemused, especially
when one knows how conscientiously he composed each of his works. Need we spec-
ify that a wood engraving such as those that illustrate this article [see page 225]

ANTIQUES, China Trade Armorial Porcelain in America, Clare Le Corbeiller. 1124-29, December 1977. An extremely interesting article written by the Associate Curator, European Sculpture and Decorative Arts, Metropolitan Museum of Art, who has used bookplates from their collection to illustrate the coats of arms reproduced on china sets. Many of these porcelain pieces date from the late 1700's.

THE O.P. BOOKLETTER (volume 1, number 1, December 1977. This new monthly will have a regular Ex Libris column written by Frank W. Allen, ASBC&D member and author of volumes on W. F. Hopson and C. R. Capon.), The Golden Age of American Bookplate Design (1890-1925), Frank W. Allen. 1:7-10, December 1977. This paper was originally presented in slightly different form before the XVI International Ex Libris Congress at Lisbon during August, 1976. This first installment deals with Sidney L. Smith and Edwin Davis French. Subsequent issues will concern Joseph W. Spenceley, William Fowler Hopson, and Arthur N. Macdonald. This article is scheduled for publication in ex libris journals in Portugal (October 1977) and Hungary (January 1978). O.P. BOOKLETTER is the first published appearance in English.

THE BOOKPLATE SOCIETY (London), Newsletter, vol. II, #19, September 1977:
    Meetings, 73. "Bookplate Forum" held October 27, 1977, and Simon Brett is scheduled to talk on his engravings and bookplates on December 6, 1977. Both meetings were held at the National Book League.
    Ephemera Society's Summer Diversion, 73. Included in events was an auction of 253 lots which contained few bookplates. Prices were high for "attic treasures" that ordinary, sensible people toss out.
    Bookplates by Jessie M. King, Brian North Lee. (2) 74-6. A sale at Sothebys in Glasgow held at the Charles Rennie Mackintosh Society on June 21, 1977 included the work of Jessie King and her husband E. A. Taylor. One bookplate design brought £2,000! Two lots of bookplate prints, totaling 15, brought £65 and £140 for an average of £13 or £14 for each print. There is a descriptive checklist of fifteen plates executed by Jessie King plus an additional five designs which may not have actually been printed for use.
    Teaser Number 1. (1) 77. Bookplates which pose problems of identification will be presented each month; contributions for this section are requested.
    Bookplates of the Inns of Court Libraries, Gray's Inn, Philip C. Beddingham, Librarian of Gray's Inn. (4) 77-81. "Gray's was certainly the first of the Inns of Court to have a bookplate. The Records of the Inn show that on 24th November 1750" an order was issued for Mr. Pyne to engrave the arms of the Society and for 2,000 copies to be printed and fixed in the books of the library.
    A Royal Bookplate, James L. Wilson. (1) 81. Illustrated is a plate for Princess Elizabeth of York, who would become Queen Elizabeth II, designed by George Perrotet, an Australian artist.
    The Ex Libris of Isaac Lemying Rebow, Brian North Lee. (3) 82-3. The first ex libris illustrated was a keepsake from the University Press in 1722; later he had two armorial plates. There are no recorded plates for earlier family members, yet Isaac Lemying Rebow had three before his death at age 30.
    New Members. 84. One hundredth member announced; nine new members include some from Switzerland, Canada, United States, Australia, and naturally England.
    Members Notes. 84. Announcement of publication by John Murray of REYNOLDS STONE; price £20 for regular edition and £50 for special edition.

THE HERALDRY GAZETTE (28 Museum St., London WC1A 1LH), Feature Page, Bookplate Collections, No. 69, 106, May 1977. Anthony Pincott, member of the [page 229]

BIOGRAPHICAL SKETCHES : Artists Represented in Official Publication
of Ex Libris Congress, Lisbon, 1976.   Translated by George S. Swarth.

VOJTECH CINYBULK / Vojtech Cinybulk, one of the best known of contemporary
                   Czech bookplate artists, was born August 10, 1915, at
Prague. Following his partents' wishes, he originally became a schoolmaster,
and at that time began to design and write fairy tales, stories, and verses
for children's magazines, designed marionettes and marionette shows, and wrote
children's plays for radio. After the Second World War, however, he returned
to his childhood love, painting, and studied at the Institute of Painting of
the School of Education at Charles University. In 1952 he began to teach, in
the Chair of Marionettes at the School of Theatre at the Academy, where his
great success was recognized by the Czechoslovak Government with the title of
laureate of the National Prize. He is also devoted to graphic art, particularly the making of bookplates, of which his earliest date from 1930. After ex-
perimenting with engraving on wood and copper, etching, and other media, he
settled on wood engraving as best suited to his style. At first he adopted the
finished and realistic manner of the 19th century masters, doing many portraits
of noted authors, musicians, and artists. Later he adopted a more stylized,
humorous, sometimes grotesque or sarcastic approach, often enhanced by the use
of a second color. The work of his third period, comprising the last ten years,
is more stylized and simplified, with strong black and white contrasts and
rhythmic torrents of whirling hatchings. During the last two years he has at
the same time made about one hundred lithographic bookplates. His motifs derive
from antiquity, the Middle Ages, and all Czech and world literature. Contrary
to most artists, he regards his other art as a sideline to his bookplates,
which for him reflect his attachment to his fellow men. In thirty years, he
has made over 500 bookplates. His plates are signed with a narrow gothic C in
a lower corner, usually on the right.

ZBIGNIEW JOZWIK / Zbigniew Jozwik, Polish scientist and bookplate artist, was
                  born in 1937. Formerly a brewer, he took a bachelor's de-
gree in chemistry, worked on the problem of bacterially derived antibiotics,
and took up oil painting, calligraphy, and wood carving. At the age of thirty,
he began to make bookplates, first in linoleum and plastic, then in woodcuts.
Simultaneously with his scientific work he has produced more than two hundred
bookplates, published five portfolios of bookplates, organized seven one-man
exhibitions, and participated in other exhibitions both in Poland and abroad,
including those in the Soviet Union, Hungary, Jugoslavia, and Denmark, and at
the XIIIth, XIVth, and XVth International Ex Libris Congresses. His bookplates
are characterized by a single symbolic image in stark black, with rustic block
lettering, and no border, on carefully chosen paper. They are signed by a
block Z incorporated somewhere in the design, typically in a fine white line
crossed vertically by a fine white line of the design.

DANIEL MEYER / Daniel Meyer was born April 23, 1908, in Alsace-Lorraine.
                He studied sculpture at the School of Decorative Arts in
Strasbourg, and in Paris. Until his retirement in October 1973, he was professor
of architectural design and modeling at the National School of Fine Arts at
Nancy. In 1959 he was decorated as Officer in the French Order of Academic
Palms. A self-taught engraver, he made his first bookplate in 1935. He has been
Secretary, and later President, of the French Association of Ex Libris Collectors, Managing Editor of the REVUE L'EX LIBRIS FRANCAIS, and Assistant Secretary
of the ARTISTES LORRAINS. His output of 280 engravings, woodcuts, lithographs,
etchings, and copperplates includes over 190 bookplates. He also does large
paintings of mountains and other subjects, and his wood carvings and busts re-

222

produced in metal have appeared in numerous French and foreign exhibitions, where he has taken many prizes. His works are included in many public collections not only in France, but also in Portugal and Italy. His bookplates are signed with a monogram: a rather wedge-shaped block D resting on a spraddle-legged block M.

LOU STRIK /   Lou Strik was born at Bindhoven, North Brabant, Netherlands, in 1921.
            After taking his bachelor's degree, he studied at the Institute of Applied Art at Bois-le-Duc and after 1945 at the Academy of Fine Arts at Amsterdam, where he finished in 1952 with a superb cooper plate engraving and was awarded the silver Prix de Rome. He was named professor of graphic techniques at Bois-le-Duc in 1954 and later at Tilburg. While specializing in engraving on wood and copper, he is also a master of lithography, etching, and recently watercolor. In his youth he was influenced by Pieter Brueghel and especially by Hieronymus Bosch, which explains his tendency toward surrealism. Among his teachers, the noted copperplate engraver Kuno Brinks influenced his technique, while in composition and design he was influenced by Willen van der Berg, Andre Verhorst, and later Jean-Paul Vroom, who instilled his love of wood engraving. He has produced a substantial number of bookplates, though by no means as many as some other artists. His bookplates are unsigned, but sometimes show an S or lower case "st" near a lower corner.

FRANK-IVO VAN DAMME / Frank-Ivo Van Damme, better known simply as Frank-Ivo,
                      was born at Antwerp, Belgium, in 1932, and attended the world-famous art schools there. He now lives in the suburb of Bkeren. He is a gifted draftsman, catching the essence of his subject in quickly sketched pencil or charcoal lines with an apparent facility produced by long practice. The more painstaking and intractible medium of wood engraving appeals to him as presenting more of a challenge; so also the limited space of a bookplate challenges his talent, more at ease on a larger field. His early linear style was soon abandoned in favor of the solidity of three-dimensional representation, achieved by bold shading. Predominant themes in his bookplates are female nudes and couples. His bookplates are unsigned but carry his emblem, a tiny circle crested with three short radiating lines and with another short line extending downward. They also show serial numbers, a helpful feature for collectors. He has produced over 170 bookplates, the most recent checklist of which appeared in Bulletin No. 59-60 of GRAPHIA (1973).

NANDOR LAJOS VARGA / Nandor Lajos Varga is a Hungarian artist born January 1,
                    1895, at Losonc. He had his first exhibition in 1919, and since then has participated in every important exhibition of Hungarian graphic art. In 1922, already holding a diploma from the Academy of Fine Arts in Budapest, he continued his studies there under Victor Olgyai, whom he later succeeded in the chair of graphic arts. In 1929-31 he spent two years on a scholarship in London, where he studied the graphics collection in the British Museum. The Royal Society of Painters, Etchers and Engravers admitted him to membership in 1940 and made him an Honorary Fellow in 1971. He is now President of the CERCLE DES AMATEURS DE LA PETITE GRAVURE. He has taught an entire generation of engravers, and has not only written but also illustrated, typeset and printed a long series of books on the techniques and esthetics of graphic art. He has produced over a thousand works, including oils, watercolors, etchings, engravings and woodcuts, of which about a hundred are bookplates. For some time he has preferred doing woodcuts, the oldest graphic technique. His bookplates are sometimes dated; they are not signed, but the plate for Gilly has a large V in the upper left corner which may be a signature.

ITALO ZETTI / Italo Zetti was born in Florence on February 18, 1913. He studied
at the Advanced Institute of Art in Florence; since 1937 he has
lived in Milan. He is both painter and engraver, preferring the latter technique, which he learned from Pietro Parigi. In his youth he assisted and collaborated with Bruno Bramanti. Since 1929 he has participated in numerous national and international exhibitions of engraving, both in Italy and elsewhere,
including exhibitions of bookplates. He has taken many prizes, was made a
Chevalier of the Belgian Crown in 1933 and Chevalier of Merit of the Order of
the Italian Republic in 1956, and is a member of the Academy of the Arts of
Design of Florence, in the class of engraving. His engravings appear in numerous public collections, not only in Italy but also in the British Museum, the
Bibliotheque Nationale at Paris, and elsewhere. His wood engravings, both
colored and black and white, include about a hundred large pieces as well as
bookplates, occasional pieces, and illustrations for several books. He was a
founder of the Italian Association of Collectors, Artists and Admirers of Black
and White and of Bookplates, of which he was President, 1948-50, and Vice President, 1965-75. His bookplates are unsigned, but sometimes a block Z can be
found somewhere in the design.

— — — — — —

BOOKPLATE LITERATURE . . . .

THE PENNSYLVANIA GERMAN FRAKTUR of the Free Library of Philadelphia, an illustrated catalogue compiled by Frederick S. Weiser and Howell J. Heaney, in two
volumes, published by the Pennsylvania German Society, Breinigsville, and the
Free Library of Philadelphia, 1976, $60, 9 1/4" x 10 1/2". These beautiful books
have 1,021 illustrations, of which 277 are in color (volume 1). One of the first
forms of Pennsylvania German folk art to be recognized and studied was the paper
work the world has come to call Fraktur. Birth and baptismal records, music
books, religious texts, tiny bookmarks, and bookplates were among the records
they created with distinctive designs and illustrations in color. All hand done,
each an original. There are numerous bookplates reproduced, some in color. Unfortunately there is no subject index though there are indexes of artists and
scriveners, of printers, engravers, lithographers, publishers, and watermarks.

GRAPHIC ARTS MONTHLY, The Book Corner, Designs and Alphabets. 49:#10:136, October 1977. FLORID VICTORIAN ORNAMENTATION by Karl Klimsch, published by Dover,
is a republication of the 19th century ORNAMENTS INVENTED & DESIGNED by Charles
Klimsch. It is suggested that some of the over 700 metal engraved designs would
be useful for posters, newspaper ads, greeting cards or bookplates.

A ARTE DO EX-LIBRIS, Notas Sobre o III volume de "Artistas de ex-libris" da
F.I.S.A.E. ou como de um chapeu sai um artista: Anthony F. Kroll, Rui Fernandes.
(4) XI:#1:7-8, 1977. The journal of the Portuguese Ex Libris Association has
a full page summary of each issue in English. The article in general concerns
the various artists represented in the third volume issued by the International
Ex Libris Congress and in particular focuses on Anthony F. Kroll, "whom (Rui)
considers a refined engraver." Tipped-in are plates for Anne Nagel, Jurupa
Mountains Cultural Center, Donald McLain, and Ernie Hovard, which features a
steer's skull and cattle brands.

A bookplate remover ($5.50/8 oz.) is offered by the Current Company, Box 46, 12
Howe St., Bristol, RI 02809. It is stated that "the removed bookplate should be
reusable after drying." Full directions may indicate whether or not the remover
is harmful to the surface from which the plate is removed.

Arjona Collection at the
University of Connecticut

The volumes in the Jaime Homero Arjona
Collection at the University of Connecticut Library bear a calligraphic bookplate
designed by Robert A. Hawley of East Hartland, Connecticut, a young designer and
calligrapher and former member of ASBC&D.
Dr. Arjona, Spanish by birth, was an internationally known authority on Lope de
Vega, Spain's most famous dramatist and
contemporary of Shakespeare. Dr. Arjona
was on the faculty of the University's
Spanish Department for a number of years
until his death. His working library was
bequeathed to his secretary Sophia Gian-
ninoto in 1956; she in turn has presented
the collection to the Library. The collection includes microfilms of all the
manuscript plays as well as a number of
17th and 18th century printed copies. Of
additional interest is that most of the

European editions were specially bound in Spain to Dr. Arjona's specifications,
so that the collection, which is housed in one place, presents an exceptionally rich
effect.   The design for the Arjona plate was produced photolithographically from
the pen and ink design onto an ungummed white stock.

1977 YEAR BOOK/LEO WYATT [continued from page 219]   Robert D. Homer, Patricia
and Donald Oresman, Boston Athenaeum, Louise and Philip Metzger. There are a
total of seven tipped-in prints; many add a touch of color, a special feature
which heightens the effect of the calligraphy. One tipped-in print was originally designed as a pressmark but now serves a dual purpose for Philip Metzger
of the Crabgrass Press.

Order your copy of the 1977 YEAR BOOK, limited to 250 copies, today - - $17.50.

JEAN CHIEZE [from page 220]   requires much more time than some large pictures
executed by certain painters? Confronted with his impressive list of works,
you will grasp the full worth of Jean Chieze's term evoking "his dog's life of
wood engraving." Also, toward the end of his life, he was to pay dearly, by very
serious eye trouble, for never having engraved with the aid of binocular loupes.
That was, alas! a very disastrous mistake. In spite of that, there was in him
neither pessimism nor self-satisfaction. He worked without rest, having for long
years, moreover, constant cares due to his wife's fragile health. He created
through need to create, to free himself, to transcend himself, and one cannot
cease to admire the least of his works, where are found no weakness, no bitter-
ness, but where is revealed, on the contrary, a rare serenity, even a powerful
vitality.

Jean Chieze understood very early the importance of European and international
exchanges of ex libris and of their collection, which are done in the same way
as postage stamps. Did he not write recently, "The ex libris is not only a
connecting link between book lovers and artists, it is also a peaceful bond be-

tween collectors throughout the world."

Numerous well illustrated articles have been published and devoted to Jean Chieze's bookplates, notably in the EX LIBRIS FRANCAIS (quarterly bulletin #5, October 1946, by Charles Forot; #16, July 1949, by Andre Jammes), as well as reproductions of his cards and illustrations of his works; an IN MEMORIAM (#117, October 1975, edited by the undersigned). We also find studies of our friend in foreign ex libris reviews: Holland, Germany, etc.

Let us add also that he was an enthusiastic and faithful member of our association from its founding in May 1939 and that, personally, we exchanged our greeting cards and bookplates with him from 1938 on. Jean Chieze participated in our national and international ex libris exhibitions where his presence, very outstanding, was always in the forefront.

Let us then not wonder that a master of such a class showed himself, as much as a man, a colleague of such pleasant relationship! We still appreciate the extreme simplicity, the spontaneous cordiality that he showed us -- although being our senior -- and we join wholeheartedly in his regrets when he deplored not having more time to devote to his friends and correspondents.

Here we are far from bookplates, but we think that in placing the man who was Jean Chieze, it better shows us his work, be it only that of bookplates. Thanks to Jean Chieze and to well-known engravers, the ex libris, which formerly was pretentious, changing later to a passe-partout label of more or less bad taste, has become an art. Jean Chieze was at once a great engraver and a great spirit, and his immense work will remain to perpetuate his memory.

— — — — — —

MISCELLANEOUS
EARLY AMERICAN BOOKPLATES / Eight early American Ex libris designed by Revere, Hurd, Doolittle and Maverick are for sale. Write: Jane B. Larus, 27 Varick Hill Road, Waban, MA 02168.

The Bard's Bookplates (Box 183 Shore Road, Westerly, RI 02891) offers a designing service. A miniature brochure, closed with wax imprinted with their seal, gives several examples of their work. "Our designs are as varied as our customer's aesthetic preferences," say Robert A. Lavelle and Hannah E. Benoit.

Some lucky cereal eaters found happy faces centered in a ten-pronged star to form a design for a bookplate. The ex libris was imprinted "Property of" or "Take Me To My Owner" with space for the owner to write his or her name. The labels were printed two-up with a pressure sensitive backing and were found in Kellogg boxes of cereal.

The Horchow Collection, Aug-Sep 1977, A Holiday Preview, is a mail order catalogue in which on page 22 appear three stock bookplates; quantities of 100 are $10. One design is Audubon's Bird, a reproduction of an 1845 study of the Lazuli Finch.

JAMES HAYES DESIGNS
PETER JOHN POWELL PLATE

James Hayes, who keeps active in his workshop nestled high in the beautiful Colorado Rockies, has executed a very simple, but symbolic plate for Peter John Powell, who is presently a scholar in residence at the Newberry Library, Chicago.

Father Powell has been a Research Associate at the Newberry Library since 1971, and has just completed a lengthy manuscript concerning the role of the Chiefs and warrior societies in Northern Cheyenne life. Prior to assuming full-time scholarly duties, he was Founder and first director (1962-71) of St. Augustine's Center for American Indians, Inc., Chicago. This Diocesan Social Agency, in which Native Americans hold all key administrative, staff, and board positions, provides supportive services for more than 15,000 American Indians residing in Chicago.

Father Powell was born in 1928 in Bryn Mawr, Pennsylvania, the son of Reverend William Powell and Helena Teague Powell. A graduate of Ripon College, Ripon, Wisconsin, in 1950, he was elected to Phi Beta Kappa. In 1953 he graduated with the Master of Divinity degree from Nashotah House Seminary, Wisconsin; in 1971 he received his degree of Doctor of Divinity.

Commencing in 1953 he worked under the Bureau of Indian Affair's Relocation Program in Chicago; however, as early as the 1940's he was engaged in field work and research among American Indians. His field work concerned the Dakota, Crow, Navajo, Blackfeet, and Cheyenne tribes. His primary field of study is Plains Indian history and ethnology, with special emphasis on the Cheyenne tribe.

In a letter Father Powell wrote about his bookplate as follows: " I am privileged to be one of the Chiefs of the Northern Cheyenne tribe. Thus the central figure of my bookplate is the sacred Morning Star symbol, given to the tribe over a century ago by Box Elder, the greatest of the old-time Northern Cheyenne holy men. That symbol is now the official emblem of the Northern Cheyenne tribe. Underneath the sacred Morning Star appears Sacerdos, the Latin word for Priest. Below that appears my Cheyenne name Hohonaa-Veahtanehe, Stone Forehead. It is the name borne by Stone Forehead, the greatest of the Keepers of the Sacred Arrows, "the Ark of the Cheyenne People", and the holiest of Cheyenne tribal possessions. The Cheyennes declare that it is Stone Forehead's supernatural power that brought about the death of George A. Custer and all his men at the Little Big Horn in 1876. The Cheyennes honored me with this name in 1961. The bookplate thus symbolizes my double vocation to be an Anglo Catholic Priest and a preserver of the sacred ceremonies and history of the Morning Star People, the Northern Cheyennes.

James Hayes will be one of several American artists represented in the publication planned by the International Ex Libris Congress for release at the Lugano (Switzerland) meeting, August 16-20, 1978. Jim designed the masthead used for BOOKPLATES IN THE NEWS and has completed a new address strip which will be seen in the April issue, which will celebrate the 8th year of publication!

- - - - - - - - - - - -

HELP INCREASE   /   Ask A Friend to Join the American Society of Bookplate
MEMBERSHIP   /   Collectors and Designers / Give a gift subscription

THE WORLD's OLDEST EXLIBRIS
by Egart Andersson
Translated from the Danish
by Rolf Erickson

In the rich literature published about exlibris it happens only very seldom that anything is ever mentioned about our oldest known exlibris. However, one would think that with the current penchant for nostalgia, it would be an obvious topic for the exlibris devotee.

The world's oldest exlibris can be found back ca. 3400 years, in the 18th dynasty of Egypt when Amenhotep III (or Amenofis III if one prefers the Greek form of the name) ruled in Thebes (1413-1377 B.C.). The documentation for this is lodged in the British Museum in London and is a light blue faience plaquette with a dark blue inscription. We know that plaquettes like this were placed in chests where the Pharoah stored his papyrus rolls. Even if such plaquettes do not measure up exactly to the exlibris of our own day, which differ mechanically since our exlibris are pasted in books to give information about the book's owner, they do belong figuratively to the exlibris category because they relate something about the book's owner, or the owner of the papyrus rolls.

Much later there were hand painted or hand drawn exlibris - among which in Denmark is the one known from Admiral Herluf Trolle and Birgitte Gjøe, a hand drawn heraldic exlibris from 1554 in the Herlufsholm Skole library. In Germany the oldest dates from the 900's and is the handpainted portrait exlibris, i.e., the one with the portrait of the emperor's widow Theofane (died 991) and her son King Otto III (983-1002), which is found in a Gotha evangelistary donated to cloister Epternach. These are figuratively exlibris in their function and successors of the world's oldest exlibris belonging to Amenhotep III. In common they all give information about who is the rightful owner to a literature collection, which can be fiction, non-fiction, or any form of written information.

It is characteristic, when one seeks information about conditions 3000 years ago, to see similarities between civilizations. There was also an enormous bureaucracy at that time and therefore many, many scribes. We tend to believe that the number of officials in later centuries has grown with steadily rising specialization; however, it should be remembered that Amenhotep III had a directress and an unbelievably large number of officials in the rule of his royal harem alone. Among these were scribes and, had these (members of the harem) had their own exlibris like their great master, later exlibris collectors could extend the boundaries of their collecting domains and include harem exlibris.

If one can assume that people with interest in exlibris have always been persons with empathy for book culture, the assumption can be proved with the example of King Amenhotep III, who is depicted as a peace loving personality with a refined cultural outlook and the most luxury loving of Egypt's pharoahs. He was married to Queen Teje, who was from Egypt's old capital city of Thebes. He found himself in a period when world trade blossomed for the first time and thereby shaped cultural bonds with Mesopotamia and the land of the Hittites north to Greece. Amenhotep III also had lively diplomatic contacts, evident from the very interesting so called El Amarna letters which are in the form of leather tablets with cuneiform in Babylonian, the diplomatic language of the day. In these Amenhotep III is mentioned six times as proposing to a prospective wife from North Mesopotamia by the upper Euphrates.

It is interesting to note that Amenhotep III, even in his old age, had a wife. She was a niece of the princess. The polygamy of the Egyptian court of that time was a practical element in securing peace and tolerance between countries. Amenhotep

III was a civilized, strong, and refined personality, who lived in an epoch where wealth and luxury poured into the capital city of Thebes in such dimensions that it must be described as having fantastic magnificence and striking elegance with imposing palaces and art works far surpassing what had existed earlier in the world and which even surpassed the renowned Ancient Rome. Under such established wealth it is not so remarkable that the world's first exlibris came into being. [From NORDISK EXLIBRIS TIDSSKRIFT, vol. #25, #1, 79-80, 1973.]

— — — — — ⸻ — — — — —

MORE BOOKPLATE LITERATURE [continued from page 221]

Bookplate Society (London), is preparing a descriptive list of bookplate collections, as these prove most helpful to the herald and genealogist. In addition to the British Museum which has a printed catalogue for its large collection, other collections numbering from 200 to 35,000 items are noted in 39 libraries in the United Kingdom. - Bookplates (3) 106,109. Illustrated are plates for Brigadier E. S. White, Jane Walkley, Gavin Walkley, and Horace N. Holbrook.

WALL STREET JOURNAL, Starting A Museum Is Easy, Raymond A. Joseph. XCVII, #123: 1, 12, December 23, 1977. Story about Mrs. Homer (Margaret Woodbury) Strong, a member of ASBC&D from 1935 to 1969, and her various collections which were originally to be housed in what was christened the Museum of Fascination.

THE PRIVATE LIBRARY, The Bookplate Designs of John Buckland Wright, David Chambers. (35) Second Series 9:#3:83-111, Autumn 1976 (published late in 1977). Alphabetical, descriptive checklist includes date of execution for 31 plates plus three which were created from book illustrations. Of these last three, one is for David and Hermione Chambers, and the other two are for Elizabeth Watson Diamond and J. Edouard Diamond from illustrations the artist engraved for the Golden Cockerel RUBAIYAT OF OMAR KHAYYAM. Each of the Diamond plates measures 8 9/16" x 4 3/16" and is suitable for framing with very wide margins. Several of the illustrations show the evolution of designs through different stages.

JARDAR LUNDE by Thor Bjorn Schyberg (Exlibristen, Box 109, 9900 Frederikshavn, Denmark), published in September of 1977 in an edition of 130 copies. Twelve pages of text, fifteen tipped-in ex libris prints, and checklist of 144 bookplates created from 1934 to 1966; format 6 3/4" x 5 1/4". There is a multi-lingual insert, including English, of a biographical sketch. Lunde is interested in oil painting, fresco painting, stained glass, and lithography; art on this larger scale has held his attention since 1966. Price: dkr 25.

EVALD OKAS with introduction by Jan G. Rhebergen (Exlibristen, dkr 125). This is a handsome portfolio of thirteen ex libris prints pulled in an edition of 150 on heavy paper with wide margins, making them ideal for framing. Each is printed in colored ink: blue, sienna, brown, green. The prints show evidence of great patience having been taken to wipe each plate carefully before pulling.

CALLIGRAPHY INK, Leo Wyatt Workshop, Pall Bohne. (9) 3:#5:6-7, July 1977. While visiting the United States in 1977, Leo Waytt gave a slide-lecture at Dawson's Book Shop, Los Angeles, on April 7, 1977, and conducted a workshop April 16 at Cerritos College for those interested in learning the methods of engraving beautiful letters. Illustrations include bookplates and the pressmark for Pall Bohne's Bookhaven Press. (If you are interested in the work of Leo Wyatt, you will want a copy of the 1977 YEAR BOOK ($17.50) published by ASBC&D.)

MORE BOOKPLATE LITERATURE . . . .

PRINCETON UNIVERSITY LIBRARY CHRONICLE, The Paul Elmer More Books in the Procter Foundation Library, Kevin P. Van Anglen. (1) 39:#1:11-17, Autumn 1977. Nearly one hundred books from More's library are now part of the Foundation's holdings. Each is marked with a distinctive bookplate which shows More seated in a comfortable chair in his cabin at Shelburne, surrounded by his books, and accompanied by his great black dog, Raj.

KOVELS ON ANTIQUES AND COLLECTABLES, Specialized Publications, page 128, July 1977. This is the beginning of a listing of publications for specialized collectors which includes as the single entry under bookplates, BOOKPLATES IN THE NEWS, published by the American Society of Bookplate Collectors and Designers. This is Part XIII of a volume the Kovels have titled LIVING WITH YOUR ANTIQUES, which will be printed sometime after original appearance in their confidential newsletter for dealers and collectors.

BOOKVIEWS, A TREASURY OF BOOKPLATES. (1) 1:#5 33, January 1977. Jack London's ex libris is illustrated in this brief notice of Fridolf Johnson's new book.

PRIVATE PRESSWORK, Frank J. Anderson (A. S. Barnes, $12.50), a bibliographic approach to the subject of avocational printing and the related book arts, includes the American Society of Bookplate Collectors and Designers among its many listings.

CATALOGO GERAL DAS EXPOSICOES, Lisbon, 1976. This is a magnificently illustrated catalogue issued for the XVI International Ex Libris Congress. Within the 175 pages are several lengthy checklists for ex libris in Portugal, heraldic ex libris of Portugal and super-libros, a listing of the various artists whose work was exhibited including from the United States Peter Fingesten, Anthony Kroll, V. O. Virkau.

EX LIBRIS LEKARZY, Andrzej Kompf and Feliks Wagner, 1972. There are 35 pages of text and checklist and 44 pages of illustration for this book which celebrates an exhibition from the collections of two well-known Polish collectors, Andrzej Kompf and Feliks Wagner.

YEAR BOOK ARTICLES   In-depth articles suitable for the YEAR BOOK are desired. Illustrative material should be available to accompany the article including bookplate prints to be tipped-in (250 copies required). Articles may be about bookplate artists, notable collectors of bookplates, or some aspect of bookplate publishing or history, exhibitions, major catalogues.

If you are planning to   INTERNATIONAL CONGRESS in LUGANO attend the Congress in Lugano, Switzerland, August 16-20, 1978, please let me know so that specific registration information may be forwarded to you when ready.

BOOKPLATES IN THE NEWS   January/April/July/October
1206 N. Stoneman Ave. #15 $7.50 US/$8.50 Overseas
Alhambra, CA 91801   Some Back Issues $2 each

AS of BC & D
Bookplates in the News

1206 N. STONEMAN AVENUE #15, ALHAMBRA, CALIFORNIA, 91801 U.S.A.
AUDREY SPENCER ARELLANES, Editor

Number Thirty-Two   APRIL 1978

EX·LIBRIS

NORMAN W. FORGUE

NORMAN FORGUE / BLACK CAT PRESS

The Black Cat Press bookplate was designed in 1934 by Calvin Brazelton, who was an associate at that time. It was originally used as a title page decoration, then as an ex libris for Norman Forgue.

When asked about compiling a checklist of ex libris he has designed and printed, Norman replied it "would take more time than I can spare. Over the years I have probably printed 300 or 400. For one client alone I was responsible for more than 50 individual plates produced in just about every form in the graphic arts."

Norman Forgue has quite a number of miniature books to his credit, and one of the latest is a two-volume bibliography of them and his printed ephemera issued between 1961 and 1977. In PURRINGS, keepsake flyers issued by the Black Cat Press, he says, "Would you believe that I made my first miniature aboard the U.S.S. Maryland, somewhere at sea in 1922! Long before there was a Black Cat Press." The bibliography will be printed in two colors and black, measure under three inches, and be in a hand-made slipcase covered in French marbled paper.

In addition to miniature books, Norman is noted for the miniature rooms he creates in his workshop including the scaled-to-size furnishings. His wife Madeline collaborates in this activity. Military miniatures are another interest.

Another frequent collaborator is G. Harvey Petty, who has calligraphed the text for several miniature books published by the Black Cat Press [8248 N. Kenton, Skokie, IL 60076].

BOOKPLATES IN THE NEWS
  U.S. $7.50
Overseas $8.50

Published
January/April
July/October

ROBERT FROST'S WOODCHOPPER FRIEND

The above is the title of a keepsake presented by G. William Gahagan, president and founder of the California Friends of Robert Frost, on the occasion of the dedication of the Robert Frost Plaza in San Francisco on March 22, 1978. The poet was born in San Francisco on March 26, 1874; Easter Sunday this year marked the 104th anniversary of his birth.

The keepsake tells of a letter to Henry Mencken in 1930 in which Frost thanked his friend for "your kindness to my woodchopper J. J. Lankes." The association of the poet and artist dated back to 1916 when Lankes illustrated several of Frost's poems published separately in magazines and a volume titled MOUNTAIN INTERVAL.

Julius John Lankes was born in Buffalo in 1884. Some of his earliest woodcuts appeared in MASSES and the LIBERATOR. In 1932 Holt published A WOODCUT MANUAL by Lankes; 18 of his bookplates are illustrated.

The above bookplate of Robert Frost is to be found in most of the 3,000 odd volumes of Frost's personal library, now housed in a special Frost Room in the library of the Washington Square campus of New York University. This well printed keepsake is the work of San Francisco printer Andrew Hoyem; a portion of the limited edition is reserved for lucky members of the Roxburghe Club of San Francisco and the Zamorano Club of Los Angeles.

GEORGE WILLIAM GAHAGAN
TELLS ABOUT HIS OWN BOOKPLATE

"My interest in weathervanes, particularly trotting horse vanes, stems from adolescent years spent in Goshen, New York - the 'Cradle of the Trotter.' My father was registrar of the standardbred horse, also secretary of the United States Trotting Association, the Hambletonian Society and the Grand Circuit from 1927 to 1946.

"Later on as a newspaper reporter in Orange County, I began to 'collect' trotting horse vanes, taking photos of them, gathering research on their history. I came to San Francisco in 1937 and worked in the advertising field. An art director friend of mine, Harry Carter, developed this bookplate with me, and I decided to use it as my letterhead as well." William Gahagan formed the California Friends of Robert Frost in 1964; he orginally became well acquainted with Frost when he was "poet in residence" at Dartmouth in the 1940s.

C.C.C. LIBRARY

Recently in acquiring a small
ex libris collection which had
been formed in the 1930's and
40's, Audrey Arellanes found a
bookplate for the C.C.C. Library.
For those of you who may not
remember, the initials stand
for Civilian Conservation Corps.
The material furnished for this
article is from Jack Vincent,
who served as an Educational
Adviser in this organization,
which was founded during the
depression years under the F.
D. Roosevelt administration.

Over three million men served in
the C.C.C. from 1933 to 1942.
During that time they planted
two billion trees, built over
40,000 bridges, constructed
hundreds of miles of minor roads,
reclaimed millions of acres of
land for our farmers, fought
hundreds of forest fires, and
laid hundreds of miles of telephone wires. But the greatest
thing the C.C.C. did was to give direction to three million young men and
provide financial assistance to their families in the great depression.

Jack Vincent remembers the bookplates used in the C.C.C. Congress appropriated money for the salary of the Educational Adviser, but none for books and
supplies. Books were scrounged wherever possible, and the donors were given
recognition through the ex libris pasted into each volume with the name of
the donor written in. The bookplate was designed by a C.C.C. boy, as "we had
artists, cooks, truck drivers, mechanics, barbers, etc., in the camps, and if
we didn't have them, we set up a school and trained them," writes Jack.

On July 23, 1977, in West Sacramento, California, the National Association of
Civilian Conservation Corps Alumni came into being. Jack Vincent pioneered
this reunion which resulted in a turnout of 452 former members of the C.C.C.
from 39 states. He has been appointed Ambassador at Large. Any interested
C.C.C. alumni may contact him at 1709 Michigan, West Sacramento, CA 95691.

— — — — — — — — — — — — — — —

JESSIE M. KING and E. A. TAYLOR: Illustrator and Designer, Joan Hughson and
Cordelia Oliver. Published in England by Paul Harris Publishing in association
with Sotheby's Belgravia, in connection with an auction held June 21, 1977, at
the Charles Rennie Mackintosh Society, Glasgow. Jessie M. King [1875-1949] and
Ernest A. Taylor [1874-1951] were married in 1908. This catalog has interesting biographical sketches of both artist and architect; there are 379 annotated
entries, many of them illustrated, some in color. A number of Jessie King's ex
libris are illustrated. The hardcover catalog is $5 plus overseas postage.

THOMAS EX LIBRIS DESIGNED BY
LOTHAR HOFFMANN

Robert G. Thomas is the senior editor at the Gale Research Company, a publisher of reference books for libraries. This house published BOOKPLATES: A SELECTED, ANNOTATED BIBLIOGRAPHY OF THE PERIODICAL LITERATURE, edited by Audrey Spencer Arellanes. Mr. Thomas also is currently president of the Book Club of Detroit. His book-collecting interests range wide, including Max Beerbohm, Christopher Isherwood, and assorted association copies of books.

Lothar Hoffmann, designer of the Thomas plate, is an Associate Professor at the Center for Creative Studies in Detroit. He teaches graphic design, calligraphy, and typography. He is also proprietor of Domus Graphica, his one-man design studio [20927 Country Club, Harper Woods, MI 48225].

Born and trained in Germany, Lothar immigrated to the United States in 1964. His free-lance association with a major art studio in Troy, Michigan, keeps him occupied between his other interests. He came to appreciate bookplates via his love for calligraphy.

— — — — — —

IDENTIFICATION SOUGHT

While attending the International Book Fair held at the Ambassador Hotel, Los Angeles, California, during February 1978, the bookplate illustrated to the right was brought to your editor's attention for identification.

Your assistance is sought in identifying the motto, the owner, and the artist, who has signed with the single letter B in cap.

Your answers will be published in the next issue, and the information will be forwarded to Samuel W. Katz, who posed the question. Incidentally the same book also contains a bookplate of David Belasco, American dramatist and theatrical producer.

— — — — — — —

INTERNATIONAL EX LIBRIS COMPETITION

There will be two competitions open to artists for the Lugano Congress: one sponsored by the city of Lugano which must bear the inscription "Ex Libris Citta di Lugano" and the other is under the patronage of the Fabio Schaub Foundation. For both the deadline is June 30, 1978. If interested write: BOOKPLATES IN THE NEWS or XVII Congresso Internazionale dell'Exlibris, Via Pretorio 20, CH6900 Lugano.

WILLIAM E. CONWAY HONORED

The purchase by UCLA's Clark Library of a collection of 17th and 18th century English theology formed in the first half of the 18th century by Thomas Cartwright of Aynhoe Park, Northamptonshire, has added significantly to the Library's holdings in that area of interest. Cartwright (1671-1748) collected contemporary works throughout his lifetime; some 1150 titles are contained in 400 volumes. The collection reflects Cartwright's deep interest in the welfare of Protestantism in England both in its theological and political aspects.

The purchase was made in recognition of William E. Conway's tenure as Librarian of the William Andrews Clark Memorial Library. A bookplate for the collection, incorporating the device of William Andrews Clark, Jr., was designed and printed by Grant Dahlstrom of the Castle Press. It was presented to Bill Conway at a ceremony following the annual meeting of the Clark Library Committee on January 25, 1978.

The Thomas Cartwright Collection
*of English Protestantism from
the private library at
Aynhoe Park, Northants.
Purchased in recognition of
William E. Conway's
devoted tenure as Librarian of the
William Andrews Clark
Memorial Library.*

— — — — — — — — — — —

Helan Halbach (116 E. De La Guerra St. Studio #3, Santa Barbara, CA 93101) bookseller, writes: "I was reading Vin Packer's SUDDEN ENDINGS (famous people who commit suicide and why, etc.) in which the account of Ivan Krueger appears; it is mentioned also that Krueger, the Swedish Match King, in his early days was a draftsman, engineer, architect, etc., and that he designed his own bookplate. It had on it the head of one of his heroes - Napoleon. I'd like to see it - if it has ever been reproduced."

Match King's
EX LIBRIS

ERCOLINI PLATES   Earl Heims, ASBC&D member, has purchased from the estate of the late Mary Alice Ercolini her treasured personalized bookplates. They are magnificent plates, usually signed by the artists. A limited number of duplicates are for sale - 10 for $5. Also purchased were Mary Alice's exceptional collection of plates with "cat and kitten" themes - 20 for $5, 50 for $10. Write Earl Heims, 6840 S.W. Canyon Dr., Portland, ORE 97225. Please, no trades.

COMPETITION IN SMALL GRAPHIC DESIGN   The Drustvo Exlibris Sloveniae (Trubarjeva 14, 61000 Ljubljana, Yugoslavia) together with Medex, the biggest Yugoslav producer of bee products and its derivatives, announces a competition for a small graphic design in any technique, but without any words, and the design should not exceed 15 cm. The picture must present the bee or a related symbol (honey, hive, apiary, swarm, etc.). Three copies of the picture should be submitted. The designs will be exhibited at the 3rd International Conference on Apitherapy at Portoroz, September 11-14, 1978. Three winners will be selected. Deadline is August 1, 1978. This competition is an interesting cooperation between an exlibris society and industry.

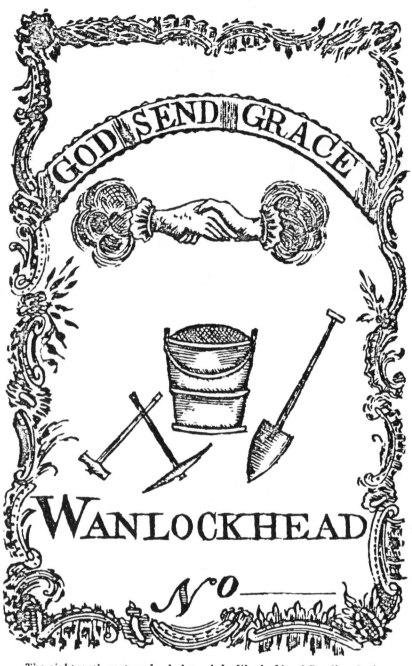

The eighteenth-century bookplate of the Wanlockhead Reading Society.

BOOKPLATE of the WANLOCKHEAD READING SOCIETY . . by George S. Swarth

Wanlockhead is a tiny Scottish village on the eastern side of the Mennock Pass, where the road from Abington to Mennock passes from Lanarkshire into Dumfrisshire. Lead mines were worked there from very early times, and in 1756 the mines, 32 in number, formed a "Society for purchasing a Collection of Books for our mutual improvement." By 1834 the Society had 196 members, out of a village of about 700, and owned over 1,000 volumes. In 1853 a small building was built to house the books, theretofore kept in the cottage of one of the miners. After 1900 the population of the village began to decline; by the mid-1950's it had dropped to 270, and is now about 170. The mines were closed in 1934, and an attempt to work them again in the 1950's was unsuccessful. In 1946 the Society dissolved and turned its library over to the Village Council, which in 1974, with outside help, formed a Museum Trust that is now restoring the village, including its renovated library, as a living museum of a past way of life in the mining district of the Lowther Hills.

An interesting account of the Reading Society, by Peter Keating, author of "The Working Classes in Victorian Fiction" (1971), appears in the London TIMES LITERARY SUPPLEMENT for January 6, 1978 (No. 3,954) at pages 16-17. The Society's ex libris is reproduced there (as above), but with no information regarding it except the statement that it dates from the eighteenth century. The plate is not listed in the catalogue of the Franks Collection.

— — — — — — — — — — — — —

Copyright 1978 by Audrey Spencer Arellanes   /   BOOKPLATES IN THE NEWS

THOMPSON DESIGNS OWN PLATE

Leon Thompson, a handicapped veteran, is a man of many interests which range from ex libris to writing. His published articles have been about post cards, valentines, ink blotters. He is a member of the Anglo-Boer War Philatelist (London), the Oceania Exchange Club of New Zealand, Wedgwood Museum in Merion, Pennsylvania, and the Bibliovermites of Seattle. Leon designs postal cards, especially for Halloween, which some of his friends are fortunate to receive.

Leon writes, "The bird on my plate carries the pen as a lance (representing writing), the newspaper in his back pocket represents the media used, the bottle of ink represents perhaps printing of the postcards I design each year, and when many people hear about the things I do and the time I spend, they sometimes remark, 'That's for the birds!'"

Born in Ranger, Texas, June 30, 1928, Leon Thompson now lives in Kent, WA.

— — — — — — — — — — — — —

FROM THE BOOKPLATE LITERATURE

DICKINSON ALUMNUS, Bookplates - Rush to Kavolis, Martha C. Slotten. (13)11-13, August 1977. Philadelphia physician Benjamin Rush was a founder of Dickinson College. The Kavolis in the article's title is Professor Vytautas Kavolis, whose ex libris was designed by ASBC&D artist-member V. O. Virkau.

ANTIQUARIAN BOOKMAN (AB), Ownership Marks on Books: Historical View, Susan O. Thompson. 61:650-et seq (about 7 pages), January 30, 1978. This well-written article was featured in the issue of AB made available to those who attended the 11th California Antiquarian Book Fair, February 2-4, 1978, at the Ambassador Hotel. Only incidentally are bookplates mentioned. Quoted is a comment by Melvil Dewey in LIBRARY NOTES, June of 1886, ". . . the experience of the world favors a book plate inside the front cover as the best indication of ownership."

FINANCIAL REVIEW, The Sword Is Mightier Than the Scissors. January 13, 1977. Pat Corrigan, associated with a freight forwarding company, commissioned thirteen artists to design bookplates for his library; they were exhibited at Prouds' Art Gallery (Sydney, Australia) under the direction of Keith James. Mention is made of a collection of 2,000 bookplates to be offered as a lot by Berkelouw's, Sydney antiquarian booksellers. (Thanks to Keith Wingate, one of our members from down-under, for this reference.)

THE PRIVATE LIBRARY, A. I. Kalashnikov: Bookplates, Book Illustrations, Graphics, William E. Butler. (15) Second Series 10:3-21, Spring 1977 (published in early 1978). This was a talk given to the [continued on page 242]

IN MEMORY OF A GRACIOUS LADY   A memorial service for Dorothy
     DOROTHY STURGIS HARDING   Sturgis Harding, 86 well-known
                                  bookplate designer of Portsmouth,
New Hampshire, was held at Christ Church in Portsmouth on February 1st.

Mrs. Lester W. Harding died January 28th at the Elmwood Nursing Home in Portsmouth after being incapacitated for several months.

While widely and best known for her bookplate designs for such world famous people as Eleanor Roosevelt and Sir Wilfred Grenfell, Mrs. Harding also illustrated and did the bookjacket design for AN ANTHOLOGY FOR THE AGELESS by Eva and Barbara Greene and other books. During most of World War II and for some years afterward, she did what she considered her duty for war service by applying her talents as an artist to the Drafting Department of the Portsmouth Naval Shipyard. Throughout all the active years of her life, and until very recently, she also designed her own Christmas cards, which became collectors' items among all her family and many friends, as her bookplates had become to collectors around the world.

The last important exhibit of her work took place recently in Denmark. Her health prevented her from attending this exhibit in person. At her request all original drawings, sketches, and files of correspondence are being left to the American Antiquarian Society in Worcester, Massachusetts.

— — — — — — — — — — — — — — —

     GLENN WYATT WOLCOTT   [Editor's note: I was sorry to hear
                                 of Glenn Wolcott's death early this
year, and share with you the letter from his widow, whose simple statements speak of a happy, full life.)

Glenn was such an unusual person - he was 84 years young and kept active until the day he died - August 17th, 1977. He was born August 27, 1893, in Friendship, New York. He was of the class of 1917 at Syracuse University and 1918 at Yale Law School. For 50 years he was an Aetna Insurance Representative. In addition to bookplates, his other interests through the years were: collecting American stamps; Civil War library; American railroading with a large lay-out of HO gauge trains; Syracuse Camera Club; matchbook covers; postcards and humorous jokes to fit every occasion; membership in the American Fox Terrier Club and American Kennel Club. He collected friends of every age, a sentimental, loving man. He loved Syracuse University and attended every football game for 59 years, except for two games when he had pneumonia in 1974!

Glenn Wolcott is survived by his second wife, former Helen Greenwood; one son, Robert A. Greenwood, and three grand-daughters. It is a pleasure to report that Mrs. Wolcott will continue the membership enjoyed for many years by Glenn.]

— — — — — — — — — — — — — — —

Mrs. Barbara Abele and Mrs. Mary   EXHIBIT AT A. K. SMILEY LIBRARY
Pew have installed an exhibit
from their collections at the A. K. Smiley Public Library in Redlands, CA., for the month of April. Each print is well documented for the interested viewer, and many are grouped under special fields such as canting, armorial, children's, etc. A portion of the exhibit is in the main lobby of the library which was built at the turn of the century; the greater part is in the Lyon Gallery where on April 23rd Audrey Spencer Arellanes will give an informal talk on bookplates - works of art in miniature.

THE FASCINATING PATH
TO EX LIBRIS COLLECTING
Verna M. S. Neuscheler

"Young man get a hobby, preferably get two: one for indoors and one for out." A. Edward Newton [1864-1940].

Collecting seems inherent to human nature, and collecting bookplates has given great pleasure to many. In other articles, the values of ex libris art, print, paper, and personalities have been related, but not for many years have there been suggestions made in the "how to collect" area. Although I consider myself in the novice class, I have encountered some tips from recognized ex librists. It is my hope that anything I write will be considered and adjusted to each person's aims and situations.

To begin, one should have great interest in this special collecting field which will lead to continuous exploration of the history, development, and esthetic values of ex libris. Then make a search of your local libraries, both public and university, for books and articles pertaining to the subject. If the libraries have a collection of ex libris, examine them. If you are not known to the library staff, it will mean viewing the collection under the scrunity of the librarian in charge. It is wise, after such a study, to draw plans for several personal ex libris which will display your personality and interests. Compare your designs with the styles you have encountered. When you have decided upon your composite design, make a preliminary sketch; if you cannot complete the plate yourself, locate an artist who will do this in the method you prefer. Your own bookplate will be the focal point of your whole collection. If you wish to collect quality ex libris, your plate must be of quality - if possible a wood, cooper, or steel engraving. Louise Seymour Jones, author of THE HUMAN SIDE OF BOOK-PLATES, wrote to me that she never believed in "an eye for an eye and a tooth for a tooth." She implied a copper dry point etching, a wood or steel engraving exchanged for the same, and a lino or zinc photogravure for the same in exchange. It is beautiful to be so positioned that you can give top ranking plates for a lesser variety. It is wonderful to encourage others with the finest you have. Alas, not many collectors have the resources either numerically or financially to so indulge the splendid side of their characters. Therefore, as a matter of thoughtful courtesy, reach to give equivalent value in all exchanges.

In developing your interest, you may have been aided by friends, who gave you copies of their ex libris, and also gave you names of their acquaintances who would exchange with you. In such a manner I encountered Dr. Robert Metzdorf, Mrs. Elizabeth Diamond, Mrs. Mary Alice Ercolini, and Mrs. Irene Pace in that order, and many others who exchanged, encouraged, and advised. The world of ex librists is peopled with wonderful individuals today, although the above mentioned are no longer with us.

It will be your pleasure to locate ex librists with the same interests. Be thoughtful about the time involved, cost of sending, and high interest. Start by sending several different plates, if possible, and responding to other sendings as soon as convenient. In 1962, Carlyle S. Baer wrote "collectors as a lot are interesting people, even the Washington lady who collected postage stamps but 'only the purple ones'. Yes, I have gotten hundreds of letters from would-be collectors of bookplates wanting advice on how to proceed, but the strange thing about all of these letters I have answered, I have rarely ever gotten a reply to them." Also, he wrote, "To be a collector of bookplates requires intelligence, considerable work which can be interesting and profitable (esthetically) to the real collector in pursuit of knowledge, and the expenditure of some money, although I have known sizable collections formed by persons who spent but little money in the building of their collections, for other than postage; building their collections was wholly by exchange." Another time he wrote, "Collecting bookplates still remains for me an interesting study. In the 50 odd years I have been collecting, I have met the world and its people. I have gotten on the side many a laugh which I have enjoyed, as the range of people interested but casually in bookplates took in a vast number of people all suffering from all the human aches and pains that the flesh is heir to. At one time we had on our rolls the man who wrecked the great Equitable Life Assurance Society of New York, and who then fled. Grover Cleveland, a past President of the United States, spent several years out of his life and, refusing all payment, saved the Society and considered it for the good of the country."

Irene Pace remarked that she allowed a two year period of time for others to respond to her sendings and was annoyed when they expected her to respond in a few months.

Mary Alice Ercolini was a true scholar of every detail of the bookplate world. She had an interest and knowledge that few could equal. Her letters of exchange were not only for collections but also for the development of the collector.

When exchanging with other collectors give information, usually on the reverse of the plate, that will make your sending more valuable to the recipient. This information should include the method of execution, year made, artist's name and country, owner's name and country if not obvious, and personal meaning of symbols used. This is to make filing and cross references more complete. When starting a collection, we have too little recognition of artists by their initials. Plates received without sufficient information can be filed only according to the country from which they were sent. This leads to error and gives no credit to a established artist or the artist's country of origin. In particular, exchanging becomes the lodestar, the encounter which expands the individual's interest, and adds the human touch to any new ex libris that is thereby acquired.

Although much of my exchanging has been through personal contact, joining ex libris societies that are active is most important thoughout your career as a collector. In the United States, the American Society of Bookplate Collectors and Designers, 1206 N. Stoneman Ave. #15, Alhambra, CA 91801, is one of the best. Among the English language societies you would find those of England, New Zealand, and Australia (only the Bookplate Society in England is now active). Most European countries have such a society, and their publications are very fine, but they pose a language barrier (though some are multi-lingual or have an English summary). It is not always possible to find a translator. The European-sponsored International Ex Libris Congress has multi-linguistic printing. The languages they use are French, German, Italian and English. If you are fortunate enough to read more than one language, then joining a European society would be most useful.

The above mentioned International Ex Libris Congress is surely the world's most fulfilling and exciting adventure for an exlibrists. I have been fortunate in attending the 1968 Congress in Como, Italy, and that of 1976 in

Lisbon, Portugal. Anyone who can manage to be in Lugano, Switzerland, this coming August 16-20 should do so. There you will meet the outstanding figures of the ex libris world - artists, authors, and collectors. There you will encounter people from some twenty different nations with their many languages. There also you will be able to exchange all the ex libris you bring with you and gather addresses for future use. Tourist-wise it is rewarding. As an ex librist, it is exhilarating. Many Europeans speak several languages and are most gracious about our language-faulty education.

Finally you should consider a way to keep your bookplates safe and easily available for your reference. I have seen ex libris beautifully mounted in books, mounted and filed in cabinets, and filed in folders kept in office files. I've gone through each plan and find the last most convenient. To have a folder for each artist listing name, country, date of birth and, if not living, date of death is helpful. Plates of unknown artists are filed by country; if unknown, by sender's country. This can create some errors, but I know of no listing of artists, their signature marks, and country. It would be helpful to have.

There is a practice of affluent collectors to buy entire collections, when available. This may seem to put the enthusiasm of many way behind those able to buy thousands, but they cannot feel the elation we small collectors do over each fine ex libris we gain. Yearly, admirable collections have been given or sold into large libraries here in the United States making the acquisition of earlier ex libris more difficult. This we will take as a fact and enjoy those we have. It is often possible to examine the rare plates housed in the special collections of institutional libraries. It is hoped that such collections will be made available for study on a continuing basis.

Acquiring books, yearbooks, and articles about ex libris is a fine help toward continuing research at leisure. The yearbooks of the societies you may have acquired by subscription, and all printed articles you can find on the subject will build your knowledge and your appreciation.

There may be other constructive suggestions, and they would be welcome. One I was given was to try always to use commemorative stamps in mailing exchanges. Even if the ex librist you write to does not collect stamps, there may a youngster next door whose day would brighten with a stamp from another country several thousand miles away. It does no harm to foster small pleasures.

Be sure your envelope will hold together on a long journey. Some people place bookplates in a plastic envelope first to insure their arrival in good condition.

It is some 500 years since the first modern ex libris was used and, therefore, collected. Ex librists are a continuing part of that historical development, and each is a part of a future of greater knowledge and growing artistic values.

[Editor's note: Other articles on the pleasures and problems of collecting would be welcomed. A project which ASBC&D members could contribute to is a compilation of artists' initials and the names they represent. While even the beginner soon knows that EDF is Edwin Davis French, not all may recognize the stylized initials MEW as Margaret Ely Webb. Please send your list of discoveries, a copy of the actual initials as they appear on a bookplate, and a Master Checklist of Artists' Initials will be published in a future issue of BOOKPLATES IN THE NEWS. In the interim, specific inqueries will be presented for immediate identification.]

— — — — — — — — — — — — —

BOOKPLATE LITERATURE [continued from page 237]

Bookplate Society in London, April 26, 1977, on the occasion of opening the exhibit of this Russian artist's work at the Flaxman Gallery, University College, London. A catalogue was issued by the college which includes a complete list of Kalashnikov's bookplates through 1976. Since 1964 he has created 438 ex libris. His first commission "came from a collector of literary curiosa . . . who ordered a bookplate for N. S. Krushchev."

— — — — — — — — — — — — —

Ex Libris

Richard D. Cohen

RICHARD D. COHEN - ENTHUSIASTIC COLLECTOR

Richard D. Cohen, a young Florida physician whose practice is limited to internal medicine and pulmonary diseases, is one of our new members, who approaches ex libris collecting with a great show of enthusiasm and energy. Other interests include book collecting and binding, stained glass construction, sundials, rose gardening. During the eight months he has been an active collector, Dr. Cohen has had several ex libris designed for him. One has a central symbol taken from an old French calendar and represents the eight corners of heaven.

The plate here tipped-in is a reproduction of a woodcut in TEXTIS de SPHAERA, published in Paris, 1538. It reflects Dr. Cohen's interest in the collection of sundials and literature related to their history and construction. The Latin inscription reads: "The scholar studied under the image of the universe."

Dr. Cohen is interested in exchanging ex libris, especially medicals (1801 Bayshire Blvd., Tampa, FL 33606). He has a plate with a unicorn, adapted from a text on heraldic symbols, printed in red.

— — — — — — — — — — — — —

EXCHANGE OF JEWISH EX LIBRIS   A collector in Israel has expressed an interest in receiving bookplates for Jewish personalities, libraries and institutions, and any ex libris depicting Jewish themes, with or without Hebrew lettering. Send exchanges to Avraham Frank, Box 7384, Jerusalem, Israel.

Modern Polish ExLibris
by Klaus Rodel from
NORDISK EXLIBRIS TIDSSKRIFT
Number 2, 1975, 27:97-101
translated from the Danish
by Rolf H. Erickson

The Polish exlibris belongs among the best of the graphic and poster art produced in Europe. In contrast to those in Denmark, consider that the leading Polish graphic artists occupy themselves with exlibris, and the result is correspondingly good.

This article will only briefly describe how devotees of exlibris art are distributed in Poland, where the exlibris centers are located, and, together with the help of some illustrations [Editor's note: unfortunately they cannot be furnished with this translation.], show how some of the more well-known artists work. Unfortunately it is not possible to use original etchings or engravings on account of this periodical's large publication.

In Poland there exists a score of so-called exlibris centers where this branch of art is cultivated with great zeal. It often happens that a number of exlibris collectors are perhaps a natural influence on the artists who occupy themselves with exlibris. This reciprocal inspiration thus results in exhibits, publications, and zealous collecting activity.

In Warsaw one has the names of Professor Konstanty Maria Sopocko, Professor Jerzy Jarnuszkiewicz, Professor Stanislow Dawski (earlier rector of the art school in Wroclow) together with Waclaw Waskowski, Czeslaw Borowczyk, Zbigniew Dolatowski, and many others who belong to the most well-known and active exlibris groups. In Warsaw wood block artists - following the tradition of artists such as Skoczylas, Chrostowski and Cieslewski - are foremost. These, however, must be set apart from S. Dawski, who often employs an etching technique.

In Cracow one is first introduced to the applied metal techniques in use at the art academy, and here you find the best artists - Stanislaw Wejman, W. Kotkowski, Jacek Gaj, and others. Wood and linoleum blocks are also turned out by a score of artists such as Adam Mlodzianowski, Krystyna Wroblewska, Stefania Dretler-Flin, Alina Kalczynska, and Jerzy Napieracz.

In Wroclaw the academy of fine arts celebrated its 25-year jubilee in 1971. The well-known S. Dawski, leader of the graphics faculty (and later rector) was here. Under his leadership came many noted artists who occupied themselves with exlibris; Zygmunt Wasniewski, Halina Pawlikowska, Alina Rogalska-Kacma, Janusz Halicki, Eugeniusz, Andrzej Basaj, as well as many others. These artists work with many different techniques. A special position is held by the world famous graphic artist Jozef Gielniak, student of Professor Dawski. For many years he has lived in a tuberculosis sanitorium. His exlibris (he has created 15) are among the best to be found. Wroclaw also has the art circle "Rys" comprised of 75 artists who concern themselves with the art of the exlibris.

Another exlibris center in Poland is in Torun at the art department of the Nikolaus Kopernikus University where two well-known and interested artists worked after the war: Professor Jerzy Hoppen and Edward Kuczynski. Both are now dead, but among their students are the familiar names of engravers Wojciech Jakubowski, Andrzej Bortowski, and Henryk Fajlhauer. In Lodz, which has had an art school since 1945, there are several interesting graphic artists: Leszek Rozga, Jerzy Leszek Stanecki, Henryk Plociennik, and Teofil Jozwiak.

In Poznan graphic artist Antoni Golebniak has been creating fine woodcuts, often with Christian motifs. Outside these exlibris centers, there are many other cities where the exlibris art has zealous adherents and where interested collectors are found.

Finally, it should be mentioned that modern Polish exlibris have many different forms ranging from simple drawings and signatures to realistic and plain "functional" exlibris. These also can be judged as independent art works without a relationship to the book. All modern stylistic forms, in which are found the free graphic style, are also employed in the exlibris art.

Poland does not have a special exlibris society organizing all of the collectors of the country, but there are, in a score of cities, small independent circles which cultivate the exlibris art as, for example, the Warsaw "Exlibris Friends," "The Society of the Friends of Art" or the exlibris section in the Polish archaeological society. Many collectors work independently from a society but do recognize one another and are in contact with collectors from abroad.

Alongside of well-known private collectors, among whom are Andrzej Ryszkiewicz, Janusz Szymanski, Antoni Brosz, Julia Mekicka, Stefan Wojciechowski, Krysztof Dzierzanowski, Przemyslaw Michalowski, Cecylia and Janusz Dunin, Andrzej Kempa, there is a constantly growing group of new collectors, often very young persons. There are also a score of official devoted exlibris collectors in museums and libraries as in, for example, the National Library in Warsaw, the "Ossolineum" Library in Wroclaw, the library in Cracow, and the museum in Malbork.

Publicity giving information about exlibris appears regularly in Poland, and there are frequent exhibits. In the years 1969-70, for example, there were over 70 exhibits arranged. These were often organized by private collectors but in conjunction with local organizations and cultural societies. In Wroclaw, for example, there have been five exhibits in the form of local biennials since 1960.

The most important exhibitions are the biennial exhibits in Malbork. Five have been held since 1963. These biennial exhibits are sponsored by the Polish Ministry of Culture, and the well-known etcher Wojciech Jakubowski working together with art historian Dr. Andrzej Ryszkiewicz, Dr. Tadeusz Przypkowski, Bogna Jakubowska, and many others for this world renowned display. Each Malbork exhibit is later shown in Warsaw, and there a very extensive and well illustrated catalog is given out. The Malbork biennial can be described today as the most important artistic exhibition on the subject of exlibris outside of the international exlibris congresses.

This topic is more fully described in an article in the EXLIBRISTEN (#100) authored by the exlibris collector and artist Jerzy Druzycki of Wroclaw. It has the title, "The Modern Polish Exlibris," and has, in addition, an historical introduction with about 30 portraits of leading Polish graphic artists. Likewise it has been possible to bring out some original exlibris executed as engravings or multi-colored prints.

AS of BC & D
Bookplates in the News
1206 N. STONEMAN AVENUE #15. ALHAMBRA. CALIFORNIA. 91801 U.S.A.
AUDREY SPENCER ARELLANES, Editor

NUMBER THIRTY-THREE   JULY 1978

COME, LET·US·LIVE THE·POETRY·WE·SING!

From the Library of EDWIN MARKHAM

BERNHARDT WALL EXHIBIT

The Ella Strong Denison Library at Claremont (California) anticipates an exhibition of Wall material from August 15 to October 15, 1978. The items to be exhibited will be from the collections of Rev. Francis J. Weber of the Archdiocese of Los Angeles and Anthony F. Kroll, a private collector.

Wall's magnum opus was FOLLOWING ABRAHAM LINCOLN, which was privately printed between 1931 and 1942 in 85 volumes.

Of particular interest to the ex libris collector are the several etched periodicals Wall created. Instead of letterpress for the text, each page of the journals was etched - text and illustrations - and then printed by hand. The periodicals with bookplate articles are ETCHED MONTHLY, WALL'S ETCHED MONTHLY, WALL'S ETCHED QUARTERLY, ETCHT MINIATURE MONTHLY MAGAZINE.

The ex libris tipped-in above appeared in ETCHT MINIATURE MONTHLY MAGAZINE for May 1948, published in Sierra Madre, California. This bookplate has been photoengraved by Anthony F. Kroll, and he used it as a keepsake for those who attended a talk he gave on Bernhardt Wall during spring 1978 before the Sierra Madre Historical Society.

Wall is well known to postal card collectors for the popular series he originated called the Sunbonnet Babies. In 1911 Wall won the title of the Postcard King.

HOFFMANN CALLIGRAPHER
of RUFFNER EX LIBRIS

Lothar Hoffmann, whose work was a feature in the April issue of BOOKPLATES IN THE NEWS, has created a very harmonious design for Frederick Ruffner's ex libris. The artist was born in Penzig, Germany, attended art schools in Berlin, Munich, and Essen, and had special studies in lettering and calligraphy under Hans Nienheysen. He immigrated to the United States in 1964, and presently resides in Harper Woods, MI.

Frederick Ruffner is president of Gale Research Company which published the Arellanes bibliography of ex libris periodical literature and more recently reprinted the Fuller bibliography of bookplate literature.

— — — — — — — — — — — — — —

FROM THE PERIODICAL LITERATURE

THE PRIVATE LIBRARY, Bookplate Designs by Richard Shirley Smith, Brian North Lee. (10) 10:84-93, Summer 1977 (received May 1978). A bookplate for James Ley Wilson, which is signed and dated in the block, is described by Lee as "among the most beautiful bookplate designs of modern times . . . ."

THE PRIVATE LIBRARY, Fifty Years, Douglas Cleverdon. (14) 10:51-83, Summer 1977. The article is based on a talk given by bookseller/publisher Cleverdon. One illustration is of a working proof with pencilled lettering by Eric Gill of a bookplate for Newman Neild.

THE PRIVATE LIBRARY, Towards a Check-list of Books Illustrated by Jessie M. King/1875-1949, Robin de Beaumont. 10:99-120, Autumn 1977. Though no bookplates are illustrated and, if at all, only mentioned in passing, the article will be of interest to those seeking additional information about Jessie King.

Yale University GAZETTE, The Osborn Collection: A Fifth Biennial Report, Stephen Parks. January 1978. A reprint was made which uses the James Marshall and Marie-Louise Osborn Collection ex libris on the cover.

JOURNAL OF LIBRARY HISTORY, Buddhist Temple Library in Japan, Philip A. Metzger. (1) 13:cover, 204-5, Spring 1978. The ex libris, apparently printed from an 18th century woodcut, is reproduced from BOOKPLATES IN JAPAN by Shozo Saito, published about 1941; this volume commands a substantial price on the infrequent occasions when it appears in booksellers' catalogues.

TIMES LITERARY SUPPLEMENT, John Retallach Ex Libris, No.3,972:552, May 19, 1978. Illustrated are both sides of a silver coin used as a bookplate by John Retallach; the design is by Richard Shirley Smith, though the illustration has omitted the owner's name and the words ex libris. The plate as reproduced has only the letters AR, which stand for argent, the heraldic color silver.

COUNTRY LIFE, The Rich World of Heraldry, Patrick Montague-Smith. CLXII: #4217:1240, May 4, 1978. One illustration shows an ex libris and a por- celain milk jug made in China for Michael Barnwell (died 1792) of the East India Company, presumably copied from his bookplate. The British Museum and British Library are holding a joint exhibition, May 4 to August 27, 1978, to show the history and development of heraldry, which suddenly blossomed and spread throughout Western Europe from the first half of the 12th century.

THE ILLUSTRATOR AND THE BOOK IN ENGLAND FROM 1790 to 1914, Gordon N. Ray. Pierpont Morgan Library and Oxford University Press, 1976. $59.50 cloth, $27.50 paper. Among the illustrators are many artists who created book- plates, such as Bewick, Edward Gordon Craig, Beardsley.

EXLIBRIS-REVUE, vol. 3:#3, 1977. There is a nice blend among the multi- lingual articles, including several in English, and a good span of ages among the artists, collectors, and editors - all concerned with ex libris. Czechoslovakian graphic artist Alena Antonova, born in 1930, works in lino cut and wood cut, with a very personal expression and "almost folkloristic tradition . . ." Many are multi-colored, though illustrations are limited to black and white. Frank-Ivo Van Damme, a Belgian artist born in 1932, has made about 180 bookplates, mostly in wood or lino, some copper engravings. A student of Mark Severin, the master's influence is apparent in the nudes illustrated in the article. Helmer Fogedgaard celebrated his 70th birthday on July 21, 1977; he is editor of the Danish ex libris journal. Artist Edmund Peter, whose Japanese-style ex libris for Fogedgaard is tipped-in, is 80 years young. ASBC&D member V. E. Vengris wrote an article in English about Lithuanian artist Gerardas Bagdonavicius, 75 on July 25, 1976, who has designed more than 150 bookplates since his first plate in the early 1920's. At the Seventh Annual Bookplate Exhibition in Los Angeles in 1931, he received the Award of Merit. Another to attain three-quarters of a cen- tury is Rudolf Koch. A young female artist is Helmiriitta Honkanen.

EXLIBRIS-REVUE, vol. 3:#4, 1977. A female artist brought to international attention is Marie-Louise Albessart of Belgium, who was awarded a top prize at the Ex Libris Congress in Lisbon in 1976. This issue has a brief review of several ex libris societies and reproduces the symbol used by each; un- fortunately the American society is not represented as the deadline was missed.

L'EX LIBRIS FRANCAIS #40, December 1977. While the King Tut exhibit made its way westward across America in 1978, Paris was visited by a Ramses II exhibit a year earlier which inspired G. Meyer-Noirel to present an arti- cle on ex libris with themes from ancient Egypt.

EXLIBRIS-REVUE, vol. 3:#4, 1977. An interesting article, probably by Klaus Rodel, which appears to have evolved from the Malbork 1977 congress, is quoted in part: "Thousand times condemned to die of old age because of its difficult identification, the ex libris revives ceaselessly despite the in- convenience of its existence, and in some parts of the world its small flame gives a warmth deeply felt. As a matter of fact it does not follow any beaten track and lays right between the graphic artist's atelier and the collector's purse. But when we study the chronicle of ex libris ex- hibitions, we can notice that this small insurgence is full of energy and collects much more than any other type of the plastic art. These exhibi- tions are particularly frequent in provinces where people have time to write letters, time to collect all sorts of things, and time to think about it. Long ago the ex libris departed for good from books. Their parting happened during the last century for many reasons, principally for an economical reason. What brought back the ex libris to a new life is the fact that it responds to the need, typical to the human nature, to possess an art work, even a small one, bearing the name and the personal identity of the ordering customer. Sheltered in an envelope, it travels throughout the world as a friendly messenger. Having parted from literature, it has found itself, unexpectedly, in an almost literary position. The ex libris was formerly created to be a guardian of property and very often an instrument of human pride. Nowadays, it is one of the last bastions and a symbol of individualism and private life, both very rare in the actual periods of mass media.

"Who are the collectors of ex libris? Exhibitions are mostly made from private collections. Created by graphic artists who give them as presents to other artists, lusted after by the last book-collectors and worshippers of images and words, the ex libris has also become an exchange object between youths who, after having collected postage stamps, are longing to raise their interests to a higher level.

"Some become collectors by chance, after having looked for something easy to keep in a box, but most of them are romantics, eccentric characters, recluses, all those who need a special language in order to understand and be understood. Therefore, envelopes containing ex libris travel in all directions, actuated by impulses which are not always clear. The trail of these travels draws on the world map a peculiar net, sometimes very thick, that psychologists, art historians, or other people interested in contemporary culture could maybe undertake to disentangle."

— — — — — — — — — — — — — —

PECKMORE COLLECTION/The bookplate collection of Harry L. Peckmore is for sale by his son, who indicates the collection numbers about 590 plus duplicates. It includes plates by French, Spenceley, MacDonald; well-known personalities such an Enrico Caruso, Andrew Carnegie. For details or to make an offer contact H. Paul Peckmore, 138 Francis Pl., Hillside, N.J. 07205.

BOOKPLATES IN THE NEWS
$7.50 U.S. & Canada
$8.50 Overseas

Published:
January / April / July / October

Copyright 1978:
   Audrey Spencer Arellanes

248

EXHIBITION   During 1977 there was an Ex Libris Display at the Tall-
               inn Pavilion in Toronto, Canada, which was sponsored by
the Estonian Art Centre. The exhibit featured ex libris from around the
world from the collection of Emil Eerme. There was special emphasis on the
work of Estonian artists.

Emil Eerme reports that from 1944 on Estonian ex libris fall into two groups:
those from Soviet-occupied Estonia, and those from the free world. The latter
ex libris display a freer form of design and a freer expression of theme and
idea interpretation and representation. These bookplates have become more compact and more individualistic, often reflecting the owner's character. A theme
which has appeared on several ex libris shows a beseiged Estonia beside a
free western nation; this has a particularly sentimental appeal for Estonians
who cherish freedom for all nations. Generally there has been a shift away
from traditional designs, with ex libris becoming more abstract in design.

—   —   —   —   —   —   —   —

THE ENCYCLOPEDIA OF COLLECTIBLES, volume 2, issued by Time-Life. This volume
includes Collectible Bookplates, comprised of a few paragraphs and seven ex
libris illustrated. A statement is made that "Great artists who have done
bookplates include Durer, Holbein, Hogarth, Manet and Toulouse-Lautrec." Specific information about the ex libris created by the last two artists would
be appreciated - please write the editor of BOOKPLATES IN THE NEWS, and if
possible include a photocopy of the bookplate, or the bibliographical reference
which backs up this statement.

—   —   —   —

JO ERICH KUHN / Jo Erich Kuhn was born on Decem-
                  ber 23, 1925 in Mainz at the Rhein-
Germany. He was trained as a draftsman, but this was not
artistic enough, so he enrolled in several art schools.
As a sailor in the German navy he became shipwrecked off
the coast of Sweden; he was picked up by Danish fisher-
men, who brought him to the city of Gothenburg, in the
Southern part of Sweden. He sustained second and third
degree burns during the sinking of his ship. After his
convalesence in a local hospital, he was sent to an in-
ternment camp. At the end of the war in 1945, Kuhn returned to Germany. After working three years at an US
Army R&R center PX in the spa city of Bad-Nauheim, he
returned illegally to Gothenburg, enrolled in the Svenska Sloedfoereningens Skola. A few years later he opened
his own advertising agency, specializing in international
trade fairs. His clintele include Egypt, Israel, Turkey,
Sudan, Greece, USSR, Italy, Holland, France. His artistic talents have brought to this part of advertising a
special note of excellence and culture.

Jo Erich Kuhn has made two dozen or more bookplates.
His own collection is a large one with prints from all
over the world except the USA. He would welcome exchanges or commissions to design ex libris. Write him
with exchanges or inqueries at Rosengartan 2A, Gothenburg, Sweden.

EX LIBRIS

HELEN & GRAHAM

HOWARTH

AUS UNSEREN BÜCHERN ~

MILT & CLAIRE CASTLE

MILTON CASTLE

It is with sadness we chronicle the passing of Milton Castle. Born in New York City, February 22, 1900, Milton has been an enthusiastic bookplate collector for several years. In 1970 he joined ASBC&D and has been a participating member through world-wide correspondence, attending most local exhibits, and using his own large collection to provide exhibitions for several institutions, including the White Memorial Hospital Library and the Doheney Library. He was a toastmaster, storyteller, and after dinner speaker of note; his memberships included the Hollywood Comedy Club. His bookplate, here tipped-in, was designed about 1930 by Roma Van Rosen. In describing his plate, Milton said, "The castle significance is obvious, the jester bespeaks professional vocation, and the glasses and big ears are personal characteristics." His collection centered around Masonic ex libris from lodge libraries and individuals using Masonic symbols in the design; bookplates from Jewish institutional or individual libraries; and college and university plates.

—   —   —   —   —   —   —

BOOKPLATE EPHEMERA for SALE / It is seldom that bookplate ephemera, including letters, notes, announcements, brochures, etc., are offered for sale; for this reason, the collection is being mentioned in some detail. Lot #1 - 4 letters by Carlyle Baer concerning etcher Bertha Gorst, $15. #2 - 10 pieces, BROTHERS OF THE BOOK to C. J. Smalley re designing his bookplate, $35. #3 - 4 pieces by De Lysle Ferree Cass, ex libris designer; letters with biographical content, $15. #4 - 15 pieces by Dr. A. W. Clark, bookplate designer; letters of considerable content, $50. #5 - 4 pieces by William F. Hopson, $20. #6 - 5 pieces by Ralph M. Pearson, who etched ex libris for Carl J. Smalley; interesting letters, $30. #7 - 100 items including designer cards, notes, letters, announcements, brochures, etc. Represented are Dorothy Furman, Dr. Hermann Radin, Helen Stearns, Winward Prescott, E. Wolfe Plank, Rev. E. H. Noll, T. B. Mosher, Archie Little, E. Valentine Kirby, O. B. Jacobson, W. R. Hays, Edwin B. Hill, Austin Hewitt, Wm. Gable, C. I. Berg, H. Alfred Fowler, Wm. Edgar Fisher, C. H. Carven, Bruno's Weekly, Goldwaite, Goodspeed; $100. EACH lot is the quoted price plus postage; lots #1 through #6 include the primary bookplate discussed in that lot as one of the items; lot #4 includes a proof copy. The collection dates from 1912 to 1916. Most letters are directed to burgeoning art dealer C. J. Smalley; as a result they are informal and informative. If interested write: Helan Halbach, 116 E. De La Guerra St., Santa Barbara, CA 93101; include a stamped, self-address envelope for reply.

REYNOLDS ✣ STONE ✣ ENGRAVINGS

Review by Pall Bohne

This book, published in 1977, is a joy to behold and to read. I have long thought that engraving letters in reverse on a block of boxwood is the ultimate in handcraftsmanship. Many try it, but few succeed, and Reynolds Stone is foremost among those who do.

The book is filled with examples of booklabels, especially the style in which the letters are white on a black or colored background, and, where quite often, the letter parts trail off into delightful flourishes. Pictorial bookplates are there too, though generally the pictorial elements are restrained to just one or two, and the lettering is the important part, which is as it should be, I think. Though most readers of this newsletter are bookplate enthusiasts, I'm certain they will all enjoy the many engravings used for illustrations or decorations in books, for this is an important part of Stone's work as a designer and engraver.

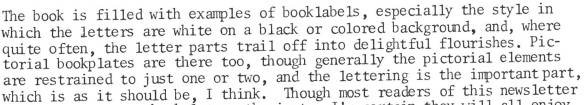

An "Introduction" by the artist and an "Appreciation" by Kenneth Clark give us some background of the man and his work, though I wish there were more autobiography from 1939, where Stone leaves off. Clark tells us that Stone and his family eventually settle in Dorsetshire after the war and that he spends his time engraving, collecting old hand presses, and wandering through the hills and dells which surround his lovely 18th century home.

There are fourteen pages of "Notes" which give information about each engraving shown in the book, which I found useful. For instance, the note for a booklabel I have long admired identified the owner, Christophere Stone, as an uncle, not one of Reynolds Stone's sons as I suspected.

The Confessions of J. J. Rousseau

REYNOLDS STONE ENGRAVINGS was printed at the Curwen Press. It suffers here and there from filled-in hairlines in certain engravings, but it is for the most part a beautiful job. The Stephen Green Press of Brattleboro, Vermont, publishes the book in the U.S. You could have bought it for $45 before the first of the year; now it is $65.

PRIVATE PRESS WORK, A Bibliographic Approach to Printing as an Avocation, Frank J. Anderson. New York: A. S. Barnes and Company, 1977, $12.50. As the title indicates, this volume, primarily for the private printer, furnishes sources for printing presses, type, paper, binding supplies, etc. The sixteen sections deal with book design, printing history, libraries and museums specializing in printing, associations for the printer, and of special interest to our readers there is a section (two pages) about bookplates, listing seven references. Frank Anderson says, "Bookplates are excellent training exercises. Bookplates can be personally useful, or can be produced for gifts."

O.P. BOOKLETTER, Ex Libris Contributions. (3) 1:37, March 1978. Illustrated are three ex libris submitted by Mrs. Robert McGlashan for the Stockholm Stadsbibliotek, Long Island Collection of the Queens Borough Public Library, and William Eyres Sloan.

O.P. BOOKLETTER, Ex Libris - Some Considerations on Arrangement, Francis W. Allen. 1:49-50, April 1978. The author of this article has been a collector for more than 30 years during which time he has accummulated 40,000 American ex libris and about 10,000 British armorials and contemporary European plates. The Augustus Franks Catalogue is used as the model for cataloguing the British armorials; Charles Dexter Allen's AMERICAN BOOKPLATES is used as the guide for the 18th century American plates. For those of a later date, the artist is the first entry, with cross references to subject, such as the various elements which may appear on the plate. Manila file folders are used to house the prints in filing cases.

O.P. BOOKLETTER, Some Bookplates Used by the San Diego Public Library. (4) 1:51, April 1978. Examples furnished by Mrs. Dorothy Hutchinson, librarian in the Wangenheim Rare Book Room.

MINIATURE BOOKS, List No. 81, 1978, Dawson's Book Shop. Item #2, Karoly Andrusko's EXLIBRISI, which contains 50 original miniature bookplates with scenes of lakes, birds, rivers, boats; 2 1/2 x 1 3/4"; $17.50.

EXHIBIT AT UNIVERSITY OF REDLANDS / A comprehensive selection of bookplates including leather, armorial, historical California, contemporary as well as some old, and a variety of pictorial ex libris is currently on display at Armacost Library, University of Redlands (California). The show will be up for at least four months, so there will be ample time for anyone in Southern California to view it. Part of the collection is loaned by Mary Pew of Redlands, who has an extensive collection built upon one formed years ago by Harry P. Dore, a Californian who taught at Berkeley and later was a rare bookseller in Oakland. Additional ex libris are from the collection of Barbara Abele, who is on the Armacost Library staff.

ex libris xvii congresso internazionale dell'exlibris

lugano 1978

V. O. VIRKAU designed commemorative ex libris for XVII International Ex Libris Congress in Lugano.

AS of BC & D
Bookplates in the News
1206 N. STONEMAN AVENUE #15, ALHAMBRA, CALIFORNIA, 91801 U.S.A.
AUDREY SPENCER ARELLANES, Editor

NUMBER THIRTY-FOUR   OCTOBER 1978

BOOKPLATE COLLECTING
IN CONTINENTAL EUROPE
G. Jan Rhebergen, President
Dutch Ex Libris Society

In Lugano, Switzerland, this year the 17th
International Ex Libris Congress will take
place. It is hoped that collectors from
the United States will plan to attend as
part of a vacation in August. It could be
useful to know a bit more about the bookplate in Europe and the artists who create
them. The attitude of the majority of the
collectors in these countries differs from
that of the English and North American ex
libris lovers.

Where the English speaking countries - and
especially the U.S.A. - have collectors
who have great interest in the owner, the
continental collector is primarily interested in the artist who made the bookplate. The artistic value of the plate is
of more concern than owner's name on the
ex libris.

The European collector, therefore, is more interested in the graphic techniques used, and usually knows the exact differences between wood engraving
and woodcut, etching and aquatint, copper engraving and dry-point, mezzotint
and vernis-mou, cliche and offset print, lithography and photo-type. This
also explains why the European collector is very much interested in ephemeral graphics. For example, great artists often make New Year cards for
close friends and print them in small editions; to receive a hand printed
greeting from the hands of, let me say, Chagall is, of course, a great exception, but it is easy to lay hand on small prints by less famous, but not
inferior artists.

This does not mean that the European collector does not value the person
for whom the bookplate is created, for there are collectors who specialize

[Editor's note: This article was written prior to the Ex Libris Congress
held in Lugano, August 16-20, 1978. We are sorry not to have printed it
earlier, but feel the content is equally timely now.]

in bookplates of famous persons and like to know as much as possible about the background of the writer, poet, statesman, composer, scholar whose ex libris is acquired. Every collector will be happy to obtain such a book-plate, but the primary focus of the European collector is on the artist.

The most "productive" countries are behind the iron curtain. Czechoslovakia should be mentioned first as there are a great number of superb artists who make ex libris in all techniques, especially the lithograph-original printed from the stone. Magnificent specimens exist in black and white; also many colored prints. Artists such as Emil Kotrba, Josef Liesler, Ludmila Jirincova, and the younger Albin Brunovsky, Vladimir Suchanek and Igor Rumansky make ex libris which every collector is eager to obtain. The artists of many of these iron curtain countries have freed themselves, more or less, from the social-realism which after WWII was admired by the governments of the satellite states. Now art is freer in these countries, and fine modern works can be found in all trends of today's art.

In Poland we find the finest modern graphic artists of this time, especially in the field of free graphic art and posters; also fine bookplates are made. A few of these artists are Wojciech Jakubowski, A. Bortowski, and A. Aszkie-towicz, who make copper engravings; Dolatowski, Barylski, and Krzywka, wood-engravers; and Zbigniew Janeczek, Leszek Rozga, and Wlodzimierz Kotkowski, who work in different "deep-print" techniques. In the Baltic Soviet states (Lithuania, Estonia, and Latvia), we find the most modern and avant-garde techniques. The most ingenious prints one can imagine come from these coun-tries. Especially deserving of attention are modern Lithuanian artists such as Kmieliauskas, Kisarauskas, Eidrigevicius, and Didelyte. While Hungary is a country with fine graphic artists of international fame (Vasarhely, Domjan, Endre Szasz, Arnold Gross), we must conclude that the great and well-known artists do not have much interest in making the bookplate. The ex libris of copper engravers, such as Bordas, Vadasz, Drahos, and Vertel, can be found in every collection. In the Soviet Union bookplate collecting and designing are very popular, and it is a good thing that the former difficult contacts no longer exist. One can write easily to Russia and quickly receive an answer.

Famous Russian artists at the moment are Kalaschnikow, Wer-cholanchew, and Frolow. Again I mention a few, but there are many more. Russia is a land of wood engravers; we do not see many etchings or copper engrav-ings, and hardly any lithographs. Newcomers to the bookplate field are Rumania, Bulgaria, and Yugo-slavia. In the last country are fine primitive painters, good graphic artists, but as a whole they are behind the other iron curtain countries. The plastic art of East Germany is heavily influenced by the Russians and still is for the greater part social-realistic. However, a graphic artist like Gerhard Al-tenbourg is, in spite of ob-

structions he had to fight, now internationally famous, and his poetic non-realistic prints are much in vogue at auctions. The ex libris art is not revolutionary, but has the disposal of good artists who can engrave book-plates in wood. It is a pity that the wonderful book illustrator Werner Klemke does not make ex libris. His colleague Karl-Georg Hirsch, however, does make the finest wood engravings.

And now the countries of Western Europe. Compared with the "bookplate activities" behind the iron curtain, one must conclude that in Western Europe the interest in the ex libris is on its return. Having a great tradition in Germany, Holland, Belgium, Austria, and France, the ex libris "bloomed" in the first half of this century. With the end of the second World War, peoples' interests spread in the widest fields, the advance of pocket-book and paper-back ousted the use of a bookplate, and the products of plastic artists found their way easily into the houses of the common many. The artist does not like to make these "small things" for "smaller money" anymore. It is a sickness that the bookplate art has to fight in nearly all the western countries. Holland and Austria were very important in the years between the two world wars, and after this time til about 1960. Artists such as Nico Bulder, Dirk van Gelder, J. W. Rozendaal, E. Reitsma-Valenca, Pam Rueter were known the world over. In Austria the famous Cossmann-school brought names like Cossmann, Teubel, Ranzoni, and Wimmer into every collector's house. Nowadays, it is more or less "silent" in these countries.

In Holland only a few artists make ex libris. The most important are Rueter (still!), Lou Strik, and Jan Battermann. In Austria the old Professor Ranzoni from time to time still makes a superb copper engraving, but no new name of any importance can be found. Austria's name is kept alive by wood engravers now. The most important are Hedwig zum Tobel; the veterinary surgeon Dr. Premstaller, who is a fine amateur-engraver; and Franz Stummvoll.

In Western Germany, once the Walhalla of the ex libris collector, it is not much better; the ex libris production is in the hands of a few. The most productive are Hermann Huffert and Herbert Ott, who both make woodcuts in a typical national tradition often "larded" with humoristic accents. Since the old copper engraver Ottohans Beier does not work anymore, the bookplate "in copper" dies out. A fine artist like Miss Elfriede Weidenhaus has made a number of lovely etchings in copper with a very personal touch.

Belgium can be called the most active country in the western countries. This is evident by the founding of the first and only museum for ex libris, the International Exlibris Centrum in the small town of Sint Niklaas in Flanders. Here the activities of Belgian and Dutch ex libris friends concentrate, and meetings regularly take place where one can visit fine exhibitions and exchange ex libris. The superb woodengraver Desire Acket (over 70) still makes his beautiful ex libris, and so does his wife Nelly Degouy. Gerard Gaudaen, the most productive bookplate artist of Belgium, provides his clients with fine engraved ex libris; therefore, he is overwhelmed with orders. Younger artists emerge, but their production is yet too small to give a judgment. A name coming more and more in the list is that of Walter Brems; he makes very nice etchings.

Denmark is the richest in collectors, and the artist Christian Blaesbjerg is famous for his nice colored bookplates, mostly drawn in pen and ink; however, he can make good woodcuts. Since Henry Schjaerven from Norway died, this country has few good ex libris. Sweden and Finland have some good artists who cut in wood, but their style is not very popular in the rest of Europe.

Switzerland has a nice tradition in graphic art, and the Swiss poster art is widely famous. One should expect good ex libris artists in this country, but since the famous Anton Bloechlinger died, there have been no Swiss ex libris artists of importance. Therefore, it is a good idea to have the International Congress this year in Lugano, as this must stimulate the Swiss graphic artists to give the bookplate more of their thoughts. If possible one would like a visit to Bern, the capital, as it is a book center where many fine books have been printed through the ages.

France does not differ from the other "western" countries. Here also a few artists have an interest in the ex libris, which is quite strange for a country with so great a tradition in plastic art. It is peculiar that two of the best known are medical doctors. Ernest Huber, MD, engraves very fine plates in wood, and dentist Michel Jamar, who prefers copper, made his name famous in the ex libris world by his magnificent copper engravings; Jamar also has a master's degree in art. A good wood engraver is Professor Daniel Meyer. His plates are often cool in style, but well engraved. The fame of the French ex libris still rests on the work of the late, Russian born, Valentin le Campion. The level of his bookplates has not been matched yet in France.

The art-nouveau gave Spain many famous artists, especially in the ex libris field. Familiar names are da Riquer, Triado, and Renart, but today Spanish ex libris art is not of great importance. There are good artists, but production is very low since artists such as Alpressa, Saez, and Botella either dies or stopped working. In Portugal collectors are quite active and stimulate their artists to make bookplates. This country has fine copper engravers; however, it must be said that the artistic standard of the bookplate in Portugal is not very high. The armorial bookplate is very popular and mostly engraved in copper; the rest are drawings, often in colors, in a very traditional way.

To conclude we look to Italy, the cradle of European civilization. Here again the activity is disappointing. A few artists create bookplates and two are wonderful wood engravers, T. Marangoni and I. Zetti, who still make bookplates which belong with the very best of the world.

The American collector is doubtless familiar with the field of English ex libris; however, the continental collectors finds it nearly impossible to get in contact with the collectors from the United Kingdom. It is a pity that in the field of bookplate collecting England still believes in the "splendid isolation."

And so I come to the end of our little journey through the European bookplate world. To summarize: The Western countries are in an impasse; produce few ex libris as compared to the countries of Eastern Europe. There are good bookplate artists, who make fine ex libris for the majority in a more or less traditional style, not much influenced by the great currents in art today. In Eastern Europe there is a great activity from both sides (collectors and artists). Graphic artists are more inclined to make an ex libris; therefore, the bookplate art in these countries is more experimental and modern than in the rest of the world. The lack of interest of the western bookowner in ordering a bookplate is the real cause of this situation; there are too many other things to buy.

FROM THE BOOKPLATE LITERATURE . . . .

THE O.P. BOOKLETTER, Milton Castle - Ex-Libran. I:90, August-September 1978. Bob Hanson prints a letter written by Milton Castle several months before his death at age 78, which reflects his friendly, unassuming nature.

THE O.P. BOOKLETTER, James Parker. (5) I:91-2, August-September 1978. Illustrated are several bookplates used by the Reverend James Parker; no text.

BOOKPLATES OF THE NINETIES, Keith Clark. Published by James Wilson and the Bookplate Society (London). Well written account of bookplates created by British artists during a period often associated with art nouveau, though other styles existed: armorial, pictorial, grotesque, and a section devoted to "ladies bookplates" with due note of today's "women's lib". Keith Clark continues to explore bookplate lore with a happy blend of readability and scholarship.

PAUL NASH AS DESIGNER, Susan Lambert. Published by the Victoria and Albert Museum, London, 1975, to accompany an exbition made possible by a gift from the Paul Nash Trust. Paul Nash [1889-1946] supported the cause of the artist's role in industry. His designs ranged from bookplates, book design, set designs for the theatre and costumes, textiles, invitations, menu cards, rugs, bookbinding, posters, china, crystal, and even a commission to design a bathroom for Tilly Losch, the dancer. This well designed and written soft-cover catalog is well worth the £1 cost.

BRITISH HERALDRY, Richard Marks and Ann Payne. Published by the British Museum & British Library, 1978. An excellent catalog published to accompany the well received exhibition on British Heraldry in the British Museum. An informative text covers early heraldry and through to the 18th century. The 268 items exhibited are well annotated, many are illustrated, some in color. Heraldry is shown as it appears in manuscripts, seals, milk and wine jugs, bookplates. Several ex libris are illustrated including the colored woodcut armorial of Sr. Nicholas Bacon (1574). Catalog priced £5.50.

BOOKPLATES SIGNED "W.P.B." 1896-1928, Horace E. Jones (President, Bookplate Society, London). Published by James Wilson and the Bookplate Society, 22 Castle St., Berkhamsted, Herts., England. This is a 12 1/2" x 9" soft-cover book with some 550 examples of ex libris signed by William Phillips Barrett which are annotated and described; 32 are illustrated in black and white; and there is an informative list of ex libris collections from which the examples were drawn. The text makes interesting revelations about Barrett, an employee of the firm J. & E. Bumpus Ltd., who was neither designer nor engraver!

The following are all Keepsakes which were part of the bounty for each participant at the 17th International Ex Libris Congress held in Lugano, Switzerland, August 16-20, 1978.

ADI ARZENSEK, portfolio of ten prints, signed and dated by the artist, several of which are for Majda Mauri of Yugoslavia.

OTROSKI EKSLIBRISI, 1978. Booklet printed in green with 27 ex libris as a keepsake from the Exlibris Sloveniae Ljubljana, Yugoslavia. One page text in three languages none of which is English.

ANATOLI KALASCHNIKOW, IL CANTON TICINO. Portfolio with ten original graphics (measuring about 9 1/2" x 13 1/2") in this artist's distinctive style, including a self-portrait. This appears to be a keepsake offered by Carlos Chiesa.

ASSOCIACAO PORTUGUESA de EX-LIBRIS. A portfolio of 22 ex libris, some tipped-in and other printed directly on the sheet from the original plate. This keepsake was made possible through the cooperation of Portuguese artists and the Portuguese Ex Libris Association. Interesting variety of techniques.

DREI SCHWEIZERISCHE EXLIBRIS-KUNSTLER. Portfolio of 8 ex libris presented by the Swiss Ex Libris Club; work of Kobi Baumgartner, Hans Tomamichel, and Hanns Studer.

EX LIBRIS - JØRGEN VILS-PEDERSEN. This keepsake is Exchange List #10 for Vils-Pedersen, who is employed in the secretariat of the Royal Library in Copenhagen. Notes about exchanging are multi-lingual, followed by a list of 327 ex libris he has for exchange. The name of the artist is given as well as the number of the plate on that artist's checklist, date and technique of execution; separately the artists' addresses are furnished. Several ex libris are reproduced and tipped-in; Jørgen is also pictured in the library.

EX-LIBRIS ARALDICI NELLA SVIZZERA ITALIANA, Gastone Cambin. This is No. 6 in a series published in Switzerland beginning in 1955. Softbound book of over 100 pages with several pages of text and the remaining devoted to reproducing a bookplate on almost every page with annotations; index by artist and owner.

APPVNTI TKINESI - EX LIBRIS by Pier Luigi Gerosa. Pen and ink designs featuring scenes in Lugano for bookplates. Printed french fold and sewn into cover stock; hand numbered and signed.

OSTERREICHISCHE EXLIBRIS-GESELLSCHAFT. This is a portfolio of 10 graphics, some of which are ex libris and one is tipped-in, presented as a keepsake by Dr. Gustav Dichler of the Austrian Ex Libris Society.

6 EXLIBRIS BY CHRISTIAN BLAESBJERG. Klaus Rodel of ExlibRisten publications, Frederikshavn, Denmark, presented this keepsake which features ex libris designed for the Lugano competitions. Text is four languages, including English.

MICHAEL FLORIAN, Vaclav Poppe. Multi-lingual text including English and 25 ex libris reproduced. The Dansk Exlibris Selskab, the bookplate society of Denmark, offered this keepsake under the editorship of Helmer Fogedgaard, whose ex libris is printed multi-color. This is a soft-cover book exceeding 80 pages.

ARTISTI DELL' EXLIBRIS, volume IV, published by the Federation Internationale des Societes D'Amateurs D'Ex-Libris. This volume is printed and bound to match in size and format the previous three volumes published in connection with prior International Ex Libris Congresses. It was under the direction of Artur Mario da Mota as editor and published by the Associacao Portuguesa De Ex-Libris. When the F.I.S.A.E. book was initiated by Gianni Mantero in 1968, it was with the purpose of "strengthening the ties that link the Associations, the artists and collectors of ex libris." The current volume of 260 pages contains articles about artists in Switzerland, Sweden, Italy, France, Finland, Hungary, Austria, Spain, Poland, Netherlands, Portugal, USA, Holland, Canada, Denmark, Rumania, Belgium, England, Russia, Czechoslovakia. There are over 100 tipped-in bookplate prints as well as many that are reproduced.

[See January 1979 issue for additional Keepsakes]

MICROBIBLIOPHILE, Ex-Libris, Anyone? II:34, September 1978. Mary T. Peterson, 412 N. Palm St., Turlock, CA 95380, "has designed and hand-printed on opaque paper, three distinctive bookplates, which while they are not miniature - 5 x 7 1/2 inches - are reasonably priced and useful to book lovers. The cost is only $3 per dozen, same design or mixed. Three samples - one of each - may be had for $.50 - one set to a customer."

SAN DIEGO HISTORICAL SOCIETY, Library Notes, Sylvia Arden. [September] 1978. Note is made of the many generous SDHS members who give books to their library and use a donor bookplate to commemorate the name of a loved family member.

HORCHOW COLLECTION, Book Guardian, August-September 1978. This catalogue offers a 'noble heraldic lion . . . on a personalized silver paper bookplate. 4" x 5 1/2". 50 personalized bookplates $12.50 + $1.25 handling/postage.' -- WALTER DRAKE, Colorful Personalized Bookplates, Autumn 1978. Another stock bookplate is a "cheerful red and yellow design" of a happy bookworm peeping at the reader, 2" x 2 1/4". Self-stick, 50 for $1.99 or 2 sets for $2.99. They also offer a golden personalized ex libris at $1.59 for 50.

A ARTE DO EX-LIBRIS, The Golden Age of American Bookplate Design (1890-1925), Francis W. Allen. (20) XI:39-51, 1977 (published mid-1978). This is a paper which was delivered by Allen on August 12, 1976 in Lisbon at the XVI International Ex Libris Congress. The article is presented in side-by-side columns in English and Portuguese. Artists discussed include: Sidney Lawton Smith, Edwin Davis French, Joseph Winfred Spenceley, William Fowler Hopson, Arthur N. MacDonald

NEWSLETTER, Bookplate Society (London), Vol. II, #22, June 1978:
    Meeting, 117. The next meeting will be Friday, September 1, 1978, at the National Book League and the speaker will be Audrey Arellanes of the American Society of Bookplate Collectors and Designers. The topic will be "Ex Libris Prints and Ephemera."
    Heraldry Exhibition, 117. The excellent exhibition at the British Museum includes bookplates for Wolsey, Bacon, Jacobean Barnwell, Dugdale, Sir Joseph Banks. Mention is also made of D. S. Howard's CHINESE ARMORIAL PORCELAIN, published in London during 1974 at £72, which contains a section on bookplates used as a pattern for armorial porcelain designs.
    Correspondence, 118. Anthony Pincott comments further on the Reynolds Stone book and the vague qualifications used to justify the excessive costs of a "special" edition. Answer to Teaser #3 is the sinister supporter of the arms for John W. Philipps is taken from his second wife's family.
    Bookplate by Eric Newton, H. R. Page, (1) 119. Newton was a journalist, art critic, and author of twelve books as well having begun work as a designer craftsman. H. R. Page asks for information concerning any other ex libris designed by Newton.
    A Note from the Editor, Brian North Lee, 119. Lee comments that the lack of contributions from members has resulted in his authoring 11 pages of the

current newsletter; this is a problem which has been lamented by editors of periodicals devoted to ex libris including Alfred Fowler, Sheldon Cheney, James Guthrie, and eventually Wright of the Ex Libris Society JOURNAL.

Some Bookplates of the Hoare Family of Stourhead, Brian North Lee, (16), 120-31. This family used a variety of bookplates through several generations from 1704 to the early 19th century. Well documented and interesting article which includes a family tree.

Books Available, 131. The Castle Bookshop (37 N. Hill, Colchester, Essex, England) offers a set of the JOURNAL of the Ex Libris Society (1890-1908) at £180. The asking price "is considered appreciably above a reasonable limit". The extensive publications of Klaus Rodel are mentioned. A paperback edition of the Kronhaussen, EROTISCHE EX LIBRIS, published in 1970, has 6 pages of German text, 200 reproductions, 8 in color, of erotic continental bookplates. "the majority highly explicit." It is available from the Bookplate Society at $3.75. The description is similar to the previous hardback editions.

The Bookplate Society Newsletter - Financial Affairs, 132-3. The balance sheet is in the black; starting in 1978 the Society receives a grant of £50 annually from the Private Libraries Association with which they are affiliated to supplement the £1 subscription for membership.

The Hodgkin Bookplate, 133-4, (1). Additional data furnished by members.

Teaser Number 4, 134. Narrative query with no illustration to assist.

Bookplate Offer, (1)134. George A. Goulty, 55 Summersbury Drive, Shalford, Guildord, Surrey GU4 8SG, England, will send his ex libris to any who send a stamped addressed envelop. (International Reply Coupons may be purchased for over-seas replies, probably allow two for air mail.) Plate is illustrated.

Our President's Eightieth Birthday, 134. Horace Jones was 80 on May 6th; he has recently completed a book on W. P. Barrett [see review page 257.]

Member's Bookplates, (4), 135. New member Peter Drummond-Murray sent two of his plates and that of Gerard Leighton which were designed by his mother, Mrs. E. I. W. Drummond-Murray, and that of Ian, his brother, by Alan Kenth-Hill.

New Members, 136. Twenty-nine new members including several from the U.S.

BOOKSELLER WEST, For Dealers with Bookplates, etc. VIII:6, June 27, 1978. Dealers with bookplate literature and/or prints are notified of the interest of the ASBC&D and to send their catalogs or lists.

A Bookplate designed by John Sutcliffe for The National Trust. Packets of 25 gummed lables bearing the design tipped in were available for sale at Chartwell, the home of Sir Winston Churchill, which is part of the National Trust. Two additional designs in silhouette were also available, the artist unknown.

EXHIBITION at Philosophical Research Society, 3910 Los Feliz Blvd., Los Angeles. CA. The exhibit from September 2 through October 29, 1978 features bookplates from a recently acquired collection and will focus on celebrities, world-famous institutions, and Californiana. Also to be shown are rare books in the PRS Library which contain unusual ex libris.

EX LIBRIS CONGRESS IN LUGANO
    -- One Member's View
by Audrey Spencer Arellanes

The XVII International Ex Libris Congress held in Lugano, Switzerland, August 16-20, 1978, attracted 265 pre-registered participants, which included 36 artists, 115 collectors, and 114 who were spouses, off-spring, and/or friends. The city of Lugano, located on a large lake, offered a breath-taking view from many of the shoreline hotels. Thus the physical setting of the Congress presented many bonus attractions for the visitor. And the site of the Congress at Il Palazzo and Villa Ciani was potentially excellent.

Initial registration, Wednesday afternoon and all day Thursday, was at Il Palazzo, but the packets of keepsakes for the participants were at another location. Only the unofficial assistance of a thoughtful gentleman from Denmark made it possible for those not understanding the official language of the Congress to find the building where the keepsakes were kept, and then to return to Il Palazzo where collectors and artists had an opportunity to mingle, exchange, and get acquainted. Facilities were to be available to give optimum opportunity for exchanging; however, something disrupted the arrangements and access to Il Palazzo was denied from noon on Thursday. Alternate rooms were inadequate and notification of even their availability did not come to the attention of all participants. Those who had attended such Congresses in the past, who had friends among the present participants, and who perhaps were fortunate enough to be multi-lingual managed to have a successful session of exchanging. As one happy collector expressed it, "All my ex libris are gone" and in exchange he had as many or more bookplates from other Congress members. But not all were so fortunate.

The Ex Libris Exhibition was in the Villa Ciani, whose rooms have been turned into display areas. Ex libris prints were in standing cases or occasionally in groupings on the wall, and there was a small representation of bookplate literature. Unfortunately the lighting was not the best for exhibition purposes and many of the prints were not shown to advantage. The hours during which the exhibit could be viewed were limited, perhaps due to rules beyond the control of the Congress.

The highlight of the Congress was a full day in the beautiful Swiss mountains and countryside. Four chartered buses, accommodating over 200 persons, left Lugano at 7:30AM. While the buses climbed into altitudes where the temperature was considerably cooler than in the valley at the lake's shore, members had a chance to chat and enjoy the truly inspirational scenery. At 2PM luncheon was served in a chalet on one of the highest passes. Everyone was eager for lunch, after such an early start, and none should have been disappointed as the repast was excellent - well planned, prepared, and served. After being generously and well fed, it was back to the bus for the continuation of the trip, mostly down-hill for the remainder of the afternoon. This was a 12-hour day that everyone enjoyed.

The third day of the Congress the banquet was held at Il Palazzo. The large banquet room was filled with members at round tables seating 8 to 10 persons. There was a lively dance band and a fair sized dance floor. Many of the participants and their spouses knew each other from prior Congresses, which made for a happy occasion. Banquets for large groups with a dance band that is worthy of dancing to are not everyone's "cup of tea", but certainly most of the crowd quite obviously found the festivities to their liking well past the witching hour.

I had looked forward to attending the Congress and the Delegates Meeting for the first time, and imagined it would be where I would

DELEGATES MEETING OF F.I.S.A.E.
and General Assembly
by Audrey Spencer Arellanes

meet the editors and officers of other ex libris organizations. However, those attending the meeting were not introduced to each other, though, I learned, there were others who also did not know everyone around the conference table.

In brief, I really don't know what business was undertaken at this meeting as not a word of English was spoken, not even a greeting! In fact quite possibly a number attending this meeting heard no word they understood. After the meeting I was told by those who understood the languages which were spoken from the head table that greetings were extended, some brief reports were made, and there was discussion about where the next Congress would be held with offers from Austria, Canada, and Switzerland, its being suggested that the French and German regions of Switzerland might host future meetings as the Italian region was doing now. Apparently no decisions were reached about the site of the next Congress, in part because both the Austrian and Canadian offers hinged upon their being able to secure official support.

Following the Delegates Meeting, which lasted about an hour, there was a General Assembly in the auditorium. There appeared to be a full turnout of members. Again the languages from the stage were limited, primarily Italian. General greetings and possibly news about the events planned for the three-day program were given. The membership was composed of sizable segments from Germany and Denmark but neither language was heard officially in the auditorium; additional groups from a variety of countries heard no official word of greeting they understood. Fortunately most attendees knew someone who did understand and could translate the most vital news. [During the banquet at least one group not represented in the official languages, gave a short toast which left the officials befuddled and uninformed and it is hoped let them experience how it feels to be left out.]

The General Assembly was followed by a reception. Like music and love, eating is a universal language unto itself, and everyone found the punch bowl very sustaining.

The old cliche about seeing one of anything and you've seen them all, does not hold for International Ex Libris Congresses. There have been Congresses at which four languages were offered, including English. Usually papers are presented; there were none at Lugano. While not lessening the disappointments occasioned by my attendance at the Lugano Congress, it must be remembered that Lugano came to the rescue in offering to host the Congress when the original ex libris organization faced insurmountable obstacles to their fulfilling their pledge. So there was bad news and good news - the official program may have left something to be desired (and to strive for at future Congresses), but on a one-to-one personal basis, the Congress was a great success!

[Editor's Note: It is hoped that this and other articles in this issue on the Congress will stimulate responses from those who were in Lugano and from members or other ex libris organizations who may have differing views to contribute.]

D·J·G

Ex Libris
Herbert Hoover

HOOVER'S DE RE METALLICA LIBRARY
YIELDS FASCINATING BOOKPLATES
David Kuhner, Librarian, Norman F.
Sprague Memorial Library, Claremont

The story has been told many times of how the young mining engineer Herbert Hoover, and his wife Lou Henry Hoover, while living in London in 1907 turned their attention to the translation of a Latin classic, the DE RE METALLICA of Georgius Agricola. A part of the story that isn't well-known is that this five-year task of the Hoovers resulted in the formation of a 1,000 volume library, now at the Claremont Colleges, which is a rich source of ex libris, autograph inscriptions, and other memorabilia of some outstanding men and women of the 16th through 19th centuries. The writer has studied the collection for several years and gathered together, largely through the bookplates, much information about the persons who owned the books before Mr. Hoover bought them.

Hoover's bookplate itself is a good place to start. The centerpiece is a reproduction of a woodcut from one of the very earliest printed books on mining, the BERGBUCHLIN VON ALLEN METALLEN of 1527. This work, whose author is anonymous, describes the locating and working of veins of ore; it served miners as a handbook which went through many editions. Later, in 1556, appeared the great DE RE METALLICA or "On the Metals" which the Hoovers translated (while raising two small sons!) three hundred and fifty years later.

The collection at Claremont, in the new Sprague Library on the Harvey Mudd College campus, presents a most interesting array of bookplate designs with emphasis on armorial types of 18th and 19th century England, but with some curious and intriguing French, German, and Spanish specimens as well. Many are still unidentified, and the writer would welcome correspondence with ex libris enthusiasts, who are interested in the history of book collecting in Europe during the period 1700 to about 1914.

The 10th Duke of Hamilton (who married William Beckford's daughter) is here with two large plates: one showing the family motto "Through" with stag supporters and another with the Knight of the Garter insignia. The well-known plate of the Duke of Sussex, who was an uncle of Queen Victoria, graces a German mining tract; and the arms of a prime minister of Spain, Canovas del Castillo, are found in a 1529 encyclopedia printed at Toledo. What's this prim diamond-shaped plate with the simple notation "Lady Davy"? It could be only the animated and wealthy widow from Edinburgh who charmed Sir Humphry Davy, the great English chemist, into matrimony in 1812 - Jane Davy, no less.

Such are just a few of the stories that the Hoover bookplates tell, a panorama of the social, cultural, political, and scientific worlds of the golden age of book collecting. What better way can we close this article than to tell this true story: inside the two-volume Gutenberg Bible that sold at Christie's in New York on last April 7th for $2,000,000 plus dealer's commission was a plate reading "Syston Park." Inside an incunabulum that Herbert Hoover purchased is the same plate. Now where were these two works united in the past? Why in the library just north of the present-day Grantham in Lincolnshire, England, the home of Sir John Hayford Thorold, a captain in the 3rd York Militia, a gentleman, and a book collector. So you see, you may not be able to touch a Gutenberg, but if you're lucky you may be able to say, "I touched the book that touched the Gutenberg."

BOOKPLATES IN THE NEWS   - -   1978 Copyright by Audrey Spencer Arellanes

AS of BC & D
Bookplates in the News
1206 N. STONEMAN AVENUE #15, ALHAMBRA, CALIFORNIA, 91801 U.S.A.
AUDREY SPENCER ARELLANES, Editor

Number Thirty-Five

January 1979

HEDWIG ZUM TOBEL
by Dr. Gustav Dichler

Hedwig Zum Tobel was born in Vienna where, after finishing grammar school, for five years she attended the Institute for the Teaching of and Research-work in Graphic Arts. Then she studied stage and costume designing with Professor Remigius Geyling, and started her career as a designer of decorations and period clothes at the Volksoper, several theatres, and for films. After 1945 she turned her interest to graphic art, lino-cut, wood-cut and woodengraving of all sizes, also to the ex libris. Hedwig has earned her living mainly as a book illustrator.

Hedwig Zum Tobel has won fame in three realms of art, which seems extraordinary. She shows real mastership in three spheres of plastic art: she has illustrated more than 150 books, made about 70 large sized engravings, and 160 ex libris. Each piece of art is most carefully planned, and conscientiously executed, so "it is a beauty forever." No wonder that experts admire her work, most of all perhaps her own colleagues, which seems, considering human nature, astonishing.

Hedwig Zum Tobel has suffered much illness and pain, but there is, besides a brilliant brain, such an overflow of affection, love, and serenity in her work that the spectator is deeply moved, and sometimes also a rare sort of humour, shocking the weak but uplifting the strong. And it proves a lasting fascination, nobody ever forgets a picture of hers. An expert, however, feels drawn back again and again to study the richness of her imagination and the perfection of her technique. The cutting is clear, but soft in effect. Everything seems so easy, so natural, so self-evident, but is, in reality, the result of clever planning and careful execution. She has chosen, moreover, the most difficult of all objects: the figures of men and animals; never painting or engraving from models, yet realistic in the highest degree.

So Hedwig Zum Tobel is not only a master of her art, but also a wonderful character. The impact of her personality is overwhelming. Her brilliance is only one part of her, the other is her self-discipline, her noble nature. Womanhood may be proud of her!

[References: Essays on Hedwig Zum Tobel in catalogues of her "One Woman" exhibitions; scientific treatises by Dr. Richard K. Donin in JAHRBUCH DER OSTER-REICHISCHEN EXLIBRIS GES. 1954/44, and Prof. Hubert Woyty-Wimmer in the same journal for 1971/72. The book POESIE DES STICHELS by Dr. Gustav Dichler, Augartenverlag, Vienna, 1977, may be translated as sonnets on the woodengravings of Hedwig Zum Tobel.

— — — — — — —

ROSCOE GILKEY DICKINSON
1894-1945

It was my fortune recently to be given the small bookplate collection of Roscoe Gilkey Dickinson, who was a professor of physical chemistry and acting dean of the Graduate School at the California Institute of Technology commencing in 1917.

After Professor Dickinson died, July 13, 1945 following a brief illness, Linus Pauling wrote a eulogy which appeared in SCIENCE, August 31, 1945.

Roscoe Dickinson was born in Brewer, Maine, on June 10, 1894. He attended the Massachusetts Institute of Technology for his undergraduate work in chemical engineering and received his B.S. degree in 1915. His original appointment to CalTech was while the school was still known at Throop College of Technology. While an instructor in inorganic chemistry he continued his graduate studies and in 1920 was awarded the doctor of philosophy degree for his work on the structure of complex crystals.

In 1917 Dickinson married Madeline Grace Haak; they had two children, Robert Winchester and Dorothy. It is believed that the bookplate reproduced above is that of son Robert; it was found among others in the bookplate collection, along with the reprint of Linus Pauling's eulogy.

During the last twenty years of his life he and his collaborators undertook research in the field of photochemistry and chemical kinetics. He was one of the pioneer investigators of the Raman spectra of ions and gas molecules, the properties of neutrons, and the use of radioactive indicators in the investigation of chemical reactions. As stated by Pauling, "His untimely death is a serious loss to science." On July 15, 1945 the New York TIMES carried his obituary.

No information is available about Robert Dickinson and Charles Allan Winter, whose name appears as the artist on Dickinson's ex libris.

THE EX LIBRIS IN JAPAN
by Hiroo Yamaguchi
Nippon Exlibris Association

Western exlibris were first introduced into Japan in 1900 by a magazine named MYOJO, in which four pieces of exlibris created by Emile Orlik, an Austrian artist, appeared. Until then signets had been used in Japan for specifying the ownership of a book - for the same purpose as that of exlibris.

The number of exlibris lovers in Japan has been increasing since it was first introduced from Europe. The first exlibris lovers' society in Japan, the Nippon Zohyokai, was founded in 1922 and lasted til 1928 when it stopped its activity. But this first society did much towards opening the way for many people to become familiar with exlibris, and the first exlibris from an artist in Japan appeared during the 1930's.

In 1933, time was again ripe for exlibris lovers to establish their society, and the Nippon Zoshohyo Kyokai was founded. But it followed the same fate as the first society and passed out of existence in 1939. Apart from these ups and downs of the societies, there has continuously been an active movement in Japan attempting to popularize exlibris among the people. In 1929, Mr. Shozo Saito published a voluminous work titled EXLIBRIS STORY. Exlibris lovers began to ask artists to make their personal exlibris, and even a few exlibris agencies started the business during the 1930's.

In the midst of this, Mr. Taro Shimo decided to establish the Nippon Exlibris Association in 1943, which has continued to this day. This association is, for the present, the only one group of exlibris lovers in Japan. Twice a year the Nippon Exlibris Association distributes among its members a special calendar with twelve pieces of exlibris attached to it. The exlibris used in the calendar have been designed by some famous artists at the request of the members.

As of 1978, the Association has 1,400 members including 120 overseas members. The exlibris for distribution are chiefly made by woodcut and printed by hand, so they can't be produced in large quantities. Therefore, this limits the further increase in number of members. Mr. Taro Shimo, the founder of the Nippon Exlibris Association, retired from the position of president in 1977 for reasons of health, and Mr. Kazutoshi Sakamoto is currently president.

The practice of exchanging exlibris among Japanese exlibris lovers hasn't been well established yet, much less with foreigners. This is partly because the exlibris has a short history in Japan and partly due to language limitation. The Nippon Exlibris Association is encouraging the Japanese members to exchange exlibris with overseas friends.

— — — — — — —

FROM THE BOOKPLATE LITERATURE . . . .

O.P. BOOKLETTER, Ex Libris. (2) 1:77, July 1978. Bookplates illustrated are from the collection of O.P.'s editor, Robert Hanson, and are for Helen E. Brown and Alexander Campbell.

AMPHORA, Caroline's Minusculae. (4) 33:34-5, 1978. Illustrated are four ex libris by Canadian artist Frits Jacobsen (522 Shanghai Allen, Vancouver,

B.C., Canada), who would welcome inqueries about bookplate commissions.

ANTIQUARIAN BOOKMAN (AB), Rudolph Ruzicka, October 23, 1978. Obituary notice for Ruzicka, who died in Hanover, NH, at the age of 95. He was an internationally celebrated graphic artist, designer, typographer, and author who was born in Bohemia on June 29, 1883, and came to the United States with his parents in 1894. At the age of 14 he was apprenticed to the Franklin Engraving Co. Ruzicka took evening classes at the Chicago Art Institute. In 1903 at the age of 20, he became affiliated with the American Bank Note Co., and later joined an advertising firm. His studio was near the Queensborough Bridge when he moved to New York. Ruzicka designed the typeface known as Fairfield in 1940 for the Mergenthaler Company; Ray Nash in an AMERICAN ARTIST article (Genius of Rudolph Ruzicka, 31:40-50, 71-3, December 1967) included seven memorial or personal bookplates designed by this versatile artist.

JOURNAL OF LIBRARY HISTORY, Los Angeles Publis Library Ex Libris. (2) 12: cover, 399-400, Fall 1977. A brief note on the library, and the ex libris is used as cover illustration and reproduced in the article.

COLLECTOR, Collecting Bookplates, Saying "This is Mine" Beautifully, Leon Thompson. (4) 9:12, October 1978. ASBC&D member Leon Thompson presents a short article for general interest; illustrations include plates for John Spencer dated 1770; George Washington; King Oscar II of Sweden; and Charlie Chaplin.

ESPOSIZIONE dell' EXLIBRIS, the catalogue of the Lugano International Ex Libris Congress, held August 16-20, 1978. The names and addresses of the participants are given, which will be a valuable resource for further correspondence; also listed with addresses are the artists who participated. Articles about the ex libris competitions appear, as well as individual articles about Anatoli Jvanovitsch Kalaschinkow, the symbolic ex libris, one titled "L-Abbazia di Einsiedeln," Remo Wolf, and Verna M. S. Neuschler's "The Fascinating Path to Ex Libris Collecting," printed in English and which appeared in BOOKPLATES IN THE NEWS earlier. [Editor's Note: I have heard that a bookseller has offered this 72 page booklet at $10; if you have the specific reference, I would like it for the record.]

GRAPHIA, publication of the Belgian ex libris society; edited by Antoine Rousseau; secretary is Leo Winkeler (Boudewijnsstraat 97, B-200 Antwerp, Belgium). The most recently received is Bulletin 71-72, 1977. The format is 7 3/8" x 10", printed two columns to the page, with good reproductions and some tip-ins. Again language is a barrier, but the lead articles seem to be on art nouveau ex libris. A bibliography accompanying the article includes references to Gleeson White's articles in THE STUDIO and other features from THE BOOKPLATE BOOKLET and THE BOOKPLATE MAGAZINE. Fritz Haans writes about the ex libris in Antwerp in 1900; Mirko Kaizl writes about Vladimir Komarek, including a checklist of his work from 1948 to 1977. [Editor's Note: This publication has excellent articles, if I may judge from the quality of the layout and illustrations. Are there any volunteers to translate a summary or an occasional article of special merit to be used in BOOKPLATES IN THE NEWS?]

EXLIBRISTEN 1967-1978, Books about Book-plates, Klaus Rodel (Frederikshavn, 1978). This is a catalogue of Rodel's publication activities from

1967 to 1978, which number 160; there is an alphabetical index by artist and the publications are in chronological order. Most of the publications are artist-monographs with a short text in three or four languages and illustrations often tipped-in or printed directly from the original wood or linocut. This makes an excellent checklist of Rodel's work and is an attractively printed booklet itself.

KARL RITTER EXLIBRIS, Klaus Rodel. (Exlibristen, 1978). The title page bears the following statement: Offset-reproduktioner efter original-raderinger udlat as exlibris-samlinger E. Jenssen-Tusch, København. The brief text by Rodel, in two languages (neither of which is English) does not appear to make mention of the article on Karl Ritter which appeared in a YEAR BOOK of the ASBC&D (1975) shortly before the artist's death in Buenos Aires in 1977 at the age of 89. The soft-cover book is in large format (8 1/2" x 11 1/2") to accommodate the size of Ritter's ex libris which frequently are the size of a frameable print. Unfortunately the poor quality of the reproductions scarcely even hints at the merit of the originals. Frequently the remarques in this edition have printed better than the heart of the ex libris.

"Bookplates," by Brian Alderson, is probably a clipping from an English newspaper that appeared mid-1978, for it reviews Fridolf Johnson's book, TREASURY OF BOOKPLATES FROM THE RENAISSANCE TO THE PRESENT; reproduced are plates for Johannes Igler; Jack London; Ellen Terry (designed by Craig); an erotic plate by Mark Severin for Claude Rolin; and a "just plain elegant" plate by Robert Gibbings for himself.

THE MODERN CZECH BOOKPLATE, Vaclav Krupa.(Exlibristen, 1978). This large format (8 1/2" x 12"), soft-cover book is well worth every bookplate collectors' consideration. The text is tri-lingual, with English represented. Each artist is pictured (whenever possible); there is a biographical/critical text; and tipped-in and/or reproduced ex libris. This is a very dramatic book visually - the variety of artists pictured (some in quite exciting poses, some seemingly caught in contemplation, some with one of their larger works as the background); the color in the prints ranges through muted, splashy, delicate, vibrant; and the textures of the engravings, etchings, lithographs, blind embossings are intriguing. It is indeed visually a very exciting book, and the text will bring the reader a wealth of information and the collector immense resources for new artists to seek out with the hope of adding their work or of commissioning a new personal ex libris. While addresses for the artists are not furnished, they doubtless may be obtained through Klaus Rodel. (The price of this volume is, at the moment, unknown, but probably at least DKr 75; for exact information contact Klaus Rodel, P.O. Box 109, DK-9900 Frederikshavn, Denmark.)

HERBERT OTT, Werner Daniel. (Exlibristen, 1978, DKr 75.) A biographical/ critical essay is given in three languages, one of which is English. In addition to 17 black and white reproductions, there are twelve tipped-in prints printed in one or more colors. This book will be a welcome addition to the libraries of all those familiar with the work of Herbert Ott.

HELGA LANGE, Norbert Ott. (Exlibristen, 1978, DKr 75.) Norbert Ott is the son of Herbert Ott and an ex libris artist himself. In the English portion of the text is the following quote: "Although the woodcut, during the time passed, has become an independent art, it never lost its historically determined role as 'art for use'. Not least this double role and the technical connection with the letterpress printing has been an essential reason for many years too that the woodcut was the leading technique of the art of ex libris - and so far still is today." Helga Lange, born in 1937, creates a wide variety of graphics including woodcut ex libris. Fifteen black and white ex libris are reproduced and five, numbered and signed, color prints are tipped-in.

- ET BERTOLT BRECHT EX LIBRYS, Klaus Rodel. In this booklet Rodel relates that German artist Hans Michael Bungter created an ex libris for his collection of Bertolt Brecht's books. The theme of the plate is taken from a Brecht poem, "Legende von der Entstehung des Buches Taoteking auf dem Weg des Laotse in die Emigration." The design shows a Chinese (?) man astride a waterbuffalo, who is reading from a book; he is accompanied by a youth.

EKSLIBRIS, E. M. Ninaev and S. P. Fortinskii (Moscow, Kniga, 1970. 239 pages, illustrated, indices, bibliography.) This volume on Russian bookplates from the 18, 19, and 20th centuries is profusely illustrated with reproductions and is priced at $20; it may be obtained from the Russica Book Shop, Mr. Valery Kuharets, 799 Broadway, Suite #301-2, New York, NY 10003. Mr. Kuharets indicates there were not many books on bookplate literature printed in pre-Revolutionary Russia nor in the Soviet Union later. The present volume, he feels, is the best book on Russian ex libris printed since WWII. When available, those published in the 1920's and earlier tend to be expensive, ranging from $50 to $400. Because of exportation restrictions, pre-1946 books are difficult to obtain. The text is in Russian and proves a barrier to most on this account, but bookplates illustrated speak a universal language which will appeal to all.

EXLIBRISY GRAFIKOW LITEWSKICH, Edmund Puzdrowski (Published in Poland, 1974, in a numbered edition, I believe, of 500. Address: Edmund Puzdrowski, Gdynska 7 B M 30, 80-340 Gdansk, Poland.) This soft-cover, 22 page booklet has a brief biography, checklist, and examples of the bookplate work of five artists: Grazina Didelyte, Stasys Eidrigevicius, Saule Kisarauskiene, Vincas Kisarauskas, Anatanas Kmielauskas; two are women artists. The checklists are numbered, in chronological order, and indicate the technique employed. The illustrations are in black and white; because of technical and/or monetary limitations the illustrations do not do justice to the originals. All of the artists show considerable imagination; however, since this reviewer does not respond well to the styles used by these artists, critical judgment is not offered.

RYSUNEK GWASZE GRAFIKA, Edmund Puzdrowskiego. (Published in Wilno, Litewska SRR, 1977.) This is basically a checklist of Stasys Eidigevicius' work as it was exhibited in Galeria Sztuki Biura Wystaw Artystycznych W Szczecinie in 1977. Six examples of the artist's work, surrealist in derivation, are reproduced in black and white. The artist is pictured with an infant.

EXLIBRIS WERELD, edited by G. Jan Rhebergen, Jr. (Minervalaan 26, 1077 NZ Amsterdam, Holland), for the Dutch Ex Libris Society. The format is 5 1/8" x 7 7/8" wide, printed three columns across. The graphics are well reproduced. The most recent issue received is #2, 1978, which contains a review of ex libris literature, much as that in BOOKPLATES IN THE NEWS under From The Bookplate Literature. There are also articles on the art nouveau influence on bookplate art in which the names of David Kindersly and Eric Gill appear along with reference to ART NOUVEAU, an annotated bibliography by Richard Kempton, Los Angeles, published by Hennessey & Ingalls, 1977; "In Memoriam" for H. G. J. Schelling, who died at age 89. [Editor's Note: This publication is not mentioned as often as some other bookplate society publications because of the editor's language limitations. Is there anyone who would be interested in translating some of the more important items from this journal, or any of the other foreign language ex libris journals, or making an English summary of the issues as they appear??

L'EX LIBRIS FRANCAIS, 40:#128, June 1978. The English summary states: "From the very beginning, man and horses have been present in history. The horse has always been the useful and inseparable friend of man's life, in the everyday life as well as in greater events, at war or in time of peace. Having been supplanted for some time by mechanics, the horse is witnessing a renewal of interest. Formerly a labouring friend, it is now becoming a playmate. If books on horses and horsemanship are numerous, bookplates on this theme are rare. Jean-Marie Cuny, a specialist on the question, presents us some of them." A tipped-in plate for Martine Cuny by Bruno Carpentier is delicately handcolored, I believe; but whether color printed or handcolored, it is a plate to attract attention. -- Germaine Meyer-Noirel described 75 chemists' bookplates, chemist in this instance meaning pharmacist. -- There are reviews of literature from ex libris societies. -- Inserted is a ten-year INDEX of the journal for 1968-1978.

INTER-EXLIBRIS 78, edited by Klaus Rodel and published by Frederikshavn Kunstmuseum (Klaus Rodel, Smedevej 20, Postboks 109, DK-9900 Frederikshavn, Denmark; price DKr20), this book is almost 5 3/4" square, softbound. Rodel in his introduction states in part: "Contrary to the art of posters or the free graphic art, the exlibris and the occasional graphic have been reserved for a narrow, unfortunately a much too small circle. . . . to reach a greater public [it] is mainly done by exhibitions open to the public, articles in newspapers and periodicals and books as well." To this end, in Frederikshavn there is an attempt to establish a bookplate collection with the purpose of exhibiting good quality ex libris both to residents of the city and to tourists. Artists were invited to participate, and this catalogue has the pictures of the artists who participated and either reproduces or tips-in an ex libris for each. The exhibition, states Rodel, "is dominated by artists from Lithuania and Czechoslovakia, which, however, only reflects that the interest in these two countries really is biggest." The only artist representing the United States is Vytautas O. Virkau of Downers Grove, Illinois, who is a ASBC&D members.

SVENSKA EXLIBRISFORENINGEN, three issues for 1978. The text is in Swedish; there are no illustrations. [Editor's Note: Again a call for help in making a translation in English of a summary or at length as appropriate.]

G. JAN RHEBERGEN

Jan Rhebergen, Secretary of the Dutch Ex Libris Society, was born in Amsterdam, February 16, 1915. He is extremely modest, but has written to me briefly about his life as follows: "After finishing high school and studying two years art-history, I went into business and became a sales manager of a factory for ready-made clothing. I enjoy now my pension. This gives me a lot of time for my hobby, the collecting of bookplates and graphic art. In 1974, the greatest part of my ex libris collection (40,000 pieces) went to the International Ex-libris Centrum in Sink Niklass, forming there the base of the property of that museum. But since then my collection has grown again and amounts already to nearly 10,000 pieces. My collection of free graphic art comprises about 3,000 large prints, and my library numbers about 5,000 books on many subjects where in the first place come the books on art (bookplates, etc.) and history in which I have a great interest, being an aquarius.

Among other official or demi-official "jobs", I sat on the council for affairs of art for the town of Amsterdam for six years. I am president and secretary of the Dutch exlibris circle, Exlibriskring der Wereldbibliotheek Vereniging (in brief E.K.W.B.V.), which is a division of the great book club "Wereldbibliotheek". I am also the editor of the magazine "Exlibriswereld" that appears four times a year. This all brings much correspondence from all over the world, but it brings me also very nice contacts and some good friends, such as Dr. Shaftel of New York City."

—   —   —   —

NOTES ON THE WOOD-ENGRAVINGS BY ERIC RAVILIUS by Robert Harling (Ariel Books on the Arts, published for the Shenval Press by Faber and Faber Ltd., 1966). This English artist died while on active service in 1942; he was an official Admiralty artist. Prior to service, Ravilius was a wood-engraver, watercolor painter, and an industrial designer of note. The biographical/critical notes make absorbing reading; the illustrations give testimony to the variety and quality of his talents. Only a few ex libris are reproduced, three, I believe. [Editor's Note: Additional information about this artist's bookplate work would be welcomed with the intent of publishing a checklist and further biographical data.]

In the course of putting together
the 1978 YEAR BOOK which features
the work of David Kindersley, it
was my pleasure to correspond
with Jerry Cole, the son-in-law
of Mrs. Kennedy. I was curious
about Weber Point and the date
1850 which appear at the center,
bottom of the bookplate which
Kindersley designed, and would
now like to share what I discovered with you. Those who have
the 1978 YEAR BOOK know the o-
riginal print is a deep brick red.

Mr. Cole wrote: Weber Point was the site of Captain Charles M. Weber's
home; he founded the city of Stockton. He arrived in California in 1841
with the Bidwell-Bartelson party and settled in San Jose. In 1843 he and
his partner petitioned Governor Micheltorena for a 48,747 acre tract then
known as El Campo de los Franceses, which was to be the future site of
the planned city of Stockton, which was founded in 1847. In 1850 he married Helen Murphy, daughter of Martin Murphy, who led the famous Murphy
party to California in 1844. He moved his new bride from San Jose to the
handsome new home he had just completed at Weber Point in 1850. It is the
house shown on the bookplate, and it was here that he founded the Weber
Library which has been carried forward by his son, daughter, and grand-
daughter. His granddaughter, Helen Weber Kennedy, for whom the plate was
commissioned, is the present owner of the continually growing collection
of Californiana. Because collection has been continuous since 1850, the
library has many items not found in any other similar collections.

— — — — — — — — — — — — — — — — —

BOOKPLATE OF ELIHU VEDDER   A recent exhibition at the National Col-
                                   lection of Fine Arts, Smithsonian Insti-
tution, Washington, D.C. (October 13, 1978 to February 4, 1979), featured
the work of Elihu Vedder. A catalogue of the 331 items exhibited is titled "Perceptions and Evocations: the Art of Elihu Vedder." Though an
American, born in 1836, Vedder lived most of his life in Italy. Joshua C.
Taylor, Director of the National Collection of Fine Arts, says in his introductory notes to the catalogue that Vedder "realized that art itself
provided a homeland, and to it he was a loyal citizen. For him, Italy was
the closest approximation of that land to be found on earth."

Elihu Vedder did extraordinary illustrations for Omar Khayyam's RUBAIYAT,
published in 1884. His work included pencil sketches; oil on canvas and
oil on wood; charcoal, chalk, and pastel on paper; Christmas cards; wall
murals; magazine covers; and at least one bookplate - his own. It is item
#263 in the catalogue and dated circa 1882. The design is the same as for
the cover of STUDIO MAGAZINE of this same period. Vedder died in 1923.

If you know of other bookplates designed by Elihu Vedder, please let your
editor know and more will be written about this artist, whom Taylor describes as "a sociable man [who] enjoyed good food, good liquor, and good
friends. . . . a lively companion and accomplished storyteller."

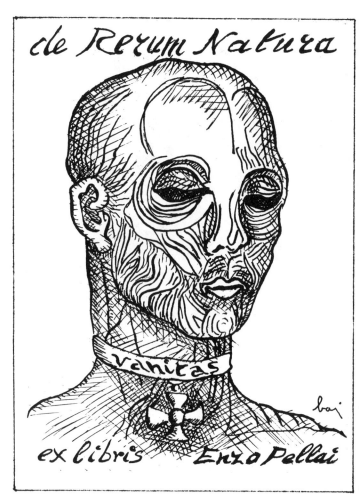

de Rerum Natura

vanitas

ex libris   Enzo Pellai

ENRICO BAJ by Dr. Enzo Pellai

Enrico Baj was born in 1924
in Milan, Italy. After ob-
taining his law degree, he
attended the Brera Academy
of Art in Milan.

In 1951 his first works were
exhibited at the San Fedele
Gallery in Milan. Since then
his work has been exhibited
in galleries and museums in
all parts of the world.

Complete bio-bibliographical
data (through 1972) are in
the book CATALOGO GENERALE
DELL'OPERA DI ENRICO BAJ,
edited by Enrico Crispelti,
Giulie Bolaffi publishers in
Torino, 1973.

Among the many exhibitions in
which his work has been shown
are the following: 1960-61,
Surrealist Intrusion in the En-
chanters' Domain held at the
D'Arch Gallery, New York; it
was directed by Andre Breton.

The Art of Assemblage which traveled as an exhibition during 1961-62 to the
Museum of Modern Art, New York (catalogue by William C. Seitz, pages 86, 104,
113); Dallas Museum of Contemporary Arts; San Francisco Museum of Arts;
The Arts Club of Chicago, a personal exhibit during 1966-67; the Hansen Gallery in San Francisco, 1969; Museum of Contemporary Arts in Chicago, 1971,
with a catalogue by Jan van der Marck.

The work of Enrico Baj is deeply ironic. He paints preferably with the assemblage technique, but he works also as an illustrator and a graphic artist.
He has contributed to CORRIERE DELLA SERA, the most important Italian newspaper.

The print reproduced above is an etching which was hand printed by Giorgio
Upiglio (Milan, 1978) on handmade paper in a limited edition which included
seven trial proofs, 100 sets, and 20 sets numbered and signed by Baj. This
ex libris is for medical books. Its motto "De rerum nature" recalls Lucre-
tius' poem by which it is inspired to signify the close connection between
science, philosophy, and art.

The ex libris imitates the anatomical drawings of the 16th century. The word
"Vanitas" that we read on the collar, from which hangs a worldly trophy, invites us to meditate about the stupidity of human behaviour. This grotesque
picture is a typical example of Baj's figurative world. He subverts in an
ironic way the obvious classicality of the subject, and he places within the
design, with a very able graphic synthesis, elements that we would judge to
be irreconcilable. The expressive sign is surreal and full of moral allu-
sions.

EX LIBRIS

HARRY

JOSEPH

HELEN M. FENTON

Bookplates are a practical application of art to everyday uses.

After all it is not size but quality that gives value to any art work. Mrs. Saunders says bookplates allow a flow of imagination rarely equalled in any other field of artistic endeavor. They may be as symbolic as sculpture - as concrete as landscapes - as patterned as textiles - as humorous as cartoons, and as photographic as portraits. Also a bookplate may express what you are, what you want to be, or what you like best.

Bookplates came into being shortly after the birth of printing from moveable type, usually set between 1440-1450 when Gutenberg printed the Bible. Books were so costly that only very wealthy people could own them. To keep books in their proper places, monasteries and churches resorted to chaining them. From this necessity of marking ownership, so that books would stay in their owner's libraries, the bookplate, as we have it today, evolved. The ex libris is a simple and convenient means of identification.

Germany then was the first country to have bookplates, then France, and finally England. The earliest known plate was a German woodcut for Hildebrand Brandenburg of Biberach, a monk of the Carthusian monastery of Buxheim, circa 1470. Incidentally, it might be mentioned that no method of keeping books where they belong has ever proved as satisfactory as chaining. Only recently Carolyn Wells wrote a lovely quatrain:
They borrow books they will not buy/They have no ethics or religion.
O would some kind burbankian guy/Cross my books with homing pigeons.

Since only the wealthier could own books, and since they marked their possessions with their arms, it naturally follows that our first bookplates were armorials. Few people could read the printed word, but they recognized the various devices of a family, so many early armorials bore no name. Some collectors only gather armorials and consider a study of heraldry the backbone of bookplate collecting. Where an armigerous plate is identified, it is given to the head of the house as the libraries as well as the lands in those days usually descended to the eldest son. Armorial plates fall into the following categories: 1500-1700 - Early armorial
1700-1740 - Jacobean (Louis XIV)
1740-1775 - Chippendale (Louis XV)
1775-1800 - Wreath and Ribbon (Louis XVI)
1800-1905 - Modern Armorial
1905-   - Contemporary

The earliest English plate, that of Cardinal Wolsey about 1525, is a simple armorial painted by hand. There were not many bookplates in England prior to the Restoration. Many believe Charles II introduced the custom when he returned from France, bringing many French fashions with him. Sir Nicolas Bacon, father of Sir Francis, the essayist, had a find handcolored armorial.

The earliest dated American bookplates are really printed labels. One is that of Stephen Daye dated 1642. Daye did the first piece of printing in the colonies in 1640. His book label is the second piece of printing. John Williams, first minister in Deerfield, had a plate dated 1679. He and his wife and children were made captive by the Indians in 1704. Most early plates for Southerners in the United States were made in England; Northern plates tended to be done by local engravers such as Paul Revere, Amos Doolittle, Dawkins, Anderson, Maverick, and Callender.

Coming forward in time we find other types of bookplates coming into use. Profound changes in society and government are reflected in the departure from the strictly armorial plate used by the wealthy, noble class to the wider use by book lovers in general to types that we classify as: pictorial, allegorical, canting, monogram, portrait, commemorative, foreign.

There are three ways for a private collector to acquire bookplates: by gift, purchase, or exchange. Exchanges are made with other collectors you know or through exchange lists issued by bookplate organizations. Dispersal of a large collection affords the smaller collector to purchase. Dawson's, Goodspeeds, and English catalogs are good sources for collections for sale. Most owners of bookplates are very gracious and kind about sending their plates to collectors.

There are two ex libris societies in the United States: American Society of Bookplate Collectors and Designers, Washington, D.C., and Bookplate Society International (Mrs. Bassett), Los Angeles.

An interesting commemorative plate is that of the Bowdoin Class of 1877 which was designed to honor the discovery of the North Pole by their classmate Peary.

The value of any collection is the value your enthusiasm places on it.

Because of its intimate association with the birth of our nation, John Adams' bookplate is considered by many collectors the most interesting of all. On the day of the signing of the Declaration of Independence, Adams was one of a committee of the Continental Congress appointed in Paris. The plate was engraved in London by Carpenter during this same trip. We may conclude it was the design he selected for the national seal, diverting it to his personal use after its rejection. While it may seem to you that many of these early American plates are merely names attached to pretty labels, just remember they belonged to many who were our governors, judges, lawyers, doctors, etc. In these old ex libris is the story of a nation's birth and progress. The William Penn armorial of 1703 has the motto: While I hold to glory, let me hold to right. In the plate the third Latin word was omitted as the engraver found the motto too long, and a blunder was made in one of the remaining words, so it made no sense. Most of the features of the Penn plate have been incorporated in the plate of the Pennsylvania Historical Society.

My interest in bookplates grew naturally out of my love of books. Some one has said that bookplates are the connecting link between art and literature. All collectors have something in common - no matter what they collect. The collecting habit like a germ is no respecter of persons - from kings to orginary folk. It's not the lure of possession but the adverture of acquiring that the collector enjoys. Once a collection is complete, the collector loses interest. This is why we have such magnificent gifts to art galleries, museums, and libraries.

- # - # -

Thus end the notes which Mrs. Fenton wrote in a sylized hand on three by five cards. For a short period of time, she kept a scrapbook about her ex libris activities. The first item is a printed newsletter which indicates that at the November 2, 1933 meeting of the Woman's Auxiliary of the American Institute of Mining and Metallurgical Engineers, Mrs. Fenton spoke on "book-plates and displayed a great number from her own rare collection."

The next clipping, dated April 27, 1934, announces the annual meeting at which officers are elected to be held in Los Angeles by the National Society United States Daughters of 1812, State of California; Mrs. Fenton is listed on the program; her topic was "Old Book Plates."

Apparently after attending Mrs. Fenton's 1812 program, Mary A. P. Johnson, State President of the National Society Daughters of Colonial Wars in Southern California, extended an invitation to Mrs. Fenton to be on their program June 12, 1934. In Mrs. Johnson's note of appreciation following the talk, she wrote: "We do not realize how very important it is to specialize in some one thing until we have squandered much time and energy in generalities and some things not so worthwhile. You have accomplished so much and consequently can impart of fund of fascinating information." So well received was the talk that the Society asked Mrs. Fenton to present "Old Book Plates" at the December 10, 1934 meeting held at the Chapman Park Hotel (Los Angeles), which appears to have been the site of their regular meetings.

A BULLETIN of the Pasadena Junior College, May 14, 1934, carried a notice of the Phylo Club Meeting on May 15 at 7:30 in the South Pasadena home of Mrs. J. Harry Fenton; she was scheduled to give an illustrated talk on "Book Plates." On the same scrapbook page is a newspaper announcement of a meeting of the Trojan Women's Club, scheduled for April 19 [1934?], when Mrs. Fenton's large collection of bookplates will be featured.

The next treasure saved in the scrapbook is a letter dated June 14, 1934 from Geraldine Kelly, assistant manager at Dawson's Book Shop, then located on South Grand in Los Angeles. She mentions the arrival of two books on bookplates - Egerton Castle's ENGLISH BOOK-PLATES at $3 and Norna Labouchere's LADIES BOOK PLATES at $4. Miss Kelly wrote: "It is difficult to get hold of book-plate books these days and we have a waiting list for nearly every arrival. There is certainly a decided interest in book-plate collecting and I am sure your article has done much to further it." [Circumstances are much the same today. Only the prices have changed!] Geraldine Kelly mentions "article" in her letter, which I have been unable to locate as published, so perhaps she meant talk.

The next clipping (November 21, 1935?) notes a bookplate display from the collection of Mrs. H. Harry Fenton at the South Pasadena Library, and the SOUTH PASADENA NEWS for November 22, 1935 announces an exhibit at the South

Pasadena Library from the collection of Mrs. Fenton, "who has one of the largest collections on the Pacific Coast." [Where is it now?]

With a date line of Arcadia (California), December 7 (1935), the headline is "Talk on Bookplates by Mrs. Fenton Features P.E.O. Meet." A penned entry on the page opposite this clipping notes that bookplate talks were given to P.E.O. chapters in North Hollywood, San Marino, three Pasadena chapters, and two South Pasadena chapters. Also in December of 1935, the California Chapter of the Daughters of Founders and Patriots of America (Los Angeles) were "favored" with the Fenton bookplate talk. Other groups to hear her talk were Scout Leaders and students at Broadoaks school in Pasadena.

Whether or not there was more bookplate activity, the rest of the scrapbook is blank. While none of the entries is dramatic nor does "Notes Toward an Ex Libris Talk" offer any new research in the field of bookplates, both show how a personal interest may be shared, bringing a sense of accomplishment to the individual who shares a personal enthusiasm and bringing knowledge of a specialized field to an audience which might otherwise never be aware of the miniature prints known as bookplates.

The editor of BOOKPLATES IN THE NEWS would welcome information about talks presented by members of the American Society of Bookplate Collectors and Designers in their local communities, and would like to publish them for our readers. Long-time member Mrs. Ione Wiechel has often presented illustrated lectures of ex libris, with emphasis on the local bookplates of her hometown, Sandusky, Ohio. We hope Mrs. Wiechel and other members will send copies of their talks for future publication in our quarterly.

— — — — — —

NEW HEIMS EX LIBRIS

Here tipped-in is a recent ex libris Earl Heims had designed which appropriately features Vishnu, the preserver god of the Hindu sacred triad. As can be seen Vishnu is applying her perservation arts on books.

Earl Heims, who is now retired and living in Tigard, Oregon, presented his design ideas to commercial artist Tom Gorman; the happy result you see here. Adding to the splendor of the oriental design is the striking use of color in the printing. The triad mentioned above includes Vishnu, Siva (god of destruction and regeneration), and Brahma (creator god).

An invitation was extended by the Bookplate Society [London] to talk before their group whenever I might be in London; so when I planned to attend the International Ex Libris Congress held in Lugano, I included London on my itinerary. The latest date possible was selected to allow for members of the British society to be home from holiday; thus Friday, September 1st was the date fixed upon, the location to be the National Book League, and the topic, "Ex Libris Prints and Ephemera."

The National Book League, housed at 7 Albemarle Street, London, is in a building first erected in 1722. It has been a private home, first of its owner, Admiral Sir John Norris; at one time it was let to a mistress of King George II; over a long period it was the Grillion's Hotel, which was occasionally home temporarily for visiting royalty. The Roxburghe Club, "founded at the suggestion of Thomas Dibdin to celebrate the anniversary of the sale of the Duke of Roxburghe's Library in June 1812 with an annual dinner," held these dinners at Grillions's in 1815, 1816, and 1823. Additionally Number Seven has been the home of the Royal Thames Yacht Club and the Royal Aetonautical Society; a combined dwelling and shop for a tailor; it suffered from bombing attacks during WWII, and for five years was uninhabitable. After months of "planning, rehabilitation and decoration, the building was formerly opened as the home of the National Book League on April 30, 1946.

Number Seven is pictured above from an engraving appropriately done by Joan Hassall for AN APPEAL TO BOOKMEN, 1945; it was used as the cover for a brief history of the National Book League. The Bookplate Society is fortunate to have quarters available in this congenial environment, and it is here they have held a number of notable exhibitions of bookplates, as well as regular meetings of the membership. The Society is also blessed with an adequate number of members who live and/or work in the City, and who by their steady attendance and enthusiasm make it possible to have reasonably frequent meetings with a variety of speakers; some like myself are travelers who make a point of visiting London so they may have the privilege of meeting Bookplate Society members.

The meeting at which I talked had about a dozen members present. A small room off the library accommodated a slide projector and comfortable seating, which didn't require a microphone for the speaker to be heard. Among those in attendance were two authors, who are especially well-known in the field of bookplates: Phillip C. Beddingham and Brian North Lee. Realizing that they would probably be present had made me ponder at considerable length upon the selection of a phase of bookplates about which to talk. While in general, English bookplate enthusiasts would know the standard sources concerning American bookplates, they might not be interested in lesser artists and talking about the better known artists might offer little new material. For this reason, I elected to talk about an aspect of bookplates not quite as often explored - ex libris ephemera and a few prints to give variety. Among the ephemeral items are exhibit catalogues; announcements of meetings and publications; printed exchange requests, letters by artists and collectors; pictures of artists, authors and collectors. Perhaps the hit of the evening was Egerton Castle pictured in fencing gear!

Following the talk, there were questions, which especially pleased the speaker as they seemed to show interest in the topic selected and further explored other aspects of the bookplate in America. As is customary with the Bookplate Society, the speaker was taken to dinner, which afforded a further opportunity to become better acquainted.

One of those attending the meeting was David Kindersley, who came to City from Cambridge and whose work is featured in the 1978 YEAR BOOK (published in December 1978); and it was a pleasure to note in the recent quarterly of the Bookplate Society that Kindersley is scheduled to speak at a meeting early in 1979.

[Continued from page 281.]

Summing up I would like to say the following: The congress in Lugano has proved how important it is that so many hours as possible are at disposal of the participants. A central place, which should be available almost 24 hours a day, enabling the participants to utilize the time as required.

An exhibition not too big, but of high standard in order to secure the clearness. - With regard to the competition it ought to be considered whether to leave a choice of subject out of account, but instead gather exlibris made during the two years since last congress. A judgment of this material should then result in a selection of about ten pieces which can be awarded. This will effect a great interest and at the same time it will not seem so straining to the artists (after the congress what shall we then do with all these exlibris made with a congress-text?)

It also ought to be investigated whether or not at least one lecture could be arranged in spite of difficulties with languages. A congress only deserves, I suppose, its name if there will be worked at a certain level - otherwise it must be a gathering.

We all hope for a meeting again in two years, - to all appearence in the friendly Austria at the river Danube at Linz. Thank you to the organizers in Lugano.

Klaus Rödel

———

Artist : Michael Rentan

#3 1978
EXLIBRIS REVUE - Volume 4

XVII International Ex Libris Congress, by Klaus Rodel

Below is reprinted the report made by Klaus Rodel, editor of EXLIBRIS REVUE and an officer of F.I.S.A.E., the official organization of the various bookplate societies which sponsor the congress.

How fast have not two years passed? Yes even ten years! With the congress in Lisbon in fresh memory, and the memories from my first congress, Como 1968, in the back of my head, my expectations to the congress in Lugano became rather high. Lugano's wonderful position, this elegant and yet rather comfortable city, the modern congress-building - and not least Carlo Chiesa's vitality contributed of course to these expectations. Just the foregoing congress in Lisbon in some way proved that a too big distance to Central Europe may act restrictive on the desire to participate, not least when you take into consideration the age of many congressists. But this year it was a question of a congress in the heart of Europe - and almost 250 participants have confirmed the thruth of this theory. 250 participants including many companions, who, to be fair, had come for more social reasons. Such a number must cause difficulties to the organizers, everything becomes more hectic, one loses (or even do not reach) the general view. In a way we all get into a strange situation: On the one hand we want so many participants as possible to get a confirmation of the interest for the art of exlibris and its vitality, - on the other hand just this big number of participants effects that one doe not get sufficient time for discussions and exchange with the individual. So, one risk to overlook participants or do not get time for exchange and so on.

Also, Lugano proved that it is necessary with more languages (which also has been aimed at by FISAE). Almost every congress till now has been dominated by a single language, a fact which always has caused that some participants have felt out of

it. (especially the English language was need very much !) Another critical point, which shall be mentioned here right at the beginning, has arised by a misunderstanding between the management of the congress-building and the organizers: There were too few rooms for exchange, and there was no flat where people could meet far into the night. When one know how "fanatic" some collectors are with exchanging and to get "returns" with them home, one understand their irritation over so many hours passing unused.

BUT: We must not forget that this congress-arrangement was organized quite spontaneous by one single person, just to keep the continuity of the congresses. It has been the intention that the congress to a wide extent also should be of social character. It will probably be difficult to find a reasonable balance between too many lectures and arrangements and on the other hand to much "leisure". It was confirmed that the theory from Elsinore (1972) about gathering the congress under one roof and concentrate the things has given the best result. It secures the highest possible utilization of all available hours.

This is, however, only theory. Till now each congress has had its own atmospere, its own distrinctive mark, and so also in Lugano. This congress was favoured with a wonderful weather, summer but not too hot and just these evenings enabling us to sit outside in a relaxed atmosphere and enjoy the being together with many friends.

The FISAE meeting of delegates was relatively fast done with. There were only a few desisions to be made - among others the question of a permanent secretariat. The undersigned had to back out here due to insufficient knowledge of French. Another proposal about making the EXLIBRIS-REVUE to an official periodical for FISAE was accepted. There will be no financial obligations, but I hope this arrangement will effect regular information from the individual societies.

The most difficult point was appointment of the placing of the next congress. Both Belgium, GDR and Hungary are interested in arranging a congress in 1984, while there were serious difficulties with 1980. A brave proposal from Svitzerland about arranging the coming congress was rejected at the following annual meating in the Swiss society. Herafter Canada offered to arrange a con-

gress, - but this was met with quite some scepticism, not least because many of the older collectors would be frightened by the long distance. While this is written, Ottmar Premstaller, St. Georgen in Austria tries to organize a congress at Linz (and it is almost certain that he will succeed).

The exhibitions of the congress were quite varied and there was a fine framing about it in the beautiful Villa Ciani. Carlo Chiesa's idea: To arrange the exhibitions with certain subjects proved to be excellent. It was impressing to note the large number of exlibris on occasion of the two competitions: The City Lugano (196) and Fabio Schaub ex musicis (273). While the jury's decision with regard to the latter seemed just, there were many collectors who found the decisions in the city-exlibris almost embarrassing. Among so many - and to a great extent quite eminent - bookplates it should have been possible to find another awarding. However, so it is with many judgments; as known, taste cannot be discussed.

One of the culminations of the congress was the excursion, a bustrip over three of the most impressive alp-passes: Nufenen, Furka and St. Gotthardt. Favoured by a perfectly weather with views over the central part of Swiss alp-peaks this experience of nature was of such a character that even the most "fanatic" collectors let their exchange material stay in their briefcases.

The festive night really was a festival, the congress danced in the true meaning of the word, - and the delight for dancing was apparently direct proportional with the age, - the older the more diligent!

The farewell dring at the Sunday proved the experiences from foregoing congresses: It is difficult to gather all participants once more after the festive night. Many had already left or stood with their trunks. It ought to be considered with future congresses to arrange an excursion as the last event of the congress (a la Bled 1974).

As at previous congresses also in Lugano, a lot of beautiful publications came as gifts from the individual societies. Also, a cooperation between the organizers and the Portuguese exlibris society has made it possible to publish the FISAE-book, Vol. IV. A summary of all publications on occasion of the congress is listed at the end of the German text.

EX LIBRIS

IN HONOR OF
OCT. 23. 1956.

NANDOR NEMETH

JOSEPH CARDINAL MINDSZENTY

NANDOR NEMETH
Nicholas G. Lipposcy

A year ago on January 30, 1978, a famous ex libris artist, Nandor Nemeth, passed away in a tragic accident. After their daily walk, his wife lit a cigarette and slept. Both burnt to death, with all the beautiful art treasures that Nemeth created through a lifetime.

Born in Hungary in 1910, he completed the Academy of Art in Budapest, as a student of F. Helbing. He was a book illustrator and as a hobby made numerous ex libris for friends. He worked with the film industry in Europe, and after his immigration to the United States in 1950, he continued to illustrate books for the Allen Wayne Publishers, and was chief designer for Audio Filmproduction and Audio Cinema Corporation.

He made about 300 bookplates, among them those for celebrities such as Pope Paul, Joseph Cardinal Mindszenty, Cardinal Spellman, President Richard Nixon, President Eisenhower, Otto von Habsburg, and they all accepted with thanks Mr. Nemeth's works. The Metroplitan Museum of Art has 200 ex libris from his own designs.

The sudden passing of the noted artist saddened his friends all over the world where his bookplates were always received very gladly. If any of our members wish to have examples of his ex libris, I can send copies free of charge to anyone - commemorating the first anniversary of the passing of this highly idealistic, great graphic artist. (Dr. Nicholas G. Lippoczy, 252 Van Houten Avenue, Passaic, NJ 07055.)

— — — — — — —

BOOKPLATES IN THE NEWS

C by Audrey Spencer Arellanes
YEAR BOOK 1978 now available - $20 :

Special : Full Membership
Both Publications : $25

Published : January/April/July/October
$8 U.S. & Canada/ $8.50 Overseas

Article by artist David Kindersley with checklist of his ex libris, nine tipped-in prints, others reproduced.
Article by Warren R. Johnston on D. D. Wiepert's Bookplate "Primitives" - three tip-ins, others reproduced.

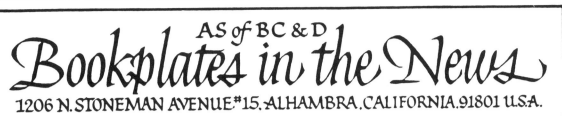

AS of BC & D

Bookplates in the News

1206 N. STONEMAN AVENUE #15, ALHAMBRA, CALIFORNIA, 91801 U.S.A.

AUDREY SPENCER ARELLANES, Editor

DAVID SERETTE of the YELLOW KID PRESS

David Serette retired, at age 40, after 20 years as a television director. Since then he has been printer-in-residence at America's oldest religious community. Printing has been a source of relaxation and exercise since 1963 when he decided it would be good therapy following a severe automobile accident. He began collecting bookplates many years ago while in grade school. As a result of childhood polio, he was always more book oriented than his peers. One day, a local antiquarian bookman, F. M. O'Brien, gave him a book with a Wentworth armorial ex libris in it. (Serette's middle name is Wentworth.) This sparked an interest that never died out but went from the engraved to the typographical. As he became more interested in the mechanics of fine printing, he started to collect printers, booksellers, and binders labels. While at Boston University, he "discovered" the work of Fred Anthoensen, and upon returning to his home in Portland (Maine) to start in the television business made himself known to this talented typographic designer. Many happy, if frustrating, hours of conversation followed the initial meeting, and over the years the two became quite good friends. What was the frustration? Mr. Anthoensen liked to talk about television instead of printing!

A frustrated sculptor, Serette began collecting old stonecarver's tools and equipment. This led to slate-carving, which led to early gravestone art, which somehow led to a series of illustrated talks that kept leaning toward the macabre and resulted in yet another collection of early embalming tools and books on the subject. Herewith is shown the plate he designed for his own use.

Serette's collecting interests are eclectic and besides bookplates, embalming gear, printing equipment, and long-haired dachshunds, he actively searches for old microscope slides both for the subject matter and the tiny owner's labels. In this limited field he has over 100 different, personalized, pre-1900 slide labels attached to over 2,500 slides. Needless to say, Serette is an ardent amateur microscopist.

His private press, The Yellow Kid Press, was named for an early comic character created by Richard Felton Outcault. (Outcault also created Buster
Brown.) Its only semi-commercial activity is miniature books and an occasional typographic bookplate. An interesting sidenote is that many years
ago, Serette advertised typographic bookplates for two months in the New York
TIMES Book Review. Right next to Antioch. He is still waiting for a response.

—   —   —   —   —   —

FRANCIS W. ALLEN
1913 - 1978

It is with sadness that
we report the passing of
Francis Wilbur Allen on
November 16, 1978. He was
65.

Born in Waterbury, CT, he
graduated from Colby Col-
lege and received a bach-
elor and master of library
science degrees from the
University of Michigan.
Frank worked in the li-
braries of University of
Michigan, LeMoyne College, Harvard, the Congregational Library of Boston, and
the Van Buren County Library of Paw Paw. He served as librarian at Western
Michigan University for 24 years before retiring August 31, 1977.

In 1963, Frank took a leave of absence for a year to serve as consultant at
the Haile Selassie I University Library in Ethiopia, under the sponsorship
of the Ford Foundation.

To his many friends in the bookplate world, Frank Allen will be remembered
not only as the author of two scholarly works on Charles R. Capon (who designed the ex libris above) and William Fowler Hopson but as a warm friend ever
ready to assist the new collector by offering plates for exchange and sharing
his own high enthusiasm and wealth of knowledge.

—   —   —   —   —   —

FRANK ALLEN - Ex Librist
by Ruth Allen

Frank's interest in ex libris was
sparked by an antiquarian book
dealer, Stanley O. Bezanson, who
was a neighbor in Needham, MA. He
conducted a mail order business out of his home, his main source of revenue
being "previously owned" books but his first love being bookplates. A deal
was struck, and for many, many months afterwards small monthly checks were
forwarded to Needham. Frank's intention was to become a dealer as well as a
collector, and from time to time--as the pressure of his library responsibil-
ities permitted--carefully typed lists were mailed to collectors in the United
States, and orders were received and filled. Frank's interest never waned in
his very special hobby, but often there was little time actively to pursue

this interest. Finally, the point came when retirement seemed desirable, and then Frank planned to devote years--he said it would take at least ten--to organizing his collection.

His enthusiasm for ex libris was tremendously spurred by his encounter with European bookplate designers and collectors whom he met at the 16th Congress in Lisbon. As a guest speaker at the Congress, Frank was introduced to many, many people who ardently shared his interest. He carried on a very rewarding correspondence with several of these people after the Congress was over.

Frank's last trip abroad, in December of 1977, was also memorable. He traveled to Denmark, where he met individually with bookplate collectors and also attended a meeting of the Danish ex libris society. A week of bookplate encounters gave him great satisfaction.

Frank's proudest accomplishments were the publication of two illustrated volumes of ex libris checklists and an article: BOOKPLATES: A SELECTION FROM THE WORKS OF CHARLES R. CAPON. (Portland, ME, The Anthoensen Press, 1950.) THE BOOKPLATES OF WILLIAM FOWLER HOPSON: A DESCRIPTIVE CHECK LIST. (New Haven, Yale University Press, 1961.) "Notes on the Bookplates of Amos Doolittle," OLD-TIME NEW ENGLAND, volume 39, #2, October 1948.

In addition, he wrote prolifically - other articles and wide-ranging correspondence with people from many parts of the world. Unfortunately, Frank's hobby did not intrigue other members of his family. So his collection lies waiting for someone who will cherish it as he did. Any inqueries should be directed to Ruth Allen, 162 W. Inkster Avenue, Kalamazoo, MI 49001.

—   —   —   —   —   —   —

IN MEMORY OF FRANK ALLEN
Verna M. S. Neuscheler

Arriving at the Lisbon Ex Libris Congress in 1976, I met the "other" attending Americans, Ruth and Frank Allen. Of course, being the only members from the U.S., we were instant acquaintances and friends. We had many opportunities to talk, eat, and do the same things together. I was impressed by the scholarly address Frank gave with dignity and assurance to the Congress. And the Europeans were also, for many inquired about him during the Lugano Congress last summer. Since the Lisbon Congress we kept in touch by letter and phone. We exchanged ex libris ideas and information and traded our duplicates. Frank never stopped developing his unusually strong interests and knowledge in the ex libris field. His willing generosity to promote and develop the knowledge of others is typical of a librarian's aims. We must feel a sadness for a world in dire need of just such fine, knowledgeable characters. And we extend a word of sympathy and appreciation to Ruth, his beloved wife, who helped him fulfill his worthwhile life on earth.

Clare Ryan Talbot

Frank Allen was an admirable correspondent and an astounding collector of our (cont. page 287)

MARK TWAIN's
BOOKPLATE
Richard Schimmelpfeng

Occasionally a handsomely etched bookplate in a Chippendale frame turns up, which is said to be Mark Twain's own. In point of fact, Mark Twain never owned a plate, using instead his signature as a mark of ownership.

The so-called bookplate was in reality the frontispiece used in volume I of several editions of Twain's collected works. It exists both in the etched state and in a photoreproduction. The signature on the left reads: W H W Bicknell sc. and on the right: Tiffany & Co. del. Which signee did which is open to question since both William Henry Warren Bicknell and Tiffany & Company designed and executed bookplates as well as other pieces of artwork. The Bicknell connection is not mentioned in C. S. Baer's article on Bicknell in the 1943/44 YEAR BOOK.

The design is an attractive one with six vignettes. The top left shows a riverboat pilot (LIFE ON THE MISSISSIPPI); top center shows a Western stage coach, reminiscent of Twain's days in Nevada and California; and top right shows a man casting the "mark" from which Twain took his pen-name (again from LIFE ON THE MISSISSIPPI). In the center is a monogram SLC for Samuel Langhorne Clemens, with a scroll beneath containing the phrase: Innocents Abroad / Huckleberry Finn. The vignettes of the ship and the railway train represent Twain's travels and the bottom vignette shows the home in Hartford on Farmington Avenue which is now restored as it was ninety years ago. At the lower left is a remarque of a cottage, probably meant to be Twain's birthplace in Hannibal, Missouri.

— — — — — — — —

THE BUFF BOOK is now in preparation by World Almanac Publications. It is to be an informative and entertaining book about people who are acknowledged experts in a broad variety of cultural, historical, recreational, and hobby fields. Members of the American Society of Bookplate Collectors and Designers are invited to participate; those interested may write to Barry Youngerman, THE BUFF BOOK, 200 Park Avenue, New York, NY 10017. You will be sent a questionnaire.

JACQUES HNIZDOVSKY
Woodcut Artist

During the bicentennial year the Smithsonian Institution Traveling Exhibition Service presented an exhibition surveying the development of the woodcut and the wood engraving in American Art. The cover for the catalogue, AMERICAN PRINTS FROM WOOD, features a print by Hnizdovsky.

Jacques Hnizdovsky was born in the Ukraine in 1915. He studied art in Warsaw and Zagreb. In 1949 he arrived in the United States, and shortly afterwards one of his woodcuts was selected for a Purchase Award at the Minneapolis Institute of Art print exhibition. This proved to be a turning point in his career, and he determined to make his livelihood as an artist.

Hnizdovsky has had numerous exhibits and print editions under the sponsorship of the Associated American Artists. His works have appeared in international invitational exhibits, as well as in US museums, libraries, and universities. His woodcuts have illustrated special editions of the works of major poets including a forthcoming Folio Society publication. Jacques Hnizdovsky has created a number of ex libris and a future YEAR BOOK will feature an article in depth about his work as well as a checklist of his bookplates. Anyone interested in inquiring about commissioning an ex libris may write Jacques Hnizdovsky, 5270 Post Road, Bronx, NY 10471.

— — — — — — —

Clare Ryan Talbot (continued) mutual subject of devotion. What a librarian he must have been, and his devotion to the bookplate was the ideal extra-curricular occupation for a librarian, for the entire world of the Book was his oyster. Our friendship was of two people with similar interests in books. When I extended my activities into the dealer's bookplate world, Frank, too, had entered a like activity with the purchase of the stocks of Stanley Bezanson. Ours was a coast-to-coast correspondence enlivened only by a single visit when he attended a library convention in San Francisco. Allen's book on Charles Capon had been published by Anthoensen Press; by 1952 his book on William Hopson was ready and it was scheduled for publication in the fall of 1952 in an edition of 500 copies by my Hilprand Press. This second imprint would have followed closely after the first successful publication of the Hilprand Press, Dr. Radbill's BIBLIOGRAPHY OF MEDICAL EX LIBRIS LITERATURE. However, tragedy entered with my husband's death, but fortunately for Allen it was arranged for the volume to be issued through the Yale University Press. This was a fitting association as Allen had known Miss Wittington, first organizer of the Hopson collections at Yale, where he took graduate studies. One of his early letters tells of a visit to Goodspeed's during his Yale Library School days when he was snapped while browsing; this picture was used in a Goodspeed catalogue. Frank Allen was a sunny sort of person and will be greatly missed by all those fortunate enough to have known him.

LESLIE CABARGA

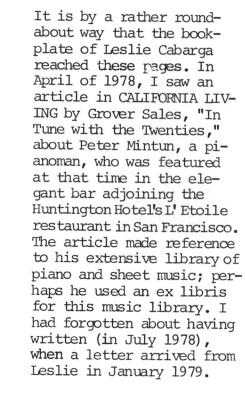

It is by a rather round-about way that the book-plate of Leslie Cabarga reached these pages. In April of 1978, I saw an article in CALIFORNIA LIVING by Grover Sales, "In Tune with the Twenties," about Peter Mintun, a pianoman, who was featured at that time in the elegant bar adjoining the Huntington Hotel's L' Etoile restaurant in San Francisco. The article made reference to his extensive library of piano and sheet music; perhaps he used an ex libris for this music library. I had forgotten about having written (in July 1978), when a letter arrived from Leslie in January 1979.

In part her note read:"Peter Mintun, for whose latest record album I designed the cover, sent me your note. He has no bookplate, but I do. I collect art books, am an artist myself, and drew this ex libris as part of a self-promotion piece, and because I always wanted a bookplate. It was done with a linoleum cut and printed the old way: letterpress. I'm always thrilled when I buy a book with the previous owner's plate, and I place mine on the opporite page - never cover up theirs. The plate shows me in the act of 'swiping' from one of my art books. Never directly, mind you."

Leslie was educated in New Jersey schools and started selling cartoon work to magazines while in the tenth grade. Her father was an art director in New York. She comments: "This exposure definitely pushed me into a career in art (actually I jumped). I wrote a book called THE FLEISCHER STORY, Nostalgia Press, 1976, about the Fleischer Brothers, cartoon pioneers who animated the BETTY BOOP and POPEYE THE SAILOR cartoons. They were right up there with Disney in the 1930's."

"Besides emulating newspaper and comic book strips, it seems I can recall at a fairly early age copying engravings and trying to make all those little parallel lines. I'm still trying to make those damn little lines parallel! In this style I'm influenced by Rockwell Kent, Lynd Ward, and Franklin Booth in particular. When I think of bookplates, I think of heroic figures, romantic images, and architectural settings: columns, arches, etc." Leslie Cabarga is interested in accepting bookplate commissions. Her price would be $100 for most plates, including roughs for approval; the designs would be pen and ink or lino cut or watercolor. Write her directly at 200 E. 16th St. Apt.1E, New York, NY 10003.

MANET

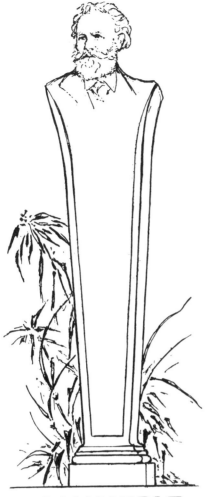

ET MANEBIT

55

An item in BOOKPLATES
IN THE NEWS, page 249,
requests information
about Manet's bookplate.
The noted artist did
have one which was cre-
ated by his friend
Felix Braquemond (1833-
1914), whose etchings
are eagerly collected
today. Braquemond also
designed twelve other
bookplates including
those for Charles As-
selineau, Aglaus Bou-
venne, and Auguste
Poulet-Malassis, author
of two bookplate books.

The Manet plate is il-
lustrated in J. Schwencke's
HET EXLIBRIS IN FRANKRIJK,
1939, page 28. The re-
production is 110 mm.
from top to bottom of the
lettering.

— — — —

LAURENCE STERNE

Mrs. Kathleen Nielsen
has a bookplate bearing
the name Lorenz Sterne,
which she would like to
offer for sale. This is
not the armorial mention-
ed by Walter Hamilton in an article in the JOURNAL of the Ex Libris Society (3:
157, October 1893). The plate in question has D. Berger in the lower right
hand corner as the designer or engraver. Any one interested in acquiring the
plate may write Mrs. Kathleen Nielsen, Sea Wave Road, R. R. #2, Campbell River
B1., Canada U9W 5T7.

— — — — — — — —

FROM THE BOOKPLATE LITERATURE

JAROSLAV FAISER, Mirko Kaizl. ExlibRisten, 1977. This booklet contains six multi-
colored, signed ex libris, which are tipped-in. Kaiser, who lives and works in
Prague, uses a technique described "as collage as here you mix the photo-lithog-
raphy and the colour-linocut to a 'pasting together' which now and then is supplemented by a pen or chalk drawing direct on the lithographic stone." To purchase,
write: Klaus Rodell, P.O. 109, 9900 Frederikshavn, Denmark.

FROM THE BOOKPLATE LITERATURE

MICHEL FINGESTEN 1883-1943, Gianni Mantero. ExlibRisten, 1977. The multi-lingual text is printed on unsewn leaves placed within a portfolio containing 21 engravings and a reproduction of what might have been his business card or ad copy. This is a thoroughly enjoyable presentation, including the translation of the text into English by Anne Eriksen, who has captured the warmth of the personal recollections of Mantero of an important artist, whose life was cut short by an infection suffered following emergency surgery for a wound received during a bombing of a concentration camp for Jews established in Southern Italy after Italy was allied with Germany. Fingesten designed between 1,500 and 2,000 ex libris. If copies of the ExlibRisten portfolio are still available, they may be obtained from Kalus Rodel, P.O. 109, 9900 Frederikshavn, Denmark. (Editor's note: YEAR BOOK 1943/44 of the ASBC&D contained an article by Peter Fingesten, "Contemporary Ex Libris," about his father Michel.)

NORMAN LINDSAY'S BEARS, selected by Keith Wingrove. Published by Macmillan Co. of Australia, South Melbourne, 1978. This selection of drawings has been made by Keith Wingrove, ASBC&D member from Australia, and in his introduction he tells briefly about the famous koala bear Lindsay created and named Billy Bluegum. Most of the drawings appeared originally in the Sidney BULLETIN and the LONE HAND, a monthly. Some of the same wit and humor which these drawings portray, also appeared in Lindsay's ex libris work. Four articles on bookplates appeared in the LONE HAND between 1910 and 1913, in one of which Lionel Lindsay, Norman's brother, is mentioned.

BOOKPLATE SOCIETY NEWSLETTER, II:24, December 1978:
Death of Our President, Arthur W. Dorling. p. 157. Horace E. Jones was President of the Society for 3 years. He had been a member of the Bookplate Exchange Club and a collector at least 20 years prior to that. He knew many of the collectors and engravers of this earlier period. -- Next Meeting, p. 158. The speaker on February 13, 1979 will be David Kindersley. -- Bookplates of Leslie Benenson, R.E., N.D.D., S.S.I., by Philip Beddingham. (2) 158-9. The two bookplates which Miss Benson has engraved are illustrated. "The first is a most magnificent and beautiful rendering of Taurus the bull and Capricorn the goat, these being the Zodiac signs of Mr. and Mrs. Arnander for whom the plate was made in 1977." The second plate for Richard Bell shows a Black Lechine Antelope and two Whale Headed Storks. -- Member's Bookplate, 159-60. Walter Schwab's plate for his Judaica collection was designed by Israeli artist Yaakov Boussidan. -- A Heraldic Bookplate Designer, P.C.B. (1) 160. N. B. Menzies (Forge House, 5 Best Lane, Canterbury CT1 2JB, England) will provide a heraldic bookplate design for between £12 and £20 from which a block can be made; the cost of having a block made and printed would be an additional cost. -- Members' Offers and Requests, 160. Bookplates offered for exchange and material sought for book on English armorial bookplates. -- Bookplates Designed by Graham Johnston - Part II, Arthur W. Dorling, 161-2. The second half of the list incorporating additions sent by Horace Jones. -- Publications, 162. Mention is made of the 1977 YEAR BOOK of the ASBC&D, Mr. Butler's list of ex libris by Kalashnikov, and Robert C. Littlewood's THE EX LIBRIS OF SIR LIONEL LINDSAY. -- Our Second Volume Completed and Other Matters, 163. The new editor is Anthony Pincott; Brian Lee has resigned after serving six years. William Butler is the new Secretary. Peter G. Summers has been invited and has accepted the office of President; Mr. Summers has been a collector since 1952 and runs the Exchange Club. --- Zelma Blakely R.D., Philip Beddingham, 164-5. This wood-engraver and illustrator died in September 1978. There is a descriptive checklist of thirteen ex libris and two are illustrated.

THE JACK OF HEARTS -
       Lawrence Stewart

Lawrence Stewart has recently joined the ASBC&D
after finding the name of our Society in Fridolf Johnson's A TREASURY OF BOOKPLATES. His
friendly letter of inquiry about membership
stated: "Last spring I started collecting ex
libris, which seemed a natural thing for a bibliophile like myself."When he discovered Fridolf's book, Stewart realized he was not the
only person with this peculiar fixation! Enclosed with his letter were three plates he had
designed. He wrote, "The old preacher is for
my professional library, I am a pastor just
fresh out of seminary. The shrunken head was
designed by the direction of my father for his
library - he is a psychologist. The card plate
was for the stuff in my non-professional library. James Branch Cabell asked, 'Why is the
Jack of Hearts the only one without a moustache?'

Cards have long fascinated me. I have designed a few and may some day try
to do an entire deck. The Jacks of Hearts and Spades both have an at-
traction. Why does the Jack of Hearts have a rose in one hand while keeping an axe behind his back? And what better card for one interested in
cards? This Jack is said to be Etienne de Vignoxes, the Knight La Hire,
who is credited with the invention of our suit signs and with the introduction of the queen to replace the oberman (still kept in some countries)."

Lawrence writes further, "My B.A. was in art, and I have a huge collection
of comic books and an interest in comic book and comic strip art. I have
interests in twice ten thousand things, but am expert in none. I study
Greek and Hebrew daily, but that is done simply to keep me from forgetting
too much. If everything goes according to schedule, I will be ordained on
May 20th. I am more single than I care to be, but living in Confidence,
population 23 (the mailing address is Melrose, but I'm in Confidence) gives
me little opportunity to change my marital status."

Lawrence Stewart is eager to exchange and correspond with members who are
willing to share their knowledge and enthusiasm with a beginner in the
field of bookplates. His mailing address is: R.F.D. #1, Melrose, IA 52569.

—   —   —   —   —   —   —   —

FRENCH and SHERBORN EX LIBRIS FOR EXCHANGE: While in Lugano during the 1978
International Ex Libris Congress, Heinz-G. Hintze made known to your editor
his interest in exchanging his Sherborn, French, and other American and
European bookplates. He specifically wants the ex libris of Michel Fingesten, Heinrich Vogeler, Emil Orlik, and bookplates of the 15th to 17th
centuries. If you are interested in exchanging, or possibly purchasing,
please write directly to: Heinz-G. Hintze, Nindorf, IM Auetal 40, 2116 Han-
stedt-Nordheide 4, Germany.

—   —   —   —   —   —   —   —

BOOKPLATES IN THE NEWS   January, April, July, October
Copyright 1979 $8 U.S./$8.50 Overseas

291

THE BOOKPLATE SOCIETY   To celebrate the opening of a major ex-
Open Weekend 6/23-24   hibition of British bookplates sponsor-
                               ed by the Bookplate Society (London) at
the Victoria and Albert Museum, there will be a series of events the weekend of June 23-24, 1979 in London. William E. Butler, Secretary of the
Bookplate Society, extends to all bookplate collectors a cordial invitation
to attend. The program will open with a reception and buffet dinner at the
Honourable Society of Gray's Inn at 5:30pm on Saturday, June 23rd. Gray's
Inn was the mediaeval center for the training of barristers located in central London. This will afford an opportunity to meet members of the Bookplate Society, to exchange bookplates, and generally chat about the subject
with new friends.

At 2pm on Sunday, June 24th, those attending the event will meet in the exhibition hall of the Victoria and Albert Museum to see 400 years of British
bookplates; the tour will be followed by tea. The Museum is publishing a
booklet for the exhibit and there will also be a handlist of the exhibits.
A charge of £10 will include the buffet dinner at Gray's Inn, tea and the
exhibition at the Victoria and Albert, and the booklet and handlist for the
exhibit. Reservations must be made in advance and requests should be sent
to William E. Butler, Secretary, 9 Lyndale Avenue, London NW2 2DQ, England.

— — — — —   — — — —

EXHIBITIONS

An international, invitational exhibition was held in October 1978 in Fred-
erikshaven, Denmark, and in the notes of the exhibit catalog, Klaus Rodel
states it is hoped the exhibit will become an annual event. He further comments that while a broad geographic representation was sought, the catalog
shows domination of graphics from Lithuania and Czechoslovakia, which "only
reflects that the interest in these two countries really is biggest." The
United States was represented by ASBC&D member Vytautas O. Virkau; he is
pictured with some of the fresh flowers which appear in numerous of his ex
libris designs.

FLOWERS IN EX LIBRIS was the title
of an exhibition held in Debrecen,
Hungary from August 10 to September 10, 1978. Ten plates designed
by Vytautas O. Virkau of the U.S.
were in the exhibit.

EX LIBRIS AT APPIANO GENTILE - an
exhibit was held from December 26,
1978 to January 2, 1979 at Appiano
Gentile, Italy. Among the artists
represented was V. O. Virkau.

Printed catalogs with a variety of
text and illustrations have been
prepared for each of the above exhibitions.

Where are the exhibits

  in the United States?

Ray
SCHULENBERG
ex libris

Signed print by V.O.Virkau

AS of BC & D
Bookplates in the News

1206 N. STONEMAN AVENUE #15. ALHAMBRA. CALIFORNIA. 91801 U.S.A.
AUDREY SPENCER ARELLANES, Editor

BOOKPLATE SOCIETY'S OPEN WEEKEND EX LIBRIS SUCCESS!

The invitation extended by the British Bookplate Society to attend the weekend of events June 23 and 24, 1979 was well received by the ex libris community as could easily be seen by the turnout of more than ninety enthusiasts.

Arrangements were made for those attending the Open Weekend to meet during Saturday morning at the National Book League, where the Bookplate Society holds its local meetings. A small exhibit was mounted of the ex libris work of Leo Wyatt for visitors to view. The NBL library offered space for visitors to chat or to use the reading tables while exchanging. Visitors were then on their own to lunch with new found friends & renewed acquaintances, or to explore London until the evening banquet at Gray's Inn.

Also on display at the National Book League was an advance copy of the new volume by Brian North Lee, BRITISH BOOKPLATES - A Pictorial History, published in Great Britain and the United States by David and Charles. This well documented and illustrated addition to bookplate history will be reviewed in October.

Saturday evening at 5:30PM historic Gray's Inn was the site for a record turnout of ninety, who had traveled from many of the European countries as well as those who had traveled lesser distances within England and your editor, who had traveled the greatest distance to participate in this momentous event. Wine was served during the social hour, though its influence was scarcely needed with such a naturally convivial gathering. Collectors had an opportunity to meet artists and other collectors. The long table at the front of the hall was swiftly utilized by collectors to spread their treasure of ex libris for exchange with other like-minded collectors. For some, who had not previously witnessed the fervor with which exchanges are made, this was a revealing experience.

A festive buffet was soon announced and all helped themselves and then sat at the long tables much as do the students at Gray's Inn during the dining term. Conversation flowed in many languages, often with bits and pieces of several including sign language.

Following dinner, Philip Beddingham, Librarian at Gray's Inn and Chairman of the Bookplate Society, called the meeting to order that he might introduce Peter Summers, President. Mr. Summers talked about the antecedents of the Bookplate Society and its current revival in conjunction with the Private Libraries Association. (It has been promised that permission to publish Peter Summers' talk will be granted; it is scheduled to appear in the October issue of BOOKPLATES IN THE NEWS.) For the enjoyment of those who do not readily understand English, Summers' talk was given in a summarized version by Antoine Rousseau, who had kindly volunteered his multi-lingual skills.

Next Mark Severin was introduced, who spoke about the differences in approach to bookplates both as personal tokens of ownership and as art works to be collected and exchanged, especially the differences between the English and those on the Continent. His wit and humor made it possible to say many things which have long needed to be voiced. (Promise has been made that this talk also will be available for the October issue.) In brief, the British Bookplate Society has made the invitation to hold the International Ex Libris Congress in London for 1982. This announcement was greeted with a wave of applause. Again, Antoine Rousseau came to the rescue to translate as he sight-read Severin's talk.

Mark Severin introduced Audrey Arellanes as the representative of the American Society of Bookplate Collectors and Designers, and she briefly extended a welcome from the United States. And affirmed that "Bookplates are indeed a passport to friendship."

Because of a curfew, it was necessary to leave Gray's Inn at 10PM. Those who wished to continue were invited to adjourn to Henekey's Wine Lodge, which was located adjacent to the Inn. And all were reminded of the Sunday activities: morning coffee at the homes of several Society members and then to the Victoria and Albert Museum for the exhibit and afternoon tea.

The weather had been beautiful on Saturday, with the unexpected summer weather of earlier in the week still prevailing. Sunday morning saw slight showers, but not enough to deter most from accepting the invitation for coffee.

Viewing the exhibition was scheduled for 2PM; however, the museum had changed its opening to half an hour later. The group made good use of the time to continue chatting, a few even took time to view the inside of the church next to the museum with its colorful stained glass windows.

"The History of the Bookplate in Britain" is a well-mounted exhibit with excellent annotations in the cases. In addition there is a printed catalogue, A HISTORY OF BOOKPLATES IN BRITAIN, listing the prints in alphabetic sequence with a symbol to the left of each entry which keys it to the exhibit case in which the bookplate appears. The catalogue annotated each print or has reference to three other publications, which are BOOKPLATES IN BRITIAN, an illustrated essay written by the Bookplate Society for the V&A; BRITISH BOOKPLATES, an historical review by Brian N. Lee (published by David & Charles, 1979); and EARLY PRINTED BOOK LABELS by Lee (Pinner, 1976). At 4PM, the group shared a pleasant tea in a separate room off the museum's coffee shop; most then returned to the exhibit and chatted with new found friends until the museum closed at 6PM.

PHILIP HAGREEN: THE ARTIST AND HIS WORK
Reviewed by Richard H. Schimmelpfeng

Of considerable interest to collectors of English 20th
century bookplates is PHILIP HAGREEN: THE ARTIST AND
HIS WORK, published in England in 1978 "At the Sign of
the Arrow" in an edition of 200 copies. The work is
illustrated with 206 wood engravings, all but three of
which were printed from the blocks personally selected
and identified by the artist.

Philip Hagreen was born in 1890, the son of the drawing master of Wellington College. In 1920 he moved to Dorset and in 1923 to Ditchling Common where he became a student of Eric Gill and collaborated in the handsome productions of St. Domonic's Press, all of which are now collector's
items. Hagreen stopped engraving in 1929.

The artist's devotional works, greeting cards,
and bookplates are end-grain wood engravings,
while his larger designs are woodcuts. None is
signed in the block which makes identification
difficult, as the similarity with Eric Gill's
work is strong. The book lables are reminiscent of labels created by Will Carter, Leo
Wyatt, and Diana Bloomfield. Items 136-167 in
the book are bookplates, a list of which follows. The Elkins Mathews label at the end is
not listed; it is found in the BOOKPLATE MAGA-
ZINE, no. 3, January 1920.

136. Joan Hagreen
137. The Corner House,
     Heathfield, Sussex
138. 8 Lansdown Place East,
     Bath

139. Shirley Dovey
140. Harrow School
141. Church of the English
     Martyrs, Haydock
142. J.A.&S. Clegg
143. Hilda Carey
144. Christopher Carey
145. G. Allsop
146. Martha Genung Stearns
147. Joseph Crowley
148. M.E. Lorkin
149. Adrian Barber
150. Richard Bagley
151. Ramsay Library
152. Prior of the College
     of St. Albert
153. Roehampton College

154. Denis & Dorothy Little
155. Pat Shaw
156. G. Blunt
157. Sign of St.Mary, Help
     of Christians, Worth
158. Society of St.Clement
159. H.&G.K. Babington Hill
160. Church of St. Mary the
     Virgin & St. Philip Neri
161. John & Muriel Simmons
162. Nora Ryan
163. College of O.S.B. Worth
164. Mary Elizabeth Hodson
165. St. Sabina in Urbe
166. Phyllis Hill
167. John L. Denman
     Elkins Matthews

The book is well-made, nicely bound, and the illustrations are carefully
printed. It is well worth the addition to any bookplate library.

KINDERSLEY'S WORKSHOP IN AMSTERDAM
by Jan Rhebergen

During the month of March in the University Library of Amsterdam, David Kindersley had an exhibition of the work of his workshop. I had the pleasure of meeting Mr. Kindersley and chatted with him about his work. He told me about his life, dedicated to the letter, and his great love for the beauty that can be found in it. Wonderful examples of his work were shown: alphabets incised in slate, engraved glass, medals, bookplates, etc. The cutting in wood does not present any difficulty for the artist, i.e. oak doors, so I asked him if he had cut bookplates in wood. "No," he said, "I am too lazy in that I prefer to draw them."

Interest in the exhibition was intense, and, of coruse, the majority of the visitors were students. Because these people have much for which to thank the letterform, it was good to give examples of lettering in its most noble form and teach them to respect it. We have Mr. Kindersley to thank for that.

Kindersley's Workshop came into being in 1946 when David was joined by Kevin Cribb. Kindersley had been apprenticed to Eric Gill during the 1930's and Cribb worked for his father, Laurie Cribb, in the Gill Workshop. So there was much in common both in training and work philosophy. In 1950 David Parsley joined them in the workshop as an apprentice.

—   —   —   — —   —   —   —   —   —

A "GRAPHIC WEEKEND" IN BELGIUM
by Jan Rhebergen

On March 24th and 25th, in the small town of Sint Niklaas, an exhibition was held during a so-called "Grafisch Weekend," a gathering of artists and collectors of ex libris. This exhibition showed the result of the first international ex libris competition offered by the town administration. There were 164 graphic artists, who sent 424 different bookplates. The artists came from Belgium, The Netherlands, Denmark, Germany, Finland, France, Hungary, Italy, Yugoslavia, Austria, Poland, Rumania, Soviet Union, Spain, Switzerland, Sweden, and Czechoslovakia. The first prize went to Czech artist Jinrich Pilecek for his etched bookplate for J. Vlasaty. Second and third prizes were awarded two Belgium artists. Many visited the exhibit opening day, and during the two-day event, many bookplates exchanged owners, thanks to the friendly environment.

—   —   —   —   —   —   —   —

METROPOLITAN LIFE STUDY: LONGEVITY OF PROMINENT WOMEN. A study was conducted of 2,352 women, who were alive on January 1, 1964 and living in the United States and whose biographies appeared in the 1964/65 edition of WHO'S WHO IN AMERICA; they were studied over a follow-up period of 12 years ending on December 31, 1975. This study should be of particular interest to members of the ASBC&D, since one of our artist-members, Miss Cleora Wheeler, is among the prominent women in the study. "Prominent women - those who have achieved distinction in a particular field of endeavor - live distinctly longer on the average than women in the general population. . . . The most favorable longevity was experienced by women archivists, librarians, and curators, as well as by artists, political leaders, government officials, and community service leaders, while the least favorable longevity was recorded for women of letters, performers and entertainers, and physicians and surgeons." (Note: Prior to the 1964/65 edition, too few women were listed to permit a statistically significant analysis.)

PHOTOGRAPHIC EX LIBRIS

Dennis Doonan, whose firm is Graphics 1,
writes a little about himself and his ex
libris: "I'm not actively seeking bookplate commissions, but I'd try to help
anyone if I could. I'm a commercial photographer by profession, and an artist/pho-
tographer by avocation. My commercial
photography is mainly advertising illustrations, newspaper ads, catalogue work,
annual reports, etc. My personal work
tends towards natural surrealism. I don't
try to create surreal pictures, I find
them. Not always the strange surrealism
of Dali, but a natural kind that allows
you to see nature and life as something
mysterious, but not totally beyond our
grasp. A single footprint of a dog on a
beach, surrounded by small pebbles and
rocks, a group of puppets in a Christmas
store display, an interesting crack in a
window of a deserted building. Surrealism
seems natural to the spirit of this area.

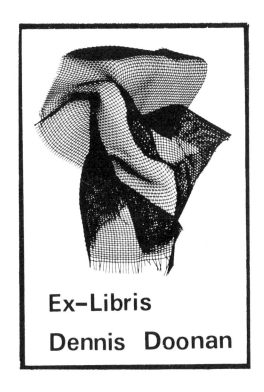

Ex-Libris
Dennis Doonan

When I was in the Southwest last summer, it was not there, as I'm certain
it's not in the West. It's very hard to describe, I guess; but it's just
something you feel and how you react to nature. I love it, but there is
something about it that is strange, surreal.

"I don't know if that comes across for the bookplates. The screen plate is
used for my general collection. I like the design, because it is a natural
development of a form, yet it is manmade.

Ex Libris

D. A. Doonan

"The Holmes plate is for my collection of Sherlock Holmes material that I collect. I have
around 500 volumes, many leaflets, and
stacks of clippings. I'm trying to accumu-
late as much information as possible on the
Sherlock Holmes motif used in both bookplates
and in advertising. I find the Holmes stories
very entertaining and a good way to unwind."

Dennis studied photography in the Layton
School of Art in Milwaukee. After working
freelance for some time, he returned to
college and earned a BA in philosophy. Following that, he took as many art courses in
college as he could and literally lived in
the art studios and the library. After getting what Dennis calls "the Bohemianism" out
of his system, he returned to freelancing.
Since 1975 he has had a studio, and finally
this year business is better and he is receiving deserved mention and recognition in
the area. (2307 Carlisle Ave., Racine, WI 53404)

FROM THE BOOKPLATE LITERATURE

MICROBIBLIOPHILE, The Golden Age of American Book Plate Design. 3:21,
July 1979. Robert Hanson's third miniature book will be the publication
of the late Francis W. Allen's paper which was presented at the International Ex Libris Congress held in Portugal in 1976. Details will be
given as soon as available.

PIPE SMOKER'S EPHEMERIS, The Green Tiger Press (7458 La Jolla Blvd., La
Jolla, CA 92037). (1) 15th Anniversary Issue:13, Summer-Autumn 1979. An
ex libris for Willard S. Morse is illustrated as used on a notecard published by Green Tiger Press.

LOUISIANA'S ART NOUVEAU, THE CRAFTS OF THE NEWCOMB STYLE, Suzanne Ormond
and Mary E. Irvine. Gretna, LA: Pelican Publishing Company, 1976, $25.
Newcomb was established in 1887 as a women's college and continued into
the 1940's as a crafts school. Illustrated are two ex libris, one designed by Myrtle A. Punjol for Mary R. Cabral in 1922 and Mary Rosenblatt
created a linoleum block for herself.

EXLIBRIS I FARVER, Helmer Fogedgaard and Johnny Kohler, privately printed
1978. Eleven tipped-in ex libris, including one on the cover, all printed in color. A few sentences of text appear about each artist, printed
in Danish.

G. M. (MIA) POT-VAN REGTEREN ALTENA, published in 1978 by Exlibriskring
der W.B.V. This is a portfolio of eight ex libris prints and one page of
text.

EXLIBRIS WERELD, Winter 1978, editor Jan Rhebergen, Jr. Report on the Ex
Libris congress in Lugano. One article has a quotation in English which
is credited to Eric Gill: "Look after goodness and truth, and beauty will
look after herself." Illustrated is an attractive plate by Marcus Beeven
with butterflies and blades of grass. An edition of Thomas Bewick vignettes
published by the Scolar Press in 1978 is mentioned; also a HISTORY OF BRIT-
ISH WOOD ENGRAVING published by Midas Books. There is an alphabetic checklist of the work of Anton Pieck, which includes the date of execution when
known.

L'EX LIBRIS FRANCAIS, September 1978. The final segment of a continuing
article on the bookplates of chemists. Report on the Lugano Congress by
Didier Kowalik. Obituary for the Italian engraver Italo Zetti (1913-78),
who died in Milan; written by Daniel Meyer.

JENSEITS DER WENDEKREISE, Paul Pfister. (ExlibRisten, 1977) Poetry text
with full page illustrations. Pfister has written on bookplates.

ALTE EXLIBRIS, Andreas and Angela Hopf. Dortmund: Harenberg Kommunijation,
1978. A small paperback, minimal text, artist and owner index, and over
200 ex libris illustrated, some in color. The reproductions range from
Albrecht Durer (1525) to the 1970's in time, and in categories such as eros,
music, allegory, ornament and symbol. Priced in England at nearly £5, it
seems expensive for a small paperback.

'79 YEAR BOOK: Severin/Landacre/Reitsma-Valenca - Fall Publication Scheduled

EX LIBRIS FOR LENDERS

One of the pleasures of owning books is sharing them
with friends; however, this
can be hazardous to a library.
Don Margo offers one solution with the special bookplate tipped-in to the right.
Not only should the plate
assist in the return of
borrowed books, but designing it gave release to Don's
skills as a calligrapher
and printer.

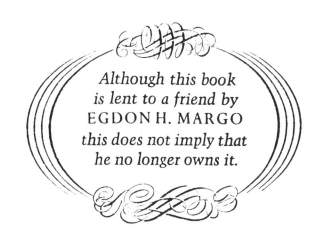

*Although this book
is lent to a friend by*
EGDON H. MARGO
*this does not imply that
he no longer owns it.*

—   —   —

GEOFF & ANN LONG

Two new members to ASBC&D are
Geoff & Ann Long, who live in
Camperdown, New South Wales.

Their joint ex libris features
their home which was built in
1892 and renovated in 1970. In
each corner is the head of the
horse of Selene, the moon goddess from the Parthenon pedi-
ment now in the British Museum,
a replica of which they have in
their garden. The side borders
have "gum nuts" (the dried seed
capsule of eucalyptus) and eucalyptus leaves; this is because
of their interest in native

flora. In the upper border is a representation of an obstetric stethoscope
since Geoff's major professional interest was obstetric anaesthesia. The
artist, who designed the bookplate, is Alan A. Gamble, a retired architect.
This was his first bookplate; several books of drawings of Sydney buildings
were recently published by Gamble; UNIVERSITY OF SYDNEY is one volume.

—   —   —   —   —   —

MORE FROM THE LITERATURE . . . . .

BELA STETTNER, Andor Semsey. (ExlibRisten, 1978, Klaus Rodel, Lyøvej 5, DK
9900 Frederikshavn, Denmark). This Hungarian artist was born in Budapest
in 1928. In connection with an exhibit of his work in 1969 at the Hungarian
National Library, a catalog was published which listed 195 ex libris by this
artist. Semsey says, "All graphic works by Bela Stettner have in common that
they focus on the human being, the human being at war and in peace...." There
is a certain tortured feeling to many of his ex libris in the current book
which features the female nude. Of his own work Stettner is quoted: "Working
with exlibris requires a special inward concentration by the artist. There-

fore I can only work within this field when I am in a relaxed and calm mood. . . . An exlibris is, however, also a help and support for my free graphic as I in this case often make a kind of preliminary study for bigger works." Twenty-six prints illustrated, some in color. (50 Kr.)

MILOSLAV NOVACEK, Stanislav Novotny (ExlibRisten, 1979). In writing about this Czech artist, Novotny says: "And so occur the unexpected meetings and imaginary lyric events, which are mysterious, brilliant, alarming, disturbing and full of inimitable poetry. Yet Miloslav Novacek is a fully contemporary artist, listening sensitively to the complicated rhythm of the present time." Seventeen prints are tipped-in, executed in silk screen technique, and many in color. (75 Kr.)

24 EX LIBRIS WITH A WINE MOTIF, G. Jan Rhebergen (ExlibRisten, 1979). The greatest specialist in collecting ex libris with a wine motif is Norbert Lippoczy, a Hungarian who lives in Poland. (Incidentally his brother, Dr. Nicholas Lippozcy, is a member of ASBC&D in the United States.) It was his idea to publish this book. Norbert comes from an old Hungarian family of winegrowers who lived in the district of Tokay. He has more than 3,000 ex libris with this specialty; he attempts to obtain three copies of each bookplate so that copies may be given to the agricultural Museum in Budapest, the Wine-Museum in Warsaw, and the third collection will go, after his death, to the municipal Museum of Tarnow, the town in which Lippoczy has lived and worked for many long years. (75 Kr.)

HET EXLIBRIS IN RUSLAND (Exlibriskring Der W.B.-Vereniging, Admiraal de Ruyterweg 545, Amsterdam-Sloterdijk, Netherlands), 8 1/4 X 11 1/2". Joh. J. Hanrath appears to have divided his text, at least in part, on geographic areas of Russia. There are two maps which show concentrations of artists by area, and two charts which appear to perhaps show the influence of certain schools of artists. It is well illustrated in black and white. (Is there a reader of BOOKPLATES IN THE NEWS who reads Russian and would offer to review the book in depth or, better yet, summarize the book in an article?)

HET EXLIBRIS IN POLEN, Joh. J. Hanrath and Cecylia Dunin-Horkawicz (Exlibriskring Der W.B.-Vereniging, Admiraal de Ruyterweg 545, Amsterdam-Sloterdijk, Netherlands), 8 1/4 X 11 1/2". There is considerable text, many illustrations including four tipped-in color prints, a map of Poland showing the boundaries originally and as changed in 1815 and 1919-37, an index of 285 artists with their dates of greatest ex libris productivity, also a chronological list of artists by birth and death dates where known.

BIBLIOGRAPHIE de L'EX LIBRIS FRANCAIS 1872-1977, G. Meyer-Noirel (Klaus Rosel, Lyøvej 5, DK 9900 Frederikshavn). There are 1,550 entries in this bibliography of ex libris literature in French. There is one tipped-in ex libris printed in color; other illustrations are appropriately the title pages of various publications, both books and periodicals.

WAPPENROLLE DOCHTERMANN, Wappenfuhrende Geschlechter der Bundesrepublic Deutschland, published in 1979 by Wappen Archiv, Stuttgart, volume XXIV. This is a beautifully created volume, 8" X 9" and an inch thick. It is a volume in a continuing series of Roll of Arms of Germany which carries on the work of Robert Steimel's RHEINISCHES WAPPEN-LEXIKON. With the exception of the index and a few text pages, the pages are printed on one side only, one coat of arms to a page, most printed lavishly multi-colored.

MORE FROM THE LITERATURE . . .

LADY, Collecting Bookplates, Keith Clark. (6) CLXXVII:#4590, March 29 1979
Personal remarks about collecting, the removal of bookplate prints from
books, housing a collection, etc. Clark offers the encouraging remark that
1,000 bookplates will take up less space that a set of ENCYCLOPAEDIA BRI-
TANNICA Two major methods of housing are in loose-leafed albums or in special file boxes. Clark comments, "There have been few books on the subject
compared with many subjects that are collected ...." Your editor questions
"few books" unless Clark is restricting the literature to volumes about
English bookplates only.

PAM G. RUETER, Dutch Engraver of Bookplates (published and available from
Arethusa Pers Heber Blokland, Bosstraat 30, 3743 GA Baarn, Holland, $20).
This private press book contains 55 wood-engravings printed from the block.

EX LIBRIS LUGANO XVII, portfolio of the work of 24 bookplate artists, issued by l'Association des Collectionneurs et Amis d' Exlibris a Praha.

AMERICAN COLLECTOR, The Conflicting History of Henry Dawkins, Engraver,
Stephen Decatur. (7) 7:6-7, January 1939. "But while Dawkins has an excellent reputation in his legitimate field, he enjoys the unenviable distinction of having been the first man in this country, as far as any
records have revealed, to be arrested for counterfeiting paper money."

INTERNATIONAL COMPETITION for two ex libris offered by Jesolo Lido, Italy;
deadline was June 30, 1979. Prizes for black and white, and color.

VENTURA COUNTY HISTORICAL SOCIETY QUARTERLY, Bibliotheca Sancti Bonaven-
turae, Msgr. Francis J. Weber. (1) 11:7-15, Summer 1976. Founded in 1782,
there are 146 tomes in a glass-fronted case as part of the Mission's observation for the bicentennial of America's freedom.

CONNOISSEUR, Beauty in Bookplates. 181:65, September 1972. Paragraph on
exhibit at National Book League's headquarters (London) by Bookplate Society, which coincides with publication of ENGRAVED BOOKPLATES 1950-70
by Mark Severin and Anthony Reid.

THE ENGRAVED WORK OF ERIC GILL, published by the Victoria and Albert Museum in conjunction with a catalogue compiled by John Physick, Keeper,
Department of Museum Services. The 220 works are briefly annotated, dimensions given, technique used (wood-engraving, etc.), and cross-refer-
enced to the companion catalogue. It is an attractive, well-produced book
at £3.50.

SVENSKA EXLIBRISFORENINGEN, #127,128-35, February 1979. Notice is given
of the Open Weekend sponsored by the Bookplate Society (London) for
June 23-24, 1979. There is a brief article by Erik Hallquist; mention of
the bookplate literature, both periodicals and books. Tipped-in on the
last page is an ex libris by Charles Behrens.

ANTIQUARIAN BOOK MONTHLY REVIEW, Book Reviews: REYNOLDS STONE ENGRAVINGS.
Reviewed by Ruari McLean. (7) 5:23-4, January 1978. Front cover has four
illustrations, and of the total illustrations two may be ex libris. McLean

writes, "Reynolds Stone, as engraver, has made himself a master of two special fields: the roman letter and country scenes, especially of woodland . . . . His best-known works are, probably, the exquisite book-plates and labels with calligraphic flourishes of which there is a superb array in this book." This is not a catalogue raisonne.

QUARTERLY NEWSLETTER (Book Club of California), Gifts to the Library. XLI: 20, Winter 1975-76. John Swingle presented "18th century book bearing the handsome engraved bookplate of John Bell," who published a 20-volume edition of Shakespear in 1785.

ANTIQUARIAN BOOK MONTHLY REVIEW, Help, please. 6:129, March 1979. Requests sources for bookplate commissions and purchase.

ANTIQUARIAN BOOK MONTHLY REVIEW, Bookplates. (1) 6:221, May 1979. Exhibit titled A History of Bookplates in Britain is in the Library Gallery of the Victoria and Albert Museum, June 6 to September 2, 1979. This is fourth exhibit of the Bookplate Society. Three publications available near time of exhibit opening: BRITISH BOOKPLATES, by Brian North Lee, hardbound book; a catalogue of the exhibit; and BOOKPLATES IN BRITAIN issued by the Bookplate Society and the V&A. Mention is made that ex libris commissions may cost from £20 for a line drawing to £300 for a copperplate. Illustration is ex libris of I. & J. Pettman's home by Michael Renton.

ANTIQUARIAN BOOK MONTHLY REVIEW, Letters to the Editor: Bookplates. 6:212-3, May 1979. Names of artists who accept bookplate commissions may be obtained from Anthony Pincott, Honorable Secretary, Bookplate Society, 3B Hurlingham Court, Ranelagh Gardens, London SW6 3UN, England.

ANTIQUARIAN BOOK MONTHLY REVIEW, Trade Notes: At the Victoria & Albert. 6: 267, June 1979. Exhibit, "The History of the Bookplate in Britain," held in conjunction with the Bookplate Society.

BiN, Bookselling Through Gale. 7:14, January-March 1979. Mentions Gale's literary calendars devoted to bookplate and calligraphic themes.

ANATOLII IVANOVICH KALASHNIKOV, Graphics, Bookplates, Book Illustrations, Ex Exhibition of Wood Engravings, 1964-76 by a Contemporary Artist from the Societ Union, introduction and checklist by William E. Butler, 1977. This catalogue was printed to accompany an exhibition at the Flaxman Gallery, University College, London, held April 25 to May 20, 1977. One tipped-in print is a wood-engraving of the University College. The checklist of ex libris numbers 428, gives technique of execution and dimensions.

L'EX LIBRIS FRANCAIS, 41:#131, March 1979. G. Meyer-Noirel describes more than a hundred ex libris on numismatics as well as those belonging to bankers on the occasion of an exhibit held during May in Nancy. Bookplates of celebrities are presented by Denise Caxtoux. Article and illustration on two ex libris for Georges Cross.

BOOK-CRAFTSMAN. No. 1, vol. 1, August 1919. Ex libris for Will Daeye Hard is illustrated.

— ⸻ — — — — — — —

PLEASE NOTIFY BOOKPLATES IN THE NEWS when you move & authorize forwarding.

NEWSLETTER (The Bookplate Society), volume 2:No. 24, December 1978. Death of Our President, 157. Horace E. Jones died October 9, 1978; he was president of the Society for three years "and was perhaps the last link with the great collectors of the past, having been a member of the old Bookplate Exchange Club as long ago as 1936 and actually having started collecting some twenty years before that." - Next Meeting, 158. David Kindersley scheduled to talk about his work the evening of February 13, 1979 at the Library Association. - "Bookplates by Leslie Benenson, R.R.,N.D., S.S.I.," Philip Beddingham. (2) 158-9. While she has only engraved two bookplates, both of which are illustrated, this young artist's talents have already won her membership in the Society of Scribes and Illuminators and she has been elected a Fellow of the Royal Society of Painter-Etchers and Engravers. Both plates feature animals. Her fees range from £20 to £50, depending upon size and complexity. Her address is: 25 Upperton Gardens, Eastbourne, Sussex BN21 2AA, England. - Member's Bookplate. (1) 159-60. Israeli artist Yaakov Boussidan designed plate for Walter Schwab's collection of Judaica. - A Heraldic Bookplate Designer, Philip Beddingham. (1) 160. N. B. Menzies (Forge House, 5 Best Lane, Canterbury CT1 2JB, England) will provide a drawing for £12-20. It would then be necessary for anyone wanting a bookplate to have a block made and printed. - Members' Offers and Requests, 160. Exchanges available from two members and one seeks signed and/or dated plates for a book in preparation on ENGLISH ARMORIAL BOOKPLATES. - Bookplates Designed by Graham Johnson - Part II, Arthur W. Dorling. Second half of list plus a few additions sent by Horace Jones. - Publications, 162-3. Among publications available are the 1977 YEAR BOOK of the ASBC&D, a checklist of ex libris by Kalashnikov prepared by William Butler, and the EX LIBRIS OF SIR LIONEL LINDSAY by Robert C. Littlewood (£18.50), which is described as being disappointing as to the quality of illustration and the typeface, but a most useful reference book. - International Ex Libris Competition 1979, 163. Competition organized by Sint Niklaas (Belgium) Ex Libris Center; unfortunately entries were required January 15, 1979. - Our Second Volume Completed and Other Matters, 163. Volume II (1976-78, No. 13-24) INDEX covers six unnumbered pages at the end of the December 1978 issue. Brian North Lee has resigned as Editor and Secretary after holding these offices for six years. New Secretary is William Butler, new Editor is Anthony Pincott. Peter G. Summers, F.S.A. was invited to accept role of President of Bookplate Society. - Zelma Blakely, R.E., Philip C. Beddingham. (2) 164-5. Two of the thirteen bookplates she designed are illustrated; nine of these are signed "ZB", probably all are wood-engravings. She was a teacher and illustrator, who died September 6, 1978. - Answer to Teaser Number 5, 166. The quotation "from detective fiction" was from Raymond Chandler's THE BIG SLEEP. - Duke of Sussex's Bookplate, 166. Report of an ex libris on a book jacket of ROYAL DUKE - AUGUSTUS FREDERICK, DUKE OF SUSSEX (1773-1843), by Molly Gillen, published by Sidgwick & Jackson, London, 1976. - New Members, 166. Nine new members.

—   —   —   — —   —   —   —

MARY PEW DIES SUDDENLY   Miss Mary E. Pew, retired Redlands high school librarian, died suddenly July 2, 1979. She had lived in the Redlands area for 54 of her 83 years. She was born in Helena, Montana on May 22, 1896, earned her library science degree from the University of Montana, and later took graduate work at USC. A member of ASBC&D, she had an excellent collection of bookplates, and was most generous with novice enthusiasts (continued bottom next page)

AN EARLY CONNECTICUT BOOK LABEL
by Richard H. Schimmelpfeng

Recently the writer was given the book label of Teiley Blaksslee, said to be of Connecticut origin. The label is unusual in giving so much information about the owner; it is too bad that he didn't give his address as well. It is a large label, measuring 80 X 178 mm. border to border, and undoubtedly came from a large quarto or folio volume. (It is reproduced in somewhat reduced size below.)

Research so far has not identified the owner. The name Teiley (Tillie, Tilla, Tilly, Tiley, Tely, etc.) Blaksslee (Blackly, Blazeley, Blakslee, Blackslee, etc.) is a common one around 17th and 18th century New Haven and Woodbury-Southbury, and turns up frequently in the vital records of the period although none is listed under 1728 (I assume the owner knew his birth year). Men of this name served in the 1756, 1767 and 1759 campaigns of the French and Indian War. None of these men apparently attend-Yale or Harvard.

In the absence of any information, it is interesting to speculate about the owner: was he a printer perhaps, or had access to a printshop? The printing is not well-done; it looks rather amateurish. The phrasing indicates somewhat that only one book was bought, and surely its purchase meant enough for the owner to have a special label in it. Was he a parson, perhaps? It would be interesting to know what the book was which the owner bought 212 years ago.

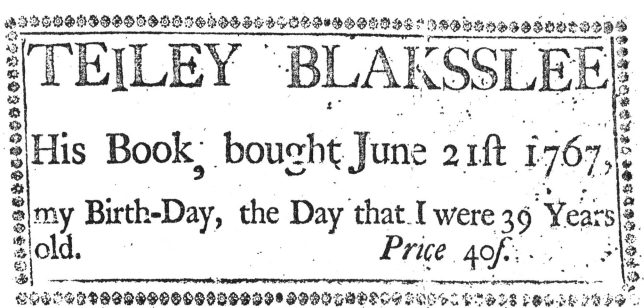

TEILEY BLAKSSLEE

His Book, bought June 21st 1767, my Birth-Day, the Day that I were 39 Years old.   Price 40*s*.

MARY E. PEW continued -) as fellow Redlands resident Barbara Abele happily discovered. Miss Pew's collection, well annotated, was on exhibit during 1978 at the A. K. Smiley Public Library in Redlands (California). Your editor was privileged to share two of her excursions in recent years to Los Angeles for a day of books and bookplates, including one of the exhibits at the Philosophical Research Library.

BOOKPLATES IN THE NEWS   JANUARY/APRIL/JULY/OCTOBER

U.S. $8/OVERSEAS $9

AS of BC & D

Bookplates in the News

1206 N. STONEMAN AVENUE #15. ALHAMBRA. CALIFORNIA. 91801 U.S.A.

AUDREY SPENCER ARELLANES, Editor

NUMBER THIRTY-EIGHT   OCTOBER 1979

PATRICK WILLIAM CROAKE'S BOOKPLATE
by   Viola L. Carlson

Patrick William Croake's bookplate is rich with detail, and given the clues
it contains, one can, with a bit of research, reconstruct the life of an
active, thinking man who made a real contribution to the quality of life
and history of Los Angeles.

The most important item in the bookplate would seem to be the copy of THE
TIDINGS, the Los Angeles Archdiocesan newspaper. A visit to THE TID-
INGS' office and the willing help of its staff quickly explained why;
Croake was the founder and first editor of the paper. The first issue was
published on June 29, 1895, and served more than half of California's Cath-
olics including the Dioceses of Monterey-Fresno, Los Angeles, and San Diego.
The first years were difficult, but Croake, a fiesty son of Ireland, was
never one to give up easily. At one time he held every job from printer's
devil to editor and publisher. When he was sure the paper was on a sound
financial footing, he turned it over to other capable hands and went into
the real estate business, but maintained a lively interest in the paper until his death, visiting THE TIDINGS' office frequently to find out how "his"
paper was doing.

Croake was born in Utica, New York in 1864 of, as he always added, Tipper-
ary parents. The family moved to Chicago where Croake graduated with hon-
or from St. Patrick's Academy. Due to ill health he came west in 1889, and
having decided on a career of writing, wrote descriptive booklets of the
states of Washington and Oregon. In 1891 he went to San Diego and engaged
in the newspaper business for four years. With that experience, he came
north to Los Angeles to start THE TIDINGS in 1895. By this time he had a
wife and three children; a fourth would soon follow.

Pride in his Irish ancestry is indicated in the Croke coat of arms in his
bookplate. When the "a" was added to the name is not known, but it is a
variant of Croc, Crok, or Croke. The Crokes are an Anglo-Irish family who
have been in Ireland since the thirteenth century. Their motto is "Buallin
se" which means "The Stroke of Peace."

There have been some illustrious members in the family. In the last century
archbishop Thomas William Croke of Cashel played an important part in the
religious, social, and political life of Ireland. Mainly through his influence, the Gaelic Athletic Association became a great force in rural life,

and the Croke park in Dublin, as well as in New York, was named for him.
Of commanding presence, he wielded an immense influence among the Irish
people.

Real estate in a booming town proved a good outlet for Croake's talents,
and by 1927 he had accumulated a fortune of $300,000. With the help of
the Irish community in Los Angeles, the only living descendant of Croake
was located - James J. Kerr, a grandson. With his enthusiastic help it
has been possible to piece together some of the activities of the later
years of his grandfather's life.

Croake was a prolific writer, using his pen and his money to champion
causes that ranged from monetary reform to the restoration of the Missions.
In 1927 he was the west coast chairman of the committee to elect Al Smith
president. He had a love and appreciation for the beauty of the columns of
trees that lined the streets and boulevards of Los Angeles. When it was
proposed that Sunset Boulevard should be widened and the pepper trees that
lined it be cut down, Croake took on City Hall with no less an ally than
Mary Pickford. A stay was granted, but eventually the street was widened
and the lovely old trees cut down. In his editorializing in the newspapers
of the day he quoted a number of poets , but none more fittingly than Joyce
Kilmer when he was trying to save the old trees of Los Angeles from the de-
velopers. Which brings us to the books on his desk; certainly they indicate
a love of poetry. Not only the famous
MISSION PLAY, but also the poems of his
great and good friend, John Steven Mc
Groarty, delighted him. Croake frequently sent letters to McGroarty requesting him to send a copy of his book,
JUST CALIFORNIA AND OTHER POEMS, to a
list of his friends whose names and
addresses he enclosed. He must at some
time have given McGroarty some of his
bookplates, for he would ask him to
place one in each of the books and indicate how he was to autograph it.

Chesterton and Belloc were high-spirited,
combative, opinionated men, whose style
and personalities undoubtedly struck a
responsive chord with Croake. F. H.
Spearman was a prolific writer of railroad stories. One of his bestselling
novels, WHISPERING SMITH, written in
1906, was filmed twice. A Catholic lay-
man like Croake, his autographed books
are to be found in Croake's library.

Kerr found among his grandfather's papers a bookplate identical to the one
here shown, but with the year 1927 printed under "Los Angeles." That was
the year the present City Hall, pictured in the window with the rising sun
behind it, was built. I think it is safe to assume that was the year Croake
commissioned his bookplate. At a later date when he needed more, he probably had the year deleted so as not to date the plate.

REYNOLDS STONE DEAD AT 70

(Following is an excerpt from obituary in
ANTIQUARIAN BOOKMAN, September 10, 1979.)

Reynolds Stone, 70, in England, one of the
leading engravers of this century. Much of
his work was for book illustration and he
also cut memorials in Westminster Abbey to
Winston Churchill and T. S. Eliot, and to
Stanley Morison and Lord Britten at other
sites. He designed the Peace stamp issued
in Britain in 1946 and various banknotes of
the Bank of England.

Born in 1909, Stone was educated at Eaton
and at Magdalene College, Cambridge. He
did an apprenticeship in printing at the
University Press in Cambridge and worked for two years at the printing house
of Barnicott & Pearce of Taunton, before settling down to a lifetime career
as a free-lance designer and engraver. He was the editor of two books on
the wood engravings of Thomas Bewick and Gwen Reverat and has contributed
articles on printing and engraving to various periodicals.

Reynolds Stone died June 24, 1979.

THE GOLDEN AGE OF
AMERICAN BOOKPLATE DESIGN

William Fowler Hopson

William Fowler Hopson,
who ranks with French,
Smith, Spenceley and
Macdonald as one of the
"big five" in American
bookplate design, was born
in Watertown, Connecticut,
and spent his boyhood in
the neighboring city of
Waterbury. In 1867 the
young Hopson was placed
by his father as an ap-
prentice in engraving with
Henry Curtis of Hartford.
When work failed in Hart-
ford, Hopson went to New

35

Another miniature book has been published in
the ever expanding field of bookplates—titled
THE GOLDEN AGE OF AMERICAN BOOKPLATE DESIGN;
it is by Francis W. Allen, who until his death
was a noted authority on ex libris and author
of two books on the subject: one on Charles R.
Capon, and the other, William Fowler Hopson.

THE GOLDEN AGE was originally given as a talk
by Allen at the International Ex Libris Congress in Lisbon (1976); then it appeared as
an article in A ARTE DO EX-LIBRIS, the journal
of the Portuguese society under the editorship
of A. M. da Moto Miranda. Now it appears as a
miniature hard-cover book, published by Robert
F. Hanson, editor of the MICROBIBLIOPHILE, at his Opuscula Press in an
edition of 300 numbered copies. The artists of this "golden age" are Sidney L. Smith, Edwin Davis French, Joseph W. Spenceley, William Fowler
Hopson, and Arthur N. Macdonald. There are nearly 50 pages of text and
five tipped-in facsimile bookplates reduced in size to fit the small pages
(sample page actual size illustrated above).

THE GOLDEN AGE OF AMERICAN BOOKPLATE DESIGN may be ordered at $18.50 or
outside USA $20 from Opuscula Press, 1627 Bob O'Link Drive, Venice, FL
33595. Make check payable to Robert F. Hanson.

GIFTS TO PRINCETON 1975-1976 - This is the 13th edition of this record of all donors who made gifts of $1,000 or more to the University during the academic year (1975-76). Rawleigh Warner, Jr., Chairman of the Council for University Resources, wrote in his introduction: "The illustrations for this edition of GIFTS TO PRINCETON suggest the importance of our university years. They are personal bookplates from alumni representing Classes back to 1860, and often revealing much about the owners' interests and backgrounds. As you will see, many of them also relate directly or indicretly to years on this campus." While the emphasis is upon the years at Princeton and subsequent achievements, the magnifying glass reveals the familiar names and initials of a few well-known bookplate artists.

JAPANESE COLLECTORS INTERESTED IN EXCHANGING   Recently Hiroo Yamaguchi wrote on
behalf of members of the Nippon Ex-Libris Association (c/o Bunka Publishing Bureau, 1-22-3 Yoyogi Shibuya-ku, Tokyo, Japan) indicating that the members listed below would welcome the opportunity to exchange ex libris with members of our Society. It is hoped that many of our members will accept this invitation and send bookplate prints for exchange; this is an excellent chance not only to establish an exchange but to develop a new overseas friendship.

  Sanzo Asanuma, 83-2262 Tomioka-cho, Kanazawa-ku, Yokohama, 236 Japan
  Peter F. Hosokawa, Ichinomiya Kyoshokuin Jutaku, 2-22, 508 Ichinomiya-cho,
    Takamatsu, 761 Japan
  Kiyomi Igi, 606-19-24-5chome, Nakano, Kakano-ku, Tokyo, 164 Japan
  Shigemaru Kishi, 3-2-3chome Higashi Hamaguchi, Suminoe-ku, Osaka, 559 Japan
  Masayuki Moronaka, 12-12 Matoba-cho, Hakodate, 040 Japan
  Hiroyuki Ogoh, 8-237 Fukudomari, Okayama, 703 Japan
  Yonejiro Sato, 9-3 Horogake, Aomori, 030 Japan
  Yoshihito Sato, 60-71 Higashiyama-cho, Hakodate, 042 Japan
  Motoi Yanagida, 60 Honen-in Nishimachi, Shishigatani, Sakyo-ku, Kyoto,
    606 Japan

The Fool and His Bookplate   Quote from Thomas Bailey Aldrich's PONKAPOG
                                  PAPERS: Every one has a bookplate these
days, and the collectors are after it. The fool and his bookplate are soon parted. To distribute one's ex libris is inanely to destroy the only significance it has, that of indicating the past or present ownership of the volume in which it is placed."

MORE BOOKPLATE LITERATURE . . . .

WESTCHESTER COUNTY TIMES, Elisha Bird, Bookplate Artist, Hailed Abroad As One of World's Best, Goodrich Bennett, July 31, 1936. Artist speaks of his work, how he happened to design plate for Jessica Dragonette, whom he enjoyed hearing sing over the radio.

LOS ANGELES TIMES (no date), Bookplate Fad Holds Interest, Neeta Marquis. Collection of Mrs. Katherine Burnham discussed and approaching exhibit and competition sponsored by the Bookplate Association International at the Museum of History, Science, and Art in Los Angeles (late 1920's, early 30's).

THE BOOKPLATE SOCIETY NEWSLETTER, 3:#25, March 1979.
Our New Device. A new masthead has been devised by Leo Wyatt, "who, with
consummate skill, has cut the woodblock . . . and has most generously presented this to the Society. . . . The small design by Diana Bloomfield, employed for the twelve numbers of Volume II, will continue to be used on the
Society's letterhead." - Meetings. David Kindersley spoke on February 13,
1979 to the combined membership of the Bookplate Society and the Private
Libraries Association; reference is made to the article appearing in ASBC&D
1978 YEAR BOOK by and about David Kindersley. Announcement is made of the
Open Weekend to be held June 23-24 which will combine Launching Brian North
Lee's BRITISH BOOKPLATES and the opening of the Bookplate exhibit at the
Victoria & Albert Museum. - Autumn Meetings. A visit by car to Hove Public Library to view collection of Frances Garnet, Viscountess Wooseley (1872-
1936), who started collecting bookplates at age 12; a second autumn meeting
is scheduled for December 4 at the National Book League. - Bookplates at
Bath. An exhibit from May 18 and continuing throughout the summer was organ-
ized by Philip Beddingham and drawn chiefly from his own collection; exhibit
at the Museum of Bookbinding adjoining George Bayntun's bindery and bookshop.
 - Junior Bookplate Society Newsletter. Emma-Rose Barber and Elizabeth Fortheringham issue their own ex libris newsletter on an irregular basis. (Editor's
Note: It was my pleasure to meet these two young collectors while visiting the
V&A exhibit on June 25, 1979.) - Bookplates of Miss C. Helard by Dr. Colin
R. Lattimore. A very interesting article about publicity-shy artist, who was
born Mary Ellen Blanche Crookes and became the wife of A. C. Fox-Davies, the
heraldic expert of the Edwardian era; she "produced many of the illustrations
for her husband's books, yet not once is she mentioned or acknowledged." A
checklist of her ex libris through 1900 is in this issue and to be continued
in a future number.

THE BOOKPLATE SOCIETY NEWSLETTER, 3:#26, June 1979.
BRITISH BOOKPLATES - A PICTORIAL HISTORY. The title of Brian North Lee's new
book. (See review elsewhere in this issue of BOOKPLATES IN THE NEWS.) - Other
Publications. V&A catalog is reproduced as part of the June Newsletter or may
be obtained as a separate. MANUAL DE EXLIBRISTICA by Fausto Moreira Rato,
published in Portugal, is available through the Bookplate Society. - Offers.
Some few volumes are still available from the bookplate library of the Society's
late president Horace Jones. David Potter will exchange his Reynolds Stone ex
libris for other plates by Stone. A catalogue of 30 bookplate designs, including a series of Zodiac bookplates, may be obtained by writing Barry Bruff,
Derwent Designs, 12 Highfield House, Arundel Gardens, London N21, England. -
Member's Bookplate. Recent Leo Wyatt plate for Dr. Colin R. Lattimore.

EXLIBRIS WERELD, #2, 1979. The lead article about artist Hubert Levigne is
by Jan Rhebergen; it includes a checklist of his ex libris from 1930 to 1952.
- Current issues of various ex libris society journals are mentioned. - Brief
note about Erich Schoner (1901-1979).

NORDISK EXLIBRIS TIDSSKRIFT, #134, 1979. Article with tipped-in color ex
libris on Bernhard Kuhlmann, Dutch-German painter and graphic artist - Polish
artist Jan Hasso-Agopsowicx has made more than 180 bookplates. - Belgian collector Josef De Belder shows some of his personal bookplates; his collection
numbers 12,000. - Current bookplate periodicals reviewed.

SUR QUELQUES EX LIBRIS MEDICO-PHARMACEUTIQUES by Professor Guy DeVaux, a reprint from REVUE d'HISTORIE de la PHARMACIE, XXV,#237, June 1978. Article in

French about the ex libris of pharmacists.

EXHIBITION OF POLISH BOOKS AND BOOK-PLATES published by the Polish Cultural Association of New South Wales for an exhibit held at the Fisher Library of Sydney University, the Maitland Municipal Library, and the Bankstown Municipal Library, from February through April of 1979. An interesting combination of Polish books and bookplates created by Polish artists. Five pages of text which include a brief bibliography.

L'EX LIBRIS FRANCAIS, #130, December 1978. G. Meyer-Noirel shows how a family geneaology can be traced through bookplates. - Michel Jamar gives his reflections on the Lugano Congress. - Marie-Claire Mangin presents some ancient ex libris. - Comments are given on several exhibitions.

EXLIBRIS-REVUE, 5:#1, 1979. New Year Graphics. Europeans tend to have New Year cards more often than a Christmas card, and bookplate collectors find these graphics very compatible with their interest in ex libris art as many of the same artists are active in both fields. Klaus Rodel reviews some of 500 greetings he received. - Ex Libris literature from many countries is briefly reviewed. - Bookplate News from England by Anthony K. Pincott. "To the British collector continental bookplates are an area which he hesitates to investigate in view of the vast numbers available. He believes that quality is more important than quantity, and that too often ex-libris are apparently commissioned for the purpose of exchange rather than being justified by use in a library." The names and addresses of eleven artists, including two women, who take bookplate commissions are given. - Editorial. At the August 1978 International Congress in Lugano, it was decided to make EXLIBRIS-REVUE the "official" publication of the FISAE. However, participation by the individual societies has been greatly below expectations. If the various societies do not contribute more news and articles, then the publication will concentrate on "yesterday's art, present the latest bookplates, and introduce tomorrow's artists." - Antoni Brosz In Memoriam. - Throughout there are illustrations and tipped-in prints.

A ARTE DO EX-LIBRIS, 11:#82, 1978. The entire issue is devoted to the ex libris of Telmo de Branganca, whose activities range from tourism and the hotel trade to archeology, ballet, stamps. The collector writes about his his collection, his fascination with ballet; he writes about the life and work of William Hogarth and the ex libris he made from a Hogarth 1749 engraving. There are numerous tipped-in prints.

A ARTE DO EX-LIBRIS, 11:#83, 1978. The major portion of the issue is devoted to Pepita Palle, who writes about her many personal ex libris with the theme of angels;she mentions her good American friend, the late Mary Alice Ercolini. - Professon Corneliu Dima-Dragan authors an article about Roumanian artist-architect Dragos Morarescu.

A ARTE DO EX-LIBRIS, 11:#84, 1978. Sergio de Oliveira writes about the second National Meeting of Bookplate Lovers at Caldas da Rainha, Portugal, October 7-8, 1978. - Gausto Moreira Rato is preparing a catalog of artists, who have created bookplates for Portuguese book collectors. - Polish collector Dr. Wiktor Dziulikowski presents an article about Polish artist Zofia Kubacka. - The worklists of three artists are presented: Johann Naha, Aulo-Gelio, and Zbigniew Jozwik.

McKibbin Bookplate, Boston Athenaeum

The artist for this bookplate is Melody Johnson Morey, a 1969 graduate of Massachusetts College of Art, who teaches pottery, sculpture, and jewelry at Tantasqua Regional High School in Sturbridge, Connecticut.

She has exhibited her work with Summerthing in Boston, The Holden Experiment (an artists' group), and at the Worcester Art Museum Sales and Rental Gallery.

A native of Waltham, Massacusetts, she has lived in North Brookfield for eight years.

Darrell Hyder is the printer of this ex libris; he returned to the craft after a start in the museum world. A native of California, he took his undergraduate degree in American History at Stanford University and his masters in the Winterthur Museum-University of Delaware Early American Cultural History Program (1961).

David
Milton Kendall
McKibbin

1906-1978

From a Fund
Given by his Friends

The Boston Athenaeum

He worked at the Stinehour Press, Lunenburg, Vermont, after a short stint in museum work at the State Museum in Albany, New York. During four years in Switzerland, he worked as compositor, proofreader in English and German, and attended a graphics art design and management course at the Zurich School of Applied Arts under the eminent Swiss book designer, Max Caflisch.

Returning to the United States in 1969 with his Swiss wife, Elizabeth, Hyder worked in Barre, Massachusetts, as production manager of Barre Publishers/Imprint Society. Since 1971 he has been in North Brookfield, running a small letterpress shop, doing work for museums, libraries, collectors, and individuals who desire careful typography.

K. SAKAMOTO AUTHOR OF MINIATURE BOOK ON JAPANESE EX LIBRIS

Mr. Sakamoto, chairman of the Japanese Ex-Libros Association, is author of a 76-page miniature, soft-cover book on Japanese bookplates. The text is in Japanese, and there are 15 black and white illustrations of plates. The copy I have contains Mr. Sakamoto's miniature ex libris. He would welcome the opportunity to exchange plates with members of the ASBC&D, and you may write him at 4-14-41 Himonya, Meguroku, Tokyo, Japan.

WANTED TO COMPLETE RUN FOR BINDING

Pages 10-11, 12-13, and 106-7 needed to complete run for binding. If you are willing to part with your originals of these pages, please contact the Editor of BOOKPLATES IN THE NEWS. Xerox replacements will be provided. All offers considered - reasonable price will be paid.

ALBRECHT DURER
1471 - 21 May - 1971
by Klaus Rodel
Translated by
Rolf Erickson
(NORDISK EXLIBRIS TIDSSKRIFT,
Nr. 3, 1971, pp. 113-7. Published on the 500th anniversary of Durer's birth.)

BOOK-PLATE OF HECTOR POMER, provost
of St. Laurence, Nuremberg. Woodcut.
Motto: "To the pure all things are pure", in three
languages.

This article has two purposes: to mark this
great artist's 500th anniversary and to draw
some parallels from his time to our own.
Surely it is not necessary to comment further on Albrecht Durer's importance for the
development of art in Germany, or even in
Europe, but in spite of the large number of
books which have appeared - in this year a-
lone nearly 20 different books have been
published in Germany, Austria, and Switzerland - only a little has been written about
his ex libris, the subject most interesting
to us.

In 1928 an offprint from which one became
better acquainted with Albrecht Durer's ex
libris and coats of arms appeared in Germany in connection with the 400th
anniversary of his death in 1528. On this occasion Walter von Zur Westen,
the well-known German collector, writer, and editor of German ex libris yearbooks, noted that it is difficult to positively ascertain which ex libris Durer
in truth himself produced and which he only had some part in producing as, for
example, drawing on the woodblock and letting another do the cutting. Added to
that, some of Durer's coats of arms were also put to use as book owner's marks
and the lines are therefore hard to draw. With existing information it follows
that the artist has created the following ex libris:

An ex libris for Durer's friend Willibald Pirckheimer the well-known German
humanist, counsel to the emperor, and Nurnberg citizen. This dates from before 1504 and is Durer's first ex libris, a wood-cut, for which he completed
the drawing. This book's ownership mark is found in two examples, one of
which bears the inscription in three languages (showing Pirckheimer's erudition):
"The fear of the Lord is the beginning of wisdom." This ex libris distinguishes itself by bearing the text "Sibi et amicis p(ositus)" or to say "for

- - - - - - - - - - - - - - - - -

(PATRICK WILLIAM CROAKE continued) With the depression of 1929 and the years
following, Croake lost his fortune. When he was 82 years old, true to his newspaper training, he wrote his own obituary and ended it with these words: "When
I am eight-five years old I shall be content with a briar pipe, a glass of good
port wine, and once in a while a few sterling loyal friends I can still call my
own." He was to live twelve years more, working in his real estate office in
his home until he died in 1958 at the age of 94.

Champion of the rights of the underprivileged, a valiant fighter who sought
to preserve the beauty of the city he loved, Croake will probably best be
remembered for being the founder and first editor of THE TIDINGS.

yourself and your friends."

After Durer's death another ex libris was created for the same owner, a copper engraving by the master J.B. from 1529 from a sketch by Durer. In addition there are some pen and ink drawings by Durer as sketches for Pirckheimer, One shows a woman's shape and a savage under an arch. And under that Pirckheimer's coat of arms which dates from between 1503 and 1505. The other, a drawing from about 1510 to 1520, shows the personification of a genius (or guardian spirit) and wings. A third sheet attributed to Durer shows three female figures in a circle. It is likely a sketch for a Pirckheimer ex libris. This dates from after 1521.

For another well-known citizen of Nurnberg, the builder and councillor Michael Beheim, Durer has made an ex libris (also employed as a coat of arms) in a wood-cut in about 1509. There is no question this is Durer's work since he has written on the back of the wood block. According to W. von Zur Westen, this ex libris did not entirely agree with Beheim's taste, and there was correspondence about it in which Durer refuted the criticism as the confident and proud artist he was.

Then there is the ex libris for Hieronimus Ebner von Eschenbach, also a prominent citizen in Nurnberg, first and foremost remembered as one who supported the Reformation in Germany. This ex libris is a wood-cut from 1516, the oldest dated German ex libris without monogram. It shows the coats of arms for the families Ebner and Furer above the inscription "Deus refugium meum." A coat of arms which with great likelihood has served as an ex libris is a wood-cut from about 1520 for Jacob von Bannissis, who was secretary at the court of Emperor Maximilian I. Another coat of arms, also used as an ex libris, is a wood-cut from around 1521 for Johannes Stabius, who was the imperial court astronomer, historian, mathematician, distinguished author, and Durer's friend.

Furthermore, there is an ex libris for Johann Tscherette, mathematician and architect to Emperor Maximilian I, also a friend of Durer's and Pirckheimer's, who in 1510 settled in Nurnberg. It is a wood-cut from about 1521 which was called "coat of arms with the wild hunter." This is a so-called "expressive ex libris" since the word Tschert means the same as devil. W. von Zur Westen characterizes the piece as follows: "The German forest devil has, under the influence of humanism and the art of the renaissance, taken on the form of a Greek Pan. The piece dates from Durer's last years and is maybe his most beautiful work within our field."

There is a pen and ink ex libris for Melchior Pfinzing, which shows a wheel of fortune with four men above which stands the goddess of fortune with scepter and crown. The drawing dates from about 1515. Finally there is an ex libris drawn by Durer, cut about 1525, most likely by Resch, for Hektor Pomer, who was dean at Nurnberg's St. Laurentius church. It shows Saint Laurentius with martyr's palms and carries the Biblical quotation, "To the pure all things are pure" (Titus 1:15).

This information must naturally be taken with reservation. There are other ex libris attributed to Durer; on the whole some doubt and undertainty prevails. Even established Durer connoisseurs do not agree on what really comes from Durer's hand. We are not talking about a scientific dissertation but merely an attempt to honor this famous artist, especially considering that Nurnberg is our common birthplace. This is also the reason that there are plans for a

Durer publication using contemporary ex libris by known artists. Some pieces in this article mark the development of the graphic art in the course of 500 years.

The Hungarian ex libris congress was in many ways rather well appointed: the ex libris competition was arranged with not less than four different themes. While three areas (Budapest, the congress, and Bartok) were international, the fourth competition was limited to Hungarian artists and the topic was "In Memoriam Albrecht Durer." Interesting work was shown and perhaps the most exciting and interesting thing was that a very young and very modern artist Dora Maurer won first prize in this competition. Naturally this created considerable sensation and some resentment among the older collectors, who have not always had sympathy for modern developments which happen and necessarily must happen - within ex libris art also. We are living in 1971 and should not think that we ought to work as though it were 50 or 100 years ago. From this spring vibrations which characterize the ex libris cause in many countries.

Unfortunately it is not technically possible to show any of Dora Maurer's ex libris, but four ex libris from widely different artists from different countries are shown here. Two of the works are by the Polish graphic artist Zbigniew Dolatowski. Both are two color linoleum cuts, and they bear the mark of the master Dolatowski. They are simple in composition, especially the one in black and gold for this article's author. The other, for book printer Vagn Clemmensen, combines a Durer memorial ex libris with a useable ex libris which is very expensive and shows the owner's profession (the illustration is of a man at a printing press) in a most beautiful way.

The well-known German artist Richard Preusse of Leipzig has, at an age of almost 83 years, made two wonderful Durer ex libris. The one made for the famous German collector Dr. Axel Leier is shown here. Unfortunately an electrotype can in no way depict the warmth and life which characterize Preusse's beautiful etchings with their prominent calligraphy. It is an unusually beautiful result at an age when most have difficulty to commit themselves to the most common, everyday happenings.

Then there is an ex libris of a completely different character, the stylized and very simple "pure" book owner's marks of the Russian Anatoli Kalaschnikow, whose works today are known worldwide and esteemed by collectors in all countries. This artist who has in only a few years made a name for himself - almost like an ascending rocket - shows here that even if the development of the art of the ex libris has been very fast, the wood is still the same living material now as well as 500 years ago to produce the most beautiful works. This ex libris, which in its simplicity and yet expressive elaboration belongs to the best Kalaschnikow has made, is found in two variations with only a few deviations. It shows how much the artist works and how little is required to yield a greatly different result.

Let us close this homage to Albrecht Durer with the thought that we today have the same joy in beautiful things only with the difference that social developments have made it possible for even "ordinary" people to possess art if they only have the interest. Conversely, in Durer's time one had to belong to the highest circles in order to find pleasure in what a master artist created. This is work emphasizing more than whether something costs 100 or 1,000 kroner and whether it has this or that artistic value. We alone, therefore, have both reason and at the same time an obligation to art, and as far as we are concerned, specifically to the art of small graphics.

BRITISH BOOKPLATES: A PICTORIAL HISTORY
by Brian North Lee. (David & Charles, Ltd.,
Newton Abbot, Devon, England; £ 12.50. David &
Charles, Inc., North Pomfret, VT 05053, USA $35.
1979. 160 pages.) REVIEWER: George S. Swarth.

From the Library of

JMB

Sir James M. Barrie

It is more than eighty-five years since the second edition of Egerton Castle's
ENGLISH BOOK-PLATES was published, and in that interval much has been written
about bookplates, as George W. Fuller's BIBLIOGRAPHY OF BOOKPLATE LITERATURE
(1926) and Audrey Spencer Arellanes' monumental BOOKPLATES: A SELECTED ANNOTA-
TED BIBLIOGRAPHY OF THE PERIODICAL LITERATURE (1971) amply testify. Until now,
however, there has not been an adequate re-examination and up-dating of the
general subject of British bookplates. That lack now has been magnificently
met by Brian North Lee, for the past six years Editor and Secretary of the
Bookplate Society, whose previous contributions to ex libris literature include
THE BOOKPLATE DESIGNS OF REX WHISTLER (1973), EARLY PRINTED BOOK LABELS (1976),
and articles in periodicals such as THE PRIVATE LIBRARY, THE BOOKPLATE SOCIETY
NEWSLETTER, MISCELLANY, and the ANTIQUARIAN BOOK MONTHLY REVIEW.

BRITISH BOOKPLATES is physically impressive. The volume measures 9 1/4 x 13"
over all, is printed on heavy paper, and has a sturdy cloth binding suitable
to a book of its size and weight. It is printed in double columns in a clear
and unobtrusive type -- 10 point Caslon old Style or the like - well leaded.
The illustrations are handsomely printed, some by photogravure, but most by very
fine-screen halftone, and reproduce with rare fidelity the quality of the various techniques illustrated, whether wood block, etching, or even very fine engraving.

The book is as impressive in content as in appearance. Departing from the
usual plan, followed by Castle and others, of using illustrations to accompany
the test, here the text is used chiefly as accompaniment to the illustrations.
After a one-page introduction, an eleven-page summary of the history of British
bookplates, and a page of advice on bookplate collecting (each page equivalent
to about four in an ordinary book), the main body of the work consists of reproductions of 207 bookplates in Part I and 54 book labels in Part II, with accompanying text. The illustrations, sequentially numbered, appear on the right-
hand pages, generally four or more to a page; but the large format permits all
plates, even some large enough to occupy an entire page, to be reproduced at full
size. The facing pages contain a correspondingly numbered paragraph about each
plate, giving extensive information about the plate, the owner, and the artist,
engraver, or printer. The plates are arranged in roughly chronological order,
and the accompanying paragraphs include very full disucssion of the stylistic
developments illustrated, of other works by the same artists, of other artists
who did related work, and of other plates made for the same owners or members
of their families. Thus the text taken as a whole does indeed provide a most
detailed history of British bookplates, beginning with Sir Nicholas Bacon's
presentation plate of 1574 and continuing to the present day. The text concludes
with a selective bibliography, Part I of which lists a dozen standard works on
the general subject of bookplates (including Audrey Spencer Arellanes' bibliography mentioned above), while Part I lists sixteen more specialized works, with
brief descriptions of their scope. The discrimination exercised in compiling the
bibliography is exemplified by the deliberate omission of two often-cited books,
J. H. Slater's BOOKPLATES AND THEIR VALUE (1898) and E. Almack's BOOKPLATES (1904)
on the stated ground of their inaccuracy.

There is an admirable index, which makes accessible much of the collateral information included in the paragraphs about particular plates. The plan of the index is that italicized numbers refer to pages of the introductory text, Roman numbers refer to numbered paragraphs accompanying illustrations, and bold-face numbers refer to illustrated bookplates of the persons named. (However, in eleven instances numbers that should be bold-face are either Roman or italic.)

The plates reproduced have been chosen with care. Some, like the Nicholas Bacon plate, are of historical importance in themselves; some exemplify the work of notable artists like Sir John Everett Millais, illustrators like Arthur Rackham, or engravers like Charles William Sherborn; some are of interest because they belonged to famous people such as Rudyard Kipling or William Ewart Gladstone; while the rest have been chosen as best typifying various stylistic developments. Of the 261 illustrations, only 22 duplicate any of the 194 plates reproduced by Castle, and even in those 22 a few differences appear. Castle reproduced a few in reduced size (without always noting that fact), he omitted Charles Dickens' name which Lee correctly shows under the crest, and he gave a smaller (or reduced) version of the Gleeson White plate, without the reversed letters in "Igdrasil" as shown by Lee. In the plate of H. G. Seaman, Castle showed, as Lee does not, a small coat of arms below the frame.

While Mr. Lee has thus duplicated few of Castle's illustrations, he has by no means produced a mere chronological supplement to Castle's work. Indeed, only about a third of the plates illustrated are subsequent to 1893 when the second edition of ENGLISH BOOK-PLATES appeared. However, no one need fear that BRITISH BOOKPLATES is merely a rehash of ENGLISH BOOK-PLATES. Mr. Lee has his own viewpoint, and the benefit of an almost incredible familiarity with the extensive research and literature that have illuminated the history of bookplates since Castle wrote. Moreover, Mr. Lee gives us, as Castle did not, extensive information about the owners of the plates illustrated and their families, all of which is interesting and which helps in understanding the place of bookplates in British social history. Supplementing these accounts there are extensive references to books or articles where further information can be found about the artists, the owners of the plates, the plates themselves, or the stylistic developments that they exemplify. The number of such works cited, many of them obscure local histories or notes or articles in esoteric periodicals, easily runs into the hundreds. In many instances we are told of collections that contain examples of the illustrated plates. In short, Mr. Lee gives for each plate the sort of information that every collector must wish he had the ability to assemble for the plates in his own collection.

As an example of the fascinating sidelights that Mr. Lee gives regarding particular plates, mention may be made of his comment on Edward Fitzgerald's plate, which was drawn by William Makepeace Thackeray. He tells us that the angel on that plate portrays the wife of William Henry Brookfield, who was depicted as Frank Whitestock in Thackeray's CURATE'S WALK.

Part II of the book, dealing with book labels, includes useful discussion of the tenuous line between decorated labels and true bookplates, a line that Lee draws according to the relative preponderance of text or decoration. See, for example, his discussion of the David Garrick label (No. 226). The 54 examples illustrated date from 1535 to 1974, and range from perfectly plain typography to borderline examples of ornate decoration. Some beautiful calligraphic woodengravings by Leo Wyatt and others are included.

BRITISH BOOKPLATES can be appreciated at many levels. As a "coffee table book" it will be a handsome ornament in any establishment. Any browser will find in it hours of fascinating reading about British artists and patrons of ex libris art. As a monumental reference work, this is a book that no serious collector of bookplates can afford to be without. Its publication will long stand as a landmark in the history of ex libris. (SPECIAL OFFER: The Bookplate Society will send BRITISH BOOKPLATES, post free, to non-members for $30. Make check payable to: Bookplate Society, c/o Anthony Pincott, 3B Hurlingham Court, Ranelagh Gardens, London SW6 3UN, England.)

'Ex libris' 'Verna'

This handprinted image is number _100_ of a limited edition of 200 impressions printed on handmade Japanese mulberry rice paper. This Ex libris was commissioned by Mrs. Verna M. S. Neuscheler.

EX LIBRIS VERNA

The bookplate illustrated to the left is one recently commissioned by Mrs. Verna Neuscheler, ASBC&D member who lives in Rochester, NY.

Mrs. Neuscheler met the artist, Michael Goscinsky, at an art show. She liked his work which was on exhibit. Though he had never designed a bookplate previously, Michael agreed and here is the attractive result, a limited edition woodcut.

Now that Michael Goscinsky has created one bookplate, he may be interested in further commissions. You may write him directly at – 69 Captain Shankey Drive, Garnerville, NY 10923.

TOM MIX'S BOOKPLATE –
AN AMERICAN ERA REVISTED
by David Kuhner

(The following excerpt is from an article as titled above which appeared in THE BRANDING IRON, #136, September 1979, publication of the Los Angeles Corral of Westerners.)

The bookplate is in the shape of an animal hide and the words on it read "The Good Book says, God helps those that help themselves, but I say God help the man that strays off the ranch with this book." And there's the signature of Tom Mix and his T.M. Bar brand.

What a place to find an echo of the cowboy-turned-movie star, this shelf in the Sprague Library at The Claremont Colleges, lined with books on the history of World War I aviation. Some friends from his circus tours of Europe probably presented this memento volume of British battleplanes. . . . He was a genuine cowboy and a sheriff before he ever saw a movie camera, . . . Born in Driftwood, Pennsylvania in 1880, he died at the wheel of his Cord roadster near Florence, Arizona on October 12, 1940. At the height of his career Tom Mix was known as "King of the Cowboys" and his horse Tony was called "the Wonder Horse."

"Published for Book Lovers:"
A Short History of American
Book Collecting Magazines
by   Lawrence Parke Murphy
BOOK COLLECTOR'S MARKET 4:
#5: 1, 4-10, Sep./Oct. 1979.

Several of the magazines survey-
ed are noted as having material
about bookplates (THE BOOK LOVER,
THE LITERARY COLLECTOR), and the
publications of H. Alfred Fowler
are given good coverage, beginning
in 1912 with THE EX LIBRAN, THE

BIBLIO, THE MISCELLANY, and BOOKPLATE BOOKLET. In writing about the BOOK-
PLATE BOOKLET, Murphy says, "which we will not go into here because the
many periodicals for the book plate collector constitute a subject in itself." Perhaps he will deal with them in a future article?

JUNIOR BOOKPLATE SOCIETY, Newsletter, vol. 1, No. 3, March 1979. Editors
are Emma-Rose Barber and Elisabeth Fotheringham. Tipped-in are ex libris
designed by each editor, one on scraper-board and the other a lino-cut. -
An Interesting Etched Bookplate by Brian North Lee. Tipped-in is "Xerox"
copy of plate for Frank Payne by Sir Charles Holroyd (1861-1917); it is the
only recorded bookplate design by Holroyd, who is credited with 300 etchings. - Briefly noted are plates for the Maynard School, Exeter, and a
stock plate which admonishes the
borrower. - Vol. 1, No. 4,
September 1979. The Youngest
Junior Member: Katy Russell of
Dale Hall, Liverpool, is 8 years
old. - John Wilson furnished a
number of original prints of
John Aspinall's Chippendale ex
libris for tipping-in. - Professor William Butler furnished
prints of his plate, details
about which appeared in the
Bookplate Society NEWSLETTER #23
for September 1978. - Tipped-in
is the ex libris of artist
Leslie Benenson, which features
a dragon. - Smallest Bookplate
In the World: Taken from MAKING
A BOOKPLATE by Mark Severin are
"small" bookplate by V. le Campion
and "smallest" by I. Zetti; both
are wood engravings.

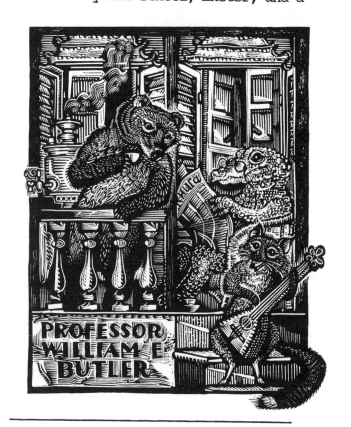

READY SOON

1979 YEAR BOOK

MARK SEVERIN - PAUL LANDACRE - ENGELIEN REITSMA-VALENÇA

Articles and checklists -   Numerous Illustrations

OPEN WEEKEND
KEYNOTE SPEAKERS
June 23, 1979 London

As promised in the report of the Open Week-end (BITN July 1979), the main talks are printed here. In reverse order of presentation, Mark Severin's appears first.

Ladies and Gentlemen, dear Friends, at last the great day has come, not only for me, but for the continental friends who are with us here, and indeed even for those who, for some reason or other, were unable to make it. For years, we have always hoped to have British collectors and artists at our ex libris congresses. As they never came, we were delighted to have this chance of coming to them.

In fact, there have always been collectors and artists hidden away in the British Isles, but they kept a little bit to themselves, they feared that any treasures trusted to the Post might never be seen again; and lastly, in recent years, they feared they would, only too often, in exchange for their choice plates, receive a batch of insignificant and badly printed lino cuts or line blocks. It is true that some continental collectors still send, as printed matter, a bunch of rubbish together with the printed notice "avec prière de'échange" expecting to receive fine proofs of wood or copper engravings. Needless to say, these individuals do much more harm than good.

One conclusive proof, among others, of the steady interest maintained on bookplates is the good price reached every time they appear in the auction room. I feel very happy today. You know that, even if I am "Belgian to the core," as an English lady once put it thirty years ago, I am nevertheless English, and very much so, in my feelings and taste. Whenever present in London, I used to ask my English collector friends if they could not put up some sort of manifestation, or could not try to send a witness to our biennial congresses. Things kept fairly quiet; then there came the joining of the Private Libraries Association by the Bookplate Society; the publication of our book BOOKPLATES 1950-1970, for which I am still infinitely grateful; and many articles relating to ex libris. But now a great move has been made with this exhibition at the V & A which is bound to prove undoubtedly that the bookplate is a lively branch of the graphic arts, with an infinite variety of wares and techniques.

British bookplates have always been of the highest standard, and indeed if the two or three first ones were not British, the quantity and quality of plates in Britain in the 16th and 17th centuries were outstanding, and this quality, apart perhaps from the "die sinkers," has been maintained up to the present day. Passing through all the phases, early armorial, Jacobean, Chippendale, etc., and confirmed in latter years by many artists among which stand out names like Sherborn, Eric Gill, Downey, Rex Whistler, Reynolds Stone, Joan Hassall, R. Shirley Smith to mention only a very few. Many of you will, no doubt, own, or remember, the special number of THE STUDIO, Modern Bookplates and Their Designers (edited by my wife's father). Indeed, THE STUDIO has often published articles on bookplates.

And so the art goes on. Many young artists now try their hands, often with success, at this fascinating branch of art. The first ex libris museum proper, in St. Nicholas in Belgium, was an audacious and original venture, and if, most certainly, their collection is modest compared to that in the British Museum (although it contains a vast selection of the work of artists of the 1920-70 period), it will also help to reveal these delightful vignettes to the public.

And now, to end with, we wish to thank our hosts for the charming idea of organizing these receptions and get together, today's as well as tomorrow's, and feel sure that this opportunity is grasped with enthusiasm and live interest by all of us from the continent. Next year's congress is to be held in Linz, Austria. If that for 1982 could be held in London, I am sure it would be supported with tremendous enthusiasm on all sides.

OPENING REMARKS by PETER SUMMERS,
President of the Bookplate Society

I feel it is a great privilege to be President of the Bookplate Society on such a happy and important occasion as this; I have a few things to say which will not take long, but first of all I wish wholeheartedly to endorse the welcome already given by our Chairman to you all. I think it may be of interest to some of you to know a little more about our Society and its origins. We started life in 1891 when the Ex Libris Society was formed by a group of enthusiasts; the number of members increased rapidly, regular meetings were held, and an excellent journal was produced. Eight years later, as an offshoot of the main Society, the Bookplate Exchange Club was formed; this enabled members to get rid of duplicate plates and to add to their own collections. The Ex Libris Society flourished for many years before closing down at the end of 1908; however, the Exchange Club, with a handful of keen collectors, carried on and still exists today. The next and most important development occurred in 1971 when members of the Exchange Club, in cooperation with the Private Libraries Association, formed the present Bookplate Society. So although the Bookplate Society, as such, is only eight years old, it has its roots back in the closing years of the last century. During the past eight years there have been three bookplate exhibitions, all organized by the Society; these have all been well attended and most successful, but this year's exhibition at the Victoria and Albert Museum, our fourth, a joint display by the Bookplate Society and the V & A, is on a much grander scale and is in fact the largest and most comprehensive bookplate exhibition ever to be held in Britain.

It covers a period of over 400 years, and contains many rarities. Those of you who are able to visit the Museum tomorrow will not, I am sure, be disappointed. A checklist of the plates on display, and an excellent illustrated booklet, are being issued free of charge to those attending. In the past few years there has not only been an increase of interest in bookplates in Britain (bookplate books do not stay long on booksellers' shelves), but there has also been an upsurge in the commissioning of personal plates. Fortunately there are many highly talented engravers able to meet this demand; among these are Leo Wyatt, Richard Shirley Smith, Simon Brett, and John Lawrence, all of whom are, I am glad to say, with us tonight, and Mark Severin, also happily present, has notably contributed to British bookplate design.

I should perhaps say something about the rarity of fine modern British plates for exchange. Here few people have more than one personal plate, to be used solely for their own books, with perhaps a few extra copies to give to friends. Some members of our Society do possess more than one personal plate, but they are the exception rather than the rule. I am under the impression that on the Continent it is not uncommon for collectors to commission many plates, and to have many extra copies printed for the purpose of exchange with other collectors. I mention these facts so that it will be understood that if a British member does not wish to exchange his plates it will probably be because he has only enough copies for his own library, with a reserve for later purchases; it is largely for this reason that a keen collector, for instance of Eric Gill's work, may not possess more than fifteen of his plates in spite of many years of collecting. Another reason for the unwillingness of some British collectors to exchange plates on a general basis is that many of us restrict our collection to particular styles, periods, or artists. As for the books on display for sale, I would strongly advise purchase now for, as I mentioned earlier, all bookplate literature tends to disappear rapidly, and in most instances is never reprinted. Finally, I would like to express a hope, which I feel sure will be realized, that this will be the first of many such gatherings; they give a splendid opportunity for bookplate enthusiasts, collectors and non-collectors alike, to get to know each other, opportunities which have been sadly lacking in the past. However such gatherings do of course involve a great deal of hard work. Almost the whole burden of this has fallen on three of our members. We have Philip Beddingham to thank for the splendid arrangements here this eveing, and what a wonderful setting, too. As for the organization of the whole weekend, we are indebted to Brian Lee and Anthony Pincott; the amount of work involved has been enormous, and this will be more easily appreciated when you see the Exhibition. It is not an exaggeration to say that without them neither the Exhibition or the Open Weekend would have taken place. We have indeed felt that we would like to pay a special tribute to Brian, who has been the mainstay of the Society since its inception, as Secretary in editing the Newsletter, writing numerous scholarly articles, and in fact being largely responsible for the considerably increased prestige that the Society holds today. His recently published book,will I feel sure, find a most worthy place on all our shelves; I have therefore the greatest pleasure, on behalf of the Society, in presenting Brian with a suitably inscribed and specially bound copy of his book.

I have no more to say except to wish you all a very happy weekend.

THE BOOK PILE

The book pile illustrated here had been used as a bookseller's label. It is very similar to the ex libris illustrated as plate 17 for James Steere of London (1760) in BOOK-PLATES IN BRITAIN, published jointly by the Bookplate Society and the Victoria and Albert Museum. In the text Brian North Lee comments: ". . . the first predominantly pictorial bookplate motif, and a curiously English one, was the bookpile. . . . it emerged about 1699 (and) was to remain in modest use for about two centuries." Lee indicates William Hewer, friend and secretary of Samuel Pepys, was among first to use the book pile.

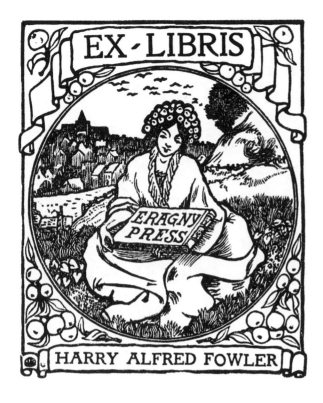

HARRY ALFRED FOWLER

Harry Alfred Fowler has a prominent place in American bookplate history as the editor of numerous journals devoted to bookplates beginning in 1912 with the EX LIBRAN.

Among his many personal bookplates is the one illustrated here, a wood-engraving by Lucien Pissarro (1863-1944), son of Camille Pissarro, the impressionist painter. The figure of the girl holding the "Eragny Press" volume was used as the Pissarro's press device between 1903 and 1914.

(Editor's Note: Information is wanted about the bookplate collection and correspondence or other papers relating to his ex libris publications and activities. Is material in the hands of a private collector or in an institutuonal library waiting, for some avid collector to discover the cache and make it the source for a research project? It will be appreciated if you will communicate any information about Harry Alfred Fowler to Audrey Arellanes, 1206 N. Stoneman Ave. #15, Alhambra, CA 91801.)

From - American Society of Bookplate Collectors and Designers

CALL for ARTICLES for FUTURE YEAR BOOKS

Interested in in-depth articles about
ARTISTS - COLLECTORS - OWNERS of bookplates

Scholarly notes concerning unusual ex libris are welcomed.

If you have a personal bookplate commissioned, why not have an overrun made so the plate could appear in BOOKPLATES IN THE NEWS along with biographical data about you as the owner and the artist ?   Institutional ex libris welcome, too, either for artistic merit or because of the importance or unusualness of the collection for which the plate was commissioned.

ALWAYS INTERESTED IN REFERENCES TO CURRENT EX LIBRIS LITERATURE

AS of BC & D

Bookplates in the News

1206 N. STONEMAN AVENUE #15, ALHAMBRA, CALIFORNIA, 91801 U.S.A.

AUDREY SPENCER ARELLANES, Editor

NUMBER THIRTY-NINE   JANUARY 1980

KIEKO TSURUSAWA - Japanese Artist
by   Ichigoro Uchida

Miss Kieko Tsurusawa was born in Hokkaido, Japan in 1942. She
graduated from Women's College of Fine Art (Department of Design)
in 1965 and worked for a company in Tokyo in its division of
graphic design for three years. After leaving that job, she
started to work on woodcut printings. She is now deeply interested in the charm of woodcut prints that she finds in the combination of Japanese paper, woodblocks, and baren.*

In 1976 she had a one-woman show
at the Yoseido Gallery in Tokyo.
In 1977 she exhibited her works
in the Veni Gallery in Kyoto in
a four print artists exhibition
called "Hanga Yonin Ten." From
1975 to 1977 her copper engravings were exhibited in the Shoun
Gallery in Tokyo. She is a member of Japan Artists Association
and is working as a part-time art
instructor in a junior high
school in Tokyo. The popularity
of her ex libris in Japan is
shown by the fact that three of
her works have been used in the
"calendar" of the Nippon Exlibris
Association.

I am impressed with Miss Tsurusawa's outstanding sense of
color, her ability to find unexpected beauty among ordinary objects and scenes around us, and

* Baren is the manual press made
of a round cardboard wrapped in
bamboo leaves, used to press the
paper onto the blocks.

her skillful handling of Japanese lettering. Her superb technique seems to be most effectively displayed in small format, i.e. ex libris. I should like to add that when I sent several Japanese ex libris by various artists to European collectors, they were all interested in Miss Tsurusawa's works most.

Checklist of Kieko Tsurusawa's Ex Libris

1. Nebuka ex libris, 86 x 57 mm, 1976
2. Uchida ex libris, 86 x 55 mm, 1976
3. Naosuke Kimura ex libris, 54 x 84 mm, 1976
4. Hattori ex libris, 80 x 70 mm, 1976
5. Ichigoro ex libris, 51 x 75 mm, 1978
6. Ex Libris Mice Raeymaekers, 47 x 75 mm, 1978
7. Ex Libris F. Ishikawa, 70 x 45 mm, 1978
8. Ichigoro's Books, 98 x 69 mm, 1979
9. Ex Libris J. Vils Pedersen, 49 x 80 mm, 1979
10. Ayami's Books, 104 x 65 mm, 1979

Any one interested in commissioning a bookplate by Miss Tsurusawa may write her at 34-12, Wakabayaski 5 Chome, Setagaya-Ku, Tokyo, 154 Japan.

INTERNATIONAL CONGRESS IN LINZ, AUSTRIA - 1980

Through the kindness of Prof. Dr. Gustav Dichler we are able to provide the following advance, preliminary details of the International Ex Libris Congress to be held in Linz from August 21 through 23, 1980. Thursday, the 21st, there will be registration from 8 to 10:30AM, then the official opening of the Congress. During the afternoon, there will be a sightseeing tour through Linz, a city of about 200,000. Friday will be the meeting of the F.I.S.A.E. and at 11AM a speech by Mark Severin, internationally noted bookplate artist and author. The afternoon and evening will be open for the exchange of ex libris. Saturday there will be a bus tour from Linz to St. Florian, an old abbey where the Austrian composer Bruckner played the organ, to Kefermarkt which is famous for a medieval woodcarved altar, to Freistadt, and back to Linz. The official banquet will be Saturday evening, the crowning event of the Congress. Those who elect to stay over on Sunday may make a trip to Steyr. Each day of the Congress the official meeting place will be open all day until midnight for the exchange of ex libris and chatting with old friends and making new friends. As soon as the registration fees and other details are known, they will be published in BOOKPLATES IN THE NEWS or if you are seriously considering attending the Congress in Linz, write to Prof. Dr. Gustav Dichler, Johann Strauss-Gasse 28, A-1040 Viena IV, Austria. For air mail reply, it would be considerate to send an international postal coupon of value equivalent to postage for one ounce air mail.

BOOKPLATE EXHIBIT -During the month of December, 1979 there was an ex libris exhibit at the LaCanada (California) Public Library from the collection of Audrey Arellanes. The exhibit was installed by Cornett Wood for the Friends of the LaCanada Public Library. A plate Cornett designed for the Boy Scouts was on display in the 1925 YEAR BOOK edited by Alfred Fowler, Kansas City, and a just-completed plate which he designed for the LaCanada library.

EX LIBRIS

Rebecca Briggs

Dream what you dare to dream :: Go where you want to go :: Be what you want to be ::

JACKY BRIGGS –
CALLIGRAPHER

One of the young artists who has come to our attention as the result of the renewed interest in calligraphy is Jacky Briggs of Jamestown, NY. As may be seen by her business card, she puts her skills to work in a number of ways. The quotation from Arthur Fiedler is from a series of quotations about music which decorate ten notes with matching envelopes which sell for $3.

The Jean Badger plate is one of two recent commissions which used the thistle, a symbol of Scottish descent. The plate, designed for her daughter, has been very popular.

Calligraphy

Hand lettered Invitations
Certificates · Verses
Bookplates
Cards

Jacky Briggs
1013 Fairmount Ave., W.E.
Jamestown, New York 14701
Phone 716·489·3496

EX LIBRIS

Margaret
Carriére
Dodds

Car Dieu a tant aimé le monde Qu'il a donné son fils unique, pour que tous ceux qui croient en lui ne périssent pas, mais aient la vie éternelle. Jean 3:16.

EX LIBRIS

Jean Carter Badger

DULCE PERICULUM

It is only with the heart that one can see rightly; what is essential is invisible to the eye ::

Jacky continues to expand her skills by attending workshops including one sponsored by the Society of Scribes in New York on the Carolingian hand, which was in use during the reign of Charlemagne, and a Cleveland workshop last spring led by the Chairman of the Society of Scribes & Illuminators in London.

THE AUSTRIAN EX LIBRIS   Austria has only seven million in-
    by   Dr. Gustav Dichler   habitants, but her ex libris society is
   President of the O.E.G.   one of the oldest in Europe. The O.E.G.
                               (Osterreichische Exlibris-Gesellschaft)
was founded in 1903, i.e. more than 75 years ago. Since then practically
all Austrian graphic artists have been members; at present O.E.G. has about
250, most of them artists, some historians, some collectors. The biggest
collector is Franz Alatter; if you want to see a special bookplate out of
his 50,000, he will show it within a couple of minutes. The O.E.G. has edited about sixty books, containing essays and ex libris; we also edit a
semi-annual paper; the Society has an archive.

Since the 15th century the essence of bookplating has been the contrast of
black and white; colored plates, mostly handcolored, exist, but are rare.
In the beginning of this century the world-famous Austrian artist Professor
Alfred Cossmann revived and improved copperplating. Of his numerous successful pupils, two are among the living: Professor Hans Ranzoni der Jungere and
Herbert Toni Schimek; both also made postage stamps. Another renowned artist
is Professor Rudolf Toth, who makes banknotes and postal stamps; among the
young artists, Werner Pfeiler (postal stamps). But copperplates are expensive
and therefore not so much in demand. The overwhelming majority of graphic
artists specialize in lino and wood. Lino ex libris are sometimes colored,
woodcut ex libris generally are black and white. Other materials one meets
very seldom. At present the best known lino artists are Professor Otto Feil
(flowers, architecture) and Dr. Ottmar Premstaller (letters, architecture);
in wood, Ella Goldschmidt (flowers, architecture), who also paints in oil and
watercolors; Leopold Hofmann (architecture, landscape, animals), who has invented a technique of his own; Erich Schoner (architecture, flowers) died a
short time ago.

Professor Hedwig zum Tobel is in a class by herself; her 170 ex libris (saints,
animals, nudes) are the collector's dream; she is also a famous book illustrator and stage decorator (costumes, decorations for the opera, etc.).

The above mentioned artists are so popular that they can scarcely fulfill all
the orders from Austria and abroad. The younger generation is represented by
Felizitas Kuhn, Helmut Kuhn, Peter Mayer, Alfred Puhrer, and Herbert Schmid.
I must point out that nearly all Austrian graphic artists (i.e. Silvia Penther)
have tried their hands at ex libris, but many of them abstained later on from
specializing in it. All our ex libris artists have one feature in common: they
strive for perfect harmony of idea and execution, and they work most carefully
and conscientiously; in short they are real artists.

. AMERICAN ENGRAVINGS to 1821   A grant has been made to the American Antiquar-
                                ian Society from the National Foundation for the
Humanities with matching funds provided by the H. W. Wilson Foundation for a
definitive catalogue of American engravings to 1821. The work will revise a two-
volume work by David McNeely Stauffer, AMERICAN ENGRAVERS UPON COPPER AND STEEL,
published in 1907, the supplement compiled by Mantle Fielding in 1917, and incorporate the research done by H. Dunscombe Colt over a 25 year period commencing in 1948, which has been turned over to the American Antiquarian Society.
The catalogue is scheduled for completion in 1982 and should be of interest to
collectors of early American bookplates.

JACQUELINE M. G. POLSTER
and the LOVEJOY PRESS
by Nathaniel Polster

Jacqueline M. G. Polster was born in 1940 in Worcestershire where she was educated in the Warley municipal school system. As an only child, her habit of "drawing with her eyes," that is of tracing objects with her gaze, sometimes brought remonstrances from her mother.

With the help of her father, who is employed in one of England's largest automotive found- ries, she found work draughting in a firm making conveyor belts. Just out of high school she pursued that work for seven years. Her meticulous output at her last post won her a lifetime offer of re-employment.

Some of her attention to detail in art de- picting flowers and other objects of nature is so thorough, and so thoroughly express- ive, that it has been termed "mysterious."

Despite the remonstrances, her mother en- couraged her to enroll in the Birmingham School of Arts and Crafts, where Jacqueline was an immediate success in life drawing. She also won attention for her water colors and oils. She continued her studies until marriage to a Turkish economics student at the University of Birmingham took them, upon his graduation, to Istanbul and Ankara.

She moved to the United States in 1969. After establishing a studio here she worked mostly in oils but soon turned to water colors and drawings. Her deep interest in Beardsley and Klimt is glimpsed in some of her current art. Her work has been hung by three Wash- ington, D.C. area galleries and has attracted purchasers from both Europe and America. It has ranged from nonrepresentational water colors awash with brilliance and movement to renditions of trees of such artistically heighten- ed realism that the trees' owners, on viewing the pictures, have remarked about owning the "original" works of art - in their gardens.

The artist lives with her second husband and nine year old daughter at her studio in downtown Washington. In recent years while continuing painting for galleries, the artist has produced line drawings for a series of book- plates. As is traditional in the field, the design elements for the ex libris have largely been ordered by clients. While execution has always been subject to client approval via proofs, she has never been requested to alter her first proof for any client. The bookplate work has drawn attention from other than bookplate collectors who have been interested in artwork of small dimension. These pieces have been reproduced for the Kennedy Center for the Performing Arts, Washington, D.C., and for several art outlets on the East Coast. Several of her drawings, as prints, have been commissioned in multiple copies, black on white, and individually watercolored in a style reminiscent of early nineteenth century book illustration.

The Lovejoy Press was founded by the Polsters in 1974 to produce fine hand printing. The primary press is a 12" x 18" platen Chandler & Price motorized hand-fed press. All composition is performed with cold type in the printing office. Output includes primarily bookplates, other artwork of small dimensions, and small books of poetry. Where clients have been interested in quality letterpress work, seldom obtainable through usual commercial channels, the press has printed ephemera such as stationery, calling cards, bookmarks, art advertising pieces, and notepapers.

Recent commissions have included letterpress prints individually watercolored. Much of the work is on art papers, often handmade papers. Included among papers stocked by the Lovejoy Press are the handmade sheets with fresh flowers embedded produced by the Richard de Bas mill founded in France in the fourteenth century and still operating. Diplomatic stationery has been commissioned on Fabriano papers from Italy by several members of Washington's diplomatic corps.

A book design by Lovejoy Press artist Jacqueline M. G. Polster has been used by a commercial offset firm.

The press is named after The Rev. Elijah Parish Lovejoy, martyred in 1837 at Alton, Illinois in defense of freedom of the press. Two series of short chapters on freedom of the press are under preparation, one a group of commentaries on the subject, the other comprising a history of freedom of the press from Gutenberg to the United States Bill of Rights. In 1980 The Lovejoy Press will publish (but not print) a two-volume edition of reproductions in full color of antique Japanese prints. The set is tentatively priced at $1,250 and will include a number of items practically unobtainable elsewhere. Extreme care has been taken in the color photo-separation work and the set is expected to become a standard reference work on Japanese prints.

The tipped-in ex libris for Richard D. Cohen, M.D., was designed by Jacqueline Polster and printed by the Lovejoy Press. Dr. Cohen, a ASBC&D member, has a number of personal bookplates, including a second design by Mrs. Polster. For their own ex libris Jacqueline and Nathaniel use the horse which is the symbol of the Lovejoy Press. (Lovejoy Press, 2128 Wyoming Ave., Washington, DC 20008.)

. CALIFORNIA'S FIRST BOOKPLATE   The La Loma Press has published an edition of fifty copies of CALIFORNIA'S FIRST BOOKPLATE. A single leaf is sewn in brown coverstock. A facsimile of the ex libris is tipped-in; it is a simple typographic plate with border and text in Spanish which translates to: I am of the ownership and use of Don Mariano G. Vallejo. Vallejo's library is said to have contained 12,000 books. Jose de la Rosa, one of the first printers in California, is credited with printing the General's bookplates, probably around 1837-39.

. CALLIGRAPHY, BOOKPLATE EXHIBIT   Mrs. Ione Wiechel, ASBC&D member, shared her hobbies of 50 years – calligraphy, bookplates, and miniature books – in an exhibit at the Sandusky Area Cultural Center (Ohio), November 4 through 25, 1979. The announcement issued by the Center was scripted by a local artist/teacher Charles Mayer and also carried a Latin instription in the hand of G. Harvey Petty. THE SANDUSKY REGISTER carried an article about Mrs. Wiechel's collection and the exhibit in the November 4th and 10th editions with several illustrations including a a warmly smiling picture of Ione herself.

ROBERT G. & ROBERT L. DENIG
by Ione Wiechel

The death of Brigadier General Robert L. Denig on July 25, 1979 at Los Altos, CA brings to a close the saga of the Denig ex libris which is witness to the beginning of the American Society of Bookplate Collectors & Designers. His father, Robert G. Denig, was a charter member of the Society, and with his aide, Lieutenant Carlyle S. Baer founded the Society in 1922 at Washington, DC. After returning to civilian life, Mr. Baer carried on the work of the Society and was editor of the Society's publications until his death in 1969.

The Denig bookplate was designed for both Robert G. Denig and his son Brigadier General Robert L. Denig. The design is enclosed within the Phi Beta Kappa Key which the Commodore was awarded while teaching at Hamilton College, Clinton, NY.

In the center of the design is the Denig coat of arms. The sketch at the top center is the USS HURON, which was wrecked at Hatteras. Commodore Denig, then a lieutenant, was the assistant engineer and one of the few saved.

The design at the left is Havana during the time of the Spanish American War. The Marine Corps device has the date 1905, the year Commodore Denig was commissioned. The bottom device represents the insignia of the U.S. Naval Academy, from which the Commodore graduated in 1873. The Distinguished Service Cross and the Croix de Guerre are noted under the Denig names.

The plate was designed and engraved by C. Valentine Kirby in 1919, and is a splendid example of bookplate design, with great personal meaning.

This is a belated tribute to two heroic Americans whose martial skills and leadership qualities were important to our country and who also enjoyed the byways of art and literature.

CHANGE OF ADDRESS - It is important that you notify the Editor at any time you change your address and as far in advance as possible. Return postage on unforwardable periodicals is costly.

. EMIL EERME – Canadian Collector

Last spring Eerme retired and now has more time to spend on his bookplate collection, which numbers some 20,000 prints. His interest was originally aroused while he was attending university in his native Estonia in 1936 when he was given a bookplate by an artist friend. Fifteen years ago Emil began planning for his future retirement and undertook three new hobbies in anticipation of the extra leisure hours he could look forward to; these hobbies were: color slide photography, stamp collecting, and bookplate collecting.

As his collection grew, Emil felt he should share these beautiful prints with others and began exhibiting in public libraries, universities, and more recently at the Ontario Legislature.

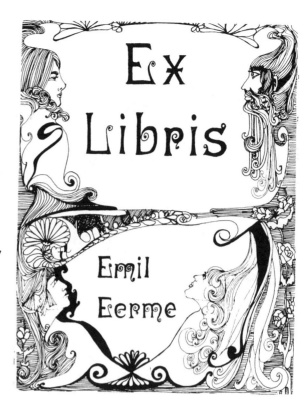

Before retirement Eerme was involved with the planning and design of freeways for the Ministry of Transportation and Communication, Ontario, Canada.

The ex libris at the top of the page was designed by Monika Uesson of Toronto in 1975; it is a pen sketch printed by offset. The Viking ship is the work of H. Seehausen in 1966, Germany. The two plates at the right bottom are an interesting reversal of the same design – one black on white, the other white on black. Those interested in exchanging may write Eerme at 20 Farmcote Road, Don Mills, Ontario, Canada M3B 2Z4.

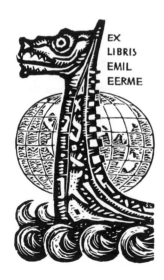

FROM THE LITERATURE . . . .

BOOK COLLECTOR'S MARKET, An Unsolved Conan Doyle Mystery, Stanley Wertheim. (1)
4:November/December 1979. The mystery is a Doyle bookplate which has appeared
in a number of volumes offered by bookdealers mostly located on the U.S. West
Coast during the past 18 months. Doyle scholars believe the ex libris may be
a forgery inasmuch as many Doyle books of indisputable provenance have never
contained such a plate. Additionally the paper on which the plate is printed
"is far newer than the books themselves" and its generally fresh appearance is
in considerable contrast to the condition of the books. The only evidence that
there might be a Doyle ex libris is contained in an article by Sir Arthur's
third son Adrian M. Conan Doyle which appeared in THE BAKER STRET JOURNAL of
September 1962. However, Professor Wertheim states that Adrian "has generally
been held in low esteem by Doyle biographers" and is considered "something of
a professional eccentric." Readers having additional information about the ex
libris are invited to write Professor Wertheim, c/o BCM, 363 Seventh Avenue,
NY 10001. Perhaps some of our ex libris authorities will have some facts to
help dispel the mystery and will write to BOOKPLATES IN THE NEWS.

LIBRARY JOURNAL, British Bookplates: A Pictorial History, 2450: November 15, 1979.
Review mentions that book is "of special interest (for) those bookplates with a
graphic link to their owners - a Kipling ex-libris that depicts a bibliophile
astride a running elephant, or a Paderewski ex-libris depicting a grand piano
on a concert stage. Helpful notes about all owners, artists, and engravers accompany black and white plates." Author is Brian North Lee.

ANTIQUARIAN BOOK MONTHLY REVIEW, Book Review, 6:385, September 1979. Review of
BRITISH BOOKPLATES: A PICTORIAL HISTORY by Brian North Lee; published by David
& Charles in England and the United States. "Mr. North Lee's introduction has
the breadth and assurance that is the mark of a thorough knowledge of his sub-
ject. The art of the bookplate, like any living thing, has evolved and reached
its heights and depths of achievement, which is all carefully traced for us here. "
The volume was reviewed at length in the October 1979 issue of BOOKPLATES IN
THE NEWS.

CHRONICLES OF THE BREAD AND CHEESE CLUB (published in 1943, Australia) devotes
chapter XIX to "The Book-Plate, The Badge of Book Fellowship," by P. Neville
Barnett, Hon. Secretary of the Australian Ex-Libris Society at that time. The
chapter (pages 103 to 125) deals briefly with the ex libris on a world basis
and more particularly in Australia. The illustrations give evidence of designs
speaking strongly of Australia - sailing ships, gum trees, penguins, the Kooka-
burras, the abo of the Out Back, and artists such as Adrian Feint.

THE EX LIBRIS OF SIR LIONEL LINDSAY (1874-1961) by Robert C. Littlewood, privately
printed, Melbourse, Australia, 1978. A hardcover book (8 x 10 1/2") in black cloth
with silver-stamped title on spine, with accompanying black cloth slip-case. The
main body of the book is an alphabetical presentation of the ex libris designs by
Lionel Lindsay; biographical details of the owner's life are given; reference is
made to publications in which the bookplate appeared. There is a chronological
list of the ex libris, a bibliography, a general alphabetical index, a brief
chronology of events in the life of Sir Lionel. It is unfortunate that none of
the qualities usually associated with a privately printed book is in evidence
(such as selection of an appropriate typeface, excellent composition, good page
design, and most essential in any volume on art - quality reproductions). Even

the frontispiece portrait of Lindsay is poorly reproduced with no accompanying note to justify such presentation. The lack of physical excellence in the book is particularly distressing considering the retail price of $60; the satin ribbon in the slip-case to make it easier to withdraw the book does not sufficiently compensate for other standards of excellence anticipated from a $60 privately printed book - even at current rates of inflation.

HERALDIC BOOKPLATES by Frank Irwin, The Hillside Press, Buffalo, NY, 1979, $12.50. This miniature book, printed from handset type, has been printed in an edition of 250 copies. The text has been drawn from three articles which appeared in THE ANTIQUARY in the 1880's, two of the authors are known: Walter Hamilton and

and again through the centuries. An ancient English bookplate for the Library of King Edward VI's Grammar School at St. Albans bears the school's arms with the motto *Mediocria Firma*. This motto also appears on the bookplates of Sir Nicholas Bacon and the Earls of Verulam. Casual

13

17

William Hogarth and a great publishing house like the Chiswick Press borrowed the Aldine dolphin and anchor for their bookplate.

Punning bookplates which have been called "canting heraldry" include the plates of "Thomas Martin whose crest is a martens; Henry

N. Bacon eques auratus & magni sigilli Angliae Custos librum hunc bibliothecae Cantabrig. dicauit.
1574.

Alfred Wallis. Above are uncut sheets printed four pages up which let you see the well-set text and the variety of reproductions. The scarlet book-cover has printed in black George Washington's heraldic ex libris. This is a handsome, informative volume to add to a growing shelf of miniature books about ex libris.

1979 YEAR BOOK together with BOOKPLATES IN THE NEWS 1980 - $27.50

Articles about and by Mark Severin - Ex Libris Checklist

Articles about Reitsma-Valença and Paul Landacre
with checklists of their bookplates

Pictures of each artist and many bookplates illustrated

WANTED: Articles for BOOKPLATES IN THE NEWS and the

future YEAR BOOKS. Please write the Editor.

BOOKPLATES IN THE NEWS   Annual Dues $10 US/Overseas
1206 N. Stoneman Ave. #15, Alhambra, CA 91801   Issued Quarterly . . .
Copyright 1980 Audrey Spencer Arellanes   January/April/July/October

AS of BC & D
Bookplates in the News

AUDREY SPENCER ARELLANES, Editor

NUMBER FORTY   APRIL 1980

THE BOOKPLATE:
A GIFT OF FRIENDSHIP

Roman Ferencevych was born in Ukraine. He immigrated to the United States as a young man in 1950, and after service with the US Army overseas during the Korean war became a printer's apprentice at Svoboda Publishers in Jersey City, N.J., established 1893. Svoboda Publishers was, at the time, strictly a letterpress firm, staffed by elderly Old World printers deeply committed to their trade as an art form. In addition to a Ukrainian-language daily newspaper and an English-language weekly, they produced other periodicals, literary and historical works, and a number of quality art books.

Eventually Mr. Ferencevych became supervisor of the printing plant. It was then that he made the acquaintance of Jacques Hnizdovsky, who occasionally used the Svoboda Publishers' press to make impressions of his larger-sized woodcuts. The bookplate is a memento of those days and of the mutual friendship that ensued, as well as of the noble profession of printing.

Mr. Ferencevych is currently with the Voice of America in Washington, DC, where for the past six years he has been a member of the editorial staff of the Ukrainian Service.

INVITATION TO THE

XVIII. INTERNATIONAL

EXLIBRIS CONGRESS

John Lloyd Balderston
Marion Balderston

The bookplate of John Lloyd Balderston was found in a translation of his BERKELEY SQUARE, a play in three acts which was originally copyrighted in 1926. This edition, translated into Arabic, appears to have been published in Cairo in 1965 and bears notice that Marion Balderston renewed the copyright in 1954.

John Balderston was born in Philadelphia on October 22, 1889. He was a student at Columbia University from 1911 to 1914; while attending the university, John was New York correspondent for the Philadelphia RECORD (1912-14) and went to Europe as a free-lance correspondent in 1915. Later he was associated with the McClure publications. Toward the end of WWI, he was Director of Information in Great Britain and Ireland for the U.S. Government Commission on Public Information (1918-19). On March 6, 1921, John married Marion Rubicam.

In addition to BERKELEY SQUARE, Balderston co-authored other plays: DRACULA (1927), FRANKENSTEIN (1931), RED PLANET (1932), and FAREWELL PERFORMANCE (1936). His writing led him to broadcasting and motion pictures. His film scripts included: LIVES OF A BENGAL LANCER, SMILIN' THROUGH, GASLIGHT, TENNESSEE JOHNSON, PRISONER OF ZENDA. During 1952 he lectured on drama at the University of Southern California.

John Balderston died March 8, 1954 and is buried at Colora, Maryland.

— — — — — — — — — — — — — — — — —

BOOKPLATE LITERATURE

CHRONICLE (Princeton University Library), Endowed Library Funds, Alexander D. Wainwright. (2) XLI:146-159, Winter 1980. Several bookplates are illustrated which are used to commemorate gifts and purchases from the Friends of the Library.

BON APPETIT, "Bon Vivant." (2) 25:13, March 1980. Under Book Talk is a brief review of Beverly Cox's MINCEUR ITALIENNE, which is "organized as a gastronomical tour through Italy's 14 regions . . .." Pictured is the author and her ex libris.

FLEURON ANTHOLOGY, Chonen and with a retrospectus by Sir Francis Meynel & Herbert Simon (Boston: David R. Godine, 1979). Included in the anthology is "D. B. Updike and The Merrymount Press," by W. A. Dwiggins (pages 111-18). Accompanying this interesting essay is a page of illustrations of commercial pieces from the Merrymount Press which include two, possibly three, bookplates. Another essay by Holbrook Jackson, "Claud Lovat Fraser: Illustrator," will be of interest to bookplate collectors even though the emphasis is on his work as an illustrator (pages 32-7).

— — — — — — — — — — — — — — — — —

BOOKPLATES IN THE NEWS   January/April/July/October
605 N. Stoneman Ave. #F, Alhambra, CA 91801   Newsletter Membership $ 10

LINZ, AUSTRIA - Site of XVIII INTERNATIONAL CONGRESS

The XVIII International Exlibris Congress is scheduled to be held in Linz, Austria from August 21 to 24, 1980. The program will start on Thursday at 8AM with registration and distribution of Congress gifts. At 11AM will be the official opening Ceremony and at 5PM the Exhibition will be opened in the Stadtmuseum Nordico. Friday morning will be devoted to the meeting of the Congress delegates with representatives from all the member societies. Professor Mark Severin will give a talk illustrated with slides at 11AM and at 2:30PM there will be a city tour. Saturday will be a full day with a bus to Freistadt for lunch and then on to Kefermarkt and St. Florian. In the evening is the official banquet, which is always a festive occasion. Each day of the Congress facilities will be provided where members may exchange ex libris 'til midnight.

The Congress fee will be S1,200, which includes the 5th volume of the FISAE book, the Congress gifts, the bus tour with lunch, and the banquet; depending on the exchange rate, it is about $90. The fee for a companion is S800 with FISAE book or the Congress gifts.

Suggested hotel accommodations range from $20 to $40 for a single, and for the Congress may be made by writing Stadtische Fremdenverkehrsburo, Postfach 310, A-4010 Linz, Austria. The Congress fee should be sent to - Dr. Ottmar Premstaller, Postfach 2, St. Georgen/Gusen, A-4222, Austria. The deadline for registration is May 30, 1980.

— — — — — — — — — — — — — — —

"Bookplates - Their Use and Design"

Friends of Literature were invited to attend a luncheon at the Chicago Art Institute on Saturday, April 5, 1980, held in the Private Dining Room. The speaker for the day was Vytautas Virkau, Professor of Art at George Williams College. To quote from the invitations sent for this event: "The use of bookplates lends an added charm and an historical record to those volumes they adorn. They come in all shapes, sizes, and conditions to delight the collector and the casual admirer alike." Illustrated to the right is a bookplate designed by Virkau in 1980; plants are a speciality, though often his designs are highly fanciful or abstract.

EX LIBRIS
CYRUS
HAPPY

— — — — — — — — — — — — — — —

MORE BOOKPLATE LITERATURE . . . . .

THE PRIVATE LIBRARY, Bibliographica, Papers on Books, Their History and Art 1895-1897, Robin Myers. Third Series:2:86-94, Autumn 1979. Interesting background to the publication of the three volumes of BIBLIOGRAPHICA, which unlike so many journals of limited duration was planned for twelve quarterly numbers. Its editor A. W. Pollard had also edited the Books About Books series for Kegan Paul which includes Hardy's BOOKPLATES. It is not too surprising to find in the new journal an article by Hardy on "The Book-Plates of J. Skinner of Bath".

Richard H. Rovere, who was a member of the NEW YORKER staff, died the day after Thanksgiving in 1979, at the age of 64.

Richard Halworth Rovere was born on May 5, 1915, in Jersey City, NJ. Later the family moved to Manhattan and he attended Stony Brook School on Long Island. During his junior year in high school he became editor of the school's newspaper, THE BULLE-TIN. His college years were spent at Bard college at Annandale-on-Hudson.

After graduation in 1937, he spent brief periods working for several magazines, including THE NEW MASSES, THE NATION, COMMON SENSE, and by 1944 he joined the NEW YORKER.

Rovere did book reviews, editorial comment, an occasional short humor piece, and covered the Washington beat from December of 1948 until his death. The obituary in the NEW YORK TIMES, written by David Bird, noted that Rovere "wrote some of the most penetrating and respected commentaries on American politics as a columnist for the NEW YORKER magazine." Rovere wrote a book, ARRIVALS AND DEPARTURES, A JOURNALIST'S MEMOIRS, which was more about the work-a-day world of a journalist than the revelation of events in his personal life. His other hardbound publications included AFFAIRS OF STATE: THE EISENHOWER YEARS (1956) and SENATOR JOE McCARTHY (1959). He called McCarthy a "barbarian," "seditionist" and "cynic" who was "in many ways the most gifted demagogue ever bred on these shores."

Mr. Rovere lived in Barrytown, NY, where he did most of his writing. His ex libris seems to show a view from Hyde Park. Perhaps a reader will know who designed the plate and send further details. (Thanks are due Francis O. Mattson for furnishing the David Bird article from the NEW YORK TIMES of November 24, 1979 and the unsigned NEW YORKER tribute in the issue of December 10, 1979.)

—   —   —   —   —   —   —   —   —   —

EX LIBRIS EXCHANGE : Wanted for exchange plates by French, Spenceley, and Macdonald. I can offer a fair range of other types. If you are interested, please write: A. B. Schofield, 12 Crofton Avenue, Walton-on-Thames, Surrey KT12 3DB, ENGLAND.

—   —   —   —   —   —   —   —

PUBLICATION DELAYED   BOOKPLATES IN THE NEWS was late this quarter due to the recent move of the Editor. The temptation to publish a double issue was overcome in view of the often expressed feeling that "double issues" herald the approaching demise of a "little magazine." An April/July issue would have saved time, postage, and possibly printing costs; however, it is hoped you too will feel a quarterly issued late is better than a quarterly in three issues!

LUCIEN PISSARRO AND ERAGNY PRESS
EXHIBIT at NEW YORK PUBLIC LIBRARY

"Lucien Pissarro and the Eragny Press" is a new exhibit which
opened at the New York Public Library's Central Building in the
Second Floor Gallery on April 25, 1980 and will run through
August 15, 1980.

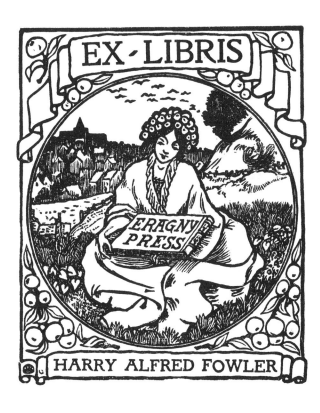

The following is from a
news release issued by the
library:

The exhibit features nearly
a complete selection of the
books printed by the Eragny
Press and has been mounted
by F. O. Mattson of the Rare
Book Division in conjunction
with "Camille Pissarro and
Impressionist Printmaking,"
the current exhibition in
the Print Gallery.

The eldest son of the noted
French Impressionist Camille
Pissarro, Lucien was primarily a painter and engraver,
but from 1894 to 1914, he occupied himself almost entirely with the printing and illustration of the books published by the Egangy Press,
which he owned and operated
with his wife, Esther Bensusan. Pissarro settled in
England where wood engraving - the form of illustration he considered most
compatible with type - was a popular medium. When he was unable to interest
commercial publishers in his illustrations, he established the Eragny Press.
Named after the Norman village where his father had lived, it flourished
during the 1890's, the golden age of the private press movement, along with
the Kelmscott, Ashendene, Vale and Doves Presses.

Pissarro's desicion to print fairy tales and French language works, in
addition to English classics, as well as his use of delicately colored
wood engravings, were unusual for their place and time. Pissarro was influenced by the English cartoonist Charles Keene, the Pre-Raphaelites
(much to his father's dismay), Japanese woodcuts and, of course, his father
(in his choice of subject matter) but his style remains quite personal and
distinctive.

The exhibition includes periodicals where Pissarro's illustrations appeared
before he began publishing his own books, some bookplates he designed, and
an original water color. One case will concern his relationship with John
Quinn, the noted New York collector of books, manuscripts and works of art,
and another his relationship with the Library's first Curator of Prints,

Frank Weitenkampf, responsible for that Division's strong holdings of Pissarro. (Editor's note: With the various bookplate associations indicated in this release, I am certain the exhibition will be of special interest to any ASBC&D members fortunate enough to view it. A future issue of BOOK-PLATES IN THE NEWS will feature the bookplate of John Quinn. See below for list of bookplates included in the exhibition.)

DIRECTORY OF AMERICAN BOOKPLATE ARTISTS   One of the many special publications issued by Alfred Fowler was a directory listing American artists actively practicing the art of designing bookplates. The directory included the name and address of the artist, the medium in which bookplates were executed, an approximate price either from sketch to finished print or for stages of the process, and occasionally other pertinent information.

Frequently inqueries are directed to the Society concerning finding an artist to design a bookplate. It would be helpful to have a listing of current artists who are interested in bookplate commissions. Please send me information about artists who have designed plates for you, either as an individual or an institution.

There is considerable documentation about artists practicing throughout Europe and England. Less is known about American artists, in part due to the fact few artists in America create any body of bookplate work today. The few who do have all the commissions they can handle. Your help in identifying artists who may be interested in bookplate commissions is needed, and any suggestions will be greatly appreciated. Write the Editor, BOOKPLATES IN THE NEWS.

LIVING ARTISTS TO FEATURE IN F.I.S.A.E. PUBLICATION

Each even numbered year there is an International Ex Libris Congress and in recent years there has been a publication containing an article from each of the member societies about a living bookplate artist. The European artists usually furnish several prints to be tipped, which means 400-500 copies of each print. The deadline for this year is past, but I am putting out a call early for American artists to represent the United States in 1982, with the idea that perhaps more than one artist would respond and each could be represented by one tipped-in bookplate print. This would require that each artist only furnish the required number of prints of one ex libris. Please write the Editor, BOOKPLATES IN THE NEWS.

BOOKPLATES in the "Lucien Pissarro and the Eragny Press" Exhibition

J. M. Andreini
J. L. Bensusan
S. L. Bensusan
Dr. Th. Gallard
Isa Taylor
"Orovida's Ex Libris" - hand colored proof for his daughter
Esther and Lucien Pissarro (not an original bookplate, but
    the cover of a leaflet, so probably printed from the original block)
Mary F. Cassola (designed by Esther Bensusan Pissarro)

ABEL LEE
AN ESTONIAN EX LIBRIS
ARTIST IN CANADA

By   Arvid Vilms

Although Abel Lee is
known mainly as a
master of monotypes,
he is creatively ac-
tive also in other
sectors of graphic
art and in painting.
At the same time he
cultivates minigraph-
ic art, which fact
is corroborated by
his numerous ex libris.

Abel Lee was born in
Estonia on the third of October 1918. He studied graphic art at the State
College of Art in Tallinn under professor G. Reindorff. The artist fled to
Finland when his native country was occupied by enemy forces in 1942 and
then moved to Sweden in 1944. The change of surroundings opened new opportunities for his inquisitive mind to discover yet untroden paths in
areas of creative expression.

In 1951 Abel Lee emigrated to Canada, where he made his home at Maple. This
small town in the vicinity of Toronto is situated in the midst of fields.
It enables the artist to retreat into a more peaceful atmosphere for his
creative work, yet at the same time be within easy reach of the lively art
center of the metropolis, where he was one of the co-founders of the art
society Colour and Form.

Abel Lee's first ex libris was completed
in 1949. His fourth bookplate was a woodcut. From there on, except for some zinc
plates and silk screens, he has favored
linocuts, which he has found to be best
suited to his kind of expression. Most of
his ex libris are di- or trichromatic,
which adds to their eye appeal. Of particular interest are his ex libris in hand
printing, which sometimes look like oil
paintings. The whole output of this mini-
art of his leaves you with an impression
that he has tried to avoid any linear an-
gularity. We sense a smooth flow of in-
tertwining forms into which the lettering
belongs as an unpretentious part. In some
instances we could associate his style as
bordering on the primitive or even absurd.
His color scheme may sometimes provoke our
disapproval. Yet the same unexpected dis-
harmonies and contrasts will challenge us

to find justification of the artist's solution of the hidden theme. Abel Lee's ex libris have a pleasant appeal, not so much arisen from humor as from playful rejoicing of beauty.

Between 1949 and 1978 Abel Lee has created 145 bookplates. [Editor's Note: A longer version of this article appeared originally in A ARTE DO EX-LIBRIS' BOLETIM trimestral da Associacao Portuense de Ex-Libris, #56, Ano XVI, vol. VII, 1971, and was accompanied by a checklist of 140 ex libris. Arvid Vilms, an Estonian by birth, has lived in Canada since 1951. He started collecting bookplates in 1963 and now numbers 9,000 prints in his collection. He has 102 personal ex libris. The portrait plate illustrated on the previous page is by Estonian artist Johann Naha, who currently resides in Munich. At 74 Mr. Vilms is still an avid collector and has had his ex libris exhibited in Portugal (1965) and Tokyo (1978).]

AMERICAN FILM INSTITUTE

When President Johnson signed the National Arts and Humanities Act on September 29, 1965, he announced that there would be "an American Film Institute, bringing together leading artists of the film industry, outstanding educators, and young men and women who wish to pursue this 20th century art form as their life's work."

In June of 1967 AFI became a reality. It is headquartered in the John F. Kennedy Center for the Performing Arts in Washington, DC, and its conservatory, The Center for Advanced Film Studies, is in Beverly Hills, California. Through these two locations, AFI serves students, scholars, professionals and those of the public whose studies, interests, or careers revolve around the moving image.

The Beverly Hills center is at Greystone, the former Doheny family estate which is owned by the city of Beverly Hills, and the research library has been named for the late Charles K. Feldman, a well-known agent and producer.

The American Film Institute
Center for Advanced Film Studies

Charles K. Feldman
Library

DARTMOUTH COLLEGE OFFER / Dartmouth College Library has numerous obsolete printed bookplates representing various donations. They do not necessarily represent the work of known designers and only two are engraved. If you would like a selection of two dozen, send $3 to: Walter W. Wright, Chief of Special Collections, Dartmouth College Library, Hanover, NH 03755. Please do not request specific plates.

PLEASE NOTIFY THE EDITOR WHENEVER YOU CHANGE YOUR ADDRESS   * * *

AS of BC & D
Bookplates in the News

AUDREY SPENCER ARELLANES, Editor

SILKSCREEN EX LIBRIS BY JOANN SAARNIIT
by Emil Eerme, Canada

Joann Saarniit is a very active Toronto-based artist. During his over
forty years as an artist, he has shown his works in more than 100 exhibitions, thirty of which were one-man shows. Before World War II, he
exhibited in Estonia, Finland, and the USSR. After the war, his showings
traveled as far as Sweden, England, Canada, and the United States.

Joann Saarniit was born in free Estonia, where he studied commercial and
fine art at the Estonian State School of Art in Tallinn, graduating in
1932 and receiving his Master of Decorative Painting diploma in 1939.
After World War II, in Finland he started painting his memories of the war
inspired mostly by the horrors witnessed during the war days and in a
prison camp. The first exhibition of works on these themes was arranged
in Stockholm, Sweden.

He arrived in Canada in 1948 and
organized numerous exhibitions of
his work in Halifax, Montreal,
Toronto, Vancouver, etc. In the
United States he exhibited in Buffalo, Baltimore, Boston, New York,
Lakewood.

Three years ago he retired from
his position of 27 years as art
director at Wolfe Bros. Industrial
Advertising Co. in Toronto. Since
then his own art has been his full
time occupation.

His works today command attention
with their powerful messages por-
traying color-rich Canadian landscapes, people in daily work and
life, with his most recent paintings based on historic Sumerian
motifs, executed in a high relief
technique.

Joann Saarniit has always been greatly interested in the graphic arts, where he especially favors silkscreen processes. From 1950 to 1980, he has been commissioned to design over fifty ex libris. In the ex libris he creates a symbolic portrait of the owner, depicting the latter's interests or profession, and combined with an innovative typographical design of the name, a fascinating composition results. Since the artist

prints these ex libris himself, he makes a limited edition of 100, thereby making them a rare and difficult item for collectors to obtain. The majority of Saarniit's ex libris have been designed for Estonian-Canadians and their various organizations; they have been displayed at special ex libris exhibitions and in public libraries across Canada. In addition to ex libris, he has done many designs and calligraphy of diplomas and honorary certificates, cards, posters, single and series editions.

His works are found in many permanent collections and in private collections alike. Some can be found in Canada House in London, England; the

Chicago TRIBUNE, USA; Canron Canada; S. J. Zacks; Albion Hanson in Sweden; The Estonian House in Toronto, and the Royal Tower in Toronto, where he has a mural 8' x 20'. His ex libris are on permanent exhibition at the Estonian House Gallery in Toronto.

Saarniit is a member of several art organizations: Ontario Institute of Painters, Multicultural Art Society of Ontario, Estonian Art Society, Estonian Arts Centre.

Joann Saarniit's studio is located at 567 Roehampton Ave., Toronto, Canada M4P 1S7.

The tipped-in prints have been reproduced offset from the silkscreen originals; unfortunately much of the

impact of the artist's work is lost without the color of the original.

The ex libris for Ernest Jaakson, Consul General in the United States for free Estonia, was done in 1972. In the same year Saarniit designed the plate for Hannes Osa, editor of FREE ESTONIAN, an Estonian newspaper in Toronto; Osa is also a writer and poet. The plate for Mati Saarniit was a gift for the artist's son on his 40th birthday. An earlier plate (1951) was designed for Ilmar Heinsoo, free Estonian Consul in Toronto, which features a viking ship and in the background the Estonian flag in blue, black, and white. (One print tipped-in bottom, left hand side page 350.)

— — — — — — — —

BOOKPLATE LITERATURE

NORDISK EXLIBRIS TIDSSKRIFT, #137, 1980. This is the first issue under the editorship of Klaus Rodel, who succeeded Helmar Fogedgaard. In the English summary, Klaus says: "N.E.T. will present new artists and deal with good quality art of exlibris from earlier periods and also present survey articles showing the art of exlibris in a wider connection. Considerable changes have been made with regard to typography, makeup, and contents. For the sake of the many foreign members of DES the articles will in future be presented in two languages, - in addition to Danish it will be either German or English." Among the articles is a lengthy excerpt from a book about one of Germany's most important ex libris artists, Willi Geiger; it is published by the Nuremberg firm of Hans Carl.

BOOKPLATE SOCIETY (London) ties are now available in two colors: navy blue and cherry red; they are 55" long and 4" wide at the base. The angel and shield design (originally borne as the device of Hildebrand Brandenburg in his early German woodcut ex libris) was selected as best representing the collecting of bookplates and interest in them. The US price is $11 each with air mail postage to North America at $3.20 or $5.50 for two ties. Payment should be made to the Bookplate Society, 3B Hurlingham Court, Ranelagh Gardens, London SW6 3UN, England.

"The Best Practitioner of The Art of Letter Writing" is a catalogue of the Frances W. and H. Jack Lang letter collection in the Department of Special Collections, Case Western Reserve Universities Libraries, Cleveland, OH. The collection was given to the Library in 1977 and includes letters ranging from 1695 (Madame Sévigné) to 1954 (Groucho Marx). H. Jack Lang was editor of THE WOLF MAGAZINE OF LETTERS for 45 years and the author of several books, including LETTERS OF THE PRESIDENTS and THE ROWFANT MANUSCRIPTS. The catalogue illustrations include Lang's bookplate which has his name as a signature as if on an envelope being hand-delivered.

"Collations and Potations" is the title of bookseller Peggy Christian's catalogue on food, drink, and related subjects. Of interest to the bookplate collector is the illustration for item #190, A COLLECTION OF ABOVE THREE HUNDRED RECEIPTS IN COOKERY, PHYSICK AND SURGERY Printed for Richard Wilkin, at the King's Head in St. Paul's Churchyard in 1714. The illustration reproduces in reduced size the bookplate of a former owner, Marion H. Hatch. The ex libris was engraved by Alfred Downey (1935) after Marion Powers; it shows a cookbook opened to a Pumpkin Pie recipe.

THE NEW REVIEW OF BOOKS AND RELIGION, 4:#6, February 1980. Ex Libris are used as illustration throughout this magazine and include those for Frederick Locker, Mysie Craig Robinson, Gordon Craig's for KD dated 1900, an Egyptian design for George Sarton, and the Club of Odd Volumes.

TINY EX LIBRIS produced by Robert E. Massmann, 1979. The open-ended slip case measures 1 1/8" wide by 1 3/16" high, and the edition is limited to 250 copies. Designs are created by Robert and Ernie Massmann and Miss Helene Sherman, calligrapher and illuminator. The label on the cover of this book, which is just over an inch square, is an ex libris for Robert E. Massmann's Non-Lending Library and is shaped like a many faceted diamond. About twenty miniature plates are reproduced; some of the designs were never executed for use. (EDITOR'S NOTE: Audrey Arellanes of the Bookworm Press has been putting aside designs and tip-ins for a book she expects to print entitled BOOKPLATES: SMALL, MINIATURE, AND TINY. If you have examples of ex libris fitting this description, please write and if possible send a print or at least a sharp copy of the bookplate. Interested owners of such plates or artists who have designed them are asked to send 250 prints for tipping-in along with biographical data and details about the collection for which the plate was designed. Those who send prints to be tipped-in will receive one courtesy copy of the book; other contributors will receive a copy at discount. Please write Bookworm Press, 605 N. Stoneman Avenue, Apt. #F, Alhambra, CA 91801.)

MARTIN R. BAEYENS, A. Coucke, published by ExlibRisten, 1979. Multi-lingual text including English. Nine ex libris are printed in earth tones and are combined with silhouettes in white for an interesting composition.

LINZ, Andrusko Karoly, 1980. This is another in the series of miniature books devised by this artist to commemorate the XVIII International Ex Libris Congress to be held in Linz, Austria, during August of 1980. There is no text, but the book consists of 24 small prints showing different buildings and scenes in Linz. (Dawson's Book Shop, 535 N. Larchmont Blvd., Los Angeles, CA 90004. $15 + 6% sales tax in California.)

NEWSLETTER (Calligrafree Corp.), 4:1, May 1980. An insert titled SCRIBE shows the work of Olof Eriksson, a Finish-born calligrapher who worked for many years in the advertising department of a large Helsinki department store.

FOOTNOTES (Northwestern University Library Council, Evanston, IL), Bookplates: Their Place in Books and Philanthropy. (12) 3 unnumbered pages, Spring 1980. A variety of bookplates are illustrated which Northwestern University Library uses to commemorate book gifts given to the library. Some collections or donors have specially designed ex libris. Helen M. Fenton is quoted; for more about her see BOOKPLATES IN THE NEWS, #35:275-78, January 1979.

WESTWAYS, Rare Edition, Ward Ritchie. (5)72:16-9, 77-8, May 1980. Ward Ritchie relates his personal recollections of Paul Landacre. Landacre illustrated Darwin's ON THE ORIGIN OF SPECIES. "One of the illustrations is of a petrel, which he did with especial loving care. Many years before he had been attracted to this bird because of its puny, almost useless legs. He made it his trademark and many of his prints are signed with a small petrel in one corner, printed in red ink. (Editor's Note: The Arellanes article about Paul Landacre in the 1979 YEAR BOOK incorrectly identified the bird as a condor.)

"The Piggott Bequest," by Burton Bernstein origin-ally appeared in THE NEW YORKER for December 18, 1978; a lengthy excerpt was carried by the Los Angeles HERALD EXAMINER late in 1979 under the title "The Hermit of Los Angeles." Charles Piggott was a miser and hermit living in a shack without electricity, gas, or plumb-ing; he was a "closet" reader who made a fortune in the stock market. He willed this fortune to the Bridgewater (CT) Library's

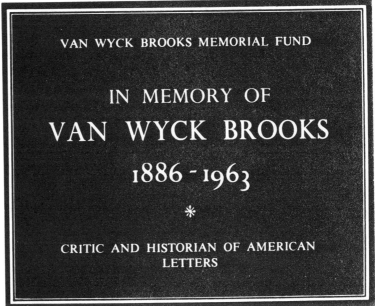

Van Wyck Brooks Memorial. An earlier memorial fund raised money to buy books in the name of the author and created the above ex libris for use in the volumes purchased. The bookplate was kindly sent by Mrs. Kay Ed-wards, librarian of the Burnham Library in Bridgewater. The Piggott Be-quest was nearly $300,000 less taxes, court costs, and attorney's fees.

New York TIMES, Book Reviews, 31, March 9, 1980. PARAGRAPHS ON PRINTING by Bruce Rogers (1870-1957) was originally published in a limited edition in 1943 and has now been reprinted by Dover Publications at $6. Roger's discussions are "illuminated with reproductions of examples of his page and letter designs, decorations and ornaments - and such miscellanea as the bookplate reproduced to the left."

EXLIBRIS WERELD, No. 1, 1980. This is a well produced journal under the editorship of Jan Rhebergen for the ex libris society of the Netherlands. An interesting bookplate for Paul Pfister is illustrated which shows a portrait of Albert Schweitzer and his signature.

DON QUICHOTE IN HET EX LIBRIS, Agatha Heeren, publish-ed in 1978/79. A small, 36-page booklet with text type-written; it is reproduced by the simplest offset method which doubtless does not do justice to many of the ex libris illustrated.

L'EX LIBRIS FRANCAIS, September 1979. Completion of an article by G. Meyer-Noirel and Guy Vaucel on "The Numismatics and Bankers' Bookplates." Articles also on Denis Cartoux's etched bookplate for novelist Robert Sabatier, in-ternational ex libris literature, The Open Weekend in London (June 23-24, 1979.

DOROTHY and JOE GLEASON EX LIBRIS

The Dorothy and Joe Gleason bookplate is an outgrowth of the Gleason created Christmas cards which depicted yearly episodes in the lives of that family. This was the greeting sent to their many friends in 1924 and was transferred to the ex libris classification by simply cutting off the line "Merry Christmas." Duncan made a pen and ink sketch 6"x12½", painted the ocean and solid parts of the vessel with black watercolor and a light shading of pale blue for the foam and more delicate parts of the sails and hull.

The Christmas series ran from 1919, the year of Dorothy and Joe Duncan's marriage, to 1959, the year of Duncan's death. The remaining years, from 1959 to 1979, have portrayed copies of his paintings, arranged by his widow, Dorothy.

Duncan's first art signature was "Joe D. Gleason" but there was another J. D. Gleason in New York so he changed to "J. Duncan Gleason" and finally dropped the J and signed his later works "Duncan Gleason." He was well known for his masterful oil paintings of square-riggers and for his fine draftsmanship and skill in line work, watercolor, and ship model building.

As a team, Duncan and Dorothy Gleason have illustrated and written five books with successful publication results, the etched book "Windjammers," "Islands of California," and "Islands and Ports of California" now being collector's items and difficult to acquire.

As a young man, Duncan Gleason excelled as a gymnast and won numerous awards including the National AAU Rings Championship (11 times between 1907 and 1922), All-Round Gymnastic Champion. He was a student at the Art Students League in New York and began his art career in 1899 with the Sunset Engraving Company. In later years he worked in the art departments of Metro Goldwyn Mayer and Warner Bros.

At the time of his death in 1959, the Los Angeles City Council passed a resolution of regret at the death of such a distinguished artist. He was further remembered by the Thirteenth District of the United States Power Squadrons by the establishment of a "Duncan Gleason Perpetual Memorial Trophy" to be awarded to the Squadron with the finest publication for that year, thus honoring the high ideals represented by Duncan's editorship of the Los Angeles Power Squadron RANGE LIGHT. A fitting tribute appeared in THE BRANDING IRON (June 1974), accompanied by pictures of Gleason as a gymnast, as an artist at the easel in his studio, and two of his paintings.

Arnold Schoenberg Institute
University of Southern California
Los Angeles, California 90007

The composer, Arnold Schoenberg (1874-1951), has been a storm center of controverst since the first performances of his earliest works at the beginning of the twentieth century, and there is no composer of our century who has not confronted the necessity of dealing with Schoenberg's pervasive influence as a force in his own creative life.

Born in Vienna to parents of limited means, if not straightened circumstances, Schoenberg's childhood passed without special notice of any musical interest. The early death of his father further reduced the possibility of providing the cultural advantages characteristic of solid middle- and upper-class Viennese families of the time. Schoenberg's developing interest in music spurred him to teach himself how to play string instruments and the piano, although he never achieved more than amateur standing on any of them. As for theoretical studies, his only teacher was Alexander von Zemlinsky, a composer and conductor, whose sister later became Schoenberg's first wife. Schoenberg considered himself an autodidact and was proud of it. He was avidly interested in literature and art as well. For some years Schoenberg devoted himself to painting rather than composing, and his paintings were shown in the company of the German Expressionists.

Out of a unique constellation of artistic and creative forces in pre-World War I Vienna, Schoenberg's way led him on a journey of discovery into the far reaches of the sound world. His mission carried him far from the comfortable neighborhoods of traditional harmony, through a landscape of increasing dissonance until, finally, with the emancipation of the dissonance, a new equality of the twelve tones of the chromatic scale, the method of composing with twelve tones which are related only with one another, emerged. Derided as a wild-eyed revolutionary, Schoenberg steadfastly clung to his self-proclaimed posture of traditionalism, a continuation of the long line from Bach and Mozart, via Beethoven, to Brahms and beyond.

Driven from Europe by the Nazis, Schoenberg came to the United States in 1933, made his way to Los Angeles by 1936, and remained there for the rest of his life. More fortunate than many of his compatriots, Schoenberg was able to keep his belongings intact and thus, when the Arnold Schoenberg Institute was opened at the University of Southern California in 1977 to house the legacy of this extraordinary man, the richness and variety of his life's accessories were soon apparent.

In addition to the thousands of pages of music and text manuscripts, paintings and drawings, programs, photographs, and newspaper clippings, Schoenberg accumulated a personal library of over two thousand volumes of printed books and music scores. He was an enthusiastic hand binder; for some volumes he even made his own endpapers, and the calligraphy of the spine lettering is often quite elaborate. He also wrote out a detailed catalogue of the books in his personal library.

Among the many objects of Schoenberg's own design, for which he made models, a small piece of paper was found mounted and poorly glued to a rough wooden frame in a box with other creations of his inventive mind. There is nothing to indicate the use for which the design was intended, but the arrangement of the lettering and the spacing strongly suggest a logo. We have adapted it as a bookplate, and we use it in the books and scroes of the collection in the Reading Room. The interlocking initial letters, "A" and "S", create space for the remaining letters of both names. Schoenberg's combinatorial genius as a master of counterpoint is as evident here as it is in his musical compositions.

Clara Steuermann, Archivist
Arnold Schoenberg Institute

-   -   -   -   -   -   -   -   -

SHERLOCKIANA

Gertrude Mahoney had the plate, which is tipped-in to the left, designed for her Sherlockiana collection by Scott Bond. Scott was originally from Plainfield, NJ, and he majored in Art History at Drew University. In 1966 he moved to Philadelphia, where he worked for several advertising agencies before starting his own freelance business. Outstanding examples of his work are the posters he made in 1974, 1975, and 1976 for Ringling Bros., Barnum & Bailey Circus. He and his wife, Sherry Rose, are active in "The Master's Class," the Philadelphia scion of the Baker Street Irregulars, an organization of Sherlock Holmes buffs.

Gertrude Mahoney grew up in Chicago where she attended Northwestern University. In 1943, she moved with her husband and three young children to Oak Park, IL, where they became active in the Art League. It was in Oak Park that they met the remarkable Carl Stephen Junge family, and it was Carl and Fanny who started her collection of bookplates. Gertrude reports that her collection is small and unmounted, but that there are some interesting plates, and of course Carl's are the jewels.

Gertrude is active in "The Red Circle," the Washington, DC, scion of the BSI, and in the "Mini Tonga Society," a group collecting miniatures of Sherlock Holmes interest, such as 1" scale replicas of the Holmes rooms on Baker Street and, of course, miniature editions of Doyle's stories. Jane Berniers and Barbara Rehab have published beautiful leatherbound, readable volumes the size of a postage stamp - but so far no micro bookplates to go in them!

This is Scott Bond's first bookplate design.

van der MUUR COLLECTIONS ON BASEBALL & JAZZ

The bookplates reproduced on the flip-side of this page represent the considerable interest of J. J. van der Muur in baseball and jazz. It was my pleasure to meet this gentleman at the International Ex Libris Congress held in Lugano, Switzerland in August of 1978, and he gave me copies of these plates. I was not familiar with the avid exchange sessions which are a vital part of any Congress and came ill-prepared to make adequate exchanges. However, many European collectors were very generous, as was Mr. van der Muur.

In response to my inquiry for details about the artists who designed the plates and about the collections they represented, Mr. van der Muur wrote as follows: "The diamond shaped baseball plate is made by Lou Strik, born in 1921. The diamond shape is the baseball field. The artist gave the umpire a fancy dress. My interest in baseball started about the time Ruth hit his 700th homer, and I stopped in 1963. I have a small collection of baseball books, including BASEBALL by Dick Siebert, BASEBALL HALL OF FAME by Ken Smith, BABE RUTH by Tom Meany, THE FIRESIDE BOOK OF BASEBALL which Mr. Lowenhaupt (Yale University bookplate collection in the Sterling Library) gave me, and some English and Dutch handbooks about the stuff.

" I have ten different jazz bookplates for my jazz library, which contains a lot of Dutch and English books and some American, such as MR. JELLY ROLL by Alan Lomax, REALLY THE BLUES by Mezz Mezzrow, JAZZMEN by Ramsey, SHINING TRUMPETS by Rudy Blesh, THE STORY OF JAZZ by Stearns, DICTIONARY OF JAZZ and biographies of Armstrong, Ellington, Billy Holiday, Bessy Smith, and others.

" In 1933 I heard Louis Armstrong and Ellington on their tours in Amsterdam; Holland was pretty jazzy then, and I tried to play the trumpet, piano, bass in dixieland bands and there were hundreds of them.

" I was born in 1912 and started my collection about 1939; it contains about 20,000 bookplates and occasional graphics, most of them European. I should like to exchange with American collectors who have good copperengravings, and I prefer ex libris above occasional graphics.

" A long time ago I sent my baseball bookplates to the Baseball Hall of Fame in Cooperstown and asked them if they might have other bookplates in their collection. They answered kindly that they had not and were not further interested. In 1970 my wife and I visited the United States and saw the Yankees beat the Cubs in 'the House that Ruth built'."

Those who may be interested in exchanging with Mr. van der Muur may write to him at Bergkloosterweg 96, 8034 P.S. Swolle, The Netherlands.

— — — — — — — — — —

ELEVENTH YEAR OF PUBLICATION
for BOOKPLATES IN THE NEWS

With this issue BOOKPLATES IN THE NEWS begins its eleventh year of publication, thus surviving longer than many of the English-language periodicals devoted exclusively to the bookplate. The continued support of the members of the American Society of Bookplate Collectors and Designers is much appreciated by the editor, and the editor welcomes contributions for future issues of the quarterly and YEAR BOOK.

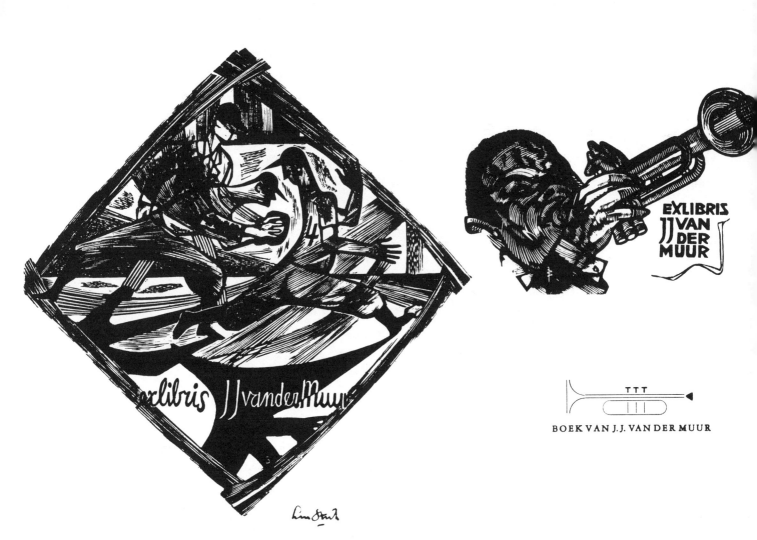

BOEK VAN J. J. VAN DER MUUR

EXLIBRIS JJ VAN DER MUUR

BEREA COLLEGE's WEATHERFORD-HAMMOND APPALACHIAN COLLECTION
AND ITS BOOKPLATE   by Alfred H. Perrin

ABOUT THE BOOKPLATE....
It was decided in 1966 that a bookplate should be designed for the books
in Berea College's extensive Appalachian Collection at Berea, Kentucky.
The artist-designer was James Hayes, then of Evanston, Illinois, now retired but still at the drawing board in Colorado. A graduate of the
Chicago Art Institute School, later a teacher of lettering and calligraphy at the Newberry Library, Chicago, and author of a book on the Roman
letter, he is nationally known as a calligrapher and lettering man.

At the college's suggestion he submitted half a dozen sketch-designs, all
incorporating the college seal as requested. The finished large drawing
was printed by a Chicago firm in 1967. It is being used in over 8,000
books in the Weatherford-Hammond Collection, which is the oldest and one
of the largest in the Southern Appalachian region.

ABOUT THE COLLECTION....
Appalachia, as Berea College has defined this region for the 125 years of
the college's existence, consists of some 240 counties of nine states -
Kentucky, Tennessee, West Virginia, Virginia, North Carolina, South Caro-

lina, Alabama, Georgia, and a small part of Ohio.
It is an area roughly 1,000 miles long and 250
miles wide. Berea College is vitally involved
in these 240 mountain counties because 80% of its
student body of 1,400 call them "home". So this
important library resource deals directly with
the students' "homeland" as well as being known
nationally as an important collection.

Historically the mountain area and its people
have been as distinctive as their regional literature. A critic of seventy years ago said of
the Appalachian people, "Very religious but much
addicted to killing each other." The Kentucky
shootings are usually family, friends, or neighbors, never strangers. Harry Caudill in his
1963 regional classic, "Night Comes to the Cum-
lands" finds the inhabitants of the Cumberland Plateau "among the earth's
most fascinating folk."

All of these things have left their mark in Berea's sixty-year old Weatherford-Hammond Collection of well over 8,000 books and many hundreds of magazine articles, tapes, and photographs. Also included are a large and growing collection of unique primary source materials, the collected Archives
of many mountain organizations and individuals.

The "earth's most fascinating folk" have been favorite subjects of fiction
writers since the 1830's and Berea has examples from all decades. Here is
evidence of how 20th century authors have fashioned a two-dimensional caricature of the mountaineer as shiftless, silent, proud, hospitable, and as
quick with his feuding gun as he was slow with his tongue. This caricatured
hillbilly mountain man like the courtly Southern planter, the woebegone
plantation hand, and the fictional cowboy and Indian is all too often the

figment of an over-active typewriter.

Mountain backgrounds and mountain folk have always provided colorful story material. In Berea's collection are more than 1,000 fiction books by mountain authors or with scenes laid in the southern mountains. It is surprising to many to note that these books were not written to be read by the people of the mountains whose traditional family library consists of one book, the Bible. The novels and short stories were written to be read by outsiders, the "flatlanders", the novel-reading public. But taken in sequence through the years, they are a remarkable example of how fiction was written and read from 1834 to 1980.

The Weatherford-Hammond bookplate, designed in 1966, is the proud symbol of a definitive regional book and manuscript collection and of a library now celebrating its 110th year in 1980.

___ ___ ___ ___ ___ ___ ___

NAPA VALLEY WINE LIBRARY

(The following is in part from BOTTLES AND BINS, 31: July 1979.)

A pamphlet was published in the early 1960's by the Napa Valley Wine Library giving the background and a bit of history of the initiation of this endeavor.

The collection known as the Napa Valley Wine Library was embodied as a department of the St. Helena Public Library (California) but with its own finances. The initial impetus to this endeavor came in 1961 when Francis L. Gould made a direct appeal to individuals and organizations in the Napa Valley and adjacent area for funds and books. Early in 1962, well over a hundred volumes and nearly as many pamphlets and periodicals had been assembled, already constituting a useful working library. A large number of these came from private collections. The University of California at Davis donated an impressive list. The broad policy of the Napa Valley Wine Library is to collect books, pamphlets, periodicals and other printed matter on the subject of wine, with emphasis on California material in general; wine labels (past and present); material from various wineries; photographs; correspondence, and all else that might be useful to research. Fiction, poetry, wine lore, history, wine cookery, viticulture and wine technology will be included.

The bookplate illustrated above was designed by the late Kate Griswold of St. Helena for the Napa Valley Wine Library.

BOOKPLATES IN THE NEWS   Published: January/April/July/October
605 N. Stoneman Ave. #F, Alhambra, CA 91801 Membership $10 / $12 Overseas

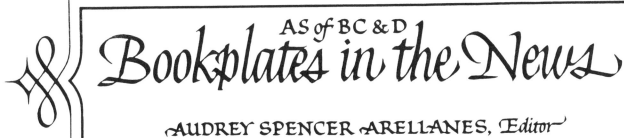

A SMALL ENGLISH LIBRARY IN JAPAN
By Cliff Parfit

Shimonoseki is on the westernmost tip of the main island of Japan and separated only by a narrow strait from Kyushu. From early times the fishing
port of Shimonoseki was important in Japanese history. Today it is a thriving
city, beautifully sited
on the south-facing coast
of the Kanmon Strait. To
sit at night in the re-
volving restaurant on the
top of Hinoyama (Fire
Mountain, where signal
fires were lighted in
olden days) is an unfor-
gettable experience. Far
below, one can see the
lights of the ships and
of the busy harbor of Moji
across the water, and
then above the ships the
graceful curve of the
Kanmon bridge outlined in
lights (one of the world's
major bridges which con-
nects Shimonoseki with
Kyushu).

It is far from the heady delights of Tokyo, but the air is pure, the people
are curteous, and the scenery beautiful. The crime rate is negligible, and
the girls are the prettiest in Japan.

One of the small places, now virtually suburbs, under the wing of Shimonoseki
City, is the ancient and comfortable village of Chofu. Here on high land over-
looking the village is the English Centre (Igiris Kan in the local dialect).
There are two buildings; one "old" building (nearly four years old now) in the
Japanese style, and a "new" building which is a functional concrete block.

The Centre is independent and entirely free from any religious or government
affiliation. The work undertaken is translation, business advice, and the

teaching of the English language at various levels. The staff is a mixture of Japanese and English nationals.

The library is in the "old" building. It is a large, quiet room lined with teak bookcases. The main collection is of books in European languages about Japan during the period 1850 to 1900, without doubt the most important and exciting half century in the history of the country. There are all the expected books, such as those by Golownin Perry and Oliphant, and then the many other books of Voyages to Japan and around Japan in the eighteen fifties and sixties.

The Meiji revolution took place with astonishing speed. In 1850 the repressive system of government designed by Tokugawa Ieyasu was still in full swing, though creaking a little. Men in armour were guarding ancient castles, and the principal weapon of war was still the sword. By 1860 the Tokugawa system was beginning to come apart, and by 1870 it was all over. Swords were museum pieces almost overnight, and the samurai changed their armor for morning coats and striped trousers. It is the object of the collection to chronicle all these changes in the original books, newspapers, and magazines of the period. One cannot but marvel at the taste and skill of the editors and publishers who produced what were, on the whole, such beautiful and interesting books.

Also included in the library are collections of English illustrated books, English classics, and, of course, hundreds of necessary reference books. Then there are collections of early postcards, early checks and bank notes, early European games, Japanese paper, etc.

The collection of ex libris was formed to give Japanese collectors first-hand experience of European and American ex libris and vice versa. With the help of part-time workers and some of the staff, we have produced hand-made books to illustrate the work of living Japanese ex libris artists and have also produced a short history of the ex libris in Japan.

Of course, bookplates are used also to embellish most of the books.

The first design of an oak tree was produced for Cliff Parfit, director of the Centre, by Maureen and Gordon Gray, a Scottish husband and wife team which illustrated many of his books for children. Originally it was printed in black but is now printed in sepia on handmade Japanese paper.

The next "oak tree" is by Henno Arrak of Estonia, who has managed to convey the youthful alertness and very feminine charm of the oak tree goddess in a signified bookplate, which he very much enjoyed making. Some further oak tree designs are in the offing and may be shown on a future occasion.

The printing press ex libris is used on a number of very old books in the library. It is designed by Peter Hosokawa, a very lively designer of Takamatsu City in Japan. Peter is a lover of incunabula as well as being a most capable and inventive designer. The plate is printed on handmade paper.

The amusing block ship bookplate was produced by Motoi Yanagida. Black ship was the name given by the Japanese to the early American steanships of Commodore Perry. These bookplates are used in many books of American voyages to Japan.

The paddle steamer bookplate, also printed on washi (Japanese handmade paper) is printed directly from a block more than a hundred years old. The plate is used for volumes of British voyages to Japan, but the age of the block shows, and an attempt is being made to produce a facsimile block from a good handpulled impression.

The leaf bookplates are the work of the Sekishu washi handcraft paper mills of Tsuwano prefecture, Japan. These plates are used for Japanese handmade books and books about folk crafts, etc.

Various other bookplates are used for special collections.

The main bookplate collection is of engraved plates and books about bookplates of the period 1890-1920 in Europe and America, and there are many duplicates in the various collections which could be made available for exchange for plates of this period.

American bookplate lovers who are visiting Japan are most welcome to call (telephone 0832-45-9285). The address for correspondence is: English Centre, Private P. O. Box, Chofu, Shimonoseki City 752, Japan.

FROM THE BOOKPLATE LITERATURE

LOS ANGELES TIMES, For Bibliophiles, the elaborate art and craft of bookplates, Nancy Belcher. (1) 3, 13, October 3, 1980. A former member of the ASBC&D, freelance writer Nancy Belcher, did a general interest article on ex libris for the Sunday Book Review section of the TIMES. The single illustration is of the plate of Rudolph Valentino, which features a crusader astride a white steed in the midst of battle; the sharp blacks and white of the plate reproduce well on newsprint, which would not be the case with an engraved or etched plate of perhaps greater artistic merit. The ASBC&D and its director Audrey Arellanes are given "good press" and the article definitely reached an interested audience as evidenced by several applications for membership.

MANUSCRIPTS, "The Household Poet" Royally Rebuffed: Bernard Barton and George IV, James D. Birchfield. (1) 32:28-34, Winter 1980. Illustrated is the bookplate for the Childhood in Poetry collection of John MacKay Shaw in the Robert Manning Strozier Library at Florida State University.

MANUSCRIPTS, News Notes, Paul G. Sifton. 32:125, Spring 1980. Through the generosity of the Mount Vernon Ladies' Association of the Union, a four-volume set of Lord Chesterfield's letters of advice to his son has been acquired for Mount Vernon. The volumes were once "owned by George Washington" and bear his bookplate.

MANUSCRIPTS, Benjamin Douglas Silliman and the Fine Art of Book Annotation, J. Kevin Graffagnino. (2) 32:191-6, Summer 1980. One of the illustrations is the heraldic ex libris of Benjamin D. Silliman.

TURNBULL LIBRARY RECORD (Wellington, New Zealand), Alexander Turnbull's Bookplates, Penelope Griffith. (10) 12:105-12, October 1979. Ten of Turnbull's ex libris are illustrated; some were printed in more than one size. The artists who designed his plates included Walter Crane, D. H. Souter, C. Praetorius, pseudonym for the artist of the Maori whale design.

Miniature
Bookplates

MICROBIBLIOPHILE, Miniature Bookplates. (1) 4:14, September 1980. Pictured to the right are the ex libris offered by Barbara J. Rahab (Dept. M, Box 7563, Van Nuys, CA 91409) at a cost of $1 for four sheets of six miniature plates each. They are printed on white gummed paper and allow space to add your name or initials.

BARBARA J. RAHEB
BOX 7563, VAN NUYS, CALIFORNIA 91409

AMERICAN PRINTING HISTORY ASSOCIATION, Bookplates Wanted for Journal Cover. No. 36,5, 1980. "Each issue of the JOURNAL OF LIBRARY HISTORY uses as a cover illustration a bookplate having some significance to the history of libraries." Usually 300 to 800 words of text explain about the cover illustration. If you have an appropriate bookplate, please write Donald G. Davis, Jr., Editor, Graduate School of Library Science, P.O. Box 7576, University Station, University of Texas at Austin, Austin, TX 78712.

THE ENGLISH-SPEAKING UNION NEWS, Books Across the Sea. 27:6, Summer 1980. Pictured is the plate designed by Diana Bloomfield for the E-SU's Books-Across-The-Sea program, founded by Beatrice Ward during World War II. It is one of the illustrations in Brian North Lee's BRITISH BOOKPLATES: A PICTORIAL HISTORY.

AMERICAN LIBRARIES, Minding the Miniatures, Edith McCormick. (5) 11:161-4, March 1980. One illustration shows "THE MARVELOUS MINIATURE LIBRARY, a collection of six classics bearing Stanley Marcus's bookplate." Each miniature is 2 by 1½" and all six are carried in a leatherette case with a pocket for each. Such a case was popular for 19th century stagecoach reading.

AMERICAN BOOKPLATES in an ENGLISH DRAWER
by J. P. T. Bury

Looking recently through some papers which had belonged to one of my god-mothers, I came across a number of envelopes variously inscribed with the words "Scrap book" or "Bookplates" or "Ex Libris." In one of them were two letters from the United States, one undated and the other of 8 March 1900, and a cache of American bookplates. The letters had been addressed to my god-mother's husband, Andrew White Tuer, and his American correspondents were George May Elwood and Wilbur Macey Stone. Eighty years later, this "find" is perhaps worth a brief note in BOOKPLATES IN THE NEWS.

A. W. Tuer (1838-1900) was a north countryman who found his way to London, and in 1863 went into partnership with a man named Robert Field as a printer and stationer. After some years, the partners branched into publishing, calling their firm Field and Tuer and, later, the Leadenhall Press. Although Field may have provided the financial backing, Tuer appears to have been the driving force behind the firm's activities. He patented a glue called "stick-phast" which had wide sales; he became the father of what has been termed the "Antique Pringing Movement;" he supplied jokes for various PUNCH artists of his acquaintance; he wrote a number of books, some of which are alluded to in the two American letters mentioned above; and he was an omnivorous collector.

Among the collectable objects which naturally enough attracted his attention as a printer and publisher, interested in design, were bookplates. He was one of the earliest members of the British Ex Libris Society and for some years served on its Council until ill health obliged him to resign. Like many collectors of bookplates, he also devised his own and, as the obituary notice printed in volume X of the JOURNAL OF THE EX LIBRIS SOCIETY recorded, "possessed several uncommon bookplates, illustrative of his own peculiar ido-syncrasies - the latest . . . . depicting a cheval glass" reflecting his name and the date 1900. Earlier, in 1895, he had presented to the Society a sheet containing two somewhat whimsical designs, one showing a broken willow plate and the other a suggestion for an Ex Libris Collectanea label. The designs for these, as for the one of the cheval glass, were executed by a well-known illustrator of the day, Ambrose Dudley.

The first of Tuer's two American correspondents, G. M. Elwood, was, I under-stand from Mrs. Arellanes, a major American collector, who also, in 1895 or 1896, became a member of the British Ex Libris Society. The address at the head of his undated letter was Box 124, Rochester, N.Y., and the letter ran as follows:

My Dear Sir:

Some time since you were good enough to send me your book-plate in exchange for several of my own, and some others, that I sent you. I have just had completed a new plate by Mr. Harry Ellis of this city and as I like it better than my old one I venture to send it to you and trust that you will like it, and I also send two or three other little plates that I do not think I sent you before. May I ask that you will favor me with two or three of your plates in exchange. I want them for a young lady collector of this city who engraved the Ellwanger plate herewith - Miss Mary Dodds.

If I have sent you any of the enclosed plates before do not

trouble to return them. You can pass them along to some other collector.

Very sincerely yours,
George May Elwood

A postscript added: I picked up at an old book stall in Norfolk recently a first edition of OLD LONDON STREET CRIES by A.W.T. It is in perfect condition and I would not take its weight in gold for the quaint little treasure. G.M.E.

The enclosures included four specimens of Elwood's new bookplate in two different sizes, one of each size printed in brown, the other two in black, and one in black of the "Ellwanger" plate. This is a splendid period piece depicting a lady voluptuously seated on a many cushioned settee, her right arm caressing a peacock whose long tail sweeps down to the inscription at the bottom of the plate - "her book Florence Cornelia Ellwanger". They also included one of Rochester Arts School, one of The Reynolds Library 1884 (which a note by Elwood on the back explained was "Rochester N.Y. Public Library" by Tiffany); one of Geo. P. Humphry of Rochester, noted as "an adaptation of an old frontier mark;" and one of Harold Chandler Kimball Jr. by Ellis. This was noted as having been reproduced and described in the "Ex Lib Journal in 1897."

The letter of 8 March 1900 from Wilbur Macey Stone, an engineer and well known writer on bookplates, of 13 Murray Street, New York City, was unhappily never seen by the man to whom it was addressed, for A. W. Tuer had died nearly a fortnight earlier, on 24 February. The letter began by paying tribute to Tuer's "very delgihtful work in preserving the memory of so much of the literature for the children of the long ago," mentioned the works by Tuer that he, Stone, possessed, and continued: "Just now I'm preparing a little paper on Children's Bookplates and ask if you will be so good as to note down any you may know of in England for me (sic) enlightenment and if you possibly have any duplicates of such I would much appreciate them. I am pleased to hand you herewith a few recent American plates, some of which I perpetrated."

The bookplates enclosed, apart from two of his own, included the following which Stone himself had "perpetrated" in the preceding two or three years: 1897 - Circulating Library of E. M. Sill of Hartford; 1898 - Gertrude Hyde and Arthur Duane Newton; Charles Burke Elliott "after an old print;" the office library of Francis H. Richards; 1899 - Isabel van Kleeck Lyon; and 1900 - George M. Stone, presumably a relation and, from the inscription, a devine or theologian.

The other American plates in the "cache" are of uncertain provenance, since some of the contents of A. W. Tuer's envelopes have become mixed over the years, and there are no conveniently pencilled notes on the backs. Two, however, were designed or engraved by Jay Chambers, one for Herbert Hale Taylor, the other for Howe Williams. Both bear the date MDCCC, which looks as though he had inadvertently gotten the wrong century! Of the remaining few, the most attractive is one bearing the name Mary Hey Shaffner.

I do not know how extensive A. W. Tuer's collection of bookplates was or how many American plates it included. Some may have been sold or given away immediately after his death, but others remained with the miscellaneous treasures of his London house in Campden Hill Square until after my god-mother's death. Then, on 27 June 1927, Sotheby's sale of books from the Tuer library included as Lot 31 a vellum album containing "over 300 book-plates, book-labels, ect. (including duplicates), mostly modern, some with autograph letters from their owners (including Frederick Locker, Linley Sambourne and Grant Allen)" and also a "large number of book-plates and correspondence referring to them loose in envelopes." The lot was purchased by someone named Thorp for £8. 5. 0. and by now its contents, including the Americana, may well have been dispersed to the four corners of the Ex Libris world.

•————————————————————•

THE JUNIOR BOOKPLATE SOCIETY, Newsletter #7, September 1980. Two junior members (under age 18) of the English Bookplate Society have published their own newsletter. This is the last issue under the editorship of Emma Rose Barber and Elisabeth Fortheringham, both of whom will be 18 shortly. Emma Rose and Elisabeth are to be congratulated. It may be hoped that both young editors will continue their enthusiasm for bookplates and write more about their discoveries of ex libris prints and artists, as represented by their articles "My Recent Bookplate Acquisitions" by E.R.B. and "Sidney Lewis-Ransom" by E.F. in the most recent issue of their newsletter. The final article in this issue is by Philip Beddingham, a senior and sustaining member of the Bookplate Society, titled "Bookplates Afloat" and tells about the White Star Line's ex libris for the OCEANIC, which pictures the launch of the steamship.

•————————————————————————•

N O T I C E S for M E M B E R S

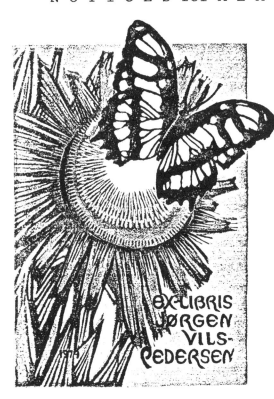

We regret to report the death of Jørgen Vils-Pedersen. A memorial note will appear in the next issue of BOOKPLATES IN THE NEWS.

Also there will be a report of the International Ex Libris Congress in Linz.

MEMBERSHIP DUES for 1981: $27.50

Includes YEAR BOOK 1980 and BOOKPLATES IN THE NEWS 1981

The YEAR BOOK features Keith Clark's article on Robert Anning Bell with a descriptive checklist of his bookplates.

•————————————————————•

BOOKPLATES IN THE NEWS
605 N. Stoneman Ave. #F
Alhambra, CA 91801
Annual Membership $10

BRITISH BOOKPLATES - Special Offer -- Members of ASBC&D may obtain a copy of Brian North Lee's BRITISH BOOKPLATES at a 20% discount from the publisher. This excellent volume was reviewed by George Swarth in an earlier issue of BOOKPLATES IN THE NEWS; 160 pages, 9 x 12 3/4, 261 illustrations, $40. At 20% plus $1 for postage and handling, you may obtain your copy by writing to Lynne Howell, Promotions, David & Charles, Inc., North Pomfret, VT 05053, identify yourself as a member of the ASBC&D, and enclose check for $33.00.

Lytton Strachey Ex Libris

The print to the left was found in Leon Edel's BLOOMSBURY - A HOUSE OF LIONS, which details the lives of this creative group including Virginia and Leonard Wolf, Maynard Kenyes, Clive Bell, Roger Fry, Lytton Strachey, and other lesser known members, such as Carrington.

"Lytton, in his education of Carrington, compared himself to the centaur Cheiron, who in Greek mythology was an immortal. Where other centaurs were primitive and barbaric, Cheiron was wise and learned. Children of famous Greeks appeared at his cave to be reared by him--Jason, Achilles, Asclepius, Actaeon. On having the Cheiron myth explained to her, Carrington designed Lytton's bookplate: the bearded centaur holds a bow with his left hand; his right hand is on the right shoulder of a young Amazonian woman. She kneels beside him and has her hand on the bow as well, and it is she who is drawing the bowstring."

Strachey is, perhaps, best known for his volume of biographies, EMINENT VICTORIANS. BLOOMSBURY is available as an Avon paperback for those who may want to know more these creative individuals who contributed to the arts, literature, and the economic/political theories of the period following the turn of the century.

PETRY BELA GRAFIKAI - This is a portfolio of eight illustrations for ancient fairy tales and three additional sheets (all 11" x 14") containing eleven tipped-in bookplates printed offset. The graphics for the fairy tales would make handsome framed prints; there is some text on each in Hungarian, which is translated into English on the back, where also is given the actual dimensions of the original drawing. Bela (Albert) Petry was born in Hungary in 1902. Educated as an artist and architect, he held an academic position with the University of Debrecen in Hungary, was a portrait painter in Munich, and came to the United States where in 1947 he settled in Boston. He has been an art designer, architect, and consulting engineer.

His publications include "100 Ex Libris by Petry" (Budapest, 1929), "Monumental Architecture Mayas-Incas-Egyptains," and Hungarian Fairy Tales. He has illustrated fourteen books; as an architect he has worked on churches, shopping centers, libraries, malls, and shrines.

To order this portfolio, please write Bela Petry, 331 Sandspur Road, Maitland, Florida 32751. Price $15 + $1 shipping for a total of $16.

AS of BC & D
Bookplates in the News
1206 N. STONEMAN AVENUE #15, ALHAMBRA, CALIFORNIA, 91801 U.S.A.
AUDREY SPENCER ARELLANES, Editor

NUMBER FORTY-THREE   JANUARY 1981

CZESLAW MILOSZ - 1980 Nobel Prize Winner

Czeslaw Milosz was born June 30, 1911 in Lithuania. His father was a civil engineer, who traveled to Siberia to work on the River Yenisey, and was drafted into the Russian army during 1914-18. After the war, the family returned to Lithuania and in 1921 Czeslaw entered high school in Vilnius, at the time the city was incorporated into Poland. His first poetry was published in 1931 and the following year he was the co-founder of the literary periodical ZAGARY.

In 1934 he received a degree of Master of Law. He continued to publish his poetry, spent time in Paris on a fellowship, and in 1937 was forced to move for political reasons from Vilnius to Warsaw. His travels extended to Italy, and it was during this time that he began work with Polish Radio. During WWII he was a writer in the Warsaw Resistance; afterwards (1946-50) he was in the diplomatic service of People's Poland.

The decade beginning with 1951 was spent in France after his break with the Warsaw government; he wrote further poetry, a novel, and his works appeared in translation in various countries. By

EX LIBRIS

CZESŁAW MIŁOSZ

1960 he was a lecturer in Polish Literature at the University of California in Berkeley. When he was offered tenure at the university, he accepted and has remained at Berkeley since then. At the time of being awarded the Nobel prize, Hugh A. Mulligan, Associated Press special correspondent, described Milosz as "awesome in front of a class. His students tend to perceive him as one of those polymathical Europeans whose intellect is so compelling that you just have to listen."

The bookplate illustrated was made as a gift for Milosz by V. O. Virkau, who says: "I distantly knew the author and he hailed from the same geographical area as I do. The church on the bookplate is that of St. Anne's, a lovely north-gothic structure in Vilnius, the capital of Lithuania, where Milosz spent much time in his youth and attended the University there. The tree is an oak, which has a variety of traditional links with the past pagan religion of that region." V. O. Virkau is a member of the American Society of Bookplate Collectors and Designers.

INSTITUTIONAL BOOKPLATES DON'T HAVE TO BE DULL

The bookplates reproduced below are examples of institutional plates which reveal the vitality which can be generated by simple graphics. These represent some of the special collections at the University of Texas, Austin. BOOKPLATES IN THE NEWS would welcome examples of good graphics for unusual collections at other institutional libraries for reproduction in future issues.

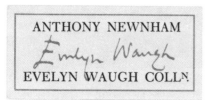

THE UNIVERSITY OF TEXAS
COLLECTION

One of the happy consequences of the recent article about the Society in the Los Angeles TIMES was a letter from John H. Stone, designer of the bookplate for Paul Sehm.

John describes Paul as appearing much the way he does on the bookplate - red-bearded, balding, chubby, 5'6", and in his mid-thirties. His interests include motorcycles, sewing, and cabinet making. He is an Egyptologist, who studied and lectured at UCLA. Paul was three years in Japan when he served in the navy, and was among the first servicemen to go to Vietnam.

The cat in the bookplate is named Michael Mouse, after a character from TALES OF THE CITY by Armistead Maupin. They are alike: both are pushy, in a likeable way. John wrote: "We thought it ironic to name a cat 'mouse.' He's an orange tabby."

John Stone, a few years younger than his friend Paul, and a few inches taller at 5"10", has a brown beard, wears glasses. By profession he is a set designer for the theatre. John and Paul have been friends for four years. In addition to friendship they share twin afflictions: hearing impairment and dyslexia.

If you are interested in writing the artist, John H. Stone's address is: 5317 Satsuma, North Hollywood, CA 91601.

Book Review: LITHUANIAN BOOKPLATES, Vitolis E. Gengris

LITHUANIAN BOOKPLATES, Vitolis E. Vengris. (Chicago: Lithuanian Library Press, Inc. and Loyola University Press, 1980. $22.00) This is a large (10¼" x 11¼"), handsomely bound book of 250 pages with more than 100 reproductions of bookplates which trace the 500-year history of this art form, and an additional 300 reproductions of ex libris designed by contemporary Lithuanian artists. Forty-four artists are represented, among them eight women, and three of the artists are Lithuanian-Americans: R. Viesulas, V. O. Virkau, V. K. Jonvnas.

There is a portrait of each artist, brief biographical text in English and Lithuanian, and examples of their bookplate designs which are coded by the international code of bookplate techniques (i.e., Cl steel engraving, C3 etching, P7 offset, T typographic, etc.). The bibliography of more than 60 items contains all major publications and writings on Lithuanian bookplates from the European, Lithuanian, and American press; even a BOOKPLATES IN THE NEWS reference!

The ex libris is a highly developed and popular art form in Lithuania, and modern artists have explored this art form through a widely varied number of styles and techniques. They frequently enter their work in international exhibitions and have achieved recognition through numerous awards.

Copies of this valuable addition to bookplate literature may be obtained by sending $22 to Lithuanian Library Press, Inc., 3001 West 59th Street, Chicago, IL 60629.

The author, Vitolis E. Vengris, is a member of the American Society of Book-Plate Collectors and Designers; a Lithuanian by birth, he currently lives in Washington, D.C. Vitolis has written a number of articles on bookplate art and has furthered interest in Lithuanian ex libris artists in the United States through lectures and exhibitions. While bookplates are a major interest, Vengris is a scientist by profession with a speciality in virology. The picture of the author which appears on the dust jacket of the book shows a handsome, bearded young man.

EXHIBIT - Bookplates by Lithuanian
Artists Featured

An unusual exhibit of miniature graphics was displated at Galerija (Chicago) from November 21 to December 6, 1980. Ex Libris is an exhibit of bookplates by 34 Lithuanian artists from the collection of Chicagoan Gintautas Vezys. Most of the artists live in Lithuania and have designed these bookplates for Lithuanian, European, and American clients.

The 20th century Lithuanian artists represented in this exhibit revealed their individual styles and the specific interests of the book owners. LITHUANIAN BOOKPLATES by Vitolis E. Vengris, a book recently published in English and Lithuanian, features the works on display along with many other examples of the art form. (See review above.)

EXHIBIT: The Whitney Halstead Memorial Exhibition was at the School of the Art Institute of Chicago Gallery, October 3-31, 1980, and at the Rockford College, November 6-23, 1980. Included in the exhibit were two prints by Vytautas O. Virkau for Whitney B. Halstead and Miyoko Ito; both are offset prints from collage.

The Green Tiger Press (7458 La Jolla Blvd., La Jolla, CA 92037) offers 20 different one-color bookplates featuring the illustrations of such artists as Arthur Rackham, Walter Crane, Margaret Ely Webb, and nine full color ex libris with examples from the work of Maxfield Parrish, Kay Nielsen, Beatrix Potter. All have the well-established Green Tiger Press quality. The print by Edwin Davis French is a well-known classic; while bookplates are seldom copyrighted, it seems out of place to see a classic created for a specific owner reappearing as a stock plate with a blank area for any purchaser to write in his or her name.

LEWIS PLATE by GOINES

Jim Lewis, a native of Los Angeles, is by profession a college instructor at Los Angeles Trade Technical College. He graduated from Art Center College of Design and, for some 15 years before entering teaching, worked as a commercial photographer.

His collecting interests include fine photography, books, bookplates, and material on 19th and early 20th century American organ building. He writes a bi-monthly newsletter for the Organ Historical Society.

One of Lewis' personal bookplates is the circular one here reproduced, which was designed and printed by David Lance Goines of the Saint Heironymous Press, Berkeley, in 1974. David Goines is well-known for his imaginative posters which he designs and prints himself in limited editions. Because of the many subtle changes in color and value, some of his posters require up to thirty separate applications of ink. Goines works in solid colors; he makes the design or drawing in line and then fills in the color on the press. "I recall one poster on which the value of a color tapers from light to dark, but this, I believe, is the only one where this happens," says Jim Lewis.

Goines' work is highly collectable and has been reproduced in many publications including an extensive spread in COMMUNICATION ARTS. In 1977 Goines had a retrospective showing at the Palace of the Legion of Honor in San Francisco. His publications include books on calligraphy and a recipe series calligraphed and illustrated.

EXHIBITION CATALOGUE - ROBERT AUSTIN, An exhibition of etchings, engravings, drawings, and watercolours, February 16 to March, 1980, Ashmolean Museum, Oxford, England. This 41-page catalogue has a brief appreciation of the artist, a biographical chronology (1895-1973), bibliography, the 102 items exhibited are annotated (#48 through #59 are bookplates and the ex libris of the Prime Minister's Library is reproduced), additional works through #153 are listed as well his work as a war artist. Copies may be obtained for $5 from Craddock & Barnard's, 32 Museum Street, London WClA 1LN, England.

ANTIQUARIAN BOOK MONTHLY REVIEW, The Library in Gray's Inn, Philip Beddingham. (8) 7:390-7, August 1980. Beddingham, Librarian for Gray's Inn and active in the English Bookplate Society, gives interesting details that led to the establishment and growth of this historic library. One illustration is the ex libris of Gray's Inn Library, showing the griffin, the badge of the Inn.

THE LANGUAGE OF GRAPHICS, Edward Booth Clibborn and Daniele Baroni. (New York: Harry N. Abrams, $35) This is a large, thick volume with an early section titled "Seal, Symbol, Ex Libris." Only ex libris reference are six Italian plates reproduced from first two decades of this century; specific artist de Carolis.

Jørgen Vils-Pedersen in memoriam

On March 16, 1980, one of the most active collectors in Denmark, indeed, all Europe, died completely unexpectedly - Jørgen Vils-Pedersen, only 44 years old. In him the Danish bookplate community lost its keenest member.

JVP - this monogram repeatedly encountered was the embodiment of the bookplate collector. It could hardly be avoided that in his eagerness for new bookplates that some of them did not measure up to the highest artistic level but mistakes of this kind fade in comparison with the enthusiasm and diligence he exercised as a collector.

He was prominent not only as a collector, but also as the author of publications, checklists, exchange lists, etc. His address register was probably the most up-to-date and comprehensive list in the north due to the precision and accuracy he gained in his work in the Personnel Department of the Royal Library in Copenhagen. His home in Copenhagen was open to collectors and artists of faraway lands.

In the short time since his death, about ten new bookplates have been created for him. Such are the two two-color serigraphs created by Eduardo Dias Ferreira of Portugal and included herein as a memorial to an enthusiastic collector. It will be difficult to see the Linz Congress without him. He will be sorely missed.

by Klaus Rodel

The above was translated by Richard Schimmelpfeng from EX LIBRIS REVUE.

COLLECTIONS AVAILABLE   COLLECTION OF MEXICAN EX LIBRIS OFFERED: Libros Latinos (P.O. Box 1103, Redlands, CA 92373) offers for sale a collection of Mexican Bookplates numbering about 300 and covering primarily the 19th and 20th centuries, though there are earlier examples; numerous famous Mexican historical and literary personalities are included. The bookplate collection is mounted between pieces of glass. For additional details, please contact George F. Elmendorf of Libros Latinos.

LARGE PAPER ARTIST'S PROOFS: About thirty large-paper prints of German-born born etcher Charles F. W. Mielatz are for sale. Mielatz, born in 1860, had his first exhibition of etchings in 1884 and was considered the "dean of American etchers." Among the bookplates being offered are those designed for Ralph and Frederica Pulitzer, Otto Kochl, and Frederica Vandervilt Webb; some of the designs are without names. For details, write directly to Mrs. Margaret B. Phelps, 8863 Via Andar, San Diego, CA 92122 or telephone (714) 455-7628. Lot Price $1,000.00.

COLLECTION of some 5,200 bookplates assembled in the 1920s and early 30s by a distinguished Portuguese gentleman, Nuno Smith de Vasconcellos, who is said to have scoured the globe for it, sparing no expense in his quest. They were sold in Cincinnati some 15 years ago from his estate. The collection is comprised of 50 uniform, custom bound volumes (7½" x 11"); most of the specimens are attached at the top of descriptive pages. In addition to an impressive number of plates from Portugal, Brazil, and the United States, most every major nation in Europe is well represented. The brilliance, variety, inventiveness, and artistry displayed throughout the collection defy a brief description. Many are signed on the plate as well as in pencil by notable artists, and they run a broad gamut of incredible sophistication, romanticism, and the macabre. Write or call - Belinda Kremer, P.O. Box 8515, Stanford, CA 94305 - (415) 497-9656 weekdays.

ROCKWELL KENT - BOOK PLATES & MARKS, Pynson Printers, April 1939, Number 6 of 1250 copies, signed by Rockwell Kent. Excellent condition, fine polished tan calf binding with inlay of the design from original blue cloth cover. Slipcase bound in color coordinated bookbinder's paper. $75. Write private owner: H. E. Stevens, 3300 Henrietta Ave., La Crescenta, CA 91214

SUMPTUOUS BOOK ON PORTUGUESE BOOKPLATES. Imprensa Nacional De Lisboa, Louis Derouet. Lisbon: 1930. CATALOGO GERAL DE PRIMEIRA EXPOSICAO DE "EX LIBRIS" EM PORTUGAL. This is a 240 page catalogue for an exhibit held October 4-31, 1927. There are numerous illustrations plus 13 actual bookplate prints on four sheets interleaved in the text. Original decorated paper wrappers bound in 3/4 floral gilt ornamented red morocco over decorated leatherette boards (minimally wormholed), with gilt ornamented spine, top edge gilt. $250.00. This is #25 of 200 copies. Initiated by the famous collector Louis Derouet, the catalogue lists not only the ex libris and their owners, but also there is a detailed list of artists and engravers, subject index. Write: Zeitlin & VerBrugge Booksellers, 815 N. La Cienega Blvd., Los Angeles, CA 90069.

FOND OF PRINTING, Gordon Craig As Typographer & Illustrator, Colin Franklin. New York: Typophiles, 1980. This is #54 in the Typophile Chap Book series and is uniform in size with other volumes in the series. Passing mention is made of bookplates as in connction with THE PAGE, which Craig published between 1898 and 1901, when Craig is quoted: "Each month we shall publish two bookplates, one already in use and one looking for a master." Among the illustrations is the title page for BOOK PLATES, Designed and Engraved on Wood or Copper by the Engravers of San Leonardo, 1907. Colin Franklin has drawn upon his own collection of Craig material, bearing the artist's annotations; as Franklin says ". . . . Craig was fun, and communicates that quality." Copies were printed for Typophiles & Book Club of California, and a paperback for Hurtwood Publications for sale in Great Britain; there are also 125 special copies signed by the author and containing two unique woodcuts by Gordon Craig.

THE JESTER PRESS (Box 2671X GPO Melbourne 3001, Victoria, Australia) plan one or two publications concerning ex libris in the coming year and indicates increased attention to the overall quality of their publications according to a recent letter from Robert C. Littlewood, whose book on Lionel Lindsay was reviewed some time ago. Specific information will be furnished as soon as it is available from the publisher.

Book Review: EX-LIBRIS OF KIEKO TSURUSAWA, Cliff Parfit

The colophon tells that this book "is produced by hand as a private publication of the English Centre, Shin-Matsubara, Chofu, Shimonoseki 752, Japan."
The production is by members of the English Centre staff. The papers used
were Hosho and Tokuchi washi specially made for this book by Seijiro Chiji-
matsu of Tokuchi village, Yamaguchi Prefecture, Japan. A picture of the
young woman artist, born in 1942, is included as well as tipped-in prints
of thirteen ex libris she has designed since 1976. The text is typed on
white paper and the prints are tipped-in on pink, which is also used for
the endpapers. In addition to many traditional plates, two of her designs
express considerable humor; one features a flared pair of blue jeans, another a single prop plane tied with a bow. The work of Miss Tsurusawa was
featured in BOOKPLATES IN THE NEWS #39.

JAROSLAV HORANEK, Frantisek Dvorak.

JAROSLAV HORANEK is another of the splendid publications of Klaus Rodel's
ExlibRisten. The text is multi-lingual; there are eight multi-color serigraphs, and a portrait of the artist. "Each work tells that the artist
knows that his exlibris also has another function than just a picture.
Therefore his exlibris also tell us something about literary themes and
takes us into a personal perception of artistic imagination." Horanek is
a Czechoslovakian artist of the intermediate generation after World War II.
Price: 100.00 Kr., published in 1980. '

M. M. WERSCHOLANZEW, Frantisck Sara

This is a 1979 publication of ExlibRisten and is priced at Kr 55.00. It
is multi-lingual, including English. Sixteen ex libris are illustrated.
Werscholanzew was born April 24, 1937 in Moscow. Surprisingly one of the
artists who influenced him was Thomas Bewick, though the Werscholanzew
work illustrated is a far cry from anything done by Bewick. " . . . he
only uses the word exlibris as a kind of visiting-card or entrance card
to the collectors' world." As with many other European artists, his ex
libris are more graphics on a small scale rather then truly functional
bookplates.

HARRY JURGENS, Klaus Rodel

This was privately printed by Klaus Rodel in 1979; price Kr 45.00. The
text is multi-lingual including English; thirteen ex libris are illustrated and there is a portrait of the artist. Jurgens is a young Estonian
born November 2, 1949. His work is very modern, perhaps erotic, and includes aphorisms. His creations, too, are in turn more and less than a
traditional ex libris.

BOOKPLATES IN THE NEWS   Quarterly: January/April/July/October
605 North Stoneman Ave. #F   North America $10/Overseas $11
Alhambra, California
United States 91801   1981 Audrey Spencer Arellanes

HOOVER CATALOGUE

A beautifully illustrated and annotated catalogue of the reference library on mining and metallurgy which former President Herbert Hoover and his wife, Lou Henry Hoover, assembled in London during their early careers has been published by the Libraries of The Claremont Colleges.

Entitled BIBLIOTHECA DE RE METALLICA: THE HERBERT CLARK HOOVER COLLECTION OF MINING AND METALLURGY, the 239-page, tall octavo volume was edited and annotated by David Kuhner and Tania Rizzo of the Libraries' staff. The catalogue was printed by the Arion Press of San Francisco, whose master printer is Andrew Hoyem.

The Hoover books, covering a broad area in the history of science as well as rare works on minerals, metals, and precious stones, were originally gathered together during the period 1901 to 1914 to assist the young mining engineer and his wife in their English translation of Georgius Agricola's Renaissance classic on mining, DE RE METALLICA. The collection was given to the libraries of the Claremont Colleges in 1970 by Herbert Hoover III, the President's grandson.

THE
HOOVER COLLECTION
OF
MINING & METALLURGY

Herbert Hoover's Bookplate.

The volume is full cloth bound with an ornamental cover design taken from one of Mr. Hoover's mining books. There are 32 full page plates with a reproduction of the famous Hoover bookplate. The catalogue is available at $125 the copy from Honnold Library, Claremont Colleges, Claremont, CA 91711.

BOOKPLATE LITERATURE

ANTIQUARIAN BOOK MONTHLY REVIEW, Leo Wyatt. 6:308, July 1979. Engravings on exhibit at the National Book League in the Mark Longman Library through August 31st; included in the display are bookplates and labels, letterheads, cards, and alphabets.

ANTIQUARIAN BOOK MONTHLY REVIEW, Some Pitfalls of Collecting George Barrow, A. M. Fraser. (7) 7:470-1, 473-5, 477, 479, October 1980. One illustration is a black bordered card in remembrance of George Barrow, which appears as if it had been used as a commemorative bookplate. The article mentions a volume auctioned at Hodgson's Rooms (England) in February 1980 bearing Lord Clarendon's bookplate.

PRESERVATION PRESS BOOKPLATE

The Preservation Press National Trust for Historic Preservation

The Preservation Press is part of the National Trust for Historic Preservation, a private nonprofit organization chartered by Congress in 1949 to encourage public participation in the preservation of sites, buildings, and objects significant in American history and culture; the Trust has a membership of 160,000.

The Preservation Press is the only U. S. publisher devoted exclusively to books on preservation of old buildings and historic architecture; it is an educational program designed to increase understanding of historic preservation through publications.

The Preservation Press bookplate for 1980 was designed by Tom Engeman of Washington, D.C. The design is a star tie rod; these rods, often with decorative ends such as the star, were used to stablize major beams in old brick and stone buildings with load-bearing walls. To secure a wooden beam to an outside wall, a tie rod (or tie bar) was passed through the wall and fastened on the exterior with a nut and an iron piece - frequently an S shape, a circle, or a star. Hand-forged iron and, in the 19th century, cast iron was used to form the decorative tie rod ends.

The bookplates may be purchased in packets of 40 gummed labels for $3.95 by writing Preservation Press, 1785 Massachusetts Avenue, NW, Washington, D.C. 20036. Funds help to support the projects of the press. The 1979 ex libris featured a Victorian storefront, the Germond Crandell Building in Washington. There is also an impressive list of publications including the practical aspects of preservation, laws covering it, preservation of wooden ships, fabrics used, the stories of various preservation projects, and five cookbooks.

PRESERVATION NEWS (June 1980) carried notice that the bookplates are available in the Preservation Shops.

MORE BOOKPLATE LITERATURE

BOOK COLLECTOR, The Library of St. Patrick's College, Manly, Unfamiliar Libraries XXIII, John Fletcher. (13) 29:179-202, Summer 1980. St. Patrick's Ecclesiatical College was built in 1885-9 about seven miles from Sydney, Australia. Among the illustrations is a bookplate for the college.

BOOK COLLECTOR, "Lefty" Wilmarth Sheldon Lewis, Mary Waldegrave. 29:239-50, Summer 1980. ". . . . by 1922, when he was twenty-seven, it was books, almost any kind of book; he collected them hoping always for a first edition, an interesting autograph or bookplate."

FROM THE PERIODICAL LITERATURE

AMERICAN BOOK COLLECTOR, The Arthur Conan Doyle Mystery: Toward a Resolution, Stanley Wertheim. (1) 1:38-40, 42, September/October 1980 New Series. Further, interesting developments to the mystery article which appeared in the November/December 1979 issue of BOOK COLLECTOR'S MARKET.

PAPER AND ADVERTISING COLLECTOR (P.A.C.), Bookplates, Josephine Roye. (9) 2:1, 4, 12, September 1980. General interest article; references include Charles Dexter Allen's AMERICAN BOOK-PLATES (one of the several reprints), Fridolf Johnson's Dover TREASURY OF BOOKPLATES, and the Arellanes bibliography.

ANTIQUES JOURNAL, Bookplates: The Vanishing Art, Paul Kandell. (9)16-9, 49, May 1980. This is less an article about a vanishing art than a picky attack on Warren's general classification of bookplates (early English, Jacobean, Chippendale, Ribbon and Wreath) and the author's theory that these classification terms turn-off the potential collector. Further that bookplates represented by these classifications do not match in design the furniture of the same name or the period. Most of the bibliography is outside the field of bookplates and Charles Dexter Allen is represented by the Hacker Art Books reprint of 1968.

Chicago SUN-TIMES, Ex Libris: The Joy of Bookplates, Nancy Belcher. (3) 13, November 23, 1980. Reprint of the article which first appeared in the Los Angeles TIMES Book Review section under a different title. The illustrations for the SUN-TIMES were selected by staff at the Newberry Library and were for DeGaulle, Woodrow Wilson, and Vincent Starrett.

L'EX LIBRIS FRANCAIS, June 1980. A variety of articles; color, glossy print of large plate (4¼" x 6¼") by Denna Gao for Le Duchat D'Aubigny is very attractive. Checklist of work of Mariaelisa Leborini from 1959 through 1962, #30 through #76, continued from March issue.

EXLIBRIS WERELD, #2, Summer 1980. Articles by Jan Rhebergen on Wojciech Luczak, Anton Pieck, Dr. Gerhard Kreyenberg.

L'EX LIBRIS FRANCAIS, March 1980. Mariaelisa Leborini checklist for 1955-59, #1 through #29; four tipped-in color prints. Different plates for Victor Hugo (1802-1885) discussed. Memorials for Antoni Gelabert (1911-1980), Catalan engraver, and Lucy Huber (1908-1980), beloved wife of French artist Ernest Huber.

Gleeson Library Associates of the University of San Francisco used the ex libris of Phoebe and Hans Barkan in their announcement for a lecture on November 9, 1980 by Marlan Beilke, "Conversations with the Future," about the Robinson Jeffers collection given by the Barkan family.

KISGRAFIKA '79/3. This is a bookplate publication from Budapest, Hungary; it measures 6½" x 9½", perfect bound. This issue has many black and white illustrations, one tipped-in color print; among the articles is one on the Japanese Ex Libris Society.

The Heirloom Library issues a Collector's Edition of the world's greatest books; each subscriber receives a bookplate special-printed for each volume with the owner's name imprinted.

EX LIBRIS
Susan K Gaylord

In the design and printing of ex libris there are unlimited possibilities with respect to subject, style, and medium. The artists with Cambridge Bookplate offer to collectors and institutions an annual limited bookplate series, as well as personalized designs. The limited series for 1981 consists initially of five plates. These plates are printed letterpress on archival quality papers with the owner's name imprinted.

Individuals who desire a personalized ex libris may select a designer from the artists represented in the limited series; upon request samples will be furnished of the artist's work. Preliminary sketches are furnished. The final print may be on white Permalife bond, 100% rag parchment, or natural 100% alpha cellulose paper. By special request, they will order Canterbury handmade paper, sheepskin parchment, or leather stock. They can provide neutral pH liquid adhesive, imported brushes, or a chromed die cast gluer, which ensures an easy, even distribution of adhesive.

As can be seen by the examples of their work reproduced here, Cambridge Bookplate offer wide variety of styles. The Cohen ex libris represents the dual careers and interests of this couple; it is printed in raised ink, in a delicate raspberry shade.

In a future issue of BOOKPLATES IN THE NEWS, there will be a story on the dynamic young man whose enthusiasm for the art of the bookplate assures Cambridge Bookplate a bright future. You may write him directly - James Keenan, Cambridge Bookplate, Box 340, Cambridge, MA 02238.

ASBC&D MEMBERS ————
1981 MEMBERSHIP DUES PAYABLE NOW:
$27.50 - Quarterly & YEAR BOOK
  10.00 - BOOKPLATES IN THE NEWS

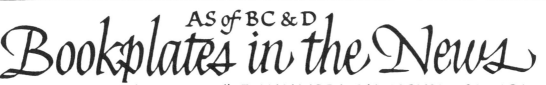

AS of BC & D
Bookplates in the News
1206 N. STONEMAN AVENUE #15, ALHAMBRA, CALIFORNIA, 91801 U.S.A.
AUDREY SPENCER ARELLANES, Editor

APRIL 1981   NUMBER FORTY-FOUR

DEREK RILEY: A SCOTTISH ENGRAVER IN WOOD
by W. E. Butler, Secretary
The Bookplate Society, London

American connoisseurs of wood engraving and bookplates will do well to become acquainted with the oeuvre of a fine Scottish artist, Derek Riley. Nestled in the outreaches of Scotland, Riley proclaims himself to be a "sculptor and engraver in wood," but it would be appropriate to add bookplate designer, private pressman, and bibliophile. He has executed thirty-two personal bookplates through 1980, all wood engravings, and has attracted the interest and patronage of collectors in Britain, Scandinavia, the rest of Europe, Australia, and North America.

Yorkshire born in 1931, Riley displayed an early interest in drawing, but wartime conditions precluded formal training in art school. An apprenticeship in the electrical industry, eventually giving rise to a position in the drawing office of a machine tool firm, provided sustenance while he attended various evening classes in art. By the mid-1950's he was sharing a studio with an artist friend. A local exhibition of the Calder Valley Arts Society of which both Riley and his studio mate were founder members, inspired Riley to take up wood sculpture. That was in 1959, and three years later Riley moved to Scotland, where he has opened his own showrooms and studios. The remoteness of Banffshire means that he rarely exhibits, but his sculpture is well represented in private collections in Scotland, England, Norway, Australia, the Bahamas, and the United States; examples of his inscriptional lettering are to be found on public and private edifices in Scotland, the motifs being chiefly abstract or symbolic carvings based on natural objects, wild life, or Celtic mythology.

In 1972 Riley was persuaded by his friend and teacher, Sam Eglinton, to try his hand at wood engraving. Making good use of a small collection of books on the subject and encouraged by one of the finest twentieth-century wood engravers, Agnes Miller Parker (1892-1980), Riley undertook as his first effort a monogram in Celtic lettering for his own subject collection on Celtic art and mythology. A year later he designed a second bookplate for his books on art and sculpture, followed in 1974 by a calligraphic label for his own general use. In 1976 two calligraphic labels were executed for his close friends Eglinton and a Scottish rare book dealer, Alex M. Frizzell, and from that beginning commissions and recognition have begun to flow. Articles have appeared on his work with illustrations and tipped-in examples in NORDISK EXLIBRIS TIDSSKRIFT (1) and THE BOOKPLATE SOCIETY NEWSLETTER (2), and he has been included in the bookplate exhibitions at the Victoria and Albert Museum (London) and the XVIII International Exlibris Congress at Linz, Austria, the latter now traveling throughout northern Europe.

Riley makes his own blocks from boxwood, and then prints them himself on a Kobold Platen press. Eight universal bookplates of special appeal to children also have been designed by Riley; these are originally wood engraved and then produced photo-lithographically and marketed by his own commercial press, The D R Press, Cullen, Scotland. More than one million have been sold.

In 1976 Riley became enamored with the private press movement and founded his own press, the Celnius Press, in order to "print selected texts & poetry which I feel I would love to illustrate" to quote from his prospectus. The first and thus far only venture is Percy Bysshe Shelley's Ode to the West Wind, with two other poems by Shelley, illustrated with three wood engravings printed from the block.

On the whole, Riley's bookplate designs have drawn upon motifs which distinguish his wood sculpture: natural objects, wild life, and his surroundings. In a nation which has nurtured the lettering standards of Reynolds Stone and Leo Wyatt, other ex libris artists have a standard of virtual perfection to match, but Riley's Celtic style letter design is especially effective in complementing his designs, and he has an evident natural affinity for the Celtic motifs.

My own bookplate, No. 28 of the Riley opus, features one of the finest examples of Scythian art which has come down to us, a golden stag found lying, when excavated in 1897, on an iron shield which it originally must have decorated. Now in the collection of the Hermitage Museum in Leningrad, the stag was exhibited at the Metropolitan Museum in New York and Los Angeles (3).

It dates from the late 7th - early 6th century B.C., perhaps the height of Scythian culture on what is now Russian and Ukrainian territory north of the Black Sea. Whether the Picts, who populated Scotland, actually originated in Scythia may or may not be fanciful history, but Riley has captured the Scythian animalism very effectively and embellished the design with a floral motif adapted from other Scythian works of the period. The bookplate is used in an appropriate subject collection. The printing has been done by Riley on his Kobold press on white paper, black over gold.

Derek Riley welcomes bookplate commissions. Prices for a single color woodengraved bookplate range from £35 to £60; quotations for multi-color plates may be obtained on application to him at Woodcarver's Shop, Bayview Road, Cullen, Banffshire, Scotland AB5 2SB. His universal ex libris may be ordered at a cost of 40 pence for 25 plus postage. Riley also is a keen bookplate collector and would be pleased to exchange modern engraved ex libris with other collectors.

CHECKLIST
1972-1980
(Unless otherwise indicated, all bookplates are X2)

1. Ex Libris D.R., 1972, 59 x 59 mm. A circular designed Celtic monogram with Celtic interlacing. The first bookplate for his books on Celtic art and mythology.
2. DEREK RILEY Ex Libris, 1973, 69 x 19 mm. Circular design for books on art and sculpture. Athene, Greek goddess of sculpture, with her owl for wisdom (books).
3. DEREK RILEY, 1974, 58 x 26 mm. Calligraphic label for general use.
4. SAM EGLINTON EX LIBRIS, 1976, 84 x 50 mm. Calligraphic label for the man who introduced Riley to printing and engraving.
5. ALEX M. FRIZZELL, 1976, 74 x 26 mm. Label in capitals for the bookseller and owner of the Castlelaw Press.
6. EX LIBRIS FRED SEELEY, 1977, 75 x 103 mm. A "memento mori" type plate depicting the origins of man and his mortality.
7. EX LIBRIS F. E. BARBER, X 2/2, 79 x 37 mm. Celtic lettering in two colors.
8. EX LIBRIS EUAN & MAIRI MILNE, 1977, 48 x 85 mm. A silhouette engraving depicting a couple in mortars and gowns (teachers), singing (members of the Edinburgh Festival Chorus) and their three dogs.
9. EX LIBRIS ARTHUR H. C. HOPE, 1977, 62 x 46 mm. A simplified version

of the Hope crest.

10. EX LIBRIS FRANK BARBER, X2/3, 1977, 59 x 109 mm. The second plate for Mr. Barber, who is a mountaineer, this time in three colors.

11. EX LIBRIS ADAM T. McNAUGHTAN, 1977, 71 x 100 mm. Depicts a Scandinavian sculptured stone. Signed with monogram "DR" on face.

12. EX LIBRIS A & M CROSBY, 1978, 51 x 75 mm. Two love bird owls on a branch. For a man and wife interested in bird watching.

13. RODNEY A. GRANT, 1978, 64 x 96 mm. "Stand Fast" is the motto of the Grant clan. The scene depicts snowcovered peaks, a castle, a loch, and two windblown pine trees.

14. EX LIBRIS BIRGIT LERCHE NIELSEN, 1978, 71 x 71 mm. Circular Celtic design with Celtic lettering.

15. EX LIBRIS HENNING NIELSEN, 1978, 75 x 38 mm. Celtic design and lettering.

16. EX LIBRIS BIRGIT LERCHE NIELSEN, 1979, 61 x 61 mm. Circular Celtic design with Celtic lettering.

17. EX LIBRIS HENNING NIELSEN, 1979, 68 x 57 mm. Celtic design with Celtic lettering. The Nielsens are keen bookplate collectors living in Greenland.

18. EX LIBRIS W. D. McHARDY, 1979, 84 x 68 mm. Cullen Auld Kirk; commissioned by Dr. McHardy for the recently retired Professor of Hebrew at Oxford University, W. D. McHardy.

19. ELAINE LOVITT, 1979. A Wyvern. 62 x 86 mm.

20. Carol Moors, 1980. Two Alsatian dogs. 67 x 100 mm.

21. Ex Libris ALDIDE JURGENS, 1980. A female nude study. 65 x 95 mm.

22. Ex Libris H. B. MUIR, 1980. Bookstalls on the banks of the river Seine, Paris. 78 x 107 mm.

23. Ex Libris MAURICE OLIVER, 1980. A calligraphic plate printed in red and in black. 47 x 83 mm.

24. ANDREW HOOD EX LIBRIS, 1980. A design based on interests: horse racing, salmon fishing, and a first edition of Robert Burns' POEMS. 70 x 95 mm.

25. Ex Libris CB & JP COTTON, 1980. Celtic design with Celtic lettering. 60 x 70 mm.

26. Ex Libris LESLEY GALBRAITH, 1980. Seascape viewed through a shell for a beachcomber. 65 x 95 mm.

27. ALISON & MICHAEL BLEANEY, 1980. Calligraphic plate. 78 x 25 mm.

28. Ex Libris W. E. BULTER, X2/2, 1980. Design taken from Scythian art printed in black and gold. 80 x 93 mm. X2/2

29. COLIN CAMPBELL, Cadet of Inverneill, 1980, X2/6. Heraldic plate in color. 102 x 113 mm. X2/6

30. Dorothy Wilson, 1980. View of cottage in Scotland. 60 x 82 mm.

31. Ex Libris Susan Hamilton, 1980. Water vole watching a butterfly. 57 x 126 mm. X2/5

32. Ex Libris Penelope Wilson, 1980. Badger in a moonlit wood. 68 x 110 mm.

UNIVERSAL PLATES (all photo-lithographic) (1) Owl reading a book, 1977, 64 x

100 mm. (2) Harvest mice, 1977, 44 x 82 mm. (3) Wren, 1978, 62 x 92 mm. (4) Boy on dolphin, 1978, 67 x 105 mm. (5) Bookworm, 1978, 67 x 105 mm. (6) Hedgehog, 1979, 60 x 62 mm. (7) Little owls, 1979, 57 x 61 mm. (8) Harebells and pansies, 1979, 64 x 70 mm.   Note: X2 = wood engraving. /2 = in 2 colors.

LEO WYATT

The many friends and admirers of Leo Wyatt will be saddened to learn that he has been seriously ill since last summer. As a consequence Leo has been unable to undertake any of the lettering or pictorial engraving for which he is so justly admired. However, Wyatt has a large body of work in print, usually in limited, signed editions, and it is hoped that a book will be published bringing a number of these works under one cover. If you have ever throught of owning one of the Wyatt alphabets or the intricately lettered aphorisms, now would certainly be the time to make that purchase directly from the artist. Prices vary according to the size of the artwork and the limitation of the edition; you may want to send a deposit of $25 or $50, keeping in mind the exchange rate (Leo Wyatt, 15 Devonshire Place, Jesmond, Newcastle upon Tyne NE2 2NB, United Kingdom).

The tipped-in bookplate above was designed by Leo for the National Book League in London to be sold as a stock plate; it is printed in several colors.

FROM THE BOOKPLATE LITERATURE

ANTIQUARIAN BOOK MONTHLY REVIEW, Catalogues, John Stephens. 8:#2, 74, Issue 82, February 1981. Randall Book's catalogue Rare Books XII contains item #3, a 1491 Venice edition of Thomas a Kempis which is annotated as "part of Syston Park's library with his bookplate." Investigation of the coat of arms which is that of a baronet, failed to list any Park baronetcy in the COMPLETE BARONETAGE. Further pursuit of Walford's COUNTY FAMILIES (1907 edition) revealed it was not a person but a place in Lincolnshire, England.

ANTIQUARIAN BOOK MONTHLY REVIEW, Ex Libris Edward Gibbon, John Turner. 8:#2: 62-3, Issue 82, February 1981. (2) Book Review of THE LIBRARY OF EDWARD GIBBON by Geoffrey Keynes (second edition) published St. Paul's Bibliographies at £12. This book gives the story of reconstructing the working library used by historian Edward Gibbon. Illustrated from two volumes are "Gibbon's label and his first bookplate, 1750," and "Gibbon's second bookplate, 1721." The dates are either switched or otherwise misquoted. The two bookplates as reproduced look similar except for a slight reduction in size for the print identified as second.

ANTIQUARIAN BOOK MONTHLY REVIEW, Top Edge Guilt (Part II), Robin Myers. (3) 8:#2:52-3, 55, 57, February 1981. Article on T. J. Wise and the forgeries uncovered by John Carter and Graham Pollard. One illustration is the Wise ex libris (slightly enlarged) with the wording: "Books Bring Me Friends, Where 'er on earth I be, Solace of solitude, Bonds of Society!"

BRITISH LIBRARY JOURNAL, Books from Japanese Circulating Libraries in the British Library, P. F. Kornicki. (7) 6:188-98, Autumn 1980. Circulating libraries were in existence during the Tokugawa period (1600-1868), and it was customary to impress in black, occasionally in red, a stamp of ownership on each book available for loan. Such stamps were easily distinguished from ex libris of private owners in that more information appeared including address of the library company, charges for borrowing, etc.

LITUANUS, The Lithuanian Quarterly, Lithuanian Bookplates, Don Anderson. (14) 26:42-4, et seq, #4, 1980. "Galerija Art Gallery can be justly proud of this outstanding exhibition which presented exquisite fine art with added appeal of ancient folklore together with an emotional message from behind the iron curtain." The exhibit is from the collection of Gintautas Vezys.

Chicago SUN-TIMES, Art, Harold Haydon. December 5, 1980. Note on the Galerija exhibition and mention of LITHUANIAN BOOKPLATES by Vitolis E. Vengris.

AMPHORA 42, Ephemera or Art? Ex Libris in Hungary at the Turn of the Century, J. E. Horvath. (11) 34-9, December 1980. "Most of these plates have one feature, however, which separates them from real art as we know it today, and that is that the chosen subject, the design, and the style reflect largely the taste and the characteristics of the book collectors who commissioned them and not necessarily that of the artist." The illustrations are from the period 1890 to 1929.

THE PRIVATE LIBRARY, Insurance and Capital Transfer Tax, David Chambers. Third Series 2:131-3, Winter 1979. Chambers, who works for Lloyd's, writes of insurance and tax situation in England. In part: "Volumes of book-plates could be valued per volume, with a note as to the number and sort of plate included in it."

NORDISK EXLIBRIS TIDSSKRIFT (Danish Ex Libris Society). Well illustrated with several multi-color tip-ins; articles about Lew Beketow, Rajmund Lewandowski, and reviews of international literature. Helmer Fogedgaard, editior of the journal for 26 years, resigns, and is being succeeded by Klaus Rodel.

EXLIBRIS-NYT (Danish Ex Libris Society) January 1980. A volunteer is needed to translate this and other Danish publications.

SVENSKA EXLIBRISFORENINGEN (Swedish Ex Libris Society), #129 and #130 for 1979. Quotation in #129: "Whilst a signature disfigures a book, a bookplate lends character and individuality and makes it akin to all the others on the library shelves, so that it at once becomes a member of the family," Marc F. Severin.

Exhibit at the Tyler School of Art of Temple University (Philadelphia) in the Penrose Gallery, October 13-31, 1980, of Contemporary Lithuanian Bookplates from the collection of Vitolis E. Vengris, who gave a talk closing day.

JOURNAL OF LIBRARY HISTORY, Bookplate of John Andrews, Katharine S. Diebl. (2) Cover, 4-7, Winter 1981. Interesting background on ex libris for circulating library about 1774 in Calcutta. Details about the artist-engraver Sheppert (Shepherd), who worked for the English East India Company's mint.

Los Angeles TIMES, Calendar Section, "When D'Eon Had His Day in Court," Lawrence Christon. A new play by David Trainer, to open at the South Coast Repertory (California) in May 1981, centers on Chevalier D'Eon, the 18th century diplomat and spy, who spent a lifetime masquarading his true gender. D'Eon had a bookplate, and his exciting activities in the service of Louis XV are documented in several bookplate publications, including BOOK-PLATE ANNUAL & ARMORIAL YEAR BOOK (1895), JOURNAL OF EX LIBRIS SOCIETY (October 1894, February 1895), NOTES AND QUERIES (August 4 and 25, 1894).

ARTFUL DODGE, Ex Libris, Jurek Polanski.(37) 2:40-47, Spring 1981. "In the past century the Ex Libris has often been the testing ground and a serious innovative stimulus for experiment in synthesizing Fine and Graphic Arts, or the achievements of Poster, Book and Advertising Art, with those of engraving and other accepted media." Illustrations are mostly pen and ink or lino cuts.

Silver in American Life, an exhibit at the Los Angeles County Art Museum, organized by Yale University Art Gallery and the American Federation of Arts. Among the silver pieces was a bookplate designed by Paul Revere.

WOMEN ARTISTS OF THE ARTS & CRAFTS MOVEMENT, Anthea Callen (Pantheon Books) New York, 1979. Illustrated is a bookplate designed by Celia Levetus for Edward R. Taylor (STUDIO, 1896). The period covered is 1870 to 1914.

ARTIST DAVID JONES (1895-1974) - A researcher in England is seeking information on woodengraver David Jones, particularly a copy of the bookplate he created for Mrs. Bertha Straight of New York. Please write directly to - Brian North Lee, 32 Barrowgate Road, London W4 4OY, England. A sharp reproduced copy of the print would be satisfactory.

LENKE DISKAY, formost graphic artist from Hungary, passed away as the result of a heart attack in December 1980; she was 52. A dear friend to the many who knew her, an excellent ex libris artist with vision, outstanding technique, and with exceptionally humanistic thinking. She won several prizes with her ex libris at various congresses. She attended the Congress in Lugano, but was unable to be in Linz last year.

F.I.S.A.E. BOOK - There will be a book featuring the work of living ex libris artists for the 1982 International Ex Libris Congress in England; as in the past the volume will be under the editor-ship of A. M. Da Moto Miranda. The volume is in an edition of 500 copies. The ex libris societies of most countries are represented by an article about at least one artist and usually there are four tipped-in prints for each artist. The American Society of Bookplate Collectors and Designers would like to hear from any artists who would be willing to furnish 500 prints of at least one bookplate or from any owners of plates by a living artist, who would be willing to furnish 500 prints to be tipped in, along with any biographical information about the owner and the artist. Write to the Editor, Bookplates in the News.

IN MEMORIAM
EARL HEIMS

Earl Heims, well-known Portland, Oregon advertising executive, died March 25, 1981 at his
home in Tigard. Born in New York City, he
moved to Oregon City with his family when he was five. His first selling
job was peddling newspapers while a grammer school student; while attending high school Earl took his first job with a local advertising agency.
By 1941 he created his own agency, in which he remained active until his
retirement in 1975. Heims was founder of the Advertising Club of Portland
and served as its president; recently he was honored for having given fifty
years of devoted service to the organization.

Earl and his wife Celia shared 43 years of a happy and fruitful marriage,
raised a daughter and three sons, and were the happy grandparents of four
grandchildren. In the eulogy given Earl Heims, Rabbi Yonah Geller said:
His home was warm and vibrant with love and affection, and there was respect and deep devotion between all the members of the family.

During the last six years, Earl underwent open-heart surgery which was
successful, but later suffered a series of strokes. With determination he
fought to regain his mobility; he was a fighter to the end.

Early in his career Heims had designed a number of stock bookplates, using
some of the same graphic and selling skills applied so well in the advertising field. His interest in bookplates expanded to collecting, and he
has been an active member in the ASBC&D for a considerable time. His own
ex libris is an adaptation from a Rockwell Kent illustration (see BOOKPLATES
IN THE NEWS pages 74, 218, 235, 278).

(Editor's Note: It was my pleasure to meet Earl and his wife Celia on one of
the many trips they made to Southern California during the winter months to
escape the rain of Oregon and enjoy the sunshine of Palm Springs. Bookplates
were always a focal point of interest whether talking with Earl in person or
over the telephone, or reading one of his newsyletters. My life has been the
richer for knowing Earl, and he will be sadly missed.)

• ── •

OLYMPIC THEME EX LIBRIS / Inquiry: I would be interested in any bookplate
with the 1932 Olympics theme. Please respond to Nancy L. Francis, 1233 Macy
St., La Habra, CA 90631. (Editor's Note: One reference is in the catalogue
of The Bookplate Association International for the exhibition held during
1932 in Los Angeles. Pictured was a design by F. Charles Blank with an
Olympic theme. Blank designed the official bookplate of the American Society
of Bookplate Collectors and Designers.

NIPPON EXLIBRIS ASSOCIATION BULLETIN, Modern American Bookplates, Audrey
Arellanes. 72:5-6, January 1, 1981. This is the third in a series titled
Western Exlibris News; the first two were "Austrian Exlibris" by Gustav
Dichler and "Modern Swiss Exlibris" by Ernest Wetter; these were translated
into Japanese by George N. Zweg. The article on American bookplates was
translated into Japanese by Ichigoro Uchida, who used as sources "Bookplates
- Prints in Miniature," written by Arellanes for an earlier Japanese publi-
cation and the article by the same author on Bookplate Societies in the
United States from the 1977 YEAR BOOK of the ASBC&D. Several illustrations
from Mr. Uchida's collection appear in the article in reduced size.

HENRY W. PRICE
by Rolf Erickson

The Henry W. Price plate was commissioned by Henry Price of Evanston, Illinois, but it is his son Edward (Ned) who is pictured on it.

The scene is the family study in the large old, comfortable Price home at 2006 Sheridan Road. Ned, who today is still practising law at eighty-one, remembers posing for it on the mission oak settee with the jade plant carefully placed nearby on the floor.

Everyone agrees it must have been done in 1910, judging from Ned's appearance, but neither Ned, nor anyone else, unfortunately, can remember the artist's name - the elusive "B.G.B.?" whose initials appear on the corner of the settee cover. Ned also questions why he was chosen to pose: "I wonder now why father chose me as a subject on his book plate or why my brother Griswold wasn't asked? He was older." Today the plates are scarce and Henry's descendants treasure framed copies in their homes. The house is no longer in the family; no one knows who now owns the oak settee, but the bookplate itself has the power to evoke many happy memories.

H. STANTON HILL EX LIBRIS (The details are as given by the owner.)

My library emphasizes the history of geology and the development of geological ideas. Perhaps the most important of these ideas was the recognition of the great length of geologic time. The scholarly Archbishop Ussher, using church records calculated in 1650 that the earth had been created in 4004 B.C., this figure coming to be generally believed. When the Scottish geoloist James Hutton in the late 18th century examined the action of present-day geologic processes and how slow-acting they were, he realized that the earth itself bore evidence of events that must have required much more than 6000 years to have taken place. At Siccard Point on the North Sea coast east of Edinburgh, he found a relationship of the rocks which proved to him that Scotland had had a long and complex history which involved the uplift and destruction of several past Scotlands. He saw that the country today, made up in part of the layered sedimentary wastes of these past Scotlands, was itself being destroyed by natural forces, processes creating vast quantities of debris which were accumulating in layers on the sea bottom and which he thought would eventually be uplifted to re-place the land that was destroyed. In all of these events that he read in the rocks, he could find, he said, "no vestage of a beginning, - no pros-pect of an end."

The view on the bookplate is an artist's conception of Siccar Point, which I myself have visited but did not see from this angle. The books below suggest the legacy of ideas which were passed along, especially from Hutton to Sir Charles Lyell to Charles Darwin, whose theory of the evolutionary development of species required a vast extent of time for accomplishment. The fossils found in the rocks which had formerly been thought to have been just "formed stones" eventually proved to be the documents of evolution. Among these the glossopetra or tongue-stones of Malta corresponded so exactly with the teeth of modern sharks that they were among the first fossils whose true origin was recognized. William Smith discovered that each geologic layer had its own distinctive set of fossils which could be used to identify it wherever it occurred and used this tool to create a beautiful, colored map that showed the rocks and patterns which underlay the landscapes of England and Wales. Lyell, Roderick Murchison, and others used fossils to divide geologic time into the units that are familiar to us today as the Geologic Time Scale.

The composition and shapes of crystals ultimately led the American mineral-ogist James D. Dana to the first meaningful classification of the mineral world.

The bookplate was created from my ideas by my daughter, Cathy, a free-lance artist who labored under the requirement that art or no-art, the rocks had to look as much like real rocks as possible. The border of crystals is from a bookplate I long admired, designed in 1907 by W. F. Hopson for the Brush Mineralogical Library of the Sheffield Scientific School, a department of Yale College which had been created largely through the efforts of James D. Dana. (Free-lance artist Cathy Hill, 374 N. Grove St., Sierra Madre, CA 91204 (213) 355-2698.)

Esther Walton has made eight different black and white drawings similar to the illustration here. Each is approximately 2" square, print-ed on ungummed paper, packed 16 in a poly bag, $2.40 + $1 handling and postage. If interested you may write E. Walton, 311-B N. Venice Blvd., Venice, CA 90291

SILHOUETTE/Calligraphic Ex Libris - An artist of proven skill in the field of silhouette cutting is Gudrun Wittgen-Schmidt, Route #1, Box 167, Sears, Michigan 49679. On average a silhouette, calligraphy, and printing of 100 bookplates would be $100, especially intricate motif somewhat higher. Please write the artist for quotations. The Silhouette bookplate has special charm!

CHURCHILL COLLECTION
by John David Marshall

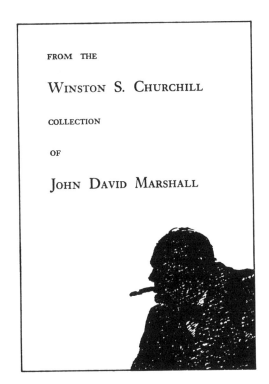

FROM THE

WINSTON S. CHURCHILL

COLLECTION

OF

JOHN DAVID MARSHALL

I've always intended to give my collection of Churchill material to the Winston Churchill Memorial and Library which is located on the campus of Westminster College in Fulton, MO, where on Tuesday, March 5, 1946, Mr. Churchill delivered what history knows as the "iron curtain" speech. I was a junior in McKenzie (Tennessee) High School in 1946, and my Father told me that if I could get a ticket for Churchill's address, we would go to Fulton. I got the ticket on the Saturday before the lecture was delivered. My Father, Mother, and I went to Fulton - they got to see Churchill and Truman in the parade through town but I was the only one who had a ticket for the address. Ticket number 1476 with my name on it is framed and hangs on the wall in my living room. Some of my friends say I have never recovered from March 5th, 1946! I agree, and I don't even want to recover from it.

My interest in Churchill goes back to the sixth or seventh grade. The girl who had the seat in front of mine in the seventh grade told me that I had a one-track mind and Winston Churchill was on both ends of the track - an observation which might still be valid! When I was in the eighth grade my Grandmother Marshall gave me a copy of WINSTON CHURCHILL: A BIOGRAPHY by Rene Kraus (Lippincott, 1942, Second Edition Enlarged) for Christmas. This book, as it turned out, is the first volume in what has become my Churchill Collection. During high school, college, and graduate library school, I acquired those Churchill items that I could manage to buy. After I went to work in the fall of 1952, I began to collect with a good bit of vigour. As the years have gone by, I've added to the collection, and it now numbers some 600 volumes (including the 350-odd books now in Fulton, Missouri). I'll continue to collect, but am glad the collection (the first installment that is) is now in Fulton.

While I was working at the University of Georgia Library (1957-67), I designed the bookplate which I use for the collection. The University of Georgia Print Shop printed some 2000 of the plates for me; needless to say I still have a goodly supply of these plates for future acquisitions. The Churchill silhouette on the plate came from a cartoon published sometime during WWII. The University Print Shop folk were able to "doctor" it a bit and I think the plate turned out very well. It is a scissors and paste-up job, but I like it, and I suppose that is what counts.

The prize item in my Churchill Collection is a first edition of SAVROLA, his only novel, which was published in 1900. Random House in 1956 published a new edition of SAVROLA with a new 76-word foreword by Sir Winston which is dated January 20, 1956. The Random House edition came out on April 16, 1956, and was reviewed by A. L. Rowse on the 15th in the New York TIMES Book Review. The TIMES indicated SAVROLA "apparently was not reviewed" in the United States; however, some considerable searching on my part discovered at least one review which appeared February 10, 1900 in none other than the New York TIMES Saturday Review of Books and Arts! I dropped a note to the TIMES and they acknowledged my find in the Book Review section of May 6, 1956.

XIX INTERNATIONAL EX LIBRIS CONGRESS: Oxford, August 18-22'82

The XIX Congress will be held at Keble College, Oxford, England under the auspices of The Bookplate Society. Both the novelty of the venue and the attractiveness of Oxford give reason to believe the Congress will be well-attended, and early registration is advisable.

DATES: Wednesday, August 18 (evening) to Sunday, August 22 (lunchtime) 1982
LOCATION: Keble College, Oxford. Accommodation of participants will be in the College, which should contribute to the sense of fellowship among Congress participants. Alternative accommodation may be arranged if desired. Oxford is 65 miles from London and served by scheduled rail and bus service. There is a rapid coach/rail link to Oxford via Reading from Heathrow Airport.
PROGRAM: Participants will assemble Wednesday evening for sherry and informal dinner. There will be talks Thursday and Friday mornings, afternoon visits to the exhibitions and tours of Oxford colleges, and a formal dinner on Saturday evening. Of course, ample opportunity for exchanging bookplates as well as optional excursions.
LANGUAGES: English, French, and German will be the three languages of the Congress. Talks will be delivered in English, and translations into French and German will be available. Translators also will be on hand for other announcements, speeches, etc. It is intended that tours and excursions will have guides fluent in French and German.
EXHIBITIONS: Two separate exhibitions are planned. A selection from collection in the Bodleian Library, Oxford, and from other public and private collections will form an historical overview of English pictorial bookplates. This exhibit will be mounted in the Ashmolean Museum. Also there will be the customary exhibit of contemporary bookplates produced between 1980-82. No ex libris competition is proposed.
Conference addresses: The President of F.I.S.A.E. is Mr. Anthony K. Pincott, 3B Hurlingham Court, Ranelagh Gardens, London SW6 3UN, England and Administrative matters, Secretary of the Organizing Committee, Professor W. E. Butler, 9 Lyndale Ave., London NW2 2QD, England. Registration forms will be available at the end of December 1981.
LOGO: The logo for the Congress was designed by David Kindersley, one of the leading lettering artists working in England.

BOOKPLATES IN THE NEWS
605 N. Stoneman Ave. #F
Alhambra, CA   91801

$10 - Published Quarterly:
January/April/July/October
Copyright 1981 A.S.Arellanes

1980 YEAR BOOK now available $22.50 separately
$27.50 with BOOKPLATES IN THE NEWS

Please notify the editor immediately when you change your address - thanks.

AS of BC & D
Bookplates in the News
1206 N. STONEMAN AVENUE #15. ALHAMBRA. CALIFORNIA. 91801 U.S.A.
AUDREY SPENCER ARELLANES, Editor

NUMBER FORTY-FIVE   JULY 1981

CAMBRIDGE BOOKPLATE by James P. Keenan

Cambridge Bookplate was founded by a small group of artisans, offering collectors and institutions individually tailored designs. It is our desire to join with the various bookplate societies throughout the world, to help renew and cultivate this too frequently neglected art form.

Most of our plates are photoengraved and printed letterpress, all on acid-free papers: white Perma-life text, ivory alpha cellulose and off-white rag parchment; other methods of printing and fine papers are available as requested.

Bookplates created by several of the artists working with Cambridge Bookplate are presented for your enjoyment.

Michael DiGiorgio

MICHAEL DiGIORGIO is a nature and wildlife illustrator. His pen and ink drawings have appeared in the publications of the Massachusetts Audubon Society, HORTICULTURE MAGAZINE, and CONSERVATIONIST.

JOHN BARNARD concentrates on linocuts and pen and ink drawings. His work is influenced by primitive and erotic art.

MARK FISHER's award-winning pen and ink illustrations appear frequently in the BOSTON GLOBE, as well as nationally. He is primarily concerned with the surreal, exotic, and fantastic.

KATHIE TODD works with oil as well as pen and ink. Her interests are in portraiture and Celtic art.

LINDA POPPER's interests are in the areas of children's art and illustrative

Kathie Todd

John Barnard

montage. Her pen and ink drawings have appeared in CHILDREN'S DIGEST and HARVARD ALUMNUS BULLETIN.

Presswork is done by Sleeth Mitchell at the Inkling Press.

For additional information and quotations, please write to James P. Keenan and Catharine W. Trembicki, Cambridge Bookplate, Box 340, Cambridge MA 02238.

(Editor's note: A future issue of BOOKPLATES IN THE NEWS will have notes on additional artists associated with Cambridge Bookplate and more tipped-in ex libris prints.)

Linda J. Popper

My Book

MEXICAN EX LIBRIS
by Barbara Abele

I recently spent the morning at Libros Latinos, the Redlands firm owned by George Elmendorf. He estimates that in the USA he is the bookseller handling the largest volume of books about Mexico and the Iberian Peninsula. Among numerous special collections is one of approximately 300 bookplates. The ex libris were wrapped in bunles of about a dozen or so in brown paper. We reviewed a group of the plates in a room used for client/visitors. He also uses the room for reference work; the walls are lined with shelves of reference books, and an atmosphere of comfort is established by carpeting on the floor and a great selection of Mexican art on the walls (which I had to ignore in order to concentrate on the bookplates). Elmendorf brought forth a reference on Mexican bookplates, EX LIBRIS Y BIBLIOTECAS DE MEXICO by Philipe Teixidor, published in 1931. During our conversation it was established that George had grown up in the Carmel area, took a college degree in Latin American studies, and spent four years working in a bookstore. Combining education and experience, he established Libros Latinos. It was obvious from the ease with which he used the aforementioned bibliography (written in Spanish) that he was well-grounded in Mexican history. He was well aware

of the identity of the majority of names of the owners of the bookplates, for he would remark "this man was in the academic world" or "he was an anthropologist" or "a scholar and a priest."

The bookplates were mounted individually under a thin piece of glass, backed with heavy paperstock and bound on the edges with brown tape; most measure 2" x 3½" or 3" x 4". Other than the name of the owner as it is printed on the ex libris, there is no identification of owner or artist. Elmendorf purchased the collection some years ago, along with a great many books, from the widow of a bookseller in Mexico City. There are probably about 250 different plates, with duplicates bringing the total to 300; most are from 18th and 19th centuries, although a few may date back to the late 17th century; some, like the example illustrated, are more contemporary. In just a brief sort through the ex libris, many were identified against entries in the bibliography mentioned above.

ARMORIALS - A collection of mainly English armorial ex libris is available for purchase. The collection includes about 19 framed ex libris (7" x 10", wood frame, glass) and 60 unframed prints of which about 17 are noted as "in Franks." Each bookplate is pasted down about ½" on 5 x 7 coverstock weight off-white. The Franks numbers are given when known; also checked were Burke and similar English references for family, coats of arms. This small collection was assembled earlier in the century. If you are interested in purchase, please send your sealed offer to The Editor, BOOKPLATES IN THE NEWS, 605 N. Stoneman Ave. #F, Alhambra, CA 91801, for forwarding unopened to the present owner, who will contact you.

FROM THE BOOKPLATE LITERATURE

OLDRICH KULHANEK (privately printed by Klaus Rodel, 1980) has a multi-lingual text and 28 illustrations of graphics by this Czech artist. Most of the illustrations are bookplates and all reflect the artist's sensitivity to the conditions of the times in which he lives. " . . . he holds a mirror against human stupidity, ill-nature, hate, lust for power, which nobody and nothing can stop, and which can change the human being into a beast." Oldrich was born February 26, 1940 in Prague.

ERIK SKJOLDBORG / KLAUS RODEL (privately printed by Klaus Rodel, 1980), text in Danish. This small booklet is innovative in design; half the book is devoted to the artist, half to the editor, and the texts meet in the centerfold from opposite directions. There is a picture of Skjoldborg at work in his studio, two poems are printed accompanied by his illustrations, there are two pages of what appear to be recipies for cooking fish. Editor Rodel is pictured in his library/office, there is text and pictures of his publications and ex libris, and something about the continuing exhibits at Frederikshavn. Silhouettes of the two men share the text at the centerfold.

ERNST GRUNEWALD, Gerhard Kreyenberg (EXLIBRISTEN, 1980, Klaus Rodel, Lyovej 5, 9900 Frederikshavn, Denmark). There are 26 pages with numerous black and white illustrations of the artist's ex libris work. The one-page English summary indicates the artist was born in 1907 and is currently living in his native city of Bremen. His work is in woodcut and metal cuts; for this publication the illustrations are lead-cuts.

BOHUMIL KRATKY (Exlibristen, Klaus Rodel, Postbox 109, 9900 Frederikshavn, Denmark). There are ten tipped-in lithographed bookplates, each with a wine motif; also frequently the owner's profession or special interests are represented. The prints are all softly tinted. There is a page of text on this Czech in three different languages.

DON QUIXOTE DE LA MANCHA, Jaroslav Vodrazka (Exlibristen). Multi-lingual text including English by the artist telling of his life-long fascination with Don Quixote; mention is made of the treatment of the tragic knight by Gustav Dore and Honore Daumier. The twenty or more ex libris are mostly printed in two colors.

LOU STRIK - TRAESNIT, Jan G. Rhebergen (Exlibristen, 1981). A large format book, 66 pages, with 28 ex libris illustrated, woodengravings. "In the first place his work shows us his interest in his fellow-man, with all his failings, his lusts and his foolishness. . . . . We are inclined to love them, in spite of their bizarre appearance, ... The erotic element is present in almost all his work, mostly done humourously, ... He is a witty conversationalist, a sharp critic who has the ability to expose the heart of the matter immediately; however, everything covered with a jovial kindness, eager to lessen the effect of his sharp remarks."

SCHRIFT GEBRAUCHS GRAPHIK, S. G. Ivenskij (Exlibristen, 1981). There are numerous illustrations plus 15 tipped-in bookplate prints by Gerhard Tag. Most are printed in color, some multi-color. Several of the prints are tipped-in in a standard and a miniature size. The miniatures include ex libris for Paul Pfister, Wolfgang Geisler, and Hanna Spiegel.

A SET of BOOKPLATES for MARY BARNARD
by Anita Bigelow

About seventeen years ago I met Mary Barnard in print, specifically in her translation of SAPPHO: A NEW TRANSLATION (first published by the University of California in 1958). Although I admired the poems at the time, only later when I had tried translating poetry myself did I realize what an awesome achievement her translation is; usually to catch the sense of another language means to lose its poetry, but Barnard's Sappho is both a faithful translation and striking poetry. Indeed, for me the Sappho so highly praised as a poet through the millennia will speak in Mary Barnard's words and cadences.

Ex Libris
Mary Barnard

hoc opus hic labor est

Amazing translation is far from the limit of Barnard's work. Her own poetry - direct, cool, quick, and deep - has appeared in such publications as THE NEW YORKER, and in various anthologies. Her COLLECTED POEMS, available from Breitenbush Publications (Portland, OR) recently won the University of Cincinnati's Elliston Award for poetry. In addition to her accomplishments as a translator and poet, Mary Barnard has shown herself to be a witty and meticulous scholar in her study of the origins of myth, THE MYTHMAKERS, just reissued in paperback by the Ohio University Press.

About two years ago I met Mary Barnard in person. Naturally I was thrilled to meet her, all the more so because she wanted me to design a bookplate for her. My only previous experience with bookplates was an ex libris I had made for my parents, but I felt confident about taking the assignment. My years of formal and informal training in art included two years as a printmaker at the San Francisco Art Institute. I had also studied typography with Jack Stauffacher and calligraphy with Lloyd J. Reynolds. Also making my job appealing was the fact that Mary Barnard had already chosen a motif, the labyrinth, and a motto, a quotation from the sixth book of the AENEID (Hoc opus hic labor est can be translated as "this is the true task, the true difficulty of the undertaking." The words are part of the Sibyl's explanation that the descent into the underworld is easy, but that the return is difficult.

My confidence and Mary's definition of the project apart, the bookplate presented several challenges. One challenge, of course, was that the bookplate had to represent Mary Barnard the brilliant translator-poet-scholar without eclipsing Mary Barnard the person. Another challenge was that the bookplate had to fit books of many different sizes. The plate also had to identify books currently in Mary's possession as well as those she had given to the Reed College Library's rare book collection.

The donated books, now-rare first editions of modern poetry by Barnard and by her friends and peers, dictated the choice of paper for the ex libris: acid-free rag paper. The dimensional variety of books involved led Mary to the idea of two sizes of plates. The classical motif and the colors used - burnt sienna and black on white - link the different sizes of plates as well as give them dignity. The handset type and the free quality of the woodcut border and labyrinth give the plates verve. The combination of dignity and elan pleased Mary Barnard and are appropriate to the bookplates' purposes.

Although reading about the bookplates is a matter of minutes, their production took many weeks. The plates evolved through dozens of sketches before I could cut the final blocks and, with the aid of Sarah Hill, set the type (14 point Bembo), and print the bookplates on an old Vandercook proof press. We only printed about 300 plates; consequently, only reproductions are possible here. All in all, I very much enjoyed the process, am pleased with the final bookplates, and I look forward to applying my skills to other such challenges.

(NOTE: If you are interested in placing a bookplate commission with Anita Bigelow, you may write her directly at 2922 Salmon Street, Portland, OR 97214.)

MAGIC and BOOKPLATES
by James B. Alfredson

From the time I was about ten years old, until I entered graduate school, I was a part-time performing magician. Since that time, my magical activities have been channeled primarily into collecting magical periodicals. I am the co-author of A SHORT TITLE CHECKLIST OF MAGICAL PERIODICALS IN ENGLISH (1976) with George W. Daily, which lists nearly a thousand separate periodicals devoted to conjuring. Somewhere along the way - and I know not when - I became intrigued by the fact that many conjurers and collectors in the field had bookplates. I started seeking them out and now have somewhat over 400 bookplates, both stock and special design, used by magicians or magical enthusiasts.

My own bookplate was designed for me in 1963 by a well-known Canadian commercial artist and magician, who, as a magician, is known the world over as "Sid Lorraine." As one of Toronto's busiest commercial artists (he is now retired), he was known by his real name, Sid Johnson.

(Note: You may write directly to James B. Alfredson, 1927 Ray St., Lansing, MI 48910.)

Catalogue - The Jester Press Pty. Ltd, P. O. Box 2671 X, GPO Melbourne, 3001, Victoria, Australia. Catalogue Number 1 by this firm was issued in April of 1981. Some forty-odd graphics are listed including ex libris by Stanley Anderson, Herbert Cole, William Dixon, Allan Jordan, Norman Lindsay, Philip M. Litchfield, Pixie O'Harris, D. H. Souter, and Henry Van Raalt. Prices range from $10 to $100. D. H. Souter (1862-1935) designed a plate for himself which features a black cat; it is reproduced as illustration for the catalogue cover. Also illustrated is Dixon's armorial for himself (Sir William Dixon) and Allan Jordan's design for Angela Boleyn appropriately featuring the platypus.

It is with great sadness that I announce the death of Leo Wyatt early in July 1981. All who knew the artistry of Wyatt will regret that no new creations will bear his signature, and all who were privileged to know Leo personally will regret not only the loss of the artist, but the loss of a sweet-natured friend.

The American Society of Bookplate Collectors and Designers has been proud to use the letterhead designed by Leo in 1973. In our 1977 YEAR BOOK was featured "The Bookplates of Leo Wyatt" by Brian North Lee; included was a comprehensive checklist of the ex libris Wyatt had designed to that time. The article reflected not only Brian's expertise in the field of bookplates but also the warmth of his personal friendship with the artist. It is anticipated that Brian will write a tribute to Leo Wyatt, and we hope to have permission to reprint it in our quarterly.

On April 18, 1981 a Memorial Tribute was held in the Margaret Brown Herrick Memorial Chapel of Occidental College for Ray Allen Billington, famed historian and Senior Research Scholar at the Huntington Library.

The tributes were presented by individuals representing key areas of Billington's life: Richard C. Gilman for Occidental College, Hugh C. Tolford for the Los Angeles Westerners and Zamoranans, James H. Thorpe for the Huntington Library, Doyce B. Nunis for his family and friends, and Martin Ridge for his students and the history profession.

Billington is perhaps best known for his espousal of Frederick Jackson Turner's theory of American history based on the Westward movement.

RAY ALLEN BILLINGTON
Memorial Tribute

His last publication was THE LIMERICK: HISTORICAL AND HYSTERICAL. Though the limerick is light, humerous, and frequently bawdy, the subject was given the scholarly approach with appropriate footnotes and bibliography.

The above bookplate was used on the cover of the Occidental College memorial keepsake; also it was used as an illustration in the Arellanes bibliography published by Gale in 1971. The ex libris was designed by Ray Billington's wife Mabel.

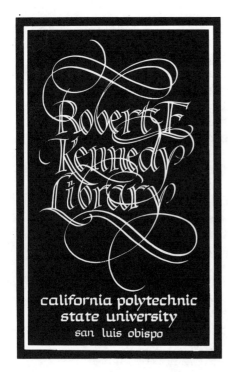

california polytechnic
state university
san luis obispo

CAL POLY BOOKPLATE COMPETITION

As part of the preparation for the opening of the Robert E. Kennedy Library of California Polytechnic State University, San Luis Opispo, there was a competition held for the design of a new bookplate for the library. This competition was under the auspices of the Library Associates, a support group formed about a year ago.

The deadline for the competition was in March 1981, and the winners were announced at the March 22nd meeting of the Library Associates held in the Special Collections Department of the Kennedy Library. In conjunction with the bookplate theme, a local member of the Library Associates, Margaret Nybak, who is also a member of the American Society of Bookplate Collectors and Designers, suggested the Director of the Society, Audrey Arellanes, as speaker for the occasion.

The Library is named for Robert E. Kennedy, president of the University from 1967 to 1979. He first came to Cal Poly in 1940 as a journalism instructor, and progressed through the years to head of the Journalism Department, then to Vice President of the University. Dr. Kennedy was instrumental in lobbying with the Calfiornia State Legislature to acquire funds for the construction of the new library building on the Cal Poly campus.

At the March 22nd Library Associates meeting, Robert Andreini, long time Cal Poly faculty member in the Speech Department and Library Associates Board Member, announced the winning bookplate designs. The winning design was by Tim Goodspeed, a graphic arts major. Second and third places went to William Taylor and Richard Schmidt. Goodspeed's design lends itself equally well to black on white or the reverse. It is shown here in two sizes which will make it suitable for books of varying dimensions.

Bob Blesse, Special Collections Librarian, and Priscilla Graham, President of Library Associates, coordinated the March 22nd meeting which was attended by about fifty members and friends. Audrey Arellanes' talk, Bookplates As A Passport to Friendship, was aimed for an audience interested in books but not particularly knowledgeable about bookplates. A variety of questions following the talk gave evidence of a lively interest. The hospitality extended to the speaker by all those involved at the University and the Library Associates, and by Priscilla and Myron Graham in particular, who acted as her local hosts, was in the best tradition of bookplate friendships.

INTERNATIONAL CONGRESS
Oxford / August 1982
Bookplates executed between 1980-82 are wanted for exhibit at the Congress.   Artists and owners may submit prints for consideration to BOOKPLATES IN THE NEWS.

AS of BC & D

Bookplates in the News

605 N. STONEMAN AVENUE #F, ALHAMBRA, CALIFORNIA, 91801 U.S.A.

AUDREY SPENCER ARELLANES, Editor

OCTOBER 1981   NUMBER FORTY-SIX

NEW BOOKPLATES for the REED COLLEGE LIBRARY
by Anita Bigelow

Last year the library of Reed College, located in Portland, Oregon, celebrated its building's fiftieth year. Last year also marked the start of
many changes for the library, such as an ambitious expansion - and a new
bookplate. I had the pleasure of designing the new bookplate. The type
is a Bembo, the motto from Horace
("The written word remains."). The
linoleum cut image represents one
of the bas-relief creatures decorating the campus's oldest dormitory
block, a 1912 gothic concoction by
architect A. E. Doyle.

LITERA SCRIPTA MANET

Reed College Library

The only constraint on the design
of the new bookplate was that it be
airy. The old bookplate was a rather
somber linoleum cut depicting the
library's western facade. Lloyd J.
Reynolds designed and cut the plate
at about the time the library moved
into its building. Reynolds had
wanted to make a new bookplate with
more white space, but he never got
around to doing do. My design does
have white space, and it comes in
two sizes, to suit the many sizes
of books in the library.

At the same time I designed the ex
libris for the library's main collection, I also designed a set of
bookplates for the books Reynolds
bequeathed to the library. This was
an awesome challenge, because Reynolds
was a formidable man. Reynolds (1902-
1978) joined the Reed faculty in 1929
as an instructor of Humanities and creative writing. He began teaching
calligraphy as a "lab" for his Humanities classes. In 1949 he offered
Reed's first formal course in calligraphy, typography, and book design. In

1972 he was named Oregon's Calligrapher Laureate. His influence was and continues to be profound, whether he is remembered as a calligrapher, a student of Asian philosophies, or a scholar of utmost integrity - one who was willing to tread on toes to stand by his judgments.

While the dimensional variety of his books led, again, to the idea of different sizes of bookplates, to pick even one motif to represent a most multi-dimensional man proved impossible for me or Judith Reynolds, his widow. We, therefore, ended with eight different bookplates, falling into three broad categories: those with poetry, those with an alphabet, and those with Chinese knots. The type, in all cases, in Frutiger 65. The poetry is that of Reynolds and written out by him; it is taken from his WEATHERGRAMS (Portland, Oregon: Society for Italic Handwriting, 1972).* The alphabets are in Reynolds' hand and are from his ITALIC LETTERING, CALLIGRAPHY, AND HANDWRITING (Portland, OR: Champoeg Press, 1963). The alphabets and the background on the bookplates with poetry are a golden brown, to evoke the kraft paper on which weathergrams are meant to be written. The Reed College Print Shop printed the Reynolds collection and main collection bookplates on their offset press. (* A weathergram is a short poem, meant to be written on a strip of kraft paper cut from grocery bags and then hung up outdoors. To make a weathergram is to make a gift to the world and to find one is serendipity.)

Reed College Library

Reed College Library

The Lloyd J. Reynolds Collection

Reed College Library

Lloyd J. Reynolds Collection

Reed College Library

Lloyd J. Reynolds Collection

The Lloyd J. Reynolds Collection

QUICK BROWN FOX JUMPS OVER THE LAZY DOG

Reed College Library

Ex Libris

G.B.

I've drawn and painted for years. Maya Moffatt asked for a generalized bookplate two families could use, so I did the Quixote on unicorn. Toni Tallman, a computer programmer with a strong interest in astrology, said do her one – hence the textured, quite dark ex libris with astrolobe, the irregular solid from Durer's "Melancholia," a sculpture Tim Coursey did (of which I did a still-life in oil she owns), and her portrait. I did a much lighter one for her eleven-year old daughter. Peggy Davis does public information for El Centro College. Her interest in cats is shown in the portrait plate for Kris Smith-Lewis; a cat is curled 'round her neck while she reads. For archaeologist Paul Larson I designed an erotic plate with satyr.

I've done magic for years, and will give three clown-magic demonstrations in November for the Hertzberg Circus Project in San Antonio. I designed my own bookplate to go on magic, literary and books

about books. I drew it on brown wrapping paper, had the drawing screened, and printed in black ink on a light parchment, which when trimmed approximates the original.

I was raised on A. Edward Newton and Holbrook Jackson, was in my teens when I read about Newton's Johnsonian bookplate, and more about the decision to apply them in ANATOMY OF BIBLIOMANIA. So I have a thorough regard for bookplate history. I'd like to etch plates but have no casual access to equipment, and I'd prefer it casual.

(Editor's Note: Gerald Burns is the very picture of a magician with beard and frock coat. He has three volumes of verse in print: BOCCHERINI'S MINUET, LETTERS TO OBSCURE MEN, and A BOOK OF SPELLS; all published by Salt Lick Press; also a volume of prose, TOWARD A PHENOMENOLOGY OF WRITTEN ART from Treacle Press. He holds a BA from Harvard, enjoyed two years at Trinity College in Dublin looking at 18th century Irish piracies and polishing Grolier bindings, and received his MA in 1969 from SMU. Burns has taught English for about ten years, and has set type five and one-half years. As can be seen his interests and talents are varied. You may write him at 2422 Vagas, Dallas, TX 75219.)

AMERICAN EXCHANGES SOUGHT   Hans-Joachim Bandilla would like to exchange with American bookplate collectors. He can write in English and German, and would welcome the opportunity to add to his small collection of American plates. You may write him at AM Krankenhaus 2, DDR-2070 Robel, German Democratic Republic.

Artists, who wish to have their work considered for exhibit at the Congress, should send original prints, which have been created since the 1980 Congress in Linz, to the American Society of Bookplate Collectors and Designers. All exhibit materials will be forwarded through the participating bookplate societies. Probably there will be a small charge to cover mounting exhibit pieces and sending them insured to England. / If you plan to attend the Congress at Keble College in Oxford send ASBC&D a self-addressed, stamped envelope for registration.

Save by paying your 1982 dues on or before December 31, 1981

1982 MEMBERSHIP DUES

$27.50 for BOOKPLATES IN THE NEWS 1982 and YEAR BOOK 1981 for Renewals received before January 1, 1982.

$35.00 for BOOKPLATES IN THE NEWS 1982 and YEAR BOOK 1981 for New Memberships commencing January 1, 1982 and late renewals.

$15 BOOKPLATES IN THE NEWS 1982 / $25 YEAR BOOK 1981 - Partial Membership

FROM THE BOOKPLATE LITERATURE

BUCKSKIN BULLETIN, In Memory of Ray Allen Billington, Paul Bailey. (1) 15:3-4, Spring 1981. Tribute by former Sheriff of the Los Angeles Westerners to Billington, "acknowledged dean of American frontier historians . . .." His bookplate, which features a covered wagon coming over the hill toward a campfire circled by other wagons, was used to illustrate the program for the memorial held for Billington at Occidental College.

AMPHORA, Armorial Bookplates, Bruce Peel. (4) #44, 18-21, June 1981. Interesting general article; of particular importance is mention of HERALDRY IN CANADA, journal of the Canadian Heraldry Society, which for the past ten years has included a feature entitled "The Heraldic Bookplate." Peel makes due note of some early women owners of ex libris: Elizabeth Pindar (1608), Dowager Countess of Bath (1671) and Alice, widow of Sir John Brownlow (1668).

BIBLIO-CAL NOTES (Southern California Local History Council), The Bookplate in California, Audrey Spencer Arellanes. (4) 11:10-12, 16, Summer 1981. A brief review of artists, owners, collectors, and editors associated with the bookplate in California. Illustrations from HISTORIC CALIFORNIA IN BOOKPLATES by Clare Ryan Talbot.

THE PRIVATE LIBRARY, Mark Severin's Book Illustrations, David Chambers. (4) Thirs Series 3:3:99-115, Autumn 1980 (published mid-1981). Among the twenty-seven books discussed and detailed in a checklist are: MAKING A BOOKPLATE, YOUR WOOD-ENGRAVING, and ENGRAVED BOOKPLATES.

VIGNETTES OF BOOKPLATE COLLECTING IN LENINGRAD, translated and edited by Professor W. E. Butler, Secretary of the Bookplate Society (England). This is the first in a contemplated series of translations and original essays on the development of the ex libris in Russia and the Soviet Union. The present volume contains reminiscences by the greatest enthusiasts of the 1930-50s, E. A. Rozenbladt and B. A. Vilinbakhov, together with an account of the Rozenbladt Collection now in the USSR Academy of Sciences Library. This study contains 13 illustrations, 58 pages, index, and is printed in a limited edition of 150 copies. It may be obtained for $2 from W. E. Butler, 9 Lyndale Avenue, London NW2 2QD, England.

ROCKWELL KENT, edited and with an introduction by Fridolf Johnson, foreword by Jamie Wyeth. This volume is to be published by Alfred A. Knopf in November 1981. It is large both as to size (9 13/16"x13 1/8") and number of pages (352); contains 96 pages of color plates; cost: $45. (Editor's Note: We hope to have a full review of this new Kent book early in 1982.)

THE PRIVATE LIBRARY, Kate Greenaway's Bookplate for Mrs. J. C. Black. (1) Third Series 3:4:141-2, Winter 1980 (published 1981). This is an addition to the plates mentioned by Keith Clark in his article which appeared in THE PRIVATE LIBRARY (Second Series, 8:3) for Autumn 1975.

THE PRIVATE LIBRARY, Walter Crane's Bookplate for the Bishopsgate Institute, James Wilson. (3) Third Series 3:4:142-4, Winter 1980 (published 1981). This is a previously unrecorded design dated 1894. The original form does not appear to have actually been used as an ex libris, but in 1903 it was redrawn by G. M. McCall and printed in four sizes. A further adaption was made, probably in the 1950s, and used for about 10 years.

NEWSLETTER, The Bookplate Society (England), Vol. 3, #33, March 1981. Bookplates of the March Phillipps De Lisle Family, Anthony K. Pincott. (3) 134-7. Current family member is attempting to reconstruct list of books originally comprising family library; many traced through various family bookplates. / Display of Contemporary Wood-engravings at Amalgam, (4), 138-39. London gallery showing work of Gertrude Hermes, John Lawrence, Sarah van Niekerk, and Anne Jope; the latter in particular is willing to accept ex libris commissions. / In Memoriam Johan Schwenke (1887-1981), G.J.R., 139. Schwenke died in February at the age of 93; he founded the Dutch Ex Libris Society in 1932. / English Artists Success in International Bookplate Design Competition, (1) 140. Leslie Charlotte Benenson and Marcus Beaven won joint first on theme of "Fauna and Flora" in competition sponsored by the International Exlibris Centrum, Sint Niklaas, Belgium. / Art of the Scribe, 140. 60th anniversary exhibition included about a dozen bookplates. / Document Repair Tape, 140. New repair tape approved for use in the Public Record Office Conservation Department and in the British Museum; marketed by Ademco Ltd., Lincoln Road, Cressex Estate, High Wycombe, Bucks HP12 3QU, England; £ 3.10p for roll 25mm x 30m or £ 25 for roll 25mm x 500m. / International Congress, 141-2. Events scheduled from Wednesday (8/18/82) evening through mid-day Sunday (8/22/82). Talks will be delivered in English and translations into French and German will be available. Registrations fees not yet set, but should be circulated at the end of 1981; registration deadline will be March 31, 1982. / "In-House" Albums, H. R. Page, 142-3. All members of the Bookplate Society may submit copies of their bookplates for inclusion in the albums; also their photographs. / Bookplate Society Postal Auction Scheme, 144. Details of new postal auction; Auction Secretary is Brian Schofield.

EXLIBRIS I. FARVER, Helmer Fogedgaard and Johnny Køhler (privately printed 1979). The bookplates of twenty-one different artists are tipped-in; most are multi-colored.

EXLIBRIS I. FARVER, Helmer Fogedgaard and Johnny Køhler (privately printed 1980). Twenty-two different artists' work represented by tipped-in prints, all multi-colored.

BLODTØRST: Martin Andersen Nexø (privately printed 1980), by Jørgen C. Rasmussen. Text in Danish; three black and white prints reproduced but do not appear to be ex libris.

VLADIMIR KOMAREK, Jiri Hlusicka (Exlibristen, 1981, Klaus Rodel, Postbox 109, DK9900 Frederikshavn, Denmark). There are ten tipped-in prints and multi-lingual biography including English; this particular monogram makes no mention of ex libris work.

GRAPHIA #80, pages 65-92. Article on Walter Wuyts with numerous illustrations of black and white ex libris, chronological checklist of 27 bookplates. By the appearance of numerous bookplates featuring the horse, the second article must concern the horse as subject of the bookplate. Articles on Axel Vater, memorial to Johan Schwenke, Paul-Francois Morvan, and news of exhibits and bookplate literature.

London TIME LITERARY SUPPLEMENT, Eulen Ex Libris, (2) 132, February 6, 1981. This is a well produced study of German Bookplates using the owl as a motif.

L'EX LIBRIS FRANCAIS, No. 138, 85-96, December 1980. Martine Desilles writes about an exhibition, Didier Kowalik lists the booklets which were distributed at the 18th International Congress in Linz; the last install-ment is given of the checklist of engraved bookplates by Mariaelisa Leboroni.

NEWSLETTER, Junior Bookplate Society (England), No. 8, December 1980. Emma Rose Barber and Elisabeth Fotheringham continue to edit a newsworthy publication. This number has 9 pages, printed one side, with several original bookplate prints, and Xerox tip-ins of several others. Articles include comments about a BBC program on Rex Whistler, an English class project on Victorian bookplates and particularly Aubrey Beardsley, letter-press printing in relation to bookplates, and some Scottish bookplates.

NEWSLETTER, Junior Bookplate Society (England), No. 9, April 1981. Heraldic Bookplates, Elisabeth Fotheringham. (4) 2-4. The article is primarily a quotation from B. C. Trappes-Lomax, whose article of the same title appeared in THE COAT OF ARMS, a heraldic quarterly. - Hieroglyphic Bookplates, David Chambers. (3) 5. The Rev. W. J. Loftie in the late 19th century designed several bookplates inscribed in hieroglyphics. Illustrat-ed are the plates for Rev. Loftie, Walter Herries Pollock, and Rider Hag-gard, author of SHE. The hieroglyphics on Haggard's plate signify "Rider Haggard, the son of Ella, Lady of the House, makes an oblation to Thoth, the lord of writing, who dwells in the Moon." - What Are They All About? Harry Page. (3) 5-7. Sir Harry Page asks "... should we have bookplates which require a short essay to enable us to appreciate them to the full?" The explanation of the various elements in his own Owl-Man plate by Dutch artist Lou Strik seems to offer justification; certainly the explanation adds greatly to the enjoyment of the print.

NORDISK EXLIBRIS TIDSSKRIFT, No. 138, 1980. Klaus Rodel writes a memorial for Jørgen Vils-Pedersen, well-known Danish collector who contributed to the international literature of the bookplate. / Rodel also writes about artist Harry Jurgens, whose work appears to be surrealistic. / The Ex Libris In Japan by Clif Parfit of the English Center, Japan, is printed in Danish and English; there are 20 black and white illustrations, many by Japanese artists well-known for their larger prints (example: Takeo Takei). Because of weather conditions, before the modern technology of adhesives, stick-on labels were impractical in Japan; thus, ownership was, and still is, marked with a seal which is inked with sticky vermilion ink and the impression then made. "To the Japanese eye, the seal impressions do not mar the beauty of a book or scroll. The seals merely provide valuable evidence of authenticy." / Vaclav Krupka writes about artist Jan Vanco, who appears to favor the female nude in his ex libris.

NORDISK EXLIBRIS TIDSSKRIFT, No. 140, 1981. Exlibris-motiver by Jan Rhebergen; numberous illustrations. Milan Erazim by Vaclav Krupka; article about young "modern" artist. Fidus (Hugo Hoppener 1868-1948) by Klaus Rodel; among the illustrations is a cover design for THEOSOPHIE (August 1910).

James Keenan has energetically put together several bookplate exhibits of work by Cambridge Bookplate artists. The Social Law Library, Boston, has an exhibit starting November 1 and continuing into 1982; St. Botolph Club in Boston has an ex libris exhibit beginning November 11, and the Concord Art Association will display 28 pieces by Cambridge Bookplate, Nov. 8-Dec. 13'81.

EXLIBRIS WERELD, Winter 1980. Articles about artist Ank Spronk, Ab Steen-voorden, Gerard Bergman (1899-1980), and something about art nouveau. (Note: Will someone volunteer to translate and/or summarize articles from this fine journal edited by Jan Rhebergen in Amsterdam? If so, please write Editor of BOOKPLATES IN THE NEWS.)

MITTEILUNGEN DER DEUTSCHEN EXLIBRIS-GESELLSCHAFT, #13, 1981. This issue contains pages 148 to 159, 8¼ x 11¼, printed on one side; text runs two-thirds the width of the page and the remaining one-third is used to re-produce ex libris. (Note: Another plea for translating and/or summarizing the articles from German.)

KISGRAFIKA, 80 1-2. This is a magazine (about 6½ x 9½, perfect bound, 80 pages) with a profusion of black and white illustrations and a variety of articles in Hungarian. There is an article about the Ex Libris Congress in Linz in 1980, several about artists, mention of bookplate literature from other ex libris societies.

THE BOOKPLATE SOCIETY NEWSLETTER (England), III:#34, June 1981. Contains following articles: The Death of Leo Wyatt, Brian North Lee; Sherborn of Gutter Land and Intriguing Questions of Bookplate Design with Notes on Edward Edwards and John Hall, Brian North Lee (147-164, 19 illustrations), Leo Wyatt by Philip Beddingham includes illustration of 13 ex libris by Wyatt including that of at least one American, William V. Hollander.

EXLIBRIS WERELD, Summer 1979. Article by Jan Rhebergen on the work of Hubert Levigne with a chronological checklist of his ex libris; reviews of ex libris literature from other societies; note on Erich Schoner (1901-1979).

SVENSKA EXLIBRISFORENINGEN, #137, 1981. This publication is issued from Stockholm. (Any volunteers with a knowledge of Swedish?) Also issued recently is an Index for Numbers 109-136.

ANATOLIJ KALASCHNIKOW (Moscow, 1981). An attractive, small (3½x5) paper-back with endpapers reproducing several volumes of fine binding with gold stamping, 87 pages which include some text in Russian, a chronological checklist of the thirty ex libris reproduced and probably their numbers in his master checklist. (Anatolij Kalaschnikow, 117334 Moskva, Leninskij, Prospekt 44-124.)

THE BOOK COLLECTOR, The Authenticity of Bookplates, Brian North Lee. 62-73, Spring 1981. "Since most bookplate collections in this country, from the British Museum Franks collection to the small lot found in a bookshop or the saleroom, contain ex-libris relating to America as well as Britain, it may be helpful to include American plates in this summary of the prob-lems involved in ensuring the authenticity of bookplates. The question has, however, less to do with deliberate forgery than questions of date and attribution, etc., for bookplates have rarely been valuable enough to give counterfeiters encouragement; even quite early examples still change hands today for pence rather than pounds, and the few collectors with enough knowledge to recognize great rarities have never wished to practise such deceit."

• ———————————————————————————————— •

AS of BC & D
Bookplates in the News

605 N. STONEMAN AVENUE #F, ALHAMBRA, CALIFORNIA, 91801 U.S.A.

ADREY SPENCER ARELLANES, Editor

NUMBER FORTY-SEVEN   JANUARY 1982

RYOZO HIRAKATA
by Cliff Parfit

Though born in Nagasaki in
1941, Ryozo Hirakata now
lives at the other end of
Japan, in Hokkaido in Northern Japan.

Hokkaido is famous for its
fine wooden Meiji buildings,
and Ryozo Hirakata has made
it his business to illustrate
these fine and well-known
buildings in many interesting
ways

Firstly he has published
sketches and woodcuts in connection with newspaper stories.
Next he has made some fine collections of woodblock postcards
in which many of the buildings
have been shown in his bold and
masculine style.

In the last year he has turned
his attention to bookplates.
The first collection of his ex
libris was published in a
limited hand-made edition by The
English Centre. In this series the printing was done in black heavy lines on a
semi-transparent kozo paper (usually Sekishu Washi), and the color was applied
by hand to the back of each plate. The resulting ex libris have something of
the appearance of stained-glass windows, though the designs are all very Japanese.

Ryozo Hirakata's style has the same no-nonsense approach which made Shiko Munakata
famous, and he acknowledges Munakata's influence in his style. He thinks and
works directly for the block rather than adapting pencil sketches to woodblock

as a more timid artist might do. As can be imagined, images of the type used by Mr. Hirakata (the family name comes first by traditional Japanese usage) show up remarkably well even on greyish newsprint, but on creamy surface of hand-made paper, the prints are magnificient. They are, of course, clearly within the Japanese "sosaku hanga" or "creative print" tradition as developed by Yamamoto Kanae and Onchi Koshiro in the early years of the present century.

The plate used to illustrate this article was printed by the artist and sealed with his personal seal, so that each ex libris is a unique work of art.

As long ago as 1964 Mr. Hirakata was a prizewinner at the Nihon Hanga-in and in 1967 he exhibited at the New Hokkaido Shindo-ten Exhibition. In 1967 also he was elected a member of the Hokkaido Hanga Association. (The word "hanga" means print or picture, but the words "sosaku hanga" or "creative print" have many overtones of meaning for Japanese artists.) In 1969 he was a prizewinner at the Ichiokai Exhibition and in 1978 the Hokkaido Hanga Association was formed with Mr. Hirakata in a leading role. In the 1980 the seal was set on his work as a professional artist by his election as a full member of the Japan Hanga Association, and in 1981 a full scale exhibition of his work was held.

Finally at the end of 1981 his first large scale book was produced with the illustrations showing many of the Meiji buildings previously seen in his woodcuts. This is a splendid first book, and we hope to see many such publications as the years go by.

Notes: Translation of the inscription on the plate: (Zoshohyo Hirakata Ryozo) Ryozo Hirakata's Bookplate.

Meiji: The first "modern" period in Japan lasting from 1868-1911.

Kozo Paper: Paper made by hand from the kozo plant. As it is very strong, it is obtainable in very thin and translucent grades. It also is obtainable in many other weights.

Washi: Any kind of Japanese hand-made paper. ("Kami" is the generic name for paper of all kinds and "Yoshi" signified European-style paper.)

Sekishu Washi: Washi from the Sekishu area.

Sosaku Hanga ("Creative Hanga Movement): A new movement in block-printing started in the early years of the present century by Yamamoto Kanae and other colleagues who wished to break away from the dying "ukiyoe" tradition.

Seal: Seal impressions are still used instead of signatures for most business and artistic purposes in Japan.

BOOKPLATES IN THE NEWS
$15/Calendar Year 1982
Copyright Audrey Spencer Arellanes
Issued - January/April/July/October

GEORGE MACKLEY, WOOD ENGRAVER
Gresham Books Limited, 1981

This is a large (8½ x 12), handsome book, with a wealth of illustration, priced at $35. The
foreword is by Sir Hugh Casson,
an introduction by Monica Poole,
a brief biography by Elizabeth
Romyn, the artist writes about
wood engraving, Ian Lowe writes
about The Collector and The Artist, Patricia Jaffe about Mackley and the Fitzwilliam. Prints
are presented in categories: sea,
botanical, commercial, waterways,
The Netherlands, commercial, and
rivers. Two letters in Mackley's
hand are reproduced; fortunately
one is from 1958 when his calligraphic hand was still beautifully
controlled.

In a Chronological List of prints
appear the following bookplates:
  1946 J. R. Toller
  1948 S.E.R.A.
       D. Keith Robinson
  1949 Elizabeth Mary Halliday
  1965 Marinus Buis
  1968 Julia Peckham
  n.d. Sally Budgen

In addition Mrs. M. V. Green of Gresham
Books indicates there are three additional bookplates. "One was for Timothy Peckham, the brother of Julia Peckham; the
other not truly a bookplate but was used
as such for the Pyt House, and the third
was for his wife Caroline Mackley. This
last is the only example of a multi-
coloured print produced by George Mackley.
Only three copies are known to me which
have not already been affixed to books.
One is in the Fitzwilliam Museum, Cambridge; the other two are the property of
the artist and Monica Poole."

If you like wood engravings, you will no
doubt enjoy this volume immensely. In
1968 Rampant Lions Press (Cambridge)
printed for the Two Horse Press in London
a selection of Mackley's prints titled
ENGRAVED IN WOOD.

A volume by George E. Mackley entitled
WOOD ENGRAVING, published by Gresham

Books, Old Woking, Surrey, England, was first published in 1948; there is now an inexpensive ($12.50) reprint. In a 1981 note of acknowledgment, Mackley wrote: " . . . my publisher, who against my inclinations to allow this book to fade into oblivion, persuaded me that my text would benefit those who had a desire to learn more about wood engraving. I trust that his judgement will prove to be sound and that, whether it is read to help those who would like to practice the art or by those who wish to acquire a better understanding of it, they will find it both instructive and informative." I feel that the artist may rest assured that the text fully justifies the publisher's decision to republish; I find his use of language, textual style no less appealing than his masterful prints. While this reprint has many of the disadvantages associated with inexpensive reprints from the visual standpoint, the text can be easily read physically and enjoyed without stint for content. The personality, wit, and humor of the artist shine through the text, and makes him seem like a person I would enjoy knowing.

Two bookplates are illustrated in WOOD ENGRAVING; the J. R. Toller by Mackley and Mark Severin's nude with sea shell for Alan Veen. (Reviewer: ASA)

EXHIBIT OF ASBC&D MEMBERS' EX LIBRIS   If you would like your personal bookplate to appear in an exhibit, it is requested that you send prints to James Keenan, Cambridge Bookplate, P. O. Box 340, Cambridge, MA 02238. Keenan has already mounted displays in the Boston area including the Social Law Library and St. Botolph Club, and he is very enthusiastic about putting together an exhibit devoted to designs used by members of the American Society of Bookplate Collectors and Designers. It is his hope that the exhibit will travel beyond the Boston area. Each print should be accompanied by the name of the artist who designed it, the date of design, technique of execution, and method of printing. It will be helpful, too, if you furnish any special details about the design, the library for which it is used, and information about your collecting interests, profession, etc. While not all the data will be utilized in the exhibit, it often helps in grouping display items and offers insight into the personalities of the owners. This is your opportunity to participate in an effort to promote interest in bookplates - to bring these miniature works of art to the attention of designers, collectors, and potential owners.

BOOKS, Gerald Donaldson (New York: Van Nostrand Reinhold Co., 1981. $14.95). This is an odd assortment of bits and snippets about books, bookmaking, the lore, love, and enemies of books. A number of bookplates are illustrated starting with a rather large stock plate by J. T. Berryman on the copyright page, others for George H. Corey Collection of Mark Twain, Frederick Willis Davis, New York Society Library, Osborn Rennie Lamb, Frances Woodworth plate by Jay Chambers, and two monogram plates; some have probably been reduced in size. A chapter titled Ex Libris is followed by this explanation: "How to choose from the far too many books available (avoiding the bad, dull, lewd, smutty and worthless), when, where, and how to read them, and advice on their care and handling." The bibliography includes two bookplate references: AMERICAN BOOK-PLATES by Allen and THE STORY OF THE BOOKPLATE by Gale Research (1971); this may be their calendar. Donaldson also authored: THE GREAT CANADIAN BEER BOOK, THE EXERCISE BOOK, THE WALKING BOOK, and THE BOOK OF DAYS.

Tom Lyons of Boston is the proprietor of T. J. Lyons Press, which for more than 50 years has specialized in "period printing." His 2,000 square foot shop houses one of the world's largest typographic collections of antique type, old stock cuts, and a great supply of ornaments, borders, and typographic bric-a-brac. Tom is quoted by Dan Solo in his article in GRAPHIC ARTS MONTHLY (May 1981): "The Depression hit me hard. I'd been in business only a few years when the bottom fell out of everything. Job shops were dying all around me. So I decided to attract attention to myself by specializing in the old fashioned. It worked." A variety of these types from an earlier period is displayed on a card for Cambridge Bookplate.

Elizabeth Chellis, ASBC&D member, had a gift plate designed for the Museum of Fine Arts. The frame and typefaces of the of the 19th century are from the Lyons collection. The frame was by J. J. Ormond, the donor's name is set in Renaissant and Museum of Fine Arts is set in Monastic. The plate has been printed letterpress with Buffalo ink on ivory alpha cellulose paper. Thus, a happy blend has been achieved by utilizing a few of the period pieces from the Lyons collection and the design talents of Cambridge Bookplate.

Though almost 90 and using a cane when he walks, Tom Lyons still has a very sprightly air. And a representative selection from his collection, about 60 different types, is now available on the headline machine, Photo Typositor, of the Visual Graphics Corp.

At the time of the American Bicentennial, Tom Lyons printed "76 Americana Type Faces to exercise fertile brains and gifted hands." This is a delightful glance at period types.

GIFT OF
ELIZABETH CHELLIS
MUSEUM OF FINE ARTS
BOSTON

Robert
Hitchman: his book.

A memorial service was held for Robert B. Hitchman on April 23, 1981 in the Episcopal Church of the Ascension, Seattle, Washington.

Mr. Hitchman died the previous Friday, April 17, in Worcester, Massachusetts, where he had attended a meeting of the Board of Councilors of the American Antiquarian Society.

Born in Denver, he moved at an early age to the Pacific Northwest where he attended the University of Washington and graduated summa cum laude in anthropology.

At retirement in 1973 Hitchman was head of Unigard Insurance Group; he also had been chairman and president of Olympic National Life. In addition to his business interests, he was an avid Northwest historian and philanthropist. He was president and board member of the Washington State Historical Society, on the board of the Seattle HIstorical Society; chairman of the Pacific Northwest Group of the New York-based Explorers' Club from 1968 to 1973, and past-president of the Seattle Society of the Archaeological Institute of America. During World War II, he was on active duty in the Army, retiring as a colonel. He had been listed in WHO'S WHO IN AMERICA since the 1971 edition.

Robert Hitchman was a long-time member of ASBC&D and frequently sent items of bookplate interest to the editor of BITN, items which otherwise might not have come to the editor's attention. His interest in bookplates dates back to the time of Frederick Starr, whom he knew well.

Robert B. Hitchman is survived by his wife Helen. And I am certain he will survive long in the memories of the many ex libris enthusiasts who knew him.

Compliments of: W. B. SAUNDERS CO.

EX LIBRIS:

←More In April

FOR THE POETRY BOOKS OF CRT

CLARE RYAN TALBOT
1899-1981

Clare Ryan Talbot, long known as the First Lady of Bookplates, died October 5, 1981 after an illness of several months. Private memorial services were held with interment at St. Joseph Cemetery, San Pablo, California.

Clare was born August 9, 1899 in Charles City, Iowa, daughter of Thomas Joseph and Margaret Ann (Darby) Ryan. She attended St. Mary's Academy and College 1914-1918, and University of Oregon 1919-20. By 1923 she had entered the antiquarian book business, a field in which she would be active through her lifetime.

It was in 1933 that Clare Talbot's first volume about bookplates appeared. IN QUEST OF THE PERFECT BOOKPLATE was published by Ruth Thomson Saunders, at her Saunders Studio Press in Claremont, in an edition limited to 300 copies, numbered and signed by the author. The attractive cover is a hand blocked design by Saunders. Paul Jordan-Smith, well-known bookman, wrote the foreword. (My copy has the original pricing label from J. W. Robinson Co. of Los Angeles showing the price to be $2! And on the page opposite the colophon is a small boxed notice of other Books About Bookplates from the Saunders Studio Press: BOOKPLATES by R. T. Saunders at $3 and THE BOOK OF ARTISTS OWN BOOKPLATES by R. T. Saunders at $2.)

In 1936 HISTORIC CALIFORNIA IN BOOKPLATES was published by the Graphic Press (Los Angeles) in both a trade and a limited edition. Robert Ernest Cowan, famed bibliographer, wrote the introduction. In a review near the time of publication, Edwin Turnbladh (CALIFORNIA ARTS & ARCHITECTURE, October 1937) said: "Whether your curiosity runs to history, art or human beings (this book) is apt to contribute well to your enjoyment of life." Prior to publication there was a charming interview with Mrs. Talbot in SATURDAY NIGHT (July 27, 1935), a Los Angeles publication. Long out of print, HISTORIC CALIFORNIA IN BOOKPLATES is sought by all serious ex libris collectors.

Mrs. Talbot was a member of three bookplate societies active in the United States in the 1930's: Bookplate Association International, California Bookplate Society, and American Society of Bookplate Collectors and Designers, and over the years she belonged to most of the ex libris societies in other countries. Also, she was founder of the Society of Ex Libris Historians.

In addition to books, she wrote a number of articles which appeared in such periodicals as AMATEUR BOOK COLLECTOR which was later titled AMERICAN BOOK COLLECTOR, PRINT, QUARTERLY NEWS-LETTER of Book Club of California, WESTERN COLLECTOR, YEAR BOOK of American Society of Bookplate Collectors and Designers. She wrote under the name of Clare Bill as well as Talbot.

Ever an innovator, Mrs. Talbot's aptly named Hilprand Press published Dr. Samuel X. Radbill's BIBLIOGRAPHY OF MEDICAL EX LIBRIS LITERATURE, 1951.

In addition to her many ex libris activities, Clare was knowledgeable in the areas of antiques and silver. She was book review editor for SILVER MAGAZINE and a contributor to WESTERN COLLECTOR and ANTIQUES JOURNAL. Mrs. Talbot is listed in the 3rd edition, 1964-65, of WHO'S WHO OF AMERICAN WOMEN and the 1978, 4th edition, of WORLD WHO'S WHO OF WOMEN; INTERNATIONAL BLUE BOOK (WHO'S WHO IN THE WORLD) 1943, published by Hyacinthe Ringrose with multi-lingual entries.

During most of her adult life Clare lived in California; Southern California in the earlier years, the Los Angeles area, and later Oakland and Berkeley. She is survived by her brother Laurence J. Ryan, who has decided to join the ASBC&D.

Clare had a number of personal bookplates, among the better known is The Candle of God plate engraved by James Webb, a variation of the Hilprand Brandenburg plate which Maxwell Noll designed and printed from a zinc cut, The Book of Kells typographical by Ruth T. Saunders, a woodcut Venetian scene by Victor Stuyvaert, and Winged Victory etched by Australian artist Ella Dwyer.

Clare Ryan Talbot has left a written legacy which will keep her name alive as long as there are bookplate enthusiasts to peruse the literature in the field.

———————————————————————————————

KOVELS' KNOW YOUR COLLECTIBLES   ASBC&D members Ralph and Terry Kovel have at least a dozen titles in print concerning antiques and collectibles to their credit. Three new titles, all in print through Crown Publishers, are: THE KOVELS' ANTIQUES PRICE LIST, KOVELS' KNOW YOUR ANTIQUES, and KOVELS' KNOW YOUR COLLECTIBLES. The last two titles contain references to the American Society of Bookplate Collectors and Designers; ANTIQUES mentions our Society under collectors' groups. COLLECTIBLES has two pages on bookplates and a brief bibliography. Two plates are illustrated which were designed in the early 1900s by Roberti Caroli Sticht. These volumes, in the sequence above, are priced at $9.95, $13.95, and $16.95.

———————————————————————————————

A TRULY LIMITED EDITION   EX LIBRIS OF YONEJIRO SATO by Cliff Parfit (Tokyo: English Centre of Japan, March 1981). This is a beautifully produced book, about 7" square, side sewn in the Japanese style; cover and flip-over slipcase have cranes imprinted in gold on a rich brown. The text papers are Hosho and Chikugo washi, a kozo paper made by Shigemi Matsuo of Yame City, Kyushu. The cover and slipcase have paper labels imprinted in silver. The colophon states book produced in an edition of six copies. This limitation is, in part, explained by fact each text page is a typed original.

There are 16 numbered bookplate items, with 19 actual tip-in; three are miniatures. Mr. Sato is known internationally for his miniature book of miniature ex libris. There is also an interesting biographical section which tells of his newspaper work as well as his art career. A color snap of the artist is tipped-in, which shows him in a library.

MITSUOMI FURUTATE
BY Cliff Parfit

Mr. Mitsuomi Furutate is described as a local artist in that he finds thousands of rewarding subjects for his art in and around his home area. But, though his paintings and drawings are made in Shimonoseki, they are popular all over Japan.

Here in Japan we are witnessing something of a consumer revolt against the pointlessness of much that is marketed as "modern art." People are not shocked any more - just bored. Artists such as Mr. Furutate find their exhibitions very well attended. The pictures sell, and we learn to look more attentively at the beauty around us.

EXLIBRIS CLIFF PARFIT

This ex libris, made in 1980, shows a venerable temple gateway in Shimonoseki leading to the ancient Kozanji Temple.

The Nippon Ex Libris Association c/o Bunka Publishing Bureau 22-1, Yoyogi 3-Chome, Shibuya-ku Tokyo 151, JAPAN

A bookplate society was first founded in Japan in 1922. The present is the third ex libris society and was founded in 1943. Total membership is over 1,500.

Membership dues - ¥2,500 per annum. Publications - Nippon Ex Libris Association Calendar published twice a year and containing six tipped in bookplates, often hand-made. A decorative album for the calendars is occasionally made available to members. Also a newsletter is sent with the calendar twice a year. On rare occasions the Association publishes a more substantial book; some years ago a handbook on Japanese ex libris was published. This is now unavailable, but copies sometimes surface at book fairs. Chief Officers of the Society - Mr. Kazutoshi Sakamoto, President, and Mr. Hiroo Yamaguchi, Secretary.

The Association's most ambitious publishing project is planned for 1982 when a full-scale handbook on Japanese ex libris will be published in English and Japanese. A few copies will be available in a "deluxe" edition with some tipped-in ex libris. The Association is planning its first major exhibition which will be shown in principal cities of Japan in Spring 1982 and in August 1982 at the Museum of Modern Art in Oxford for the International Congress. In October, the exhibition will travel to Sint Niklas Exlibris Centre.

George Mackley : Wood Engraver

See page 403.

NUMBER FORTY-EIGHT   APRIL 1982

ADRIAN FEINT DESIGNER OF JOHN GARTNER BOOKPLATE

The John Gartner plate, #199 on Adrian Feint's checklist, is a woodcut, though the tipped-in here is a more recent offset print.

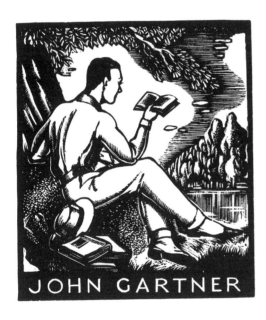

Adrian Feint is a well-known and greatly admired Australian artist, who designed his first bookplate in 1922. By 1944 his checklist total 221; by that time he had become a recognized painter in oils and his bookplate era had come to an end. Three times the YEAR BOOK of the American Society of Book-plate Collectors and Designers has featured Feint's work. First in 1930 when the Honorable John Lane Mullins, then president of the Australian Ex Libris Society, wrote about Feint's bookplates; five tipped-in prints accompanied the article; there was a portrait of the artist and a checklist to 100 covering the years 1922 through part of 1931. The first plate was a process plate, but most of the other early ex libris (1922-25) were etchings; during 1926 the woodcut became the preferred technique; some were handcolored and some were printed in two colors.

The 1938 YEAR BOOK contained an article on Feint by Sydney Ure Smith, Vice President of the Australian Academy of Art. There were seven tipped-in ex libris prints, a photograph of the artist, and the checklist was continued from #101 to 192, covering the balance of 1931 and into 1938. Carlyle S. Baer, Secretary and editor for ASBC&D, had a woodcut, which was #79 on the checklist.

A final checklist which included the earlier prints as well was published in the YEAR BOOK 1963/64. It was in chronological order #1 through #221 for 1922 through 1944, with a brief note from Thelma Clune, a long-time friend of the artist.

John Gartner was first a member of the ASBC&D in 1960; while his general interest in graphics continued over the years, he was not an active member of the American society again until 1979. Two additional bookplates used by John Gartner will be featured in a future issue of this quarterly.

In Tribute to Phoebe Brown Baker
June 27, 1914 - December 17, 1981

We are saddened to report the death of Phoebe Brown Baker, wife of Louis Stannard Baker, of Locust Lane, Kennett Square, PA. Mrs. Baker was a member of our Society from 1946.

Born in New Brunswick, New Jersey, the daughter of Dr. Frederick Lane Brown and Esther May Suydam Brown, she graduated from Bradford Junior College in 1933 and earned her A.B. from the New Jersey College for Women, Rutgars University in 1935. She also did graduate work in Library Science at the University of Michigan. Mrs. Baker worked as a bookbinder at the Longwood Gardens Library, Kennett Square. She enjoyed and lectured on bookplates, book collecting, and early American decoration.

Mrs. Baker was a member of the Unionville Presbyterian Church. She was past president of the Penn's Grant Chapter, National Society of Colonial Dames XVII Century; past regent of the Wissahickon Chapter, National Society Daughters of the American Colonists, and a member of the Chester County Chapter of the Daughters of the American Revolution. Earlier in her life she was active in the Girl Scouts of America including directing day camps, and during World War II she was a hospital nurses' aid and worked in disaster relief service through various organizations.

In the ASBC&D Membership Directory 1973 (issued as YEAR BOOK 1971/72) Mrs. Baker indicated that her bookplate was designed by Jeannette C. Shirk and reproduced offset. The design incorporates her father's bookplate (which was designed and engraved by C. Allen Sherwin in 1937) as she inherited his collection. The flower and bird symbolize a love of nature, the hourglass - a lack of time in which to do all that she would like to do.

Too often other family members do not share a special interest such as ex libris; happily Phoebe and Louis Baker did share this interest. Louis will continue membership in the Society and, we hope, continue to reap the many and varied pleasures which come to those fascinated by these miniature treasures.

INSTITUTE OF PAPER CHEMISTRY

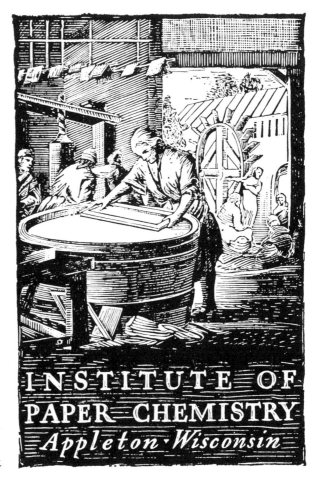

The Paper Museum was established in 1939 with the hope of stimulating interest in the craft of papermaking and promoting understanding of present-day paper and its relation to the Graphic Arts. The original museum was located at Massachusetts Institute of Technology until October of 1954 when it was acquired by and moved to Institute of Paper Chemistry in Appleton, Wisconsin.

A pamphlet issued by the museum briefly outlines the history of papermaking and the extensive displays detailing the development of paper throughout the ages. "Paper was invented during the second century A.D. by the Chinese eunuch Ts'ai Lun but it was not until the year 770 that Japanese artisans, under the sponsorship of the Princess Shotoku, first conceived the idea of printing upon paper. For the craft of papermaking to reach the Occident after its invention in China required more than a thousand years, no paper was made in Europe until the establishment of a mill in Spain about the year 1144. In Europe the art of printing did not have its inception for almost three centuries after the introduction of papermaking in the Occident.

The bookplate used by the Institute of Paper Chemistry is from an engraving in BOOK OF TRADES by Abraham van St. Clara published in Amsterdam in 1717. Dard Hunter was director of the Paper Museum, which contains many of the source materials Hunter used in writing his monumental works on paper.

MEMBERSHIP ACTIVITY   Deceased: Alexander S. Mikhalevsky,
                             January 23, 1981.
Resignations: John R. Jensen, Saint Louis Public Library, Dr.
    Norman Shaftel.
Moved, No Forwarding Address: Dr. Mario G. Fiori, John Lath-
    ourakis.
NEW MEMBERS:
    Mrs. Agatha Heeren, Boerhaaveln 53, 5707 SG Helmond, Nether-
        lands.
    Mr. Louis S. Baker, Locust Lane, Mounted Route, Kennett
        Square, PA 19348.   (See Memorial to Mrs. Baker, p. 412.)

BOOKPLATES IN THE NEWS   Copyright 1982 Audrey Spencer Arellanes
$15 Calendar Year   Quarterly: January/April/July/October

MICHAEL HARRISON'S BOOKPLATE

Russell Hastings, an architect in Arizona, made a wood block and printed the first 100 copies of Michael Harrison's bookplate. The ex libris is a combination of Hopi and Navajo—a Hopi bird symbol and one of Harrison's Navajo names which means "Little Mexican."

The original is printed in black and hand-colored in red.

(Note: Print and details furnished by Mrs. Anna Marie Hager of San Pedro, CA.)

WEDGWOOD EX LIBRIS DESIGN

The ex libris to the right was generously sent to your editor after the owner saw a write-up about the Society in the Collectors' Directory.

Mr. and Mrs. William B. Childs are Wedgwood collectors, so it was natural to incorporate a Wedgwood design into the bookplate Mr. Childs had made for his wife Emily.

ESTONIAN ARTIST SILVI VALJAL

Emil Eerme of the Estonian Art Centre has several bookplates by Silvi Valjal. Two are illustrated here; the original for Emil is printed in black and that for Linda in sienna.

Emil Eerme is interested in exchanging bookplates; also postage stamps. (Emil Eerme, 20 Farmcote Road, Don Mills, Ontario, Canada.)

414

FROM THE LITERATURE . . . . .

ITALIX, James F. Hayes. (18)12:10-19, Winter 1982. The illustrations include a portrait of the artist and ten ex libris. "Hayes has worked his magic with letters on stone, glass and wood. He writes them freely, for he considers spontaneity to be an essential quality of calligraphy. His thousands of jobs range from quarter-inch square bookplates to the 9 x 14 foot memorial wall panel for the Michigan College of Mining and Technology." This article as well as all the others in ITALIX are written in an italic hand and reproduced offset. This is a good biography; single copies of ITALIX are $4.

EARLY AMERICAN LIFE, Early American Bookplates, Patricia Johnston. (10)52-4, April 1982. "Bookplates by nature are prideful things. Few of them stick to the business of naming a book's owner. Instead, they elaborate on his lineage, formulate his philosophy, and in myriad ways point up his character. On colonial bookplates, a man's patriotism often showed as well." Good overview of the primary artists of the period.

MEDISCHE EXLIBRIS, Agatha Heeren. This is a booklet, 5 3/4 x 8, stapled, 20 pages, 19 illustrations, reproduced from typewritten copy on duplicator. There is a checklist of 150 medical ex libris which gives the owner's name, country of origin, design technique, and year of execution when known.

DON QUICHOTE IN HET EXLIBRIS, Agatha Heeren. This booklet is similar in size and production to MEDISCHE EXLIBRIS; 36 pages, 30 illustrations. There is a listing of the artists by country, and each plate illustrated, name of artist and country; design technique and date of execution given when known. Pictured are a wide variety of designs which each touch on the Don Quixote theme.

EXLIBRIS, Agatha Heeren (Boerhaavelaan 53, 5707 SG Helmond, Holland). Similar to above booklets, 16 pages and 37 illustration; like the other booklets the text is in Dutch, I believe. Considerable variety in illustrations; part of text appears to be about artist Johan Jacobs. (Editor's Note: Mrs. Agatha Heeren has just recently joined ASBC&D, though she obviously is no stranger to the world of ex libris. She has numerous personal bookplates and would welcome exchanges with other ASBC&D members.)

Bookplate Collection for Sale: Librarium, RD 190, Black Bridge Road, East Chatham, NY 12060-9730. This dealer has issued a 12-page mimeographed catalog listing bookplates, with size in centimeters. The collection is housed in three 3-ring binders with a plate pasted on each page and a typed description below. In addition there is a binder of letters but no artists seem to be included. Four manila folders contain loose bookplate prints. The collection is priced at "$750 postage paid and insured. Other offers will be considered."

NORDISK EXLIBRIS TIDSSKRIFT, #144, No. 4, 1981 (Klaus Rodel, P.O. Box 109, 9900 Frederikshavn, Denmark). Articles about two women artists: Nadezda Cancikova and Alena Laufrova; also Uriel Birnbaum, Lajor Kamper, Tomas Bim. Numerous ex libris reproduced and some prints tipped-in.

Reports for 1981, Boston Athenaeum, by the Director Rodney Armstrong. Mention is made that named book funds are established at $2,500 and a special bookplate is designed for each volume purchased from a named book fund.

A ARTE DO EX-LIBRIS, #92, vol. 12, No. 4, 1980. Ex-Libris Camonianos, 107-18. annotated checklist numbering 139. Several other articles with numerous ex libris reproduced and some tipped-in, 119-34.

A ARTE DO EX-LIBRIS, #95, vol. 12, No. 7, 1981. The English summary mentions article on Ex Libris Dedicated to Roumania's President Nicolae Ceausescu by Dr. Cornelius Dima-Dragan. "In today's world, tormented by questions and in search of forms, the ex libris of hommage here presented, bring in a breath of trust and humaness. The Book regains its sacred rights - -of symbol and Instrument of Peace."

EX LIBRIS EX LIBRIS EX LIBRIS EX LIBRIS EX LIBRIS EX LIBRIS EX LIBRIS EX LIBRIS EX LIBRIS LIBRIS

HENRIETTA VEPŠTAS

VYTAUTAS O. VIRKAU

THE BOOKPLATE, OR EX LIBRIS, A PRINTED LABEL INTENDED TO INDICATE OWNERSHIP, USUALLY PASTED INSIDE THE FRONT COVER OF A BOOK

APRIL 13 - MAY 2, 1982   OPENING RECEPTION FRIDAY, APRIL 16, 5 - 9   GALLERY HOURS TUE. - SAT. 11 - 6, SUN. 1 - 4

Funded in part by the Illinois Arts Council, a State Agency

THE PRIVATE LIBRARY, On Austin Dobson and Some of His Books, Claude A. Prance. (3) Third Series 4:116-132, Autumn 1981. Illustrations include a portrait of Dobson and copy of his bookplate designed by Alfred Parsons. W. D. Orcutt, American bookman, called Dobson "interpreter-in-chief of the eighteenth century." Among his many writings is a short biography of Frederick Locker-Lampson, which includes an illustration of the Kate Greenaway ex libris for Locker.

TIME, Essay: Would You Mind If I Borrow This Book? (Roger Rosenblatt). (1) 82, April 5, 1982. An amusing essay mostly on the hazards of lending books from your personal library; contains passing reference to bookplates, which Rosenblatt feels have slight, if any, impact on bringing books back to their rightful owners. The illustration by Cathy Hull pictures a book with Ex Libris on it much as if it were a headstone with a kneeling, weeping man bringing flowers to the dearly departed.

ANTIQUARIAN BOOK MONTHLY REVIEW, Collecting Books for Their Design. III - Daniel Berkeley Updike and the Merrymount Press, Ruari McLean. (5) 8:382-5, October 1981. One illustration shows bookplates designed by Updike for Theodore and Caroline Foster Sizer, Simon de Vaulchier, and for Ernest L. Gay (class of 1897) Collection at Harvard.

ANTIQUARIAN BOOK MONTHLY REVIEW, Reynolds Stone 1909-1979. 8:319, August 1981. Exhibit at Dorset County Museum, Dorchester, England. "A very pleasantly-printed booklet" produced by Dorset Natural History and Archaeological Society in connection with exhibition. Two essays by Stone and essays by J. W. Goodison and Ruari McLean; wood engravings reproduced include bookplates, colophons, and book illustrations. The booklet was designed by the artist's son, Humphrey Stone. For copies (no price quoted) write: Dorset Natural History and Archaeological Society, Dorchester DT1 1XA, England.

ANTIQUARIAN BOOK MONTHLY REVIEW, In Memoriam: Leo Wyatt. 8:319, August 1981. Leo Wyatt died July 6, 1981 and the memorial service was at Newcastle-upon-Tyne on July 14, 1981.

Antiquarian Book Fair, Los Angeles, February 18-20, 1982. There seemed to be more than the usual number of bookplate items at this Book Fair. Among them: The John Dreyfus ex libris appeared on a bookmark advertising the Dinkytown Antiquarian Bookstore of Minneapolis. Kenneth Karmiole (Los Angeles) had ABOUT BOOKPLATES by Doan ($35) and Frank Allen's book on Hopson ($30, Yale 1963). Arthur H. Minters (New York) displayed Kent's BOOKPLATES AND MARKS ($225). John Barrymore's ex libris appeared in a science book offered by Daniel E. Guice (Santa Barbara). Gail Klemm (Ellicott City, MD) featured a copy of the Mark Holstein ex libris signed by the artist, Allen Lewis ($20). Gary Steigerwald (Bloomington, IN) displayed the bookplate of Albert Sperisen. Bromer Booksellers (Boston) had a copy of MINIATUR EXLIBRIS by Abraham Horodisch, published in an edition of 200 in Amsterdam in 1966 ($250). This has a multi-lingual text including English, 95 pages plus 14 miniature etchings.

Oak Knoll Books (New Castle, DEL), Catalog #33, listed both the 1926 original and the 1978 Gale Research reprint of George W. Fuller's BIBLIOGRAPHY OF BOOK-PLATE LITERATURE at $60 and $20 respectively.

SVENSKA EXLIBRISFORENINGEN, 42 (1982) 1. Ten pages; one tipped-in print for Gunnar Aldor by Leo Halmgren.

EXHIBIT OF MEMBER'S EX LIBRIS   The response to the request by James Kee-
                                   nan that member's send copies of their ex
libris for a future exhibit has been most pleasing and James Keenan wishes
to express his thanks for the prompt and generous replies received; in time
he will write individually. He hopes that members, who have not yet sent
copies of their bookplates, will do so now. It would really be wonderful
if the exhibit could includes a bookplate from each member!

MELISSA
HOUSTON

BOOKPLATES OF P. HAGREEN, Introduction by John Bennett Shaw (Nappanee: The
Private Press of the Indiana Kid, 1982. James Lamar Weygand, 852 E. Marion,
Nappanee, IN 46550.) This is in an edition of 65 copies; write the publisher for price. The frontispiece is a 1939 portrait of the artist at work.
About 120 of Hagreen's ex libris are reproduced in black and white or color
(red, blue, gree, sienna). The cover and title page are decorated with a
woodcut by Philip Hagreen for a Garden Party broadside. The spine is gold
stamped; some copies use Roman gold stamping with a deep-cut brass stamping
type; the others use a printing type.

In his introduction John Bennet Shaw wrote from Santa Fe, New Mexico in January of 1982: "Hagreen's work is imaginative, precisely designed, executed
with a strong and firm hand and often with a flair of grace and even humor.
These wood cuts and wood engravings certainly can stand as art. They reflect
the man who created them: an artist, a thinker, a man with respect and understanding for all peoples, a loyal and informed citizen, a Christian of ex-
emplary devotion and influence, but most of all a true artist."

The Printer's Forward by James Lamar Weygand gives a biographical sketch of
Philip Hagree, and an assessment of the artist's work and philosophy.

THE BOOKPLATES OF EDWARD B. HEFFERNAM is to be published by The Jester Press,
690 2978 P.O. Box 2671X, G.P.O. Melbourne 3001, Australia. It will be 8vo
Imperial, 48 pages printed letterpress with approximately 20 plates tipped-in.
The edition will be limited to 100 copies with about 20 deluxe bound in Kan-
garoo hide. Further details will be available in June through a printed flyer.

1922 - 1982   1982 marks the 60th anniversary of the founding of
60th Anniversary   the American Society of Bookplate Collectors and
                     Designers. It would be nice to hear from individuals
and institutions with reminiscences of early artists and collectors.

AS of BC & D

Bookplates in the News

605 N. STONEMAN AVENUE #F, ALHAMBRA, CALIFORNIA, 91801 U.S.A.

AUDREY SPENCER ARELLANES, Editor

Number Forty-Nine   JULY 1982

BELA PETRY

Bela (Albert) Petry was
born in Hungary on
March 31, 1902.

His education includ-
ed attending Academy
of Fine Arts, Budapest;
Architectural Academy
in Vienna; Rome Academy
of Fine Arts; Munich
School of Architecture;
and Boston Architecture
Center. He started his
career as a professor
at the University of De-
brecen, Hungary (1930-36).
During the war years he
was in the Hungarian Mil-
itary Engineer Corp. Dur-
ing 1946-47 he was a por-
trait painter in Munich,
following which he moved
to Massachusetts where he
was an art designer for an
engraving company in Worcester. For ten years commencing in 1948 he was art de-
signer for United Publishers in Boston, and then moved into the field of architecture as a practicing architect and as a professor at the Boston Architecture
Center. He has designed numerous churches, shrines, libraries, and shopping
malls. In 1961 he received first prize from the A.I.A.

Bela Petry's interest in bookplates dates from early in his career. In 1929
the Antheneum, Budapest, published his 100 EX LIBRIS BY PETRY. Several of
his bookplates will be included in the exhibit of the International Ex Libris
Congress to be held during August of 1982 in Oxford, England; the exhibit is
limited to bookplates designed since the last Congress in 1980 in Linz, Austria.

An article and partial checklist
of the bookplates of Bela Petry
appears in A ARTE DO EX LIBRIS,
volume 12: No. 8, 1981, #96. The
text is in English and Portuguese;
twenty-six ex libris are reproduced, and there are 13 pages of
text by Jose Vicente de Braganca.

Some time ago Bela Petry created
a portfolio of fairytale illustrations which was printed in an
edition limited to 200 copies. A
few are still available at $20.

This artist's work displays the
old-world charm and romance of
his personality as well as touches
of subtle humor. You may write
directly to Bela A. Petry, 331
Sandspur Road, Maitland, FA 32751,
concerning bookplate commissions.

BOOKPLATES

IN THE NEWS

The October issue
of our quarterly
will carry news of
the International
Ex Libris Congress held in Oxford dur-
August, 1982. Your Editor will give
a firsthand account of the Congress
and hopes to have news from all of the
participating bookplate societies, individual artists, and collectors.

420

FROM THE LITERATURE . . . .

BOOK COLLECTOR, Bain's Bewick. 31:7-18, Spring 1982. Reassessment of Bewick's importance. Iain Bain has written two volumes: THOMAS BEWICK: AN IL-
LUSTRATED RECORD OF HIS LIFE AND WORK (published 1979) and THE WATERCOLOURS
AND DRAWINGS OF THOMAS BEWICK AND HIS WORKSHOP APPRENTICES (published 1981).
Suggests a catalogue raisonne should be compiled of surviving work of Bewick
workshop "including book-plates, engraved billheads and letterheads, silver
plate, even the dog collars, if any still exist."

HERE AND THERE IN TWO HEMISPHERES, James D. Law (Lancaster, PA: Home Publishing Co., 1903). This autobiography includes reference to Rev. Dr.
Joseph H. Dubbs, Audenried Professor of History at Franklin and Marshall
College and famed as collector of Americana and bookplates. Included in his
collection is print of Durer plate for Pirkheimer (1521), excellent representation of German, French and Italian artists, English plates date from
times of James VI with Jacobean series up to Sherborn, American plates from
Colonial times. The following quote is from Dr. D. McN. Stauffer, one of
editors and proprietors of New York ENGINEERING NEWS as well as an ex libris
artist and authority: "Dr. Dubbs' entire list is of high quality, without
any padding merely to swell the numbers, so that it can be safely said his
Book-plate Collection is without many equals anywhere." (page 433)

JOURNAL OF LIBRARY HISTORY, University of Chicago Library, Philip A. Metzger. (1) 17:cover, 78-80, Winter 1982. "One would be hard put to imagine
a greater contrast between the bookplate featured on the cover of this
issue and the library it identified: the one 'dull, uninspired, and otherwise undistinguished;' the other, 'one of the greatest book-deals ever made.'"
The curator of the Special Collections of the University of Chicago library
is quoted as saying, "I guess one can now say that you can't tell a book by
its bookplate." The bookplate reflects the character of the donors who were
"self-made unadorned men." The nine names on the ex libris of the Berlin Collection (purchase made in German capital in 1891 by University's president
from bookselling firm of S. Calvary & Co.) included Cyrus McCormick, C. R.
Crane, H. H. Kohlsaat.

1800 WOODCUTS BY THOMAS BEWICK AND HIS SCHOOL, edited by Blanche Cirher (New
York: Dover Publications, 1962). A chapter on Graphic Arts includes bookplates, heraldic devices - coats of arms, shields. Ten ex libris are reproduced including J. Bewick, J. Grech, M. Anderson, three with initials
and balance with shield or other device where name might be entered.

THE BEWICK COLLECTOR, A DESCRIPTIVE CATALOGUE OF WORK OF THOMAS AND JOHN
BEWICK, Thomas Hugh (London: Lovell Reeve & Co., 1864). One chapter is on
Cuts Done for Private Gentlemen for Book-Plates and Other Purposes; these
are items 1928 through 2123 on pages 303 through 322. Some of the items
merely indicate print on different type of paper.

JOURNAL OF LIBRARY HISTORY, Ex Libris for Genaro Garcia, Philip A. Metzger.
(2) 12:cover, 70-2, Winter 1977. This is the first of a series about bookplates of significance to library history. Plate featured is for eminent
Mexican lawyer-scholar Genaro Garcia (1867-1919), whose collection center-
ing on Mexican independence formed the nucleus of the University of Texas'
Latin American Collection.

JOURNAL OF LIBRARY HISTORY, Library Company of Philadelphia, Anna Lou Ashby. (2) 12:cover, 187-88, Spring 1977. Benjamin Franklin was the father of subscription libraries in America. In 1731 the Library Company of Philadelphia was formed by fifty members, each pledging ten shillings per year and contributed 40 shillings each to get the library started.

JOURNAL OF LIBRARY HISTORY, Public Record Office of Great Britain, Philip A. Metzger. (1) 12:cover, 285-6, Summer 1977. Tower of London appears in this ex libris. The Public Record Office was established in 1838 and has become "one of the world's greatest repositories of archival material." An early Keeper of the Records had his quarters in the Tower. The bookplate is a copperplate engraving by J. Mynde from about 1770.

JOURNAL OF LIBRARY HISTORY, Los Angeles Public Library, Philip A. Metzger. (1) 12:cover, 399-400, Fall 1977. After several short-lived efforts, the Los Angeles Library Association was formed December 7, 1872, first as a subscription library and then in 1878 it was officially renamed Los Angeles Public Library. Outstanding early librarian Tessa Kelso did away with the "ladies reading room." The bookplate was adopted in 1889 and used until 1903; this first LAPL bookplate features an angel holding a torchlight over the city.

JOURNAL OF LIBRARY HISTORY, Buddhist Temple Library, Philip A. Metzger. (1) 13:cover, 204-5, Spring 1978. Ex libris illustrated was used in the Zojoji Temple in Shiba, Tokyo prefecture. The temple was destroyed during WWII. Example of the plate was found in copy of THE BOOKPLATE IN JAPAN by Shazo Saito (Tokyo: 1941).

JOURNAL OF LIBARRY HISTORY, Connecticut State Library, Philip A. Metzger. (1) 13:cover, 323-5, Summer 1978. The motto on this plate translated: "He who transplants sustains."

JOURNAL OF LIBRARY HISTORY, College of Fort William, Katharine Smith Diehl. (2) 13:cover, 466-8, Fall 1978. Interesting tale of surgeon turned linguist and two bookplates furnished courtesy of the National Library of India at Calcutta. Fort William is in Bengal, India.

THE BOOKPLATE SOCIETY NEWSLETTER, vol. IV, #37, March 1982. The Bookplate Society Independence, 1. Ballots were returned by 76 members with the majority voting for independence from the Private Library Association after ten years of partnership. / Television Ex-Libris, 3. A children's program under the direction of Tony Hart, artist, used bookplates as a theme on his series "Take Hart". / The Bookplates of Reg Boulton, W. E. Butler. (2) 4-5. Painter, engraver, and art teacher, Frederick Reginald Boulton retired in 1978 and began engraving bookplates in 1981. He has designed nine to date and would welcome bookplate commissions, which start at about £25. Write: 30 Broomy Hill, Hereford HR4 OLH, England. / The Moscow Bookplate Society, W. E. Butler. 6-9. Review of the Society's activities from about 1902 to 1921. / A Few Russian Wood Engravers, John R. Biggs. (3) 9-12. Some historical background, then specific artists discussed: Vladimir Andreyevich Favorski, Leonid Hizhinsky, Nellie Lvova, Vasily Lopata, Vasily Chibanik. / Some Bristol Book Labels, Brain North Lee. (15) 13-20. Ever the thorough sleuth, Brian Lee shares his research results with his readers, documenting the lives of artists and owners of the Bristol area in the 18th century; his easy writing style has the warmth of conversation.

EXLIBRIS-NYT, Dansk Exlibris Selskab (P.O. Box 1519, 2700 Copenhagen, Denmark), April 1982. Yngve Forsbolm In Memoriam (Feb. 11, 1906 - Jan. 11, 1982). Ex Libris of Daron De Selby, and other brief articles (pages 781-8).

GRAPHIA, 1982/1, March 1982. Luc De Jaegher, by Antoine Rousseau. (21)151-69. Article plus chronological checklist (1938-1981) and alphabetical list of owners of the plates. Five prints are tipped-in. / Numismatische Exlibris, J. Fortuyn Droogleever. (8)170-4. Text and update of checklist of bookplates featuring numismatics (#234-279). / Jacqueline Verbist-Maanen, A. Vermeylen. (6) Portrait of woman artist; original multi-color graphic tipped-in; checklist of her plates #1-20, 1974-81. / In Memoriam Leo Wyatt, Brian North Lee. (3)179-81. Illustrations include portrait of Wyatt at work and two of his prints for David and Hermione Chambers, and Dr. Colin R. Lattimore. This is a fitting tribute to a great artist and a kindly man by a person who admired the skills of the artist and enjoyed the friendship of the man. / L'exlibris Charles Baron de Selby, A. Collart. (1)182.

MITTEILUGEN DEUTSCHE EXLIBRIS-GESELLSCHAFT, December 1981, #14,160-177. This publication is perfect bound, 8 1/4" x 11 3/4", printed one side only, with two columns of print or variations with reproductions of bookplates. Interesting variety of bookplates.

EXLIBRIS-REVUE. This is the first appearance of the Official Bookplate-News for F.I.S.A.E. in its new format measuring 5 7/8" x 8 1/4". Vol. 6, 1980 1/2, 1-12. Includes story and photographs from the International Congress in Linz, Austria in August 1980. Vol. 6, 1980 3/4, 3-24. Variety of articles, reproductions of ex libris and some tip-ins. Vol. 7 - 1981 1/2, 25-36. One brief article is in English by Heikki Lahi about Exlibris Clubs in Estonia.

NIPPON EX-LIBRIS ASSOCIATION publishes a bookplate calendar twice a year. January through June of 1982 are represented by a flower print by Hideo Hagiwara, Yasushi Omoto's snow scene, a unicorn by Hitoshi Karasawa, a two-color print with a blind embossed chicken by Sumiko Ueki, a multi-colored fish by Takeo Takei (whose work frequently appears in the calendars), a grasshopper by Yoichi Kenmoku.

BOOKSELLER, published by ASBC&D member Mary T. Peterson, quotes a bookplate verse and has a good word for the publications of the Society.

Miniature Books, List No. 114 from Dawson's Bookshop, offers Abraham Horodisch's MINIATUR EXLIBRIS at $175.00. This is a 95 page miniature with an English summary of the German text; it was published in an edition of 200 in Amsterdam during 1966.

1981/82 YEAR BOOK Features

. Lynd Ward
. Jacques Hnizdovsky

Articles / Checklists / Tipped-in Prints

$25 separately or with 1932 Membership
$35 including BOOKPLATES IN THE NEWS

LARGE BOOKPLATE COLLECTION TO BE SOLD   ; Below is a news release from
FOR MORGAN LIBRARY BY SWANN GALLERIES   : New York City, May 17, 1982.

One of the world's largest collections of bookplates ever assembled, more
than 150,000 individual plates, is being offered for sale by Swann Galleries
in behalf of the Pierpont Morgan Library. The Morgan Library, to whom the
collection was bequeathed in 1969, recently appointed Swann to act as their
agent. In accordance with the preference of the Morgan Library, Swann will
first explore the possibility of finding a single buyer for the entire collection before dispersing it at one of its regular Thursday book auctions.

The collection, built by the late Margaret Woodbury Strong of Rochester,
New York - the largest single shareholder of Eastman Kodak - represents
some of the finest English, American, and German engravings as well as excellent examples of Japanese, French, Italian, and Portugese plates, many
going back to the 16th century. Included in the vast accumulation of armorial, pictorial, and institutional bookplates, filling nearly 20 filing
cabinets, are handcolored bookplates, proofsheets, original sketches, and
copper plates, as well as both mounted and unmounted plates. Artists include D. Y. Cameron, Arthur Rackham, Rockwell Kent, Bruce Rogers, Von Bayros
and Wengenroth. Prominent names of owners include Paul Revere, Theodore
Roosevelt, John Philip Sousa, and Lord Byron.

The bookplate collection is accompanied by more than 450 books on the subject (approximately 250 titles, many of which are in multiple copies).
These include both standard references and rare books in many languages,
plus nearly 100 volumes of periodicals.

The Strong collection is actually a spin-off from a much larger collection
of over 300,000 collectibles. Prior to her death, Mrs. Strong directed
that her estate create an endowment of $60 million to establish and maintain
a museum to house her 19th century Americana collection in Rochester. The
Strong Museum is scheduled to open this coming fall.

Swann Galleries is now accepting bids, either separately for the bookplates
or together with the bibliographic collection. The entire collection is
available for private viewing at Swann, by appointment. For further information, interested parties may contact Ms. Betsy Pinover, Vice President,
at Swann Galleries, 104 E. 25th St., New York, NY 10010; (212) 254-4710.

(Editor's Note: With the opening of the Strong Museum this fall, I would
like to have an article on Margaret Woodbury Strong. Some of our members
doubtless knew her and/or exchanged with her; I would welcome hearing from
all individuals who might have something to contribute to such an article.)

• —— •

Cesi Kellinger, Bookseller (735 Philadelphia Ave., Chambersburg, PA 17201)
recently offered EX LIBRIS, Buchkunst und agewandte Graphik, Berlin, 1911,
in three volumes (21, 22, 23 for 1911, 1912, 1913) but not all numbers of
each volume for $75, and also Walter Hamilton's FRENCH BOOK-PLATES, London,
1896: Chiswick Press, $37.50.

• —— •

BOOKPLATES IN THE NEWS   Published January/April/July/October
$15 Calendar Year   Copyright'82 Audrey Spencer Arellanes

Ex Libris

Various comments are heard when a library of golf information in mentioned. Yes, a Golf Library does exist and the Ralph W. Miller Golf Library is one of two of its kind in the United States. While one such facility is located at the headquarters of the United States Golf Association in Far Hills, New Jersey, the other can be found at the Industry Hills and Sheraton Resort in the City of Industry.

Industry Hills is situated on top of historically recognized "P" Hill; in addition to the Library, it encompasses two golf courses, facilities for conventions, four restaurants, a tennis and swim center, an equestrian center with 15 miles of trails, and a Sheraton Hotel.

The holdings of the Golf Library center round the game of golf, and all are noncirculating reference and research materials, including more than 4,000 books, 1,200 bound and unbound periodicals, 2,000 articles from non-golf magazines, 3,000 golf course and clubhouse postcards, 2,000 score cards, 2,000 photographs, 500 artworks, and 500 museum-type objects, all of which have been identified and cataloged.

RALPH W. MILLER
Golf Library

Industry Hills
City of Industry, California

Much of the material was collected over a forty-year period by the late Ralph W. Miller, a prominent Los Angeles attorney. In 1974 the collection was purchased from his estate by the City of Industry for Industry Hills, since then the collection has expanded appreciably due primarily to the interest of golf enthusiasts. Six employees staff the library - two full-time and four part-time.

The Ralph W. Miller Library is a unique compilation of information not only directly connected to golf but also relates to Scottish and local history, cultural, physical and psychological societal influences, turf-grass and soil maintenance and golf course management, as well as regional geography.

The vast collection of books contains more than 400 pre-1911 volumes including the first book published on golf, THE GOFF, a story describing a golf match which was written in 1743, and the 1597 edition of THE LAWES AND ACTES OF PARLIAMENT, which forbade golf to Scotsmen and advised them to take up activities such as archery, which is useful to self-defense.

The ex libris tipped-in above has been furnished through the courtesy of Jane Mueller, Librarian at Industry Hills. The plate has been printed on stock which is pressure-sensitive and has a "crick and peel" backing for easy application of the bookplate to a large number of books. At the present the library is considering the design of a more artistic bookplate. though the current one identifies the special collection at a glance. The Library is open to the public seven days a week between 8:30AM and 5PM, and had approximately 3,500 visitors during the last half of 1981.

IONE K. WIECHEL (1897-1982)

Ione K. Wiechel, a lifelong resident of
Sandusky, Ohio, died January 30, 1982 at
the age of 85.

Her daughter Ellen Amstutz says Ione was
"an inveterate collector of books, book
marks, bookplates, calligraphy, greeting cards, miniature books, postcards,
and had a far-flung correspondence. She
had a strong love of gardening, and flowers were an important part of her life.
Daily walks through her garden sustained her during the last years of her
life. She received her first bookplate in 1930; from that small beginning
52 years ago, her collection grew to be quite large. Portions of her collection were on display at the Western Reserve Museum, Cleveland, for a
period of time. She also had slides of some of her collection. Besides
everything else, she raised a daughter who has a long way to go to catch up
with her mother!"

Ione graduated from the University of Wisconsin in 1918 and worked as an
accountant for the Ingersoll Watch Co. in New York City from 1918 to 1923,
when she returned to Sandusky as a self-employed accountant. She was married in 1934; divorced in 1942.

Ione, with her wealth of knowledge about bookplates and her generosity in
sharing this knowledge and sharing her duplicates with beginners in the
field, will be greatly missed by the many fortunate enough to be the bene-
ficiaries of this sharing and to have corresponded with her.

DEREK RILEY - Engraver in Wood

Since the last article about Derek
Riley, he has moved to Lyndale,
Chapel Road, Necton, Norfolk, Eng-
land

Additions to the checklist in BITN
for April 1981 are:

    33 - R. A. K. Watt
    34 - Lars C. Stolt
    35 - H. B. Muir
    36 - Maria Tratsaert
    37 - A. K. McHardy

MANCHESTER HERALD (CT), Bookplates can be plain or fancy, Russ MacKendrick.
(1) January 20, 1982. A column titled Collectors' Corner gives a boost
for bookplates. Pictured is a simple landscape through a window for Henry
Russell Movey. The address of the ASBC&D is given, though a jumble of an
old number and a misspelled street name. (EDITOR'S NOTE: When you see any
reference to bookplates, please send the full item to me for use in BITN.)

AS of BC & D
Bookplates in the News

605 N. STONEMAN AVENUE #F. ALHAMBRA, CALIFORNIA, 91801 U.S.A.
AUDREY SPENCER ARELLANES, Editor

HARRISON COLLECTION EX LIBRIS BY JAMES HAYES

The San Francisco Public Library has a number of notable collections within its Special Collections. The History of the Printed Book combines the resources of the Max J. Kuhl Collection (1926), the Robert Grabhorn Collection (1956), and the Jane Hart Collection of Book Design (1966). Other special collections include the George M. Fox Collection of Early Children's Books, California Authors, Robert Frost, Schmulowitz Collection of Wit and Humor, Sherlock Holmes, The Panama Canal, and the Richard Harrison Collection of Calligraphy and Lettering.

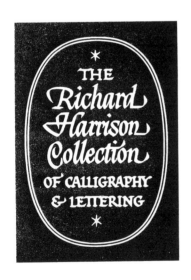

The Richard Harrison Collection of Calligraphy and Lettering has fittingly had an ex libris designed to identify it by a leading American calligrapher, James Hayes.   The San Francisco Public Library first housed the Harrison Collection in 1963, though it had been in formation for a number of years and Harrison continues to add to it. In addition to more than 500 works of reference and instruction manuals, there are more than 400 pieces of original calligraphy and lettering; while most are contemporary, there are a few old manuscript leaves.

Susie Taylor, curator of the Harrison Collection, says the SFPL has become more active since 1976 in presenting public programs and demonstrations of calligraphy, which are enthusiastically received by library patrons. Exhibits are held, presentations are made to visiting calligraphy classes (averaging about two a month), and visitors from all over the world are welcomed.

Richard Harrison, now 72, has led an active and interesting life, which is related by Don M. May in the FRIENDS OF CALLIGRAPHY NEWSLETTER (1976). May says, "If Harrison has had an abiding love for letters, his passion was tennis." To leave his days free for tennis, he chose to become a waiter and eventually a bartender, in which capacity he served for 25 years at the Stock Exchange and Olympic Clubs of San Francisco. Art was a part of his life from childhood, with commercial art classes in high school; later he won a scholarship to attend night classes at the California School for Fine Arts. It was in 1949 after seeing an exhibit of calligraphy by Byron Macdonald that he was exposed to writing with a broad-edged pen. A number of years later (1954), Harrison was among the pioneers to grind fountain pen nibs into the chisel shape; mostly he improvised with Esterbrook pens. An attempt to factory tool Esterbrook nibs for the Chancery writing proved to be much less satisfactory than the hand-ground and polished nibs.

James Hayes, the designer of the Richard Harrison Collection ex libris, is featured in the current issue of FINE PRINT (The Bookplates of James Hayes by Don Moy, 8:126-7, October 1982), which has several articles focusing on calligraphy. Hayes has been retired for several years in Woodland, Colorado; however, retirement has not meant an end to calligraphic endeavors, only a more selective acceptance of commissions. Among the black and white reproductions of his ex libris in the FINE PRINT article are plates for Ruth Cummings, Alfred H. Perrin, Gerald T. Banner, Joseph E. Fields (with a reproduction of George Washington's signature), William Stout, C. A. Hurt, and the Richard Harrison Collection; the black and white illustrations do not do justice to the originals which are frequently printed in color, as is the Harrison plated tipped-in on the reverse side of this page.

In discussing his calligraphic ex libris, Don Moy writes: "It should be added that Hayes puts a lot of work into his bookplates - more than a lesser craftsman would bother with and sometimes more than his fee justifies. Even a bookplate with only a name is a painstaking enterprise." To quote Moy further: "However, his reputation does not stand on his longevity but on his achievements as the quintessential Johnstonian calligrapher, the rare bird who makes straight-forward and distinctive letters without resort either to deliberate imitation of Johnston's letterforms or to the hocus-pocus commonly invoked by penmen to dress up their alphabets."

•───•

TALKS at XIX INTERNATIONAL CONGRESS   Five talks were given during the XIX International Ex Libris Congress held in Oxford, England, August 18-22, 1982. All were well delivered, informative, and the prints presented in the slides were a visual delight.

Brian North Lee delivered the opening talk titled "British Pictorial Bookplates," which was slide-illustrated and given in two parts on Thursday and Friday mornings. It has been published as the Summer issue of THE PRIVATE LIBRARY with 78 ex libris illustrated. The second talk on Thursday was by Cliff Parfit of the English Centre in Tokyo; his subject was "Ex-Libris in Japan" and the Centre has published a hardcover book expanding on the talk entitled EXLIBRIS JAPAN. These first two talks were also represented in Oxford exhibitions; The Eldon Gallery of the Ashmolean Museum presented "British Pictorial Bookplates" (August 5-September 12, 1982) and "Ex-Libris Japan" was at the Museum of Modern Art (August 16-October 3, 1982). On Friday following the second part of Lee's talk, Gerard Gaudsen spoke on "Contemporary Ex-Libris." His talk centered on Continental plates. The fifth and last talk, "Lettering in Bookplates," was delivered by David Kindersley.

The selection of topics provided a diversified view of bookplates. While the basic idea of an artistic means of proclaiming ownership is evident in the bookplates of every country, each country has its own special style.

MUSINGS ON MY MOTHER'S BOOKPLATE COLLECTION
by Ellen Wiechel Amstutz

At the moment, the predominate thought in my mind is "Why, oh why, did I not ask more questions when she was still with us." I grew up hearing the names of the Diamonds (vaguely remember visiting them in Cleveland when I was very young) and Sarah Blake - and I knew that the long shelf full of black binders with the alphabet letters on them contained her collection - and I had my very own bookplate which I always loved, but that was the sum of my knowledge. As a teenager I was not too interested in all her books and voluminous correspondence, then went to college, married, and followed my own interests.

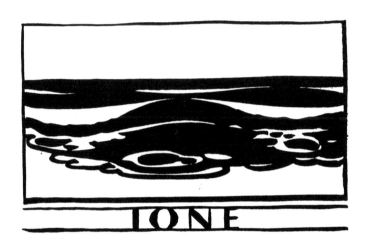

And today I sit in her living room with her books strewn around me and the fragrance of the Peace rose from her garden on the desk, and I must try to sum up her collection. How do you summarize a life filled with the love of finer things, a constant search for more knowledge, and an interest in so many things?

I am estimating that there may be 3,000 ex libris prints. The largest number of them are in looseleaf binders, 9 x 6½". Some have been removed for exhibits and talks and are mounted on heavy gray paper. They are well annotated for the most part; I think if she knew anything about the owner or the artist, she noted it.

The following are the original plates and blocks in her collection:

Blocks: "IONE" by Paul McPharlin, 1930, 3½ x 2¼". (see tip-in above)
       "IONE" Typographical border from a French type specimen book,
          about 1810. Lettering by Paul McPharlin, printed on

a handpress, 2 x 1½", n.d.

"Madeline Lillie" - I think my mother designed this; I remember her
working on a lily drawing when I was young. Madeline was a
friend of my mother's, 3 3/4 x 2 1/8", probably 1940's.

Plates: "Ex Libris, Ione Klenk Wiechel" by V. Flessig, copper plate, 3 1/8
x 3", 1948.

"Ex Libris, Ione Klenk Wiechel" by V. Flessig, copper plate, 2¼ x 3",
1948. A scene with flowers, a book, and butterfly.

"Ione Klenk Wiechel" by Sarah Eugenia Blake, aluminum plate, 1945.
A floral bouquet.

"Ellen Marguerite Wiechel" by Sarah Eugenia Blake, aluminum plate,
1944. After a design by Kate Greenaway.

"Dwight Remington" by Sarah Eugenia Blake, aluminum plate, 3½ x
5¼", 1952. Believe San Marco horses are featured.

"Mary Lou Cranston" by Sarah Eugenia Blake, 2 3/8 x 5", n.d.
Oriental lady.

In addition to the five personal plates mentioned above, my Mother had two
more. Of these two, she has the artists' design progression (Paul McPharlin)
and the mock-up changes in the other design (G. Harvey Petty, calligrapher).
She used these to show the progression in making a bookplate. There are no
plates or blocks for these two designs:

Design of snail and opening fern with initials i and k in
upper corners, well concealed, 2 7/8 x 2½", 1933, by McPharlin.

"Ione Wiechel" by G. Harvey Petty, silhouette of open book
under the name, 2 3/4 x 1 5/8", typographic.

In several of her garden books I find the plate "From the Garden Library of
Ione" which looks very much like some of the things the Diamonds might have
done on their press.

There are five scrap books with plates, possibly her earliest efforts at
the collecting game. There is a box with plates mounted on heavy paper;
these prints were used in her exhibit at the Western Reserve Museum in
1961. These are divided into categories, i.e. Rockwell Kent, Famous People,
Cleveland, Punning, The Art of the Book, Children, Miniatures. There are
also several boxes with loose plates; these last several years she did not
have the energy to keep current with bookplate activities.

There are five portfolios of bookplates by Sarah Eugenia Blake.

It was my Mother's wish that the collection be kept whole, so I do not wish
to break it up. In addition to the bookplate prints, there is bookplate
literature, many of the essential reference works (books and periodicals)
which provide information to add to the collector's enjoyment.

(If you are interested in the collection of Ione Wiechel, write Ellen Amstutz,
235 Webster Avenue, Van Wert, OH 45891. What a wonderful start for a
beginner; the many annotated prints would be an introduction to the magic
world of bookplates, the books and periodicals would provide the historical
background for the international field of ex libris. It is important that
a collection which was put together with love and care also be cherished by
the next owner.)

FROM THE BOOKPLATE LITERATURE

BRITISH STATIONER, A Chat on Bookplates, Frank G. House. (2) 351-53, January 10, 1923. Mentions Major Alfred Fowler and American Bookplate Society in Boston

THE GRAPHIC, "Ex Libris": The Modern Bookplate, Frank G. House. (3) 496, June 8, 1929. "Today these little 'marks of ownership' have developed into works of art, sought after by the collector and prized by the owner."

"600" MAGAZINE, Ex Libris, S. H. Clarke. (6) 26:#120, 1-3. Mention is made of Severin's HOW TO MAKE A BOOKPLATE at 15 shillings.

COUNTRY LIFE, This Book Belongs To . . . , Christopher Neve. (9) 1596-97, June 7, 1973. One bookplate illustrated shows a vintage Bugatti designed by Italo Zetti for Rudy Haller.

TRANSACTIONS OF CAMBRIDGE BIBLIOGRAPHICAL SOCIETY, Bibliographical Notes: The Origin of Sir Nicholas Bacon's Book-plate, E. R. Sandeen. 2:373-6, Part V, 1958. Well documented article.

ANTIQUE DEALER & COLLECTORS GUIDE, The Varied Delights of Book Plate Collecting, J. B. L. Allen. (5) 98, 100, March 1974. Pleasant article; just what the title indicates.

FEDERATION OF BRITISH ARTISTS QUARTERLY, Art and Craftiness, Frederick Skinnard. (2) 3:10-11, Spring 1974. Illustrations are of plate for First Lord St. Levan by F. W. Skinnard and E. D. French plate for Henry Blackwell.

THE LADY, Collecting Bookplates, Keith Clark. (6) #4590:566-7, 575, March 29, 1973. Practical hints for the beginning collector.

BIBLIONOTES (Transactions and Proceedings of the Society of Antiquarian Booksellers' Employees), Second Series, No. 4, Autumn 1961. Bookplate or trade-card? It may be a printer's trade card. Liverpool City Library has largest collection after British Museum.

BIBLIONOTES, Book Labels. Second Series, No. 6, 11-12, Winter 1962. Sale at Puttick and Simpson's rooms in 1897 lasted 5 hours; 278 lots realized ₤300. Marshall Sale of 1906 realized ₤2,844. DAILY CHRONICLE of February 29, 1897 quoted: "We are inclined to think . . . that the rage for bookplates has overstepped the bounds of common sense, and degenerated into a mere craze, which is only a trifle more absurd than the postage stamp mania."

ARCHAEOLOGIA CAMBRENSIS (Welsh Bookplates), Sir Griffith Book Plates, W. J. Hemp. (5) 197-201, December 1941. Heraldic sleuthing and changes in name.

NATIONAL LIBRARY OF WALES JOURNAL, Book Plates in the National Library of Wales, Herbert M. Vaughn. (8) 1:#3, 130-5, Summer 1940. Mentions Vaughan's book on the Aneurin Williams collection.

LIVERPOOL BULLETIN, English Book-Plate Styles, J. F. Smith. (11) 1:#3, 18-29, February 1952. Liverpool Public Library has collection of 60,000 ex libris prints from collections of James Carlton Stitt, bequeathed in 1934, and George H. Viner recently presented additional bookplate prints.

COLLECTIBLES ILLUSTRATED, Display Case - Ex Libris: Margaret Woodbury Strong, (2) 1:14, September/October 1982. This notice of the 150,000 bookplate collection of Mrs. Strong to be sold by Swann Galleries is illustrated - in color, no less - by two ordinary stock plates, one with the owner's name written in an undistinguished hand.

AMERICAN BOOK COLLECTOR, A Curious and Uncommon Man: Henry Spencer Ashbee Reconsidered, Charles Farrell. (3) 3:2-18, July/August 1982. This is Part II of a three part article. Ashbee indeed lives up to the title of this article. Mention is made of the portrait bookplate Paul Avril designed for Ashbee showing him with a beard; his membership in the Ex Libris Society is noted. Incidentally the JOURNAL of the Ex Libris Society carried an obituary in the June 1892 issue.

ANTIQUARIAN BOOK MONTHLY REVIEW, Ex-Libris in Japan, Cliff Parfit. (13) 9: 132-35, April 1982. The black and white reproductions make one aware of how much color adds to the Japanese bookplate. This is a brief review of the ex libris in Japan and the exhibit to be held in Oxford in conjunction with the XIX International Ex Libris Congress during August 1982.

THE PRIVATE LIBRARY, Pictorial Bookplates in Britain, Brian North Lee. (78) Third Series 5:58-116, Summer 1982. The entire issue, devoted to Lee's article, details the exhibit mounted at Ashmolean Library, Oxford; it presents the close attention to artistic nuances and biographical detail that result from Lee's research and fine turn of phrase. Another must for your library.

REYNOLDS STONE, 1909-1979, An Exhibition Held in the Library of Victoria and Albert Museum, July 21 - October 31, 1982 (London: Victoria and Albert Museum, 1982). Ruari McClean writes an introduction, there is an Autobiographical Essay and Note on Wood Engraving by the artist himself, a chronology (1909-1979), a catalog of the exhibit which included 1005 items, and a 3-page select bibliography. Illustrations are printed in sepia and black. This is an 84 page paperback, 5½ x 8½. Bookplates are included in a section titled Engraved Letterheadings, Bookplates, Christmas Cards, Devices, Illustrations and Coats of Arms. Stone also designed typefaces, alphabets, postage stamps, coins, and bank notes.

OXFORD MAIL, Undercover Art Form of the Jealous Bookworms. (5) No. 16,260, p. 6, August 17, 1982. "The charm of bookplates lies partly in the fact that they're small, and usually intricate, but also that they are personal. . . . . It's one area where someone without a lot of cash to throw about can put themselves in the position of a patron of the arts in the 18th century manner, commissioning a personal work of art."

EXLIBRIS JAPAN, A Study of Japanese Bookplates, Cliff Parfit. (Published by the Nippon Exlibris Association, Tokyo: 1982, and is available from the English Centre, P. O. Box 11, Chofu, Shimonoseki 752, Japan). This is a hardback book with a colorful dust jacket, 100 pages of which the first 18 are an introductory text, pages 22 through 92 are color reproductions of Japanese ex libris, somewhat reduced in size but with original dimensions given, arranged alphabetically by artist, and pages 93 through 100 give biographies of some of the artists and include addresses for anyone who may want to commission an ex libris. This volume is a must for all who are interested in the international aspects of the bookplate. Earlier volumes on Japanese ex libris command high prices on the rare occasions they appear on the market.

COLLECTOR'S LIBRARY of the CIVIL WAR

Time-Life Books' most recent offering in theme collecting centers on the Civil War. They say "each new volume of this landmark series will be an exact reproduction of the first edition, with the same typography, title pages, maps and illustrations that lent such distinction to the rare and beautiful originals." In addition to gilt edges, antique-style endpapers, and a textured satin ribbon marker, there is a specially designed collector's bookplate.

Pictured to the left is a copy of the ex libris which has been designed with ample space at the bottom for the owner's name to be printed.

ROBERT CLARENCE LESTER 1910-1982

For several years Robert Lester had been a member of ASBC&D and his brother Ron has furnished a brief biographical sketch to share with his friends. Robert was born in Watertown, New York, December 31, 1910 and died in his sleep on April 13, 1982 at the age of 71¼ years, in Burbank, California.

During the Great Depression in the 1930's, after a variety of experience's, Bob served for several years as General Manager for an automobile sales and distributing company. In the spring of 1941, he followed his two brothers to California. After graduating from Western Air College, he served Lockheed Aircraft for the next 5 years as a sheetmetal worker. Moving up the ladder he was a Chief Inspector and Manager of Quality Control for Westmont Corp. for 17 years. As a complete change of pace, he transported cars coast to coast for several years, seeing and enjoying the scenery of the USA. For the 14 years before his retirement in 1982 he was Inspector for Barry Controls; he was much revered by his co-workers and upon his retirement, the director of his department "retired" Bob's personal inspection stamps at the same time on the grounds that "there will never be another so qualified to use those particular stamps."

Since 1963, Bob was co-organizer and charter member of the Southern California Campanology Club, the Southern California Chapter of the American Bell Association. During these 19 years he managed to amass an enviable collection of both metal and porcelain bells of all sizes and descriptions.

During the past ten years, Bob was a member of the 107-year old National Amateur Press Association with 400 to 500 members worldwide; he was an accomplished printer with handset type on his hobby letter press. Probably his interest in printing led to bookplates. After retirement he started work on the design of his personal bookplate, but did not complete it. Though a bachelor, Bob will long be remembered by his many friends and his family - two brothers, five nieces, three nephews and their families.

Photo-created Bookplates
by Henrietta Vepstas

Henrietta Vepstas has created more than
fifty ex libris using color-toned photo-
collage technique. Born in Siauliai,
Lithuania, she is a graduate of University of Illinois at Urbana-Champaign and
also studied photography and printmaking
at the Art Institute of Chicago.

Exhibits of Vepstas' work have appeared
at Ciurlionis Art Gallery, Chicago; 2nd
Street Gallery, Charlottsville, VA; and
Galerija, Chicago. Her work also is included in LITHUANIAN BOOKPLATES (published by Lithuanian Library Press, 1980)by
V. O. Vengris.

John Alderson in his column Focus, which
appeared in the CHICAGO SUN-TIMES July 16,
1982, wrote: Not only are there a wealth
of personal associations that can suggest
images suitable for individual book owners, but plates can also be designed
to suit a particular genre of books someone likes - mysteries, science
fiction, romance, adventure. Noting her teenage son's interest in sci-fi,
Vepstas made a special edition of plates featuring a playfully bug-eyed
transformation of his picture with the immortal word "Ssshhzam!"

If you are interested in a photo-created bookplate by Henrietta Vepstas,
she would need to know something about the owner of the plate - profession,
hobbies, and some informal photos if the owner wishes a self-likeness in
the ex libris, and the name as it is to appear on the print. A charge of
$50 will provide 5 signed originals and 100 offset printed copies; addi-
tional copies at $10 per 100. You may write the artist, a new ASBC&D mem-
ber, at 9432 S. Longwood Drive, Chicago, IL 60620.

EXCHANGE WITH AMERICAN COLLECTORS SOUGHT   Recently a letter
                                             was received from
Holland expressing a wish to exchange bookplates with American collectors.
The writer is Daniel De Bruin, who has plates by Zwiers (C25X, C3, X2),
Strik (C2, C3, X2), Severin (C23X), Rueter (X23X), Battermann (X2/2), and
Westselaar (P13X, C2). He would like to collect good bookplates in all
techniques of all countries, and especially heraldic bookplates after 1890.
You may write his directly: Daniel DeBruin, Meidoornhf 30, 2923EL Krimpen,
Aan Den Ijssel, HOLLAND.

FISAE CONGRESS IN OXFORD

Oxford, England was the site of the XIX International Ex Libris Congress and the Bookplate Society (England) was host to over 200 participants for this first Congress held outside continental Europe. As might be expected, most of those attending came from Europe and England, but there were several who journeyed from Australia, Japan, and the United States.

Keble College was the headquarters for the Congress. Most participants took advantage of this opportunity to stay in "college digs" which offered charm and reasonable rates. In addition, having a headquarters for the Congress brought and kept members together; there were shared meals in the college dining hall, conversation and exchanging in the Exchange Room, an opportunity to buy bookplate literature in the Book Shop, and multilingual sociability in the college bar until closing time, when the hardy enthusiasts continued conversation and exchanging in each others' rooms.

No matter how well organized the host group, there is always a short period when everyone descends upon registration. However, the wait in line is most often pleasantly passed in conversation, renewing old friendships and making new friends, and the wait was well repaid by the packet of ex libris literature given each participant, which was provided by the ex libris societies of various countries. (Individual titles will be found in this and subsequent issues of BITN in the section FROM THE LITERATURE.) The major book for the Congress was Volume VI published under the auspices of FISAE, the official governing body which sponsors the Congress. As in the past there are articles about and tipped-in and reproduced ex libris created by artists from all the participating ex libris societies; this is a book everyone interested in the work of contemporary artists will want; a book, well-worth the price, that gives a sampling of the international aspects of ex libris.

During the Congress a meeting was held for FISAE Delegates. There was considerable discussion about the languages to be used at future Congresses; English, French, and German are official languages plus the language of the host country if it is not one of the three mentioned. Short of facilities like the United Nations where there can be simultaneous translations, the host country will continue to set the language for talks and in some instances a much-sought speaker will be accepted to talk in the speaker's native tongue. A Delegate from Finland summed up the situation very nicely by stating that the international language of the Congress is the bookplate print itself. One has only to see the activity in the Exchange Room, where avid collectors, having no common language, negotiate satisfactory exchanges. As at the Oxford Congress, mimeographed copies of the talks in French and German can be provided for those who don't understand the language of delivery, in this case English.

The major point of business at the Delegates meeting was the acceptance of Professor Lang's offer that Weimar, East Germany, be the host for the Congress to be held in 1984. Several sites for future meetings were discussed, but no conclusions were reached. Anthony Pincot has been the president of FISAE and William Butler has been secretary; FISAE officers are selected by the ex libris society of the host country.

ATTENTION ALL ARTISTS
INTERNATIONAL EX LIBRIS COMPETITION
The International Exlibriscentre of the city of Sint-
Niklaas has organized a com-
petition among graphic artists from all countries for the execution of a
bookplate with the theme of Science Fiction.

All entries must have the owner's name, the word Ex Libris or equivalent,
and center on the theme of Science Fiction. All graphic art techniques
are permitted. Artists may submit one or more ex libris; two copies of
each must be entered and entries addressed to: Internationaal Exlibriscentrum van de Stad Sint-Niklaas, Stedelijk Museum, Zamanstraat 47, B-2700
Sint-Niklaas, Belgium. A letter should accompany each entry giving the
artist's name, short curriculum vitae and full address, name of the titleholder (owner), technique used, year of execution; this information
needed for the catalogue, which is to be prepared. Only printed ex libris
are acceptable; drawings, photocopies, etc. cannot be accepted. All entries must be received by January 14, 1983; the jury will meet on the 31st
of January. There will be separate ranking for three main techniques:
xylography, chalcography, and lithography. All entries become the property
of the International Exlibriscentre.

The competition is being held in conjunction with the Ministry of Dutch
Culture and the following awards have been established: Award of the
City of Sint-Niklaas for xylography, chalcography, and lithography with
related techniques; three equal awards of 15,000 Belgium francs; Victor
Stuyvaert Award, GRAPHIA Award, Award of Ministry of Dutch Culture, Pro-
vince Oost-Vlaanderen Award, Public Works Loan Board Award, Award of the
Vriendenkring der Oud-Atheneumstudenten (Old Boy's Association), and
Award Paribas.

The jury will be composed of members of the Advisory Board of the Exlibriscentrum; final selections and awards will be made by the Court of Burgo-
master and Aldermen. A selection of the entries will be exhibited at the
12th Biennal of Small-sized Applied Graphics to be. held at the Ex Libris
Centre from March 12 to May 8, 1983. The results of the competition and
the inauguration of the exhibition will be at 11:30AM on Sunday, March 13th,
1983.

Editor's Note: I sincerely hope there will be American artists among the
participants of this competition, and that American artists will be considering a greater participation in the work to be exhibited at the International Congress in 1984.

MORE FROM THE LITERATURE

NORDISK EXLIBRIS TIDSKRIFT, #145, #1, 16 pages, 1982 (Klaus Rodel, editor).
An article on ex libris of doctors; work of Charlotte Anderson reproduc-
ed; Rodel writes about Charles Baudelaire; extensive article by Gianni
Mantero on Michel Fingesten (1883-1943).

JUST RECEIVED - A List of Fine Books on Book Plates, 2 74-item list from
Kenneth Karmiole, Bookseller, 2255 Westwood Blvd., Los Angeles, CA 90064.
If you are interested in a copy, write the bookseller directly.

AS of BC & D
Bookplates in the News
605 N. STONEMAN AVENUE #F, ALHAMBRA, CALIFORNIA, 91801 U.S.A.
AUDREY SPENCER ARELLANES, Editor

FIFTY-ONE   January 1983

SARAH CHAMBERLAIN : WOOD ENGRAVER

It is our pleasure to present the first two bookplates designed by a young Oregon artist for an old, prestigious Boston library. The artist is Sarah Chamberlain and the library is the Boston Athenaeum, whose 175th anniversary was noted in TIME (November 15, 1982).

BOSTON ATHENAEUM

From the fund given in memory of
Elsie Livingston Johnson
1904-1981

BOSTON ATHENAEUM

From the fund in honor of
Ola Elizabeth Winslow
1885-1977

Teacher, Author, Humanitarian

Sarah Chamberlain has prepared well for her chosen field starting with a BA in book illustration and design from Hampshire College, Amherst, MA., followed by a year's apprenticeship with Barry Moser of the Pennyroyal Press and a tutorial under the direction of Leonard Baskin. In addition she studied printing under Harold McGrath of Hampshire Typothetae.   The skills thus learned were subsequently taught to others in a full art program, which included drawing, printmaking, painting, sculpture, pottery, and batik, at South Kent School (CT); later batik and letterpress at the Multnomah Art Center in Portland (OR). Commencing in the fall of 1981, Sarah taught letterpress and wood engraving at the Oregon School of Arts and Crafts. Also during the past six years Ms. Chamberlain has designed, illustrated, and printed limited edition children's books. Thus far, she has produced nine books, two of which were commissioned. She markets the books herself to collectors, libraries, and rare book dealers.

The two commissioned books were miniatures done for Bromer Booksellers; one titled A Bestiary shows her special skill in depicting animals.

One of her more recent books, The Pied Piper of Hamelin, was selected for the 1981 Western Books Exhibition sponsored by the Rounce & Coffin Club. Chamberlain had one-woman shows at the Image Gallery in Portland in 1981, at the House of Books in Kent (CT) in January 1980, and her work was included in Seventy Books of the Seventies at the New York Public Library.

The two bookplates commissioned by the Boston Athenaeum are for special book funds in memory of Ola Elizabeth Winslow (1885-1977) and Elsie Livingston Johnson (1904-1981). If you are in interested in commissioning an ex libris from Sarah Chamberlain, please write her directly at 7219 S. E. 41st Avenue, Portland, OR 97202.

BOOKPLATE COLLECTION BRINGS $20,000 AT SWANN GALLERIES
(Press Release January, 1983)

A collection of more than 150,000 bookplates, together with related bibliography, was sold to a London collector for $20,000 by Swann Galleries in New York City. Filling nearly 20 file cabinets, the collection was assembled by Margaret Woodbury Strong of Rochester, who bequeathed it to the Morgan Library in 1969. According to George S. Lowry, President of Swann, "it was the preference of the Morgan Library that the collection be offered to a single buyer who would keep it intact, rather than disperse it at public auction." Lowry was particularly pleased with the results in view of the limited market for bookplates and the disordered state of this vast collection. He explained that it is the only bookplate collection of similar magnitude and quality to appear at auction in recent years.

William E. Butler, Professor of comparative law at the University of London, is the new owner. He intends to transfor his new acquisition into a working collection ("a marvelous spare time occupation"), and from it plans to mount exhibitions and write articles. Butler became a bookplate collector as a result of his combined interest in books and graphic arts. He began his collection in 1976 and has been an active member of the Bookplate Society (U.K.) since.

The Strong collection is comprised primarily of turn-of-the-century Anglo-American bookplates. It also contains fine representations of modern Japanese, 17th century German, French, Italian, and early American examples. Accompanying the bookplates were 100 volumes of periodicals and 250 related book titles. The entire collection was actually a spin-off from Mrs. Strong's much larger assemblages of Victoriana and dolls which form the basis of the newly opened Margaret Woodbury Strong Museum in downtown Rochester. (Editor's Note: If you knew or corresponded with Margaret Strong, please write the editor of BITN and share your recollections of this collector with our readers.)

A PAIR OF BOOKPLATES for the BOSTON ATHENAEUM by Anita Bigelow

It is fitting for these bookplates to appear in BOOKPLATES IN THE NEWS; they were commissioned after Rodney Armstrong, Director and Librarian of the Boston Athenaeum, saw the bookplates I designed for the Reed College Library in the October 1981 BITN. He wrote me in late March of 1982 with an offer of a commission. Naturally, I felt honored and delighted, and I accepted the commission.

BOSTON ATHENÆUM

From the fund
in memory
of
Edward A. Taft

I turned to Hellenic motifs, which - surprisingly - had not been overused, according to Mr. Armstrong, in the Athenaeum's large set of bookplates. (The Athenaeum has just celebrated its 175th year, so one can imagine how very many ex libris it must have accumulated in that time.)

I came up with several ideas. By mail Mr. Armstrong narrowed down choices to two designs. One is a drawing based on a vase painting depicting Athena making a horse out of clay. The other is a woodcut version of an Attic coin. The type is 12 and 14 point Times Roman, set by Irish Setter of Portland, Oregon. John Laursen of Press-22 printed the bookplates offset on Curtis rag paper. (Irish Setter and Press-22 do much of the limited edition and fine book work in Portland.)

Enough bookplates were printed for the Athenaeum to receive about 1,500 each, and for there to be a set for BITN. The bookplates were sent from Portland to Boston in early October - almost a year after the appearance of the article which occasioned their commission.

(To contact the artist write: Anita Bigelow, 2922 S.E. Salmon, Portland, OR 97214.)

•————————————————•

CHANGE OF ADDRESS ??

Please notify BITN immediately.

•————————————————•

Boston Athenæum

FROM THE LITERATURE

WALL STREET JOURNAL, Neither a Book Borrower nor a Book Lender Be, Toby Smith, November 3, 1982. Interesting essay quotes Charles Lamb on book borrowers - "mutilators of collections, spoilers of the symmetry of shelves, and creators of odd volumes." Smith also mentions the futility of hoping a decorative label ("I enjoy sharing my books as I do my friends, asking only that you treat them well and see them safely home") will bring books home.

THE LESTER DENT COLLECTION
by Lawrence M. Stewart

Lester Dent (1904-1959) was one of Missouri's most prolific authors. He was working as a telegraph operator in the late 1920s when he decided there might be more money to be made by writing fiction, especially for the pulp magazines. In 1929 he made his first sale, to the magazine TOP NOTCH and shortly afterwards he was selling enough to become a full-time author.

The Street and Smith Company had a great success with THE SHADOW and in 1932 decided to bring out another hero title. Dent was hired and created the gadget-minded hero Doc Savage under the pen name Kenneth Robeson. Dent wrote 165 of the 181 Doc Savage stories to see print. In addition to adventure tales, Dent also wrote mystery novels, western stories, etc., and was published by such magazines as the SATURDAY EVENING POST.

Norma Dent, his widow, is presently considering which university library will one day house Dent's collection of manuscripts and writings.

The drawing on the bookplate is of Doc Savage as he appeared on the cover of the first DOC SAVAGE MAGAZINE, "The Man of Bronze," March 1933.

INSTRUCTIONS FOR MOUNTING BOOKPLATES

1. Mix paste with water in mixmaster, if possible, or with a spoon, stirring until a smooth, heavy mixture is reached. Strain to remove lumps.
2. Place bookplate face down on a clean piece of paper and apply paste to plate thinly and evenly.
3. Let plate set for about one-half minute for expansion.
4. Place plate in position. After putting piece of clean white paper on top, rub it down with a roller, bone folder, or fingers.
5. Surplus paste around edges may be removed by using a small piece of slightly wet cotton wound around a small stick - such as a swab stick.
6. Keep book open and expose plate to air for about two hours.
7. If desired, remaining paste may be kept in refigerator for several days for reuse. Always stir well before applying

(Above submitted by calligrapher James Hayes. Paste is any good grade of wheat flour paste such as Peerless Dry Paste #6 distributed by Samuel Schweitzer Co., 600 West Lake Street, Chicago, IL 60606.)

BOOKPLATES IN THE NEWS

Quarterly: Jan./April/July/October

Calendar Year - $15.00

1983 Membership / $35
to include
BOOKPLATES IN THE NEWS 1983
and
YEAR BOOK 1983

The print tipped-in to the right
is a double first for BOOKPLATES
IN THE NEWS - the first ex libris
with Chinese characters and the
first plate designed by two artists. The two artists are Wang
Hui-Ming and Jacques Hnizdovsky;
the Chinese symbols by Wang and
the red monogram in English by
Jacques.

In a letter Wang Hui-Ming writes:
"The Chinese always write their
family name first, then their
given names. I used the Chinese
way before I came to the United
States. When I first came to the
United States,my American friends
always asked me what is my English
name; so I adopted an English
name, Hui-Ming Wang, for their
convenience. My friend Jacques
Hnizdovsky ia a clear-thinking man.
He used the initials of my name
in Chinese order, which when in-
verted are my initials in English.
As we Chinese say, all roads lead
to Beijing, even if you fly upside

down, backwards and forward! You can write Chinese from top to bottom or
from bottom up, from left to right, or the other way around. I am rather
a conventional man, so I adopt currently the most conventional way of arranging two characters horizontally, left to right. These two characters meaning storage or collection and books or calligraphical writings are tradi-
tionally used in Chinese seal carving for ex libris."

"Seal carving is also as old as Chou Bronze, that is, more than two thousand years old. In the Chinese tradition, a painter has to be also a poet,
a calligrapher, and a seal designer, if not a carver; because he has to in-
scribe his painting with poetry in calligraphy and authenticate it with his
seal. Collectors also have their own seals on works of art and books. The
most notable collector was the Emperor Chien Lung of Ching Dynasty (1736-95).
He literally filled the 'negative space' of paintings in his collection with
his over-generous comments and numerous personal seals saying 'being seen and
appreciatively examined by His Magesty Emperor Chien Lung.' Here is a collection of my personal seals:

Hui-Ming
Ex Libris

H. M. W.

Wang
Hui-Ming

Hui-Ming
(ying)

Hui-Ming
(yang)

"The ex libris I carved for my friend Jacques Hnizdovsky is half ying and half yang because all human beings are half ying and half yang in nature; to put it another way, that is to say there is womaness in every man and manness in every woman. The harmony of ying and yang is the supreme attainment of humankind."

Wang Hui-Ming is a painter, woodcutter, and calligrapher in both Chinese and Western calligraphy. The name of his studio is Epoh, which is not a misspelling of epoch but rather the reverse of "hope." The steed in his studio logo is a Chinese Pegasus with the wings clipped; he has hoofs to strike the fountain of the Muses to well forth, but no wings to hover over the commercial world of art. If you are interested in commissioning a bookplate, you may write the artist directly: Wang Hui-Ming, Epoh Studio, Montague, MASS 01351. / Jacques Hnizdovsky, 5270 Post Road, Riverdale, NY 10471.

EXHIBITION: Hnizdovsky
              Four Decades of Visual Art

The Ukrainian Institute of America had an exhibit from December 5, 1982 to January 15, 1983 featuring the work of Jacques Hnizdovsky. The works exhibited included paintings, tapestry, watercolors, drawings, and posters. The brochure for the exhibit listed 82 items and included a brief text, which in part said: "Hnizdovsky has also designed and illustrated many books and created numerous bookplates, which are regularly included in the international Exlibris exhibitions. The 1981-82 Yearbook of the American Society of Bookplate Collectors and Designers has devoted twenty pages to his bookplates. Today, at 67, Hnizdovsky is working as hard as ever, dividing his time between painting, woodcutting and etching. He also finds time to illustrate books, primarily poetry, and to design books and bookplates." The Ukrainian Institute is at 2 E. 79th St., New York, NY 10021.

FROM THE LITERATURE

NEWS LETTER (Private Libraries Association), Bookplates by New Zealand Artist for Sale. No. 100, Winter 1982. Eurosearch Holdings, 1/50 Amy St., Ellerslie, Auckland 5, New Zealand, have approximately 1,000 bookplates by the New Zealand artist and designer Hilda Wiseman, which were acquired in 1982 following the artist's death. Prices range from £2 -5 sterling per plate. Plates date between 1923 and 1972 and are linocuts, woodblocks, zinc and aluminum blocks. The condition is described as being in "gallery AA" condition.

With the financial assistance of the
W. K. Kellog Foundation, the Library
of California State Polytechnic University, Pomona has developed a comprehensive collection of retrospective
and current materials on the Arabian
horse. The collection, among the
finest in the world, is heavily used
by researchers and breeders, as well
as by students and faculty of the
University. Collector's items and
rare books are featured, in addition
to the working materials used in tracing pedigrees or in researching specific problems such as immunodefi-
ciency disease, which is endemic to
the Arab breed. The collection is made
available, upon request, to persons
outside the academic community.

THE

W. K. KELLOGG

ARABIAN HORSE LIBRARY

of

California State Polytechnic University

Pomona

KROLL FECIT 1982

The collection, housed in a special
reading room, is of particular im-
portance to the University which is located on the site of the W. K. Kellog
Arabian Horse Ranch founded in 1926. In addition to materials on the Arabian Horse, the collection also includes the Ranch papers and copies of the
papers of Kellogg dating from his purchase of the stock herd from Lady Judith
Wentworth of Crabbet Stud.

Arabia of the 18th and 19th centuries is also featured in the collection,
mainly in the books of European and American travelers who included descriptions of the "horse of the desert" in their writings. Official studbooks
from more than twenty countries, numerous private studbooks, histories of
the Arabian horse, and backfiles of serial publications are also important
segments of the collection. Staff members are available to assist users in
translating foreign language materials.

The logo of the bookplate is the weathervane which is on the tower of the
original stables. It is designed by Anthony F. Kroll and is printed in
black and gold.

MORE FROM THE LITERATURE

NEWBERRY LIBRARY BULLETIN, Rudolph Ruzicka, Artist and Craftsman, Philip
Hofer. 6:328-38, August 1978. Ruzicka, born in Bohemia on June 29, 1883,
moved to Chicago in 1894, and in 1897 was an unpaid apprentice in a LaSalle
Street wood engraving shop. He made an ex libris for Hofer, which is described as "a wood-engraved round bookplate, printed in seven colors, after
a watercolor drawing by Hans Halbein, the Younger."

Editor's note: It would be appreciated if Institutional Members would let
me know about bookplate items in their publications or exhibitions.

Elmer J. Porter designed an ex libris for his daughter in Hawaii and gives the following description of the design: "I choose to use the Mosher's front door. The house is a large, rambling type with several Oriental characteristics, of which the front door is one which is patterened after a Chinese moon gate. The door opens into a hallway which is all glass on one side, and you can see some of the plants in the atrium. On each side of the door are bonsai. The plate is signed on the left side just under the bonsai tub. The house is in Honolulu, high on top a mountain back of Diamond Head."

The Mosher library is general in character as they have wide interests.

Elmer J. Porter, a long-time member of ASBC&D, is a professor emeritus and former chairman of the Art Department of Indiana State University in Terre Haute. His interest in collecting bookplates dates back to his childhood when he had a neighbor who was a collector. Mrs. Porter is also an artist. Both are retired now and share an interest in painting and travel. Their summers are spent on the coast of Maine where they have a summer place.

Elmer Porter has designed ten bookplates, here listed in chronological order:

Katherine Bryan (armorial)
Elvada Thompson (pictorial)
Paul L. Faulker (pictorial)
The James Lawrence Porters (armorial)
Thomas R. Jackson (pictorial)
The Griswolds (armorial)

Laura Baker (pictorial)
The Stephen Ballentines (pictorial)
The Allan Moshers (pictorial)
Cunningham Memorial Collection,
  Cunningham Memorial Library
  Indiana State University
  Terre Haute, Indiana

FROM THE LITERATURE

MANUSCRIPTS, The Adventure of the Arthur Conan Doyle Bookplate, Stanley Wertheim. (1) 34:279-89, Fall 1982. Portions of this article originally appeared in BOOK COLLECTOR'S MARKET (Nov/Dec 1979) and AMERICAN BOOK COLLECTOR (N.S.1 Sep/Oct 1980).

ACHT NEDERLANDSE EXLIBRIS IN HOUTGRAVURE OP HET THEMA VERZAMELEN. A portfolio of eight ex libris, printed on cream colored cardstock; appears to have been published in Budapest in 1970. Includes work by Andriessen, Battermann, Altena, Roemburg, Rueter, Sins, Strik, Vossebeld. A similar portfolio with work of eleven artists was published for Ex Libris Congress in Linz, 1980.

AS of BC & D

Bookplates in the News

605 N. STONEMAN AVENUE #F. ALHAMBRA, CALIFORNIA, 91801 U.S.A.

AUDREY SPENCER ARELLANES, Editor

NUMBER FIFTY-TWO   APRIL 1983

PIXIE O'HARRIS - Australian Artist

Ex Libris

Ann & Geoffrey Long

Pixie O'Harris was born in Wales in 1903, one of nine children, whose father, George F. Harris, was a noted portrait painter. At the age of 14 she became the youngest member ever selected by the Royal Art Society of South Wales.

Arriving in Australia with her parents and other members of the family she became known in Sydney for her drawings for children. She has illustrated fourteen books by other authors; she has decorated more than fifty children's hospital wards, day nurseries, baby clinics, and schools. One of her nursery pictures was hung in Buckingham Palace.

Pixie also occupies a place in the adult art world and has exhibited widely. She is also well-known as the author of books for children, as well as plays and poetry. The Coronation Medal, the Jubilee Medal, and an MBE have been awarded to Pixie O'Harris. In 1977 she was made a Patron of the Royal Alexandra Hospital for Children.

Pixie is married to Bruce Pratt, who was editor of the AUSTRALIAN ENCYCLOPEDIA for many years before his retirement. They live at Vaucluse, Sydney. Mrs. O'Harris writes: "The art of bookplates in Australia is reviving slowly again after being very much to the fore in the 1920's and 1930's. Unfortunately I have not kept count of the bookplates I have designed, but counting from memory they would probably be near the fifty mark. I began when I was 18 and new to Australia, and was spurred on by Percy Neville Barnett. My work in illustration, oil painting, and poetry is often written about in Australia, but so far very little about my bookplates. A short autobiography comes out in April (1983) published by Rigby's of Adelaide, and they are including a few."

MATTHEW da SILVA

Pixie O'Harris 1982

Pixie O'Harris has created a series of bookplates for Geoffrey and Ann Long and their children. The joint plate for the parents is featured on the front page of this issue. The Long's are Australian booksellers and members of ASBC&D.

Plates for two of their children appear on this page; those for Toby and Naomi.

Reproduced also is a signed plate created in 1982 for Matthew da Silva.

Almost all her work has a certain fairy tale quality.

She has designed a diamond jubilee plate for the Englist Association: Sydney Branch 1923-1983. Her design incorporates English and Australian native flowers.

Naomi Long

Toby Long

A Huck Finn Bookplate by Marshall Glasier
by Richard H. Schimmelpfeng

In recent years Dr. Robert W. Stallman gave his manuscripts and working papers to the University of Connecticut Library. I was the go-between, as it were, dropping by his house to pick up more material as time went on; in all the spirited discussions (Dr. Stallman was a fascinating and voluble conversationalist) I remained unaware that he had a bookplate. This turned up after his death in late 1982 when his wife Virginia gave me more items and casually asked if we wanted the bookplate too.

Robert Wooster Stallman (1911-1982) was active in the field of English literature his whole life as teacher, author, editor, and reviewer. His biography takes a full page in CONTEMPORARY AUTHORS (New revised series, v. 3) published by Gale in Detroit. He was perhaps best known for his works on Stephen Crane and his editions of Crane's writings; indeed, Dr. Stallman was the Crane scholar. His STEPHEN CRANE: A BIOGRAPHY (1968, rev. ed, 1973) received critical praise as the first thorough documentation of Crane's life. What is not widely known is that Stallman wrote poetry, some of which has been recorded by the Library of Congress. One volume of poems was THE FIGUREHEAD AND OTHER POEMS, 1944-1977, published in 1977, which contained "Come back to the raft" about Huck Finn's fake drowning. The poem, first published in the SEWANEE REVIEW in 1954 remained one of Dr. Stallman's favorites.

A friend of the family was Marshall Glasier, a New York painter and a teacher at the New York Art Students League. He created the pen and ink sketch sometime during 1955 or 1956. The owner's signature is, of course, a facsimile. The tip-in is through the courtesy of Mrs. Virginia Stallman.

FROM THE LITERATURE

PRIVATE LIBRARY, Third Series 5:3, Autumn 1982. GEORGE MACKLEY - WOOD ENGRAVER, CONFESSIONS OF A WOODPECKER, and WOOD ENGRAVING are all reviewed by Brian North Lee, who admires Mackley's work, but none of the books escapes unscathed, though the deed is done with well chosen words. "Though the book is richley bound in quarter leather with marbled boards, perhaps a simpler binding would have better accompanied the work of a printmaker whose creations celebrate the magic of man's artefacts and the natural world they serve. But it occurs to me that it may be churlish to overcriticize an elaborately produced book doubtless intended to honour and emphasize the importance of George Mackley, whose skill we may wonder at and admire. (See page 448 for another reviewer's opinion.)

MATRIX 2, A review for printers and bibliophiles. No. 2, Winter 1982. Wood-engraving in Russia, John R. Biggs. 1-15, numerous illustrations. Thanks to Arthur Goldsmith, Jr., this article was brought to the editor's attention. He indicates ex libris are mentioned throughout the article and a number are reproduced. The books costs about $30 US.

Several volumes honoring or reprinting the work of the British master wood engraver George Mackley have been published in the last two years. One of them, CONFESSIONS OF A WOODPECKER (Old Working: Gresham Books, 1981. 250 copies) reprints an illustrated lecture Mackley presented at the Print Collectors Club in London in 1967. All the wood engravings by prominent artists shown in the lecture are included in the text. In addition, a pocket at the end of the volume contains numerous plates of Mackley's own owrk; his wood engravings are truly exquisite. One of the plates contains four ex libris on it; those of Julia Peckham, S.E.R.A. (Surrey Education Research Association), J. R. Toller, and D. Keith Robinson. (Review by R. H. Schimmelpfeng)

PHILATELIC LITERATURE REVIEW, Philatelic Bookplates, George T. Turner. (29) 4:43-59, Second Series No. 16, Third Quarter 1954. The author of this article gives considerable detail about each ex libris as well as biographical details about the owner and philatelic activities. Some interesting information is furnished about the Collectors Club of New York (its librarians from 1896 to 1950, locations of the club, and notes about the Club and its library). (Thanks to Stanley M. Bierman, M.D., for this article.)

FINE PRINT, The Book Art of Valenti Angelo: An Homage, Abe Lerner. 9:27-9, January 1983. The article adheres to the subject of the title, but all who are interested in Valenti Angelo (1897-1982) will want to know about his book illustration.

LEAFLETS, Massachusetts Civic League, A Village Library, Mary Anna Tarbell. No. 3, 1909. The Brimfield Public Library ex libris is on the cover. "The design on the book-plate is Steerage Rock, an immense boulder resting on the highest point of land in Brimfield and in the original Bay Path, the route taken by the settlers of the Connecticut Valley in their journey from the Bay. The motto accompanying the design is 'Books give the far view.'"

THE CONNECTICUT COLLEGE LIBRARY BULLETIN, To Honor a Friend: Endowed Book Funds and Gift Funds. (12) 11-16, Number Three, Fall 1977. A minimum of $5,000 establishes a named endowed fund. "Many of the newer funds have their own special bookplates. Illustrations include ex libris for several Yale University Library funds, Connecticut College Library, and Harvard.

EXLIBRIS-REVUE, Official Bookplate-News for F.I.S.A.E., vol. 8, 61-88, #2/3, 1982. This issue is devoted to the Congress during August of 1982 held in Oxford, England. Primarily pictorial, including scenes at Keble College inside and out, the bar, lecture auditorium, members exchanging, the council meeting. The European contingent missed the "Congress dance" but otherwise extended priase to the British Society which hosted the Congress.

EXLIBRIS-REVUE, vol. 8, 89-96, #4, 1982. The entire issue is devoted to literature published mostly in 1982. English-language bookplate literature output is very small compared to the European countries.

EDWARD FRANCIS SEARLES
by Jim Lewis

In 1887, Edward Francis Searles created somewhat of a stir when he married the widow of California railroad
baron Mark Hopkins. Searles was an
interior designer with the prestigious
New York City decorating house of
Herter Bros. and had supervised several design projects for Mrs. Hopkins.
Searles was in his early 40's when
he married the 67 year old widow, a
union that the newspapers had a field
day with, referring to Searles as the
"New York paper hanger."

Over the years following his wife's
death, Searles used the fortune to
expand his family home at Methuen,
Massachusetts, into a huge rambling
Tudor affair containing over seventy
main rooms, a collection of books,
sculpture and antique musical instruments, and six pipe organs.

Searles' bookplate was designed using Gothic elements that include tracery,
quartre-foils, and a pointed arch. It is unsigned, undated, and no artist
has ever been associated with the plate. Searles' collection of books was
extensive and one of the last additions he made to his home was an exquisite
library in the Italian renaissance style, built especially to house his collection of Bibles.

FROM THE LITERATURE

Published in the late fall of 1982, in time for Christmas, I assume, was
ROCKWELL KENT ; An Anthology of His Works, edited with an introduction by
Fridolf Johnson (New York: Knopf, 1982). It is a sumptuous volume, somewhat on the coffee-table size (13" high), and one which should delight all
Kent aficionados. It is beautifully printed, as might be expected from
Knopf, with exceptionally clear illustrations on well-laid-out pages. As
might also be expected, reproductions of some bookplates are included, principally one page with twelve designs, another page with Dan Burne Jones'
plate, and several other bookplates scattered at random through the volume,
usually in a vignette placing. The volume is hefty, 358 pages, and bookplates occupy only a brief space. The cost is $60, which is not expensive
today for such a lovely piece of work, but probably most bookplate collectors
would want to see the volume first.   (Reviewed by Richard H. Schimmelpfeng)

THE INNOCENT BYSTANDER, New Bookplate Designed for Library. August 13, 1982.
This publication is the weekly newsletter for the University of Connecticut
Libraries. Illustrated is the linoleum cut executed by Editha Spencer, a
local print maker, whose work was featured in the F.I.S.A.E. volume published
in connection with the International Ex Libris Congress, Oxford, 1982.

AUGUSTINUS VIRGILIUS BURBA. 16 ex libris (Privately printed by Klaus Rodel, Postboks 109, DK 9900 Frederikshavn, Denmark, 1982. Softcover, 8½ x 8¼, 39 pages, 3 pages of multi-lingual text including English, ex libris are printed one side of page only in muted green. Price: 60 Danish kr.) "Through all the years the art of exlibris has been 'the quiet' branch of the art, one could be tempted to say that it almost has been a marginal note to the graphic art altogether. On the other side, the exlibris has always been an expression of what is going on within the artistic life, especially from the beginning of this century and quite particularly in the time between the two world wars. The small graphic of the inter-war period, including the exlibris, is an expression of a political engagement which probably will never get a similar intensity." Symbolism is a strong theme throughout Burba's etchings.

JANA KREJCOVA EX LIBRIS, Alena Nadvornikov. (Published by ExlibRisten, 1982. Klaus Rodel, Postboks 109, DK 9900 Frederikshavn, Denmark. Softcover, 9 x 6¼, 10 pages of multi-lingual text including English, 19 ex libris reproduced including one on cover. Price: 90 Danish kr.) Jana, born in 1946, is self-taught. "She is not making book-plates for order but as presents for dear people, to express her affection, admiration or tenderness in this way. The traditional graphic kind of an ex libris is for her rather a pretext for a small medallion in which her inclination to simple expression can be applied very successfully." Her graphics are lino cuts.

EDUARDO DIAS FERREIRA, Farveserigrafier, 6 ex libris for Jørgen Vils Pedersen, by Klaus Rodel. (Published by ExlibRisten, 1982, Postboks 109, DK 9900 Frederikshavn, Denmark. Soft cover, 8 3/4 x 6½, 6 pages of multi-lingual text including English, 6 tipped-in bookplates, all multi-colored prints. Price: 50 Danish kr.) Ferreira's name can now be added to the small list of artists using serigraphy. His use of color comes naturally as an extension of his glassmaking. "The present series of exlibris works was made for Jørgen Vils Pedersen, probably the most dedicated collector of exlibris works in Denmark. Tragically, the series is also a beautiful memorial to him, as the works came in only a few days after his death. Let us therefore use Eduardo Dias' beautiful colour prints to commemorate a dedicated and tireless collector."

HANS GEORG ERLER by Klaus Rodel, Postboks 109, DK 9900 Frederikshavn, Denmark. (Published 1982, softcover, 11 x 8½, 125 pages including 7 pages of multi-lingual text including English, 55 ex libris printed on one side of page only. Price: 110 Danish kr.) "The exlibris art reflects the history of art - in any case the German exlibris which has, during the last 100 years, mainly been a branch of art for collectors. In the development of the exlibris, one can follow the taste of the time and see the various attitudes to exlibris as an object of art and of collection. Especially exlibris from the twenties and from the early thirties, before the National Socialists began their unification ("Gleichschaltung") of the art, gives an exact picture of the period in which it was created." Women and death have been chief among the subjects of Erler's ex libris. " . . . in his women's exlibris there are many attitudes toward women. The attitude of society, of men. Material that every feminist and sociologist could use for causes of research. The old exlibris have their own charm. It is women - and it is much more. Woman as sphinx, as demon, as sexual object. Woman as the predominating creature and as the oppressed toy. Amazing, fascinating, and typical of the period!"

BOOKMAN (University of Portland), Book Memorials. (1) 5:#3, Whole #19, Cover, 24, April 1953. "Book memorials not only aid the deceased by serving to call to silent prayer those who read the names of the departed on the Memorial book-plates, but they aid the Library as well."

NORDISK EXLIBRIS TIDSSKRIFT, #140, 1981. Exlibris-motiver by Jan Rhebergen. Milan Erazim by Vaclav Krupka. Hugo Hoppener (1868-1948) by Klaus Rodel. A four-page insert has four tipped-in prints by Kobi Baumgartner of Switzerland. No English summary.

EXLIBRIS I FARVER, 9 examples, by Helmer Fogedgaard and Johnny Køhler. Privately printed, 1982; softcover with multi-colored ex libris pasted down, 8 more tipped-in with paragraph of text about each; each print by a different artist.

THE EX-LIBRIS OF SIMON BRETT, Brian North Lee (published by ExlibRisten, Klaus Rodel, P.O. Box 109, DK-9900 Frederikshavn, Denmark, 1982). Simon Brett has been fortunate indeed to have this book written by a person not only knowledgable in the field of bookplates but one who knows both the individual and the artist.

CONTEMPORARY SOVIET BOOKPLATE DESIGN, Catalogue of an Exhibition in the Flaxman Gallery and Cloisters of University of London, August 1982, compiled and edited by Professor W. E. Butler, Secretary, The Bookplate Society (London: 1982). Of Studies on Bookplate History, this is Russia Series 2, published in a numbered edition limited to 350 copies. It may be obtained from Professor Butler, 9 Lyndale Ave., London NW2 2QD, England, £2 plus mailing costs, 95 pages, 8¼ x 11 3/4, 2 page introduction, index of artists and owners, pages 1-89 are each devoted to an artist, whose name is printed in cyrilic type also. There is at least one ex libris reproduced for each artist along with some biographical data, and a listing of all that artist's ex libris represented in the exhibit, date of the commission and technique of execution. Eighty-nine artists are represented; work mostly of 1970-80 period. The inexpensive off-set reproduction of the illustrations cannot show to full advantage the variety of printing techniques, but this is an excellent introduction to current achievements of bookplate artists in the Soviet Union and updates the 28 artists included in the Severin/Reid volume on ENGRAVED BOOKPLATES: EUROPEAN EX LIBRIS 1950-1970 (published in 1972).

BRITISH PICTORIAL BOOKPLATES, The Ashmolean Museum, 1982. This is a handlist, edited by Brian North Lee, of the exhibit at the Ashmolean Museum in Oxford from August 5 through September 12, 1982, which was installed in conjunction with the XIX International Ex Libris Congress, August 18-22. The exhibit is arranged in chronological order with the earliest plate that of Bishop John Hacket (1592-1670). Birth and death dates are given, when known, for both the owner and the artist, as well as brief identification of the owner or the scene depicted. As with all of Brian Lee's undertakings, careful research is evident, which added to the viewer's enjoyment of the exhibit and makes the catalogue reader want to explore further the lives of the owners and the art of the bookplate designers.

CONTEMPORARY EX-LIBRIS 1980-1982, Catalogue of the Exhibition in the Central Library, Oxford, August 1982 (published London: The Bookplate Society, 1982, on the occasion of the XIX International Ex-Libris Congress held in Oxford during August 1982). This catalogue represents ex libris comissions executed by artists since the last FISAE Congress in 1980; there are 610 works by 365 artists from twenty countries. The catalogue is arranged by country, by artist, and lists the owner's name, year of execution, and technique of production. There is a cross reference of all the artists, and a key to the techniques of production. The countries sending exhibit material are: Austria, Belgium, Brazil, Bulgaria, Canada, Czechoslovakia, Denmark, Finland, France, German Democratic Republic, Holland, Hungary, Japan, Poland, Portugal, Romania, Union of Soviet Socialist Republics, United Kingdom, United States, Yugoslavia.

THE GRAPHIC WORKS OF ANATOLII IVANOVICH KALASHNIKOV, translated and edited by Professor W. E. Butler (London: 1982, Studies on Bookplate History, Russia Series 3, 8¼ x 11 3/4, 250 numbered copies, 92 pages, alphabetic index of bookplate owners, 6 pages of selected bibliography 1965-80 with emphasis on Russian publications which Prof. Butler is fortunate to be able to read in the original.) There is a list of exhibitions from 1964 to 1980, international prizes from 1967 to 1979, designs for pictorial stamped envelopes from 1957 to 1981, postage stamp designs, stamped postcards, pictorial commemorative postcards, first-day cover envelopes. Ex libris from 1964 to 1982 number 600. Kalashnikov was born in 1930, a Moscovite by birth. A woodengraver, his work came to the attention of the USSR Ministry of Communications for whom he has done 65 postage stamps and hundreds of envelopes, postcard, and other commemorative designs. He has also created book and music dust jackets and cover designs. Of the 30 illustrations, most are ex libris, with the balance showing examples of his other work.

Another Leo Wyatt: Richard Schimmelpfeng reports that he deals with an English bookseller, Keith Hogg, who handles almost exclusively books on the printing arts. Recently he acquired a stunning book called SIXTEEN CONTEMPORARY WOOD ENGRAVERS: A COLLECTION OF WOOD ENGRAVINGS PRINTED FROM THE ORIGINAL BLOCKS TO ACCOMPANY AN EXHIBITION (Newcastle, England: David Esslemont, 1982). Limited to 250 copies. Artists include Simon Brett, David Esslemont, Monica Poole, Peter Reddick, and others. The foreword does not state where the exhibit took place; however, the interest to a bookplate collector is that Leo Wyatt's exquisite calligraphic ex libris for Dudley Wilson is printed on the colophon, as a tribute to Wyatt. Dudley Wilson is one of the names signed to the foreword.

NEWS LETTER (Private Libraries Association), Bookplates by New Zealand Artist for Sale. No. 100, Winter 1982. Eurosearch Holdings, 1/50 Amy St., Ellerslie, Auckland 5, New Zealand, have approximately 1,000 bookplates by the New Zealand artist and designer Hilda Wiseman. These ex libris were acquired in 1982 following the artist's death. Prices range from £2 - 5 (sterling) per plate. Dates of the plates are from 1923 to 1972, and are linocuts, woodblocks, zink and aluminum blocks. The condition factor of the overall collection is described as "gallery AA."

AMERICAN BOOK MONTHLY REVIEW, Ex-Libris in Japan, Cliff Parfit. (13) 9: 132-35, April 1982. The earliest Japanese bookplate dates from 1470. "Even today, bookplates are regarded as something of an exotic luxury in Japan and only dedicated booklovers are likely to use them."

In Fond Memory : Philip Beddingham

It is with sadness that I report the sudden death of Philip Beddingham during January of 1983. Most recently Philip Beddingham was the Chairman of the Bookplate Society (U.K.) and among the hosts for the International Ex Libris Congress held in Oxford, England during August of 1982. Philip has been active in the English society and held different posts including that of editor for their quarterly.

Beddingham was Librarian at historic, world renowned Gray's Inn, London. The Bookplate Society's Newsletter featured an interesting article on the various ex libris used by Gray's Inn in one of its issues. Philip wrote a number of monographs on bookplates; occasionally these appear in book-sellers' catalogues.

Philip Beddingham was probably the first person in England with whom I corresponded concerning bookplates during the period more than 20 years ago when I was working on my bibliography. Philip was most generous in making available to me bibliographical notes he had made on periodical literature appearing in England. It was a particular pleasure meeting Philip on my first trip to England, being given a personally escorted tour through the legendary Gray's Inn, and best of all receiving the personal invitation of Philip and his wife Kathleen to visit their home. An added dividend was a ride into the English countryside and stopping at a local country pub. The evening we were there the pub was filled with the happy celebration of the local soccer team.

Philip will long be remembered by his many friends. Perhaps my fondest memory of Philip will always be his fine sense of humor and the merry twinkle in his eyes.

The bookplate above was designed by Diana Bloomfield; she also designed the logo for the Bookplate Society. (Audrey Arellanes)

•————————————————————————•

Additional Notes on Ex Libris of Boston Athenaeum   Below are additional notes on Elsie Livingston Johnson and Ola Elizabeth Winslow, whose ex libris by Sarah Chamberlain appeared in the January 1983 issue of BITN.

Mrs. Edward C. Johnson II (1904-1981) was a great gardener; hence the motif of flowers on the bookplate, and she had a particular fondness for cats; hence the feline on the bookplate. Her daughter, Mrs. Mitchell, says her mother fell in love at 16, was married to Mr. Johnson at 19, and thereafter her life was domestically inclined, though with a great deal of attention paid to her garden, one of the great ones of the Boston area.

Ola Elizabeth Winslow won the 1941 Pulitzer Prize for biography with her life of Jonathan Edwards. She had a distinguished career as teacher, author and historian, but it was as "a genius in human relations" that she had her greatest talent and success.

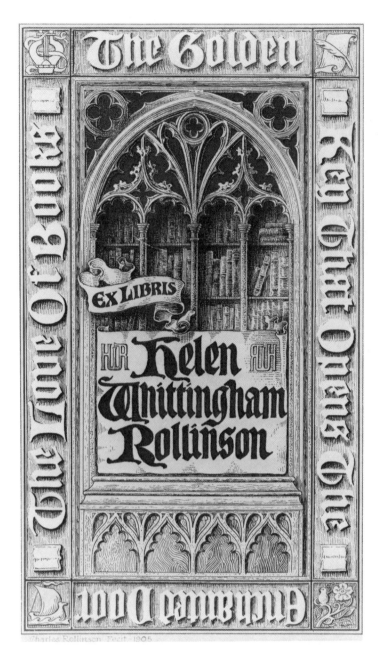

The Golden Key that Opens The True Book I

EX LIBRIS

Helen Whittingham Rollinson

Charles Rollinson Fecit 1905

HELEN WHITTINGHAM ROLLINSON
by Richard H. Schimmelpfeng

In 1977 a gift of two illuminated manuscripts was made
to the University of Connecticut Library, one by Helen
Rollinson and one by the Amer
& Rollinson Studio in New York.
For some years I had been aware
of the firm of Amer & Rollinson, specialists in fine lettering, designing and illuminating of scrolls of honor,
certificates, diplomas, family
trees, and the like, and so
was aware of the exceptional
quality of these two manuscripts. Not much was known
about Miss Rollinson except
that her father was Charles
Rollinson, that she had lived
in nearby Willington, CT, and
that she had created these
Prayers for a New Year in exquisite calligraphy with jewel-
like illuminations in glowing
color, bound in blue morocco,
and encased in a watered silk
envelope. The donor had been a
friend of the artist.

There the matter rested until
last December when the manuscript was displayed along
with other gifts. It caught
the attention of a lady who
wanted to know all about it
and anything we knew about
Helen Rollinson since she and
her husband were living in the house that Miss Rollinson built. Two fascinating pieces of information surfaced. "Helena Countryman" wrote an article entitled "The home that came true" for the September 1927 McCALL'S in which she
described the trials and tribulations she encountered in building her "little
place" which she expected to cost $2,400 but which actually cost $4,985. It
is a fascinating article and also makes the artist more real.

The second item of information was that the present owners had the original
design by Charles Rollinson, dated 1905, for his daughter's bookplate. The
original is enormous: 12 3/4 x 7 1/2 inches. What is not known is whether
a bookplate was actually cut from the design.

BOOKPLATES IN THE NEWS
 Copyright 1983
 Audrey Spencer Arellanes

January/April/July/October
Calendar Year $15/Single $4
or Quarterly/YEAR BOOK $35

AS of BC & D

Bookplates in the News

605 N. STONEMAN AVENUE #F, ALHAMBRA, CALIFORNIA, 91801 U.S.A.

AUDREY SPENCER ARELLANES, Editor

NUMBER FIFTY-THREE   JULY 1983

Hui-Ming Wang: Artist

The work of this multi-talented artist was featured in an earlier issue of BITN (#51), and it is a pleasure to again have tipins, each printed in color.

The ex libris to the left is for Michael Paine, a friend of Hui-Ming Wang, who reads widely in philosophy, history, political thoughts, and literature, East and West, old and new. He has a fine collection of books. Out of admiration the artist designed this plate.

Wang says, "I carved a line in classic Chinese which says:

> My only wish in life is to read all the great books and to see all great paintings and calligraphy, East and West, ancient and modern.

This seemingly immodest saying is not out of line with traditional Chinese art of seal carving in which one often carves a whole poem or an essay in a group of seals by one or several artists. Besides, a wish is only a wish."

Hui-Ming Wang was the subject of an article in the June-July 1982 issue of CONTACT, in which are revealed his vibrant spirit, a fertile imagination, a creative

In loving memory of F. Ward Paine and for lasting friend= ship between the Chinese and the American people, we present this book to Zhejiang University.

Michael and Victoria Paine

and joyful sense of humor as well as his status as scholar-artist.

Zhejiang University is one of the leading universities in China, established in 1897. Originally it was named "Quishi" (truth seeking) Academy. It is situated by the beautiful West Lake in Hangchow and is jointly run by Chinese Academia Sinica and the Zhejiang Provencial government. The well-known physicist Professor Qian San Qiang is also the vice-president of Chinese Academia Sinica. Zhejiang is now an institute of science and technology. It has fifteen academic departments, and in 1979 had over 6,000 undergraduate students and 421 graduate students. It has four research institutes, twenty-one research laboratories; in addition, there are six independent research laboratories. Six factories provide students with on-the-job training. The university library has over 750,000 books and 10,000 journals in Chinese and other languages. The campus has 247 acres. Hui-Ming Wang was moved by the Paine's generosity in donating books to the university and made this ex libris for their presentation.

Michael Paine's gracious wife Victoria, who prefers to be called Tori among friends and relatives, is also an avid reader. She has her own collection of books.

The artist says, "I think the letters of the word 'Tori' are graphically beautiful, so I made this plate for her, and I feel this color green reflects her personality."

Hui-Ming Wang has recently has an exhibition titled Work-on-Paper which was featured at the Thronja Art Gallery in Springfield, MA. It ran from May 31 to June 25, 1983.

QANTAS EMPIRE AIRWAYS, Art in Books. (7) 8:8-9, August 1981. P. Neville Barnett of Sydney, Australia, is pictured in his library tipping-in bookplates; he has authored five books of ex libris with concentration on Australian plates. For many years Barnett was librarian at the Bank of New South Wales.

PFIZER SPECTRUM. Ex Libris. (16) 4:14-5, January 1, 1957. Harvey Cushing's ex libris by E. D. French included initials of other Cushings and dates of their doctorates. A psychosomatic ex libris dated 1784 reads, "The Gift of Dr. Nash to me In Hopes of my Improvement."

PUBLISHERS' WEEKLY, Obituary Notes. 192:36, October 23, 1967. Warren H. Lowenhaupt, curator of ex libris at Yale since 1951, died September 29, 1967 in Brussels, Belgium, at 76. He was on a European trip looking for acquisitions. Yale has largest ex libris collection in Western hemisphere. Lowenhaupt created the Lowenhaupt Bookplate Trust which was designed primarily to provide for a curator of bookplates and bookplate literature.

PENNSYLVANIA DUTCH AMERICAN FOLK ART, Henry J. Kauffman. Revised & Enlarged Edition. New York: Dover Publications, 1946, 1964. The Pennsylvania Dutch term for bookplate is bucherzeichen, which usually indicated the owner's name, date of ownership, and sometimes the name of the donor. Two ex libris are illustrated.

HUGH WYNNE, FREE QUAKER, S. Weir Mitchell. (2 volumes) New York: Century Co., 1898. The grey cover of each volume has William Penn's ex libris in blind relief.

THE STEWARTS BOOK PLATES, C. E. Stewart. n.d., n.p. However, this copy has an inscription by the author to Lady Isobel Stewart dated February 8, 1911; the author's address is given as London. This is a paperback of 19 pages with 28 ex libris reproduced.

ALBUM EX LIBRIS MEDICORUM, One Hundred Fifteen American and European Book Plates Past and Present, Wasyl Luciw, MS, PhD. Toronto: Slavia Library, 1961. There are 18 pages of text and index of ex libris by subject (nudes, bookpiles, portraits, etc.). Plates have all been reproduced on ivory color paper and tipped-in to portfolio about 5" x 8".

13 DEVICES, Peter Fingesten. Introduction by Antoinette K. Gordon. New York: Pax-Press, 1952. Edition limited to 300 copies; $1 prepublication price. These are devices commissioned as "Ex Libris, seals, and covers."

THE MAVERICKS, AMERICAN ENGRAVERS, Stephen De Witt Stephens. New Brunswick, N.J.: Rutgers University Press, 1950. The bookplates of Peter and Peter R. Maverick are items #101 through #211 (pages 96-105). Includes those signed by the Mavericks or "attributed to" or "very like."

AN EARLY CONNECTICUT ENGRAVER AND HIS WORK, Albert C. Bates. Hartford, CT: 1906. This concerns primarily the work of Richard Brunton, who is perhaps best remembered as involved in the counterfieting of Spanish milled dollars.

JOURNAL OF THE WEST, Catalogue by Peggy Christian on American Artists and

Illustrators reproduces a C. M. Russell ex libris which is signed and dated 1909; it is item #114. The illustration is titled "Medicine Man" for Albert Forrest Longeway.

CHICAGO JEWISH FORUM, Books. 15:56-7, Fall 1956. Leah Yablonsky Mishkin reviews EXHIBITION OF JEWISH BOOK PLATES published by Graphic Archives and Museum. The catalog has 99 pages; priced $2.50. Eight hundred ex libris prints are described from Jerusalem exhibit sponsored by National Union of Printing Workers of Israel; catalog prepared by Avrom Weiss, archivist and librarian. Printed in Hebrew and English, covers period 1720 to 1955, and mentions other catalogs back to 1887.

BULLETIN of NEW YORK PUBLIC LIBRARY, A Cursory Survey of Maledictions, Lawrence S. Thompson. 56:55-75, February 1952. Wide variety of warnings to possible biblioklepts with quotations in numerous languages.

ACCESSIONS 1960, Winterthur, Delaware. Paintings and Prints section mentions Richard Brunton, American Revolution era engraver, and N. Hurd's ex libris for Wentworth family.

PRINCETON UNIVERSITY LIBRARY CHRONICLE, An Early American Book Label, M. Halsey Thomas. (2) 22:36-7, Autumn 1960. Label is for John Cotton (1658-1710) and is dated June 5, 1675.

AMERICAN ANTIQUARIAN SOCIETY PROCEEDINGS, Seventeenth Century American Book Labels, R. W. G. Vail. 43:304-316, 1933 (New Series).

MAUGHAM, A BIOGRAPHY, Ted Morgan. New York: Simon and Schuster, 1980. On page 274 there is a reference to the Queen's Doll House which was built in 1923, designed by noted architect Sir Edwin Lutyens on a scale of 1" to 1'. "The books, one inch high and bound in yellow calf, with Queen Mary's bookplate on the inner cover, included two hundred works by authors of the period, who had been asked to contribute an original composition or a passage from a published work, writing it by hand in a volume the size of a postage stamp." (Editor's Note: Does anyone have a copy of this ex libris which they would send for reproduction in a future issue of BITN?)

L'EX LIBRIS FRANCAIS, No. 146, December 1982. This special number is devoted entirely to Italian engraver Luigi Gercsa and includes a checklist of his work in chronological order from 1974 to 1980; it totals 359 items. Born near Como, he is an architect and president of B.N.E.L. (Bianco e Nero dell Ex Libris, the Italian association). Eight prints are tipped-in and two are reproduced.

GRAPHIA, #86, March 1983. Article on artist Elsa Courtoit by Leo Winkeler which pictures artist at work and ten of her plates, two of which are tipped-in. Bookplates with the theme of Pinocchio (12). Article by L. Van Den Briele about Karol Izakovic, who specializes in portrait bookplates. Fourteen ex libris reproduced and a picture of the artist. Articles also on Andre Noels, Oskar Roland Schroth, Eduard Albrecht Intrigeert, Henri Coppez (1869-1946).

MITTEILUNGEN DER DEUTSCHEN EXLIBRIS-GESELLSCHAFT, #1, 1983. Dr. Norbert Nechwatal gives an interesting impression from the International Congress in Oxford titled "Oxford von A bis Z."

THE BOOKPLATE SOCIETY NEWSLETTER (England), Vol. No. 1, March 1983. This is the first issue as an independent organization from Private Libraries Association; it is also in a new, smaller format with justified margins printed from type. Articles included: "Bookplate Centre of the German Democratic Republic." "The Bookplates of J. Walter West," Emma-Rose Barber. (2) 3-8. Emma-Rose Barber was co-editor and producer of the Society's junior newsletter. As the result of her research at the British Museum, the Tate Gallery, and the Victoria & Albert Museum, the article provides a brief biography of the artist and a checklist of the 33 bookplates he designed. West lived from 1860 to 1933. "News of the Society and Its Members." (1) 8-9. The Society's first auction and exchange meeting was held February 25, 1983. Friends of John Gartner will be distressed to learn that he lost his home, private library, and entire bookplate collection in a fire that ravaged vast areas of Australia in February. He has begun to rebuild his bookplate collection. Any who wants to assist in rebuilding his collection, may send personal plates and duplicates to: John Gartner, Viewfield, Mount Macedon Road, Mount Macedon, 3441 Australia. "Leslie Beneson Wins Prize." (1) 9. The competition was sponsored by the Ex-Libris Centrum in Sint Niklaas; theme was science fiction. "New Bookplates." (2) 10-11. Illustrated are new plates for Kenneth Langford and Anthony Howard Stacey designed by Derek Riley and H. N. Eccleston, respectively. "Publications." Mention is made of article in February 1983 issue of ANTIQUARIAN BOOK MONTHLY REVIEW and publications for sale by James Wilson and W. E. Butler.

THE BOOKPLATE JOURNAL (England). This is volume 1, number 1 for the new journal of the English bookplate society; it is a handsome publication measuring 5 7/16" x 8½" with three sewn signatures totaling 48 pages. Subscription in the U.S. is $20, which includes the BOOKPLATE JOURNAL, quarterly NEWSLETTER, and a free book.

THE BOOKPLATE JOURNAL, Comment. 1:1-2, March 1983. "After prolonged soul-searching, a poll of the membership, and ten years of nuturing while attached to the Private Libraries Association, The Bookplate Society decided to assume the risk of independence in order to enlarge the scope of its activities and improve services to members. Publication of a proper journal was high on the priorities of the restructured Society."

THE BOOKPLATE JOURNAL, Lettering on Bookplates, David Kindersley. (30)1: 2-15, March 1983. This article was adapted from an address delivered by the author at the XIX International Ex Libris Congress at Oxford in August 1982. "There are many more superb bookplates just with letters than there are artists' designed with applied lettering. In other words, whilst letterers produce lettering of a very high standard, yet do not consider themselves to be artists, the artists often produce very fine engraved or drawn designs with appalling lettering. Artists often leave the impression that lettering is of less value or importance than their designs." In conclusion, Kindersley writes: ". . . the bookplate is a marvellous inspirer of inventiveness in direct proportion to its apparent uselessness. Not only can it be easily removed from someone else's book, but it is even easier to put one's own bookplate in other people's books. In spite of this, the idea of a bookplate has flourished for about four centuries and has given great joy to the designer and the owner. Long may this gentle art continue." The forthright insight and charm of Kindersley's talk has successfully transferred to the printed page.

THE BOOKPLATE JOURNAL, Geometrical Typographic Bookplate Design, Hellmuth Weissenborn. (10) 1:15-25, March 1983. This article originally appeared in TYPOGRAPHISCHE MITTEILUNGEN in Berlin in July 1929; it has been translated by his widow Lesley MacDonald. There is a checklist of Professor Weissenborn's 49 bookplates which gives technique, subject, dimensions, and indicates when signed.

THE BOOKPLATE JOURNAL, Reflections on Disposing of Bookplate Collections, W. E. Butler. (2) 1:26-34, March 1983. ". . . most bookplate collections presented to institutions cease to become living collections. Unlike the book or graphic art holdings, they rarely enjoy an acquisitions budget and virtually never have a curator knowledgeable about bookplates and in a position to enlarge or upgrade the bookplate collection. The alternative is to sell the collection." Professor Butler details the sale of three collections. The Harold Mortlake collection of about 28,000 ex libris prints was purchased by a syndicate of four London collectors. Dr. Arthur Brauer's continental collection of about 30,000 bookplates was acquired by A. K. Pincott. The collection of American Margaret Woodbury Strong was at her death given to the J. P. Morgan Library; a dozen or more years later Swann Galleries in New York City was appointed to dispose of the collection. The Strong Collection was said to contain 86,000 prints in 1969; Swann gave an estimate of 150,000. Whatever the amount, the Strong Collection is now in private hands in England.

THE BOOKPLATE JOURNAL, A Memoir of C. W. Sherborn, R. H. R. Brocklebank. (1) 1:35-39, March 1983. Lt. Col. Brocklebank (1881-1965) penned this sketch of Sherborn (1831-1912) in January of 1944 for circulation to other collectors; Brocklebank was a member of the Exchange Club for many years.

THE BOOKPLATE JOURNAL, Profile of An Artist: Mark Severin, Brian North Lee. (2) 1:40-2, March 1983. "Though Mark was born in 1906, in his friendship one quickly discovers that the sane and kindly adviser is endowed equally with a spirit of most refreshing youthfulness." About his work: "He has a particular flair for disclosing the nude, and, whether seductive or simply naughty, his girls reveal both his and their assurance and are much sought after to be held captive within the boards of books."

THE BOOKPLATE JOURNAL, Portrait of A Bookplate: I - Willen Library, Brian North Lee. (1) 1:43-5, March 1983. The donor of the Willen Library was Dr. Richard Busby (1606-95). Unfortunately the books were moved from the parish library to the vicarage, and all were destroyed in a fire May 1, 1946.

THE BOOKPLATE JOURNAL, Review, David Knott. 1:46-8, March 1938. THE BOOK-PLATES OF PHILIP HAGREEN with an introduction by John Bennett Shaw was printed at the Private Press of the Indiana Kid by James Lamar Weygand. An edition of 65 was printed; if still available copies are $25. Hagreen was an English artist, who made a complete turn-about in the approach to his work after being invited by Eric Gill to work in the St. Dominic's community at Ditchling. An earlier book titled PHILIP HAGREEN: THE ARTIST AND HIS WORK (Southport, CT: At the Sign of the Arrow, 1975) had only a fourth of the bookplates (116) illustrated in Weygand's publication. Unfortunately the bookplates are printed from zinc cuts made from artist's proofs in the John Bennett Shaw collection in the University of Notre Dame, Indiana.

Linda Wenzel
1726 Galena Street
Aurora, Colorado 80010
May 12, 1983

The American Society of Bookplate
Collectors and Designers
605 N. Stoneman Avenue, No. F
Alhambra, CA 91801

Dear Bookplate People:

My name is Linda Wenzel, and I have just formed a new company named BookBytes. Its purpose is to make custom designed medical bookplates and to utilize the graphics capabilities of my computer to do computer graphics imbedded in medical or technical papers. I also do any kind of off-set design; for instance, I do business cards, especially if they require some imagination.

I started this business after being in the hospital for a long time--over six weeks at this particular stretch (not my record, by any means)--and I started sketching to while away the time. One doctor saw my rather technical style and asked me to do a set of bookplates for him, and, as things will, my requests kept growing until I had done about ten sets of medical bookplates as gifts for my doctors. At that time, I didn't even charge for printing--I paid for that myself. Some time later, one of these doctors sent me an article from the January 1983 issue of _Diversion_ magazine and urged me to stop giving away expensive freebies.

A couple of months ago I was again in the hospital for five weeks,(I have a degenerative disease), and started taking commissions for bookplates. I have four designs delivered--all of them quite amusing, utilizing the doctors' wants and desires for motifs, and putting those ideas into my own conception of a motif--and I am quite pleased with the results. The commissioned bookplates have a quite different quality from the earlier ones, because of the diversity of ideas used in them, plus my extra care to produce a quality printed product since I was being paid. I only charged $50.00 for 75 copies of each drawing, but again, these doctors are my friends. In the future, my rates will go up to $75.00 for $75 copies. Additional copies are easy to reproduce, and will not cost nearly as much.

I will enclose some examples of my work, and perhaps you can put me in touch with customers who desire talents similar to mine. The enclosed business card will also give a good idea of the scope of my business. I hope to hear from you soon.

Sincerely,

Linda J. Wenzel

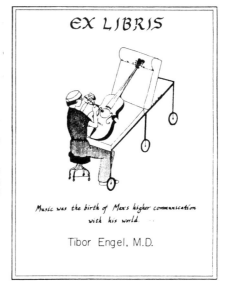

Dr. Roger is an orthopedic surgeon. He wanted a combination of orthopedics, computers, and music. Anyone familiar with Beethoven's Fifth will get the joke. Dr. Roger loved the idea.

Dr. Engel is an OB/GYN specialist. His plate combines obstetrics and music.

Dr. Lewis is a pediatrician and left me to my own devices. Professionally he sees children up to 18 years of age.

(Note: The letter and bookplates have been reduced in size somewhat to fit the space available.)

MORE FROM THE BOOKPLATE LITERATURE

CZECHOSLOVAK LIFE, Ex Libris, Pavel Koranda. (5) 46:188,28-9, June 1981. Prague geologist Karel Zizkovsky has an ex libris collection of 10,000 prints. He specializes in heraldic ex libris, those by particular artists, and all bookplates with the motif of the rat catcher. Karel is quoted: ". . . the Ex Libris Collectors' Club is one of the oldest hobby clubs in this country. It was founded in 1918. Today, we are affiliated to the Czechoslovak Society for Aesthetics, of the Academy of Sciences. We hold meetings every week, to make exchanges, and discuss the latest news. Our annual conventions are attended also by collectors from other countries, with whom every member maintains extensive correspondence."

THE KOVEL'S COLLECTORS' SOURCE BOOK, Ralph and Terry Kovel. Crown Publishers, Inc., New York, 1983. Chapter 12, Books and Bookplates, page 21, lists the American Society of Bookplate Collectors and Designers and BOOKPLATES IN THE NEWS.

NORDISK EXLIBRIS TIDSSKRIFT, #150, #2 of 1983. Jurgen Nemetz, Klaus Witte. (12) 83-5. Young-looking artist (born 1944) who has a distinctive and interesting style. - Exlibrissituationen 1983. Klaus Rodel, editor of the journal for the Danish society, has made an extremely interesting article and layout using the masthead page of the journals of the bookplate societies of all known countries, fifteen in all including BOOKPLATES IN THE NEWS. - Zbigniew Dolatowski, Klaus Rodel. (16) 94-6. This artist tends to use predominant masses of black in his ex libris designs.

ANTIQUARIAN BOOK MONTHLY REVIEW, The Bookplate Journal. (1) 10:189, May 1983. Illustrated is Reynolds Stone ex libris for Rosamund and Elliott Viney. THE BOOKPLATE JOURNAL is the new periodical of the English society; £10 includes the journal, NEWSLETTER, and a free book.

ANTIQUARIAN BOOK MONTHLY REVIEW, News from Sotheby's. (1) 10:174, May 1983. Illustrated is the Igler ex libris which appears in at least one volume in London's Sotheby sale May 17-18, 1983. This hedgehog bookplate is one of the earliest 15th century ex libris and "among three earliest known." The scroll at the top of the bookplate is translated as: "Hans Igler may a hedgehog kiss you."

ANTIQUARIAN BOOK MONTHLY REVIEW, A Rare Book's Odyssey, George D. Gupen. (3) 10:52-55, February 1983. Book under discussion is the Baskerville HORACE with the ex libris of Richard Dennis Hoblyn (died 8/22/1886).

A ARTE DO EX-LIBRIS, Ex-Libris Heraldicos Portugueses, O Ex-Libris Do Dr. Jorge Preto. 66-7, #100, 1982. Engraved ex libris with St. George and the dragon and heraldric device tipped in. - For another article there is an engraved tipped-in ex libris for Jose Sainz-Trveva. - Giuseppe Mirabella. (8) 74-7. Artist is pictured in his library, a checklist of 43 prints is given in chronological order with technique of production. - Bela Petry. (6) 78-9. Checklist is continued for Bela Petry with 61 ex libris designed during 1980 through 1982. (Editor's Note: In addition to having engraved tip-ins there are three ex libris reproduced using color. Are there any ASBC&D artist or collector members who will furnish engraved prints (225 needed) for tipping-into BOOKPLATES IN THE NEWS? Or any institutions with engraved or etched plates they would furnish?)

FOLGER LIBRARY EX LIBRIS
and
Engraver: S. E. Scantlin

The world-famous Folger Shakespeare Library in Washington, D.C. came into being as the result of an interest aroused in Henry Clay Folger while he was a student at Amherst College. He attended a lecture by Ralph Waldo Emerson and read his essay on the tercentnary of Shakespeare's birth; thus began a life-long interest in Shakespeare and his world.

Folger graduated from Amherst College in 1879 and later received his law degree from Columbia University. Starting as a clerk, he eventually became President and eventually Chairman of the Board of Standard Oil of New York. In 1885 he married Emily Jordan of Elizabeth, New Jersey, a Vassar graduate who shared his enthusiasm for Shakespeare.

Over the years the Folgers acquired 79 of the 240 First Folio editions known to exist. Without the First Folio edition of Shakespeare's works, almost half of the plays we know today would have been lost, as they do not survive in the single play/quarto form.

The corner stone of the library was laid in 1930 by the Folgers. It was their gift to the American people; a library built to house the magnificent treasure of some 93,000 books, 50,000 prints and engravings, and thousands of manuscripts which they had assembled. Two weeks after the corner stone was laid, Henry Folger suffered a fatal heart attack. Mrs. Folger oversaw the completion of the building and its dedication April 23, 1932, appropriately on Shakespeare's birthday. President Hoover, scholars, and ambassadors from all over the world attended the ceremony.

The building includes an exhibition gallery known as the Great Hall, a theatre styled to suggest an Elizabethan innyard threatre, and reading rooms. The Folger Reading Room is reminiscent of a Tudor/Stuart banquet hall with carved dark oak panelling and Elizabethan motifs in the plasterwork. A replica of the bust of Shakespeare in Stratford's Trinity Church, where Shakespeare is buried, stands at one end of the Reading Room; at the other end is a magnificent stained glass window by Italian glassmaker Nicola D'Ascenzo, depicting the Seven Ages Man - infancy to old age - as enumerated by Shakespeare's character Jacques in AS YOU LIKE IT.

The Folger bookplate was designed by Peter Cocci using Shakespeare's coat of arms; the engraved work was shared by Thomas R. Hipschen and Stanley E Scantlin.

Stanley Scantlin was born in Benton Harbor, Michigan on March 8, 1949; he attended local schools and graduated from high school in 1967. He attended Western Michigan University at Kalamazoo for four years, but left before graduation to become an apprentice engraver for the Colonial Williamsburg Foundation in Williamsburg, Virginia in 1971. While apprenticing under Master Engraver James J. Kinsey at Colonial Williamsburg, Stanley went to the College of William & Mary to study art and printing. At this time he also had an interest is calligraphy. In 1975 he moved to Northern Virginia to apprentice with sculptural engraver Eqesto A. Ligi, and finished his formal apprenticeship in 1981.

Scantlin specializes in engraving ex libris, personal and business station-

ary, specialty cards, Christmas cards, invitations, certificates, embossed seals, and presentation silver. Depending on the nature of the commission he works with associates, who are specialists in the art and engraving fields.

Scantlin has six handpresses on which he does wet paper plate printing and hand die stamping.

This young engraver says, "Every March I have a booth at the Antiquarian Book Fair in Washington, DC. At this fair I exhibit a collection of engraved ex libris and writing papers. The commissions gained from this show keep me busy throughout the year." However, if you are interested is commissioning an engraved bookplate, you may write indicating what you want and request a quotation: Stanley E. Scantlin, 2786 Patrick Henry Dr., Woodbridge, VA 22191.

LIMUR

464

NEFERTITI EX LIBRIS

by Keith Wingrove

KEITH WINGROVE

I chose the bust of Nefertiti and the scroll for several reasons. I have always been interested in Egyptain temples and art. I have also been deeply interested in art and have a large collection of art books, prints, drawings, etc.

The bust of Nefertiti is one of the most beautiful and satisfying works in the whole world of art. She is not called the beautiful one for nothing! Her names means "The beautiful one has come." She has been claimed by some authorities as "one of the most beautiful women of any period in the world's history." An opinion I heartily agree with. Louis Stanley in his THE BEAUTY OF WOMAN (1955) writes of this bust as "the work of a talented sculptor for nothing short of a touch of genius could have moulded the line from the lower eyelid, skirting the cheek, to the arc of the mouth with the sealed, full lips. The flesh could still be warm, soft, pulsating, and any woman of today would envy the languorous eyes, the shapley nose, fastidious lips, and face of esquisite sensibility."

To me she represents a symbol of beauty, both womanly beauty and beauty in the wider meaning. She is a symbol of art. These are the reasons I chose her as the main theme for the bookplate. She was the wife of Akhnaton (1364-47 BC), the heretic pharaoh; his reign is of particular importance in that it marked an attempt to establish monotheistic religion in Egypt. He abolished the old gods and substituted the worship of the life-giving sun. The bust was found in Amarna in the house of a sculptor, who is known as Thutmose. This is said with reasonable but not absolute certainty as to his identity.

Derek Riley, the English artist, has made an excellent representation of the bust. The scroll beneath the bust relates to books and literature. The first books were scrolls.

JAPANESE ARTIST: Yoichi Kenmoku
    by   Keith Wingrove

The above bookplate was designed, cut, and printed by Yoichi Kenmoku of
Tokyo. He is an artist whose work ranges through oil and water color
painting, wood engraving, ceramics, and copperplate engraving. He had
executed fourteen ex libris up to 1981 when he did this plate.

The design was taken from a well-known woodblock print by Utamaro. His
full name is Kitagawa Utamaro, famous for his prints of beautiful women.
He was born in 1753 and died in 1806. The ex libris is based on his
print published circa 1790-94, as far as I can ascertain.

As a book collector and also a collector of Japanese prints, I thought
the subject a most suitable one for a bookplate.

XXth CONGRESS OF FISAE in WEIMAR   The XXth International Ex Libris
                                    Congress will be held in Weimar
                                    during the second half of August
in 1984 for five days.   The program will consist of three lectures and three
bookplate exhibitions.   The exhibitions will be The Bookplates of the German Democratic Republic, International Exhibition of Bookplates, and International Contest of Bookplates.

At the same time the oldest German collection of bookplates will be presented; it is a collection from the 18th century, which a collector living in
Berlin acquired.   Several excursions are planned including a visit to the
Goethe-Schiller Memorial Houses at Weimar, trips to Erfurt for an exhibition
of Lithunian bookplates, and to Eisenach (Wartburg). Another excursion by
boat will cross the Sea of Thuringia to the Bookplate Centre of GDR, the
State Museum of Burgk Castle.   Here will be viewed the Paul Heinicke Collection, Soviet and Czech Bookplates.   There will be time also to exchange
ex libris.

Artists are requested to submit bookplates designed in 1982-83 for the In-
ternational Bookplate Exhibition.   Submissions should be made on or before
January 10, 1984. (If you are interested, please write the Editor of BOOK-
PLATES IN THE NEWS for further details, as it is not known at this time
whether submissions may be made directly to Weimar or only through the
Society to which you belong.)   A catalogue will be issued.

The International Contest is dedicated to the 225th anniversary of Friedrich
Schiller.   Artists are requested to create bookplates for literature collections of Schiller.   The deadline for submission is April 15, 1984.   All
submissions will be retained by the GDR Bookplate Centre.

Further details may be obtained from Prof. Dr. Lothar Lang, President of
FISAE, Staatlichee Museum Schloss Burgh, DDR-6551 Burgk/Saale, Germany.

THE NORMAN F. SPRAGUE
MEMORIAL LIBRARY
HARVEY MUDD
COLLEGE

A GIFT OF

SPRAGUE LIBRARY at CLAREMONT

A functional bookplate, designed to
provide space for registering book
donor names, is a new addition to
the beautiful Norman F. Sprague Memorial Library at the Claremont
Colleges. The Tom Jamieson Design
Office of Claremont created the ex
libris.

The library is the home of several
internationally famous rare book
collections.   Built in 1972 and designed by Wendell Mounce AIA Assoc.
of Glendale, the building commemo-
rates the distinguished Los Angeles
medical educator and physician. The
donors were Dr. and Mrs. Norman F.
Sprague, Jr.   The late Mrs. Sprague
was a daughter of Harvey S. Mudd.

EXCHANGES WANTED   European collector Christian Selle, Bad Godesberg, Muffendorfer Strasse 4, D-5300 Bonn 2, Germany, would like to exchange with American bookplate collectors. He lists a variety of plates by different artists, which have been designed between 1961 and 1980.

• ── •

MORE BOOKPLATE LITERATURE

DIVERSION, Doctors' Bookplates, Christiane Bird. (18) 244 et seq, January 1983. Interesting article in part drawing upon information furnished by Dr. Norman Shaftel and Dr. Theodore Schultz. DIVERSION offers, in the article, to act as a clearinghouse for physicians who want to exchange commissioned ex libris; they will attempt to exchange each plate for a plate from a physician of the same specialty. (Editor's note: Small correction; the article indicates membership in ASBC&D has dropped from 250 members; to the best of my knowledge the Society never had that many members.)

NORDISK EXLIBRIS TIDSSKRIFT, #149, 1983. Articles on Kaj Welsch Riis (1917-1982), Henry Carlo Skov, Paul Boesch (artist is pictured at work with his Siamese cat sitting near the block being cut), Hans Volkert whose work seems to be of the period 1900-30. An article from THE BOOKPLATE MAGAZINE for 1921 about Garth Jones appears in Danish (?) as well as English. There are three pages of bookplate literature reviews.

L'EX LIBRIS FRANCAIS, #147, March 1983. Les ex-libris savernois with alphabetic checklist. In memoriam Charles Favet (1899-1982). Three pages of literature and exhibition reviews.

• ── •

WANTED   I D E A S   and   S U G G E S T I O N S

for articles for future YEAR BOOKS -

Please write:

American Society of Bookplate
  Collectors and Designers
605 N. Stoneman Ave. #F
Alhambra, CA 91801

Also - In 1932 when the Olympics were held in Los Angeles, the Bookplate Association International sponsored an exhibit of bookplates and included some specially designed with an Olympic motif. Would any artists interested in submitting ex libris designed for the 1984 Olympics please write ASBC&D.

• ── •

BOOKPLATES IN THE NEWS   January/April/July/October
605 N. Stoneman Ave. #F   Calendar Year $15
Alhambra, CA 91801   (C) Audrey Spencer Arellanes

AS of BC & D

Bookplates in the News

605 N. STONEMAN AVENUE #F, ALHAMBRA, CALIFORNIA, 91801 U.S.A.

AUDREY SPENCER ARELLANES, Editor

NUMBER FIFTY-FOUR   OCTOBER 1983

Hui-Ming Wang again has been generous in providing handpulled, color printed bookplate prints to be tipped-in BOOKPLATES IN THE NEWS. They are ex libris for his sons and daughter.

James Wang, the second son, is a research geophysicist, who lives in Southern California. He likes the sun, seas, mountains, and deserts, and above all the earth formations of rock and sand. Hui-Ming says his son "enjoys solidute and reflective thinking, so I printed his plate in green.

Kathleen Wang is a student of mathematics. Hui-Ming writes that his daughter wanted him "to carve her Chinese name on her plate. She likes all kinds of birds, especially humming birds, which often hover over the azaleas in front of the house. I carved her ex libris with the shape of birds and printed it in the color of our azaleas."

Dennis, the oldest son, is interested in astronomy. To fit his interests Hui-Ming carved the sun and the moon, yin and yang, night and day, and printed it in black and white.

If you are interested in having a personalized bookplate designed by Hui-Ming Wang, please write to him directly:

> Hui-Ming Wang
> Epoch Studio
> Montague, MASS 01351

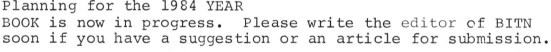

WANTED: Articles for

1984 <u>YEAR</u> <u>BOOK</u>

If you have an idea for an article about a bookplate artist or collector, a particular phase of collecting, a history of an editor, author, or publication devoted to ex libris, please write Audrey Arellanes, the editor of BITN, with your suggestions.

Illustrations and tip-ins are an essential part of any publication about ex libris.

Planning for the 1984 YEAR BOOK is now in progress. Please write the editor of BITN soon if you have a suggestion or an article for submission.

1984 DUES - Again next year the dues are being kept at $35. This makes the third year without an increase. It will be especially appreciated if you will <u>send</u> your <u>payment</u> for dues <u>before February 1, 1984</u> or at least indicate your intention of continuing your membership by that date.

LOS ANGELES TIMES, San Gabriel Valley "At Home" section, p. 6, August 20, 1983. San Bernardino Library Seeking Book Donations. The San Bernardino County Library has a brochure titled "Books: as tributes .... as memorials" which describes how citizens may establish a book endowment or donate a single volume. Beginning with an endowment of $150, the annual interest is used to purchase a book each year and a bookplate is placed in each book indicating who the donor was or in whose memory the book is given. "A book memorial is a fitting expression of sympathy and a lasting tribute that continues a person's influence in the community."

L'EX LIBRIS FRANCAIS, No. 148, June 1983, p. 250-60. Article illustrating numerous ex libris of comte Aime Mottin de La Balme. Article and two clever cartoons about the Oxford Congress participants exchanging. In memoriam: Emil Kotrba (1912-1983).

MITTEILUNGER DER DEUTSCHEN EXLIBRIS-GESELLSCHAFT e.V, #2, 1983, p. 17-32. The lead article is a tribute to Lucas Cranach (1472-1553) illustrated with bookplates by a variety of artists including a nude by Mark Severin.

EXLIBRIS WERELD, #2, Summer 1983, p. 433-48. One article gives several examples of essentially the same design adapted by different artists for different owners.

SVENSKA EXLIBRISFORENINGEN, #145, 3, August 1983, p. 42-7. The cover carries the emblem for the XX International Ex Libris Congress to be held in Weimar during 1984. There is a tipped-in bookplate for I. B. Colmeill which reproduces open pages from an illuminated manuscript.

ANTIQUARIAN BOOK MONTHLY REVIEW, Book Reviews. EDWARD GORDON CRAIG: THE LAST EIGHT YEARS 1958-1966, Letters from Ellen Gordon Craig. Edited with introduction by Edward Craig, two wood engravings by John Craig. Published by Whittington Press in edition of 345 copies; £ 20. Ellen is sister to Edward and daughter of Edward Gordon Craig. Reviewed by Colin Franklin.

ANTIQUARIAN BOOKMAN (AB), BRIDESHEAD REVISTED - The Page Proofs, P. William Filby. 72:1286,88,90, September 5, 1983. A fascinating account of page proofs sent by his publisher to Evelyn Waugh via 10 Downing Street and in the Prime Minister's post bag to Italy, flown to Croatia, and dropped by parachute to an isolated "resistance" area where Waugh had been sent as a member of a British liaison mission to Yugoslovia partisans fighting Nazis. The proofs, given to Loyola-Notre Dame Library in Baltimore by the author, were bound by Zaehnsdorf in red crushed morocco with Waugh's coat of arms in gold on the front cover. "The grey end paper was Waugh's bookplate, a coat of arms, with the motto: Industria Ditat (Industry Enriches)."

ANTIQUARIAN BOOK MONTHLY REVIEW, Leonard Smithers, A Publisher of the 1890s, Part II, George Sims. (6) X:294-7, 299, August 1983. Smithers launched THE SAVOY in 1896 to rival THE YELLOW BOOK from which Aubrey Beardsley had been dropped. Beardsley did designs for all eight issues of SAVOY. One illustration is ex libris for Harry Pollitt (Herbert Charles Pollitt 1872-1942), who was an undergraduate at Trinity College, Cambridge. "Smithers started THE SAVOY chiefly to give Beardsley a chance without much hope of making money out of it" according to Vincent O'Sullivan.

QUEEN MARY'S DOLL's HOUSE EX LIBRIS
By Doris Frohnsdorff

EX LIBRIS

Ernest Howard Shepard (1879-1976) designed the ex libris for Queen Mary's Doll's House library. The artist is perhaps best known for the incomparable illustrations he created for A. A. Milne's four "Pooh" books - WHEN WE WERE VERY YOUNG, WINNIE-THE-POOH, NOW WE ARE SIX, and THE HOUSE ON POOH CORNER. He was also associated with PUNCH magazine, making steady contributions to it over a period of fifty years.

The bookplate is shown larger than the final version. It was probably reproduced from Shepard's original drawing in pen-and-ink. The bookplate depicts a view of Windsor Castle with Queen Mary's monogram on a banner at the top and the words "Ex Libris" at the bottom. Shepard has signed the plate with his initials E S at the lower right corner of the Windsor view. This is rather unusual, for he always used E H S (I can't recall any other time he used E S).

For further information on Queen Mary's Doll's House, please see THE BOOK OF THE QUEEN'S DOLL'S HOUSE and THE BOOK OF THE QUEEN'S DOLL'S HOUSE LIBRARY. Both are edited by E. V. Lucas and published by Methuen & Co. Ltd (1924); both volumes in an edition of 1,500 copies.

MORE BOOKPLATE LITERATURE . . .
FDR REPORTER, Bookplates, Norman Lawson. (2) 2:4, April 1970. John Valentine's Book Shop was located in Glendale, CA; he published the FDR COLLECTOR until his death in 1955. The quote on his ex libris is from FDR's message to Booksellers on May 6, 1942. E. R. Underwood's plate was designed by his son-in-law.

A LOS ANGELES TYPESTICKER: WILLIAM M. CHENEY, A Bibliography of His Printed Work, Mary Lutz Jones. Los Angeles, 1981, printed by Richard J. Hoffman, 4 3/4 x 6 1/4 high. There is a biographical note, listing of articles and books about Cheney, and the bibliography. Included is the miniature SOME MINOR BOOK PLATES, published in 1975 with an introduction by Audrey Arellanes. From the introduction, the bibliographer quotes: "The miniature bookplates in this volume, designed by William Cheney, aptly meet the criteria set by Craig; in addition they possess two elements associated with Cheney - perfection in graphic design & subtle touches of humor."

California Book Auction Galleries held a sale October 1, 1983 in San Francisco of 467 items from the Library of Valenti Angelo, author, illustrator, and printer. The only bookplates were a five volume series, EX-LIBRIS ITALIANI MODERNI, which was published in Bologna, no date given. An estimate of $70 - $100 was given by the auction house for the 500 plates. Catalog issued, $5.

NOTICE   The 1983 YEAR BOOK is currently at the printers and is expected to be ready for delivery toward the end of the year. Articles on Editha Spencer - Josiah Wedgwood - European ex libris - Carl Oscar Borg.

HISTORIC CALIFORNIA IN BOOKPLATES
Reprint of Talbot Classic

The Ohio University Press has produced a handsome reprint of the 1936 printing by Graphic Press of Los Angeles of Clare Ryan Talbot's interesting volume on the bookplates by California artists or for owners living in that state. The dark green library binding bears the gold stamped impression of the author's ex libris by Victor Stuyvaert of Belgium on the cover.

The reprint was prepared with the assistance of Clare's brother Laurence J. Ryan, whose efforts were instrumental in achieving publication of this reprint. It can only be regreted that Clare did not live to enjoy the appearance of the reprint, which she had long hoped for. Naturally, the first edition, trade or limited, is preferred, but the availability of a reprint now makes it possible for bookplate enthusiasts to have a copy for their own reference.

Copies may be ordered from Ohio University Press, Scott Quadrangle, Athens, Ohio 45701. Reprint 1983, $15.95.

PAUL LANDACRE: A LIFE AND A LEGACY

Since the article on Landacre's bookplates in the 1979 YEAR BOOK of the ASBC&D, there have been a number of publications about his larger prints and some books illustrated with his prints. More recently has appeared a full length biography with an excellent bibliography and an update on the Landacre bookplates. PAUL LANDACRE: A LIFE AND A LEGACY by Anthony L. Lehman has been published as Number 15 of the Los Angeles Miscellany Series by Dawson's Book Shop, Los Angeles, 1983 ($45). Each chapter heading is a landscape printed in a different color; other illustrations are black and white. The cover has a repeated printing of the black petrel, which has long been associated with Landacre; the endpapers print in miniature a variety of his larger prints. Appendix B is devoted to a listing of Paul Landacre's ex libris

designs in chronological order with dimensions. Exact dating was not available at the time of the YEAR BOOK article. Also an additional plate has been documented for Otis Art Institute as of 1954, ten years later than the other bookplates, which ranged from 1926 through 1944. Two are still undated; perhaps you can offer information to establish dating for the ex libris for Florence Russell and Dr. Shuman.

Printed by Richard J. Hoffman and bound by Bela Blau, the publication has all the best features to be desired in a book-quality reading in a physically handsome volume.

· ─────────────────────────────────────── ·

LANDACRE EXHIBIT   The Los Angeles County Museum of Art has mounted an exhibit of Landacre prints, which will be shown August 25 to November 6, 1983. While no bookplates are included in the exhibit, it will be of interest to those who appreciate Landacre's prints, whatever their form. To accompany the exhibit, a catalogue has been issued, PAUL LANDACRE: PRINTS AND DRAWINGS. The foreword is by Ebria Feinblatt, Senior Curator of LACMA, Jake Zeitlin writes "Recalling Paul Landacre," and "The Art of Paul Landacre" is by Sally R. Bourriex of the J. Paul Getty Museum. The 44-page catalogue is well illustrated, includes a brief chronology, listing of selected prizes and exhibitions, and a bibliography which includes reference to the Arellanes article from the 1979 YEAR BOOK of ASBC&D.

· ─────────────────────────────────────── ·

MORE BOOKPLATE LITERATURE

MITTEILUNGEN DER DEUTSCHEN EXLIBRIS-GESELLSCHAFT e.V., March 1982, pages 178-88. Many small articles; the page layout is about 2/3 of the width for text and 1/3 illustrations. Among the artists whose work is featured are: Ellen Beck, Mark Severin, Diana Bloomfield, Reynolds Stone.

DET MODERNE EXLIBRIS I SLOVAKIET (The Slovakian Bookplate), Ivan Panenka. Published in 1981 by Exlibristen, Klaus Rödel, Postbox 109, Dk 9900-Frederikshavn, Denmark. Multilingual text including English. Biographies of about a dozen artists, including three women, mostly born in the 1940's. Each artist is pictured and usually two ex libris or other graphics are reproduced.

A ARTE do EX-LIBRIS (Portugal), XIII:2/#98, 1982. Articles on Henry Gris; continuing checklist of Portuguese artists (F through J); checklist for Christian Blaesbjert (1977-81, #401-518), with three multi-color tip-ins; checklist for Zbigniew Jozwik (1979-82, #288-346).

A ARTE do EX-LIBRIS, XIII:3/#99, 1982. Mikhail Verkholantsev by Sveltana Mironova with English translation in side-by-side columns with Portuguese. Artist born in 1937 in Moscow. He has designed 90 ex libris. -- Inge Look by Toivo Asikainen also has complete English translation. Born in Helsinki in 1951, Inge studied horticulture and passed her examinations in 1974. In 1977 she switched careers from gardening to free-lance graphic artist, primarily illustrating children's books. The several bookplates tipped-in could easily be book illustrations, brightly colored as in a child's book. -- Ruxandra (Didi) Alexe by Dr. Cornelius Dima-Dragan. "The Cross, that symbol of crucification and salvation, became the central element of the ex libris dedicated to Ronald Reagan, the President of the USA. It indicates the world of today symbolically living the prophecy In hoc signo vinces written in the sky."

CHRISTA JAHR
by Lothar Lang

(This article is from F.I.S.A.E.,
Federation Internationale des Soci-
ietes d'Amateurs d'Ex-Libris Artists,
volume VI, Portugal, 1982, and has
been translated by George Swarth for
ASBC&D. The original article was in
German, which Thomas Walter-Bonini
translated into French.)

Christa Jahr, born in 1941 at Qued-
linburg in Harz (East Germany), after
her artistic development belongs to
what is called the third generation
of the famous and highly regarded
school of wood engraving of Leipzig
which rather should be called the
school of engraving of Leipzig. It
is in that city of Leipzig that engraving on wood and on copper have
made their home.

At the Leipzig upper school of
graphics and the making of art books,
Heinrich Ilgenfritz taught engraving
on copper from 1955 to 1961; at the
same time the young Gerhardt Kurt
Muller was influencing the upper school by his engravings on wood (outside
the academy, this was Hans Schulze).

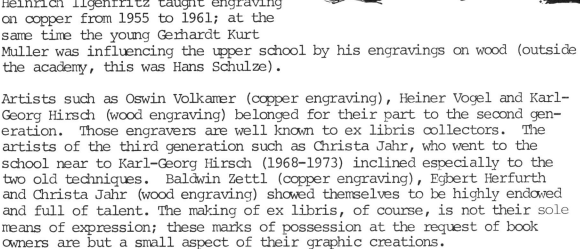

Artists such as Oswin Volkamer (copper engraving), Heiner Vogel and Karl-
Georg Hirsch (wood engraving) belonged for their part to the second generation. Those engravers are well known to ex libris collectors. The
artists of the third generation such as Christa Jahr, who went to the
school near to Karl-Georg Hirsch (1968-1973) inclined especially to the
two old techniques. Baldwin Zettl (copper engraving), Egbert Herfurth
and Christa Jahr (wood engraving) showed themselves to be highly endowed
and full of talent. The making of ex libris, of course, is not their sole
means of expression; these marks of possession at the request of book
owners are but a small aspect of their graphic creations.

Christa Jahr has been established since 1973 as a free-lance worker at
Leipzig (38 Dinterstr., 7 022 Leipzig, DDR). She is making a series of
book illustrations as well as separate engravings worthy of interest.
Certainly, in her style the impression of her master Hirsch is discovered. The personality of Christa Jahr reappears less in the graphic structure of her works than in her power of creation and artistic invention.
This graphic structure is at once dense and full of force; she keeps a
little of the artless and sincere heaviness of the artisan interpreted
by an unsophisticated approach and a work of "patine."   Christa Jahr's
creations bear witness to her inclination for fabling which at times
makes one think of unconstrained and carefree folkloric representations.
These characteristics appear notably in the six ex libris we have chosen

for this volume.

The readers of the ex libris collections of the
Pirckheimer Society, at the heart of the cultural federation of East Germany, will be able to
recall that in volume III (1980), we presented
two ex libris by Christa Jarh: those of Dr. Ort-
win Dankert and that of a lyric poet Wulf Kirs-
ten. In volume II (1978) of that annual, we
reproduced the ex libris of Uli Eichhorn, which
appears in the form of a rebus. The original ex
libris of Dankert and Eichhorn figure in this
volume of FISAE. Dankert is professor of athletics at Berlin. His ex libris shows this with the
bear appearing in the coat of arms of Berlin,
just like the relationship existing between the
engraver and professor of Bernburg on Saale and
the bear tamer of that place. Eichhorn's ex
libris is intended for a collection of books
illustrated by Karl-Georg Hirsch; it appears, as
we have mentioned above, in the form of a rebus,
something very rare in ex libris art, where there
appears the explanation "the work honors the
master." The ex libris of the Russian collector
Ivensky is rather due to chance, as Christa Jahr
has told me: he wanted "something having a touch
of rococo art." Just like that of Dankert,
Piepenbring's ex libris makes reference to the
city of Bernburg: Elisabeth Piepenbring, like
the artist's mother, came from Bernburg, city in
which Christa Jahr grew up after Leipzig. The
owl and the mirror make one think of Till Eulen-
spiegel at Burnburg. The last ex libris deserves an explanation: it is
intended for the photographer Fred Schindler. The elephant makes one

think of the different trips that the
photographer has made to the Indies;
the acrobat on the rope makes us ob-
serve that the commissioner of this
ex libris is a free and independent
worker; therefore, without fixed place.

We have described these marks of possession with language charged with
images to let us shed some light on
the peculiarity of Christa Jahr's ex
libris. Her ex libris give evidence
not of graphics of complaisance for
the collector, but of a graphic usage
in the proper sense of the term of
which the content is adapted each time
in a perfect way to the collector. These
precise graphics are a connecting link
between the collector and his collection.
For that reason, Christa Jahr's ex libris
show two points: beautiful creations characteristic of her art as well as an
an exchangeable "identification card" for the collector.

WILLIAM MORRIS IN PRIVATE
PRESS AND LIMITED EDITIONS:
A Descriptive Bibliography
of Books By and About William Morris 1891-1981, John J.
Walsdorf. (Phoenix: Oryx
Press, 1983, $74.50, 602 p.,
clothbound and slipcased.
Index of names, titles, and
presses; five page chronology.) This is a magnificent
reference work on Morris,
perhaps a little far afield
for the bookplate collector,
but the indexes reveal many
names well-known in the ex

libris field. (Under the title of THE POEMS OF JOHN KEATS is mention of an
inscribed copy, "in the hand of William Morris to Edward Burne-Jones . . . ."
Further, it notes that the volume carries the book
label, printed at the Kelmscott Press in Golden type,
which is reproduced to the right.

FROM THE LIBRARY OF
EDWARD BURNE-JONES
THE GRANGE NORTH
END ROAD FULHAM.✿✿

In the introduction to Section I, The Kelmscott Press
Books: William Morris in Inscribed and Association Copies, the author tells
how the idea of his Morris collection crystalized and it involved a bookplate.

The descriptions accompanying the bibliographical entries are expansive and immensely educational in themselves, flesh-
ing out the persons, whose familiar names
we recognize, who knew Morris in his life-

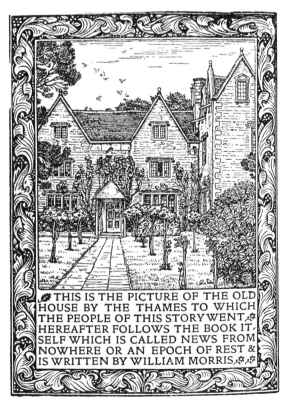

☙ THIS IS THE PICTURE OF THE OLD
HOUSE BY THE THAMES TO WHICH
THE PEOPLE OF THIS STORY WENT.✿
HEREAFTER FOLLOWS THE BOOK IT.
SELF WHICH IS CALLED NEWS FROM
NOWHERE OR AN EPOCH OF REST &
IS WRITTEN BY WILLIAM MORRIS.✿✿

time or wrote about him afterwards.

As can be seen by the illustrations here,
Alfred Fowler, who was very active in the
bookplate world both before and after WWI,
paid tribute to Morris in the plate S. L.
Smith engraved for him.

Among my happy discoveries in browsing
through this book was the printing of an
address given by Morris on THE ART OF THE
PEOPLE, which was published in Chicago by
Ralph Fletcher Seymour, whom I recognized
as having designed bookplates; an annota-

477

tion here gives reference to a 1945 autobiography, with Ralph Fletcher Seymour also as publisher, SOME WENT THIS WAY, A FORTY YEAR PILGRIMAGE AMONG ARTISTS, BOOKMEN AND PRINTERS. It is pleasant to find that the "greats" in the little world of bookplates really had a very active role in the "real" world.

FAC-SIMILE OF WASHINGTON'S ACCOUNTS (from June 1775 to June 1783), during the Revolutionary War from the original papers in the Library of Congress and in the National Archives. This facsimile was published in 1983 in recognition of the Bicentennial of the successful conclusion of the Revolutionary War. The back cover of this folio has a tipped-in reproduction of George Washington's bookplate. This keepsake was published for members of the Manuscript Society by Dr. William R. Coleman.

COLLECTION FOR SALE   William P. Wreden, Books & Manuscripts, of Palo Alto, California is offering for sale the ex libris collection of Nuno Smith de Vasconcellops of Brazil, which consists of over 5,500 bookplates. Most of the plates in the collection are mounted, usually one per leaf, and the leaves clothbound in 50 volumes. In eight volumes the leaves are loose; likewise, 375 bookplates, some duplicates, are loose.

Ex libris of both individuals and libraries are included, primarily from Europe, the United States, and Brazil. Among the European countries well represented are Germany, Czechoslovakia, and Hungary. The plates range in date from approximately 1890 to 1940, many in an Art Nouveau or Art Deco style. Both the bound and the loose leaves are arranged alphabetically by owner's name; two of the loose leaf volumes are devoted exclusively to Brazilian ex libris. Each plate may be further classified by country, artist, reproduction process, legend, format, etc. The condition of the plates in this unique and valuable collection are uniformly fine, although some of the leaves on which they are mounted show wear. The price for the collection is $3,250.00. All inqueries are to be directed to William P. Wreden, P. O. Box 56, Palo Alto, CA 94302 or telephone (415) 325-6851.

MORE BOOKPLATE LITERATURE

NORDISK EXLIBRIS TIDSKRIFT, #3, 1983. Article on Ladislav J. Kaspar (in English and Danish), Czech artist born April 29, 1915 in Travnik, which at that time was part of Austria-Hungary. His techniques include woodcut, linocut, copper and lithography. Two ex libris feature soldiers of earlier centuries in elaborate uniforms and with weapons of the period; another has a portrait of Admiral Lord Horatio Nelson. Another article features ex libris honoring Pope Paul II.

MICROBIBLIOPHILE, Big and Little, Kathryn Rickard. (1) 7:cover, 15-7, March 1983. Author relates her experiences of collecting miniature books; each book is now catalogued and carries her bookplate.

MICROBIBLIOPHILE, Auction Action, Robert Hanson. 7:13-4, March 1983. Prices quoted from AMERICAN BOOK PRICES CURRENT for 1982 for some of the 44 miniature volumes included. Among them MINIATUR EXLIBRIS by Abraham Horodisch, published in Amsterdam in 1966, brought $130. (Editor's Note: Same volume seen at a 1982 Book Fair with an asking price of $200.)

BARRY MOSER - Wood Engraver
By James Keenan

ΕΚ ΤΩΝ
ΒΙΒΛΙΩΝ
ΤΟΥ
ΜΩΣΗΡΟΣ

Barry Moser was born in Chattanooga, TN, on
October 15, 1940. Barry was educated at
Auburn University, University of Tennessee
at Chattanooga, and did graduate work at
University of Massachusetts. He studied also
with George Cress, Leonard Baskin, Jack
Coughlin, and Harold McGrath. He works outside of Northampton, MA, at his studio and
the Hampshire Typothetae with master printer
Harold McGrath on the Pennyroyal Press im-
prints.

Barry Moser's first
wood engraving was
produced in 1968, and he is now considered to be one
of the finest engravers of our time. At 43, he has
illustrated over sixty books which include Melville's
MOBY DICK, Lewis Carroll's ALICE'S ADVENTURES IN WON-
DERLAND, Dante's DIVINE COMEDY, and Homer's ODYSSEY.
His work has been exhibited internationally and is represented in numerous collections in the United States and
abroad.

Barry welcomes bookplate commissions and inqueries should be addressed to:
Barry Moser, c/o Lisa DeLisle, 2 Linseed Road, West Hatfield, MA 01088.

XX. INTERNATIONALER EXLIBRIS-KONGRESS

WEIMAR
1984

XX INTERNATIONAL EX LIBRIS CONGRESS

The 1984 Congress will be held in
Weimar from August 24 through 28th
at the Burgk Castle.

The emblem for the Congress was
designed by the well-known book illustrator Prof. Dr. Albert Kapr of
Leipzig. The design was adapted
from a symbol standing in Goethe's
garden near his summer house in Weimar; often the poet described it as
an expression of harmony of contrasts.

The international ex libris contest
will have the theme of the 225th
anniversary of Friedrich Schiller.

For direct information you may write:
    Prof. Dr. Lothar Lang
    President of FISAE
    Staatliches Museum Schloss Burgk
      Exlibris-Zentrum
    DDR-6551 Burgk/Saale
      East Germany

September 29, 1983

Audrey Arellanes
Director
American Society of Bookplate
 Collectors and Designers

Dear Ms. Arellanes

In reply to your letter, ordinarily I supply only finished drawings in pen & ink or scratchboard; however, I am willing to see to the printing as well – naturally, the cost would reflect this.

I work in other media as well: pencil, wash, charcoal, Conté crayon, pastels, & Spectra color, but always with an emphasis on drawing. My favorite medium is pen & ink because they are portable and reproduce well. I illustrate books as well as bookplates, & I've never drawn a line that I didn't imagine in print.

So far, I've illustrated a textbook, a cookbook, innumerable t-shirts, a few ads and business cards, and several Christmas cards. Currently I am working on a children's book.

My work tends to fantasy, wildlife, portraiture and cubism. I can't remember a time when I didn't have a callus on my hand from drawing, but before I attended art school in my thirties, I worked as a proofreader, editor & columnist for a chain of community newspapers.

I can't think why it would interest your readers, but if you are desperate for biographical copy you are free to mention that I have two grown children, two grand children, a husband, & a cat; my hobbies are reading English texts & endlessly writing the alphabet on scraps of paper; and I write poetry that I never imagine in print.

I hope that will do, because whenever I'm faced with the necessity of producing a 'bio, I become hopelessly flip! Forgive me. And thank you for your kind comments.

Sincerely,

Adrien Rain
10656½ Russell Ave.
Sunland, CA 91040
213-353-7316

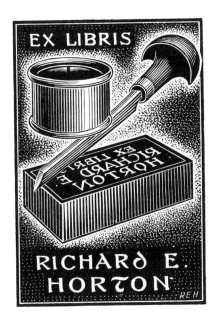

I started getting serious about wood engraving only three years ago after a lapse of some forty years. My body of work is not yet very large, but a small number of engravings are reproduced to give an idea of my work.

I learned about wood engraving as a very young man and am probably the very last of the old-time trained engravers. My real love has been in pictorial engraving as opposed to the stiffness and formality of most commercial work.

There is currently much good work **being done** by artists using wood engraving as their medium. Barry Moser is one of the better ones; however, none of these artists has been trained in the old traditions as I have. It is my objective to combine the best of the old with the best of the new and perhaps develop a unique contribution to the art of wood engraving. I do not know how well I will succeed, but it is great fun trying.

I have been hesitant to make too successful an effort to advertise myself these past few years since retiring, but I am now beginning to reach out to make contacts and would welcome bookplate commissions. (Richard Horton, 2983 W. 235th St. No. 1, Torrance, CA 90505.)

Two designs by Richard Horton

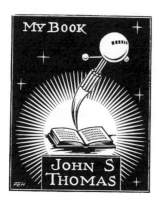

See FDR REPORTER, page 472.

AS of BC & D

Bookplates in the News

605 N. STONEMAN AVENUE #F, ALHAMBRA, CALIFORNIA, 91801 U.S.A.

AUDREY SPENCER ARELLANES, Editor

NUMBER FIFTY-FIVE   JANUARY 1984

Ex Libris

ALICE CULLER

ALICE MOONEY CULLER : Collector

The tipped-in print of one of Alice Mooney Culler's bookplates has been provided through the kindness of her neice Mary Bingham Roach.

Alice Mooney Culler, wife of William Herbert Culler, was born in Wilkes Barre, PA on August 16, 1902 and died in San Marino, CA on October 26, 1982. She had been a resident of California for 67 years, and had lived in Honolulu, Hawaii for ten years. While in Hawaii, Mrs. Culler was librarian for the Kamehameha School for Girls and the Iolani School for Boys. In the Los Angeles area she held library posts with the West Los Angeles Public Library, was branch librarian for Allendale in Pasadena, and also at that city's main library. She had attended UCLA and USC and held degrees as Bachelor in Science and Library Science. Mrs. Culler also had been a school principal and was associated for a time with Pacific Chemical Co.

Mrs. Culler belonged to a number of organizations including the Daughters of the American Revolution, Daughters of the American Colonists, National Society U.S. Daughters of 1812, was California State President of Las Camadres, charter member of American Legion Auxiliary, member of the Friday Morning Club (Los Angeles), American Library Association of School Librarians, California Library Association, and the San Marino Women's Republican Club. As a member of the Friday Morning Club she may have been introduced to bookplates through their publication or an exhibition.

An interest in bookplates was shared by other family members, who also had personal bookplates: her mother, Mrs. Alice B. Mooney, to whom the Kenneth Roberts' ex libris on a postal card was sent, and her aunt, Helen Mooney Fenton, one of whose bookplates was tipped-in and accompanied by an article in BOOKPLATES IN THE NEWS (#35). In addition to the plate featuring her home, Mrs. Fenton had an attractive ex libris engraved by James Webb.

The postal card below in the format of a bookplate is from Kenneth Roberts, born December 8, 1885 in Kennebunk, ME. He received B.A. from Cornell in 1908 and Ltt.D. from Dartmouth in 1934. Roberts was reporter and columnist on the Boston POST (1909-17); on staff of LIFE (1915-18); European correspondent for SATURDAY EVENING POST (1919-29); on PUCK (1916-17); was Washington correspondent (1921-26); and then retired from journalism. During WWI he served as captain in the Intelligence Section of the Siberian Expeditionary Force (1918-19).

In 1930 Kenneth Roberts' first novel ARUNDEL was published; it brought

early American history alive and was followed by THE LIVELY LADY (1931), RABBLE IN ARMS (1933), CAPTAIN CAUTION (1934) which was filmed by Hal Roach, NORTHWEST PASSAGE (1937) filmed by MGM, OLIVER WISWELL (1940), LYDIA BAILEY (1947) filmed by 20th Century-Fox. In 1957 Roberts received a Special Pulitzer Prize.

Kenneth Roberts married Anna Seiberling Mosser February 14, 1911 and she worked with him on a translation of Moreau St. Mery's American journal 1793-98, which was published in 1947.

Roberts died July 21, 1957 and was buried in Arlington National Cemetery.

• ————————————————— •

EXHIBITS - Dennison Library at Scripps College, Claremont, CA
    an Ex Libris exhibit from the Louise Seymour Jones collection, Feb. 20 to March 29, 1984.

Exhibit of bookplates by current American and European artists is scheduled March 6 -April 13, 1984 at the Boston Athenaeum.

Dear Mrs. Mooney:
I made it up
Kenneth Roberts.

ELENA ANTIMONOVA by Arnold Salenieks
from Federation Internationale des
Societes d'Amateurs d'Ex-Libris
Volume VI, ARTISTAS de EX-LIBRIS
Portugal, 1982

Elena Antimonova is seen as one of the most gifted and most interesting of Latvian artists; it is already almost ten years since all her friends of the Beaux-Arts were pleasantly surprised by her miniatures and her etched ex libris; this sentiment is shared even beyond the boundaries of Latvia. The artist taught herself to master the technique of graphic art; at the Academy of Beaux-Arts of the S.S.R. of Latvia, Elena Antimonova studied painting. Nevertheless, only once has she exhibited an oil painting of her composition. One wonders what could have decided the artist to turn to graphic art. Right after her baccalaureate in 1964, E. Antimonova found a place as professor of design while beginning her studies at the Beaux-Arts in 1965. Design has a preferred place with her, and she learned to master that art well. To devote herself to painting did not suffice for E. Antimonova; many of her inner aspirations remained unsatisfied. Every book read awoke in the young artist a desire for very expressive formats abounding in ideas. E. Antimonova was the first artist whose ex libris figured beside graphic works at the exposition of the Beaux-Arts.

In E. Antimonova's ex libris as in her other engraved plates, Man is omnipresent, frequently represented in the form of nude women intertwined in various positions, seen from different angles.

The designs of her ex libris often include a symbolic meaning, writing playing only a minor role, but always in perfect harmony with the whole composition without becoming, apart from a few cases, a separate part of the composition. During these latter years, etching (C3) has given place to aquatint (C5) in the choice of techniques.

And it is precisely for her ex libris created in this period that E. Antimonova has seen herself awarded the title of Laureate and the medal of the IId Biennial of Ex Libris at Vilna in 1979.

The work of the artist is not limited to interpreting her graphically. Already during her studies she illustrated some books; this mode of expression took on such proportions that little by little it became her principal occupation. She has made the illustrations for about thirty works, principally collections of poems as well as works of Lucian, Blake, Shakespeare, books dealing with ancient times and strange lands, in a word books that have touched her by their romantic side and that allowed giving free course to fantasy. Lately, E. Antimonova has leaned toward books for children where she finds joy and satisfaction in creating gay, brightly colored pictures.

E. Antimonova's first ex libris dates back to 1964. The few ex libris executed during the years of her studies were cut on linoleum. After having completed her studies at the Beaux-Arts (1971), the artist undertook etching; it was at that time she took part in the expositions where she met with great success with the public with her miniature etchings as the sole graphic art; she has also mastered the art of bookbinding and happily practices painting on porcelain. Her love for books roused in her the wish to demonstrate some handwritten specimens; "The Count of Nulin" by A. Pushkin is an example of them. A poem by F. Villon has been illustrated in the style of the old miniatures.

In tracing the work of E. Antimonova, one feels that the artist experiences a deep need to fill herself with the feeling of the world's most loved literary works, to live them, to be able in her turn to express them and to render them according to their own artistic possibilities. Lately, the artist has set herself to painting portraits. But be assured, graphic art and particularly ex libris will continue to occupy a principal place in the work of Elena Antimonova.

(Translated from the French by George S. Swarth.)

GUNĀRS BALTIŅS

BOOKPLATES IN THE NEWS
January/April/July/October
$15 Calendar Year Basis

© Audrey Spencer Arellanes

1983 YEAR BOOK now at
the printers. Sorry
for the delay.

INTER-EXLIBRIS '83, Klaus Rodel (Frederikshavn, June 1983). This is the catalogue of the 6th international small graphics exhibition held in the Frederikshavn Art Museum (Denmark). In the brief introduction, Rodel indicates that the exhibit is dominated by East-European artists, especially Czechoslovakia. He also notes a "pronounced tendency towards the etching technique . . . while there are few colour exlibris at the exhibition (perhaps because of rising costs of printing)." Each artist is represented by one ex libris and a portrait. It was particularly interesting to see the increasing number of women artists. The personalities of the artists as revealed in their pictures was almost as interesting as the content and techniques of the bookplates. This is an oblong booklet approximately 8 3/4 by 6½" and contains 108 pages.

KAERLIGHED: BOHUMIL KRATKY, 18 litografiske exlibris (ExlibRisten, 1983, Klaus Rodel, Postbox 109, DK 9900 Frederikshavn, Denmark). Multi-lingual text includes English. This Czechoslovakian artist has created a series of bookplates with the theme of love, all in color using three different stones for the lithographs. In addition to the love theme common to all, each print also features the profession of the owner or objects expressing special interests of the owner.

HANNU PAALASMAA, Klaus Rodel (ExlibRisten, 1983). There are eight signed, tipped-in ex libris prints and a multi-lingual text. "Finland is becoming an important place in terms of developments within contemporary exlibris. The number of collectors is rising, the Finnish exlibris society has started to print the text in their annual portfolio in a foreign language too, and an increasing number of Finnish participants attend the international exlibris congresses." Hannu Paalasmma is a calligrapher, who has applied his calligraphic skill to the design of more than 100 ex libris; he is also responsible for many of the program titles on Finnish television. He lettered a long banner that was presented to the participants at the Congress in Oxford in 1982. His prints are reproduced by the silk screen process and in size and simplicity are in the best tradition of the functional ex libris.

CHRISTIAN BLAESBJERG 6, Klaus Rodel, 1983. There are twenty ex libris, 19 of which are multi-color tip-ins. This is the sixth volume about this outstanding Danish artist, who has designed nearly 600 ex libris. The current volume, in celebration of his eightieth birthday, mixes "sex and sex together - sex seen as an expression of love without pornography."

EX LIBRIS BIBLIOGRAPHY, H. C. Skov (Randers, 1980, published by Klaus Rodel, Postbox 109, DK 9900 Frederikshavn, Denmark, 1983). This is an international bibliography of bookplate literature which includes books and periodicals. England is represented by 27 items and the United States by 16; Denmark by over 400; in all thirty-two countries are represented. While I cannot read the brief introduction, I imagine the bibliography was compiled from Skov's personal collection of ex libris literature.

GRAPHIA #88 (1983/3), September 1983. Most of this issue is a directory of artists which includes name, address, picture of the artist, and at least one bookplate reproduced; a few sentences of biography also appear. This is an easy way to see the work of numerous artists and select those whose work appeals to you to write concerning commissioning a bookplate.

PULITZER WINNER DESIGNED
    BOOKPLATE
    By Robert Lee

This bookplate was drawn
for me by the late Bruce
Russell, political car-
toonist for the Los Ange-
les TIMES for many years.
Bruce and I were class-
mates at UCLA, Class of
1927, where he drew car-
toons for the campus daily
and I was news editor of
the publication.

I thought my bookplate
might be of special in-
terest to collectors in-
asmuch as it was executed
by a winner of a Pulitzer
Prize for editorial car-
tooning. It possibly may
be the only bookplate by
a winner of that presti-
gious national award.

The verse by John Wilson
was selected by me, as
being most appropriate
for a collector of books. I am not a bookplate collector.

MORE BOOKPLATE LITERATURE

AMPHORA, A review of the 1982 Calligraphic Year: A Flourish of Scribes,
Martin Jackson. (5) 51:12-15, March 1983. Four of the illustrations are
from the Society for Italic Handwriting Bookplate Competition - 1982.

PALM BEACH POST, Bookplates Collectors' Status Symbol, Anne Gilbert. (1)
October 23, 1983. "Sometimes bookplates are more important than the books
themselves, such as when it contains a celebrity name. The recent Gloria
Swanson Estate auction is a case in point. Several lots of books, otherwise rather inconsequential, got a big play from bidders because they contained bookplates designed by the actress and bearing her full name."

SPAHR LIBRARY NOTES (Dickinson College, Carlisle, PA 17013), Ex Libris -
The Vengris Collection, M.S. (3) 8:#2, 1 page, December 1983. Vitolis
Vengris, who is a scientist by profession, gave a slide lecture at the
Seminar on the Art of the Book, held September 29 to October 1, 1983, at
Dickinson College. The three-day seminar included talks by Henry Morris,
Richard J. Wolfe, Maurice Sendak, Walter Hamady, Fritz and Trudi Eberhardt,
Dan Carr, David Godine, Timothy Barrett, and Vitolis Vengris. An exhibit
of bookplates was presented in the Sharp Room of the library. Vengris has
given a gift of 1,150 ex libris prints to add to the college's collection.

FISAE BOOK - VII - 1984   This is volume seven of the book printed in
conjunction with the International Ex Libris
Congress held every other year in the even numbered years. It will contain
384 pages with more than 300 ex libris of which 120 will be tipped-in, and
forty-five artists will be represented from about thirty countries. The
work of Bela Petry will represent the United States. The volume is priced
at 80 Swiss francs on orders received before February 29, 1984 and 100 Swiss
francs commencing March 1, 1984. Order and payment should be directed to
A. M. da Mota Miranda, Casa do Outeiro, 4890 Celorico de Basto, PORTUGAL.
The Congress for 1984 will be held in Weimar, East Germany, but due to possible distribution difficulties, sales will be handled through Mr. Miranda
rather than through Professor Lang, who is president of the Congress this
year.

SMALL THINGS CONSIDERED, The Art of the
Bookplate, is a booklet by Jonathan Held,
Fine Arts Division, Dallas Public Library,
which was published for the exhibit of ex
libris, October 24, 1983 - January 6, 1984.

The bookplate prints exhibited are from a
collection given the Dallas Public Library
by Cloyd M. McClug in 1983. McClug, born
in Waco, Texas, attended Baylor University
and received his MLS from Florida State
University.

The attractive booklet was designed by
Paula Barber and the cover illustration is
by Michael Sours. The cover design was enlarged as a poster to advertise the exhibit.

MORE BOOKPLATE LITERATURE

THE BOOKPLATE JOURNAL (English ex libris
Society), 1:#2, September 1983:

Comment, 49-51. A copy of the Hans Igler-
Knabensberg ex libris given a pre-sale
estimate of £3-5,000 by Sotheby's actually
was purchased for £8,250 by New York dealer
B. H. Breslauer.

Contemporary Trends in Bookplate Design,
Gerard Gaudaen. (26) 52-64. This article
is based on an illustrated lecture read at the XIX International Ex Libris
Congress held in Oxford during August 1982. "The most exciting aspect of
the contemporary bookplate is the treasure of ideas, the content, the spirit,
the expression of each bookplate. Colour has brought an enrichment in the
sense that the same elements of style of the black and white bookplate have
been stressed and made more expressive or the poetic element has been in-
tensified. Contemporary bookplate design has something for everyone, be they
proponents of the 'avant-garde,' the traditionalists, the devotees of 'letter

bookplates' or the aesthetics of design, the poets of content, or the athletics of technique." An article based on the same lecture, but in a different format, will be included in the 1983 YEAR BOOK of the ASBC&D.

The Adventure of the Arthur Conan Doyle Bookplate, Stanley Wertheim. (1) 65-74. Portions of this article appeared originally in BOOK COLLECTOR'S MARKET for November/December 1979, AMERICAN BOOK COLLECTOR (new series) for September/October 1980, and MANUSCRIPTS, XXXIV, 1982. The evidence presented leaves little doubt that the bookplate was devised by the author's son Adrian and was not used by Arthur Conan Doyle, further that books in which it has been pasted are not necessarily from Doyle's library.

John Keyse Sherwin, Brian North Lee. (5) 75-83.. Sherwin (1751-90) was a pupil of Bartolozzi for three years and in 1785 was appointed engraver to the King. Article includes interesting biographical details of this little known artist, and gives considerable information about six variations for Blackburne family bookplates.

Profile of an Artist: Joan Hassall, Brian North Lee. (1) 84-6. "Her work as a bookplate engraver is distinguished, and these days prints of her ex-libris are both prized and hard to come by. In a little under forty bookplates she has demonstrated her versatility, and it is evident that she approaches this art with the seriousness and integrity which mark her book illustration." A book of her engravings is in preparation by David Chambers, which will be published by the Private Libraries Association.

Portrait of a Bookplate: 2 - Unrecorded Dobuzhinskii Design, W. E. Butler. (1) 87-9. The unrecorded design was purchased by the article's author at a Sotheby's sale held March 3, 1982. The plate is for Lt. General Count D. N. Mavros, signed with the initials MD in Russian, and is dated 1905.

Bookplate Bibliography: In Search of the Ideal Reference Tools, W. E. Butler. 90-6. Two Russian bibliographies are discussed; one by M. Iu. Panov (126 pages, published in 1971) lists 423 works primarily from publications wholly devoted to bookplates and another compiled by Iu. P. Martsevich under the auspices of the Nebrasov City Public Library in Moscow, also since 1971. The latter bibliography attempts to be exhaustive, including not only books, catalogues, mementoes, and all the literature gathered by Panov, but every single publication where a bookplate is mentioned or illustrated. "In 1980, there were 1,112 entries, up from 1,041 in 1979." "Two questions will arise at once in the Western collector's mind. More than eleven hundred published items a year about bookplates even in a large country is astounding! How is it done? The answer is simple: bookplates enjoy substantial sustained support from the press and media. The great majority of entries are journal and newspaper articles. Several journals and newspapers give weekly coverage to bookplate exhibitions, artists, or new plates. How does Mr. Martsevich succeed in compiling such a massive listing, for he is not a professional bibliographer and does this in his spare time? He enjoys support from fellow enthusiasts who send items for inclusion, but he also has access to a press-clipping service which doubtless supplies many of the references to provincial publications. . . . . But for all the institutional support it enjoys, one should not lose sight of the fact that there, as here, publications about bookplates are chiefly generated not by professional art historians, bibliographers, librarians, or curators of collections, but rather by those who love, collect, and research bookplates."

KOBI BAUMGARTNER
by Ernst Wetter

Switzerland has at present but few artists who also create bookplates. Most of them are draughtsmen; that explains the predominance of wood engraving. To my eyes at least, their profession really forces draughtsmen to produce either symbols or designs of a communicative nature which clearly expresses their message. As to painters and engravers, they have more freedom of expression.

What makes Switzerland a "bad market" for bookplates is that there they are primarily objects for collection. It has been a long time since anyone pastes them in their books, which are primarily numerous paperbacks; who would think of decorating them with bookplates? Besides, collecting bookplates is hardly a widespread interest. This is shown by the paucity of members in the Swiss bookplate society (some 80 at the present time), of whom moreover many are interested only in specific subjects.

Thus one must rejoice to see emerge some artists who devote themselves to this sort of work. One among them is the draughtsman Kobi Baumgartner, of Zurich, who signs his works "Kobi B." The prize won by his design in wood engraving in color (X1 - X6) at the XVIth International Ex Libris Congress at Lisbon deserves to make him known beyond his own country. Thus, Klaus Rodel devoted a special pamphlet to him (ExlibRisten 1973, Klaus Rodel, Postbox 109, DK 9900, Frederikshavn, Denmark).

Kobi Baumgartner was born in 1916. A serious accident forced him to give up secondary school, and he turned to the graphic arts. Soon, his drawings and his articles began to appear in various journals and reviews. It is at this time that he made his first wood engravings. Already twenty-eight years old, he entered the Geneva School of Fine Arts where he found excellent teachers such as Guinand, Theurillat, and Hornung. After rather long sojourns at Florence and Rome, Kobi Baumgartner settled in 1949 at Zurich where he still lives.

Included among his works are a whole series of frescoes, inscriptions, mosaics, and stained glass windows intended for public buildings and private homes. Apart from painting, he came to turn more and more to wood engraving in color. Baumgartner is much sought as an illustrator of reviews, special numbers of journals, and also of books. We mention, by way of example, the fairy tale "Funfe und ein fliegendes Bett," illustrated with wood engravings in color. Proclaimed one of the most beautiful Swiss books in 1967, it received, at the Sao Paulo Biennial the prize awarded to the best group of illustrations of a work outside a series. Postage stamps and sheets for congratulatory telegrams produced by his hand have likewise been outstanding.

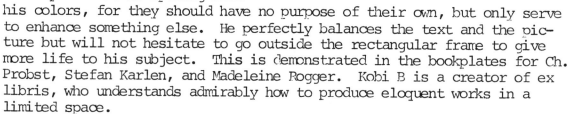

Kobi Baumgartner's bookplates are conspicuous for their clarity. The artist knows perfectly how to express the essentials in a limited space. He is sparing with his colors, for they should have no purpose of their own, but only serve to enhance something else. He perfectly balances the text and the picture but will not hesitate to go outside the rectangular frame to give more life to his subject. This is demonstrated in the bookplates for Ch. Probst, Stefan Karlen, and Madeleine Rogger. Kobi B is a creator of ex libris, who understands admirably how to produce eloquent works in a limited space.

NB: Translated into French by Georges N. Zwez and into English by George S. Swarth. The article is from FISAE (Federation Internationale des Societes d'Amateurs d'Ex Libris Ex-Libris Artists), volume VI, 1982, Portugal.

492

WILLIAM TARG
Bookman

In response to an inquiry about his bookplate, William Targ wrote: "This plate was made for me by my old friend from Chicago, John Gorth, when I lived at 25 Fifth Ave. (about 25 years ago), NYC. I smoked a pipe then - no more. I still have about 6,000 books - many quite rare - about me. I've shifted gears, and no longer work for a commercial publisher. My activities are centered about the Targ Editions. My wife is Roslyn Targ, the literary agent. John Groth still works from his studio on East 57th St., NYC. Being self-employed and autonomous is a joy few editors ever achieve. I still buy books (got a batch in Paris when I was there last October), and I still have a small supply of the bookplate which I stick in some of my favorite volumes. Last fall I published a novel, SECRET LIVES, in England; also in Brazil, Argentina, and Holland; coming soon in Turkey!"

Targ is perhaps best known for his "books about books" - BOUILLAIBAISSE FOR BIBLIOPHILES (1955) and BIBLIOPHILE IN THE NURSERY (1957); he was also the editor for L. C. Powell's BOOKMAN'S PROGRESS (1968). Targ was born March 4, 1907 in Chicago. He was editor-in-chief and vice president of World Pub. Co. (1942-64); editor-in-chief at G. P. Putnam's Sons (1965-67); and from 1974 has been senior editor and vice president of Targ Editions. For more details of an exciting life in the world of books, you might read his anecdotal autobiography, INDECENT PLEASURES (1975)

GERMAN COLLECTOR
TO VISIT USA

Claus Wittal, Fliednerstr. 27, 6200 Wiesbaden, Germany, writes as follows:

"I am a member of the German Exlibris Society and want to make contact with American ex libris collectors, specially people in or near New York and Detroit. I am planning a trip to USA around April - May."

Mr. Wittal has a variety of personal plates including engravings, multi-color prints, which do not reproduce as clearly as the humorous plate he designed for Christa. (Editor's note: I hope some of our members in the cities mentioned will write Claus Wittal and extend the friendship of the international ex libris circle.)

HERALD & CHRONICLE (San Francisco), Review: California's Bookplates, James Silverman. January 1, 1984. " . . . (HISTORIC CALIFORNIA IN BOOKPLATES) deserves attention. It is an invaluable source for stories about Californians and books: artists, writers, lawyers, doctors, theatre people, teachers and other bibliophiles, churches and universities, with separate chapters about San Francisco and Los Angeles." Reprint by Ohio U Press.

CALIFORNIA MAGAZINE, Review, p. 141, September 1983. Brief review of C. R. Talbot's HISTORIC CALIFORNIA IN BOOKPLATES, a reprint of 1936 classic.

THE APHA LETTER (American Printing History Association), Exhibits, Winter 1984. Bookplate exhibits are scheduled at Houghton Library, Harvard University, "Marks in books illustrated and explained," during February, and Chapin Library, Williams College, "Marks of Ownership," through February 5, 1984.

L'EX LIBRIS FRANCAIS, #149, September 1983. The entire issue is devoted to an international juried exhibit held in May 1983, which featured about 800 prints by a large number of artists representing most countries in Europe, Japan, and two artists from the United States (H. Fanny Kouzan and Vytautas O. Virkau).

PRINCETON UNIVERSITY LIBRARY CHRONICLE, New & Notable, (1) XLV:97-9, August 1983. Illustration is bookplate used for Grabhorn Press Collection presented by Isabel Shaw Slocum to Princeton University in the name of her late husband Myles Standish Slocum, class of 1909.

AMERICAN BOOK COLLECTOR, Fun and Fellowship: The Amenities of Early Lincoln Collecting, Mark E. Neely, Jr. (3) 4:2-8, November/December 1983. One illustration is the ex libris of one of the Big Five Lincoln collectors, Judd Stewart, a mining executive who lived in Plainfield, NJ, and whose collection is now at the Henry E. Huntington Library of San Marino, CA.

NOTES (Alcuin Society, Series II), No. 14, Christmas 1983. AMPHORA's First Fifty is a keyword index to the articles in the first fifty issues. Three articles appear under the keyword "bookplates" by A. S. Arellanes, B. Peel, and S. X. Radbill; two under "ex libris" by J. E. Horvath and C. Parfit; and one under "exhibition" by G. A. Spencer. / Under Bulletin Board is a note by Capt. P. A. Fournier of Quebec; he asks for Alcuin Society members to send him copies of their personal bookplates.

The Bookplate Society NEWSLETTER (English), V:#3, September 1983. Mention is made of a tribute to Philip Beddingham in GRAYA, journal of the Honourable Society of Gray's Inn (No. 86). / Bookplate by Mervyn Peake for Nehemiah Asherson, eminent surgeon in the field of ear, nose, and throat medicine. The ex libris incorporates bones found in the ear. Peake (1911-68) was poet, playwright, and book illustrator. / Huguenot Bookplates by Stephen de Crespigny. Within the last six years, the article's author has collected over 200 hundred bookplates with Huguenot connections representing about 130 different families. / New Bookplates by Jacques Hnizdovsky. Reproduced are plates for Benoit Junod and Sylvie Stoyanka Junor. / The Eno Sale by Wilbur Macey Stone. This is the publication of a manuscript from the Butler Collection written by Stone at the time of the November 16-17, 1916 sale of American and foreign ex libris owned by Dr. Henry C. Eno in New York City.

AS of BC & D
Bookplates in the News
605 N. STONEMAN AVENUE #F, ALHAMBRA, CALIFORNIA, 91801 U.S.A.
AUDREY SPENCER ARELLANES, Editor

Number Fifty-Six   APRIL 1984

A Note from Laurence J. Ryan

I was born in Sanborn, Iowa on July 15, 1902. My father was Thomas J. Ryan; my mother, Margaret A. (Darby) Ryan. Our family moved to Portland, Oregon about 1908, where I attended high school and in 1920 enrolled in the University of Oregon in Eugene. We moved in 1923 to Los Angeles where I attended University of California at Los Angeles and later at Berkeley. My college studies were terminated in 1924 due to recurring eyesight problems.

Before World War II, I held several jobs and then helped Uncle Sam build ships for three years when the war broke out. In 1945 I became a civilian employee for the Navy and retired after 26 years in 1972.

I am a bookworm but not a writer like my late illustrious sister, Clare Ryan Talbot. In addition to membership in ASBC&D, I belong to the Alcuin Society, Augustan Society, California State Library Foundation, Gleeson Library Associates of University of San Francisco; Friends of the J. Paul Leonard Library of San Francisco, Friends of the Berkeley Library, Friends of the Alameda Library, and the American Film Institute.

My interests include reading biographies and autobiographies; also reading movie history books. I have been a movie buff ever since the Ryan family went to nickelodeons about 1910 in Eugene, Oregon.

(Maxwell Hamilton Noll designed a plate showing Laurence Ryan's interest in cartography. The map used for the design was adapted from the frontispiece in the first volume of Venegas' NOTICIA DE LA CALIFORNIA. Originally the plate bore the name Laurence Darby Ryan; when Anthony F. Kroll rephotoengraved the plate for a new run, Darby was dropped for the middle initial J.)

Hearst Castle, a California State Historic Monument, is located atop a mountain about 45 miles northwest of San Luis Obispo. William Randolph Hearst (1863-1951) named the estate San Simeon and called the house <u>La Casa Grande</u>. While the main house is referred to as a castle, it perhaps more nearly resembles a Spanish cathedral. Hearst built <u>La Casa Grande</u> with the idea it one day would be a museum.

Of particular interest to bookplate collectors would be Tour 2 at Hearst Castle. This tour includes the upper level of the mansion, Hearst's personal libraries, his bedroom suite, and the kitchen. As you walk into Hearst's bedroom, to your right on the wall by the door is the original artwork from which was printed the bookplate here reproduced. As is usual, the original artwork is several times larger than the finished print. The plate was designed by William H. Wilke and printed by John Henry Nash.

William Wilke designed a variety of bookplates, including those for James Duval Phelan, an early mayor of San Francisco; one for Yehudi Menuhin commissioned by a group of music admirers; John Francis Neylan; Alice and J. B. Levinson; Ethel Moore Hall of Mills College; Aurelia Henry Reinhardt, president of Mills College; Herbert Brenon; Noel Sullivan; and the artist's own ex libris.

Henrietta Vepštas
Vytautas O. Virkau
EX LIBRIS*

* The bookplate, or ex libris, a printed label intended to indicate ownership, usually pasted inside the front cover of a book.

April 2 - 30, 1984
Reception 7 - 9, Friday, April 6
BEVERLY ART CENTER
2153 W. 111th St. Chicago, IL 60643

This project is supported by a grant from the Illinois Arts Council, a state agency

HUGH THOMSON
by George S. Swarth

Hugh Thomson (1860-1920) was one of the foremost illustrators of his time. His skillful draftsmanship and outstanding ability to suggest in small compass and with a few deft lines infinite detail of landscape, architecture or character are well exemplified by his illustrations for many volumes of the series "Highways and Byways" of various British counties. His drawings of horses and dogs are masterful, but he probably is best remembered for the charming eighteenth century scenes with which he illustrated such books as SHE STOOPS TO CONQUER and THE VICAR OF WAKEFIELD by Oliver Goldsmith, CRANFORD by Elizabeth Gaskell, EVELINA by Fanny Burney, QUALITY STREET by Sir James Barrie, and the works of Jane Austen. Less well known are his contributions to the field of ex libris. However, according to M. H. Spielmann and Walter Jerrold in their biography, HUGH THOMSON. HIS ART, HIS LETTERS, HIS HUMOUR, & HIS CHARM (A. & C. Black, London, 1931), he did make seven bookplates for friends or relatives, five of which are here reproduced. We may regret that he did not do more in an area to which his special abilities were so well suited.

Hugh Thomson was born on June 1, 1860, in Coleraine, County Derry, Ireland, the eldest of three children of John Thomson, a successful business man. From earliest boyhood Hugh liked to draw, and after a brief apprenticeship with a firm of linen manufacturers in Coleraine, his artistic ability came to the attention of John Vinycomb, head of the art department of Marcus Ward & Co., a firm pre-eminent in the field of color printing, in Belfast. This led to his employment with that firm, which lasted from 1877 to 1883. There he was one of about forty artists under Vinycomb's supervision, doing various sorts of commercial work, including Christmas cards in which the firm were said to be pioneers. He and Vinycomb became fast friends, and such interest as he had in bookplates may be traceable to Vinycomb, who later published his well-known ON THE PROCESSES FOR THE PRODUCTION OF EX LIBRIS (A. & C. Black, London, 1894; reprinted from the JOURNAL of the Ex Libris Society), as well as FIFTY BOOKPLATES

(printed for the author by W. & A. Baird, Belfast, 1906), and J. VINYCOMB: HIS BOOK OF BOOKPLATES (Otto Schulze & Co., Edinborough, 1908).

In November 1883, following the advice of Vinycomb and other friends, Thomson moved to London, where there were greater opportunities for original work. In 1884 he married Jessie Miller, whom he had known in Belfast; they had one son, John, born in 1886.

In London, Thomson worked briefly for the firm of McClure, Macdonald & Macgregor, but soon moved to Macmillan's, where Comyns Carr, editor of the recently founded ENGLISH ILLUSTRATED MAGAZINE, had immediately recognized his outstanding ability.

Thereafter he worked primarily for Macmillan, who published 34 of the 66 books that he illustrated, though he also illustrated books published by many other firms as well as doing illustrations for periodicals and other miscellaneous work. Between 1887 and 1931 there were twenty-four exhibitions of his drawings: two at the Victoria and Albert Museum,

five at the Fine Art Society, and others at various galleries, mostly in London but also in Paris, Birmingham, Newcastle-on-Tyne, Ulster and Folkestone.

Beginning late in 1899, Thomson suffered from recurrent illnesses of increasing frequency and severity, which often interrupted his work for considerable periods. In 1915 he was found to be suffering from angina pectoris, which greatly limited his activity thereafter, though he continued to work as he was able. From 1917 to 1919, when the war brought a suspension of most publishing, he took a position in one of the wartime offices of the Board of Trade. In 1918, thanks to the representations of a group of his friends, including the Earl of Crawford and Balcarres, Lord Plymouth, Sir E. J. Poynter, Sir Herbert Samuel, Sir Herbert Maxwell, Sir Frederick Macmillan, Mr. John Burns and Mr. M. H. Spielmann, he was put on the Civil Pension List in recognition of his outstanding artistic work. On May 7, 1920, while he was talking with a friend, his heart stopped.

Hugh Thomson was a shy and unassuming man, but one with great personal charm, who quickly established warm and lasting friendships with most of the people with whom he came in contact. Writing of him after his death, Sir James Barrie said: "He was a man who drew affection at first sight, so unworldly so diffident, you smiled over him and loved him as if he were one of his own delicious pictures. What the man was came out in his face and in all his modest attractive ways; it might be said of him that he was himself the best picture he ever made. His heart was the gentlest, the most humorous, and so was he."

The seven bookplates made by Thomson were for J. Comyns Carr, Canon Alfred Ainger, Ernest Brown, Rose Thomas (Mrs. Carmichael Thomas), Dale Thomas, William Edward Frank Macmillan, and the artist's son John Thomson. Those for Macmillan and Mrs. Thomas are dated 1901, that for John Thomson 1909; the dates of the others do not appear. The motto on John Thomson's plate, "Labor improbus omnia vincit," taken from Virgil, may we translated "Ceaseless work conquers all," and well characterizes Hugh Thomson's steadfast devotion to his own work.

FROM THE BOOKPLATE LITERATURE

THE PRIVATE PRESS, second edition, Roderick Cave (R. R. Bowker Co.: New York & London, 1983). One illustration is the 1736 ex libris for the Parish Library of Reverend Francis Blomefield of Norfolk, England.

ANTIQUARIAN BOOK MONTHLY REVIEW, California Bookplates, Brian North Lee. 11: 65, February 1984. "This is a somewhat curious but intriguing book, the labour of love of a noted bookplate collector who clearly relished the chance to tell the story of California through illustration of bookplates of residents of that State. . . . .the opportunity to examine how another generation contrived to introduce personality and pride in history to ex-libris design is well worth our taking today. . . . . that the work was worth reprinting there is no doubt."

ANTIQUARIAN BOOKMAN, In Quest of Harry Clarke: A Collector Turned Publisher, Keith Burns. (2) 73:1879, et seq, March 12, 1984. Harry Clarke was born in Dublin in 1889 and died in Switzerland in 1931; he was an illustrator and created stained glass. "Harry Clarke was turning out dozens of theatre programs, stock certificates, bookplates, memorial cards, advertising booklets, musical recital covers, magazine covers, and even handkerchiefs."

BOOKPLATES IN THE NEWS
605 N. Stoneman Ave. #F
Alhambra, CA 91801

QUARTERLY: January/April/July/October
Calendar Year Dues: $15
Copyright Audrey Spencer Arellanes

William J. Krupinski was born and raised in Milwaukee, Wisconsin. He started drawing as a child with crayons on old shelving paper. By sixth grade he had moved up to ball point pen on lined paper, and graduated to pen and ink on bristol board by high school. At the present, he is working in commercial art as well as signwriting.

Krupinski says his favorite medium remains pen and ink in making posters, logos, cartoons, bookplates, labels, and greeting cards.

In writing about his drawings, the artist said, "Our rural setting inspired these nature oriented designs. Each one portrays a plant common to this area. The original drawings are done with a crow quill pen on #200 crescent illustration board." Rights to the series are owned by the artist.

Krupinski has lived in the Colby area since 1977, a small town in rural Wisconsin, the original home of colby cheese. You may write him at P. O. Box 362, Colby, WI 54421.

MARKS OF OWNERSHIP is a poster from an exhibit at Chapin Library in the Milton C. Rose Gallery, Williams College Museum of Art, Dec. 11, 1983 to Feb. 5, 1984. Seventeen ex libris are reproduced including those for David Garrick, Elisha Brown Bird, Jack London, Gardiner Chandler by Paul Revere; a wide range of styles and techniques are represented. Copies of the poster may still be available from the university $5.

Donald Hall is a poet, a good one. He is the author of REMEMBERING POETS; HENRY MOORE, THE LIFE AND WORK OF A GREAT SCULPTOR: a collection of short stories STRING TOO SHORT TO BE SAVED; and a play about Robert Frost. Among his books of poetry are THE YELLOW ROOM: LOVE POEMS; A ROOF OF TIGER LILIES; and THE ALLIGATOR BRIDE: POEMS NEW AND SELECTED.

Thronja Art Gallery is one of the best galleries in New England, directed by Janice Throng, a delightful lady with good eyes for art and a good mind for business. The gallery is located in Springfield, MA and specializes in paintings, sculpture, and prints.

(Note: Artist Hui-Ming Wang and his wife Anna, who is a sculptor, had a joint show of paintings and sculpture at the Thronja Art Gallery during the spring of 1983. Hui-Ming will have a one-man show of prints and paintings in Tokyo during July and August this year.)   Hui-Ming
             Box 212 Greenfield Road
             Montague, MASS 01351

XXth Congress of FISAE   The XXth International Congress of FISAE will be held August 25 - 28, 1984 at Weimar, East Germany. The Congress fee is 200 marks and should be transmitted to Deutsche Aussenhandelsbank AG Berlin for the GDR travel agency Account-number 6835-16-72824, FISAE Congress, Code number 24290884.

On August 25th the congress will open with exhibits and a meeting of the FISAE delegates. On the 26th an excursion to Eisenach is scheduled which includes visits to Bach's birth place, Luther-House, and the Wartburg. The Congress continues on the 27th with an excursion to Burgk Castle for a viewing of the National Exlibris Collection of the GDR. The final day's activities include visits to the Memorial Places of the Classical German Literature at Weimar (Memorial houses of Goethe, Schiller, Herder, and Wieland) and an evening party will bring the Congress to a close. The President of the congress is Prof. Dr. Lothar Lang e.h., Direktor, Staat-liches Museum Schloss Burgk ExLibris-Zentrum, DDR-6551 Burgk/Saale, Germany.

EXLIBRIS-KUNSTLER, ARTISTAS DE EX-LIBRIS, Vol. VII (1984). This volume is published in connection with the XX International Ex Libris Congress to be held in Weimar during August of 1984; it is perhaps the largest edition at 381 pages and limited to 500 numbered copies. Forty-five artists are represented from about twenty-six countries. Several bookplate prints are either reproduced or tipped-in for each artist. The participating countries include East and West Germany, Spain, England, Scotland, Hungary, Yugoslovia, Bulgaria, Sweden, Finland, France, Austria, Japan, United States, Holland, Romania, Portugal, Czechoslovakia, Russia, Poland, Italy, Belgium, Switzerland, Canada, Denmark, and Greece. A number of the articles are in English including those on Enric Clusellas (Spain), Leslie Benenson (England), Angela Lemaire (Scotland), Ivan Razborsek (Yugoslovia), Hannu Paalasmaa (Finland), Yonejiro Sato (Japan), Iwami Furusawa (Japan), Bela Petry (US), Eduardo Dias Ferreira (Portugal), Miroslav Houra (Czechoslovakia), Segismundo Pinto (Portugal), Gregory Bosenko (Moldavia), Vladimir Sheffer (Kazakhstan), Pantelis Pantelopoulos (Greece), Vilko Cekuta (Canada), and Borge Nees (Denmark); a few of these also appear in the native language of the artist. Even when you can't read the text, there is a strong message to be gained from the illustrated ex libris prints themselves. (The cost of FISAE Volume VII is 80 Swiss francs and it may be ordered directly from Artur Mario da Mota Miranda, Casa do Outeiro, 4890 Celorico de Basto, Portugal.)

MY LIFE WITH EXLIBRIS, Kazutoshi Sakamoto (Chofu, Shimonoseki City, Japan: The English Centre of Japan, 1983.) This small, almost square volume, is in a beautifully made fold-over slipcase. There are two color snapshots; one of Kazutoshi Sakamoto, the other with Mrs. Sakamoto (I believe) in front of an ex libris exhibition. There are over thirty tipped-in ex libris prints from among his 140 personal plates; mostly of Japanese design, multi-color; a few are etchings. Mr. Sakamoto became interested in bookplates in 1927 while in junior high school, and has been very involved in the field of ex libris as an owner of personal plates, a collector, writer on the subject, and in 1977 he accepted the position of head of the Japan Exlibris Association. "I'm finding purpose for my life in exlibris, and will continue the love of exlibris I inherited from those who taught me about them. I will particularly remember with respect Mr. Shozo Saito and Mr. Taro Shimo who helped me understand these small, but precious, art objects. In one of my books I called them 'paper jewels', and still think that this is an appropriate description."

EX LIBRIS, Notes on My Family's Bookplates, Lawrence Clark Powell (Tucson: Press on the Bajada, 1984). This small volume was printed for the Friends of Fay and Larry Powell. In the preface, Powell writes: "To those benighted souls who regard bookplates and other marks of ownership as needless sentiment, this booklet is not addressed." Bookplates provide a framework for a brief family biography beginning with Powell's father, whose plate was made by Brock and Co., a leading Los Angeles jeweler-engraver between 1912 and 1920. There is a personal plate for Gertrude, his mother, and a gift plate in her name at UCLA, Larry's own first ex libris, several designed by Ward Ritchie including a joint plate for Fay and Larry and one each for their sons Wilkie and Norman, a series of personal bookplates by notable printers (Gregg Anderson, Thomas Perry Stricker, Grant Dahlstrom, Richard Hoffman). (A copy of this privately printed book appeared in a recent Dawson's Book Shop catalogue at $30.)

BOOKPLATE of C. W. G. BELL
Designed by Joy Weygand

EX LIBRIS
C·W·G BELL

My son, Charles William Gordon Bell, for whom
this plate was made, was born on January 15,
1953 in Newcastle upon Tyne, England. He was
educated at the local grammar school and graduated from the University of Leicester, where
he majored in politics. He now has a manage-
rial post at British Telecommunications in
London.

Whilst at university he became friendly with
a Nigerian student. The friendship has continued and Charles has twice been hosted by
Remi and his wife at their home in Lagos,
where Remi is employed in one of the leading
banks, formerly Barclay's, of Nigeria.

Because of his travels through the country,
Charles has developed an interest in things
Nigerian, and so, when I happened to find a
book on African embroideries, I was sure he
would appreciate the petit-point canvas of a head based on a Benin Bronze.
The head which is in the Metropolitan Museum of Art is a superb example of
the bronzes, made by the lost wax technique, for which the people of Benin
in Nigeria have been famous for the last 700 years.

The canvas, which now hangs on a wall in my son's home in Enfield, I embroidered in shades of cream and brown tapestry wool, the background being
in a strong green. It is fifteen by fifteen inches and contains approximately 72,900 stitches.

Charles, who has never been known to discard any book either bought or
acquired is a great admirer of the books printed by my husband, James Lamar Weygand, who is proprietor of the Press of the Indiana Kid. It was
possibly seeing THE BOOKPLATES OF PHILLIP HAGREEN that prompted the request to James for some bookplates for his own library. He asked that
the plates be based upon the embroidered head. James consented to print
the plates if I cooperated by drawing the design. This I did.

The brown of the design was printed from a zinc etching made from the
drawing, and the green background from a linoleum block which I cut.
The name C. W. G. Bell was printed from handset Goudy Hadriano.

The latter was very appropriate as for several years we lived in the
village of Corbridge in Northumberland. Half a mile along the road is
the Roman fort of Corstopitum built by the Emperor Hadrian, who also was
responsible for the Roman wall four miles to the north. Nearby, a lovely
drive to the southwest through the rolling Northumbrian hills, lies
Cherryburn, the home of the famous wood engraver Thomas Bewick.

My life changed radically after taking a bus tour of Yugoslavia. It was
on this that I met James, whom I later married. I left the hills of my
native land, to live in the flat Amish country of Nappanee, Indiana. I

exchanged the exhausting job of a teacher in a very tough town school for the tranquil and enjoyable life as the wife of a printer of miniature books.

(Mrs. James L. Weygand, 852 E. Marion St., Nappanee, Indiana 46550.)

ARTHUR NELSON MACDONALD   For an exhibition (at Montclair Art Museum, Montclair, New Jersey, of bookplates by Arthur Nelson Macdonald (1866, Attleboro, Massachusetts - 1940, East Orange, New Jersey), I am interested in locating the following:

1) Private, library, or museum bookplate collections with significant numbers of Arthur Nelson Macdonald bookplates, or other memorbilia.
2) Information about his personal life and family, and his professional career.
3) Reminiscenses about Arthur Nelson Macdonald from anyone who knew him or commissioned work from him.

Please address all replies to: Edith A. Rights, Librarian, LeBrun Library, Montclair Art Museum, P.O. Box 1582 Montclair, New Jersey 07042

1984 DUES - If you have not already paid 1984 dues of $35, please send your check today, or please send notification of cancellation.

FROM THE BOOKPLATE LITERATURE

A ARTE DO EX-LIBRIS (Portugal), vol. XIII, No. 5, #101, 1983. Issue is almost entirely devoted to 200 bookplates of Juan Catasus Torralbas (1911-1971) and is beautifully illustrated with tipped-in prints, some etchings, printed in color. Two especially attractive ex libris feature circus characters. (Pages 81-106). One plate was designed by American Sally Blake. - Illustration and article about the War Service Library plate which was designed for books provided by the American people through the American Library Association for soldiers and sailors.

INTERNATIONAL EXLIBRIS COMPETITION   The City of Sint-Niklaas, in conjunction with the Ministry of Dutch Culture, is organizing an International Exlibris Competition on the theme of The Scenic Dramatic Arts (theatre, opera, musical comedy, ballet, musical).

There will be more than BF 65.00 in prizes including three awards by the City of Sint-Niklaas in three disciplines (xylography, calcography, lithography). The Victor Stuyvaert Award will be given to the artist under 30 years of age, who makes the best woodengraving.

All graphic techniques are permitted; the maximum size is 13 cm. Each submission must mention the owner's name and the word "ex libris" or a similar formula. A maximum of three designs may be submitted, and two copies of each printed ex libris must be forwarded to: Internationaal Exlibriscentrum van de Stad Sint-Niklaas, Sedelijk Museum, Zamanstraat 49, 2700 Sint-Niklaas, BELGIUM. Entries will not be returned. The deadline is January 1, 1985.

BOOKPLATES FROM CHINA   This is a sampling of bookplates from
                                         China which are being sent to Weimar
                                         for exhibit during International Ex
Libris Congress in August of 1984.   Credit is extended to Mr. Li Ping Fang,
editor of BAN HUA SHIGIE in China, who forwarded the prints through Hui-Ming
Wang.   Only the briefest information is available about the artists, which
is shared with you below.

Tao Po Ching, born 1946 in Wuzi; he works in Wuxi Library.

Wu Chang Chiang, born 1954 in Tiejin; he is a teacher in the National
Central Academy of Fine Art and is a member of the National Association
of Woodcut Artists.

Wang Tieh Chuan, born 1938 in Szechwan; he is a member of the National
Association of Woodcut Artists and is a faculty member of Szechwan Academy of Fine Art.

Cheng Shu Fang, born 1941; he is a graduate of the National Central
Academy of Fine Art, an art editor of The People's Literature magazine,
and a member of the National Association of Woodcut Artists.

Wang Tung Hai, born 1938 in Fu Ning, Hopei; he is a graduate of the
National Central Academy of Fine Art, an art editor of The Beijing Review, and a member of the National Association of Woodcut Artists.

Li Hua, born 1907 in Kwangchow; he is a faculty member of the National
Central Academy of Fine Art and chairman of the National Association of
Woodcut Artists.

Wang Chun Li, born 1941 in Tangshan, Hopei; he is a teacher in the Beijing
School of Fine Art and a member of the Beijing Art Association.

Chang Kwei Lin, born 1951 in Beijing; he is a member of the National
Association of Woodcut Artists, a faculty member of the department of
woodcut at the National Central Academy of Fine Art, Beijing.

Chiang Chih Lin, born 1944; he is an art teacher in Chengtze Middle
School.

Chang Tsp P'eng, born 1937 in Tangashan, Hopei; he is a lecturer at
the National Central Academy of Fine Art and a member of the Association of Woodcut Artists.

Yu P'eng, born 1922; he is a secondary school art teacher.

Kang Hsin Sheng, born 1950 in Beijing; he is a worker in Chengtze Coal
Mine, Beijing.

Tan Chuan Shu, born 1936 in Beijing; he is a lecturer at the National
Central Academy of Fine Art and a member of the National Association
of Woodcut Artists.

Liang Tung, born 1926 in Liaoning; he is the Director of Beijing Watercolor Society, associate editor of Banhua Shgie (The Woodcut Interna-

tional), and a faculty member of the National Central Academy of Fine Art.

Chen Ching Yun, born 1944 in Beijing; he is a lecturer at the National Central Academy of Fine Art and a member of the National Association of Woodcut Artists.

Chang Kwei Lin

(Editor's Note: Perhaps it is unfair to reproduce these bookplates only in black and white; the colors of the originals and the textures of the papers on which they are printed add considerably to their appeal.)

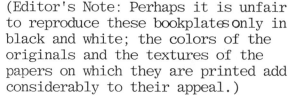

Tao Po Ching

Cheng Shu Fang

Yu P'eng

Wang Chun Li

Chen Ching Yun

Wang Tung Hai

Wang Tieh Chuan

Li Hua

Liang Tung

Chiang Chih Lin

Chang Tsp P'eng

Wu Chang Chiang

Kang Hsin Sheng

Tan Chuan Shu

Wang Tieh Chuan

With renewed interest in bookplates spreading through this country, I have been asked frequently whether or not I "do" such work. Truly, producing a bookplate would seem well within the skills afforded a wood engraver such as I. And even though I did represent England's Leo Wyatt in this country for a few years, obtain commissions for him and print his bookplate engravings at my own Penmaen Press, I personally have done only about three bookplates for clients which use my own engravings. Others have been strickly typographical. I did a small engraving and a small bookplate for the Boston Public Library in 1974, then a plate for a private individual soon after. I also did a wood engraving for the California University Law Library, but I don't believe it was ever made into an actual bookplate. Currently, I am creating a bookplate for my old friends at the Boston Athenaeum Library.

BOSTON PUBLIC LIBRARY

The
John A. Lewis
Collection of
Americana

Purchased from the Fund established by Mrs. Lewis

In fact, this miniature art is becoming increasingly appealing to me, and I would like very much to explore its possibilities as a designer and engraver. The woodcut and wood engraving marries well with any typographic message, pieces of type being themselves akin to miniature woodcuts. Besides, cutting a plate in boxwood allows me to print the design directly from the block onto the bookplate itself, thus each bookplate becomes an original print.

My main vehicle over these many years, as designer, illustrator, editor and publisher, has been the book. I have been active in the publication of contemporary poetry, fiction and translation --part of that growing fraternity of book arts presses that take pride not only in producing work of editorial merit (I have published the likes of William Saroyan, Joyce Carol Oates, Allen Ginsberg, Robert Coover, Vicente Aleixandre, and Richard Eberhart), but books that, one hopes, have redeeming aesthetic and production values. The title pages designed for these publications strike me now as employing characteristics similar to what is required for successful bookplate design. I've always used original art on my

In Memory of
Edith West Wetsel

title pages, mainly because I am an illustrator at heart, and the title page is a kind of barometer for the whole book. The print is designed in such a manner as to reflect the basic feeling of the book itself. Sometimes the engraving has been designed to be a potpourri of images from the entire body of text, or it can illustrate one specific poem, perhaps the title poem. Bookplate design should likewise reflect the person or place for which it is to be used. A client in Toronto to whom I have recently sent sketches for a bookplate is a case in point. How to get across the client's interest in music (especially the voice), his interest in hand bookbinding and books themselves; the client is a librarian. The same applies to the Athenaeum bookplate in progress, designed to reflect the interests of a deceased former literary editor, lover of the pianoforte, a connoisseur of fine wines, and a lover of his pine-shrouded home west of Boston. All this in a space of about $1\frac{1}{4}$ x $1\frac{1}{4}$ inches allowed for the woodblock's size!

So the challenge is there. And I'd like to take it up. My prices vary depending on the size of the engraving and the pressrun involved. As I am in a position to print bookplate as well as to design and illustrate them, the price depends on paper and printing time, whether one color, two, or several. A wood engraving will be at least $150-200. But again, as these special items of this fascinating art in miniature are so completely individual, prices must be resolved individually. Whatever the result, the client does have something unique, something that is most certainly a reflection of his or her private or public collection. And that's the fun of it!

THE CONCORD ART
ASSOCIATION

(Michael McCurdy has illustrated and designed many books for both the fine press and the trade. His Penmaen Press is well known as a small literary press, and his new work as co-publisher of Penmaen/ Busyhaus Publications is oriented toward art publishing with its first planned publication a collection of thirteen original wood engravings by renowned American wood engravers. McCurdy's book TOWARD THE LIGHT, a collection of his selected wood engravings, was published in 1982 in Canada and has won the 1983 Bronze Medal at the Leipzig book competition known as Die Schonste Bucher aus aller Welt.

If you are interested in commissioning a bookplate, write the artist at RD #2, Box 145, Great Barrington, MA 01230.)

AS of BC & D
Bookplates in the News
605 N. STONEMAN AVENUE #F, ALHAMBRA, CALIFORNIA, 91801 U.S.A.
AUDREY SPENCER ARELLANES, Editor

BOOKPLATES IN NEW ZEALAND
by Philip F. Prescott

It reasonably could be said that the most noteworthy feature of the Auckland Ex Libris Society is its longevity. It was founded in 1930 and started
life as the Auckland branch of the New Zealand Ex Libris Society, which
was headquartered in Wellington, the capital of the country. Although nom-
inally a branch of the New Zealand Society, the Auckland body functioned
independently and in 1954 it broke away and changed its name to the Auckland Ex Libris Society. Shortly after this the New Zealand Society ceased
to function; the Auckland group remains
the only bookplate organization in the
country

The Society maintains a low profile;
membership is limited and by invitation only. The restriction on membership makes it possible for all meetings
to be held in the homes of members. No
doubt this has played a part in the continuing existence of the Society. At
the founding of the Society in 1930 the
principal object was defined as "to
promote and extend the use of bookplates"
together with several ancillary goals
relating to bookplates. In 1932 these
aims were extended to include the "writing, printing, illustration, publication
and reading of books." In the 1930s the
membership consisted largely of artists
who designed bookplates and of ex libris
collectors; in the 1980s, while member-
ship still has a core of bookplate designers and collectors, it would be
more accurate to describe it as a literary society.

The existence of the Society was contemporaneous with the career of one
particular person, Hilda Wiseman. She was born in Australia in 1894, but
at a very early age came to Auckland, New Zealand, where her father practiced as an architect. She received her art education at the Elam School
of Art, now part of the University of Auckland. As early as 1925 she was
engaged in designing and cutting blocks for bookplates and in correspond-

ing with collectors overseas. She was an accomplished watercolorist and illuminator, but her special talent lay in printmaking from linocut, and partically all of the bookplates she designed were in this medium. She was one of the prime movers in the foundation of the New Zealand and Auckland Ex Libris Societies and was secretary of the latter society for 37 years. Unfortunately no definitive checklist of Hilda Wiseman's bookplates exists, but the writer of the present article has over seventy in his collection and has knowledge of nearly as many more. Her total output must have been well in excess of one hundred. A feature of her work was the frequent introduction of the indigenous flora and fauna of New Zealand and the motifs of Maori carving into her designs. It was largely through her influence that the Auckland War Memorial Museum Library was able to acquire the large and important bookplate collection of the noted Australian collector P. Neville Barnett, while she presented her own large collection to the Auckland Public Library shortly before her death in 1982.

The bookplates illustrating this article have either been designed by members of the Auckland Ex Libris Society or have been commissioned by members.

The Prescott bookplate showing the wingless bird turning the page with its bill depicts the Apteryx or Kiwi. Seldom seen, as it lives in the depths of the New Zealand bush and is nocturnal of habit, the kiwi remains nevertheless the most familiar symbol of New Zealand, so much so that New Zealanders are frequently referred to as "kiwis." The tipped-in print is from a linocut by Hilda Wiseman.

Two further Hilda Wiseman linocuts show the artist's interest in indigenous themes. The Lawrence plate shows a Tui, a popular forest bird, also known as the Parson Bird from the ruff of white feathers suggestive of a clerical collar. The plate also incorporates one of the basic designs of Maori carving. The Russell Duncan plate depicts a Maori warrior taking part in a war dance or "haka." The motto in Maori translates as "In knowledge is strength." The original is printed in two colors.

Robert Langholm is well-known in New Zealand as a bonsai grower and lecturer. His several bookplates are all designed around this theme. The tipped-in print above is a linocut by Hilda Wiseman and uses one of his own trees as a model. A second plate for Langholm, which is reproduced on the next page, has a rather

Art Nouveau design in a line block by
Vanda McWilliam.

The Rodger bookplate, incorporating the
armorial bearings of Sir William Rodger, was designed by David Wood, best
known in New Zealand as a calligrapher.
Sir William is President of the New
Zealand branch of the Heraldry Society.

EX LIBRIS

P. F. PRESCOTT

The bookplates reproduced for P. F. Prescott and Jean & Graham Dawson are the work of E. Mervyn Taylor, who was the leading New Zealand exponent of the art of wood-engraving and enjoyed an international reputation.

OFFERED FOR SALE - Nineteen bookplates from the 18th and 19th centuries offered for sale at $75. For full details write Len Schulman, P.O. Box 212, Downey, CA 90241.

INTERNATIONAL EX LIBRIS COMPETITION 1985

The International Exlibriscentre of City of Sink Niklaas has organized an International Ex Libris Competition in conjunction with the Ministry of Dutch Cultural Affairs to be held as the 13th biennal of small graphics from March 16 through May 5, 1985. Deadline for entires is Janaury 1, 1985. The theme: The Scenic Dramatic Arts (theatre, opera, musical comedy, ballet, musical). All graphic techniques are permitted. The design must mention the owner's name and contain the words "exlibris" or a similar formula; the maximum size is 13 cm.

Artists may submit a maximum of three ex libris, two copies of each must be sent to International Exlibriscentrum van de Stad Sint-Niklaas, Stedelijk Museum, Zamanstraat 49, 2700 Sint-Niklaas, Belgium. Accompanying the prints should be a letter with the artist's complete name and address, short curriculum vitae, name of the titleholder and the technique used, and year of design. Only printed ex libris are acceptable; all submitted become the property of the International Exlibriscentre. Interested artists should write the center directly for more details.

X INTERNATIONAL EXHIBITION AT MALBORK

ASBC&D member Vytautas O. Virkau had twenty-six ex libris on exhibit; he was prize winner with the highest, regular distinction, the Honorary Medal. The exhibit takes place in the Castle Museum between June 14 - 17, 1984.

BOOKPLATES IN THE NEWS

Quarterly: January/April/July/October

Dues: Calendar year basis $15

(C) Audrey Spencer Arellanes, 1984

Ex Libris

An Exhibition of Selected BOOKPLATES

February-March 1984

THE MELBERT B. CARY, JR. GRAPHIC ARTS COLLECTION

There is hardly a wall in the Weil home that is not hung with at least one Jacques Hnizdovsky print - some with as many as six, so in 1983 when James L. Weil needed a logo for his new publishing house, he naturally asked his "resident artist" to design it. Each credits the other with the original design concept, but they agree the felicity of letter forms deserves no small thanks for the result, which was accomplished in less than four hours.

EX Libris

James L. Weil

Publisher

Actually, they had worked together before. Years earlier they were introduced by their friend Aleksis Rannit, the Estonian poet and Yale art historian. In 1979 James Weil, publisher of the Elizabeth Press, commissioned Jacques Hnizdovsky to cut two wood blocks for Dr. Rannit's book of poems SIGNUM ET VERBUM; two years later the book was printed by the Mardersteigs' Stamperia Valdonega in Verona. In all, the Stamperia printed some seventy Elizabeth books over the years. Several of these were included in the Mardersteig exhibition mounted in 1984 by the New York Metropolitan Museum of Art.

The beautiful books the Mardersteigs made for the Elizabeth Press were often admired for their format as much as for their contents - contemporary poetry, essays, and new translations from the ancient Greek and Latin. Weil explains it was never his wish to embellish a text, but by fine workmanship and materials to show respect for a text and to honor it. In 1982, to celebrate their twelfth year of friendship, Martino Mardersteig printed a keepsake of Weil's own poems on the Officina Bodoni hand press. Weil names it "among my cloudy trophies hung." Elizabeth books were noticed in the little magazines and the big ones as well. The trade edition of the Press' last title, LIFE SUPPORTS by William Bronk, won the 1982 American Book Award for Poetry. After twenty years, Weil chose to turn his attention to other literary lands, particularly the corners of corrupt and forgotten texts. Hnizdovsky will cut a wood block for one of the three Keats studies in progress.

A new imprint was occasioned, and a new imprint occasioned a new logo. For the present ex libris, the artist has incorporated his logo together with copy from the letterhead designed and printed by Carol J. Blinn at the Warwick Press in Easthampton, MA. Blinn apprenticed to Howard McGrath at the Gehenna Press, then in 1973 established Warwick. She printed the Weil bookplate on the 12 x 18 Kluge, on archival paper, and from Jan van Krimpen's Spectrum, her house type. Blinn's colleagues confess there are few who can match her work with Spectrum. Her collaborators in the present project agree to that heartily.

Hnizdovsky's bookplates are familiar to readers of BOOKPLATES IN THE NEWS, with their earliest appearance in the July 1977 issue, again in April 1980, and more recently in a joint plate with Hui-Ming Wang. His work, together with a complete checklist of his bookplates, was featured in the Society's 1981/82 YEAR BOOK with an essay by Aleksis Rannit. Last year a Peking magazine BAN HUA YI SHU published an article about Hnizdovsky's woodcuts, and in a recent number of another Chinese periodical, BANHUA SHIJIE, there was published an interview with the artist and several pages of reproductions of his woodcuts.

PANORAMA OF CZECH LITERATURE (Prague, #3, 1981). There is no text about the bookplates or the artists; eight ex libris are reproduced, mostly as tail-pieces. There are two prints each by Karel Svolinsky, Vojech Cinybulk, Frantisek Tichy, and Anna Grmelova.

AB (ANTIQUARIAN BOOKMAN), News Notes. A.P.H.A. to Honor Dreyfus. 72:4345-6, December 19-26, 1983. John Dreyfus, eminent English printing scholar, was selected as 1984 laurate of American Printing History Association. (Note: his personal bookplate reflects his typographic interests.)

MATRIX 2 (Whittington Press, 1982). (Note: this publication has not been available to the editor, but it is believed to contain material of interest to bookplate collectors.)

THE WHITE HOUSE LIBRARY, A Short-Title List (The White House Historical Association, Washington, D.C., 1967). The foreword by James T. Babb, Librarian Emeritus, Yale University, states because of shelf-space the library is limited to twenty-five hunded volumes. Tipped-in is a print of the simple label used to identify the volumes. The official eagle emblem is blind embossed on the ex libris.

POP CULTURE MANIA, Stephen Hughes (McGraw-Hill, 1984/$8.95, 330 pages). This paperback is subtitled "Collecting 20th-Century Americana for Fun and Profit." Among the fifty-two collectibles mentioned are bookplates (pages 119-121). Members of the bookplate collection fraternity might question the statement that the "most popular items (are) photo-mechanically produced bookplates" even when "drawn by popular late 19th and 20th century artists." Overall this is a good guide for beginners with many references, sources, addresses.

JAN HALLA, Klaus Rodel (Privately printed, 1983). Multi-lingual text and 16 ex libris reproduced. Although the subtitle indicates all 16 reproductions are bookplates, only one actually shows any name. The artist was born in 1926, studied art in Prague, and has designed about 150 ex libris.

DIRECTORY OF BOOKPLATE DESIGNERS (The Bookplate Society: London, 1984). Twenty-six artists are represented, all from England or Scotland, except Mark Severin from Belgium. A bookplate is reproduced for each artist, followed by a biographical paragraph, the artist's birth date. The address for each artist is provided for any who want to write concerning commissioning a bookplate.

NEWSLETTER (The Bookplate Society), VI, No. 1, March 1984. Announcement of the members' book for 1983: J. A. C. HARRISON by Brian North Lee. / There is a Notes and Queries section available to Bookplate Society members and scholars.

NEWSLETTER (The Bookplate Society), In Search of Mary Lawson, James L. Wilson. (4) 6:4-9, March 1984. One of the excitements of bookplate collecting is the search into the life of an elusive artist; such is the case with Mary Caroline Lawson, whose work was featured in the JOURNAL of the Ex Libris Society (1905-08). The last of her plates was dated 1911; after that nothing. Wilson traced her through her last known address in 1906, to a Vicarage, a convent, marriage in 1911, after which she moved to Calcutta. Printed also is a handlist of her ex libris, originally compiled by Horace Jones.

THE BOOKPLATE JOURNAL (London), Comment, 2:#1, 1-2, March 1984. Note is made that the excellent reference DICTIONARY OF BRITISH BOOK ILLUSTRATORS: THE TWENTIETH CENTURY (London: John Murray, 1983) makes no mention that at least one hundred of the artists listed have designed bookplates.

THE BOOKPLATE JOURNAL (London), The Early Bookplates of Paul Nash, Clare Colvin. (28) 2:#1, 3-18, March 1984. Clare Colvin, of the Tate Gallery, writes in detail of 28 extant bookplates, nearly all of which were designed between 1908 and 1910. The illustrations are reduced in size, but the checklist gives the actual dimensions.

THE BOOKPLATE JOURNAL (London), Bookplates of the Institution of Mechanical Engineers, Benoit Junod. (12) 2:#1, 19-28, March 1984. The author, Cultural Attache at the Swiss Embassy in London and a member of the Swiss Society of Heraldry, follows the documentation available from the Institute's archives about the commissioning of its several bookplates including one by J. R. G. Exley in the style of G. W. Eve's plate for the Institution of Electrical Engineers and a design by Stephen Gooden which was not actually used as a bookplate.

THE BOOKPLATE JOURNAL (London), Bookplate Designs and Chinese Armorial Porcelain, David S. Howard. (11) 2:#1,29-40, March 1984. The author compares bookplates from the Franks and Viner collections in the British Museum (35,000 and 5,000 respectively) with armorial designs on Chinese porcelain. An extensive list is offered giving the Franks or Viner number and indicating where procelain design is identical, similar, derived, or copied.

THE BOOKPLATE JOURNAL (London), Profile of An Artist: Will Carter, David Chambers. (2) 2:#1, 41-2, March 1984. "His lettering flows very sweetly, cut in lead or wood for an inscription, or drawn for printing. The letters in his book labels are firmly drawn, and bold enough to print well despite being so greatly reduced in size, the consequent variation in relationship between thick and thin lines being nicely allowed for in the original. The colouring is the label's final glory, for the cunningly mixed reds, greens, blues, and browns have a softness about them, and yet a strength which is given full vigour by the double inking which he finally gives to each impression."

THE BOOKPLATE JOURNAL (London), Portrait of a Bookplate: Caesar Ward & Richard Chandler, Brian North Lee. (2) 2:#1,43-6, March 1984. The bookplates discussed served half as bookplates and half as trade cards for the bookselling activities of Ward and Chandler; one from about 1734, the other not before 1740.

THE BOOKPLATE JOURNAL (London), Review, Lesley Weissenborn. (1) 2:#1, 47-8, March 1984. Reviewed is THE EX-LIBRIS OF SIMON BRETT by Brian North Lee which was published in Denmark under Klaus Rodel's imprint ExlibRisten. "It is heartening to read how Brett describes his approach to a commission to make an ex-libris: 'The challenge of bookplate design is to tune oneself into another's feelings and carry them to the greatest possible depth.'"

GERARD GAUDAEN (Catalogue for exhibit March 24 to April 23, 1984 at Sint Niklaas). A variety of graphics are reproduced in the catalogue with text material from several authors, including poetry. There is a section on his ex libris, a biographical chronology, list of publications about him.

THE MICROBIBLIOPHILE, A Unique Periodical, Msgr. Francis J. Weber. 8:#2, 2-3, May 1984. The unique periodical is THE ETCH MINIATURE MONTHLY MAGAZINE which was etched and published by Bernhardt Wall (1872-1956). It was published for the year 1948; three of the issues (February, March, and May) had articles or illustrations of bookplates.

FRANCIS J. WEBER, The Monsignor of the Archives, Doyce B. Nunis, Jr. (Los Angeles: Dawson's Book Shop, 1983). The cover illustration by Anthony F. Kroll is a variation of the miniature bookplate designed for Msgr. Weber.

THE BOOK COLLECTOR, Bibliographical Notes & Queries. Note 453. The Bookplate of Charles Dickens, Dick Hoefnagel. (5) 32:349-51, Autumn 1983. Dickens' ex libris has received attention because of "alleged improper use of the heraldic crest it displays." There are two varient versions including differences in lion's eyes, mane, tongue. sweep of end of tail, contour of hindquarters, torse of the crest. Both versions illustrated are from Dartmouth University. J. A. Gere, Keeper of Department of Prints & Drawings identified two versions as 8619 and 8618 in Franks; 8618 is further identified with Henry Sotheran Ltd., which purchased Dickens' library "complete and outright." Prints made for subscribers to Lombard Street Edition of Charles Dickens novels published in 1932; reprints made on cream paper.

THE LAKEVILLE JOURNAL and THE MILLERTON NEWS (CT), November 17, 1983. Old Bookplates. A collection of old bookplates was displayed at Scoville Memorial Library in Salisbury; lent by Lou Burgess, some of ex libris belonged to George May Elwood of Rochester.

———————————

SHARE YOUR BOOKPLATE

Do you have a bookplate you would like to share with other ASBC&D members? If you do, please send a print along with some biographical data about yourself and the artist who designed it; if you would like to furnish enough prints to tip-in, 225 would be needed. This is an opportunity to share your bookplate and the artist who designed it.

VIRGILIO TRAMONTIN
by   Albert Collart

Born in 1908, at San Vito al Tagliamento (Italy), Virgilio Tramontin followed the courses of the Venice Academy of Fine Arts. It is there that he made his first campaign.   It is in this temple of art that he received instruction from the master Virgilio Guido for painting and from E. Brugnoti and G. Giuliani for engraving.

As an artist, he has remained faithfully attached to his native land, to that green plain of Friuli bounded by the waters of the Tagliamento and Livenza. It is in the midst of this rustic region that he draws the best of his inspiration, an inspiration always renewed, which his artistic sensibility, lover of nature, translates in idealized notations by a burin at once firm and light.

It is above all in his large plates that the subtle art of Tramontin takes on its full dignity. His burin knows how to translate with mastery the imposing serenity of a vast landscape or the intimacy of an old sanctuary lost in the midst of trees denuded by autumn. If his landscapes cry out with truth, he nevertheless knows how to put there that poetic touch – light and silence – that draws attention and holds the dream to which the artist invites us.

But, here it is a matter of ex libris, engravings of small size, where the hand of the engraver runs the risk of feeling imprisoned by too restrictive a frame. However, one realizes, in admiring the proofs that illustrate the present article, the facility with which Tramontin plays with this tight frame of the ex libris which is far from being a minor art as is too often thought. Whatever these be of landscapes, of animals, of flowers, of human figures, or of whatever objects, the ensemble of the composition forms a harmonious whole that no false note comes to disturb. Examination of a long series of ex libris conceived by the Friulian engraver is like an art gallery where many different works follow one another without giving rise to boredom or provoking satiety. None of the signs is disclosed there that sometimes make one say before the work of certain artists: he repeats himself.

Virgilio Tramontin has participated in his country, in numerous expositions; he has likewise displayed abroad and notably at Berlin, Birkenfeld, Bruges, Graz, Helsinki, Istanbul, Leningrad, Moscow, Nancy, New York, Oslo, Sint Niklaas, Tallinn, Teheran, Valence, Zurich, etc. His works are spread in the art museums and print collections of his country and abroad. It must be added also that in the course of a career already long, Tramontin has gathered in various places numerous engraving prizes. The later came to repay justly the labor and virtuosity of an artist who has known how to interpret successfully, by the magic of his burin, the deep love devoted to his native land and the benevolent curiosity with which he inclines toward the beings and things that compose his enchanted universe.

(Translated by George S. Swarth from volume VI FEDERATION INTERNATIONALE DES SOCIETES D'AMATEURS D'EX-LIBRIS, EX LIBRIS ARTISTS; Portugal, 1982.)

. ———————————————————————————————————— .

BOOKPLATE EXHIBIT AT BOSTON ATHENAEUM   The exhibit will open September 20 and run through October 10, 1984.   About 500 contemporary ex libris prints have been brought together by James Keenan through the generous response from the ASBC&D membership and additional prints have been drawn from the collection of the Boston Athenaeum.

Opening day at 6PM Michael McCurdy will talk on "The Illustrator as Publisher." Toward the end of the exhibition James Keenan will give an illustrated talk at 12noon on October 4; the talk is titled "Commissioning A Bookplate." If you will be in the Boston area during the period of the exhibition, you will have an excellent opportunity to see some of the best of contemporary bookplate design, not only from the United States but also the British Isles, Europe, and Japan.

. ———————————————————————————————————— .

EX LIBRIS DAL MONDO
PER PINOCCHIO

CENTENARIO DI
PINOCCHIO
1883-1983

This catalogue reproduces all the ex libris of artists, who participated in an International Competition of ex libris designs, held in 1983, under the auspices of the Italian National Foundation "C. Collodi" of Pescia, together with the Society of Friends of Ex Libris BNEL, Aretine Branch. An exhibit of the entries began November 25, 1983.

The book may be ordered from: Libreria Salimbeini s.r.l., Casella Postale 1450 Via Matteo Palmieri, 14 - 16 r. 50122 Firenze, ITALY.

Size of the book is 17 x 24 cm, 270 pages each with one reproduction of an ex libris.   The price is L28.000.   In his Introduction, Fernanco Tempesti says: "Pinocchio would seem at first to be a mechanical and dated figure from the 19th century, but in these ex libris it is wonderfully clear that he continues to inspire an enormous quantity of diverse, strong, and stunning visual images."

AS of BC & D
Bookplates in the News

605 N. STONEMAN AVENUE #F, ALHAMBRA, CALIFORNIA, 91801 U.S.A.

AUDREY SPENCER ARELLANES, Editor

NUMBER FIFTY-EIGHT   OCTOBER 1984

JAMES HUMPHREY WILKINSON (1893-1984)
by
Eileen Boyle, Librarian
Wangenheim Room - San Diego Public Library

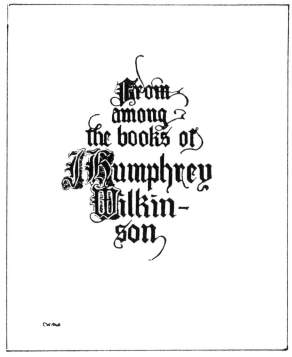

J. Humphrey Wilkinson was a member of the American Society of Bookplate Collectors and Designers for over forty years. He began collecting bookplates about four decades ago after acquiring plates of Frederick Garrison Hall at auction. Humphrey amassed over 500 books and periodicals on ex libris. about one-third of the monographs and periodicals were foreign publications representing several European countries. His international interest is also evident in his collection of over 6,500 bookplates.

Mr. Wilkinson, a native of St. Paul, Minnesota, worked in the invenment business with the Wells Dickey Company and the Caldwell-Phillips Co. His father died when Humphrey was young, and he developed a close relationship with his maternal grandfather, James Daniel Humphrey. As a tribute to his grandfather, Mr. Wilkinson, at the age of 32, financed, built, and equipped a hospital wing for the Children's Home Society of Minnesota. His interest in children and young people continued throught his lifetime. The cottage he designed and had built in Rockport, Massachusetts, served as a gathering place for Humphrey's family from the time his daughter was a teenager until his grandchildren reached adulthood. Mr. Wilkinson moved to La Jolla, California, with his wife Cecelia in 1957. His many interests included art, music, literature, chess, photography, and architecture.

In accordance with Mr. Wilkinson's wishes his daughter, Joann, presented the Wangenheim Room of the San Diego Public Library with his exceptional collection. Mr. Wilkinson had requested that it be given in memory of his grandfather, James Daniel Humphrey.

521

The Wangenheim Room is a special collection on the development of the book and the history of printing. The collection was begun by Julius Wangenheim, a San Diego banker and bibliophile, and bequeathed to the city of San Diego by his widow Laura Klauber Wangenheim. The collection is housed in a room that resembles a private library with matched teak paneling and oriental rugs creating an atmosphere of calm and serenity. In illustrating the development of the book through the ages, the collection ranges from Babylonian clay tablets, Egyptian papyrus, medieval manuscripts to contemporary fine press books. Examples of fore-edge paintings and unusual bindings are on display.

During September and October a sampling of Mr. Wilkinson's collection is on exhibit and includes the plates of Herbert Hoover, Henry Cabot Lodge, Walter P. Chrysler, Arthur Ochs Sulzberger, Ellen Terry, Isadora Duncan, and Charlie Chaplin. However, visitors are always welcome and the Librarian would be pleased to show member of ASBC&D items from the J. Humphrey Wilkinson bookplate collection. The Wangenheim Room is open Tuesday through Saturday from 1PM to 5PM, but it is advisable to telephone ahead (619/236-5807).

Among artists who designed personal bookplates for Mr. Wilkinson are Oscar T. Blackburn and Cleora Wheeler. The Blackburn plate, designed in 1958, was specifically for his bookplate literature. In 1960 a lettered label was created by Cleora Wheeler.

. ⸺⸺⸺⸺⸺⸺⸺⸺⸺⸺⸺⸺⸺⸺⸺ .

Exhibition   The Bookplate Society (England) has mounted their sixth exhibition titled "London Bookplates," which are on display from October 1 through November 30, 1984 in the Whittington Room of Guildhall Library, London. Camden Morrisby's ex libris illustrates the flyer.

XX International   The Bookplate Society's NEWSLETTER (vol. VI, No. 3, September 1984) reports on the congress at Weimer,
Ex Libris Congress   August 24-28, 1984. There were about 270 participants from nineteen countries. Three talks were given, each in German with English and French translations: "The Art of the Bookplate in the GDR: Issues and Problems," by Professor Lothar Lang; "Dresden Bookplates ca. 1900," by Dr. Albert Scholz; and "The Rediscovery of the Oldest German Bookplate Collection," delivered by Mr. H. Patzke. There were a variety of exhibitions including one in connection with Prof. Lang's talk; the usual two-year retrospective of plates designed since the last Congress; an exhibit of bookplates designed in honor of the German writer Schiller; medical bookplates 1900-30; and exhibits centered around the other two lectures. The Netherlands has offered to host the XXI Congress in Utrecht in 1986, and elected as president of FISAE was Mr. Ph. van Praag, author of SOCIALE SYMBOLIEK OP NEDERLANDSE EXLIBRIS (1983).

The NEWSLETTER also included the text of Prof. Lang's from which I quote: "This is the first problem: the bookplate is not accorded attention by art historians, although the bookplate has a 500-year history. At the turn of the century, the bookplate attracted heraldry specialists and genealogists. But thereafter the bookplate, which has flourished since 1900, became a field for unprofessional scholars, gifted dilettantes, who have undertaken research with devotion, diligence, endurance, and enthusiasm, but who chronicled rather than researched the bookplate."

J. A. C. HARRISON, ARTIST & ENGRAVER, by Brian North Lee (The Bookplate Society and Forlaget Exlibristen, 1983). Reviewer: George S. Swarth.

It is the pleasant custom of The Bookplate Society (that is, the British society, which so styles itself) to publish each year a book on a subject of ex libris interest, which is distributed free to members. This year's publication is Brian North Lee's admirable monograph on the work of John Augustus Charles Harrison (1872-1955).

The volume consists of fifteen pages of text interspersed with ten pages of illustrations, followed by a one-page bibliography, a forty-eight page checklist of Harrison's 352 known bookplates, a list of nine drawings for bookplates of which no prints have been found, and fifty pages of reproductions of bookplates. A print of the bookplate for Ian Mackenzie is tipped in as a frontispiece (over a reproduction of the same plate which includes a thistle remarque and signature lacking on the actual print). The book is 7 3/4 by 11 inches, printed on coated paper which permits very high quality reproductions, though a little fine detail is necessarily lost in any reproduction. It is softbound but sewn; the cover design and title appear only on the loose jacket.

The book is a splendid example of the extensive and painstaking research and scholarly presentation that have characterized Mr. Lee's other works, including THE BOOKPLATE DESIGNS OF REX WHISTLER (The Bookplate Society's volume for 1973) and BRITISH BOOKPLATES: A PICTORIAL HISTORY (1979).

Mr. Harrison's private life appears to have been uneventful, and is dealt with only briefly. The text is devoted chiefly to his professional career and a critique of his work as it developed through the years. Harrison's father was an engraver, and the boy became his pupil at an early age; Lee reproduces two very competent engravings that he made at the age of fourteen or fifteen. From the age of nineteen onward he worked as an engraver, either employed by or associated with London stationers who, among other things, provided engraved bookplates for their clients. As Lee explains, a confusing aspect of this situation was that plates so made bore either the name of the company or the initials not of the engraver but rather of the company officer who was in charge of the engraving aspect of the business and who sometimes participated to some degree in designing the bookplates: William Phillips Barrett during the twelve years that Harrison was employed by John & E. Bumpus, Ltd., and F. G. House during his later association with Truslove & Hanson. Thus their initials rather than Harrison's will be found appended to many plates in the Harrison checklist, even though Harrison was chiefly or wholly responsible for the designing as well as the actual engraving.

In addition to bookplates, Harrison engraved many postage stamps and portraits for banknotes and government bonds, both British and foreign, several of which are reproduced. The reproductions, even of very tiny portraits, are excellent and well show the high quality of Harrison's work. He did only two book illustrations: one after Van Dyck's portrait of Charles I, the other after Holbein's portrait of Sir Thomas More, the latter of which is reproduced. Harrison had a lifelong interest in the stage, both amateur and professional, both as actor and producer, and did many pencil or pen and ink sketches and gouache paintings of actors. A splendid painting of Sir Henry Irving as Richard III is reproduced, and even in the black and white reproduction shows the great ability of the artist.

The checklist gives Harrison's 352 bookplates in alphabetical order, indicating the plate number of those that are reproduced. The reproductions are also in alphabetical order, but as only fifty plates are reproduced, the numbers, of course, do not correspond to those in the checklist. The checklist describes each plate, with the date when known and a few lines of information about the owner when that is available. It would have been interesting if the reproductions could have been put in chronological order, so that one could trace more easily the development of Harrison's technique, but since the dates of many plates are unknown, that, of course, was not possible. An unusual feature of the checklist is that names and other lettering quoted from the plates are printed in solid capitals when they so appear on the plates. Asterisks mark the few plates of which no print could be examined to learn the type face.

The high esteem in which Harrison was held is amply shown by the eminence of the people for whom he made plates: George V, when Prince of Wales; Edward VIII, when Prince of Wales; George VI, when Duke of York (wreathed initial "A" for his first name, Albert); Queen Alexandra, when Princess of Wales; Queen Maud of Norway; Princess Helena Augusta Victoria of Schleswig-Holstein-Sonderburg-Augustenburg, the third daughter of Queen Victoria; her daughter, Princess Helena Victoria; Grand Duke Michael of Russia; the Duke of Portland; the Duke of Northumberland; the Duchess of Bedford; the Marquess of Anglesey; Field Marshal Roberts, Earl of Kandahar and Pretoria; and many other peers and persons of note. Following the arrangement of the catalogue of the Franks collection, plates are listed by family name, with cross-references under titles. Royal plates are, of course, under given names, as shown on the plates.

The plates illustrated are of many styles. About half are purely armorial, mostly with elegant mantling that stands comparison with Sherborn's best. There is one rococo plate, that of Mildred Boynton, executed with delicacy and taste often lacking in that rather floridly fanciful style. There are many pictorial plates, some with incidental heraldry: landscapes, library or other interiors, gardens, an alert and lifelike horse's head, a view of an African plain from a library window, and on the plate of Herbert John Gladstone a fine picture of his father, the Prime Minister, bent over his desk. The plate of Florence Leach shows an impressive Egyptian arch, with a figure standing in bright sunlight beyond, dwarfed by the magnitude of the framing arch. The selection strikingly shows the versatility of the artist who handled these diverse styles and subjects all with equal skill.

Until now there seems to have been no published material about Harrison's bookplates, except to the extent that they may be included in Horace E. Jones' work, BOOKPLATES SIGNED 'W.P.B.' (i.e., William P. Barrett, of John & E. Bumpus, Ltd.) 1896-1928. Everything else listed in the bibliography deals with Harrison's work on stamps or banknotes. Brian North Lee, with his usual ability, has presented a valuable introduction to the ex libris work of an outstanding artist, about which little information has been heretofore generally accessible.

BOOKPLATES IN THE NEWS
ISSN: 0045-2521

Calendar Year Dues /$15
Quarterly: January/April/July/October

FROM THE BOOKPLATE LITERATURE

GRAPHIA, No. 90, June 1984. A portion of the issue appears to be devoted to brief memorials to deceased artists: Cornelis-Andre Vlaanderen (1881-1955), Maurits Van Coppenolle (1910-1955), Jeb Boudens (born 1926), Gerard Schelpe (1906-1973), Arthur George Stainforth (1893-1954), Albert Setola (1916-1981), Albert Isselee (born 1903). As usual, this is a well-produced publication under the direction of Andre Vercammen of Sint-Niklaas, Belgium.

MICHEL FINGESTEN, DAS GRAPHISCHE WERK, Norbert Nechwatal. For those interested in this artist, the book may be ordered from Dr. Norbert Nechwatal, Querstrasse 1, D-8640 Kronach, Germany. Published in 1983 (?), there is an English summary; cost DM 69.

NIPPON EX LIBRIS SOCIETY. Twice yearly they issue calendars with each month printed on a separate sheet and with an ex libris printed tipped-on. Usually the prints are multi-colored, sometimes as many as eight colors. The Japanese society also publishes an 8-page newsletter. A recent issue reproduced in reduced size several bookplates for Klaus Stiebeling and printed in Japanese and English a listing of the international symbols for the various techniques by which bookplates are made (such as C for intaglio printing, X1 for woodcut, P7 for offset, and E for calligraphy).

L'EX LIBRIS FRANCAIS, No. 151, 1984. Robert Kugel writes about artist Robert Kuven (1901-1983) and gives a checklist of twenty-two ex libris he designed from 1934 through 1980. - Germaine Meyer-Noirel tells of a curious bookplate belonging to books given by the French government to the Catalonian Library of Barcelona in 1916. There is a memorial note on Colette Pettier (1907-1983).

MITTEILUNGEN DER DEUTSCHEN EXLIBRIS-GESELLSCHAFT e.v., p. 13-28, 1984. Helmer Fogedgaard writes about ex libris literature. Dr. H. Kretschmer has an article about the brothers Hans and Leo Frank. Numerous ex libris reproduced in reduced size for all articles.

NORDISK EXLIBRIS TIDSSKRIFT, #153, 1984. Article on Petr Hampl by Josef Tresnak with several ex libris reproduced. Memorial to Emil Kotrba with some of his bookplate illustrated. Graphics of Victor Schapil by A. A. Sidorov.

NEWSLETTER OF THE IMBS (International Miniature Book Society), The Greatest Miniature Book Artist, Dr. Martin Znidersic. (3) 1:7-9, 1984 (this is volume 1, number 1). The artist is Karoly Andrusko, who has created 150 various miniature book in a twenty year period. Several of his miniature books were as keepsakes for International Ex Libris Congresses, the first in 1972 when the Congress was held in Helsingor. Andrusko has also designed a great number of ex minilibris of a suitable size for his miniature books. Two of the illustrations are minibookplates which are smaller than many stamps.

ENDOWED BOOK FUNDS AT HARVARD UNIVERSITY. This is a twelve page booklet introducing potential donors to the possibility of establishing a book fund with a gift of $5,000 or more. The income is used to purchase books. For many of the funds bookplates are designed for use in the purchased volumes; a number of attractive plates are reproduced. Inqueries to Joan Nordell, Harvard University Library, Wadsworth House, Cambridge, MA 02138.

Ex·LIBRIS

Sid Chaplin.

GIN–GANG EX LIBRIS for SID CHAPLIN
by Joy Weygand

Sid Chaplin was born in County Durham, England. He left school at fourteen years of age to enter the coal mines of his native county. Being an intelligent, resourceful young man he studied hard and gained a scholarship to Ruskin College. Later he was sent to the Pennsylvania mines to study American techniques.

For several years he worked as a public relations officer for the British National Coal Board; contributions to their magazine helped to hone his undoubted skill as a writer.

For many years he contributed articles to the prestigious Manchester Guardian; his knowledge of current events and local history made these articles interesting to a wide readership. He drew on his memories of life in the mining villages of his youth to produce some delightful, poignant short stories. One notable collection in THE LEAPING LAD was adapted to make a highly successful play CLOSE THE COAL–HOUSE DOOR. This was performed not only on the London stage but on BBC television.

Newspaper articles, lectures, television scripts and novels keep him fully occupied and his worth has been recognized, not only by the University of Newcastle-upon-Tyne, which awarded him an honorary master's degree, but by the nation. It was a proud day when he and his family set off for Buckingham Palace where he received the Order of the British Empire from a member of the royal family.

Sid is a very private person, an author of repute, and an art collector. Pride of place goes to his watercolor sketch by Thomas Bewick, though he has many beautiful paintings by well-known north country artists.

He is passionately interested in the history of his native Durham and the neighboring county to the north, Northumberland, and in the ancient city of Newcastle, where he has lived for the past twenty-eight years. He has an encyclopedic knowledge of customs of the towns, villages, and countryside.

As he had taken an interest in the bookplate which my husband (James Lamar Weygand) and I had produced for my son, Charles Bell, I offered to design one for him if he would choose a subject. I was not at all surprised therefore when his choice fell upon a typical north country subject. The gin-gang was a round shed in which two horses moved round and round, furnishing the motive power for a threshing machine housed in a nearby barn. Coal was too expensive to haul up to the outlying farms and timber was scarce.

Sid's younger son, Michael, has inherited his father's skill with words and communication, though they take a different form; he is a producer of documentaries for London Weekend Television.

(The Sid Chaplin bookplate designed and printed by Joy and James Lamar Weygand, 852 East Marion Street, Nappanee, Indiana 46550.)

MORE FROM THE BOOKPLATE LITERATURE

JOHN & MARY'S JOURNAL, Bookplates: Past, Present, and Future, Vitolis E. Vengris. (20) #8:4-14, Winter 1983. A good survey article. "Bookplates, both in their content and their method of production, are reflections of history. In all their varieties, bookplates reveal with great fidelity the prevailing taste in decorative art of different periods, show the influence of the fashions of the time in art, architecture, and heraldic practices. In parallel fashion, the production techniques for making bookplates have changed with advances in technology, from woodcuts and copper engravings to lithographic and photoengraving processes."

QANTAS EMPIRE AIRWAYS, Art in Books. This article was referenced on page 457 of BOOKPLATES IN THE NEWS as appearing in August 1981. The correct date is August 1951. (Thanks to the efforts of Dr. Geoffrey Long, a ASBC&D member from Australia, this correction is presented.)

CALLIGRANEWS, Dr. Ottmar Premstaller's Carvings. (8) 8:7, May/June 1984. Illustrated are eight stamps carved by Dr. Premstaller of Austria; he used a razor blade sliver on erasers, wood, and linoleum.

GRAPHIA, #89, February 1984. A portion of this issue is devoted as a memorial to Leo Winkeler.

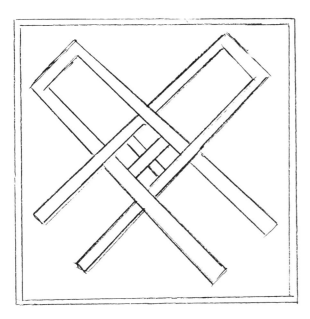

DO YOU RECOGNIZE THIS PLATE?
by Dirk Cable

In a nice copy of Bret Harte's LUCK OF ROARING CAMP, bound in a red crushed morocco, I think in England for Brentano's in New York, I discovered on the front paste down endpaper what I take to be a label of ownership of curious design: two intertwined capital A's tooled in gold upon what appears to be Japan vellum and bordered in gold. The border is a weak 1/16" and the entire label, including border, is 1" vertically by 1 1/6" horizontally. Perhaps it was intended to be 1" square. The crossbars of the A's form an X, by chance or design.

If you can identity this label, please contact Dirk Cable, 350 S. Lake Ave., Pasadena, CA 91101.

FOR SALE / GERMAN EX LIBRIS   Collection of over 200 German bookplates mostly etchings (nudes, symbolic, scenic, humorous, and armorial) from 1915-1940's and including some from the late 1800's. Artists include Herman Hirzel, Morisot, Georg Jilovsky, O. Barth, Karl Blossfeld, Senfferheld, and many others. For details contact Diana Sowder, 1809 Columbia Avenue, Ft. Wayne, IN 46805.

DON HUBBARD

Commander Don Hubbard is a retired Naval aviator currently
residing in Coronado, CA. Following the termination of his 24
year career in 1967, he founded
a successful marine business
specializing in inflatable boats
and small craft. This business
was sold in 1977 when he turned
his efforts full time to marine
art and writing.

His first book, SHIPS-IN-BOTTLES:
A STEP-BY-STEP GUIDE TO A VENER-
ABLE NAUTICAL CRAFT, was published by McGraw-Hill in 1971 and
subsequently translated into German and published by Verlag Delius,
Klasing & Co. in 1973. In 1982
he became the first president of
the Ships-in-Bottles Association of America and is now editor of their quarterly journal, THE BOTTLE SHIPWRIGHT. (The ex libris reproduced above is
for Dane Per Christensen, who is a graphic designer and also a ship-in-
bottle builder who specializes in putting figures in bottles, hence the design for his linoleum cut plate.

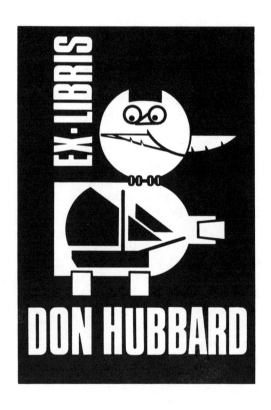

Hubbard is a marine watercolor artist.
He served on the board of directors of
the 800-member San Diego Watercolor
Society for a number of years and is an
active member of the American Society
of Marine Artists. His paintings depict
scenes both above and below the sea's
surface. He is also a member of the Nature Printing Society and specializes
in creating watercolor Gyotaku (Japanese
fish prints) on rich paper and cloth.

His interest in bookplates stems from a
signed and numbered edition of the late
Rockwell Kent's bookplates which he inherited from his father in 1972. With
only one exception all of Hubbard's ex
libris have been executed in linoleum
and relate in some way to his interest
in the sea. Through ship-in-bottle contacts in Denmark he has become acquainted with other bookplate enthusiasts in
that country and become a member of the
Danish Bookplate Society. Hubbard's
plate to the left was designed by Per
Christensen in 1983 and shows his particular interest as a ship-in-bottle
builder. (Don Hubbard, P.O. Box 550, Coronado, CA 92118.)

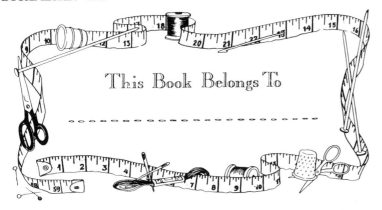

"Stitcher Stickers" are the creation of Craftways of Berkeley, CA. and may be found in needlecraft shops. The labels may be used for identification of treasured books about various aspects of your favorite needlework.

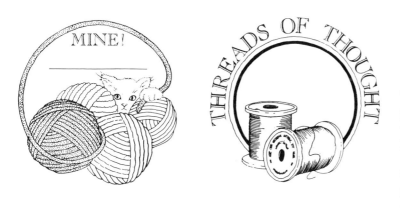

The rural scene is a stock plate offered to support the National Trust for Scotland

The Hedgehog Workshop in England portrays a number of different animals on its stock ex libris.

This book belongs to

ROBERT G MENZIES

The Directors of Prouds
cordially invite you and company
to preview their second

Book Plate ⎤
Ex libris ⎦ *Exhibition*

at

Prouds Art Gallery

on

Thursday, 13th September, 1984

8.30 a.m. - 7.30 p.m.

Duration of Exhibition 14 days.

PROUDS ART GALLERY
Cnr. King and Pitt Streets, Sydney
Phone: 233 4488

Gallery Director:
Keith James

SECOND BOOK PLATE EXHIBITION   Above is the announcement of the recently
held exhibition in Sydney, Australia, at
Prouds Art Gallery, which used the bookplate Lionel Lindsay designed for
Robert G. Menzies, Australian prime minister during World War II, as illustration.

A thirteen page catalogue of the 270 prints exhibited was produced accompanied by a reprint of an article from AUSTRALIAN BUSINESS by Robert
Holden on "Ex Libris . . . The Australian Bookplate." Holden is librarian
at the James Hardie Library of Australian Fine Arts; his article is a good
review of the rise, fall, and resurgence of the bookplate in Australia.

The catalogue is by artist with the name of the owner, technique, how the
plate is signed, and the price. All of the 270 prints are priced, with a
low of $20 and a high of $250 for a Norman Lindsay etching. A hand-colored
woodcut by Adrian Feint for Carlyle S. Baer, long-time Secretary of the
ASBC&D, is printed at $150.00. Some listings are by subject.

Artists represented include Norman Lindsay, Pixie O'Harris, Harold Byrne,
William Hunter, Adrian Feint, Lionel Lindsay, Gayfield Shaw, George D.
Perrottet, Sydney Ure Smith, D. H. Souter, Roy Davies, etc. (It is hoped
to have a follow-up article on how well the sales went at these substantial prices.)

CONTEMPORARY EX LIBRIS: AN EXHIBITION
September 20 through October 10, 1984

"The Illustrator as Publisher"
A talk by Michael McCurdy, proprietor of the Penmaen Press
Thursday, September 20 at 6:00 p.m.

"The Art of the Contemporary Bookplate"
A talk by James P. Keenan, member of the American Society of
Bookplate Collectors and Designers
Thursday, October 4 at noon

For reservations, please telephone 227-8112.

The Boston Athenaeum • 10½ Beacon Street • Boston, Massachusetts
Monday through Friday   9:00 a.m. to 5:30 p.m.
Saturday, beginning October 6   9:00 a.m. to 4:00 p.m.

bookplate designed by Michael McCurdy

James P. Keenan Reports on
Contemporary Exhibit

The show of contemporary ex libris at the Boston Athenaeum has been an outstanding event. We hope this will be only the first of many exhibitions and that bookplate exhibits will again become an annual happening.

Opening night, September 20, 1984, Michael McCurdy presented an illustrated talk on "The Illustrator As Publisher." He discussed his work as a wood engraver, some current projects, and the history of his own Penmaen Press. On October 4th, I have an illustrated talk on "The Art of the Contemporary Bookplate." This talk included a brief history of the bookplate and of ex libris societies. Also covered were collecting and exchange procedures, and a variety of ideas for a personal ex libris using slides of selected pieces from the show.

Many of those who attended the show saw, for the first time, the limitless scope of the bookplate. There were 444 pieces on display in eleven cases and arranged by artist's nationality. Fridolf Johnson's introduction to A TREASURY OF BOOKPLATES FROM THE RENAISSANCE TO THE PRESENT is reprinted as the introduction to the thirty-page checklist accompanying the exhibit. The plates are listed by country and alphabetically by artist within each country. Under the artist's name is the bookplate's owner, its date, when known, and the medium used. The medium is identified by the symbols approved by the International Congress of Ex Libris, Barcelona, 1958. To encourage new bookplate designs, a directory of addresses for 105 of the 200 artists represented is included at the end of the checklist.

An annual exhibit will help to further the art of the modern bookplate. Some years ago there was a traveling show which visited cities across the country. It is my hope we can do this once again. In future shows the focus will be on a theme or the ex libris designs of specific artists. The show can be tailored to suit the needs and space of an institution interested in hosting the exhibition.

I look forward to receiving inquiries and suggestions from ASBC&D members concerning future exhibitions. Please write to James Keenan, P.O. Box 340, Cambridge, MA 02238. (Copies of the checklist are available for $4 through the Boston Athenaeum; write Mr. Donald C. Kelley, c/o Boston Athenaeum, 10½ Beacon St., Boston, MA 02108-3777.)

MORE BOOKPLATE LITERATURE

ASBURY PARK PRESS, Drumthwacket's Library Rich in Everything Except Books, Jill Hand. September 30, 1984. Drumthwacket is the official executive mansion of New Jersey near Princeton; it will house a working library for the governor and members of his administration. A special bookplate will be designed which may include symbols from the state seal and an exterior view of the house.

ASBURY PARK PRESS, Bookplates Still Appearing for Private Libraries, Jill Hand. (9) September 30, 1984. Antioch Publishing Co. of Yellow Springs, OH, designs custom-made bookplates starting at $150 for 200; forty stock designs are available starting at $2.95 for a box of 50. G. P. Putnam's, publishers of ". . . And Ladies of the Club," special ordered bookplates with the author's autograph for a special promotion. THE FINAL ENCYCLOPEDIA was distributed at the 42nd World Sicience Fiction Convention and "the company decided to put bookplates in some of the volumes, rather than release a limited edition . . . ."

1984 YEAR BOOK

  Clare Leighton

   Bella Landauer

    Kazutoshi Sakamoto

     and perhaps more

It will be end of the year before it is ready for delivery.

THE NIPPON EXLIBRIS ASSOCIATION
FIRST CONGRESS
by Cliff Parfit

The massive Washington Hotel in Shinjuku Tokyo made an excellent venue for Japan's first Exlibris Congress. Just across the road from the hotel are the buildings of the Bunka Publishing Company which, under the guidance of its bibliophile president Mr. Isao Imaida has supported the association for many years.

The congress exhibition opened on October 13th at one of the Bunka exhibition halls. It was planned by the association's secretary Mr. Koichiro Kozuka and supported by well-known Tokyo collector Mr. Ichigoro Uchida. The plates were beautifully mounted and hung, and there was a useful catalogue with notes supplied by Mr. Uchida. The major part of the exhibition was a superb retrospective collection of Japanese exlibris. Some very rare and beautiful plates from private collections were shown, but the bulk of the exlibris were from the unique collection of the Association. There was also an interesting collection of new Chinese exlibris. It is obvious that there are some talented artists already making exlibris in China.

The foreign section of the exhibition was from the English Centre collection. There were small collections by the Estonian artists Vive Tolli and Silvi Valjal. These ladies are book illustrators and are both in the forefront of exlibris design in Estonia. The major display in this section was of exlibris by von Bayros, and there was also a general collection of exlibris from 1900 to 1925.

The lecture program was held on October 14th at the Washington Hall on the third floor of the Washington Hotel. The session was opened by the President Mr. Katsusaburo Hasegawa. Greetings were extended to well-known artists present in the hall and mention was made of exlibris artists who had died in recent years. Short financial and administrative statements were made before the first lecture.

The opening lecture was given by Mr. Kazutoshi Sakamoto, the former president of the Association who retired last year for reasons of health. Mr. Sakamoto spoke of the history of the Association from the early years of the century to the present. Mr. Saito Shozo, who did so much to put the Association on its feet, was, of course, mentioned.

The second speaker was the award-winning artist from Aomori, Mr. Yonejiro Sato. He also talked about the early days of the Association, then of his college art classes in Aomori and showed some of the excellent books of exlibris made by his students. Next was Mr. Ichigoro Uchida, who spoke about this year's F.I.S.A.E. congress held in East Germany and showed a number of interesting slides of the Congress. The last lecture was by Cliff Parfit of the English Centre Japan; it concerned the exlibris of the "Golden" age (ca. 1900-25) in Europe. The lecture was illustrated with seventy slides.

The lectures were followed by an exchange and purchase session; the sale was very successful owing largely to the support of Mr. Imamura of the famous Gohachi Gallery in Kanda (Tokyo's book town). In addition to the superb books of exlibris on sale from many sources, the Nippon Exlibris Association's fine Congress keepsake was presented to each member with a free copy of Japan's oldest bibliophile magazine KOSHOTSUSHIN.

Next on the program was a lavish reception at the Washington suite served by a corps of charming hostesses. (The Japanese spare no pains to make these occasions a success.) Many members continued to exchange exlibris while listening to some further talks, while Mr. Iwami Furusawa, the surrealist artist sat at one side of the room making convincing sketches of lady members and of some of the charming hostesses. Mr. Imaida stood in another part of the room radiating goodwill and giving copies of his superbly handsome bookplates to all comers.

So ended the first congress of the Nippon Exlibris Association, but arrangements are already in hand for a second congress at Utsunomiya (north of Tokyo), which was the home of well-loved exlibris artist Kawakami Sumio, and is also the present home of his student, Mr. Katsusaburo Hasegawa, the president of the Association.

AS of BC & D
Bookplates in the News
605 N. STONEMAN AVENUE #F. ALHAMBRA, CALIFORNIA, 91801 U.S.A.
AUDREY SPENCER ARELLANES, Editor

NUMBER FIFTY-NINE   JANUARY 1985

PAUL LEMPERLY AND HIS BOOKPLATES
by Dean H. Keller, Assistant for
Collection Development and Management
University Libraries, Kent State

Paul Lemperly, the noted Cleveland, Ohio, book collector, had an international reputation for the outstanding library of association copies he assembled during his career. He described some of these volumes in two books publish-

ed by Cleveland's book collector's organization, The Rowfant Club, of which Lemperly was a charter member. AMONG MY BOOKS was issued in 1929 and BOOKS AND I appeared in 1938. His books were sold at auction on January 4 and 5, 1940, in New York City by the Parke-Bernet Galleries, Inc. One thousand sixty lots were sold in four sessions during the two days of the sale.

Lemperly was born in 1858 on the near West side of Cleveland, and it was there he was raised and went to school, graduating from West High School. His long business career was spent with the wholesale drug firm of Hall-Van Gorder Co. His home on Clifton Boulevard in Lakewood, a Cleveland suburb, housed his library and was a gathering place for friends, scholars, fellow

book collectors, and such literary figures as Eugene Field, De Witt Miller, William Allen White, Francis Wilson, and others. It was at his Clifton Boulevard home that he died on May 4, 1939, at the age of eight-one.

In his "Foreword" to the Parke-Bernet Galleries' catalogue for the Lemperly sale, Noel Lawson Lewis described Lemperly, the collector, this way:

> Paul Lemperly's especial interest as a collector began and con-
> tinued to the end of his long life, with the most human of all
> bookish attributes, Association. He loved his books for their
> contents, for their binding, their type, their illustrations
> and for their features but, above all, he loved them for their
> association -- in countless cases, personal association of the
> closest kind -- with their authors.

Lemperly collected, for the most part, modern authors, recognizing the merits of many of them before they became generally known or popular. Among the authors he collected were Joseph Conrad, Stephen Crane, Norman Douglas, A. E. Housman, Thomas Hardy, Rudyard Kipling, John Masefield, and Robert Louis Stevenson. He corresponded with many of them and many inscribed copies of their books to him. The auction catalogue is filled with quotations from inscriptions or letters of Paul Lemperly.

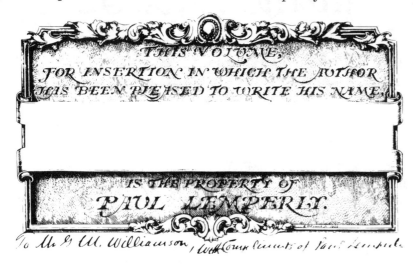 

It seems that in a great many cases Mr. Lemperly first wrote to the author asking permission to send him a book, or several books, to be inscribed. If the response from the author was positive, the book would be sent with the proper postage for its return. At least one author appreciated Lemperly's thoughtfulness for A. E. Housman wrote to Lemperly on December 11, 1899, in part, "I think yours is the only letter containing no nonsense that I have ever received from a stranger, and certainly it is the only letter containing an English stamp that I ever received from an American Your countrymen generally enclose the stamps of your great and free republic." The letter was quoted in connection with item 470 in the auction catalogue, Housman's A SHROPSHIRE LAD, London, 1896.

Given Lemperly's intense interest in association copies, it is not surprising to learn that he had a great interest in bookplates. One of his close friends and frequent visitors to Cleveland and the library on Clifton Boulevard was the great American designer and engraver of bookplates, Edwin Davis French. Lemperly collected bookplates designed by French, and other bookplates as well, and in 1917 Mr. and Mrs. Lemperly donated their bookplate collection to Western Reserve University (now Case Western Reserve University) in Cleveland in memory of their daughter Lucia, who died in 1915. In 1911 Lemperly arranged an exhibit of his collection of bookplates, and other engravings, of French at the Rowfant Club in Cleveland and the Club published a catalogue of the exhibit entitled BOOK-PLATES AND OTHER ENGRAVINGS BY EDWIN DAVIS FRENCH, with a Foreword by Charles Dexter Allen, Cleveland, 1911. Allen was also a friend of Lemperly.

Paul Lemperly used several different bookplates in his books and at least two of them were designed by French. The first, dated 1897, depicts a monk seated in a library, framed in elaborate scroll work with a quotation from Thomas a Kempis, "Here you have heaven and earth and all that goes to make up life." "Paul Lemperly, His Book" appears in a panel at the bottom of the plate. This bookplate was printed in both black and brown ink.

A second plate designed by French is most unusual and related directly to Lemperly's association collection. Instead of always sending books to authors for their inscriptions, a costly and hazardous practice, Lemperly had French design a bookplate that could be sent to an author for his signature. The

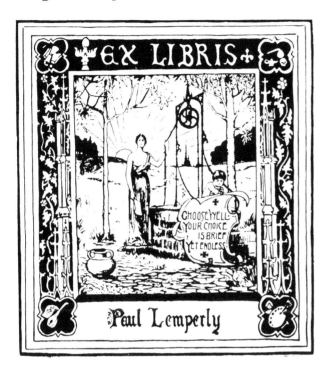

signed plate could be returned to Lemperly for insertion in the appropriate book. The plate, which is dated 1900, is a rather large one, measuring 4½ inches by 2 5/8 inches. It consists of a panel surrounded by scroll work, with a rather large space at the center in which the author was to write his name. The plate is lettered, "This volume,/for insertion in which the author/has been pleased to write his name,/is the property of/Paul Lemperly." Lemperly used this plate liberally, and he was most successful in persuading authors to sign and return them to him for insertion in their books. Ample evidence of his success may be found in the auction catalogue for the sale of his library, where books with this bookplate are usually described as "With (the author's name) signature on Mr. Lemperly's bookplate."

The Kent State University Library's Department of Special Collections has two volumes containing this bookplate. One is in Sheila Kaye-Smith's scarce first book, THE TRAMPING METHODIST, London, 1908, and the second is in IF WINTER COMES by A. S. M. Hutchinson, London, 1921. In a note to Lemperly inserted in the Hutchinson volume, the author volunteers that "I think your bookplate is quite delightful."

Lemperly also used two different bookplates designed by Edmund H. Garrett. One is an open book surrounded by a serpent on a field of stars, framed with holly leaves. It is lettered simply, "Ex Libris / Paul Lemperly." The plate is dated 1893. The other Garrett plate is Lemperly's initials, "PL" intertwined, and it is lettered "Ex Libris / Paul Lemperly." This plate is undated.

One other bookplate that we have identified as having been used by Paul Lemperly was designed by Bert K. Canfield. The center panel depicts a woman at a well with the motto, "Choose well. Your choice is brief yet endless." The two sides are decorated with Gothic spires and leaves, at the four corners are symbols representing literature, science, music and art, and the lettering is "Ex Libris" at the top, and "Paul Lemperly" at the bottom.

While Paul Lemperly was probably not the only collector to employ the "association" or "autographed" bookplate, he was undoubtedly one of the most successful. The rich collection he assembled over many years with diligent and personal attention, which is so well documented in his sale catalogue of 1940, is ample proof of that success.

RUDYARD KIPLING

EX LIBRIS

Frederic Remington

LVX·SVMMA· LEX·MEA·

EX·LIBRIS·
HENRY·VAN·DYKE·

He lovèd much on bookes day and night to pore,

Richard Le Gallienne

But yet he loved his wifie more.

THE LEMPERLY BOOKPLATE COLLECTION
AT CASE WESTERN RESERVE UNIVERSITY LIBRARIES
by Sue Hanson, Special Collections Librarian

In 1917, Mr. and Mrs. Paul Lemperly of Cleveland, gave their bookplate collection to Western Reserve University. The gift was given in memory of their daughter, Lucia, who had attended the College of Women and died in 1915.

The Lemperly collection, now housed in the Department of Special Collections, consists of over 600 bookplates, bookplate literature, catalogs and some materials relating to Edwin Davis French. The bookplate collection is in two sections; one part consists of 82 celebrity bookplates, the other is made up of bookplates and engravings by Edwin Davis French. French's skill as a designer and engraver, blending etching and engraving to create the intricate compositions, was in great demand. He was approached by many prominent persons and institutions to design bookplates: The Grolier Club, Harvard College Library, Vassar, Princeton University, and others. He began designing bookplates in response to a request from his sister-in-law who was a librarian at Columbia College. Nearly all of the bookplates on the list compiled by I. H. Brainerd for the Grolier Club Exhibit are in the collection. These often include two or more impressions of the plate, trial proofs, and print proofs, some signed by the artist.

WESTERN RESERVE UNIVERSITY

THE GIFT OF
MR · AND MRS · PAUL LEMPERLY
IN MEMORY OF THEIR DAUGHTER
LUCIA LEMPERLY

French was born in 1851, in North Attleboro, Massachusetts. He began as an engraver of silverware. From about 1893 to his death in 1906, he designed bookplates. A portion of a letter he wrote to Paul Lemperly in January, 1898, is quoted from papers in the collection,

"Yes, my dear Mr. Lemperly, I should consider myself fairly fortunate in my present situation, if I only had my health, although I fancy my very modest 'competency' would seem very insufficient to many people, however sufficient it may be for my simple manner of living. I had, however, before I commenced engraving book-plates, five years ago, an experience of twenty-five years in a noisy, ill-ventilated factory, trying to do careful work and taking charge of the engraving department, located in the same room with the silversmiths, amid hammering and filing, the rattle and shriek of machinery, the air full of gas and fumes of acid, -- well, I am not surprised that my health is no better now, and I am thankful that I was able to leave the factory when I did. They paid me fairly well there, but I had to be there ten hours each day, and evenings during the holiday season, say from November 1st to Christmas. And what worried me very much for the last few years I was there, I saw the demand for engraved work steadily diminishing and what we had to do becoming of a cheaper grade, until there was nothing that I could take interest in, and the force of thirty men who were in my department had got reduced to two or three. Of course, I could not earn my salary but they kept me, as I suppose, for what I had done, and in the hope that work would revive again. When I began to engrave book-plates, I

asked for leave of absence for a few weeks, until I could finish
what orders I had received, so unexpectedly, but fortunately, I
never had to go back again."

There are 82 celebrity bookplates in the collection, representing mostly
British and American personalities, notable for their vocations and avoca-
tions: lords and ladies, actors, poets, artists, historians, politicians,
and others. Some of the bookplates have additional significance because
of the artists who created the designs. On many, Mr. Lemperly has written
a line or two on the back of the mounting, identifying the owner or the
artist or contributing information on the history of the plate.

Oliver Wendell Holmes' bookplate pictures a chambered nautilus. Mr. Lemperly has written on the back, "A
plate which could have been identified
had owner omitted his name."

The bookplate of Henry Van Dyke shows
a young fisherman reading instead of
tending his line. Van Dyke's signature,
with Princeton and the date are written
at the bottom of the plate. On the
back of the mounting, Mr. Lemperly
has added a verse,

"Diplomat, scholar, poet, divine –
Professions varied, in which he
    doth shine –
But as angler, a failure, for 'tis
    long sine –
Fish could be caught with so loose
    a line!
Feb 24, 1917   P L

There is another poem, this one cut from a dealer's catalog, and is apparently Van Dyke's answer to a question regarding the designer of the plate:
    "Siddons Mowbray drew this lad/And James D. Smillie etched him:
    You can see his book; likewise his brook/But his fish? He hasn't ketched him."

Rudyard Kipling's bookplate depicts a man perched in elegant luxury aboard an
elephant, reading and smoking a narghile held by a retainer. Mr. Lemperly notes
the bookplate was designed by Kipling's father and adds a line from the author's
letter of May 14, 1896, " I enclose a specimen of a rather badly printed bookplate of mine."

Richard Le Gallienne's bookplate presents a charming scene, the man is kneeling before a pile of books with the woman resting her arm on his shoulders.
The legend reads, "He loved much bookes day and night to pore, but yet he
loved his wifie more." A poignant note is added by Mr. Lemperly, "Gift of
Mr. Le Gallienne shortly before the death of his wife."

William Morris, publisher of the Kelmscott Press books, surprisingly, has a
simple bookplate in contrast to the elaborately decorated books for which
he was known. Mr. Lemperly adds that the plate was printed in Morris's

Clement Shorter, journalist and critic, has a bookplate designed by Walter Crane.

"Golden" type at the Kelmscott Press.

Alfred Tynnyson's bookplate bears his autograph signature and a motto in Latin. Mr. Lemperly writes that the bookplate was the gift of Mrs. Locker-Lampson, Frederick Locker's second wife. His daughter, Eleanor, from his first marriage was the wife of Tennyson's son Lionel.

Frederick Locker's Rowfant Library was the inspiration for the name of the organization of Cleveland bibliophiles, the Rowfant Club. Mr. Locker and his family have six bookplates in the Lemperly collection. All six bear the same legend, "Fear God and fear nought." One of the plates was designed by Walter Crane and three of the others by Kate Greenaway.

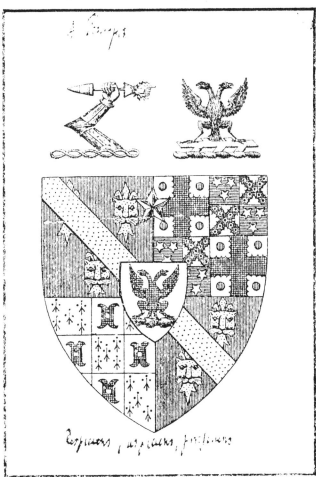

The only plate designed by Randolph Caldecott, according to Lemperly, is one for Owen Seaman, editor of PUNCH.

Edward Fitzgerald's bookplate was designed by his friend, William Makepeace Thackeray. Lemperly had been given the plate by Julian Marshall, the London Collector and Authority on bookplates. Edmund Gosse is quoted as saying that Fitzgerald wrote him in a letter that Thackeray designed the plate in 1842. The angel may have been intended to portray Mrs. Brookfield.

Lemperly notes that another bookplate was given to him by Julian Marshall, this one of Thomas Carlyle. He says further that the plate was designed by Henry T. Wake, Quaker bookseller and dealer in curiosities.

The bookplates are illuminating, not only because they reflect their owners' personalities, but also because the artists, combining insight and skill, created fitting symbols of ownership. The University is grateful for the Lemperly bequest, a valuable and fascinating collection of fine examples of the art of the bookplate.

(Editor's Note: A special thanks to the two institutions which have provided the interesting articles about Paul Lemperly and his bookplate collection. We would welcome articles about other collectors of the past and where their collections found a permanent home.)

BOOKPLATES IN THE NEWS
January/April/July/October
ISSN: 0045-2521
(C) Audrey Spencer Arellanes
Quarterly & YEAR BOOK:
Calendar Year Membership $35

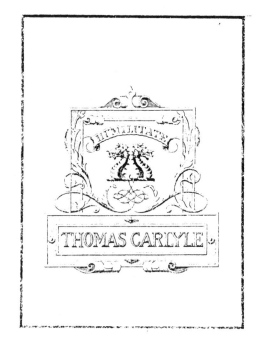

FROM THE BOOKPLATE LITERATURE

THE PRINCETON UNIVERSITY LIBRARY CHRONICLE, "Dear Charles": A. Edward Newton's Letters to Charles Grosvenor Osgood, Maxwell Luria and Richard E.
Brewer. (2) XLVI;5-48, Autumn 1984. One of the illustrations is Newton's
bookplate. "Before the end of 1909, Osgood designed a bookplate for Newton
with a Johnsonian assertion from the LIFE."

GRAPHIA #91, p. 65-96, 1984/3. Articles about Japanese artists: Iwami
Furusawa, Toshio Kajiyama, Toshio Sekine, Genshichi Tsukagoshi, Minoru
Yokota. Other articles about Gerard Schelpe, the International Congress
in Weimar, a series of artists whose designs are fantasy, a tribute to
Bela Stettner (1928-1984).

IN MEMORIAM LEO WINKELER 1919-1983 (Sint-Niklaas, GRAPHIA, 1984). Eleven
bookplates designed in tribute to Leo Winkeler, each printed on a separate
sheet, contained in a gray folder with portrait of Winkeler on the front.

FINE PRINT, American Calligraphy Revisted, 1945-1965, Charles E. Skaggs. 10:
155-163, October 1984. Among the artists mentioned are Raymond DaBoll and
James Hayes, both of whom executed numerous bookplates.

THE PRIVATE LIBRARY, Designing Engraved Booklabels, Reynolds Stone. (1) 6:
146-7, Winter 1983. "In a mark of ownership like a booklabel the name is
the important thing. . . . But I tend to discourage the customer who wants
all his interests and hobbies crammed into one small block. However, his
name alone or with a simple device, motif, or rebus, can often be made into
something worth sticking into a book."

THE PRIVATE LIBRARY, Reynolds Stone's Bookplates, David Chambers. (24) 6:
148-172, Winter 1983. Stone produced some 350 bookplates from the early
1930s to 1979, the year he died at age 70. The checklist is alphabetic and
includes the dimensions of the plate and date of execution when known.

THE PRIVATE LIBRARY, Working with Reynolds Stone, Michael Harvey. 6:173-6,
Winter 1983. Interesting first-hand account by young artist who worked
with Stone for six years. "Designs for bookplates were often sketched out
on the client's letter or envelope, then drawn in pencil and white gouache
on the end grain of the boxwood block."

L'EX LIBRIS FRANCAIS, #152, 1984/3. Article by Germaine Meyer-Noirel about
Mme. de Stael, who in 1804 began a long stay in Weimar, the site of the Ex
Libris Congress in 1984; it is illustrated with the bookplates of some of
the people she knew or met there. Bernard Francois, a Burgundy bookseller,
explains the poem-bookplate of Charles Esnault. Romuald Luczynski of Poland
writes about the oldest Polish bookplate, that of Maciej Drzewicki, dated 1516.

THE PRINCETON UNIVERSITY LIBRARY CHRONICLE, Recent Acquisitions - Western
Americana, Alfred L. Bush. (1) XLV:97-9, Autumn 1983. Illustrated is bookplate of Myles Standish Slocum, class of 1909, whose Grabhorn Press collection
was given to Princeton by his widow, Isabel Shaw Slocum. " . . Mr. Slocum's
net was thrown wide enough for the obscurer products of the Grabhorn Press:
for high school annuals from schools discriminating (and rich) enough to commission them from such caring craftsmen, for Bohemian Grove plays, for exhibition catalogues, eulogies, broadside invitations, tributes, bookplates."

EPHEMERON (The Book Collectors), John Payne, 2 unnumbered pages, 2:#5, January 1985. Payne is a librarian who has been associated with the Lily Library as a Fellow under David Randall and the Humanities Center at the University of Texas; his publications include a definitive bibliography of W. H. Hudson and more recently he co-authored a John Steinbeck study. His calligraphic ex libris illustrates an announcement of his talk on book appraising and the tax reform act of 1984.

THE BOOKPLATE JOURNAL, volume 2, #2, September 1984. Comment, 49-50. Notes about the article to follow on printing processes and a new publication from Leipzig: JUGENDSTIL-EXLIBRIS (includes at least one American artist: Jay Chambers). -- Printing Processes for Bookplates: A Critique, Otto M. Lilien. (10) 51-60. Lilien, son of artist E. M. Lilian (1874-1925), takes exception to the scheme of symbols for printing processes adopted in 1958 by the Federation of Exlibris Socities. -- Heraldry and Bookplates, Colin R. Lattimore. (15) 61-74. "Heraldry is the twelfth-century version of the car number plate. It is simply a means of identifying one individual from a large group of apparently similar individuals. As such, its use on bookplates is ideal for individuals legally entitled to bear arms." -- Theatrical Bookplates in the Tenin Collection, E. I. Makedonskaia (translated from the Russian by William Butler). (9) 75-87. Boris Tenin, a noted Russian actor for some 60 years, is also a bibliophile and bookplate collector. -- Profile of An Artist, Gerald Cobb, Brian North Lee. (1) 88-90. Cobb is a fine heraldic artist and doyen of the heraldic designers on the staff of the College of Arms. -- Portrait of A Bookplate, Louis Michaud. B. Junod. (1) 91-4. Paul Klee (1879-1940) etched one bookplate, that for Louis Michaud (1880-1957), whom he met during the period 1886-8; the plate was executed in 1901. -- Wood engraving by Derek Riley for Peter J. L. Scott reproduced. -- Review. Mark Severin reviews J. A. A. HARRISON, ARTIST AND ENGRAVER by Brian North Lee. "His style belongs to the turn of the century in being very detailed, often heavily ornamented, but he is undoubtedly one of the few artists who gave England her reputation for being the mother country of engravers."

THE BOOKPLATE SOCIETY NEWSLETTER, vol. VI, #3, September 1984. Weimar 1984, 25-30. International Congress, August 24-28, was attended by 270 registrants from nineteen countries. The exhibit of International Bookplates 1982-84 "marked the debut, thanks to the American Society of Bookplate Collectors and Designers, of modern Chinese bookplates. 15 Chinese artists were represented ..." -- XXI Congress (1986) in Utrecht, 30-1. Mr. Ph. van Praag, author of SOCIALE SYMBOLIEK OP NEDERLANDSE EXLIBRIS (1983) was elected the new FISAE president. -- Bookplates in the GDR: Issues and Problems, L. Lang. 32-6. This is a translation of the lecture delivered by Professor Long at the Weimar Congress.

A ARTE DO EX-LIBRIS, vol. XIII, #7, #103, 1984 (pages 153-214). A big issue with numerous tip-ins. Articles about the FISAE book for the 1984 Weimar Congress; artist Andre Gastmans; artist Oriol M. Divi; artist Petr Melan; artist Christian Blaesbjerg; checklist for Ricard Marlet I. Saret (1896-1976); continuation of a checklist for Mariaelisa Leboroni Pecetti; article on several Japanese artists; article and checklist for Helmut Arndt.

NORDISK EXLIBRIS TIDSSKRIFT, 36:#3, #155, 1984. Articles on ex libris in Holland, artist Per Christensen, bookplate literature.

THE HOOVER COLLECTION AT SPRAGUE LIBRARY,
HARVEY MUDD COLLEGE
David Kuhner, Librarian

The central science library for the Claremont complex, the Norman F. Sprague Library at Harvey Mudd College, contains a very fine history of sciences private collection, the personal library of the late President Herbert Clark Hoover and his wife, Lou Henry Hoover. This collection of about one thousand volumes came to the Colleges in 1970 as a gift from Herbert Hoover III and the Hoover family.

Herbert Hoover, who traveled the world in the early 1900's as a consulting mining engineer, early acquired a love for rare books, especially titles in the fields of mining, mathematics, astronomy and alchemy, natural history, and geology. He and his wife patiently searched book stores and catalogues and added, volume by volume, such important items as Euclid's ELEMENTA GEOMETRIAE (Ratdolt, 1482), William Gilbert's great work on the magnet (DE MAGNETE, London, 1600), a geography by Strabo (Venice, 1472), Barba's ARTE DE LOS METALES (Madrid, 1640), and other works by Gesner, Borelli, Dana, and Montalbano - prime names in the history of mineralogy and crystallography.

The works of Georgius Agricola especially intrigued the Hoovers. His monumental work DE RE METALLICA (Basel, 1556) had never been translated into English, and Lou Henry Hoover commented, "The task has been doubly difficult . . . because, in using Latin, the author availed himself of a medium which had ceased to expand a thousand years before his subject had . . . come into being." But in 1912 the Hoover translation appeared in England, and it remains a collector's item to this day.

The Hoover Collection on the History of Science and the Metallic Arts, now open to all interested scholars at the Sprague Library in Claremont, constitutes a very special kind of tribute to President and Mrs. Hoover that is long overdue. Some of the bookplates in the Hoover books include the one above for Lady Davy, a widow of wit, beauty and wealth, who married noted chemist Sir Humphry Davy in 1812. When Sir Humphry wished to travel in Europe during 1813-15, Lady Davy was permitted by Napoleon himself to travel on the Continent unhindered and unharmed.

Another plate of interest is that of Sir John Hayford Thorold (1733-1831) who amassed at Syston Park in Lincolnshire, England, one of the great collections of the 19th-century. Two of his books, a Gutenberg Bible and a Mainz Psalter, became the costliest volumes ever exchanged for money when the library was sold in 1884. The Bible made headlines again in 1978 when it was auctioned in New York City for two million dollars. His 1472 Strabo geography book eventually came to Mr. Hoover.

The Tenth Duke of Hamilton, Alexander Douglas-Hamilton (1767-1852) was among the elite of the Scottish peerage; his honors included Knight of the Garter, Fellow of the Royal Society, British Museum Trustee, and Member of Parliament. He married his cousin, Susana Beckford, "one of the handsomest women of her time" and the daughter of dilettante-author William Beckford. The Duke thus acquired the noted Beckford Library in addition to his own. The Hamilton book which has come into the Hoover Collection is Robert Plot's NATURAL HISTORY OF STAFFORDSHIRE (Oxford, 1686). Plot was called "the father of county natural histories in Britain."

Sir John Thorold (above).

Alexander Douglas-Hamilton (left).

Sir Henry Bartle Edward Frere (1815-1884), British colonial administrator in India and South Africa, was a bookish and gentle soul caught up in the travails of mutiny and riot and war. He served as Governor of Bombay, negotiated a treaty with the sultan of Zanzibar to halt the slave trade and was sent to the Cape Colony as high commissioner in 1877. There he attempted to deal with "spear fidgeting" Zulu tribes but failed; there was a massacre of troops, and he was recalled to England.

Eight of his books survive in Mr. Hoover's library. The bookplate to the right is in a nicely bound set of the history of Herodotus (1862). Other Frere volumes are Roman classics of such authors as Martial, Statius, and Valerius Maximus. When he lost one library in a shipwreck he started to build another at once.

NOTES FROM AN ARTIST
James Michael Dorsey

The plate to the left is for a professor at the University of Georgia at Atlanta. He is a world authority on medieval and renaissance English literature, and his first work was a bibliography of Sir Gawain and the Green Knight. Thus, my design speaks for itself.

The plate below is for a Certified Public Accountant, who recently became a partner of her firm; thus the clock to show her newly acquired hours, and to balance the desk, plus the tools of her trade, and the single rose which is always present on her desk.

The third ex libris is my own and will thus advertise for me whenever I lend a book. I am seeking commissions in all forms of illustration. My work is in ink, colored pencil, and oils. Mostly I have illustrated magazines and done oil portraits.

Recently I completed a large Olympic mural on the west wall of the Original Pantry Cafe in downtown Los Angeles. (James Michael Dorsey, 3034 Reid Ave., Culver City, CA 213/836-4439)

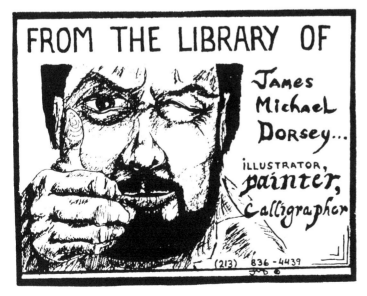

AMERICAN HISTORICAL PRINT COLLECTORS SOCIETY, AHPCS and California Historical Society Hold Joint Regional Meeting. P. 5, November 1984. On October 28, 1984 presentations were given focused on California prints: Rose Tisdel spoke on DeLongpre; Jean Roshal presented California on post cards; Audrey Arellanes' talk featured California artists who executed bookplate prints: Mallette Dean Carl Oscar Borg, Paul Landacre. Bookplate prints by these and other artists were mounted on matboard for display.

THE WOOD ENGRAVINGS OF JOHN FARLEIGH, Monica Poole, RE, foreword by H.R.H. The Duke of Edinburgh.   Gresham Books, Henley-on-Thames, Oxfordshire, England. Pages 128, over 150 wood engravings, 9 in color.   Publication date: February 8, 1985; price £29.50.   Size: 360 x 250 mm; binding: casebound in art canvas with head and tail bands.

In writing this book, Monica Poole has the advantages of having studied under John Farleigh and of being an accomplished wood engraver herself.

There are a dozen pages of biographical text, a concise chronology, and detailed lists of books illustrated with wood engravings, wood engravings created as original prints, bookplates, editions taken from commissioned wood engravings, books by Farleigh, books illustrated in other media, and a master index.

Monica Poole writes: "John Farleigh's work is completely outside the English pastoral tradition which has influenced so many printmakers; the school which draws life from the countryside, whether expressed with the earthiness of Bewick or the glorious excesses of Samuel Palmer. He is closer to the Blake of the biblical and mythical illustrations, and, like Blake, searches for a great theme, not a visual one but one of ideas."

Though John Farleigh (1900-1965) executed only a few bookplates, his work should be of interest to ex libris collectors, especially those who admire wood engraving. If you want to purchase the book write directly to Gresham Books, P.O. Box 61, Henley-on-Thames, Oxfordshire RG9 3LQ, England.

1984 YEAR BOOK

. Clare Leighton

. Bella Landauer

. Notes from Japan

Ready soon for delivery.

AS of BC & D

Bookplates in the News

605 N. STONEMAN AVENUE #F, ALHAMBRA, CALIFORNIA, 91801 U.S.A.

AUDREY SPENCER ARELLANES, Editor

NUMBER SIXTY

APRIL 1985

TWO EUROPEAN ARTISTS

. Jurgen Dost

and

. Anatoli
   Kalaschnikow

by

Helmer

Fogedgaard

Jurgen Dost is a German graphic artist, who has created several ex libris for me. Above is a humorous bookplate with the sun and a horse; it is a lino-cut in three colors. Dost works both in wood-cut and lino, always with fine results, and most of his prints are multi-colored.

Jurgen Dost was born in 1939. He studied to be an art teacher. To date Dost has created about 150 ex libris in a variety of styles but predominantly modern; he is one of the most versatile bookplate artists in Europe.

Anatoli Kalaschnikow is one of the many bookplate artists in the Soviet Union, and he also has made numerous Russian stamps. His ex libris are all wood-engravings; the motifs are both naturalistic and abstract. He

has created several hundred bookplates, all of them numbered. The
plate tipped-in to the right is
number 54 and belongs to a German.

Anatoli Kalaschnikow was born in
1930. He studied at the academy
of art in Moscow. For some years
he worked as a free artist, but
in 1957 he was appointed to the
ministry for the postal system,
where his stamps were highly esteemed.

Kalaschnikow has created bookplates for collectors in many
countries and is known and admired
on an international basis.

(Helmer Fogedgaard is well-known
internationally by all those interested in bookplates. He is
currently editor of EXLIBRIS-NYT,
one of the bookplate publications
in Denmark.)

•——————————•

MATRIX 2, Wood-engraving in Russia,
John R. Biggs. (15) 2:1-15, Winter
1982. Because of difficulties in
exporting wood blocks, engravings
are printed from line blocks. "It
is the fact of the artist engraving his own block which is at the
heart of the revival of creative
wood-engraving. . . . There is a charming custom for engravers to produce an Ex Libris as a compliment to somebody they admire or otherwise have
an interest in. I was myself pleasantly surprised, many years ago, to be
presented with an Ex Libris specially designed for me by artists I had
met. . . . Vinyl engraves quite sweetly."

MATRIX 1, Leo Wyatt, David Burnett. (1) 1:64, Autumn 1981. From obituary which
appeared in THE TIMES (London): "He was unique among modern bookplate art-
tists in being a superb exponent of both copper engraved armorials & book
labels engraved on wood . . .."

MATRIX 3, Wood-engravings of John Lawrence, Peter Gray. (21) 3:21-41, Winter
1983. Numerous multicolor, fanciful illustrations from books are tipped-
in; one is "Brian North Lee Juvenilia" bookplate.

MATRIX 3, An Engravers Apprentice, Michael Renton. (7) 3:126-36, Winter 1983.
Ex libris for Elisabeth Brayne, Mary Vincent, Robin Densem reproduced.

MATRIX #1, Autumn 1981, Ad: "We can supply anything ... from a bookplate to a
map." E. Walters & G. Miller, 360 Oppidans Rd., Primrose Hill, London NW3.

THE GOLDEN BALL TAVERN
Weston, Massachusetts
by   James Keenan

The Golden Ball Tavern is located on
the old Boston Post Road in Weston,
MA. The Tavern is included in the
National Register of Historical Places
and has membership with the Society
for the Preservation of New England
Antiquities.

The inn "at the Sign of the Golden
Ball" was built in 1768 by Captain
Isaac Jones, who operated it from
1770 to 1793. It then became a residence and stayed in the Jones family
until the death of Ralph Jones in
1963. The inn was purchased from his
estate and donated to the Golden Ball
Tavern Trust.

Isaac Jones was an early Tory sympa-
thizer and his patriot neighbors had
little appreciation for his views. In
1773-4 he ignored the patriot boycott
of tea and sold it in Weston and surrounding Massachusetts towns.   In March
of 1774, three months after the Boston Tea Party, his tavern was raided; the
entire house was ransacked by angry colonists.

In January and April of 1775, scouts from General Gage's army made their
headquarters at the Golden Ball Tavern while exploring the possibility of
sending the army through Weston to seize the military supplies in Worcester.
Jones' advice and the hostility the scouts experienced along the Boston Post
Road influenced Gage's decision to make his attack by way of Lexington and
Concord.

Jones' conversion from Tory to accepted patriot took place sometime in 1777.
In 1778 we find him a Selectman of Weston and for nine different years until
his death in 1793. His earlier Tory views overlooked, he lived and died a
respected Weston citizen.

In 1980, the Trustees of the Golden Ball Tavern were interested in having a
bookplate designed for the museum collection. A simple design was chosen
by the committee similar to the signboard which hangs in front of the tavern: "at the Sign of the Golden Ball." The tipped-in print is printed letterpress on 100% rag parchment.

CHARLES F. LUMMIS CENTENNIAL
SYMPOSIUM – Southwest Museum
February 1985
Included in an exhibition ac-
companying the Lummis sympo-
posium was a book whose top edge was branded with the Lummis signature.

THE VIRGINIA STEELE SCOTT COLLECTION

The Huntington Library, Art Collections and Botanical Gardens in San Marino, California, has been the recipient of a three-part gift from the Virginia Steele Scott Foundation: fifty American paintings, funds to erect a separate gallery to display the paintings and house related activities in American art, and an endowment for operating the professional side of the new facility. For its part, the Huntington furnishes maintenance and security. The agreement for the gift was signed in 1979 and the Gallery, described as a "post modern" building designed by Santa Barbara architect Paul Gray, was opened to the public in 1984.

The American paintings comprising the collection have been selected since 1975 by Millard Sheets, painter, designer, and art administrator, and Maurice Bloch, professor emeritus of art history at the University of California at Los Angeles, retired curator and director of the Grunwald Center for Graphic Arts at UCLA, and a leading scholar of nineteenth century American painting. The collection is not static or fixed, but free to grow and be refined, thus enhancing its value to the general public and the scholar alike. There are no stated chronological boundaries imposed upon the collection; current holdings date from the 1740s to 1930s.

Virginia Steele was born in Pittsburgh, PA, in 1905, to Harry and Grace Steele, the first of six children. Her father, an industrialist, made his fortune and retired before the age of forty to California. Within a year he was back in business with U.S. Electrical Motors and had accumulated another fortune by the time of his death. Virginia attended the Carnegie Institute of Technology where she studied set designing for a year. Later she transferred to Yale University and studied playwriting in George Pierce Baker's famous Drama Workshop. Following the university years, Virginia traveled, lived abroad, and in Florence met Jonathan Scott, a British painter. They were married in 1938 in Oxford, and moved to Pasadena, California, where Scott painted and Virginia devoted her time and energy to collecting and philanthropic activities in connection with the Pasadena Art Museum.

Small in stature, Virginia Steele Scott was described by friends as doll-like, but credited with enormous energy and enthusiasm, and impulsive in her generosity.

In 1973 she started building a private museum adjoining her Pasadena home; this was completed in September of 1974, just four months before her death. The Virginia Steele Scott Foundation was established in February 1974. The bookplate used for the reference volumes accompanying the art collection is an adaptation made by Anthony F. Kroll from a bronze medallion created by Leonard Baskin.

(Source: THE VIRGINIA STEELE SCOTT GALLERY: A GIFT TO THE HUNTINGTON ART COLLECTION by Robert R. Wark, Curator of the Huntington Art Collections.)

FROM THE BOOKPLATE LITERATURE

SEA FRONTIERS, Ex Libris: Neptunus Rex, Don Hubbard. (19) 31:83-5, March-April 1985. "Once in place on the flyleaf, the bookplate becomes a part of the book's personality as it passes down to future readers." As the title of the article implies, the bookplates reproduced all have something to do with the sea.

AB (ANTIQUARIAN BOOKMAN), William P. Wreden, Books & Manuscripts. 75:1001, February 11, 1985. A page ad includes "Bookplates. Ex Libris collection of Nuno Smith de Vasconcellos of Brazil. Over 5,500 bookplates primarily from Europe, the United States and Brazil, ca 1890-1940. Most mounted and arranged alphabetically by individual or library name in 50 cloth bound volumes. Many Art Nouveau or Art Deco, some signed by the artists. $1,950."

AB (ANTIQUARIAN BOOKMAN), Memorial Tribute: Warren Howell and the World of Rare Books, Jacob L. Chernofsky. 75:945, February 11, 1985. World famous antiquarian bookseller was born November 13, 1912 in Berkeley; died January 11, 1985.

ANTIQUARIAN BOOK MONTHLY REVIEW, Diary. 12:69, February 1985. Sir Harry Robertson Page died New Year's Eve 1984. He was collector of Victorian scrapbooks, ephemera, and bookplates. He was City Treasurer of London, served on numerous government commissions; he wrote the Page Report on National Savings.

ANTIQUARIAN BOOK MONTHLY REVIEW, Spoiled Bookplates. 12:27, January 1985. A reader's letter concerning the ravages of a member of the auctioneer's staff at Philips & Jollys Auction Rooms in Bath, England, who used a black felt-tip pen to obliterate the names on bookplates in some offered volumes. The ex libris were for Corsham Court Library and Methuen family.

ANTIQUARIAN BOOK MONTHLY REVIEW, Classified. 11:335, August 1984. "James Wilson, books & bookplates. The Corner Bookshop, Camden Loch, Chalk Farm Rd., London NW1."

ANTIQUARIAN BOOK MONTHLY REVIEW, Oxford Book Auctions. 11:218, June 1984. Page ad for auction June 15, 1984 illustrates the lion Charles Dickens ex libris and a printed library ticket reading "From the Library of Charles Dickens, Gadshill Place, June, 1870."

AMERICAN ARTIST, Educated Hand, Fridolph Johnson. (18) 21;42-7, 75-6, September 1957. Five of the illustrations are ex libris. Excellent tribute and assessment of work of Allen Lewis by fellow artist Norman Kent.

THE SCRIPTURE (Scripps College, Claremont, CA), Bookplates in the Library. 19:#29, unnumbered page, May 19, 1949. About Louise Seymour Jones collection. "In a simple yet artistic manner, a bookplate lets the reader know that the owner has cared enough to mark his book with a permanent label of affection and ownership."

JOURNAL OF LIBRARY HISTORY, The Cover, Philip A. Metzger. (1) 17:78-80, Winter 1982. Dull bookplate for an exciting collection. Berlin Collection, named for the city where it was purchased, of some 57,000 books and 39,000 dissertations is identified by a label which lists the names of the nine donors.

JOURNAL OF LIBRARY HISTORY, The Cover, Philip A. Metzger. (1) 17:186-8, Spring 1982. Ex libris featured was used by the library of the Royal Academy of Surgery in eighteenth century Paris; contrary to the usual practice of the times, it appears to be a woodcut rather than a copper-plate engraving.

JOURNAL OF LIBRARY HISTORY, The Cover, Mary Bell. (1) 17:343-5, Summer 1982. Bookplate of Henrietta Cavendish Holles (1693-1755), wife of Edward Harley, for her personal library at Welbeck; it was designed by George Vertue in 1731.

JOURNAL OF LIBRARY HISTORY, The Cover, Katharine Smith Diehl. (1) 17: 474-6, Fall 1982. The ex libris featured is a plain label for A.B.C.F.M. Mission in Singapore.

JOURNAL OF LIBRARY HISTORY, The Cover, John P. Chalmers. (1) 18:74-6, Winter 1983. Reverend Thomas Bray (1656-1730) founded earliest public libraries in British North America which were established by the Society for Propagation of the Gospel; ex libris for these libraries was en-graved by Simon Gribelin (1661-1733). Records of the Society show that 8,000 impressions of two bookplates were provided in 1709.

JOURNAL OF LIBRARY HISTORY, The Cover, John P. Chalmers. (1) 18:190-2, Spring 1983. The bookplate reproduced is perhaps the earliest of ten or more bookplates used in libraries of Christ Church. This early armorial uses the arms of Cardinal Wolsey, who founded the college in 1525.

JOURNAL OF LIBRARY HISTORY, The Cover, John P. Chalmers. (1) 18:322-4, Summer 1983. Armorial plate for family library of some 200,000 volumes started in late 16th century by Lindsay family of Balcarres; library dispersed in sales in 1887, 1889, 1900, 1924, and 1947/48.

JOURNAL OF LIBRARY HISTORY, The Cover, John P. Chalmers. (1) 18:473-5, Fall 1983. Bookplate reading "Gift of the Society for Propagation of the Gospell in Foreign Partys 1704" was engraved by William Jackson and produced in several states including omission of the date.

JOURNAL OF LIBRARY HISTORY, The Cover, Renee Lemaitre. (1) 19:183-6, Winter 1984. Following WWI a children's library was formed by an American committee in France for which a bookplate was designed by Helen Stowe Penrose.

JOURNAL OF LIBRARY HISTORY, The Cover, Margaret F. Dominy. (1) 19:306-8, Spring 1984. Bookplate of Adrienne and Julien Peridier, French as-tronomer who left his library and astronomical instruments to the University of Texas, Austin. Ex libris engraved by Adolpe Giraldon (1855-1933).

JOURNAL OF LIBRARY HISTORY, The Cover, Les Gronberg. (2) 19-426-30, Summer 1984. Illustrated is bookplate Albrecht Durer designed for Willibald Pirckheimer in 1501. "Pirckheimer may perhaps have originated the use of portrait bookplates by placing his portrait at the end of his books." The portrait was done by Durer in 1524.

JOURNAL OF LIBRARY HISTORY, The Cover, John Richardson. (2) 19: 541-4, Fall 1984. Two ex libris are printed: one for Pierce and Ruth Butler by R. Hunter Middleton; the other for The Pierce Butler Collection by James Hayes. Brief article about the collectors and the artists who executed their ex libris.

NEWSLETTER (Nippon Ex-Libris Association), #80, January 1, 1985. A brief English summary of this 16 page Japanese journal indicates it contains messages from artists and owners of ex libris, a report from the 20th FISAE Congress in Weimar by Ichigoro Uchida, notes from the editor, and articles by NEA president Shozaburo Hasegawa on the First General Meeting of the NEA held October 14, 1984 in Shinjuku (250 participants and 24 artists) and accompanying the meeting was the Paper-Jewel Exhibition of Japanese ex libris old and new, European to 1900, and Chinese ex libris; about 1,000 viewed the exhibit. The annual calendar issued by the Society appears in two parts; January through June and July through December.

L'EX LIBRIS FRANCAIS, #153, 1984. Article by Robert Kugel about the "golden number" and Germaine Meyer-Noirel reports on the Weimar Congress.

AMERICAN BOOK COLLECTOR, Philip Hofer, A Personal Recollection, Con Howe. (3) 6:3-6, January-February 1985. The illustrations are ex libris; among printed ephemera which Hofer collected were bookplates.

AMERICAN BOOK COLLECTOR, Philip Hofer, Scholar, David P. Becker. (1) 6:6-7, January-February 1985.

SVENSKA EXLIBRISFORENINGEN, #151, February 1985, pages 107-118; text in Swedish. Several imaginative bookplates reproduced.

EXLIBRIS WERELD, #3, 1984, pages 521-544. Articles on collector F. G. Waller (1867-1934), the Weimar Congress, a tribute to Cyril Bouda (11/14/1901 – 8/29/84). Article in English on Russian artist Yuriy Lukshyn, "whose small graphics contain a unique atmosphere similar to that in Marc Chagall's paintings . . . ."

NORDISK EXLIBRIS TIDSSKRIFT, #156, #4, 1984, pages 33-48. Article with English translation about Yvonne de Vries, who designed her first bookplate at age 13; now has 4 etched and 17 printed bookplates to her credit.

JOURNAL OF LIBRARY HISTORY, The Cover, Philip A. Metzger. (1) 16:543-5, Fall 1981. Charles Theophile Guichard, renamed Quintus Icilius for a centurian in the Battle of Pharsala formed a library which became part of the Royal Library of Prussia under Frederick the Great. A bookplate dated 1780 identified his collection within the library.

JOURNAL OF LIBRARY HISTORY, The Cover, John Buechler. (1) 16:607-10, Fall 1981. Interesting, brief article on Charles Whittingham (1785-1876) and Chiswick Press. Bookplates for three surviving members of family probably cut by Mary Byfield; original block at St. Bride Printing Library.

NEWSLETTER (The Bookplate Society, London), 4:#4, December 1984, pages 37-48. Bookplate Exchange Club, after being in existence for 85 years, has suspended activities because of dwindling interest. -- David J. Chambers preparing checklist of Joan Hassall's bookplates; asks for details about any bookplates which may have been made from engravings originally intended for other purposes. -- James L. Wilson writes about two versions of a bookplate for the Bank of England. -- Remarks about bookplates featuring Dr. Samuel Johnson (1709-1784).

DIRK VAN GELDER, Henk van Buul (Arethusa Pers Herber Blokland Baarn, 1984). This is a softcover book of about 75 pages devoted to Dirk Van Gelder, who was born in 1907. There are fifteen truly wonderful prints, mostly bookplates; there is a list of his bookplates, #44 to #66, created between 1948 and 1980. The text includes what appear to be assessments from other artists, such as Cees Andriessen, Gerard Gaudaen, Pam Rueter, Wim Ziers, Mark Severin. There is no text in English, but the prints can be enjoyed regardless of language. To purchase write: Exlibris Wereld, Minervalaan 26, 1077 Amsterdam, Nederland.

AMERICAN ARTIST, Happy Birthday, Fridolf. (1) 50:26, March 1985. Former editor of AMERICAN ARTIST, Fridolf Johnson, celebrated his 80th birthday on February 24, 1985. Johnson attended Art Institute of Chicago; is author and editor of seven books; the most recent is an anthology of Rockwell Kent's work published by Alfred A. Knopf.

AT THE SIGN OF THE SILVER HORSE (Trovillion Private Press), A New Bookplate. 12:#1, Autumn 1952 (unnumbered page). Review of Louise Seymour Jones' HUMAN SIDE OF BOOKPLATES. " . . . this author purposely avoids that angle (art-tist's viewpoint), producing an intimate narrative that booklovers will find full of literary surprises."

PUBLISHERS WEEKLY, Western Books 1952. 161:1580-4, April 5, 1952. Exhibit starts two concurrent tours. HUMAN SIDE OF BOOKPLATES included among 33 entries.

EXLIBRIS WERELD, #4, Winter 1984, pages 545-552. Includes index from 1977 through 1984 as an insert. Article and checklist for A. H. Saaltink. -- Illustrated is ex libris by G. T. Friend for Acton.

LOS ANGELES TIMES, Percival: A Woman Ahead of Her Time, Miv Schaaf. Part 5, 6, March 27, 1985. Olive Percival was "the first woman underwriter ever hired" by an insurance company for which she worked 38 years until retirement in 1929. But she is best known in the Los Angeles area for her collections, including her bookplate collection at UCLA.

GHEORGHE RADU by Dr. Emil I. Bologa
from ARTISTA DE EX-LIBRIS VI, FISAE
Portugal, 1982/Translator-G.S.Swarth

Gheorghe Radu was born in Brasov, Romania, on March 28, 1935. After completing a course of graphic art at the Technical School in Jassy he took up engraving, but when infantile paralysis left him paralyzed on his right side, he was obliged to give up engraving in favor of design.

Returning to Brasov, he worked as a retoucher, while participating in several graphic exhibitions. At the urging of Dr. Emil I. Bologa, president of the ex libris and bibliographic club of Brasov, he undertook the making of bookplates and participated in exhibits,

beginning with the first Brasov exhibition of Dr. Bologa's collection in 1972. Since 1972 he has made more than fifty vignettes, responding to requests from Portugal, Sweden, the Soviet Union, and Czechoslovakia. His favorite themes include nudes, horses, Don Quixote, as well as children's ex libris.

His designs in black and white are characterized by simplicity and economy of line, executed rapidly and with great elegance. He never corrects or retouches his work, having the capacity to capture quickly the true essence of his subject. His ex libris have a lyric quality, rejecting violence and evoking an atmosphere of profound calm. He is able to create a veritable "coloration" in black and white, notably for the landscapes that serve him as background and sometimes even as actual subject. The soft and undulating lines with which he accomplishes his compositions produce a rhythm of convex and concave forms, a music.

Gheorghe Radu's professional qualities, the lapidary line of his designs, eliminating everything

superfluous, the pure atmosphere pooled with graceful silhouettes are characteristics of his work that explain the appreciation of and demand for them from numerous connoisseurs and collectors of ex libris. In the art of graphic

PROF. C.T. JIGA

EX-LIBRIS

miniature, called also the "epigram" of the design arts, Gheorghe Radu proves again that what is great is not necessarily monumental.

For devotees of graphic art relating to books, the ex libris remains, without reference to its possessory statement, an important cultural act showing our attachment to a literary work. It shows an attachment to the printed word, for all those for whom the love of books remains an esthetic passion, a noble preoccupation and objective.

BOOKPLATES IN THE NEWS
Quarterly: January/April
               July/October

ISSN: 0045-2521

(C) Audrey Spencer Arellanes

THE QUARTERLY NEWS-LETTER (Book Club of California), John Henry Nash: A Collector's Reappraisal, Norman H. Strouse. XLVII:59-74, Summer 1982. Article originally appeared in the GAZETTE of Grolier Club (N.S.) #19, December 1973. Mentions library label reading: John Henry Nash Library, Presented to the University of California by Mr. and Mrs. Milton S. Ray and Members of Their Family." Interesting article about a printer whose career has suffered ups and downs.

PLEASE SHARE YOUR EX LIBRIS
with ASBC&D members
Send a copy of your plate-
Information about yourself,
the artist and the bookplate.

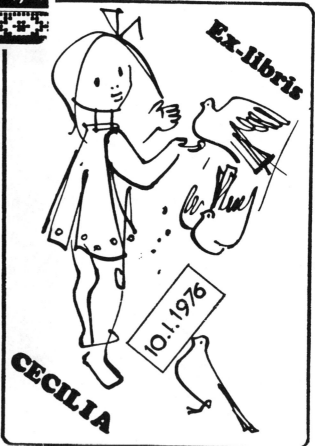

THE ALBERT ALPHIN
MUSIC LIBRARY of
Boston Conservatory
of Music
by James Keenan

The Boston Conservatory of Music was founded in February of 1867. Its founder was Julius Eichberg, a violinist and composer of fine repute. Under his leadership the Conservatory gained a standing among the foremost music schools and attracted students from many parts of the country.

In 1933, the Conservatory came under the direction of Albert Alphin, who had been both a student and teacher at the school. He was responsible for reorganizing the school as a non-profit institution, acquiring its present complex of buildings on The Fenway in Boston, and constructing the theatre in 1949. With his guidance the Music Education Department was formed and the Theatre and Dance Departments were established. This was unique in making the Boston Conservatory one of the first institutions in the country to provide professional training in three performing arts.

Albert Alphin retired from his position as the fourth Director of the Conservatory in 1967. In this same year, the Albert Alphin Music Library was founded and named after this energetic leader. The library started as a small collection of 12,300 volumes and over the past eighteen years has increased to hearly 40,000 volumes.

The Albert Alphin Music Library staff wanted a bookplate to represent the collection in 1980. A 19th century engraving that illustrates an assortment of musical instruments was selected for use with these books. The tipped-in bookplate is printed letterpress on Permalife Text paper.

MORE FROM THE BOOKPLATE LITERATURE

A ARTE DO EX-LIBRIS, Vol. 13, #8, #104, 1984, p. 215-258. An unusually large issue with additional unnumbered pages on which bookplates are reproduced. Articles on Antonio Gomes Da Rocha Madahil (Dec. 10, 1893 to June 27, 1969), Alexandru Radulescu with a checklist #1-119 from 1975 through 1984, M. Fils (Dr. Otakar Marik) with checklist #1-208 from 1969 through 1984.

CONNOISSEUR, Traveline. 215:128, January 1985. Reprinted from PASSPORT, the Newsletter for Discriminating Travelers: "Elegant bookplates. In Paris there's an unusual little shop called Agry that's world famous for its bookplates ... ." Agry, 14 Rue de Castiglione, 75001 Paris, France.

Milan Humplik
Gagarinova 21
360 09 Karlovy Vary
Czechoslovakia
(Artist: P. Rolcik
X2, 1983)

ELLA STRONG DENISON LIBRARY

SCRIPPS COLLEGE

LOS ANGELES TIMES article (page 556) mentions the Mcpherson Society.

Discovered in the Louise Seymour Jones Collection in Denison Library at Scripps a plate of early movie star Monte Blue.

EXCHANGE: Clifford P. Firmbach has prints of Arthur Macdonald bookplates which he is happy to exchange for ex libris by E. D. French, A. J. Brown, J. W. Spenceley, Frederick Spenceley, and C. Gallaudet. Please write: Clifford P. Firmbach, 4500 S. 31st St., Apt. #103, Arlington, VA 22206.

EXCHANGE: Edwin Jewel is interested in Australian bookplates and literature. either to exchange or purchase. Please write: Edwin Jewel, C/- 11 Barkly St., Warragul, Victoria 3820, Australia

HAVE YOU PAID YOUR 1985 DUES? $ 35

General Index

General Index

A

General Index

General Index

O

P

T

U

V

Illustrations Index

Illustrations Index

In the issues of Bookplates in the News that subscribers receive, many illustrations are tipped-in. To designate those not tipped-in, the page number is preceded by the abbreviation "facsim."

A

B

C

Illustrations Index

N

O

P

U

V

639

W

Z